The Shorter Works
of
1763

The New Century Edition
of the Works of Emanuel Swedenborg

Jonathan S. Rose
Series Editor

Stuart Shotwell
Managing Editor

Lee S. Woofenden
Annotation Editor

EDITORIAL COMMITTEE

Wendy E. Closterman

Lisa Hyatt Cooper

George F. Dole

Jeremy F. Simons

Chara Smith

The Shorter Works of 1763

The Lord
Sacred Scripture
Life
Faith
Supplements

EMANUEL SWEDENBORG

Translated from the Latin by George F. Dole
With an Introduction by Jonathan S. Rose
And Notes by Susanna Åkerman-Hjern, Glen M. Cooper, Lisa Hyatt Cooper,
George F. Dole, R. Guy Erwin, David N. Gyllenhaal, Robert H. Kirven,
Jonathan S. Rose, Fitzhugh L. Shaw, Stuart Shotwell, Richard Smoley,
and Lee S. Woofenden

SWEDENBORG FOUNDATION
West Chester, Pennsylvania

Originally published in Latin (Amsterdam, 1763) as five separate works:
The Lord: *Doctrina Novae Hierosolymae de Domino*
Sacred Scripture: *Doctrina Novae Hierosolymae de Scriptura Sacra*
Life: *Doctrina Vitae pro Nova Hierosolyma ex Praeceptis Decalogi*
Faith: *Doctrina Novae Hierosolymae de Fide*
Supplements: *Continuatio de Ultimo Judicio: Et de Mundo Spirituali*

© Copyright 2020 by the Swedenborg Foundation, Inc.
All rights reserved. No part of this publication may be reproduced or transmitted in any form or by any means, electronic or mechanical, including photocopying, recording, or any information storage or retrieval system, without prior permission from the publisher.

Printed in the United States of America

ISBN (library)   978-0-87785-503-3

The translations collected in this volume also appear separately in Portable editions without prefatory and introductory matter, annotations, tables of parallel passages, and indexes.
The Lord: ISBN 978-0-87785-412-8
Sacred Scripture: ISBN 978-0-87785-414-2 (under the title *Sacred Scripture / White Horse*)
Life: ISBN 978-0-87785-413-5 (under the title *Life / Faith*)
Faith: ISBN 978-0-87785-413-5 (under the title *Life / Faith*)
Supplements: ISBN 978-0-87785-416-6 (under the title *Last Judgment / Supplements*)

Library of Congress Cataloging-in-Publication Data

Names: Swedenborg, Emanuel, 1688–1772, author. | Dole, George F., translator. | Rose, Jonathan S., 1956–, writer of introduction.
Title: The shorter works of 1763 : The Lord, Sacred scripture, Life, Faith, Supplements / Emanuel Swedenborg ; translated from the Latin by George F. Dole ; with an introduction by Jonathan S. Rose ; and notes by Susanna Åkerman-Hjern, Glen M. Cooper, Lisa Hyatt Cooper, George F. Dole, R. Guy Erwin, David N. Gyllenhaal, Robert H. Kirven, Jonathan S. Rose, Fitzhugh L. Shaw, Stuart Shotwell, Richard Smoley, and Lee S. Woofenden.
Description: West Chester, Pennsylvania : Swedenborg Foundation, 2020 | Series: New century edition of the works of Emanuel Swedenborg | "Originally published in Latin (Amsterdam, 1763) as five separate works: The Lord: Doctrina Novae Hierosolymae de Domino; Sacred Scripture: Doctrina Novae Hierosolymae de Scriptura Sacra; Life: Doctrina Vitae pro Nova Hierosolyma ex Praeceptis Decalogi; Faith: Doctrina Novae Hierosolymae de Fide; Supplements: Continuatio de Ultimo Judicio: Et de Mundo Spirituali." | Includes bibliographical references and indexes. | Summary: "The four main short works in this volume by Swedish theologian Emanuel Swedenborg (1688–1772) form the basic foundation of his thought. They have commonly been published together in other editions under the collective title "The Four Doctrines." The Lord discusses the nature of the man known as Jesus Christ, his divine nature, and the meaning of his crucifixion. Sacred Scripture is about the Word, by which Swedenborg means the parts of the Bible that he feels reflect a deep spiritual teaching. Life discusses how we ought to live a religious life. Faith talks about faith as an acknowledgment of inner truth and the necessity of expressing such faith through good actions rather than simply holding beliefs. In addition to these short works, the volume includes a fifth work, which consists of two supplements to previous works by Swedenborg: a brief addition to Last Judgment and a longer addition to Heaven and Hell"— Provided by publisher.
Identifiers: LCCN 2019021705 | ISBN 9780877855033 (cloth)
Subjects: LCSH: New Jerusalem Church—Doctrines—Early works to 1800.
Classification: LCC BX8711.A7 D65 2020 | DDC 289/.4—dc23
LC record available at https://lccn.loc.gov/2019021705

Senior copy editor, Alicia L. Dole
Cover designed by Caroline Kline
Text designed by Joanna V. Hill
Ornaments from the first Latin editions, 1763
Indexes by Alicia L. Dole, Sarah Dole, Skye Kerr Levy, and Chara Smith
Typesetting by Alicia L. Dole and Sarah Dole; charts by Alicia L. Dole

For information about the New Century Edition of the Works of Emanuel Swedenborg, contact the Swedenborg Foundation, 320 North Church Street, West Chester, PA 19380 U.S.A.
Telephone: (610) 430-3222 • Web: www.swedenborg.com • E-mail: info@swedenborg.com

Contents

Translator's Preface, by George F. Dole	1
Works Cited in the Translator's Preface	7
A Note on Editions and Translations, by Jonathan S. Rose and Stuart Shotwell	9
Selected Works Cited in the Note on Editions and Translations	13
Seeking Greater Engagement: Swedenborg's Shorter Works of 1763, by Jonathan S. Rose	15
Appendix 1: A Brief Summary of Swedenborg's Methods of Distribution	93
Appendix 2: Analysis of References to *Secrets of Heaven* in Swedenborg's Works between 1758 and 1763	97
Appendix 3: Internal Evidence for the Publication and Presentation Order of the Shorter Works of 1763	101
Appendix 4: Swedish Bishops, 1760–1772	103
Works Cited in the Introduction	104
Short Titles and Other Conventions Used in This Work	109

The Lord

Preface		123
[1]	§§1–7 / The Entire Sacred Scripture Is about the Lord, and the Lord Is the Word	125
[2]	§§8–11 / To Say That the Lord Fulfilled All of the Law Is to Say That He Fulfilled All of the Word	141
[3]	§§12–14 / The Lord Came into the World to Subdue the Hells and to Glorify His Human Nature; the Suffering on the Cross Was the Last Battle by Which He Completely Defeated the Hells and Completely Glorified His Human Nature	146
[4]	§§15–17 / The Lord Did Not Take Away Our Sins by His Suffering on the Cross, but He Did Carry Them	152
[5]	§18 / The Imputation of the Lord's Merit Is Nothing More nor Less Than the Forgiveness of Sins That Follows upon Repentance	158

[6]	§§19–28 / The Lord as the Divine-Human One Is Called "The Son of God" and as the Word Is Called "The Son of Humanity"	161
[7]	§§29–36 / The Lord Made His Human Nature Divine out of the Divine Nature within Himself, and in This Way Became One with the Father	170
[8]	§§37–44 / The Lord Is God Himself, the Source and Subject of the Word	188
[9]	§45 / God Is One, and the Lord Is God	198
[10]	§§46–54 / The Holy Spirit Is the Divine Nature That Emanates from the Lord and Is the Lord Himself	199
[11]	§§55–61 / The Athanasian Statement of Faith Agrees with the Truth, Provided That We Understand It to Be Referring Not to "a Trinity of Persons" but to "a Trinity within One Person," Who Is the Lord	212
[12]	§§62–65 / The New Jerusalem in the Book of Revelation Means a New Church	219

Sacred Scripture

[1]	§§1–4 / Sacred Scripture, or the Word, Is Divine Truth Itself	229
[2]	§§4–26 / There Is a Spiritual Meaning in the Word, Which Has Been Unknown until Now	232
[3]	§§27–36 / The Literal Meaning of the Word Is the Foundation, the Container, and the Support of Its Spiritual and Heavenly Meanings	253
[4]	§§37–49 / Divine Truth, in All Its Fullness, Holiness, and Power, Is Present in the Literal Meaning of the Word	258
[5]	§§50–61 / The Church's Body of Teaching Is to Be Drawn from the Literal Meaning of the Word and Is to Be Supported by It	267
[6]	§§62–69 / By Means of the Literal Meaning of the Word We Unite with the Lord and Form a Companionship with Angels	275
[7]	§§70–75 / The Word Is in All the Heavens and Is the Source of Angelic Wisdom	279
[8]	§§76–79 / The Existence of the Church Rests on the Word, and Its Quality Depends on the Quality of Its Understanding of the Word	281

[9]	§§80–90 / There Is a Marriage of the Lord and the Church in the Details of the Word and a Consequent Marriage of Goodness and Truth	285
[10]	§§91–97 / It Is Possible to Wrench Heretical Ideas from the Literal Meaning of the Word, but What Is Damning Is to Convince Ourselves [That They Are True]	294
[11]	§§98–100 / The Lord Came into the World to Fulfill Everything in the Word and So to Become Divine Truth or the Word Even on the Outermost Level	300
[12]	§§101–103 / Before the Word That We Have in the World Today, There Was a Word That Has Been Lost	302
[13]	§§104–113 / By Means of the Word, There Is Light Even for People Who Are outside the Church and Do Not Have the Word	305
[14]	§§114–118 / If There Were No Word, No One Would Know about God, Heaven and Hell, Life after Death, and Least of All, about the Lord	309

Life

[1]	§§1–8 / Religion Is All about How We Live, and the Religious Way to Live Is to Do Good	315
[2]	§§9–17 / No One Can Do Anything Genuinely Good on His or Her Own	321
[3]	§§18–31 / To the Extent That We Turn Our Backs on Evil Deeds Because They Are Sins, the Good Deeds We Do Come Not from Ourselves but from the Lord	325
[4]	§§32–41 / To the Extent That We Turn Our Backs on Evils Because They Are Sins, We Love What Is True	332
[5]	§§42–52 / To the Extent That We Turn Our Backs on Evils Because They Are Sins, We Have Faith and Are Spiritual	335
[6]	§§53–61 / The Ten Commandments Tell Us Which Evils Are Sins	339
[7]	§§62–66 / All Kinds of Murder, Adultery, Theft, and False Witness, Together with Urges toward Them, Are Evils on Which We Must Turn Our Backs Because They Are Sins	344
[8]	§§67–73 / To the Extent That We Turn Our Backs on All Kinds of Killing Because They Are Sins, We Have Love for Our Neighbor	347

[9]	§§74–79 / To the Extent That We Turn Our Backs on All Kinds of Adultery Because They Are Sins, We Love Chastity	350
[10]	§§80–86 / To the Extent That We Turn Our Backs on All Kinds of Theft Because They Are Sins, We Love Honesty	353
[11]	§§87–91 / To the Extent That We Turn Our Backs on All Kinds of False Witness Because They Are Sins, We Love Truth	357
[12]	§§92–100 / The Only Way to Abstain from Sinful Evils So Thoroughly That We Develop an Inner Aversion to Them Is to Do Battle against Them	359
[13]	§§101–107 / We Need to Abstain from Sinful Evils and Fight against Them As Though We Were Doing So on Our Own	362
[14]	§§108–114 / If We Turn Our Backs on Evils for Any Other Reason Than That They Are Sins, We Are Not Turning Our Backs on Them but Are Simply Making Sure They Are Not Visible in the Eyes of the World	365

Faith

[1]	§§1–12 / Faith Is an Inner Recognition of Truth	371
[2]	§§13–24 / The "Inner Recognition of Truth" That Is Faith Is Found Only in People Who Are Devoted to Caring	374
[3]	§§25–33 / Our Knowledge of What Is True and Good Does Not Become Faith until We Are Engaged in Caring. Once We Have a Faith That Is Born of Caring, Though, That Knowledge Becomes a Resource That Gives Form to Our Faith	379
[4]	§§34–37 / The [True] Christian Faith in One All-Encompassing View	382
[5]	§§38–43 / The Present-Day Faith in One All-Encompassing View	383
[6]	§§44–48 / The Nature of a Faith Divorced from Caring	386
[7]	§§49–54 / The Philistines Mentioned in the Word Represent People Devoted to a Faith Divorced from Caring	388
[8]	§§55–60 / The Dragon Mentioned in the Book of Revelation Symbolizes People Devoted to a Faith Divorced from Caring	391
[9]	§§61–68 / The Goats Mentioned in Daniel and Matthew Symbolize People Devoted to a Faith Divorced from Caring	395
[10]	§§69–72 / A Faith Divorced from Caring Destroys the Church and Everything It Stands For	400

Supplements

Supplement on the Last Judgment

[1]	§§1–7 / The Last Judgment Has Taken Place	405
[2]	§§8–13 / The State of the World and the Church before and after the Last Judgment	408
[3]	§§14–31 / The Last Judgment on Protestants	412

Supplement on the Spiritual World

[4]	§§32–38 / The Spiritual World	419
[5]	§§39–47 / The British in the Spiritual World	421
[6]	§§48–55 / The Dutch in the Spiritual World	425
[7]	§§56–60 / Roman Catholics in the Spiritual World	429
[8]	§§61–67 / The Catholic Saints in the Spiritual World	431
[9]	§§68–72 / Muslims and Muhammad in the Spiritual World	434
[10]	§§73–78 / Africans, and People of Other Religions, in the Spiritual World	436
[11]	§§79–82 / Jews in the Spiritual World	439
[12]	§§83–85 / Quakers in the Spiritual World	441
[13]	§§86–90 / Moravians in the Spiritual World	442

Notes and Indexes

Notes	447
Appendix: The Reference of the Word *Canaan* in the Bible and in Swedenborg's Theology, by Lee S. Woofenden	529
Works Cited in the Notes	531
Index to Preface, Introduction, and Notes	541
Index to Scriptural Passages in the Shorter Works of 1763	567
Table of Parallel Passages	587
Index to the Shorter Works of 1763	593
Biographical Note	629

Translator's Preface

Outline

   I. *The Lord, Sacred Scripture, Life,* and *Faith*

  II. *Supplements*

 III. Problematic Material

 IV. Acknowledgments

THE present volume consists of five works. All were published by Swedenborg in 1763; they are "the shorter works" of that year in contrast to Swedenborg's far longer 1763 publication, *Divine Love and Wisdom*.[1] They are best considered under two heads: (I) *The Lord, Sacred Scripture, Life,* and *Faith;* and (II) *Supplements*.

I. *The Lord, Sacred Scripture, Life,* and *Faith*

In 1766 Swedenborg looked back on the first four works presented here and offered the following overview:

> There are four sets of teachings that are now in print—one on the Lord, the second on Sacred Scripture, the third on living by the commandments of the Decalogue, and the fourth on faith—which may establish the following: that the Word has now been opened and that it bears witness to the fact that the Lord alone is God of heaven and

---

1. In the first editions, *Divine Love and Wisdom* runs to 151 pages, *The Lord* to 64, *Sacred Scripture* to 54, *Life* to 36, and *Faith* to 23. It should be noted that in a sense *Sacred Scripture* has two dates of publication, since the entire work recurs in an edited version as the fourth chapter (§§189–276) of Swedenborg's final published work, *True Christianity*.

I

earth, that we are to live by his commandments, and that the faith of the present day needs to be dismissed.²

The Latin term here translated "sets of teachings" is *doctrinae,* and thus the passage just quoted encouraged later editors and publishers to apply the title The Four Doctrines to these works, though they were never formally so designated by Swedenborg.³

The first three "sets of teachings"—on the Lord, Scripture, and how we should live—deal with what are identified in *Divine Providence* 259:3 as the "three essential principles of the church: belief in the divine nature of the Lord, belief in the holiness of the Word, and the [way of] life that we call 'charity.'"

Faith, the fourth and shortest of these "Four Doctrines," effectively denies faith the status of a *separate* essential principle of the church, which Swedenborg saw as an error in existing Christian doctrine. Faith must be accompanied by the performance of caring acts: as Swedenborg has already told us in *Life,* faith must exist in a union with the way we live (*Life* 44), because "believing in the Lord is not simply thinking that he exists but is also doing what he says" (*Life* 48). Chapters 4 and 5 of *Faith* (§§34–43) contrast an overview of "the [true] Christian faith" with an overview of "the present-day faith," much to the detriment of the latter; and subsequent chapters equate people devoted to a faith devoid of caring with the Philistines, the goats of Daniel and Matthew, and the dragon of Revelation in the Bible.⁴ All this is summed up in the first sentence of the work's closing chapter:

> A faith divorced from caring is no faith at all, because caring is the life of faith, its soul, its essence; and where there is no faith because there is no caring, there is no church. (*Faith* 69)

In effect, then, *Faith* constitutes a negative epilogue to the affirmatives of the previous three treatises.

All four teachings are based on Scripture, but the methodology does not, as in common text-proofing practice, place heavy emphasis on a few

---

2. *Revelation Unveiled* 668. This and the other translations in this preface are by George F. Dole.

3. Another mention, in *Draft of "The Lord"* (= Swedenborg 1994–1997) §2, refers to them as "four treatises" (the Latin in that case is *4 tractatibus*).

4. For discussion of these symbols, see the following notes: on Philistines, page 471 note 148; on goats, page 515 note 455; on the dragon, page 510 note 420.

selected verses. Rather, the approach is encyclopedic. Section 4 of *The Lord* cites one hundred and one passages on "the day of the Lord," followed by twenty-one on the Coming of the Lord in §6 and thirty-two on the glorification in §32.[5] Section 2 of *Life* contains thirty-nine passages on the general theme of keeping the Lord's commandments, and the remainder of the work is organized around the Ten Commandments.

It is noteworthy, given Swedenborg's usual focus on inner meaning, that these passages are to be understood literally.[6] Even in *Sacred Scripture,* where the intent is to demonstrate the presence and use of spiritual meaning in the Bible, chapters 3–6 (§§27–69) insist on the fundamental importance of the literal meaning. Thus these four works are clearly addressed to readers who take the Bible seriously and who understand it literally. We might well read *Sacred Scripture* first and regard *The Lord* and *Life* as carrying out the policy that it advocates—drawing the church's teachings from the literal meaning of the Word (§53).

II. *Supplements*

In a sense, we could say that the present volume contains not five works but six. The title *Supplements* is subdivided into two: one supplement on the Last Judgment and one on the spiritual world.

The *Supplement on the Last Judgment* can be understood as filling a lacuna in Swedenborg's 1758 work on the Last Judgment, which focuses on the judgment of Roman Catholicism and largely ignores the judgment of Protestants.[7] The supplement on the Last Judgment does seem to follow quite naturally on the critique of "faith alone" that is central to *Faith*.

It begins with a half-page title, embellished with ornaments and with the title itself in very large type. Following §31, there is a new half-page title, *Supplement on the Spiritual World,* which typographically quite precisely parallels the first half-page title, *Supplement on the Last Judgment,*

---

5. On the concept of "glorification," see page 449 note 8.

6. Note that in *Revelation Unveiled* the wall of the holy city is said to represent the Word in its literal meaning, representing the fact that the literal sense contains the entire theology of the new church (§§898, 902, 914).

7. This focus accords with the complete main title of the book, which is *The Last Judgment and Babylon Destroyed.* The Babylon of the Book of Revelation has often been interpreted as a symbol for the Roman Catholic Church; see page 471 note 148.

ornaments and all, but continues with §§32–90. It begins by calling attention to the previously published *Heaven and Hell* (1758), and describes the condition of the British, the Dutch, popes, Catholic saints, Muslims and Muhammad, Africans and other non-Christians, Jews, Quakers, and Moravians in the spiritual world following their judgment. The unstated premise of these portraits is the folly of any religion's claim to be in sole possession of absolute truth, and a pervasive theme is the presence of both heavenly and hellish individuals in every religion. It is, then, a continuation of *Last Judgment*'s postmillennial theme, but it brings that theme down to earth, or more properly, grounds its exposition in the spiritual world.

All of these works are clearly addressed to a biblically literate, Christian readership. In the eighteenth century, though, many of the most creative minds saw Christianity as a major obstacle to the quest for understanding; and at times it must have seemed that the churches were doing all they could to foster that impression, citing biblical authority against the claims of scientific empiricism.

For Swedenborg, the Bible and empiricism were not at odds. In his extensive paranormal life, he remained the empiricist;[8] and the other work of 1763, *Divine Love and Wisdom,* immediately appeals to the common experience of love and goes on to build an empirical case for the same "essential principles" that in the shorter works have just been argued on biblical grounds. It may require a stretch of the mind to keep the contents of *Divine Love and Wisdom* in mind while reading *The Lord,* and vice versa; but they were evidently written by someone whose mind stretched that far.

III. Problematic Material

With remarkable consistency, Swedenborg's theological works are composed in gender-neutral Latin.[9] Those few passages where usage in this respect is markedly different from our own are significant as exceptions that point up the rule rather than as evidence to the contrary.

---

8. Embedded in Swedenborg's massive exegetical work *The Old Testament Explained* (traditionally titled *The Word Explained*), written between 1745 and 1747 but published only posthumously, one can read an "autobiographical subtext" following a strenuous dialog between Swedenborg's beloved childhood faith and his impressive scientific empiricism, leading to a surprising and paradoxical resolution. See my forthcoming work on this topic.

9. With apologies to the reader, the discussion of problematic material here repeats the treatment in the translator's preface to *The Shorter Works of 1758*.

Gender-neutral language is one thing, however, and gender-neutral thinking is another. Swedenborg's understanding of the universe is expressed in conceptual pairings—for example, understanding and will, faith and love, truth and goodness—and male and female align with these pairings in a complex manner.[10] To a twenty-first-century reader coming "cold" to his theology, the alignments taken by masculine and feminine principles may at first seem stereotypically patriarchal. But Swedenborg was not a patriarchalist. In fact, the foremost of his strictures on relations between the sexes is that neither party should dominate the other (for example, *Heaven and Hell* 380:1–2; *Marriage Love* 248). To the new reader, then, one can only make a plea that Swedenborg's distinctions between the sexes stem from something better considered and more complex than an unthinking adherence to classic gender roles (though Swedenborg himself on rare occasions appears to make exactly such classic statements). Patience in tracing the pattern of his thought on these matters will reward the reader with a stimulating perspective unlike that of either the eighteenth century or the reader's own times.

Further, Swedenborg's era did not concern itself with political correctness in speech or writing. Instead, it highly valued polemics. It did not shrink from what we would find blunt and even offensive statements of opinion about particular groups, especially—as in Swedenborg's case—when there was a point to be made about something those groups symbolized to the writer. In the course of his exposition of theology in the shorter works of 1763, Swedenborg finds cause to denigrate in their various turns Jews, Muslims, and Christians of various stamps; not to mention the nonreligious. Thus one will find him insisting that the religion of Muslims is not an "inward" one (*Supplements* 71) and that "from very early on, Quakers started straying more and more into evil practices" (*Supplements* 84). But these groups are important to Swedenborg's argument only insofar as they symbolize, to his way of thinking, certain religious attitudes; they are not objects of personal hatred. Never, for example, does he call for violence against any group or individual. In his works he repeatedly states

---

10. Contrast, for example, *Marriage Love* 33, 91, 160, 187, 218:2, 296:1, where women are said to align with volition and love, while men are said to align with intellect and wisdom, with *True Christianity* 37:3, 41:3, where these alignments are reversed. In yet another passage these alignments are said to be different in one part of heaven than in another (*Secrets of Heaven* 8994:4). See also, and especially, *Marriage Love* 155B, in which some wives in heaven make it very clear to Swedenborg that they know a great deal that he is incapable of appreciating.

that any effort to coerce others into adopting particular religious beliefs is doomed to failure.

These flights of symbolic exposition have to be seen in the larger context of Swedenborg's works, where he does address salvation at the personal level. He there declares in strong terms, and without exception, that

- Every human being is the neighbor who is to be loved, and we are not to despise anyone (*True Christianity* 406–411).
- All people are created and predestined for heaven, and none for hell (*Divine Providence* 329–330).
- A multiplicity of religions is absolutely necessary (*Divine Providence* 326:10).
- All the world's religions include rules for life that when followed have the power to bring salvation to their adherents (*Divine Providence* 253–254).

These points, it should be noted, were striking departures from the general Christian perspective of Swedenborg's time. On this matter, then, not one but three pleas need to be made to the reader: "Context, context, context."

IV. Acknowledgments

The present translations were handed to their critical readers in essentially first draft form, and the meticulous and sympathetic attention given them by Chara Cooper Daum has saved me from any number of embarrassing moments. The supportive and discerning spirit of the entire Editorial Committee has been exemplary and, if academic rumors are correct, virtually unprecedented. I have felt very much in harness with Lisa Hyatt Cooper as she proceeds year after year through *Secrets of Heaven,* and as Series Editor Jonathan Rose plots the course (with time out for his own translating) and Managing Editor Stuart Shotwell holds the reins.

Over the years, the New Century Edition has been supported by the Asplundh, Brickman, Elder, Glencairn, Iungerich, and Rotch Foundations, and by the many individuals who have given to the Swedenborg Foundation. Without them, the New Century Edition would not be possible.

GEORGE F. DOLE
Bath, Maine
May 2020

Works Cited in the Translator's Preface

Swedenborg, Emanuel. 1927–1951. *The Word of the Old Testament Explained.* Translated and edited by Alfred Acton. 10 vols. Bryn Athyn, Pa.: Academy of the New Church.

———. 1994–1997. *Concerning the Lord and Concerning the Holy Spirit.* Translated by Samuel Worcester and revised by John C. Ager. In vol. 6 of *Apocalypse Explained,* edited by William Ross Woofenden. West Chester, Pa.: Swedenborg Foundation.

A Note on Editions and Translations

JONATHAN S. ROSE
and
STUART SHOTWELL

THE present edition of *The Shorter Works of 1763* is based on the first printed Latin editions of the five works included.[1] Each was issued separately in Amsterdam sometime after the beginning of June 1763,[2] most likely in the order in which they are printed here.[3] The following titles were republished in facsimile by the Swedenborg Institut of Basel, Switzerland: *The Lord* (1959), *Sacred Scripture* (1960), *Life* (1960), and *Faith* (1961).

The second Latin editions of the same four works, edited by Ludwig Hofaker and Gustav Werner, were published by Guttenburg in Tübingen in 1834–1835 as sections 1–4 of the series *Scripta Novae Domini Ecclesiae* (Writings of the Lord's New Church); a third Latin edition of the same, edited by Samuel H. Worcester, was published jointly by the American Swedenborg Printing and Publishing Society in New York and the Swedenborg Society, London, in 1889 under the title *Quatuor Doctrinae* (Four Doctrines); a fourth Latin edition, edited by N. Bruce Rogers, was

---

1. The information in this sketch of publication histories is drawn from Hyde 1906, Wainscot 1967, and Ryder forthcoming; additional research was conducted in the Swedenborg Library, Bryn Athyn, Pennsylvania, with the invaluable assistance of its director, Carol Traveny, and director of Swedenborgiana, Carroll Odhner.

2. Swedenborg, who oversaw the printing of his theological works, did not leave Stockholm for Amsterdam until early June 1763.

3. The order of the works in this volume corresponds to the order found in Swedenborg's own lists. The works were evidently composed and very likely printed in the same sequence. For a summary of the evidence concerning the order in which they were published, see appendix 3 of the introduction, pages 101–102; see also Hyde 1906, 366 item 1717. It should be noted that this order also matches the listing of the three key doctrines of Swedenborg's theology in *Divine Providence* 259:3: see the translator's preface in this volume, page 2.

published by the Academy of the New Church, Bryn Athyn, Pennsylvania, in 2016, again under the title *Quatuor Doctrinae*. And an edition with Latin and English on facing pages, edited and translated by John Elliott, is forthcoming from the Swedenborg Society.

Because *The Lord* was grouped by Swedenborg himself with *Sacred Scripture, Life,* and *Faith* under the informal title "the four teachings" (*Revelation Unveiled* 668), these four works have often been published together. Thus the publication history of *Sacred Scripture, Life,* and *Faith* closely follows that of *The Lord,* and it seems best to cite the history of *The Lord* as representative of all four works, rather than to repeat four times over the same information with minor variations.

The first English translation of *The Lord* of which we have record was that of Peter Provo, printed by Robert Hindmarsh in London in 1784. With it began a cycle of revising and republishing the work that is typical of English editions of Swedenborg.[4] Provo's translation was revised and reissued five times until a new translation was made by Charles Augustus Tulk and published in London in 1812.[5] Thereafter the work was reissued over sixty-five times, sometimes with revisions, but more often simply as a reprint of another edition. The known revisions include those of Tilly B. Hayward (1833); Hayward and John Worcester (1868); Samuel H. Worcester (1880); John C. Ager, Charles H. Mann, and Samuel S. Seward (1880); Arthur H. Searle (1896); and John Faulkner Potts (1904). The first American edition was a reprint of a 1791 revision of Provo's translation, issued in Boston in 1795 by the printer Thomas Hall. The new and original translations include those of George Harrison (1860), William C. Dick (1954), and N. Bruce Rogers (2014). It has also been translated into Czech, Danish, Dutch, French, German, Hungarian, Ilokano, Japanese, Korean, Latvian, Portuguese, Russian, Spanish, Swedish, Welsh, and Zulu. English versions were issued in Braille in 1928, 1954, and 1967.

---

4. As indicated in the note on editions and translations in *The Shorter Works of 1758,* during the eighteenth and nineteenth centuries and into the first half of the twentieth century, publishers of Swedenborg's works often referred to what we would now call a "reprint" as a new "edition," and what we might now call a light "revision" as a fresh "translation." In fact, it seems to have been the general practice that a "translator" in this era would base his or her text on some earlier published version, presumably for expedience and to avoid introducing new errors. For an example of the changes inserted in one such "translation," see *The Shorter Works of 1758* (= Swedenborg [1758] 2018), pages 24–25 note 5.

5. Tulk, a friend of the poet Samuel Taylor Coleridge, supplied him with a copy.

This general model having been given, a few divergences in the early publication history of *Sacred Scripture, Life,* and *Faith* remain to be noted. *Sacred Scripture* and *Life* were revised by Samuel M. Warren in 1862 and 1864, respectively. At around the same time, J. C. Rowlatt of the University of Cambridge, a presbyter of the Church of England, left a lively manuscript translation of *Sacred Scripture* among his papers at the time of his death, which others then published in 1863; he had dedicated the translation to the archbishops, bishops, presbyters, and deacons in the Church of England, which seems fitting, given the way Swedenborg himself promoted this title (see the introduction, pages 48–50; see also pages 57–65, 93–96). The work *Life* is remarkable for having been translated into English for the first time by William Cookworthy, who had actually met Swedenborg;[6] this version was published in the year of Swedenborg's death, 1772. This was followed in 1786 by a rendering by the great British Swedenborgian translator John Clowes. Although Clowes translated a considerable amount of Swedenborg's corpus, *Life* was to be the only one of the "Four Doctrines" to which he set his hand. *Faith* was not published outside of Latin until 1792; another of the early British Swedenborgians, William Cowherd, was the translator.

Sacred Scripture was translated into most of the languages into which *The Lord* was translated, but was also rendered in Sotho; and both *Sacred Scripture* and *Life* were translated into Italian. *Life* was also translated into Esperanto, Finnish, Gujarati, and Tamil.

The history of *Supplements* is both less complicated and less repetitious than its four predecessors. The second Latin edition, edited by J.F.I. Tafel, was published in Tübingen by Verlagsexpedition in 1846. It had the honor, unusual for the time, of being printed simultaneously in two sizes: an octavo and a quarto, the latter on better paper. A third Latin edition, edited by Samuel H. Worcester, was published jointly by the American Swedenborg Printing and Publishing Society in New York and the Swedenborg Society, London, in 1889.

The first translation into English was that of Robert Hindmarsh; it was printed by Hindmarsh himself in London in 1791. Thereafter the work was issued over forty times in various forms—by itself, with *Last Judgment,* and in collections of minor or miscellaneous works. The major revisions (sometimes labeled translations) were undertaken by James John Garth Wilkinson (1839), Jonathan Bayley (1875), John Worcester (1899),

---

6. For very brief accounts of the meeting, see Tafel 1877, 539, 1061.

and John Whitehead (1913). The first American edition was a reprint of a London edition of Hindmarsh's revision of his own translation; it was published in Boston in 1828 by Hilliard, Gray, Little, and Wilkins, and Adonis Howard. New and original translations by P. H. Johnson (1951), Doris H. Harley (1961), and John Chadwick (1975) were published in London by the Swedenborg Society.

Supplements has also been translated into Czech, Danish, Dutch, French, German, Korean, Latvian, Portuguese, Russian, Spanish, and Swedish.

We are grateful to the late Norman Ryder for his massive bibliography of Swedenborg's works, three volumes of which have appeared and others of which are forthcoming; and to the Swedenborg Society, for granting us an advance glimpse of the relevant material in Ryder's volume 4, which was helpful to us in numerous ways as we assembled this material.

Selected Works Cited in the Note on Editions and Translations

Hyde, James. 1906. *A Bibliography of the Works of Emanuel Swedenborg, Original and Translated.* London: Swedenborg Society.

Ryder, Norman. Forthcoming. *A Descriptive Bibliography of the Works of Emanuel Swedenborg (1688–1772).* Vol. 4. London: Swedenborg Society.

Swedenborg, Emanuel. [1758] 2018. *The Shorter Works of 1758.* Translated by George F. Dole and Jonathan S. Rose. West Chester, Pa.: Swedenborg Foundation.

Tafel, R. L. 1877. *Documents Concerning the Life and Character of Emanuel Swedenborg.* Vol. 2, parts 1 and 2. London: Swedenborg Society.

Wainscot, A. Stanley, comp. 1967. *List of Additions to the Bibliography [of the Works of Emanuel Swedenborg, Original and Translated, by the Rev. James Hyde] since Its Publication in 1906.* London: [Swedenborg Society]. Mimeographed.

Seeking Greater Engagement

Swedenborg's Shorter Works of 1763

JONATHAN S. ROSE

Outline

I. The Five Works in This Volume
    a. The Identity and Sequence of "The Four Sets of Teachings"
    b. The Self-Declared Purpose of "The Four Sets of Teachings"
    c. *The Lord*
    d. *Sacred Scripture*
    e. *Life*
    f. *Faith*
    g. *Supplements*

II. Key Elements of Context before 1758
    a. Swedenborg's Drive to Publish
    b. Swedenborg's Role in the Swedish Government
    c. An Initial Attempt at Engagement: *Secrets of Heaven*
    d. Swedenborg's Efforts to Preserve His Anonymity
    e. The Unsatisfactory Response to *Secrets of Heaven*

III. Key Elements of Context in the Years 1758–1763
    a. Targeting Leaders of the British Clergy and Nobility
    b. The Unsatisfactory Response to the Works of 1758
    c. The Impact of Years of War and Inflation
    d. The Five-Year Pause in Swedenborg's Theological Publishing
    e. Targeting Leaders of the Swedish Clergy and Nobility
    f. Swedenborg's Seven Memorials
    g. The Distribution to Various Leaders
    h. Reviews and Notices of the Works of 1758 and *Secrets of Heaven*

IV. Signs of Further Experimentation and Changes in Approach
   a. A Change in the Size of Publications
   b. A Change in the Place of Publication
   c. The Sudden Halt to *Revelation Explained*
   d. The Decline in Swedenborg's References to His Magnum Opus
   e. Separate Approaches for Clergy and Nobility

V. Contemporary Responses to the Shorter Works of 1763
   a. Five Contemporary Reviews and a Notice of the Shorter Works of 1763
   b. Response from the Swedish Royal House

VI. Conclusion

Appendix 1: A Brief Summary of Swedenborg's Methods of Distribution

Appendix 2: Analysis of References to *Secrets of Heaven* in Swedenborg's Works between 1758 and 1763

Appendix 3: Internal Evidence for the Publication and Presentation Order of the Shorter Works of 1763

Appendix 4: Swedish Bishops, 1760–1772

Works Cited in the Introduction

I am grateful for the conversations I was able to have with the following scholars and friends who contributed insights for this introduction: George F. Dole, John E. Elliott, Frank S. Rose, Jane Williams-Hogan, James F. Lawrence, Stuart Shotwell, Lisa Hyatt Cooper, Morgan L. Beard, Kristin King, Guus Janssens, Stephen McNeilly, Chelsea R. Odhner, and Christopher Dunn. I also enjoyed and benefited from input from members of the New Century Edition editorial committee not already listed above: Wendy Closterman, Chara O. Smith, and Jeremy F. Simons. Heartfelt thanks for their kindness and expert help go to Maria Asp at the Royal Swedish Academy of Sciences; Jan Mispelaere and Olof Holm at the Swedish National Archives; Evan Boyd at the Charles Porterfield Krauth Branch of the United Lutheran Seminary Library; and Carol Traveny, Carroll Odhner, and other staff at the Swedenborg Library in Bryn Athyn, Pennsylvania. I am thankful to Göran Appelgren for his help with Swedish translations and to Alain Nicolier for his help with French. And in writing this introduction I felt heavily indebted to scholars who are no longer with us, but whose names and works remain.

IN 1763, Emanuel Swedenborg[1] (1688–1772), at seventy-five years old, was not content to rest on a lifetime of considerable achievement. Decades earlier he had become a respected scientist and philosopher, accomplished in a number of fields and well known in his native Sweden and across Europe. He could therefore have justified some leisure and repose toward the end of his long day in this world. But when he was in his midfifties, longings that he had had since childhood for a deeper understanding of humankind and its relationship to the physical and spiritual worlds had begun to be fulfilled in new ways. He reports that he had a vision of Jesus Christ and was given a lasting consciousness of the afterlife while he was still alive and functioning in this world. This was a new, dynamic field for his research and exploration and one to which he devoted himself with a passion.

Over the course of the two decades leading up to 1763, he wrote and published many books about his extraordinary experiences and new insights, yet it was difficult for him to find an audience. Entrenched ideas, age-old dogmas, distraction, apathy, and even some vigorous opposition squelched interest in what he had to say. He had ambitious goals and a visionary's hope for the future of humankind; but how could he foster a heaven on earth if he failed to engage with anyone here? Thus the shorter works that he published in 1763 came at a turning point in his theological publishing, after some disappointment with earlier results. In a number of respects, these works constitute a new approach and a new effort to increase the world's engagement with his theology.

1. The Five Works in This Volume

Swedenborg's theological publications generally appeared at intervals of a year or less. However, in the middle of the span of his theological publishing, which occurred between 1749 and 1771, there were four consecutive calendar years in which he produced no theological work in print: 1759, 1760, 1761, and 1762. In fact, from the point at which he left off in the fall of 1758 to the point at which he resumed in the fall of 1763, almost five years elapsed in which he issued no new books.

---

1. Throughout this introduction the author will be referred to as "Swedenborg," even though that was not his name for the first thirty-one years of his life. His name at birth was Emanuel Swedberg (also spelled Svedberg) and remained so until May 23, 1719, when his family was ennobled and nonclerical members of the family were given the last name Swedenborg (also spelled Svedenborg).

After this long gap, the first five works that were published were those contained in this volume: *The Lord, Sacred Scripture, Life, Faith,* and *Supplements.* These are quite slender works—in fact, these five are among the eight shortest theological works he published (see figure 1).

Work	Pages	Date
Secrets of Heaven	4,563	1749–1756
Heaven and Hell	272	1758
New Jerusalem	156	1758
Last Judgment	55	1758
White Horse	23	1758
Other Planets	72	1758
[Five-year interval]		
The Lord	64	1763
Sacred Scripture	54	1763
Life	36	1763
Faith	23	1763
Supplements	28	1763
Divine Love and Wisdom	151	1763
Divine Providence	214	1764
Revelation Unveiled	629	1766
Marriage Love	328	1768
Survey	67	1769
Soul-Body Interaction	23	1769
True Christianity	542	1771

Figure 1. Swedenborg's theological works, their lengths in pages, and their years of publication

Despite their small size, the topics the first four works address are central to Christianity—the nature of Jesus' divinity, the nature of the Bible, how we are to live, and the nature of faith. The fifth, *Supplements,* is a collection of specifics about life after death; it contains sequels to two works about the spiritual world published in 1758, *Last Judgment* and *Heaven and Hell.*

The theological works that were published before the five-year interval and those that came after it differ to such an extent as to represent two distinct phases. As figure 1 shows and we will see further below, there are twice as many titles in the second phase, but the works tend to be smaller. Harder to quantify, but also noticeable, are the changes in the tone and approach of the second phase. The core theological message remains strikingly consistent throughout, but the presentation becomes more pointed. These five fallow years, then, appear to have represented something much more significant than a long break.

The author apparently thought of the first four of these new works as a kind of subset in themselves—and the creation of such a subset within his works was itself an innovation in Swedenborg's published theological corpus.

a. The Identity and Sequence of "the Four Sets of Teachings"

As George F. Dole points out in his preface to this volume, Swedenborg later referred to *The Lord, Sacred Scripture, Life,* and *Faith* as a collective whole:

> There are four sets of teachings that are now in print—one on the Lord, the second on Sacred Scripture, the third on living by the Ten Commandments, and the fourth on faith. . . .[2]

The collective term here translated "the Four Sets of Teachings" is *Quattuor Doctrinae;* it has traditionally been translated "the Four Doctrines." Although all of Swedenborg's published theological works after the first, *Secrets of Heaven,* refer repeatedly to one another,[3] they never refer to another subset.

A special affinity between these four books is suggested as well by the similarity of their titles: each indicates that these are *teachings for the New Jerusalem:*

> *Teachings for the New Jerusalem on the Lord*
> *Teachings for the New Jerusalem on Sacred Scripture*

---

2. *Revelation Unveiled* 668:1; JSR's translation. Unless otherwise indicated, in this essay the quotations from the theological works published by Swedenborg are drawn from the translations of the New Century Edition. The initials of the author of this introduction indicate his original translations of source material.

3. On this point, see Rose 2013, 98–111, especially figure E on page 103 and figure F on page 105.

Teachings about Life for the New Jerusalem: Drawn from the Ten Commandments

Teachings for the New Jerusalem on Faith

Swedenborg's description of the set of four teachings just quoted on page 19 also confirms that the sequence he intended for them is *The Lord, Sacred Scripture, Life,* and *Faith.* This sequence is also corroborated in a passage in *Spiritual Experiences,* the lengthy manuscript in which Swedenborg recorded events he witnessed in the other world. Here he records a conversation in the afterlife with a former British bishop, of whom we will hear more on pages 53–54 below:

> A bishop wanted to see me with the intention of refuting the things I had written about the nature of faith when it is separated [from caring]. When we met, he told me that people in Britain were going to be receptive to the first work, which concerns the Lord, including its point that the New Jerusalem means a new church. They were also going to accept the second work, which concerns the sanctity of the Word,[4] and the third as well, which contains teachings regarding life. But they would utterly reject the fourth work, which concerns faith.[5]

This is clearly an allusion to the four sets of teachings, and again they are referred to in the order *The Lord, Sacred Scripture, Life,* and *Faith.*

In fact, in the case of all five of the shorter works of 1763, the precise ways in which they refer to each other, even down to the tense of verbs and the presence or absence of references to specific section numbers, entirely bear out that they were published, and are consistently presented, in the order *The Lord, Sacred Scripture, Life, Faith,* and *Supplements.*[6] By contrast, the five works of 1758 were published in one order *(Other Planets, Heaven and Hell, Last Judgment, New Jerusalem, White Horse)* but are consistently listed by the author in another *(Heaven and Hell, New Jerusalem, Last Judgment, White Horse, Other Planets).*[7]

---

4. By "the Word," Swedenborg generally means the Bible or those parts of it he considered to be inspired. For a more complete and nuanced discussion of his use of this term, see pages 449–451 note 11.

5. *Spiritual Experiences* [= Swedenborg 1998–2013] §[6098:1]; JSR's translation.

6. For detailed evidence for this sequence, see appendix 3.

7. On this "presentation order" of the works of 1758, see the editors' preface to *The Shorter Works of 1758* (Rose and Shotwell 2018), pages 29–33.

b. The Self-Declared Purpose of "The Four Sets of Teachings"

The question of how the target market of the four sets of teachings reveals their purpose will need to be deferred until later in this introduction (see part IVe below), after we have explored the circumstances under which they were composed and how they were presented to the world. Here we will deal with what the works themselves, and other works by Swedenborg, have to say or at least hint about the purpose of these four.

The first of the five shorter works of 1763, *The Lord,* immediately shows signs of its difference from the preceding portion of the corpus: it begins with an author's preface that marks the first time Swedenborg provided his readers with some sense of his theological publishing program.[8] Because this preface contains valuable and intriguing information, it seems worthwhile to quote it here in full:

> Some years ago, I published five small works:
>
> 1. *Heaven and Hell*
> 2. *The New Jerusalem and Its Heavenly Teachings*
> 3. *Last Judgment*
> 4. *White Horse*
> 5. *Planets, or Earthlike Bodies, in the Universe*
>
> Many things were presented in these works that had previously been unknown. Now the following works are to be offered to the public at the command of the Lord, who has been revealed to me.
>
> *Teachings for the New Jerusalem on the Lord*
> *Teachings for the New Jerusalem on Sacred Scripture*
> *Teachings about Life for the New Jerusalem: Drawn from the Ten Commandments*
> *Teachings for the New Jerusalem on Faith*

---

8. Such information is quite rare in Swedenborg's published theological works; there are only two other examples. Five years later, he included a page at the back of *Marriage Love* (1768) listing all his prior works, and announcing a future work that was to appear within the next two years. Given that *Marriage Love* was the first of his works to bear his name on its title page, his purpose in including this list of other works on the back page was no doubt to communicate his authorship of works that had originally been issued anonymously. The following year, in the preface to *Survey* (1769) he discussed how the work related to a promised forthcoming title mentioned also in the list in *Marriage Love*, namely, *True Christianity*. His works contain other prefaces than these, but they are focused on theological and spiritual content rather than on his own past and future publishing program.

> *Supplements on the Last Judgment [and the Spiritual World]*
> *Angelic Wisdom about Divine Providence*
> *Angelic Wisdom about Divine Omnipotence, Omnipresence, Omniscience, Infinity, and Eternity*
> *Angelic Wisdom about Divine Love and Wisdom*
> *Angelic Wisdom about Life*
>
> "Teachings for the New Jerusalem" means teachings for the new church now to be established by the Lord. The fact is that the old church has come to its end, as can be seen from what is said in §§33–39 of the booklet *Last Judgment* and from more that will be said in the forthcoming booklets just listed.
>
> The twenty-first chapter of Revelation tells us that after the judgment the New Jerusalem will come. As you will see under the last heading below [§§62–65], this New Jerusalem means a new church. (*The Lord* preface)

This preface, brief though it is, points to a number of things worth noting: (1) The five shorter works of 1758 contain "many things . . . that had previously been unknown." For example, the reader will learn that immediately after death we find ourselves in a spiritual world that is in many ways remarkably like our physical world. (2) The Lord has been revealed to the anonymous author. (3) The Lord has commanded the author to offer nine more works to the public. (4) The titles of four of these works contain the words "Teachings for the New Jerusalem." (5) The titles of another four of these works contain the words "Angelic Wisdom about," followed by various topics. (6) The "New Jerusalem" means a new church.[9] (7) The "old church" has come to an end.[10] (8) It is predicted in Revelation 21 that after

---

9. Swedenborg uses the term "the church" in a variety of ways; it can at times be difficult, therefore, to pin down what he means. *New Jerusalem* 246:2, in its chapter on the church, says that "the Lord's church includes all people in the world who are living a good life according to their own religion," but the previous subsection there notes that the church "takes a particular form where the Word [that is, the Bible] exists and the Lord is known by means of it" (*New Jerusalem* 246:1). So according to Swedenborg, "the Lord's church" in its broadest definition is multinational and multidenominational, but the church in the past two millennia has taken a particular form on earth as Christianity, just as it did in Old Testament times as ancient Judaism. For more on the use of this word in Swedenborg's theological works, see page 448 note 5.

10. In the context of Swedenborg's other works, it appears that by the "old church" he means especially Protestantism and Roman Catholicism as formerly spiritually central among world religions. The sense in which these have "come to an end" is nuanced, though; apparently the

the Last Judgment (which is depicted in previous chapters of the Book of Revelation), the New Jerusalem will come.[11] (9) The predicted Last Judgment has in fact happened, and therefore the predicted new church will now begin to come about. (10) These booklets have been written to serve that new church.

These "four sets of teachings," then, small as they are, can be seen as four cornerstones on which this new religious edifice is to be founded. What else would or could be more important for the launching of a new religious (and specifically Christian) era than a new understanding of God and the nature of Jesus' divinity, a new understanding of the Bible and how to read it, a new understanding of the importance of living a religious life and what that life entails, and a new understanding of what faith is, how we acquire it, and what it does—and does not do—for us?

In fact, as pointed out in George F. Dole's preface to this volume, Swedenborg's subsequent work *Divine Providence,* published in 1764, the year after these shorter works of 1763, identifies the first three of these topics as the "essential principles of the church" and shows how the fourth aligns with them:

> There are three essential principles of the church: belief that the Lord is divine, belief that the Word is holy, and the [way of] life that we call caring. For each of us, our faith is determined by that life that is caring; our recognition of what that life must be comes from the Word; and

---

change in them that he is predicting is an internal one. In *Last Judgment* 73:2, after saying that the state of the world, with its times of war and peace, will remain "much the same" after the Last Judgment as before, Swedenborg writes:

> As for the state of the church, though, this is what will not be the same from now on. It will be similar in *outward* appearance, but different with respect to what lies *within.* Outwardly, the churches will continue to be divided as they have been, each will continue to put forward its own body of teaching as it has in the past, and the religions among non-Christians will continue to be much the same as they have been. However, from now on the people in the church will have greater freedom of thought concerning matters of faith and concerning spiritual things that have to do with heaven because their spiritual freedom has been restored. (*Last Judgment* 73:2, emphasis added)

So it seems that the "oldness" and "newness" of "the church" here refer especially to individuals' freedom of thought about religion and spirituality.

11. Swedenborg does not necessarily mean that the New Jerusalem will come about immediately after the Last Judgment. Toward the end of *The Lord* he speaks of "the *recent* founding of a new kind of church in the spiritual world and the *eventual* founding of a new kind of church in the earthly world" (*The Lord* 62:2, emphasis added).

reformation and salvation come from the Lord. (*Divine Providence* 259:3; JSR's translation)

This passage has an ABCDDCBA pattern: The first part descends from the Lord through the Word to the way we live, assigning faith a place only at the end of that sequence. The second part returns up the chain, showing that our faith depends on the way we live, that our life in turn depends on the Word, and that the transformation that is our goal comes from the Lord. Some such insight as to where each fits in no doubt underlies the sequence of *The Lord, Sacred Scripture, Life,* and *Faith.*

The sequence is striking, because in the Protestant Christianity Swedenborg grew up with, faith would have been placed higher on the list than it is here, perhaps even at the top (compare, for example, the anecdote related in *Faith* 41–42); and "life" or "caring" (that is, living a life of actions impelled by care for others) might not have appeared on the list at all. The doctrine of virtually all Protestant denominations at the time asserted that "works," or the manner in which one lives, contributed nothing to one's salvation.

Now let us take up and examine each of these cornerstone books in turn, and also give similar consideration to their companion volume, *Supplements.*

c. *The Lord*

Swedenborg's own texts provide two distinct opportunities for determining the purpose behind these works. One is provided by statements in a given work about itself, and the other by statements that other works of Swedenborg's make about it.[12] Let us start with what *The Lord* says about itself.

The work not only opens with the program statement[13] just quoted, but also closes with a list of the work's six main contributions:

> The new principles that are in this booklet are, in general terms, the following:

---

12. Whichever of these viewpoints we choose, the amount of material it shows us roughly decreases in order of publication. That is, there is much to say about *The Lord,* quite a lot about *Sacred Scripture,* but not much at all about *Life, Faith,* or *Supplements.* Where a work does not reflect on its own purpose, a summary of key points will be provided.

13. "Program statement" is a term commonly used in literary studies for passages in a text in which the author's purpose is made explicit.

1. God is one in person and in essence, and is the Lord.
2. The whole Sacred Scripture is about him alone.
3. He came into the world to subdue the hells and to glorify his human nature. He accomplished these two goals by allowing himself to undergo trials; he accomplished them fully by the last of these trials, which was the suffering on the cross. By this means he became Redeemer and Savior, and by this means he alone has merit and justice.
4. He fulfilled all of the law, meaning that he fulfilled all of the Word.
5. He did not take away our sins by his suffering on the cross, but he did carry them like a prophet—that is, he suffered in order to be a representation of how the church had abused the Word.
6. The imputation of merit is nothing unless we understand it to be the forgiveness of sins after repentance.

These principles have been presented in this booklet. In forthcoming works—on Sacred Scripture, on teachings about life, on faith, and on divine love and wisdom—there will be more that is new. (*The Lord* 65)

These points are in accordance with the theological nature of the work. Although most of these six points are stated positively, the new perspective they contain involves rejections of prevailing teachings in Christianity and could be reworded as follows:

1. There is no trinity of persons in God; "the Son" is not a separate person from "the Father."
2. Sacred Scripture is not to be taken merely literally.
3. Jesus' suffering on the cross did not redeem the human race and was not an exercise in gaining merit in order to cloak our sins.
4. The Lord did not do away with the Ten Commandments; that is not what "the law" means in Romans 3:28 and other similar passages.
5. The conventional idea that the Lord took away our sins is erroneous. Instead he demonstrated ("carried") them representationally to show how the church had abused the Word, just as prophets before him had shown Israel's sins by demonstrating them representationally.

> 6. The imputing of his merit to us is not something that does or can occur, unless we understand it to mean his forgiveness of our sins after we actively repent of them.

In an earlier passage as well, Swedenborg provides a brief summary statement that prefigures the first point made just above: "God is one both in person and in essence, in whom there is a trinity, and . . . that God is the Lord" (*The Lord* 60).

Immediately after the words just quoted, Swedenborg adds a note reflecting about the moment in spiritual history during which his works are appearing and clearly affirms the centrality of one particular teaching for the church of the future—the teaching that the resurrected Jesus is the one God, in whom is a divine trinity:

> The reason these facts about the Lord are now being made known for the first time is that in Revelation 21 and 22 it was foretold that a new church would be established by the Lord at the close of the former one, *a church in which this teaching would be first and foremost.* This church is what is meant in Revelation by the New Jerusalem [Revelation 3:12; 21:2] into which only those who recognize the Lord alone as God of heaven and earth can enter. . . .
>
> The reason this has not been seen in the Word before is that if it had been seen too early it would not have been accepted. That is, the Last Judgment had not been carried out yet, and before that happened the power of hell was stronger than the power of heaven. . . . This state of hell's power was decisively broken by the Last Judgment that has now been carried out. Since then—now, that is—anyone who wants to be enlightened and wise can be.[14]

The key teachings of *The Lord,* then, are hard to miss; they are stated at the outset, repeated in the middle, and summarized at the end.

In addition, during its brief course *The Lord* addresses other core issues of Christology and Christianity such as the following: how and why Jesus

---

14. *The Lord* 61:1–2, emphasis added. The importance of this passage is confirmed by *Divine Providence* 263, where Swedenborg amplifies an ongoing discussion of the Trinity by inserting *The Lord* 60–61 as a four-paragraph block quotation. The idea that wisdom has become more accessible takes a visual form in a later work: Swedenborg describes seeing a magnificent temple in the spiritual world with the inscription "Now it is allowed," and explains that these newly revealed teachings make it safe to investigate the mysteries of faith, whereas it was not safe before (*True Christianity* 508).

became one with God the Father; the nature of his divinity; the nature of his unity; what his being the Word means; why Scripture sometimes refers to him as "the Son of God" and sometimes as the "Son of Humanity,"[15] and what those terms mean in context; and what the Holy Spirit is and what role it plays. As a bonus, Swedenborg quotes the Athanasian Creed, an early statement of certain principles of the Christian faith, and then boldly rewords it to better reflect his doctrine.

As for what message other works of Swedenborg's identify as the main thrust of *The Lord,* their statements could be summarized and paraphrased as follows: The approach the work takes is that it presents material from the Word and supports it with reasoning (*Faith* 40). It teaches that believing in the Lord is one of two essential elements of Christianity (*Faith* 37). What we are to believe is that God is one in both person and essence and consists of a trinity; and the Lord is that God; that is, the Father and the Lord are one (*Divine Love and Wisdom* 146, 151; *Divine Providence* 157:9, 262:7). This is because the Lord's divine and human natures constitute one person (*Divine Providence* 122). Faith in *this* God would make the church truly Christian (*Divine Providence* 262:2). The fact that our notion of God became distorted is our own fault, because the Word teaches the truth about God clearly (*Divine Providence* 262:7). In fact, the Word is solely about the Lord, and teaches that he alone is the God of heaven and earth (*Revelation Unveiled* 642:2, 668:1, 958).

d. *Sacred Scripture*

Sacred Scripture, too, contains open assertions of its purpose. At a time when doubt about the value of the Bible was rapidly increasing in Europe, Swedenborg writes that the Lord has revealed the inner meaning of the Bible to him in order to allow him to resolve people's uncertainties about its true nature. Under the right circumstances that meaning can convince even earthly-minded people of the Bible's value.

> The Word is divine truth itself, containing both divine wisdom and divine life. . . . There is something holy in every statement, even in every word, even at times in the letters themselves; so the Word unites us to the Lord and opens heaven. . . . The Word fills us with good

---

15. This is the term traditionally translated "the Son of Man." For more on this term, see pages 454–455 note 39.

desires that come from love and truths that lead to wisdom, provided we read it with the help of the Lord and not just on our own. . . . *To free people from any doubt that this is the nature of the Word,* the Lord has revealed to me an inner meaning of the Word, a meaning that is essentially spiritual and that dwells within the outer meaning, which is earthly, the way a soul dwells within a body. This meaning is the spirit that gives life to the letter; therefore this meaning can bear witness to the divinity and holiness of the Word and be convincing even to earthly-minded people—if they are willing to be convinced. (*Sacred Scripture* 3, 4, emphasis added)

In fact, fairly early in this work Swedenborg explicitly expresses its purpose as preventing the spread of skepticism about the holiness of the Bible.

[Looking at the literal meaning of the Word alone, people] think, "Is *this* holy? Is *this* divine?" To prevent this kind of thinking from spreading to more and more people and then gaining strength and so destroying the Lord's union with the church where the Word is, it has now pleased the Lord to unveil the spiritual meaning so that we may know where in the Word that "holy material" lies hidden.[16]

Whereas the striking and colorful nature of Swedenborg's spiritual experiences might suggest to the casual reader that they were the most significant part of his theological message, he indicates numerous times that his primary focus is actually on salvaging and uplifting the Bible's sagging reputation. The retelling of his spiritual experiences plays a role in showing the Bible's true heavenly and spiritual nature, but only a supporting one. Here in *Sacred Scripture* he says that such experiences showed him, and allowed him to show others, that the Word exists in heaven—with the implication that it is therefore spiritual and heavenly at its core. The first of two related statements actually concerns the purpose of the work *Heaven and Hell:*

Until the present time, people have not known that the Word exists in heaven . . . and that it [is] read both by angels there and by spirits who live underneath the heavens. . . . To keep this from remaining hidden

---

16. *Sacred Scripture* 18:1. This passage echoes the beginning of *Heaven and Hell* (see the end of *Heaven and Hell* 1, which is quoted below on pages 48–49).

> forever, I have been granted companionship with angels and spirits, to talk with them, to see what their circumstances are like, and then to report many things that I have heard and seen. This reporting was done in the book *Heaven and Hell* (published in London in 1758). That will enable you to see that angels and spirits are people and that they are abundantly supplied with everything we have in this world. (*Sacred Scripture* 70)

The second such statement occurs toward the end of *Sacred Scripture;* there Swedenborg mentions the threat of extinction of "any real understanding of the Word" as a primary motivation for the work *Sacred Scripture* as well:

> It was foretold that at the end of the present church darkness would rear up out of the lack of recognition and acknowledgment of the fact that the Lord is the God of heaven and earth and out of the separation of faith from caring. Therefore, *to prevent this from leading to the death of any real understanding of the Word,* it has now pleased the Lord to unveil the spiritual meaning of the Word and to make it clear that in that meaning—and thereby in the earthly meaning—the Word is all about the Lord and the church. In fact, it is about those subjects alone. He has also unveiled many other things that may serve to restore a light of truth from the Word—a light that has almost been snuffed out. (*Sacred Scripture* 112:1, emphasis added)

Crucial to understanding Scripture, then, is the realization that its primary teachings are (1) that the Lord is the only God (that is, the divine Son and the Father are not separate persons); and (2) that faith cannot exist apart from a life of caring. These teachings are, again, diametrically opposed to the more prevalent understanding of Jesus as but one of three persons in the Godhead and of faith as the solitary factor in our salvation, to the exclusion of our actions.

Along the way, *Sacred Scripture* explores the nature of the Bible's inner meaning but also emphasizes the importance, holiness, and power of the literal meaning. It has a deft explanation for the many paired expressions, seemingly redundant, that fill the Bible, such as joy and gladness, mountains and hills, and so on. It includes a chapter on the largely lost "ancient Word" and its nature. And it cites divine revelation, whether past or present, as the ultimate source of all the wisdom in the world.

The work ends with a warning to people who esteem their own thoughts highly and the Bible lightly, and in effect implores them to have a change of heart:

> Let me say in closing what people are like after death if they have attributed everything to their own intelligence and little if anything to the Word. At first they seem to be drunk, then foolish, and finally brainless; and they sit in darkness. So beware of this kind of insanity in yourselves. (*Sacred Scripture* 118)

As for how other works by Swedenborg characterize the purpose of *Sacred Scripture,* they describe it as follows: *Sacred Scripture* teaches that the Lord is the Word and that all the teaching of the church should be based on the Word (*Divine Providence* 172:1). We are joined to the Lord and the Lord is joined to us through the spiritual meaning of Scripture (*Divine Providence* 219:6). Every detail in the Word has a spiritual meaning that has the Lord alone as its subject (*Revelation Unveiled* 642:2, 958). As a consequence, everything in the Word is in touch with heaven (*Divine Providence* 172:2), and angels become aware of these details when people in the physical world read the Word with devotion (*Divine Love and Wisdom* 280). In summary, the Word is now open, and testifies that the Lord alone is the God of heaven and earth (*Revelation Unveiled* 668:1).

e. *Life*

The opening heading of the work *Life* reveals the essence of the work:

> Religion is all about how we live, and the religious way to live is to do good. (title of *Life* 1)

Again, such a statement stands in contrast to prevailing contemporary Protestant views that religion is all about what we believe.

The work goes on to teach that if we are following the lead of our own lower selves, we are incapable of doing anything genuinely good; but if we turn our backs on, that is, abstain from, evil acts of various kinds, particularly those mentioned in the Ten Commandments, our actions can actually come from the Lord and be genuinely good (title of *Life* 18). It is important to know whether the good we do is genuine or not, because nothing less than our salvation is at stake. It does not matter how much we know about Christianity; if we have not turned our backs on evil, we will slough off all that knowledge after death (*Life* 27).

In addressing the Protestant doctrine of salvation by faith alone, Swedenborg asserts that our faith does play a role in our salvation, but not the exclusive role it has been assigned. Our faith comes to life only when our sins have been forgiven because we have done active repentance, and not before; our faith cannot save us unless we repent and change our ways (*Life* 51).

These principles apply not only to Christianity but to other faiths as well, according to Swedenborg. All religions have something akin to the Ten Commandments. Everyone who lives by principles like these, of whatever religion, is saved; everyone who does not is damned (*Life* 65). This is a significant departure from the view that only Christians are saved.

The work then singles out four of the Ten Commandments for special consideration: those against killing, committing adultery, stealing, and bearing false witness. As it explores these, it both takes them literally and adds that there are also deeper and subtler ways in which one may either break or keep these commandments. For instance, in the case of the commandment against killing:

> All kinds of killing means all kinds of hostility, hatred, and vengefulness, which yearn for murder. Killing lies hidden within such attitudes like fire that smolders beneath the ashes. That is exactly what hellfire is. It is why we say that people are on fire with hatred and burning for vengeance. These are types of killing in an earthly sense; but in a spiritual sense "killing" means all of the many and varied ways of killing and destroying people's souls. Then in the highest sense it means harboring hatred for the Lord. (*Life* 67)

Likewise in the case of the other three commandments on which he focuses, Swedenborg describes layers of meaning and of areas in which they apply. Because these evil actions have roots that extend beyond our reach, only God is able to uproot them in us; this is not something we can do for ourselves without divine assistance.

The work teaches that our motivation is centrally important as well. If we follow these commandments and abstain from these evil actions for any other reason than their sinfulness before God, we are merely hiding them from others while we are alive in the world, and they will burst forth into view after death (*Life* 110). Despite its brief scope, then, the work manages to lay out detailed mechanics regarding salvation and what one has to do (and not do) in order to be saved.

The work ends with a coda (*Life* 114) that hints that these principles have application to the workplace as well and even to society as a whole—something the author goes into in more detail in a later work (see *True Christianity* 422–424).

The way other works of Swedenborg's summarize the approach and core teachings of *Life* is as follows: Like *The Lord, Life* consists of material from the Word presented and supported with reasoning (*Faith* 40). Again, a vital point it makes is that living a good, useful life is one of the two essential elements of Christianity; the other (as we have seen above) is believing in the Lord (*Faith* 37). The essence of the Christian religion is to lead a good life, and a key part of that life is abstaining from evil actions as sins; faith apart from good action does nothing except get in our way (*Divine Providence* 265:1). We are saved if we live by the Ten Commandments (*Divine Providence* 254:2; *Revelation Unveiled* 668:1), that is, if we abstain from the evil acts mentioned in the Ten Commandments, on the grounds that they are sins against our religion and against God (*Divine Providence* 326:8). We need to think these truths and do these good actions with apparent autonomy and independence (*Divine Love and Wisdom* 425). When our earthly self is purified in this way, our whole self becomes purified (*Revelation Unveiled* 49:5).

f. *Faith*

Although the first three of the four sets of teachings lean heavily on scriptural quotations, *Faith* takes quite a different approach: it depends to a greater extent on the authority of reason to make its case. The few biblical allusions it contains are negative: for example, people who espouse salvation by faith alone are compared to the Philistines in the Old Testament (*Faith* 49–54) and the dragon in the New (*Faith* 55–60). This avoidance of scriptural quotation is an interesting choice in an age in which theology was obsessed with "proof-texting," or the heavy citation of Scripture passages as proof of a thesis. Perhaps Swedenborg adopted this method in order to bypass the hardened fortresses of stock interpretation.

Some crucial points of the work are that faith is an inner recognition of truth (title of *Faith* 1). This is quite the opposite of blind faith and mere trust in someone else's say-so. Faith, rather, has everything to do with what makes sense:

> Real faith is simply recognizing that something is so because it is true. This means that people who are devoted to real faith both think and

say, "This is true, and that's why I believe it." That is, faith is dependent on truth, and what is true is the object of faith. So if we do not understand that something is true, we say, "I don't know whether this is true or not, so I don't believe it yet. How can I believe something that doesn't make sense to me? It may be false." (*Faith* 2)

In these words, Swedenborg signals his intention to bring faith and rationality, which had become much distanced from one another in contemporary Europe, into the same orbit. Swedenborg finds this "faith apart from truth" in the doctrine of Roman Catholics and Protestants alike (*Faith* 8–9). He then strongly warns against taking things on someone else's authority and seeking to provide support for them retroactively, a caveat with obvious applicability to the interpretation of Scripture.[17]

Genuine faith arrives by a different path: it comes only to people who devote themselves to a life of caring and treating others well (title of *Faith* 13). Swedenborg takes issue with a well-worn Christian saying to the effect that faith brings forth good works as a tree bears fruit.[18] Swedenborg argues that it actually works the other way around: caring is the active entity; it brings forth faith in order to accomplish something useful. Faith, then, is just "caring in its middle phase" (*Faith* 17)—that is, it is caring manifesting itself in particular thoughts and realizations as it moves toward doing someone some good.

Knowledge is a good thing to acquire, but it is not the same as faith, and only becomes faith as we become "engaged in caring" (title of *Faith* 25).

After setting his views on faith side by side with contemporary views, Swedenborg uncharacteristically declines to argue point for point against the prevailing views and instead tells two stories of his experiences in the spiritual world regarding faith (*Faith* 41–43).

He asserts that the faith of contemporary Christianity is actually blocking people's interaction with angels; the difference in understanding between the two groups functions like a language barrier (*Faith* 48). The

---

17. *Faith* 11. Toward the end of the work Swedenborg returns to this theme in a brief lament to the effect that blind faith shuts down the mind (*Faith* 71).

18. Compare Matthew 7:15–20; and, for the classic statement of Protestant treatment of this theme, see Martin Luther's *The Freedom of a Christian* (for an English translation, see Luther [1520] 1957, 333–377, especially pages 360–364; for a recent annotated treatment in English, see Luther [1520] 2016, especially pages 513–519; and for the Latin original behind both of the above, see Luther [1520] 1897, 49–73, especially pages 61–64).

final heading declares that such a faith "destroys the church and everything it stands for" (title of *Faith* 69). But as he closes, he clarifies that he is criticizing only people who both believe in and practice faith alone; people who in actuality avoid doing evil things and treat others well will be saved no matter what they profess to believe (*Faith* 72).

The work is summarized by a few statements in Swedenborg's other works as teaching that, contrary to popular opinion, faith by itself—that is, faith that is not the result of love and caring—cannot save us; the notion that it can is to be rejected, along with other beliefs that constitute contemporary faith (*Divine Providence* 242:1, 258:1; *Revelation Unveiled* 668:1).

g. *Supplements*

As for *Supplements,* early in its pages it provides us with an explicit reason for its existence, or at least for the existence of the first of the two parts of the work:

> The primary purpose of this supplement to *Last Judgment* is to make known what the state of the world and the church was like before the Last Judgment and how that state has changed after it, and also how the Last Judgment was carried out on Protestants. (*Supplements* 2)

Swedenborg begins the work by urging its readers to set aside the generally held view of the soul in the afterlife as breath or wind that lacks a body and sense organs. He also warns against the accompanying notion that souls will regain sensory abilities only at the time of the Last Judgment, at which time they are to be reunited with their physical flesh to live again in the material world. He asserts that instead the soul is clothed after death with a *spiritual* body that is much like a physical body, only better; whereas the physical body will decompose and become uninhabitable. For support Swedenborg appeals to his readers' intuitions—specifically, to the widespread expectation that we will see our lost loved ones after death, a hope that is voiced in eulogies that depict the recently deceased surrounded by angels and enjoying beautiful gardens in heaven (*Supplements* 6).

Once this correct view of the afterlife is grasped, it becomes clear that the Last Judgment will not be an event in the physical world; in fact, Swedenborg asserts that it has already occurred in the spiritual world, where all but those who are still alive in the physical world are gathered. He explains that the Last Judgment on Protestants in particular affected only Protestants who had an inward devotion to evil, and one that was well hidden behind an outward goodness. Groups of such Protestants constituted pseudo-heavens that were closely attached to the outermost realms of the real heavens just above them. These pseudo-heavens are what the Bible means by "the first heaven and the first earth" that passed away (Revelation 21:1). Then Swedenborg briefly describes how the inner evil qualities of these hypocritical Protestants were brought to light and their pseudo-heavens were dismantled in cataclysmic ways, allowing good people who had been trapped nearby to rise in joy to freedom.

As the first part of the work ends, Swedenborg admits to its succinct nature, hinting that there was much more that could have been said about what happened to Protestants during the Last Judgment: "This provides a general outline of their fate. The details of what I saw are more than can be described here" (*Supplements* 29).

In the second part of *Supplements,* the longer of the two, the work takes us into territory Swedenborg had never explored in print before: a series of sweeping characterizations of the inner natures of whole nations and groups of people from our world. To explain how he was able to, and why he did, include this material, he mentions that the "spiritual light" to which he had been granted access made people's inner nature "plain to see" (*Supplements* 39). He then says of that light:

> Since I have been granted the opportunity to be in that light and to see by that light what the inner selves of people from various nations are like—this through associating with angels and spirits for many years—I have a duty to reveal this information; it is important. (*Supplements* 39)

The list of groups covered, which he collectively refers to as "nations," but which includes religious groups and geographical areas as well, is curiously uneven. A group as large as a whole continent is given a chapter alongside something as small as a breakaway Protestant sect. The groups he discusses are: the British; the Dutch; Roman Catholics; Roman Catholic saints; Muslims; Africans and people of religions other than Christianity, Judaism, and Islam; Jews; Quakers; and Moravians. It seems strange that the most populous part of the world then and now, the entire Asian continent, goes without specific mention. Australia, New Zealand, and North, Central, and South America are also absent or else lumped in with Africa. The work is also silent about the population of areas where the Orthodox Church predominated, such as Russia. Even the coverage of nearby Christian western Europe is spotty; it is curious to note that in the first part of the work, Swedenborg talks about the location of Germans,

Swedes, and Danes in the world of spirits (*Supplements* 20; see also *Life* 4), but in the second part does not mention these peoples or discuss their character.[19]

Rather oddly placed in the work are brief treatments of leading Protestant reformers Martin Luther (1483–1546), Philipp Melanchthon (1497–1560), and John (or Jean) Calvin (1509–1564) in the spiritual world. Although Melanchthon and Luther were Germans and Calvin was a French-born Swiss, Melanchthon is placed at the end of the chapter on the British (*Supplements* 47), and Calvin and Luther appear at the end of the chapter on the Dutch.[20]

One surprise in the book is a fleeting mention of the apostle Paul. It appears in *Supplements* 87, on the second to last page of the first edition. The context concerns how Moravians viewed various parts of the Bible. Ordinarily, a reference to Paul by a Christian writer of the time would not be unusual in the least. Yet Swedenborg had avoided using Paul's name on any of the previous 5,344 printed pages of his theological works.[21] Although what is said about Paul in *Supplements* 87 is in itself unremarkable, the use of the name nevertheless seems to reflect a subtle change in approach on Swedenborg's part. This mention is followed by another in

---

19. Eight years later, Swedenborg copied much of the second part of *Supplements* (§§32–90) into the end of *True Christianity* (§§792–845), although he edited the material quite a bit for its new context. The two most noteworthy additions in *True Christianity* are an entire chapter on Luther, Melanchthon, and Calvin and one on Germans in the spiritual world. For a chart of the major differences, see the translator's preface to *True Christianity* volume 1 (= Rose 2006), page 20.

20. See *Supplements* 54, 55; see also note 19 just above. In the largely parallel passage in the author's additional material in *True Christianity* (§§792–845), Luther, Melanchthon, and Calvin are not only given almost fifteen times as much space as their treatment in *Supplements* receives, but they appear in their own chapter, which takes pride of place ahead of all the other nations and religions treated. What it contains sometimes contrasts with what we find in *Supplements,* perhaps because Swedenborg meant to describe a situation in the spiritual world that had changed during the intervening eight years. In *Supplements* 55, Luther is still unable to give up faith alone; in *True Christianity* 796 he has succeeded in giving it up and has gained a new perspective. In *Supplements* 47, Melanchthon is not doing well; in *True Christianity* 797, we learn that he eventually started rethinking some of his former positions and moving in a more positive direction. Calvin's circumstances, though, seem to have deteriorated over time. In *Supplements* he is "in a community of heaven" and is considered welcome there by its governor because he is honest and causes no trouble (*Supplements* 54). In *True Christianity,* however, angels and "servants of the Lord" abandon him because of his beliefs in predestination, and we last see him hurrying down a road toward an underground cave (which in Swedenborg's accounts of the spiritual world usually means a place in hell) that holds and restrains people who are devoted to such beliefs (*True Christianity* 798:2, 11).

21. Swedenborg's lack of mention of Paul up to this point was a matter of bafflement for Swedenborg's contemporaries. Swedish theology professor Gabriel Beyer directly questioned him about

Divine Providence 115, which includes a pointed discussion of the meaning of Romans 3:28, 31. In Swedenborg's theological works that were published after that, the name comes up more frequently; it occurs sixty-eight times in Swedenborg's final published work, *True Christianity*.[22] This seems to signal a greater willingness to meet contemporary Christianity on its own ground.

The sole reference elsewhere in Swedenborg's corpus to characterize these supplements as a whole, *Divine Providence* 27, cites them in support of Swedenborg's thesis that all the citizens of both heaven and hell were once alive in the physical world.

II. Key Elements of Context before 1758

Despite their novel and intriguing content, these shorter works of 1763 have been somewhat neglected, even by those familiar with Swedenborg's works. This may be a result of their brevity, or because readers felt put off when they opened the pages of the first work, *The Lord,* and were immediately confronted with a barrage of largely unexplained biblical quotations. Whatever the reason, their story has not been told.

And their story is valuable, both because the works represent a new beginning in Swedenborg's theological publishing and because the circumstances of their birth and the methods of their early distribution illustrate the passion that Swedenborg felt and the sustained, creative effort he made to give this information to the world. Let us first explore his publishing and his public life up until that time.

a. Swedenborg's Drive to Publish

Throughout his life (1688–1772), Swedenborg was apparently driven by a voracious and wide-ranging appetite for learning. Furthermore, in early

---

why he did not quote the Epistles of the apostles (for the relevant portion of Beyer's letter of March 18, 1766, see Acton 1948–1955, 608–609; and for Swedenborg's response, see Acton 1948–1955, 612–613). German author and clergyman Friedrich Christoph Oetinger (1702–1782), too, wrote Swedenborg a letter in which he notes briefly that Swedenborg never quotes the Epistles; see Acton 1948–1955, 625. Although Beyer, writing in early 1766, is technically incorrect, in that two verses from Paul's Epistle to the Romans were quoted and discussed in §115 of the 1764 work *Divine Providence,* he may be forgiven for his mistake, since that is the only passage in Swedenborg's published theological works to quote or cite the Epistles up to that time.

22. For more on the increase in Swedenborg's use of Paul's name and references to the Epistles over time, see Rose 2013, 100–101 and figure A on page 99.

adulthood he developed a zeal to publish his innovative thinking and to share in compendium form the information he had gathered in his researches. His attitude is captured in a quotation from a work he published late in life, in 1769:

> I am obliged by my conscience to make these things known. What good is it for one person to know something unless what that person knows, others too may come to know? Otherwise, gathering knowledge is like collecting and storing valuables in a vault and only looking at them now and then and counting them over, without any intention of ever making use of them. It is a form of spiritual avarice. (*Soul-Body Interaction* 18:2; JSR's translation)

A sense of obligation to publish seems to have been operative in Swedenborg since his early twenties; it may have started even earlier than that.

His father, Jesper Swedberg (1653–1735), established a printing press at the seat of his bishopric in Skara (Acton 1948–1955, 442 note 4) and published many works of his own, so Swedenborg grew up in a print-oriented household. Swedenborg's first works to appear in print were two poems he had written in his native Swedish at the age of twelve. One was a forty-line poem celebrating a marriage; the other was a four-line poem saluting a graduation essay. From the age of nineteen on, he published frequently, issuing works in a variety of genres and lengths, from poems and learned articles of just a page or two to a scientific work in three folio volumes that contained almost seventeen hundred pages.

In fact, from the age of twelve to the age of sixty he published 4,590 pages of material.[23] He issued new works virtually every year. Although at different times during his adult life he worked in a wide variety of fields, from anatomy to mathematics, from mineralogy to philosophy, the drive to set his thoughts down on paper, see them through the press, and present them to the world can be seen in all his scholarly endeavors.[24]

It appears that his urge to publish only increased as he aged. In 1743, when he was fifty-five, he submitted a formal petition to the president

---

23. This figure does not include second, third, and fourth editions of works written during this period and issued then or at later times.

24. He also wrote many pages of manuscript that did not end up in print; we know of over 28,000 pages (Rose 2005b, 388); and we know there was more that has not survived.

of the Swedish board of mines for permission to go abroad in order to research and publish a series titled *The Soul's Domain;* he indicated that he anticipated the work would fill 4,000 pages.[25]

b. Swedenborg's Role in the Swedish Government

Another critical part of the context of the works of 1763 is the role Swedenborg played in the Swedish government. This was a role he was not born to; two formative events in his life placed this mantle upon him.

One was a death: in 1696, when Swedenborg was just eight years old, his oldest brother, Albrecht, died of a fever. Through this loss Swedenborg became the oldest male child in his family.

The other was his ennoblement in 1719 at the age of thirty-one. After the sudden death of Charles XII (1682–1718), Ulrika Eleonora (1688–1741) became queen, and in an effort to gain new supporters, she conferred nobility on 148 families (Metcalf 1987, 116). Swedenborg's family was one of them.

Since Swedenborg was now the oldest male in the family, his ennoblement granted him a seat in the House of Nobles, which was one of the four estates of the Swedish parliament, referred to in Swedish as the Riksdag, and in English sometimes called the Diet. There were three tiers within the Swedish nobility, which in descending order were the counts, the barons, and the untitled nobility. Swedenborg and his family were in the last of these categories and had no title.[26]

The titles of counts and barons remained in use during Swedenborg's lifetime, but after 1719 the distinctions among the categories of nobles were no longer strictly observed in the practical functioning of the House

---

25. Acton 1948–1955, 498 and note 2; as it turned out, only three volumes, or "parts," were published; but the first of these did proclaim to the public that the completed work would have seventeen parts, that is, seventeen volumes (Swedenborg 1744, iii–iv).

26. In Britain, and in literature written there, Swedenborg was often referred to as a baron, which was the equivalent level in that country, insofar as the baronage was the lowest rank of the English peerage, which at that time made up the House of Lords. In Sweden itself he would never have been referred to as a baron, since he had no title; but in Britain the label seemed appropriate because, like British barons, Swedenborg held the lowest rank of those who sat among the nobility in the government. (The comparison of the systems is made further confusing because, unlike the Swedish nobility, the British nobility had two titled ranks beneath the baronage [that of baronet and knight], though they were not in the peerage.)

of Nobles (Metcalf 1987, 118–119). Thus his seat there gave him as much of a voice as any other member.

The other three estates in the Riksdag were the House of the Clergy (in which Swedenborg's father sat until his death in 1735); the House of the Burghers; and the House of the Peasants. The Swedish government was unique among European governments at the time for granting a voice and a vote in the government to members of the peasant class (Metcalf 1987, 5, 59).

The largest and most powerful of the four estates was that of the nobles, and this superiority was attested in many ways. The Estate of the Nobility had more representatives than the other estates: the meetings of the Riksdag during Swedenborg's lifetime generally consisted of fifty members of the clergy, eighty-five or ninety burghers, one hundred fifty peasants, and as many as a thousand members of the nobility (Metcalf 1987, 118–119). Nobles also held much of the power in the government. The sixteen-member Privy Council (or *Riksråd* in Swedish, also known as the Senate or the Council of the Realm), which together with the monarch governed the country and also acted as the supreme court, consisted exclusively of members of the nobility (Metcalf 1987, 41). The Estate of the Nobility also had twice as many representatives as the other estates on all the key committees and deputations, and the chairs all had to be members of the nobility (Metcalf 1987, 119, 122). There was, moreover, a Secret Committee, the most powerful committee of the Riksdag; it dealt with foreign policy, defense, and national finances. Consisting of a hundred people, it was made up of twenty-five members of the Estate of the Clergy, twenty-five members of the Estate of the Burghers, no one from the Estate of the Peasants, and fifty members of the Estate of the Nobility (Metcalf 1987, 114, 122).

Although the Estate of the Clergy had significant power, especially in areas related to the church and theology, by itself it could not determine the law of the land, a limitation to which Swedenborg himself refers in a letter late in his life; the agreement of three of the four estates was required to pass a law (Acton 1948–1955, 710–711 and note 5).

The Riksdag did not meet every year. It was envisioned as meeting every third year (Acton 1948–1955, 677), but its timing could be adapted to meet the needs of the moment. It met fifteen times during the fifty-two years between Swedenborg's ennoblement and his death. Some of the meetings fell within one calendar year; after 1738, many of them started late in one year and ended in the next; and one particularly intense set of meetings stretched across three calendar years: 1760, 1761, and 1762—a period of importance to this introduction.[27]

Perhaps because Swedenborg had a stammer that was particularly noticeable when he was nervous,[28] as far as we know he never stood up and addressed the Riksdag. But he occasionally wrote position papers, referred to as memorials; these were copied and distributed to those in attendance. It appears that before 1760 it was not Swedenborg's custom to write memorials for the sessions of the Riksdag.[29] He wrote quite a few formal letters to the king and wrote two or possibly three letters to the Secret Committee (we have such letters that he wrote in 1719 and 1734, and a draft in 1755 that he may or may not have sent). But before 1760 he wrote memorials for only one meeting of the Riksdag, that of 1723 (Acton 1948–1955, 289–314).

c. An Initial Attempt at Engagement: *Secrets of Heaven*

Now that we have established this context, we can direct our attention to Swedenborg's later life in print. Upon experiencing what could be termed a shift in consciousness around the age of fifty-five (Smoley 2005, 19–24), Swedenborg turned to writing biblical exegesis and theology. But this change in focus did not slow his written output; he continued to write with as much energy and application as ever. After creating his own indexes to the Bible, which covered 2,623 manuscript pages, and writing a draft of a work explaining much of the Old Testament, which filled 1,951 pages,[30] in 1749 he began publishing what was to be his magnum opus, *Secrets of Heaven*. (The Latin title, often retained in English translations, is *Arcana Coelestia*.) This ambitious undertaking began with a startlingly new explanation of the inner meaning of the first chapter of Genesis, expanded its

---

27. After the meeting of the Riksdag at which Swedenborg was ennobled in 1719, there were meetings in 1720, 1723, 1726–1727, 1731, 1734, 1738–1739, 1740–1741, 1742–1743, 1746–1747, 1751–1752, 1755–1756, 1760–1762, 1765–1766, 1769–1770, 1771–1772.

28. Sigstedt 1981, 93, 452 note 140; Acton 1948–1955, 334; Tafel 1875, 34, 57; Tafel 1877, 545, 695.

29. This statement is based on the cumulative testimony of Acton 1948–1955. The exhaustive nature of Acton's researches is attested in his preface, pages xiii–xv.

30. Referred to as *The Old Testament Explained* in this edition, and published in an English translation by Alfred Acton under the title *The Word of the Old Testament Explained* (Swedenborg 1927–1951), this work contains lengthy commentaries on the books of Genesis and Exodus, with briefer commentaries on the books of Joshua, Judges, Ruth, 1 and 2 Samuel, 1 and 2 Kings, 1 and 2 Chronicles, Leviticus, Numbers, and Deuteronomy, in that order.

exegesis through the rest of that Bible book, and continued through Exodus as well, growing into a multivolume series in the process. The work is highly self-referential: Swedenborg indexed it separately as he worked and used the index to incorporate abundant cross-references among the volumes. There are indications he intended to include study of other books of the Bible as well,[31] but he called a halt in 1756, after eight years of labor and the completion of his treatment of Exodus.[32]

During these years spent on *Secrets of Heaven,* Swedenborg produced an average of 570 large printed pages annually. In its completed form, *Secrets of Heaven* filled 4,563 printed pages, a total strikingly close to the 4,590 pages he printed in the first six decades of his life; that is, between the ages of sixty-one and sixty-eight he published almost the same number of pages as he had between the ages of twelve and sixty—a sixfold increase in the rate of output of an already prolific writer, doubling his lifetime output of publications and pushing it past 9,000 printed pages.

In contrast to his publications before 1745, which had been printed in various cities in Sweden, the Netherlands, and Germany, these volumes were published in London. Publishing them in his homeland would have been impossible: not only was the state of the art of printing there well behind that of London and Amsterdam, but religious restrictions on publishing in Sweden would not have allowed him to print these radical theological works. And, as we will see, it would have been much harder for him to maintain his authorial anonymity in his home country, where he was a well-known figure.

d. Swedenborg's Efforts to Preserve His Anonymity

Swedenborg did not print his name on the title pages of the eight volumes of *Secrets of Heaven.* This decision to publish anonymously followed a pattern that can be observed before his theological period at those points when he moved into new fields of study. One biographer conjectures that his resort to anonymous publication at these times stemmed from his awareness that he lacked credentials in the particular field he was entering

---

31. See the reader's guide to *Secrets of Heaven* (Woofenden and Rose 2008), pages 23–24, 24–25 note 14.

32. Swedenborg writes that the last six chapters in Exodus actually repeat much of what he had already explained in Exodus 25–31, and therefore he draws the exegesis to a close after Exodus 35:3; see *Secrets of Heaven* 10733, 10750, 10767, 10782, 10807, 10832.

(Sigstedt 1981, 156). Since his name added no credibility to the endeavor, there was no point in compromising his privacy. If, however, his insights were well received, he would acknowledge his authorship in later works in the same field. In the case of *Secrets of Heaven,* he may have withheld his name for the same reasons; but in this case the stakes were arguably higher. It was one thing to publish on chemistry; but in those days, to publish a work that went against the prevailing religious orthodoxy, which was also the religion of the state, was to court censure and punishment.[33]

But whatever we may conjecture about his reasons for preserving his authorial anonymity, his efforts to protect it are a matter of record. His London publisher, John Lewis (died 1755), reported that he was "positively forbid" to disclose Swedenborg's identity.[34]

e. The Unsatisfactory Response to *Secrets of Heaven*

Despite his anonymity as the author, Swedenborg, along with his publisher Lewis, made efforts to get the word out about *Secrets of Heaven.* At the time, a common way in which people learned of new books was through notices and reviews in periodicals. Notices ranged in size: minimal ones would do no more than state the title, the price of the book, and where it was for sale; but in those days books often had long, descriptive titles, which conveyed far more information in the setting of these meager listings than would the relatively terse titles of books today. Longer notices were still diminutive, but would include the place of publication, size (quarto, octavo, etc.),[35] and brief mentions of chief selling points.

Reviews in those days, like the reviews of today, consisted of opinion about and analysis of the work in question, but they tended to be longer than they are now. In the book-oriented world of eighteenth-century

---

33. As an example of the interest in maintaining orthodoxy, in 1755, toward the end of the years in which *Secrets of Heaven* was published, a new chair of theology was created at the University of Uppsala for the express purpose of finding out and combating heretics. Nils Wallerius (1706–1764), to be further mentioned below, was the first person to hold this chair (Frängsmyr 1975, 665).

34. Tafel 1877, 494. Compare Acton's conjecture that Swedenborg must have communicated such injunctions to his printer, John Hart (around 1701–1762), as well (Acton 1948–1955, 528); see also the asterisked note at Tafel 1877, 232.

35. A quarto is about 7 inches by 10 inches (18 centimeters by 25 centimeters), depending on how the pages are trimmed; an octavo is approximately 6 inches by 9 inches (15 centimeters by 23 centimeters).

Europe, many journals provided such information, sometimes lifting it from other journals.

The timing of notices and reviews differed as well. Notices were easily assembled and therefore appeared much more promptly after publication than reviews, which of course involved reading, reflection, and composition.

When Swedenborg completed *Secrets of Heaven,* volume 1, in September 1749, copies were apparently sent out internationally for review, and meanwhile two brief notices were placed in London journals (*The London Magazine,* September 1749; *The British Magazine,* September 1749). Although the notices contained little more than the bare title, one of them caught someone's attention. Bristol accountant, author, and poet Stephen Penny (around 1711–1780) purchased a copy of *Secrets of Heaven,* volume 1, read it, and on October 15, 1749, wrote a brief but enthusiastic response to publisher John Lewis, asking to be notified when other volumes appeared and whether the same author had written other works. John Lewis in turn was so delighted with Penny's response that he published it, along with further information about where the book was available, on Christmas Day on the front page of the *Daily Advertiser* (Lewis and Penny 1749).

However, we gather that Lewis was not happy that there was so little other response to the volume. Swedenborg mentions in his journal of spiritual experiences, as quoted just below, that he received a letter, which must have come from Lewis, reporting poor sales. As far as we can tell, the letter was written around November 1749 concerning the first volume, which had been published just two months earlier.[36] The situation, he writes, led the angels with him to reflect on the Christian world's receptivity to this material:

> I received a letter saying that only four copies had sold within two months. When I told this to some angels, they were surprised, but said that this

---

36. Though Acton 1948–1955, 510, presents as certain the dating of this letter to November 1749, that dating and the application of the letter to volume 1 are conjectures based on the following considerations. *Spiritual Experiences* (= Swedenborg 1998–2013) §4422, in which the letter is mentioned, is not itself dated, but in the most recent Latin edition it comes fifteen pages after *Spiritual Experiences* 4389, which is dated September 15, 1749, and 133 pages before §[4831a], which is dated November 18–19, 1751. If Swedenborg was writing fairly steadily in his journal at that time, this passage would have been written in early December 1749. Given this estimation as well as the more aggressive marketing that was given to the second volume in 1750, as described just below, it seems most likely that the reference to poor sales concerns volume 1 and was written around November 1749.

must be left to the Lord's providence; and it is in the nature of providence that it does not compel anyone. It could of course do so, but the first people to read this work should be those who live by their faith. . . . There was then a demonstration [in the afterlife] of how things stand with the rest of the people in the Christian world. Such people were brought back into the state they had been in during their lives in the flesh, and were then given an opportunity to think about the things that have been written [in *Secrets of Heaven*] about the other life and the explanations [there] of the inner meaning [of the Word]. They seemed as though they were about to vomit, rejecting all of it with disgust, as they themselves admitted. (*Spiritual Experiences* [= Swedenborg 1998–2013] §4422; JSR's translation)

Swedenborg presumably agreed with the angels' perspective and the importance of reaching people who felt inwardly drawn to the material as a result of "living by their faith."

The early lack of response may have increased Swedenborg's sense of urgency to get the word out as widely as possible, so that the small percentage of people who were ready and hungry for the message might have a chance of finding it. From the evidence that survives we gather that Swedenborg and his publisher made a more complex, concerted effort to let the British public know about the second volume of *Secrets of Heaven* than they had for the first. One new thing they tried was to issue the exegesis of the next six chapters of Genesis in separate pamphlets, chapter by chapter at an affordable price of eight or nine pence each, rather than in book form; and they had the material translated into English, and the English versions too released chapter by chapter. And to give people an impression of the work and characterize the author more fully, in early 1750 Lewis wrote a fairly substantial pamphlet about *Secrets of Heaven* (Lewis 1750). In it he lauded the anonymous author's learning and generosity, the uniqueness of his approach, and the elegance and profundity of his writing, and he quoted both Stephen Penny's letter and a verbal affirmation from a "grave, judicious, and learned" gentleman who had visited Lewis's bookshop. Lewis mentioned that each chapter would be available in both Latin and English, and said that notices would be placed in the newspapers when each new chapter was published. In the pamphlet Lewis also extended an invitation for people to come to his print shop, which was right by Saint Paul's Cathedral and the busy thoroughfare of Cheapside, and peruse the book at their leisure before deciding whether to buy or not (Tafel 1877, 492–497). And to make the free pamphlet and the Latin and English versions of *Secrets of Heaven* more widely available, Lewis placed them not only in his own print shop and two others but also in pamphlet shops in London and Westminster. He placed two notices in the *Daily Advertiser* in February letting the public know about the appearance of the first of these chapters, the one on Genesis 16, as well as the availability of the free pamphlet and where the chapter and the pamphlet could be found (*Daily Advertiser,* February 5, 1750; *Daily Advertiser,* February 12, 1750). He issued another notice in a different periodical in April when Genesis 17 became available (*General Advertiser,* April 20, 1750), and two more in June when Genesis 18 appeared (*General Advertiser,* June 18, 1750; *General Advertiser,* June 19, 1750). The notices for Genesis 18 also included mention of the fact that "the latter part," meaning the nonexegetical essay that makes up the end of the chapter, concerns what happens in the afterlife to young children who die.

However, for some reason Lewis placed no notices when Genesis 19 and 20 were published, as far as we know. And a notice that appeared in November 1750 when Genesis 21 was completed did not mention that chapter by itself, but instead advertised the *first* volume in Latin again, and added that a second volume, meaning Genesis 16–21 now bound together, was now available in either Latin or English (*Whitehall Evening Post,* November 10, 1750).

To the best of our knowledge, although Lewis's pamphlet had promised them, no notices appeared for *Secrets of Heaven* volumes 3–8; neither were any of these volumes translated into English during Swedenborg's lifetime.

We do not know why this more aggressive marketing campaign was discontinued after just three chapters and the English translations were halted after just six; but their abandonment strongly suggests that they did not have the desired effect (Acton 1948–1955, 511).

So much for the notices of *Secrets of Heaven;* but there was also a lone review of volume 1, which appeared on the Continent in May 1750—a four-page review in German in the much-read weekly philosophical and scientific journal *Neue Zeitungen von gelehrten Sachen* (New Tidings of Learned Affairs), published in Leipzig (*Neue Zeitungen* 1750, 313–316). *Neue Zeitungen* had reviewed virtually all of Swedenborg's pretheological publications; but it seems clear that the reviewer did not recognize the writer of the anonymous *Secrets of Heaven* as Swedenborg. In fact, he asserts that the author, as any reader of the work would readily discern, was a Roman Catholic writing in a state of ecstasy. The contents of the review mainly cover the spiritual experiences described in the work rather than its exegesis or its theological program; the reviewer does briefly conclude, however, that the work's theological content is full of errors. The author of *Secrets of Heaven,* he opines, suffered from an overheated imagination, but the work may nonetheless provide a suitable diversion for the idler and the crank.

We do not know what effect this negative review had on sales, but no increase in reader interest seems to have resulted from it. No other journal picked it up, and although volumes of *Secrets of Heaven* kept appearing year after year, the work was apparently not reviewed again by any periodical until a full decade later, four years after the last volume had appeared (see pages 72–73 below).

III. Key Elements of Context in the Years 1758–1763

The reasons behind Swedenborg's decision to bring his exegesis of *Secrets of Heaven* to a close at the end of Exodus are not known. Something can be conjectured from the shape of what followed, however. The last volume of *Secrets of Heaven* appeared in 1756, and in 1758 he issued five significantly smaller titles: *Heaven and Hell, New Jerusalem, Last Judgment, White Horse,* and *Other Planets.* Their total page count was about the same as an average volume of *Secrets of Heaven.* Given that a decade earlier he had launched a series that ultimately totaled eight massive quarto volumes, this reduction in the length of his works is a remarkable change in strategy. Since these works of 1758 were heavily oriented toward *Secrets of Heaven,* to such an extent that they can be seen as a series of topical indexes to that work,[37] we can reasonably conclude that he was discouraged by the response to *Secrets of Heaven* and that he shifted to issuing shorter books in the hope that they would catch the attention of potential readers of his magnum opus.

---

37. See the introduction to *The Shorter Works of 1758* (Smoley 2018), pages 48–49, and the editors' preface to the same volume (Rose and Shotwell 2018), pages 33–34. The production of the references to the earlier work must have taken an enormous amount of effort; they required, in effect, a threefold indexing of *Secrets of Heaven;* see Rose and Shotwell 2018, 34–37.

a. Targeting Leaders of the British Clergy and Nobility

When Swedenborg finished publishing the works of 1758, his publisher[38] placed notices in London newspapers, listing their Latin titles and prices, and adding at the end a composite title for *Secrets of Heaven* with one price for all eight volumes as a set.[39] As we will see further below, Swedenborg's efforts seem to have been concentrated primarily on the potential audience in Great Britain, and to have been directed particularly toward religious and secular leaders there, although review copies were apparently again sent to some journals on the Continent.

This does not mean that the content of Swedenborg's theological works was primarily intended for an elite audience, or included flattering dedications to those in high places—a literary feature common at that time.[40] To the contrary, his theological texts are frequently critical of the ecclesiastical leadership and scholarly thinkers of his times and assert that common people tend to have more wisdom than do those in the upper echelons. For example, in his 1758 work *Heaven and Hell,* a work initially distributed to leaders of the clergy and nobility in Great Britain, the author indicates at the very outset that the purpose of the work is to protect "people of simple heart and simple faith" from foolish, corrosive ideas that are being put forward by those of advanced learning:

> Church people these days know practically nothing about heaven and hell or their life after death, even though there are descriptions of everything available to them in the Word. In fact, many who have been born in the church deny all this. In their hearts they are asking who has ever come back to tell us about it.

---

38. Mary Lewis (1705–1791) was the publisher of Swedenborg's works of 1758; she had taken over the business after her husband, John Lewis, died in 1755 (Rivers 2018, 33).

39. *Whitehall Evening Post,* March 28, 1758; *Whitehall Evening Post,* March 30, 1758; *Lloyd's Evening Post,* April 5–7, 1758; *Lloyd's Evening Post,* April 10–12, 1758; *Public Advertiser,* April 10, 1758.

40. Before 1735 Swedenborg himself had included flattering dedications of his scientific and philosophical works to a king, a queen, a duke, three counts, an astronomer, his own father, and his brother-in-law. For example, volume 1 of his 1734 *Philosophical and Metallurgical Works* (traditionally known as the *Principia*) was dedicated to Ludwig Rudolf, duke of Brunswick-Lüneburg (1671–1735); volume 2, to William VIII, regent of Hesse-Kassel (1682–1760); and volume 3, to Frederick I, king of Sweden (1676–1751).

> To prevent this negative attitude—especially prevalent among *people who have acquired a great deal of worldly wisdom*—from infecting and corrupting *people of simple heart and simple faith,* it has been granted me to be with angels and to talk with them person to person. I have also been enabled to see what is in heaven and in hell, a process that has been going on for thirteen years. Now I am being allowed therefore to describe what I have heard and seen, in the hopes of shedding light where there is ignorance, and of dispelling skepticism.[41]

Swedenborg did write in Latin, though, which was a language of the educated. Presumably he did so in order to have the greatest impact across the broadest international area.[42] In eighteenth-century Europe Latin was still alive; it was a spoken language that was constantly acquiring new vocabulary. Swedenborg had been trained in it from childhood; from the age of nine on, all the lectures he had heard in classrooms, whether in Sweden, Germany, or Italy, had been given in Latin. As a result, it was a language he and other educated Swedish men knew as well as they knew Swedish; in fact, Latin was considered a better language than Swedish for matters of philosophy and science—it had a vocabulary for such things that contemporary Swedish lacked.

Swedenborg's original readership and initial target audience will thus have consisted almost exclusively of well-educated males, although he was no doubt hoping that the good news his theological works were intended to convey would spread beyond that limited circle.

Swedenborg mentions specifically that he distributed (presumably again without compromising his anonymity) free copies of his works of 1758 to

---

41. *Heaven and Hell* 1, emphasis added. For other passages on the theme that the wisdom and faith of the simple and uneducated often exceeds that of those who are well educated, see *Secrets of Heaven* 196, 3482, 3747, 4760:4, 5089:2, 6316, 10492:4; *Heaven and Hell* 74, 313, 602; *Divine Love and Wisdom* 361; *Revelation Unveiled* 812:2; *Spiritual Experiences* (= Swedenborg 1998–2013) §2663. Swedenborg's life as well as his texts demonstrated a care and concern for ordinary people. Swedenborg scholar Frans Gustaf Lindh (1871–1960) pored over eighteenth-century records and concluded that people who had worked as Swedenborg's servants were left remarkably well off (Lindh 1921, 171).

42. The Swedish royal librarian, Carl Christoffer Gjörwell, in speaking of Swedenborg's choice of language for his theological publications, referred to Latin as *werlden almännaste Språket,* that is, "the most universal language in the world" (Gjörwell [1782], 222). For more on Gjörwell, see pages 74–75 below.

all the British archbishops, bishops, members of the House of Lords in the British Parliament, and priests at Oxford University.[43]

A passage in *Supplements* may shed some light on why Swedenborg chose the British in particular as the focus of his initial distribution. The combination of freedom of the press and open-mindedness—which is reflected in the location of the British in the world of spirits as he observes it—made that nation a particularly promising audience for his work:

> The better individuals among the British people are at the center of all Christians [in the world of spirits]. . . . This is because they have a profound intellectual light. This trait of theirs is not noticeable to anyone in the earthly world but it is obvious in the spiritual world. They owe this light to their freedom of thought and consequent freedom of speech and writing. (Among other peoples who have no such freedoms, the intellectual light is smothered because it has no outlet.)[44]

b. The Unsatisfactory Response to the Works of 1758

In several manuscripts of around 1759 that have come down to us, Swedenborg makes comments that suggest he was disappointed by a lack of response on the part of these British leaders. One appears in a draft Swedenborg wrote for what would later be reworked and published in 1763 as *The Lord*:

> The Lord has given a revelation concerning heaven and hell, concerning the fact that the Last Judgment has already been carried out, and concerning the spiritual meaning of the Word;[45] and therefore the way to salvation has been revealed, along with the state people are in after they die; and all this has been done fully and openly so that anyone

---

43. See *Spiritual Experiences* (= Swedenborg 1998–2013) §§[6098], [6101:2], portions of which are quoted on pages 53–54 below. On this point, it is interesting that *New Jerusalem*, published in 1758, ends with a seemingly incongruous chapter (§§311–325) on ecclesiastical and civil governance, which, unlike the rest of the work, has no references to *Secrets of Heaven* (no doubt because the chapter itself was copied whole and entire from *Secrets of Heaven*), and seems rather randomly placed after a chapter on the Lord. Was it aimed at the clergy and the nobility? Indeed, that particular chapter seems to have caught the eye of Count Tessin, a Swedish nobleman whom we will meet below; on March 25, 1760, he copied §§318–325 word for word into his diary. He also wrote out the table of contents of the entire work. For both of these passages, see the transcript in Academy Documents 795.11.

44. *Supplements* 40; the point is repeated in *True Christianity* 807.

45. Swedenborg is referring in a general way here to the works he just published in 1758: *Heaven and Hell*, *New Jerusalem*, *Last Judgment*, *White Horse*, and *Other Planets*.

who understands the Latin language can know it. And this was done just a year ago and copies were distributed—and yet the church does not care. In heaven it is a matter of great astonishment that the church is in such a state that its people will not even consider things that constitute its essence, instead rejecting them as inconsequential. This is an indication that there is no room in their minds for things that are heavenly, and even when these are revealed directly to them, they do not see them. (*Draft of "The Lord"* [= Swedenborg 1994–1997c] §1; JSR's translation)

The description of the works published in 1758 as having appeared "a year ago" dates this passage to 1759. And it is noteworthy that this was a draft of the work *The Lord,* with which he began publishing once more in 1763, after the five-year intermission that has been mentioned. That is, the passage shows that he felt the need to point to the works he had issued previously and explain why he is moving in a somewhat new direction in *The Lord.*

It is intriguing that Swedenborg made this statement after having completed at least two chapters of his ambitious, promised exegesis of the Book of Revelation, titled *Revelation Explained* (traditionally titled *Apocalypse Explained*).[46] This is of interest because it may help to explain a mystery explored in appendix 2: In those opening chapters of *Revelation Explained* Swedenborg took much the same exegetical approach as he had in *Secrets of Heaven,* and included many cross-references back to *Secrets of Heaven,* as well as to the works of 1758. That approach changed dramatically as the manuscript of *Revelation Explained* unfolded, perhaps in response to these disappointments. Swedenborg may have started writing *Revelation Explained* at a time when he still felt hopeful of some engagement and response to his works of 1758 from readers in Great Britain; but we can conjecture that by the time he was working on the third chapter, he was already beginning to think that there was no hope of such a response and turning his aim in a new direction.

We gain a further understanding of Swedenborg's disappointment from another manuscript passage, also datable to mid-1759, which occurs

---

46. Nine times in the 1758 work *Last Judgment* Swedenborg promises a fuller explanation in a work on the Book of Revelation, once adding that it is to be published within two years, that is, around 1760; see *Last Judgment* 42, 43, 44, 47, 50:2, 60 (twice), 61:9, 72. Apparently two chapters of *Revelation Explained* had already been completed by the time Swedenborg wrote *Draft of "The Lord"* because there is a cross-reference in *Draft of "The Lord"* (= Swedenborg 1994–1997c) §63 to *Revelation Explained* (= Swedenborg 1994–1997a) §183 (at the beginning of his explanation of Revelation chapter 3).

in a draft called *Commentary on the Athanasian Creed*. It confirms that Swedenborg was not content with merely distributing his works to various ecclesiastical and political leaders in Britain; he was in fact hoping for some sort of active response from them. Like the passage from *Draft of "The Lord"* just quoted, this statement suggests his amazement over receiving none:

> The Lord has brought to light mysteries concerning heaven and hell, our life after death, the Word, and the Last Judgment—topics that the church is to teach. They have been written down in Latin and distributed to all the archbishops, bishops, and political leaders of this kingdom—and yet not a word of response has been heard. This is a sign that these individuals actually have no love within themselves for things related to heaven and the church, and that the church is at its end. In fact, there is no church anymore, because the church exists [only] when the Lord is worshiped and the Word is read with enlightenment. . . . (*Commentary on the Athanasian Creed* [= Swedenborg 1994–1997b] §2; JSR's translation)

Another passage written in approximately that same period, 1758–1759, but in yet another manuscript, may help us further understand what particular type of response Swedenborg was hoping for and did not get from these leaders, and why it was so important. He was looking for some form of endorsement that would lead to wider dissemination of his ideas, since apparently in his view the British public was very much influenced in such matters by the leadership:

> It is in the nature of the British that if they read a book that has not been recommended by someone they respect, they see in it only the words on the page and their literal meaning, and not the gist of what is being said. This would be like hearing someone speak but paying attention only to the person's vocabulary and eloquence and not to the topic the person is speaking about. But when they read a book that has been recommended by someone they respect, they are able to rise above the literal meaning and see the import of the work. They then apparently gain enlightenment about the topic under discussion. So the recommendation of someone they respect is needed before this enlightenment can occur. As a result, when a book is recommended, they will buy thousands of copies; if a book is not recommended, no one buys it—almost no one whatsoever in the entire kingdom. The British are all alike in this respect. (*Spiritual Experiences* [= Swedenborg 1998–2013] §5951; JSR's translation)

A passage from *Supplements* mentioned earlier, about the spiritual excellence of the British, contains an additional thought that was not quoted above. It is expressed in milder terms than the statement from the unpublished *Spiritual Experiences* 5951 just above, but the thought is nonetheless similar:

> The better individuals among the British people are at the center of all Christians [in the spiritual world]. . . . This is because they have a profound intellectual light. . . . This light is not automatically activated in them, however; *it is stimulated by others, especially by those who are famous or powerful among them.* As soon as people *hear statements from these authorities or read something they have recommended,* then this light blazes forth; it rarely happens before [such stimulation].[47]

From these hints we can conclude that the silence of British leaders led to disappointing sales, and those sales convinced Swedenborg in 1759 that his current approach was not working. It is surprising, however, that just one year after publishing the five works of 1758 Swedenborg was apparently ready to declare the British campaign a failure.

As an aside, it is worthy of note that some four years later, after Swedenborg had published works in 1763 and 1764, he reported an interaction in the spiritual world in which a recently deceased British bishop gave specifics of how Swedenborg's efforts had been thwarted in the late 1750s in Britain:

> . . . that Bishop, who died three years ago,[48] disclosed what method he used to nullify those things written prior to this about Heaven and Hell and other matters, [which he had done] both among the Nobility and

---

47. *Supplements* 40, emphasis added. This passage is repeated in *True Christianity* 807.

48. From the surrounding context we learn that the British bishop in question—the same bishop we met briefly on page 20 above, who thought people in Britain would utterly reject Swedenborg's views on faith—must have died around 1761, according to Swedenborg's report. *Spiritual Experiences* [6098], like many sections in the later part of *Spiritual Experiences,* was not assigned a specific date by Swedenborg, but it must have been written between December 30, 1763, and December 3, 1764, coming as it does between entries with those dates (§§[6097] and [6107] respectively). Putting these facts together, the resulting story seems to be that between the time Swedenborg's works of 1758 were published and distributed and the time of the bishop's death in 1761, the bishop cast aspersions on them; then, upon meeting Swedenborg in the spiritual world in 1764, he confessed what he had done, even while actively denouncing the work titled *Faith* that Swedenborg had published in 1763 (see the quotation from *Spiritual Experiences* [6098:1] on page 20). In his published works, Swedenborg generally suppresses names in reports about individuals in the spiritual world, but that is not the case in *Spiritual Experiences,* which he left unpublished. Nevertheless, he does not give us a name here. A possible candidate is the opinionated, popular, and much published Bishop Thomas Sherlock (1678–1761).

through the priests at Oxford, and that he had accomplished this, so that now there is silence about them. (*Spiritual Experiences* [= Swedenborg 1998–2013] §[6098:2])

Another part of Swedenborg's conversation with this bishop is reported in *Spiritual Experiences* [6101]:

> Afterwards the aforementioned Bishop told about the 5 works about heaven and hell and the other subjects that had been given as a gift to all [of them] and to all the Protestant Lords in Parliament, how he had especially scoffed at them, reviling and blaspheming them, and along with the rest in the end had put a stop to the reading of all of it, to the point that they entirely rejected them. He told what he had said to them and something of what he had said to others, and the various false arguments [he had given] against those [works]. . . . How other priests were suborned for the purpose of destroying that work[49] was also disclosed which also had the effect that it had been entirely rejected, when nevertheless these things are from the Lord out of heaven. (*Spiritual Experiences* [= Swedenborg 1998–2013] §[6101:2, 4])

We may conjecture that it was at least in part Swedenborg's discouragement over this lack of response, in addition to other factors still to be discussed, that compelled him to leave London in June or early July 1759 and go home to Sweden.

As we will see below, there are several signs that he went on to make adjustments, first in the targets of his distribution, and then in the nature of the works he subsequently produced.[50] But before we get to these

---

49. By "that work," Swedenborg seems to mean the same body of work to which he previously referred in the plural, namely, the five titles he published in 1758.

50. This is not to say that Swedenborg gave up on the British clergy from then on. From a letter written by Johann Christian Cuno (1708–1796) to Swedenborg we learn that Swedenborg sent copies of his 1766 work *Revelation Unveiled* to "each and every one" of the British bishops (Acton 1948–1955, 651). That work contains material likely to have caused a stir; specifically, accounts of spiritual experiences that portray British bishops in the spiritual world in a very poor light (*Revelation Unveiled* 341, 675, 716). And in 1769 he again employed an English translator and published *Survey* and *Soul-Body Interaction* in both Latin and English. Yet the reaction seems to have remained minimal for some years; this we gather, ironically, from a letter that Swedenborg eventually received from an Anglican priest, Thomas Hartley (1708–1784). Hartley wrote a cordial letter to Swedenborg on August 14, 1769, and included a deferential apology for the lack of Britain's response:

> On behalf of my country, may I, though an obscure man, be allowed, distinguished Sir, to give you due thanks for your love towards us, for your migrations, your abidings in England, and your indefatigable labor in the cause of our salvation (for who else

adjustments we should touch on those other, more impersonal factors impinging on his life at that time.

c. The Impact of Years of War and Inflation

During the years of Swedenborg's publishing hiatus, Sweden was embroiled in the Seven Years' War, a multinational, even multicontinental conflict, in which Britain, Prussia, Hanover, and Portugal battled against an alliance of France, the Holy Roman Empire, Russia, Spain, and Sweden. Despite the name of this war, fighting began in 1754 and did not come to an end until the spring of 1763; it played out from North America to Europe, southward to West Africa, and eastward to India and the Philippines.[51] Sweden, which had been significantly weakened by the Great Northern War of 1700–1721 (Metcalf 1987, 109), played a relatively minor role in the conflict. Still, it suffered generally from the war as other nations did, and in particular by sending its troops into battle against the ruthless strategic genius Frederick II, king of Prussia (1712–1786). By the time the war was over, Sweden was badly humiliated and its hopes of regaining land it had previously lost were dashed (Szabo 2013, 384).

During this period Swedish currency also experienced raging inflation, which doubled prices between 1755 and 1765 (Metcalf 1987, 111). The Swedish rates of exchange with other European currencies fared even worse and doubtless had a significant impact on Swedenborg's ability to publish in Britain and the Netherlands.[52] Foreign currencies at that time were usually

---

will give them, if not poor me?). The offices of such great charity most surely deserve this of us; but, sorrowing, I am silent as to how little as yet, the fruit thereof appears on our side. The Lord most High grant that from this sowing a gladsome harvest may flower and mature at home among the British. (Acton 1948–1955, 683)

51. The impact of the war on its era is almost forgotten today, but its severity was attested in a letter the French writer and philosopher Voltaire (1694–1778) wrote in English on November 4, 1758, to George Keith, the tenth Earl Marischal (1692 or 1693–1778):

This present war is the most hellish that was ever fought. Yr lordship saw formerly one battle a year at the most, but nowadays the earth is cover'd with blood and mangled carcasses, almost every month. Let the happy madmen who say that all what is, is well, be confounded. 'Tis not so indeed with twenty provinces exhausted and with three hundred thousand men murdered. (Voltaire [1734] 2003, 150)

52. Lars Bergquist's biography of Swedenborg includes a chapter on Swedenborg's finances. It reports that his highest known level of annual income was 5,000 riksdalers, and his theological publications altogether cost 198,000 riksdalers to publish (Bergquist 2005, 353–354), or almost forty years' worth of income. Given that these works were so expensive to produce, inflation will have had a sizeable impact on his plans.

quoted in Swedish marks kopparmynt (there were then several Swedish currencies in circulation at once). In January 1755, the exchange rate between Swedish marks kopparmynt and Dutch rijksdaalder was thirty-six marks kopparmynt to one rijksdaalder; by October 1762, that rate had soared to a high of 102.5 marks kopparmynt per rijksdaalder (Edvinsson 2010, 267), an inflation of 185 percent. Similarly, over that same period the rate of exchange between Swedish marks kopparmynt and British pounds sterling rose from 40.44 marks kopparmynt per pound sterling to 110.5 marks kopparmynt per pound (Edvinsson 2010, 270), an inflation of 173 percent.[53]

When Swedenborg finally returned to publishing in 1763 and 1764, then, publication of multiple large volumes like *Secrets of Heaven* would have required considerably more of his resources. This may in part explain his turn toward shorter works. This phenomenon will be explored further below, but here it can be noted that in the nine years from 1749 to 1758, he published six titles totaling some 5,300 pages, whereas in the eight years from 1763 to 1771, he published twelve titles totaling only about 2,100 pages.

d. The Five-Year Pause in Swedenborg's Theological Publishing

The Seven Years' War may also suggest a solution to another mystery. Why did Swedenborg not stay a little longer in London in 1759 and publish the first volume of *Revelation Explained*? After all, he had prepared a fair copy[54] for the printer complete with a title page giving "London 1759" as the place and date of publication. But as a member of the Swedish government, he may have found that remaining in London had become uncomfortable or even dangerous, since Great Britain and Sweden were on opposing sides of the Seven Years' War. And once he had arrived safely home, to return by sea to London or Amsterdam would have been contraindicated, given the naval battles that raged between Britain and France in the English Channel.[55]

---

53. Although these exchange rates did descend from their wartime heights, throughout the remainder of Swedenborg's lifetime they never returned to their former levels. For example, at the time he passed away, the rate of exchange with the Dutch rijksdaalder was 65, and the rate of exchange with the British pound sterling was 67.25 (Edvinsson 2010, 267, 270). So this financial disadvantage affected the entire second phase of his theological publications.

54. A fair copy is a second copy of a manuscript, written more carefully and legibly, that omits the corrections and deletions that generally accumulate in a draft version.

55. On September 1, 1759, a Swedish merchant living in Amsterdam named Joachim Wretman wrote a letter to Swedenborg expressing relief and joy that Swedenborg had recently arrived safely

This enforced absence from the centers of publishing in London and Amsterdam suggests a solution for the larger mystery of why Swedenborg did not publish anything theological between the fall of 1758 and the fall of 1763. It is noteworthy that within just a few months of the signing of treaties ending the war in February 1763, Swedenborg traveled to Amsterdam and resumed his publishing.

e. Targeting Leaders of the Swedish Clergy and Nobility

Although in the case of Swedenborg's earlier published theological works it seems to have fallen largely to his publisher to do what we might now refer to as marketing, in 1760 we see Swedenborg himself taking the lead in this role.

From three sources—a memoir and two letters—all written by fellow members of the Swedish nobility during or shortly after March 1760, we gather that by then Swedenborg had formed and initiated a new plan. As we will see, this plan necessitated the sacrifice of his anonymity, in Sweden at least. It consisted of two tactics: distributing books and evoking interest in them by conversing more freely about his spiritual experiences.

The memoir was written by Count Carl Gustaf Tessin (1695–1770). Although for much of his adult life Tessin had been an eminent politician and had been confidant and advisor to Queen Lovisa Ulrika (1720–1782), as well as President of Chancery (which was equivalent to prime minister), member of the Privy Council, ambassador, and tutor to the future king Gustav III (1746–1792), by 1754 he had alienated the current Swedish king and queen and withdrawn from public life.

Tessin reports that he went to Swedenborg's house on March 5, 1760, and he and Swedenborg openly discussed Swedenborg's spiritual experiences and his book *Heaven and Hell*. We do not know if his visit was in response to an invitation from Swedenborg, but it seems clear that Tessin had already learned of the book and Swedenborg's authorship of it. As he says:

> I began at once by talking to him about the work *Heaven and Hell*. He said that besides his own copy he had only two others, which he

---

in Sweden, and added, "Present conditions are like to be dangerous, especially for Swedish shipping. If the Danish court commences estrangement from the Swedish by recalling its Ambassador without his taking leave, it looks like utter madness, and in such a case the whole North will be involved in a war for the sake of France and England" (Acton 1948–1955, 527–528). (Little information about Wretman is available, including the dates of his birth and death. The dates of his extant letters to Swedenborg range from November 25, 1749, to March 21, 1767 [Tafel 1877, 223, 263].)

had intended at the next Diet to hand over to two bishops; but as he had heard that one copy of it had come into the country without his knowledge, and that it had been sold to His Excellency Count Bonde, he had reconsidered the subject, and given one of the copies to the Senator, Count Höpken, and the other to Oelreich, the Censor of books and Councillor of Chancery. He expects fifty more copies from England this spring, when he will send more.[56]

The other people Tessin mentions in this passage from his memoir were also members of the Swedish nobility and were active in its government. Count Gustaf Bonde (1682–1764) was a longstanding friend of Swedenborg's who had recently rejoined the Privy Council, having formerly been Lord High Treasurer of Sweden and president of the board of mines, on which Swedenborg had also sat for many years; in 1722 Swedenborg had dedicated volume 1 of his *Miscellaneous Observations* to him (Swedenborg 1722, 3–4). Count Anders Johan von Höpken (1712–1789), too, was a Swedish statesman; he had been Tessin's successor as President of Chancery, and remained a prominent and active member of the government. And Swedenborg's lifelong friend Niklas von Oelreich (1699–1770) had recently become Censor of the Realm.

Tessin tells us that Swedenborg had brought with him from Britain just three copies of *Heaven and Hell*. Presumably, he had as many copies of the other works of 1758 as well. He kept one set for himself and planned at first to give the other two to bishops for consideration at the next meeting of the Riksdag; but when he learned that a prominent member of the nobility already had a copy, he decided instead to target the nobility first. The fifty copies soon to come were presumably intended for distribution to other members of the clergy and nobility.

As Swedenborg would have known—the schedule was set years in advance—the next session of the Riksdag would begin on October 15, 1760. So in March he had some seven months in which to launch a conversation and interest leaders of the Swedish government in his works prior to the Riksdag.

Tessin also gives us an idea of the content of his conversation on March 5 with Swedenborg. Swedenborg told him that he had been having spiritual experiences for sixteen years, and apparently mentioned having

---

56. Tafel 1877, 399, with corrections; a translation of Tessin 1819, 356.

recently spent a full day in the spiritual world with a mutual acquaintance of theirs. Tessin reports:

> Last Wednesday Senator Ehrenpreus was with him the whole day. He fills the office of judge in his society, but was ashamed of the little insight he formerly had compared with the light he has now.[57]

The "last Wednesday" referred to here must be Wednesday, February 27, 1760, since that was the Wednesday before March 5, 1760 (which was itself a Wednesday); so on February 27, Swedenborg reportedly spent a whole day in the spiritual world with Ehrenpreus. This was Count Carl Didrik Ehrenpreus (1692–1760), chancellor of the University of Uppsala, who had passed away just six days earlier, on February 21.

The news Swedenborg was relating was thus of particular interest to Tessin. Not only did it concern a colleague of Tessin's who had died less than two weeks earlier, it told him the shape of that man's afterlife: after only a few days in that world, Ehrenpreus was already playing a prominent role there and had quickly come into a deeper understanding than before.

After mentioning the lot of their friend in the spiritual world, Swedenborg was then apparently so bold as to make a prediction to Tessin about Tessin's own future life and role in the spiritual world:

> He assured me that as soon as I came into the other world, I should certainly be appointed to the Privy Council. I thanked him and assured him that I had enough of it in this life.[58]

Swedenborg was in effect promising Tessin that when he passed on into the afterlife he would immediately be restored to the position of power and influence on a privy council there like the post he had held in former times. Although Tessin replied that he had had enough of politics, it must have made an impression on him, because he specifically mentioned this detail to another nobleman in the government, Baron Daniel Tilas (1712–1772).

Tilas sat on the Swedish board of mines as a governor and councilor. Ten days after Tessin met with Swedenborg, on March 15, Tessin

---

57. Tafel 1877, 399, with orthographical corrections; a translation of Tessin 1819, 356–357.

58. Tafel 1877, 400, with orthographical corrections; a translation of Tessin 1819, 357.

met with Tilas, and the next day Tilas wrote somewhat bemusedly about what he had learned to his protégé Axel Fredrik Cronstedt (1722–1765), a fellow member of the board of mines and prominent mineralogist.

> Some years ago I had the honor to take part in a correspondence on magic and mystical philosophy. We have now got hold of the right man [for this purpose]. A very short time ago the whole town was almost in alarm about it; and the affair spread surprisingly fast; for not a breath was heard respecting it before my departure.[59] It is Swedenborg, who has communication with the dead whenever he chooses, and who can inquire after his former departed friends when it pleases him, whether they are in heaven or hell, or whether they hover about in a third, nondescript place. He has had many conversations with Senator Ehrenpreus; likewise with Count Gyllenborg, about whose condition he gives satisfactory accounts. He called on Baron Hårleman in order to get from him the plan for some building, and he found him taking a walk in his garden. For Broman he looked for a long time in heaven and on earth, and also in hell, and found him at last in a third place. Queen Ulrika Eleonora is doing well; she is now married to another noble gentleman, and lives in a state of happiness. I am all in a flutter before conversing with him and hearing whom my late wife, Hedvig Reuterholm, has married; I should not like it, forsooth, if she had become sultaness.
>
> All this he reports without a screw seeming to be loose in the clockwork in any other respect. He has also written a book upon communication with spirits, which has been printed in England; I have not yet seen it. Nor would I have lent any credence to all this stuff, had I not heard it yesterday from Count Tessin's own mouth. He assured me that in the other world one amuses oneself with such things as bear

---

59. The first paragraph of Tilas's letter to Cronstedt, which has not been quoted with the portion presented here, indicates that he had just returned from a three-week journey: "On Friday, I came back from Svavelbruk after a three-week trip" (Bergianska Avskriftssamlingen 10:670; JSR's translation). Tilas must have left Stockholm some three weeks before the previous Friday, that is, around Friday, February 22, 1760. Therefore when Tilas refers to "the affair" spreading "surprisingly fast," he means that news of Swedenborg's experiences had become the talk of the town in less than three weeks in late February and early March 1760. (I am grateful to Maria Asp, archivist at the Center for History of Science at the Royal Swedish Academy of Sciences, for affording me a look at the contemporary handwritten copies of Bergianska Avskriftssamlingen.)

a likeness to our affairs in this world; and for this reason Swedenborg promised that Count Tessin should one day sit again in the Privy Council; but the Count answered him smiling, that he had so much of this in the world below, that he did not desire anything but rest above.[60]

This account catalogs some extensive name-dropping on Swedenborg's part. In addition to the aforementioned Count Ehrenpreus (and Tilas's own late wife Hedvig Reuterholm [1719–1741], whom Swedenborg presumably did not bring up) there is reference to:

- "Count Gyllenborg," which could refer to either of two brothers who had been prominent in the contemporary Swedish nobility: Carl (1679–1746) or his much younger brother Fredrik (1698–1759). Fredrik seems the more likely referent since (a) he was a close friend of Swedenborg's, and (b) after outliving his brother by fifteen years, he had just died some six months earlier, toward the end of the previous August, and thus might have been more present in the minds of these noblemen than the elder Count Gyllenborg.
- Baron Carl Hårleman (1700–1753), who had been the architect of the royal palace in Stockholm, and is reported here to be involved in plans for a building in the spiritual world.
- Erland Carlsson Broman (1704–1757), a controversial figure who rose from a lower rank to become a favorite and confidant of King Frederick I (1676–1751). He had been called on to manage, of all things, the king's love affairs.
- Queen Ulrika Eleonora, who had been queen regnant from 1718 to 1720 and then queen consort to her husband, Frederick I, for the rest of her life.

A particularly striking aspect of Tilas's statement is that it shows Swedenborg's news being taken more seriously because it has been heard from a respectable source.

So from this slender but intriguing evidence we gather that it was almost as if a switch had been flipped on. Swedenborg suddenly began

---

60. Daniel Tilas to Axel Cronstedt, March 16, 1760; translation from Tafel 1877, 395–396, with corrections. For handwritten copies made from the original letters, see Bergianska Avskriftssamlingen 10:670–673.

discussing his books and spiritual experiences with numerous members of the Swedish nobility some time in late February or early March, 1760.[61]

The particular content of these conversations is also worth noting. This letter and Tessin's suggest that each conversation included Swedenborg's sharing with members of the nobility news concerning recently deceased members of the nobility in the other world.[62] This information and his willingness to share it seems to have quickly and effectively created a particular interest in his claims. As we have seen, Tilas expressed surprise at the rapidity with which the news spread and at the emotional response it evoked ("the whole town was almost in alarm about it").

Tessin's visit with Tilas prompted Tilas to meet with Swedenborg to hear more for himself. He did so at some point in the next seven days, because on March 24, 1760, he writes another letter to Cronstedt on the same topic. This time his tone is a bit more sober:

> Since writing my last letter I have been in company with this wonderful man. Many consider him crazy; but I desire to scan the matter more thoroughly before expressing myself upon it. Senator Höpken has visited him for three or four hours; likewise Senator Tessin. He has digested his theses in five books, but I do not recollect the names of all. One treats of heaven, another of hell, another of the New Jerusalem, and the Last Judgment, etc. Only three copies of these works have been introduced into the country; one for his own use and another for the censor; the third copy Senator Bonde has procured for himself from abroad. He has now asked, and likewise obtained permission, to import fifty copies, with the proviso that he send in a list of those who receive copies. He intends to submit them to the judgment of the bishops at the Diet. Just hear this surprising news: The Last Judgment has already taken place in 1757, and he talks about it as familiarly as if he had been the secretary there, and taking down the minutes. Since that time the judgment board is constantly in session, and parties are judged as soon as they arrive.

---

61. It is probably no coincidence that the three most famous anecdotes regarding Swedenborg's clairvoyance all date from this era of his life, or from July 1759 through November 1761. He had shed his anonymity and interest in him was running high. The sheer number of versions in which the anecdotes are related attests to the breadth of their dispersal as rumors. For discussion of these anecdotes, see Sigstedt 1981, 269–281; Smoley 2005, 33–36.

62. These types of conversations may be what Swedenborg is referring back to in 1768 when he writes, "I have given thousands of reports to people about the deceased, as for example what the situation in the other life of their siblings, married partners, and friends was like" (*Marriage Love* 28; JSR's translation).

> This information must not be spread abroad, since I do not desire to be accountable for it. These things are known to thousands here; but I do not think it advisable they should become generally known. Yet I do not object to your having allayed the suspicions of the gentleman of whom you write in your last, since this was quite proper. But to take just one topic, what he says about the Last Judgment, this is such an extraordinary statement, that it seems quite necessary to move carefully in the matter.[63]

Several things are worth noting in this letter: (1) It indicates that Swedenborg had been visited in the past few days by several top members of the Swedish government, whom we have met before. And these visits involved some lengthy conversations; it seems safe to assume that a three- or four-hour exchange with Senator von Höpken went beyond a polite social call. (2) It is striking that the letter refers to Swedenborg's five works of 1758 as "digests" of his theology; we might wonder if Swedenborg himself presented them that way. (3) Here we also learn that Swedenborg has received permission for the importation of the fifty sets of the works of 1758 he had requested earlier. (4) Although Tessin's memoirs told us that Swedenborg gave his first few copies to noblemen, here we see that as of late March he still planned to submit his works to the *omdöme,* the verdict or judgment, of the bishops at the Riksdag. (5) Along with news about friends in the spiritual world, the information conveyed by Swedenborg included the fact that the Last Judgment had already taken place. (6) We glimpse the danger of espousing new religious concepts in that period; Tilas was fearful of being quoted as having even mentioned Swedenborg's idea that the Last Judgment had already happened. And finally, (7) it is noteworthy that Tilas says, "These things are known to thousands here." Even if this is something of an exaggeration, word seems to have spread rapidly in Stockholm in March of 1760.[64]

---

63. Daniel Tilas to Axel Cronstedt, March 24, 1760; translation from Tafel 1877, 397, with corrections. For a handwritten copy made from the original letter, see Bergianska Avskriftssamlingen 10:672–673.

64. Tessin's memoirs also indicate that such meetings were still going on as of June 3, 1760: Tessin reports that on that date he and five or more members of his extended noble family visited with Swedenborg; and Swedenborg told the group that he had "often" visited their mutual friend Countess Hedvig Elisabet Sack in the spiritual world, who had just died a month earlier on May 3, 1760. Tafel 1877, 401, quotes this passage from Tessin's memoirs, but in a footnote gives the date of her death as 1778, which is not correct and does not make sense in context.

And all the above bespeaks not an accidental release of information at a dinner party or its gradual leaking out over time, but a planned and deliberately executed campaign on Swedenborg's part to inform members of the highest nobility and clergy in Sweden of his books and the spiritual experiences on which they were based.

Interestingly, at that time Swedenborg was still at pains to preserve his anonymity in other countries. We learn this from a letter written a few months later, on August 7, 1760, from Count Bonde, whom we met earlier, to Swedenborg on behalf of a Baron Louis von Hatzel, who was then residing in Rotterdam in the Netherlands.[65] From Bonde's letter we gather that the subject of Swedenborg's works must have come up in a conversation between Baron von Hatzel and Count Bonde, and the Count must then have told the Baron that he knew who the author of these books was but could not reveal it to him. He did, however, suggest that he could write to the author on the Baron's behalf and see if the author would be willing to respond directly. Swedenborg accordingly wrote back to Count Bonde on August 11, but his answer is surprising, given that knowledge in Sweden of his authorship had become widespread over the previous four months:

> As to the accompanying letter from Herr Baron Hatzel of Rotterdam, I ought to answer it in accordance with his desire, but since it concerns the Writings which last came out in London, on which my name is not printed, I must not let myself into any literary correspondence with any one in foreign lands, and so myself give my name as the author. But not so within my own country. Yet those who are in foreign lands can be answered through others. . . . (Acton 1948–1955, 533)

This strongly suggests that though Swedenborg's works themselves and the concepts they contained were intended for the widest possible distribution, the strategy of presenting his works to the highest members of the clergy and nobility under his own name was at that time limited to Sweden alone.[66]

---

65. The dates of von Hatzel's birth and death are not known, but for a few biographical details about him, see Acton 1948–1955, 530 note 5.

66. Swedenborg's efforts to keep his identity from being known by other Europeans appear to have been short-lived and unsuccessful. For example, a memorial to the Swedish government by Anders Nordencrantz dated February 10, 1761, responding to what Swedenborg had written about his book (see pages 66–67), complains that one "gets to hear in the whole of Europe, talk of the Swedenborgian dreams, etc., and this with unbecoming ridicule on the part of men lacking

It was obviously necessary for Swedenborg to sacrifice his anonymity in order to take advantage of his many connections with the upper echelon in Sweden. This was clearly costly to his reputation.[67] On the other hand, the opportunity to talk face to face with people and tell stories of mutual friends who had passed on must have given this latest approach some advantages over the British campaign, which had been conducted, as far as we can tell, in absolute anonymity.

f. Swedenborg's Seven Memorials

During this five-year pause in Swedenborg's theological publishing, the only new writing of his that was made public consisted of seven memorials, or proposals to the Swedish government: these were on political and financial topics such as the exchange rate, the exporting of copper, political freedom, and a defense of the Swedish government. Given that there had been many previous meetings of the Riksdag for which Swedenborg wrote no memorials, it is striking that he was so active in the meetings of 1760–1762.

Swedenborg seems to have had mixed feelings about politics. On the one hand, he showed a great affection for his native land throughout his life and writes about the importance of love of one's country a number of times in his theological works.[68] He also took his work for the government quite seriously, as can be seen by the praise for his memorials that appears in a later statement about him from Count von Höpken:

> The most solid memorials, and the best penned, at the diet of 1761, on matters of finance, were presented by him. In one of these he refuted a

---

understanding" (Acton 1948–1955, 572). In addition to oral reports concerning him, some information also appeared in print, and it reached people in high places both at home and abroad. An example of one such mention with particularly significant impact is given in an anecdote summarized in Sigstedt 1981, 278–281: Sometime before October 1761, Princess Philippine Charlotte of Prussia, duchess consort of Brunswick-Wolfenbüttel (1716–1801), encountered a journal article reporting that there was an unnamed man in Sweden who was pretending to have spiritual experiences and converse with the dead. This news led the duchess to correspond on the subject with her sister, Lovisa Ulrika, queen of Sweden, and in turn led the queen to inquire after the identity of the man and ultimately to meet Swedenborg. The actual source of the duchess's information is not known; the original article was said to have appeared in the *Göttingische Anzeigen von gelehrten Sachen* [Göttingen Gazette of Learned Affairs], but no such article has been found in it.

67. See, for example, the quotation from Carl Nyrén in note 78 below.

68. See, for example, *Secrets of Heaven* 6821; *True Christianity* 305; *Sketch on Goodwill* (= Swedenborg 1996) §§83–86.

> large work in quarto on the same subject, quoted all the corresponding passages of it, and all this in less than one sheet. (Tafel 1877, 408)

But his having made an earnest and careful contribution to the work of the Riksdag does not mean he relished attending its meetings. The memoirs of Carl Robsahm (1735–1794), a friend of Swedenborg's and treasurer of the Bank of Stockholm, indicate that Swedenborg disliked, and preferred to avoid, the divisiveness, power struggles, self-centeredness, and partisanship that often characterized the sessions of the Riksdag in general and the Estate of the Nobility in particular in the second half of the eighteenth century:

> During the session of the Diet he was interested in hearing news of the House of Nobles, of which he was a member by virtue of his being the head of the Swedenborg family. He wrote several memorials; but when he saw that party spirit and self-interest struggled for mastery, he went rarely up to the House of Nobles. In his conversations with his friends, he inveighed against the spirit of dissension among the members of the Diet; and in acting with a party he was never a party man, but loved truth and honesty in all he did.[69]

It might be tempting to see Swedenborg's government activities in 1760 to 1762 as a temporary replacement for his theological writing. But given the information from two sources that he had plans to submit his works to leaders among the clergy and nobility at that very meeting of the Riksdag, and given that those works openly spoke of his lively, daily interactions with spirits and angels and were based at least in part on them, his papers to the government might also have been intended to serve another function: to show that he was without question a competent, mentally balanced human being. It is noteworthy that his memorials contain nothing about angels or spirits or spiritual experiences or knowledge gained by any extraordinary or extrasensory means. They reason systematically on a material and secular basis about the problems of the day.

For example, as mentioned by Count von Höpken above, one of the tasks Swedenborg undertook during that time was to give a thorough reading to a controversial work by the Swedish nobleman Anders Nordencrantz (1697–1772); it described the Swedish system of government in over seven

---

69. Tafel 1875, 42, with orthographical corrections. See also the apparent restatement of this passage by Antoine-Joseph Pernety (1716–1796) in Tafel 1875, 63–64.

hundred quarto pages (Nordencrantz 1759; see Metcalf 1987, 140, 142). This is not the place to weigh in on that debate, or explore the friendship, mutual appreciation, and cooperation between Swedenborg and Nordencrantz that grew out of it, but one thing that does seem relevant is that Swedenborg went the extra mile, so to speak, in volunteering to take on a reading and analysis of this sizeable tome and report back to other members of the government about it. He was partly driven in all this, no doubt, by an honest desire to be of service to his country; but being helpful, proactive, and rational in making political contributions to the Riksdag might also forestall any judgment that he was mad or hallucinating, and thus allow him to serve the higher purpose of disseminating his theology.

This part of his strategy seems to have worked: he remained a trusted member of the government (Acton 1948–1955, 571). During that same session of the Riksdag, he was formally asked by the Secret Committee to serve as one of its eight representatives on the Secret Exchange Deputation, an ad hoc committee made up of members of several different estates that was to discuss the financial crisis (Acton 1948–1955, 557–558). This was hardly a position that would have been offered to someone believed to be insane.

g. The Distribution to Various Leaders

We do not know what Swedenborg did with the fifty sets of the works of 1758 he was granted permission to import (assuming he did receive them). We have no information about to whom he may have distributed them, or with whom he may have discussed them during the Riksdag of 1760–1762. It is unfortunate that a list of recipients, which Swedenborg was ordered to provide as a condition of importation, has not come down to us. Nevertheless, later examples of his methods of distribution suggest some possibilities, which we will explore briefly below and in somewhat more detail in appendix 1.

There are two main approaches Swedenborg took or contemplated taking in later years to distribute his works to government leaders; one was a public or group approach—a formal, collective presentation that would become part of an official record. The other was a private or individual approach to various leaders, in order to create awareness and perhaps pave the way for a more public discussion in the future.

There was nothing to stop Swedenborg from officially presenting his works himself to the Estate of the Nobility at the Riksdag of 1760–1762.

As a member of the government he had this right. In fact, so many of the estate's over one thousand members were bringing pet projects and self-serving issues to the floor that the business of government was becoming bogged down with them.[70] Swedenborg could, then, have added consideration of his own theological works to the docket, but, as far as we can tell, he chose not to. The records of the Riksdag of 1760–1762 survive to this day, and contain no hint that the Estate of the Nobility, or any of the other three estates for that matter, was given a proposal concerning Swedenborg's theological works of 1758.[71] Instead, as we have seen, Swedenborg did bring before the House of Nobles seven papers of a secular nature on the urgent political and financial issues facing Sweden at the time.[72]

However, the lack of evidence from the Riksdag of 1760–1762 does not necessarily mean that Swedenborg wrote no memorial about his works to the Estate of the Clergy or any other estate. He may have done so and it may have been blocked. An event in 1769 shows how this might have occurred. In that year he wrote a memorial to the Estate of the Clergy concerning problems with the importation into Sweden of his 1768 work *Marriage Love* (Acton 1948–1955, 689); although the memorial was eventually considered by the so-called ecclesiastical committee, it was in some way blocked so that it never reached the estate as a whole and was not entered into the minutes.[73] Because we know of it, however, it remains as evidence of Swedenborg's willingness to bring to the Estate of the Clergy the issues posed by his works.

---

70. Swedish historian Michael F. Metcalf points out that in the Riksdags during the Age of Freedom (1718–1772) there was a "tendency for the Estate [of the Nobility] to concern itself with even the most narrow of private interests. . . . Thanks to the immediate representation of each noble family in this Estate, nothing prevented the individual member from unabashedly seeking his own advantage or that of his nearest relatives and friends at the expense of the expeditious consideration of public business" (Metcalf 1987, 119).

71. I am grateful to historians Jan Mispelaere and Olof Holm at the Swedish National Archives in Stockholm for checking the minutes for each estate of the Riksdag from 1760 to 1762 on this point.

72. One of these seven secular memorials by Swedenborg, the one concerning Nordencrantz's book, was read before the Estate of the Clergy as well, but the clergy declined to discuss it, characterizing the matter as a private dispute (see Academy Documents 842.12).

73. Carl Robsahm wrote about Swedenborg's efforts to import his works for distribution at the Riksdag of 1769, and indicates that it was not just the House of the Clergy that Swedenborg had in mind to target; he "desired to distribute the books among the members of the various Houses of the Diet" (Tafel 1875, 46).

Another, later incident shows him contemplating an even bolder and more comprehensive approach. On April 30, 1771, Swedenborg wrote to his friend Gabriel Beyer (1720–1779), bemoaning the ongoing heresy trial of his works in Göteborg[74] and presenting his plan of action for the Riksdag that was to begin six weeks later:

> I am astonished that they are still going on with the matter in Gothenburg—of which I am going to complain at the next Diet when I will send over *Universa Theologia Novi Coeli et Novae Ecclesiae* [Comprehensive Theology of the New Heaven and the New Church = *True Christianity*] which will at last leave the press in June. Of this work, *I will send two copies to each Estate with the request that a Deputation of all the estates be set over it* and so bring the matter to an end. (Acton 1948–1955, 735, emphasis added)

A deputation was an ad hoc committee consisting of deputies from more than one estate; it would meet when the Riksdag was in session in order to facilitate communication between estates. Here Swedenborg would like a deputation to be established that would include members from all four estates; so his plan was for representatives from across the government to have a group discussion of his latest theological work. Although the book in question, *True Christianity,* did indeed "leave the press" very shortly before the Riksdag began, as far as we know this plan was not carried out, and Swedenborg departed for Great Britain instead and died there the following spring.

These two later examples, then—writing a memorial to the clergy and a planned proposal for all four estates to appoint a committee to discuss his work—show that at some point in his career he took or at least considered some public or group approaches. Most of the distribution efforts on his part that we know about, though, were of the private or individual variety, although many of them involved letting people know the names of others who were receiving a copy and summarizing positive responses he had received concerning the books (see appendix 1).

Assuming, again, that Swedenborg received the fifty sets of his works of 1758 he was granted permission to import into Sweden in early 1760, we can conjecture that he used those fifty sets to make private, individual approaches of some kind from 1760 to 1762.

---

74. For discussion of this trial, see Sigstedt 1981, 387–409.

The list of recipients Swedenborg was asked to provide to the authorities—if in fact that list was ever drawn up—surely would have included some of the clergy. We can assume this from the fact that he planned to distribute his works to the clergy in 1760. And no matter how well Swedenborg's works might have been received among his fellow noblemen, the opinion of the leadership of the church would carry more weight in matters of theology.

Furthermore, the Riksdag would have provided a tempting opportunity. The bishops were ordinarily in their own dioceses throughout the country, so the meeting of the Riksdag, when most if not all of the bishops were gathered in one place, would provide an ideal moment to reach a number of them at once. The opportunity would have been all the more attractive because supplying even the complete list of bishops with copies would have been an easy matter. They formed a much smaller group than the nobility. There were just thirteen of them; besides the single archbishop, who was the head of the church of Sweden and in effect the bishop of Uppsala, there were a dozen bishops immediately below him serving the other dioceses.

Although what Swedenborg wished to communicate to the bishops was a revolutionary departure from Lutheran theology, nonetheless many of the bishops were his close personal friends and relatives, and therefore he may have had reason to hope for at least a fair hearing from them.

Of course, from this distance in time it is impossible to reconstruct every facet of Swedenborg's relationships with the contemporary bishops in Sweden, but we do know some details. Swedenborg himself was born into what could be called a highly episcopal family. His father Jesper Swedberg was the bishop of Skara and an influential force in the church of Sweden. His older sister Anna (1686–1766) married Erik Benzelius (the younger, 1675–1743), who became bishop of Göteborg, then bishop of Linköping, and finally, for a few months, archbishop of Uppsala. Swedenborg lived with Anna and Erik while he was attending the University of Uppsala, and became close then as well to Erik's younger brothers Jacob (1683–1747), who became bishop of Göteborg and then archbishop of Uppsala, and Henrik (1689–1758), who became bishop of Lund and then archbishop of Uppsala.[75] While Swedenborg was living with Erik and

---

75. Three Benzelius brothers, Erik, then Jacob, then Henrik, held the position of archbishop consecutively from 1742 to 1758.

Anna, a fellow boarder there was Andreas Rhyzelius (1677–1761), who later became bishop of Linköping; when Charles XII needed a character reference for Swedenborg before working on a project with him, he turned to Rhyzelius, and Rhyzelius apparently gave a good report (Acton 1948–1955, 126). When Swedenborg was on his tour abroad after his university years, he met and became friends with Eric Alstrin (1683–1762), who later became bishop of Strängnäs. Swedenborg's nephew Lars Larsson Benzelstierna (1719–1800) became bishop of Västerås; he was the son of yet another brother of Erik Benzelius's, Lars Benzelstierna (1680–1755), whose spouse was Swedenborg's younger sister Hedwig (1690–1728). Erik and Anna's daughter Ulrika (1725–1766) married Petrus Filenius (1704–1780), who became bishop of Linköping after Rhyzelius passed away. Swedenborg's father mentored Jacob Serenius (1700–1776), who became bishop of Strängnäs after Alstrin passed away. Swedenborg met and became friends with Bishop Mennander of Åbo (1712–1786), apparently at the Riksdag of 1760–1762 (Acton 1948–1955, 598). And Swedenborg knew Bishop Halenius of Skara (1700–1767) well enough that the bishop came to visit him at his home, though he subsequently criticized the bishop's lifestyle and the content of his preaching.[76]

Quite a few letters survive that were exchanged between Swedenborg and various Swedish bishops and other clergy both in Sweden and abroad after 1760, and most of these exchanges were focused on his theology.[77]

Whatever efforts Swedenborg may have made, though, seem to have had little lasting effect. Although ending his anonymity did seem to allow him an opportunity to commence a conversation about his theology in

---

76. Acton 1948–1955, 599–600; Tafel 1875, 67–68. For a full list of the Swedish bishops who were in office between 1760 and 1772, and who were therefore potential targets of Swedenborg's marketing and distribution efforts, see appendix 4.

77. Assuming *The Letters and Memorials of Emanuel Swedenborg* (Acton 1948–1955) is as exhaustive as it purports to be, Swedenborg's correspondence with members of the clergy greatly increased after he gave up his anonymity in March 1760. Although Acton's work cannot give a complete picture, because Swedenborg apparently had a practice of not keeping copies of letters he himself either sent or received, we nonetheless find in it forty-four letters that Swedenborg exchanged with members of the clergy in Sweden and elsewhere after 1760. By contrast, Acton presents only one letter from Swedenborg to a member of the clergy between 1749, when he began publishing his theological works, and 1760, and that is a brief note he wrote to his nephew Carl Jesper Benzelius (1714–1793).

Sweden, the resulting publicity did not achieve what he desired.[78] This may help explain why he changed his publishing program after 1762.

h. Reviews and Notices of the Works of 1758 and *Secrets of Heaven*

Although the leaders of the Swedish government may not have been very responsive to Swedenborg's overtures or to his actual books, his works of 1758 did successfully attract the attention of two prominent theologians—one in Germany and one in Sweden—as well as that of the Swedish royal librarian. Their responses deserve a brief look.

In 1760, for the first time in a decade, *Secrets of Heaven* was reviewed. The reviewer was Johann August Ernesti (1701–1781), professor of rhetoric and theology at Leipzig and a renowned Bible scholar who was one of the founders of the historical-grammatical school of biblical exegesis; he had just taken the editorial reins of the *Neue theologische Bibliothek* (New Theological Library), a journal of biblical interpretation and reviews of works on the Bible. At the outset of his thirteen-page review, Ernesti notes that his attention was first drawn to *Secrets of Heaven* by the works of 1758 (though he does not name them):

> Inasmuch as a number of little works have come to our notice, containing wonderful explanations of certain parts of the Revelation of John . . . and as in these treatises we are on almost every page referred to a fundamental work called the *Arcana Coelestia,* we became anxious to come into possession of this latter work in order to find out what kind of *arcana* from heaven are therein reported, although, on the whole, we care as little for *arcana* as do the gentlemen of the medical profession.[79]

After presenting a fairly dispassionate and balanced summary of the contents of this massive work, Ernesti then changes his tone and passes judgment on it:

---

78. The few responses that have come down to us from individual members of the clergy and nobility were mixed, as we have glimpsed in the material from Tessin and Tilas. For another example, see the anecdote related by Carl Nyrén (1726–1789), an author, priest, and economist, in his autobiography. Nyrén describes a reception to celebrate the installation of Bishop Filenius at *Den Gyldene Freden* ("The Golden Peace") restaurant in old Stockholm in November 1761. It was attended by priests and noblemen, the latter including Swedenborg, whose niece was married to Filenius. There Nyrén saw Swedenborg "being praised by some and ridiculed by others" (Academy Documents 844.15; for the Swedish original, see Nyrén 1836, 128–129).

79. Odhner 1912, 138, with orthographical corrections; a translation of Ernesti 1760, 515.

We hesitate to trouble our readers by giving any further extracts from this work. It is not difficult to see that the author under this fantastic form endeavors to present naturalism[80] and his own philosophical opinions. It is a romance of a new kind such as may perhaps be compared with Klimm's subterranean journeys.[81] But while the latter is harmless fiction, the former—because it abuses and perverts the Sacred Scriptures by the pretension of an inner sense—is in the highest degree worthy of punishment.[82]

Though Ernesti's concluding judgment is harsh, his preceding lengthy and balanced summary of the work stands out in contrast to the silence Swedenborg's works had, for the most part, elicited to that point.

In 1763, Samuel Johansson Alnander (1731–1772), a Swedish theologian and bibliographical author, became associate professor of literary history at the University of Uppsala. In 1762 he had published a very popular summary of theological works from a variety of Christian perspectives, titled *Anvisning til et Utvaldt Theologiskt Bibliothek* (A Guide to [Collecting] a Select Theological Library), which appeared in many volumes and editions over the next two decades. The second part of the work came out in 1763 and included something new: for the first time ever, as far as we can tell, Swedenborg's name was printed next to the titles of his anonymously published works.

The notice of Swedenborg appears in a peculiar way, however. At the end of a list of commentaries on the Bible, Alnander places a lengthy footnote of almost four pages listing further works on the subject. Most of the entries in this list, which include a work by Gabriel Beyer, one by Bishop Andreas Rhyzelius, and one by Bishop Jesper Swedberg, are given

---

80. By "naturalism" here, Ernesti may be referring to Swedenborg's portrayal of life in the next world, which Swedenborg frequently insists bears strong resemblances to life in the material world. He may also, however, be referring to a system of religious belief that derives from nature rather than revelation. If this is the meaning, the exact reference of the charge is not clear (Swedenborg himself often expresses opposition to naturalism in this sense), but presumably Ernesti is referring to Swedenborg's use of his own spiritual experiences to support his theology. Compare the comment below by Gjörwell concerning this "new revelation" of Swedenborg's that derives "from things seen and heard."

81. The reference is to the utopian fantasy novel *Nicolai Klimii Iter Subterraneum* (Neil Klim's Underground Travels), written by Ludvig Holberg, Baron of Holberg (1684–1754). It was published in Latin in 1741 and translated into several European languages.

82. Odhner 1912, 145, with orthographical corrections; a translation of Ernesti 1760, 527.

the briefest of notices: simply a title, place and date of publication, and indication of format ("4" for quarto, for example); but then Alnander breaks this pattern and devotes an entire page to Swedenborg. His boldness in doing so apparently caused him some uncertainty; he pretends to ponder whether to include the titles of Swedenborg's works or not:

> But should I include or simply avoid Assessor[83] Emanuel Swedenborg's unusual and odd works, which have been rather ambitiously printed in London in several tomes in quarto size, and, at least according to the contents of the titles, are supposed to be counted among exegetical writings? Their odd nature may excuse my boldness in making their titles known, although I cannot imagine what use there might be in presenting material that so completely transcends my and others' understanding. (Alnander [1763] 1772, 285 note; JSR's translation)

We can speculate that this deprecatory comment is meant as a protection from any theological censure to which Alnander might be exposed.[84]

Alnander then proceeds to quote the full original Latin titles and dates of the following: the five original volumes of *Secrets of Heaven* concerning Genesis; the three original volumes of *Secrets of Heaven* concerning Exodus; *Heaven and Hell, Last Judgment, New Jerusalem, White Horse,* and *Other Planets;* and Swedenborg's 1745 transitional work *Worship and Love of God.*

Alnander's mention of these works, buried though it was in a footnote, was picked up by Carl Christoffer Gjörwell (1731–1811), the young, progressive royal librarian. In January 1764, he published a similar mention of Swedenborg's name and the titles of his works in the periodical *Svenska Mercurius* (The Swedish Mercury),[85] a literary journal of which he was the editor. Though he leaves out *Worship and Love of God,* he otherwise explicitly plays off of and responds to Alnander's comments:

> Assessor Em. Svedenborg . . . in these enlightened times has taken upon himself to explain and interpret the revealed Word through a new

---

83. "Assessor" was Swedenborg's title on the Swedish board of mines.

84. Whether as a result of this precaution or not, Censor Niklas von Oelreich did give his official imprimatur to Alnander's work.

85. The name of this publication is found spelled in several different ways in the periodical itself: *Swenska, Svenska,* and *Svenske Mercurius.*

revelation of his own, namely, "from things seen and heard," which is how he characterizes the source of his new light on religion. Swedenborg's works on physics and mineralogy are familiar; but not those in exegetical theology, which he published in several quarto volumes printed in London. As these volumes are quite unusual, and have already been mentioned by Professor Alnander on his page 285 . . . , I do not hesitate to mention their titles for the benefit of our readers who do not study theology but are nonetheless interested in acquiring rare and unusual books for their collections. And I say this with great confidence because I can . . . attest that their content also exceeds my limited understanding. (Gjörwell 1764a, 73–74; JSR's translation)

Then Gjörwell lists the titles of *Secrets of Heaven* and the works of 1758 exactly as Alnander does. In a footnote he adds that the works in question can be seen at the Royal Library in Stockholm. In combining both a notice of where one could see the books with a disclaimer that the material was completely over his head, and recommending the works to book collectors but not to those who study theology, the reviewer, we can conjecture, was walking a fine line to avoid censure.

These three responses in print, while far better than silence, obviously still fell short of the full engagement Swedenborg was hoping for. Clearly, some sort of escalation was desirable, but what would that look like? What was he to try next? The best clues we have concerning his plans take the form of his subsequent manuscripts and published works themselves, including the shorter works of 1763. So let us examine these for any hints they may provide.

IV. Signs of Further Experimentation and Changes in Approach

The manuscripts that Swedenborg wrote during the period between 1758 and 1763 and the works he published in 1763 and 1764 give evidence of experimentation and change in several ways: he reduced the size of his published works; shifted their place of publication; abruptly brought a lengthy manuscript explaining the Book of Revelation to a halt; decided for some reason not to refer to *Secrets of Heaven* as much as he had before; and perhaps most importantly, issued two different sets of works at the same time, apparently with different audiences in mind.

a. A Change in the Size of Publications

As mentioned earlier in this introduction, after this five-year period Swedenborg began to publish shorter works.[86] Between 1749 and 1758, he published six theological titles that totaled 5,141 pages; the average volume length was 857 pages and the median length was 114 pages. After these years he published twelve theological titles that totaled 2,159 pages; the average volume length was 180 pages and the median length was 66 pages.

We do not have any letter or manuscript statement from Swedenborg suggesting why, after issuing what were in many respects summaries of *Secrets of Heaven,* he continued to shrink the length of his works even more. One is left to conjecture, as discussed above, that the effect of inflation may have played a role and the results of previous efforts may have been seen as still insufficient.

b. A Change in the Place of Publication

Another minor enigma concerning this period in Swedenborg's life is why, even after the Seven Years' War officially came to an end in February 1763, he did not return to London and resume publishing his works there. With one exception, all his theological works subsequent to his five-year hiatus were published in Amsterdam.[87] In this case as well, no statement survives from the author himself to explain the change, but Swedenborg scholars have put forward some conjectures.

To Cyriel O. Sigstedt (1888–1959) and more recently to Guus Janssens, the question is not why Swedenborg turned from London to Amsterdam in 1763, but why he originally turned from Amsterdam to London in 1749; and the answer to that question probably has to do with his determined effort at that time to preserve his anonymity.[88] By 1763, Swedenborg's

---

86. Though the works were shorter, he still published them in the same quarto size as before.

87. The exception is *Soul-Body Interaction,* a very short book published in London in 1769. Swedenborg's works were still sold primarily in London, however, as a contemporary advertisement at the end of *Marriage Love* indicates (Swedenborg 1768, 328).

88. Although Swedenborg had had at least as long an association with London as with Amsterdam, having visited the former many times beginning in 1710 and the latter many times beginning in 1711, both Sigstedt (1981, 224) and Janssens (2010) plausibly maintain that Swedenborg was better known in the latter.

authorship of these works was known, and he may have no longer felt a need to avoid publishing in Amsterdam.

Another possible explanation is mentioned by R. L. Tafel (1831–1893): Swedenborg left for Amsterdam in the spring of 1763 "for the subsequent publication of his theological works in Holland; probably on account of their rejection by the clergy and the leading men of England" (Tafel 1877, 995). As evidence, Tafel cites two unpublished manuscripts (the relevant passages are quoted above on pages 50–51 and the top of page 52). If this was indeed a factor, here again Swedenborg had nothing to lose by returning to Amsterdam. After all, publishing and selling his works in London had done little to help him break into the British market. From this time on, he seems to have directed a greater share of his efforts toward the Continent; perhaps the shift in place of publication was part of that.

c. The Sudden Halt to *Revelation Explained*

Other evidence of Swedenborg's change of plans can be seen in the manuscripts that survive from this period. The most striking of these is the sudden cessation of the lengthy exegetical manuscript titled *Revelation Explained*, already mentioned above. After 2,590 manuscript pages of rough copy and a parallel fair copy that reached 1,958 pages, the rough manuscript mysteriously comes to a halt in explaining Revelation 19:10, about three quarters of the way through the Bible book.

Whatever the reasons for the abandonment of *Revelation Explained*, suffice it here to say that the sudden cessation of work on the book is surely a sign of a drastic about-face or change of plans of some kind.

d. The Decline in Swedenborg's References to His Magnum Opus

Another compelling sign that a change was underway is the role that references to *Secrets of Heaven* played in his works during this period. As mentioned above, the works of 1758 functioned more or less as a series of topical indexes to *Secrets of Heaven*. Its presence in them is inescapable. Yet this program of inserting abundant pointers back to the major work came to an end in the manuscripts Swedenborg wrote during the five years without a publication.

The technical details of the research demonstrating this trend have been relegated to appendix 2. For our current purposes, we can say that in the works of 1758, the number of statements pointing to topics in *Secrets of Heaven* starts at a high level and more than triples by the end. However, the frequency of such references in *Revelation Explained,* a work of 1758–1759, commences at a lower level and diminishes as the book proceeds. In the manuscripts written between 1759 and 1763 there are very few such references, and in the shorter works published in 1763, almost none.

Besides the overall pattern of disappearing cross-references to topics in *Secrets of Heaven,* we find one particular omission of any reference to the work that is especially surprising. Given the years of effort required to produce *Secrets of Heaven* itself—which, as has been mentioned, is a heavily cross-referenced work of 4,563 pages—not to mention the labor of indexing it three times over in the course of producing *New Jerusalem* and the other works of 1758, it is a shock to see that in the preface to the first work of 1763, *The Lord,* the author lists his previous works . . . but omits mention of *Secrets of Heaven* altogether, as if it never existed.[89] Indeed, the first mention of *Secrets of Heaven* in the shorter works of 1763 occurs toward the end of *The Lord,* not as part of the main text but in an author's footnote (*The Lord* 64 note a). Thereafter we find only a few topical references to *Secrets of Heaven* in these works. The shift in strategy marked by this paucity of references is truly remarkable, although the reasons behind it are unclear.[90]

e. Separate Approaches for Clergy and Nobility

The list of projected works in the preface to *The Lord,* quoted in full above in part Ib on pages 21–22, contains something of a puzzle. It proclaims that Swedenborg intended to publish two works "about Life": *Teachings about Life for the New Jerusalem: Drawn from the Ten Commandments* and *Angelic Wisdom about Life.* If printing costs were effectively greater for Swedenborg because Swedish currency had been devalued, how could, and why would, he have planned to produce two works with such similar titles at more or less the same time? Not long after this statement appeared in print, Swedenborg decided not to publish the second of these, so we cannot compare the two texts themselves; but we do at least have the two titles and one of the works in full.

The differences in title may at first seem to tell us little. But each belongs to a group of four titles in that list in the preface to *The Lord*

---

89. See the list on page 21 above, or see the preface to *The Lord* itself.

90. It is worth noting, however, that when Swedenborg first put his name on a title page of a theological work in *Marriage Love,* he included at the end of the book a list of theological works he had previously published, and in that instance *Secrets of Heaven* is indeed mentioned; see Swedenborg 1768, 328.

that starts the same way: *Teachings* versus *Angelic Wisdom.*[91] (Indeed, as we have seen above on page 19, *Revelation Unveiled* 668:1 lists the first four together and collectively refers to them as "four sets of teachings.")

What can be said about the difference between the extant works labeled *Teachings* and the extant works labeled *Angelic Wisdom*? For one thing, the works labeled *Teachings* tend to cite and quote the Bible far more than do the works titled *Angelic Wisdom*. *Teachings for the New Jerusalem on the Lord* and *Angelic Wisdom about Divine Love and Wisdom* are both ostensibly about God, and yet the former quotes Scripture forty-five times as much as the latter (Rose 2013, 102). And the works labeled *Teachings* make frequent use of Christian terms such as *Father, Son,* and *Holy Spirit* and quote from the Christian Creeds; the works labeled *Angelic Wisdom* speak instead of "God," "the Divine," and "the Divine-Human One" and rely heavily on argumentation and analogy. The underlying teachings are consistent, but the tone and manner are quite different.[92]

Swedenborg even seems to use a different term for a work on angelic wisdom than he does for other works: he calls it a *transactio,* or "treatise." In the mid-eighteenth century this was a term used of works that were juridical, historical, or argumentative in nature. Swedenborg's general practice from the beginning of his theological publishing was to refer to a sizeable

---

91. The first group of four titles is *Teachings for the New Jerusalem on the Lord; Teachings for the New Jerusalem on Sacred Scripture; Teachings about Life for the New Jerusalem: Drawn from the Ten Commandments;* and *Teachings for the New Jerusalem on Faith*. All these were published and all are contained in the present volume. The second group of four titles is *Angelic Wisdom about Divine Providence; Angelic Wisdom about Divine Omnipotence, Omnipresence, Omniscience, Infinity, and Eternity; Angelic Wisdom about Divine Love and Wisdom;* and *Angelic Wisdom about Life*. The first and third titles in this latter group were published, albeit in reverse order; the second and fourth were planned for but never appeared in print.

92. To put this another way, in the first editions, the first 33 pages of *The Lord* contain more biblical quotations than all 578 pages of the works of 1758 put together. And unlike *Revelation Explained,* in which there is abundant explanation of every biblical quotation, many of the quotations in *The Lord* are presented one after another with no intervening commentary, a method that seems to presume great biblical literacy on the part of the reader. In fact, if we take three bodies of Swedenborg's published texts and compare them in this regard, we see a similar pattern. The three bodies of texts are: (1) the five works of 1758, (2) the five shorter works of 1763 (four out of five of which are labeled *Teachings*), and (3) *Divine Love and Wisdom* and *Divine Providence* (which are both labeled *Angelic Wisdom*). If we continue to use the pages of the first editions as units of comparison, the first of these three bodies of text cites or quotes an average of 178 biblical verses for every one hundred pages; the second body, 1,610 verses; the third body, 129 verses. To put it another way, the shorter works of 1763 collectively cite or quote Scripture over twelve times as much per first edition page as do the works of 1758, and over fourteen times as much per first edition page as do the works labeled *Angelic Wisdom*.

book as an *opus* ("a work") and a short book as an *opusculum* ("a small work"),93 but in 1763, in the preface to *The Lord* we have been discussing, he introduced *transactio* as a new term for "the works to be drawn from angelic wisdom":

> These are mysteries familiar to heaven's angels that will be unfolded, as far as possible, in the treatises mentioned in the preface to *Teachings on the Lord* that are to be drawn from angelic wisdom: namely, *About Divine Providence; About Omnipotence, Omnipresence, Omniscience; About Divine Love and Wisdom;* and *About Life.* (*Sacred Scripture* 32; JSR's translation)

Of the nine items in that list, Swedenborg uses the term *transactio* only of the four works whose titles begin with the words "*Angelic Wisdom.*" This is borne out in other passages as well.94

There are even passages in which Swedenborg lists several titles of his works and uses *transactio* for *Divine Love and Wisdom* and *Divine Providence,* but other terms for other works. For example:

> . . . in the treatise *About Divine Love and Wisdom* and earlier in this treatise *About Divine Providence,* and also in the work *Heaven and Hell* . . .95

Given that Swedenborg's two initial target audiences were leaders among the clergy and leaders among the nobility, as we have seen in the case of both Great Britain and Sweden, it seems sound to conjecture that the works labeled *Teachings* are for the former, whereas the works labeled *Angelic Wisdom* were oriented more toward the latter. Indeed, *Sacred Scripture* 115 refers to people, such as Deists, who believe in God but not the authority of the written Word, and says how one needs to approach them:

> But then there are people who propose and then prove to themselves that without the Word we could know about the existence of God,

---

93. These two terms are used most often, but Swedenborg also occasionally uses the terms *liber* (book), *libellus* (short book), or *codicillus* (small volume) to refer to his works.

94. See *Sacred Scripture* 100; *Life* 15, 36, 107; *Divine Love and Wisdom* 4, 130; and ubiquitously in *Divine Providence.* (Because the term *transactio* is translated variously, the reader may need to resort to the Latin to see it clearly in these passages.)

95. *Divine Providence* 163; JSR's translation. In the later theological works *Marriage Love, Survey,* and *True Christianity,* however, Swedenborg shifts to using the term *transactio* in internal cross-references to refer to a chapter.

about heaven and hell, too, and something about other things that the Word teaches. They then use this assumption to undermine the authority and holiness of the Word, if not out loud, then in their hearts. *There is no dealing with them on the basis of the Word. We must appeal to the light of reason* because they do not believe the Word, only themselves. (*Sacred Scripture* 115, emphasis added)

Although this is expressed in a way that was no doubt insulting to that readership, the material in italics in these last two sentences could serve as a motto for the approach taken in the treatises labeled *Angelic Wisdom;* they lean heavily on the light of reason, and only lightly on Scripture references.[96]

All this suggests a solution to the puzzle of how Swedenborg could have planned to issue two works "about life" in the same year: one (the one that was actually published) was apparently geared toward the clergy and those readers steeped in the principles and traditions of the Christian church; the other (which was not published after all) would presumably have been written, like the other *Angelic Wisdom* books, as a treatise for an audience that appreciated philosophical rather than scriptural reasoning. And because the term "life" as Swedenborg uses it in his theology has a number of different meanings,[97] the very topics to be covered in these two works may have been quite different from each other as well—whereas Swedenborg wrote *Teachings about Life* on how and why people are to practice the Ten Commandments, he may have intended *Angelic*

---

96. Since two works that were to have been titled *Angelic Wisdom* were never published, it is a matter of interest whether Swedenborg ever used that label for other works or projected works; that is, was this conceived of as a series, and if so, which works were to be considered part of it? There is indeed one other work that has these words in its projected title: the work on marriage. See the early versions of its title in *Revelation Unveiled* 434:1 (*Angelic Wisdom about Marriage*) and the letter to Beyer of February 1767 (*Secrets of Angelic Wisdom Concerning Marriage Love;* compare Acton 1948–1955, 631). In the final wording of the title of *Marriage Love,* to which these both evidently refer, there is mention of "wisdom," but not "angelic wisdom." Given this circumstance and certain other features *Marriage Love* shares with the *Angelic Wisdom* series, it seems fair to conclude that even though in its finished form *Marriage Love* was not titled *Angelic Wisdom about Marriage Love,* it shows an affinity of approach with *Divine Love and Wisdom* and *Divine Providence.*

97. Chadwick and Rose 2008 give ten meanings for Swedenborg's term *vita* ("life"): (1) the state of being alive, life; (2) life on earth (as opposed to life after death); (3) life after death; (4) life on earth as regarded as a period of time, lifetime; (5) a person's life on earth as regarded historically, the events of one's life, biography; (6) a person's life regarded as a series of actions, way of living; (7) life as a faculty possessed by a person; (8) the state of being spiritually alive, real life; (9) life regarded as a force derived from the Lord; (10) the vital principle or vivifying force of anything.

Wisdom about Life to cover something quite different, such as how the Divine is operative in living things in the physical world.

This is not to suggest that there was something wrong with the works Swedenborg had published before, but rather that he may have designed his various works about the New Jerusalem to act as so many points of entry to their core theology (Rose 2013).

V. Contemporary Responses to the Shorter Works of 1763

Nothing survives in the way of direct evidence from Swedenborg himself on his method of distributing the shorter works of 1763, but one thing he must have done was to send the five works *The Lord, Sacred Scripture, Life, Faith,* and *Supplements* collectively to a number of journals in Sweden and elsewhere on the Continent. This is clear from the five collective reviews of these works that appeared in four different languages between 1763 and 1765. Additional evidence can be seen in a brief notice that appeared in a Swedish journal in August 1764; it mentioned the five shorter works as well as *Divine Love and Wisdom* (published in 1763) and *Divine Providence* (published in 1764).

a. Five Contemporary Reviews and a Notice of the Shorter Works of 1763

During the first few years after the shorter works of 1763 were published, five reviews and a notice appeared in various places; let us take these in chronological order of their date of publication.

Two reviews were dated 1763. The first was written by the same theologian who reviewed *Secrets of Heaven* in 1760. In late 1763, Ernesti published a nine-page review in German of all five of the shorter works of 1763. It appeared in the periodical he edited, *Neue theologische Bibliothek* (New Theological Library).[98]

---

98. Although Ernesti later published a review of *Revelation Unveiled* (Ernesti 1766), he never reviewed *Divine Love and Wisdom* and *Divine Providence,* which can be seen as evidence, however weak, to support the theory that those works were intended for a different audience than were the shorter works of 1763 (see part IVe). That is, perhaps Swedenborg did not send the philosophical works *Divine Love and Wisdom* and *Divine Providence* to Ernesti because he was a biblical scholar and those books do not directly interpret Scripture.

Ernesti begins by summarizing the teachings in a fairly balanced way, taking only occasional potshots at the anonymous author.[99] Then, writing in the first person plural as a member of the clergy himself, Ernesti says:

> He accuses us of teaching a faith without love, blames us for teaching that good works do not bring salvation, and generally condemns the teaching that the understanding must be subjected to the obedience of faith . . . and he tries to make this [teaching] ridiculous by a story which is supposed to have taken place in heaven.[100]

Clearly, Ernesti took these works as being aimed at the clergy. In his conclusion, his tone becomes angrier and more dismissive:

> We hesitate to detain our readers with any further extracts. It is deplorable that a person, who in other respects is a learned man, should have gone so far astray, and that he should plague himself and his readers with such fantastical digressions, which also must be very expensive to himself (for he, of course, must print these books at his own expense, and they are all printed in a sumptuous manner). It would cost less to present his Sabellian and naturalistic system in a straightforward manner, and be through with it in a few sheets. . . .[101]

Ernesti's sarcastic conclusion, then, is that these works, some of the shortest theological works Swedenborg had written to date, are still too long; Swedenborg could have saved himself some money by stating his views even more baldly—views that Ernesti finds unorthodox and heretical. But even while dismissing them, he admits that the works are nicely printed.

The other review of the shorter works of 1763 to be dated to that same year is a four-page account found in the Hague edition of the *Bibliothèque des sciences et des beaux arts* (Library of the Sciences and Fine

---

99. Ernesti apparently knows the writer's identity, but insists "we must not mention it" (Odhner 1912, 146; a translation of Ernesti 1763, 725).

100. Odhner 1912, 150; a translation of Ernesti 1763, 732; the last phrase here is presumably referring to *Faith* 41–43.

101. Odhner 1912, 151, with corrections; a translation of Ernesti 1763, 733. The Sabellians were followers of a third-century heretic who believed that the Father, the Son, and the Holy Spirit were not separate persons of the Godhead but instead simply three modes of divine manifestation. In making this charge, Ernesti was correct insofar as there are at least superficial similarities between Sabellianism and the Swedenborgian concept of the Trinity. On the charge of Swedenborg's system being "naturalistic," see note 80 above.

Arts).[102] In it the reviewer lists the titles, and in fact presents the two parts of *Supplements* as separate titles, yet refers to the works collectively as a single volume of two hundred pages.[103]

In a light and somewhat doubting tone, the reviewer notes that the author presents these works as things not before known, written by direct command of the Lord, and inspired by immediate revelation, and adds that the author claims he brings nineteen years of spiritual experience to his work.

Unlike Ernesti's careful summary of the theology, this review skips over the contents of the four main books of teachings and turns to summarizing the spiritual experiences in the second part of *Supplements*. As just one example, it notes the interaction that Swedenborg reports in *Supplements* 60 between Louis XIV (1638–1715), then in the spiritual world, and Louis XV (1710–1774), who was reigning at the time, and adds disingenuously, "Without a doubt, Louis XV will remember this apparition" (*Bibliothèque* 1763, 553). The only passage quoted in the review appears in a footnote and in its original Latin; it is a portion of *Supplements* 32:

> We are still human beings after death—so much so that we do not realize we are not still in the physical world. As we used to in the world, we see, hear, and talk. As we used to in the world, we walk, run, and sit. As we used to in the world, we eat and drink. As we used to in the world, we sleep and wake up. As we used to in the world, we enjoy making love to our spouse. Briefly put, we are still human in every way. This makes it clear that our death is simply a continuation of our life. Death is just a transition. (*Bibliothèque* 1763, 552 note; translation of Swedenborg's text by George F. Dole)

In the last two sentences of the review, we are given a reason why the theology is not discussed:

> We will say nothing about the author's theological opinions of the Last Judgment, the Trinity, the Atonement of Jesus Christ, justification,

---

102. *Bibliothèque* 1763. The *Bibliothèque des sciences et des beaux arts* came out in two parallel editions: one was published in Paris under tight censorship, and the other in the Hague, where there were fewer restrictions on content. As a result, the content of the two sometimes differs. Swedenborg's works are mentioned only in the Hague editions: in addition to the review just mentioned, a brief notice of the publication of *Divine Love and Wisdom* and *Divine Providence* was included in the July-to-September 1764 issue (*Bibliothèque* 1764).

103. The reviewer's description of the works as appearing in a single volume suggests that Swedenborg had them bound for reviewers in that format. In this connection, it may be relevant that the notice by Gjörwell in *Svenska Mercurius* mentioned above (Gjörwell 1764a, 73–74) reports that all the works of 1758 together form but a single volume.

and so on, because we would be afraid of attracting negative attention to him. It would be best, if possible, to keep Holtius and Comrie from hearing about this. (*Bibliothèque* 1763, 554; JSR's translation)

The final reference, facetiously stated, points to Nicolaas Holtius (1693–1773) and Alexander Comrie (1706–1774), who were Calvinist defenders of orthodoxy, persecutors of those perceived as heretics, and authors of dozens of books vigorously opposing the Enlightenment thinking that had taken hold of many theological schools at the time. The reviewer's supposed lack of desire to draw attention to the author's theology is of course somewhat undercut by the existence of the review itself, as well as by the attention-getting list of things the reviewer will not cover. It is further subverted by a footnote the reviewer includes on the very mention of the Last Judgment just quoted, which says:

He believes that the Last Judgment has already taken place, but what he says about it is rather obscure. It must be explained more clearly and in greater detail in one of the treatises he has previously published. (*Bibliothèque* 1763, 554 note; JSR's translation)

Two footnotes in the review, then, communicate some of Swedenborg's most astounding claims in these works.

In 1764, the London *Monthly Review* published a review in English of the five shorter works of 1763.[104] This review is clearly influenced by the review in the *Bibliothèque des sciences et des beaux arts*. For one thing, it too presents only one quote, in Latin, from the works, and that is exactly the same passage from *Supplements* 32; the only differences are that it presents the quotation in roman font instead of italic and italicizes the phrase "we enjoy making love to our spouse," ending the quotation after that point with an "etc." In addition, it too avoids the theology and focuses on the spiritual experiences in the second part of *Supplements*. And many of the same highlights are mentioned. It is not a mere copy of the French review, however, and the British reviewer has clearly seen the works for himself. He is also aware of Swedenborg's works of 1758, about which the French reviewer seems to be in the dark.

In making similar points, the English review has taken the light tone of the French one and made it more sarcastic, dismissive, and presumably entertaining to its readership. For example, on the point concerning Louis XIV's visit with Louis XV the reviewer says:

---

104. *Monthly Review* 1764. The review mistakenly gives 1764 as the publication date of the books.

> We have, in this circumstance, another instance of the secrecy with which matters are carried on at the court of Versailles. Not a syllable transpired, or got into any of the Gazettes, about the apparition of Louis the XIV having paid a visit to his present Christian Majesty. And yet this conference happened on the 13th of December 1759, at eight a clock in the evening precisely; of which all future compilers of the French history are by us desired to take particular notice. (*Monthly Review* 1764, 574)

The reviewer concludes by saying he cannot tell what the author's motives were in publishing this strange material, but feels that a jury of "literary coroners" who held an inquest on this body of work would no doubt hand down a unanimous verdict of lunacy.

In Sweden the first notice in print of the works of 1763 was published by Gjörwell in the August 1764 issue of the *Svenska Mercurius* (Gjörwell 1764b), the same reviewer and periodical that had just dealt, as we saw, with Swedenborg's works of 1758 in the January 1764 issue (see pages 74–75 above). As we will see further below (on pages 89–91), Gjörwell acquired copies of Swedenborg's works of 1763 and 1764 in late August of the latter year. He immediately posted a notice of them in the issue of his journal for that month. The tone is markedly more favorable than that of the reviews outside Sweden.

The notice begins with Swedenborg's name (something not included in the French and British reviews) and the information that he had recently returned from Amsterdam, where he had published several new books. It gives a cross-reference to the recent review in the same periodical of Swedenborg's works of 1758, then lists the Latin titles in the following sequence: *Divine Providence* (perhaps listed first because it was published in that very year), followed by *Divine Love and Wisdom* and then each of the shorter works of 1763 in sequence. The notice concludes as follows:

> All these are in large quarto, and superbly printed, like the longer and shorter works published in London from 1749 to 1758. The whole collection is in the Royal Library of Stockholm, as a present from the author. (Gjörwell 1764b, 651; JSR's translation)

Again we find that contemporaries judged the quality of the printing to be high. Although this notice is more substantial than some of the others, it does not rise to the level of a review; as we will see below, Gjörwell would publish a review of the shorter works of 1763 the following year.

In October 1764, another French-language journal published in the Netherlands, the *Journal des sçavans* (Journal of the Learned), published what amounts to a French translation of the English review that had appeared in the *Monthly Review,* with only minor changes. Most notable of these is the ending; the translator stopped short of including the reference to a literary coroners' verdict of insanity and instead ended with this distancing but not nearly as damning statement:

> We are at a loss to know how to judge or even guess what the motives were behind the publishing of this work, or rather this jumble of reveries. (*Journal des sçavans* 1764, 533; JSR's translation)

In February 1765, Gjörwell published his review of the shorter works of 1763. Although his earlier notice of the works had also mentioned *Divine Love and Wisdom* and *Divine Providence,* they were not included in this review. Gjörwell must have seen the text of an earlier continental review, because he opens his review by saying, "The Journalists abroad announce a singular work," and then follows the talking points established by the other nontheological reviews, including the truncated quotation from *Supplements* 32.[105] Gjörwell mostly sidesteps the sarcasm of those reviews, however; the closest he comes to it is his statement concerning the account involving Louis XIV: "This is a very important anecdote in French History" (Tafel 1877, 706; a translation of Gjörwell 1765, 169). And he dodges the theological concepts even more deftly and completely by saying merely this in his conclusion: "The author's remaining ideas on the subject of the articles of our faith are entirely passed over."[106]

---

105. Because the review in the *Bibliothèque des sciences et des beaux arts* formed the template for the review in the *Monthly Review,* and because that in turn was translated to become the review in the *Journal des sçavans,* it is hard to tell which of the three Gjörwell took as his model; the truncation of the quotation of *Supplements* 32 arguably narrows it down to one of the latter two.

106. Tafel 1877, 706, with orthographical corrections; a translation of Gjörwell 1765, 169. Gjörwell makes one factual mistake in his review: unlike the other reviewers, he concludes that Swedenborg's statements about sexual intercourse in the spiritual world actually mean that there is a begetting of children there. Swedenborg expressly says this is not the case, however (*Marriage Love* 44:9, 51). It is an interesting sign of a growing awareness of Swedenborg's works at the time that a professor of Greek and oriental (Middle Eastern) studies at the University of Lund, Jakob Jonas Björnståhl (1731–1779), wrote directly to Gjörwell on March 25, 1765, to say that he, Björnståhl, had "read Swedenborg's works well" and felt the need to correct him on this point (Academy Documents 896.11).

All the reviewers except Ernesti, then, seem leery of engaging with the theological content. Nonetheless, now that Swedenborg had published the shorter works of 1763, his theological works were finally being noticed in print, and in forums where their titles were spelled out and their key points mentioned and even quoted.

Swedenborg apparently expected and even welcomed a negative response. We gather this from a letter he wrote to Beyer in 1769 concerning a controversial document that Swedenborg had authored and given Beyer permission to print and circulate:

> I have also received the printed letter, about which, in the beginning, a large number in the House of Clergy made a great noise; yet such noise does no harm, for it acts in the same way as ferment in wine when it is being made, of which it later clears itself; for if that which is unright does not come to be ventilated and so driven off, that which is right cannot be seen and received. (Acton 1948–1955, 701–702)

b. Response from the Swedish Royal House

Perhaps the most remarkable new approach to distribution Swedenborg took with his works of 1763 and *Divine Providence* was to give them to kings and queens; as far as we know, he had not done this with his theological works before.

On his way home from printing the works of 1763 and 1764 in the Netherlands, in July or August of 1764, Swedenborg stopped in Copenhagen. From Gjörwell [1782], 223, we learn that he there presented *The Lord, Sacred Scripture, Life, Faith, Supplements, Divine Love and Wisdom,* and *Divine Providence* to Frederick V, king of Denmark (1723–1766).

Swedenborg then traveled on to Stockholm, arriving on August 12, 1764, and made a presentation of the same works to the king and queen of Sweden. It seems that Swedenborg and his gift of books were well received. The king extended an invitation (technically known as a command) for Swedenborg to dine in Drottningholm, the queen's castle, with the royal family around August 19, just a week after he had returned. In attendance at this dinner were King Adolf Frederick (1710–1771) and Queen Lovisa Ulrika; their children Gustav (1746–1792), Charles (1748–1818), Frederick Adolf (1750–1803), and Sophia Albertina (1753–1829); five present or former members of the Privy Council including Count Tessin, Count Bonde, and Count von Höpken; and Swedenborg (Acton 1948–1955, 724). Two sources indicate that the topic of conversation the whole evening was Swedenborg's spiritual experiences. One of these sources was a letter Swedenborg himself wrote:

> That our Savior revealed Himself before me in a visible way, and commanded me to do what I have done and what further is to be done; and that He then allowed me to come into conversation with angels and spirits—this I have declared before the whole of Christendom in England, Holland, Germany, Denmark, as also in France and Spain, and likewise on different occasions here in this Kingdom, before their Royal Majesties, and, in particular, when I had the grace to eat at their Majesties' table when the whole Royal family was present, and also 5 Privy Councillors, when nothing else was talked of but this. (Swedenborg to King Adolf Frederick, May 25, 1770; Acton 1948–1955, 724)

Although this letter was written by Swedenborg, and therefore might be doubted, it was written to King Adolf Frederick, the very monarch with whom he had dined. It seems very improbable that Swedenborg would have exaggerated the account of an event his majesty had hosted and experienced for himself. His version accords with that of Gjörwell, who communicated about the dinner in a letter to Swedish author Johan Hinric Lidén (1741–1793):

> Eight days ago, Assessor Swedenborg was at Drottningholm, presenting his new books to the king, who commanded him to eat at his table, whereupon he captivated the royal family with news from the other world.[107]

This royal dinner must have left quite an impression on Swedenborg; in a three-page autobiographical account of his long life written for Thomas Hartley (1708–1784) and Dr. Husband Messiter (1731–1785) in 1769, he devoted a whole paragraph to that evening with the royal family (Acton 1948–1955, 678, 681–682).

A week and a half later, on August 28, 1764, just two and a half weeks after Swedenborg had arrived home, Gjörwell paid a visit to Swedenborg at his home for the purpose of officially requesting copies of his latest

---

107. Gjörwell to Lidén, August 27, 1764; JSR's translation. In a letter written to Lidén a week earlier, on August 20, Gjörwell had provided him with a list of Swedenborg's seven "new books": *Divine Providence, Divine Love and Wisdom,* and the five shorter works of 1763. Presumably Gjörwell was referring again to these seven when he informed the same person a week later that Swedenborg presented "his new books" to the king. For both letters, see Academy Documents 886.11.

published works for the Royal Library, and secondarily to learn more about the content and background of Swedenborg's works for himself. Gjörwell shortly thereafter wrote a careful and quite formal, signed account of his visit, which was eventually published.

Royal Library, August 28, 1764, afternoon.

> A little while ago I, the undersigned, returned from a visit to Assessor Emanuel Swedenborg, on whom I had called in order to request, on account of the Royal Library, a copy of the works he has lately published in Holland.
>
> I met him in the garden adjoining his house in Hornsgatan in the southern part of Stockholm *(Södermalm),* where he was engaged in attending his plants, attired in a simple garment. . . . Without knowing me or the nature of my errand, he said smiling, "Perhaps you would like to take a walk in the garden." I answered that I wished to have the honour of calling upon him, and asking him, on behalf of the Royal Library, for his latest works, so that we might have a complete set, especially as we had the former parts he had left with Wilde, the royal secretary.
>
> "Most willingly," he answered, "besides, I had intended to send them there, as my purpose in publishing them has been to make them known, and to place them in the hands of intelligent people." I thanked him for his kindness, whereupon he showed them to me, and took a walk with me in the garden. . . .
>
> His mission consists in communicating this new light to the world; and whoever is willing to accept it, receives it; the Lord also has granted him this revelation, that he may make it known to others. . . . Its object really is, that a New Jerusalem is to be established among men; the meaning of which is, that a New Church is at hand, about the nature of which, and the way to enter it, his writings really treat. . . .
>
> When a man dies, his soul does not divest itself of its peculiarities *(böjelser);* these he takes with him: when I could not refrain from asking him what Professor Dr. Nils Wallerius[108] busies himself with; "He still goes about," he said, "and holds disputations."
>
> His former works were printed in London, but his latter in Amsterdam. He has, nevertheless, been over to England, in order to present

---

108. Nils Wallerius was born in 1706 and died on August 16, 1764, just twelve days previous to the writing of the report. He was the hunter of heretics mentioned in note 33 above.

them to the Royal Society;[109] and on his return home he presented them in Copenhagen to the King of Denmark; even as last week he presented them to both their Majesties in Drottningholm. They have been favourably received everywhere. He had only twelve copies of the works with him in this country, four of which are intended for the public libraries, and four more for our most prominent bishops.[110]

Here we see several of the themes of Swedenborg's program at once: (1) his desire to pass along the "new light" of his revelations, (2) his sharing some "news from the other world" about a mutual acquaintance who had recently passed away, and (3) his supplying copies to Sweden's chief libraries and most prominent bishops.

Though these elements of his program are now familiar to us, the dynamic visible in this meeting with Gjörwell is new. Whereas all the effort and energy had to this point been going out from Swedenborg over and over again, here at last someone has instead come to him, asking for his works. Gjörwell's visit may well be said to mark a turning point in the history of Swedenborg's dissemination campaign. From now on, it would not be unidirectional; increasingly in the years and, beyond his lifetime, in the decades ahead, interested readers and thinkers would seek out his works.

VI. Conclusion

As we have seen, in 1759 Swedenborg was dismayed by the lack of response on the part of the leaders of the British clergy and nobility to *Secrets of Heaven* and his works of 1758. Giving up his anonymity in early March 1760 in Sweden, he sought to engage the leaders of the Swedish clergy and nobility during the Riksdag of 1760–1762. We do not know exactly how this effort played out or what resulted, though it is clear that the response again appears to have been muted: a conversation briefly flared up, but no lasting change seems to have occurred. As Swedenborg pondered his next move, his homeland of Sweden became engulfed in a multinational war and suffered severe monetary inflation.

---

109. This visit to England in the spring of 1763 is otherwise unattested, but a quick round trip from and to the Netherlands might not have taken more than a week.

110. Tafel 1877, 402–405, with corrections; a translation of Gjörwell [1782], 220–224.

As soon as the storm of war had passed, Swedenborg returned to publishing his theological works, but they were cast in a different mold. Reshaping the same essential substance, he crafted smaller works that were more focused in theme and precisely targeted. In this new kind of writing, he dialed back the references to *Secrets of Heaven* and arguably created his first-ever works specifically for clergy, "the Four Sets of Teachings," as well as his first works targeted expressly at readers who thought in less scriptural terms, namely, *Divine Love and Wisdom* and *Divine Providence*.

Despite their brevity, topically the five shorter works of 1763 confront the monolith of accepted Protestant thought. To the clergy, and others who would listen, *The Lord* asserts that contemporary Christian ideas of Jesus are wrong; it makes the case, both with reasoned argument and through the presentation of scriptural quotation, for a more fundamentally unified view. *Sacred Scripture* claims that contemporary Christian ideas of the Bible are wrong; there is far more to Scripture than its literal meaning. *Life* says that contemporary Christian ideas of how our lives and good deeds relate to our salvation are wrong; it offers a bold new emphasis on works, and is accompanied by practical advice on how to live by the Ten Commandments. *Faith* holds that contemporary Christian ideas of faith, especially the notion that faith should be blind and accept ideas even if they make no sense, are wrong; it makes an eloquent case for the alternative. And finally, *Supplements* extends the challenge of the works that precede it by illustrating in vivid terms the fate of Christian leaders in the spiritual world who had seemed intensely religious outwardly, but were inwardly evil.

At the beginning of 1760, Swedenborg's work as a theological author was universally unknown. Less than five years later, in August 1764, as the result of a systematic campaign of engagement with religious and secular leaders in Sweden, he found himself invited to visit the king and queen of Sweden, specifically for the purpose of presenting his latest works and explaining his views. He dined not only with them and their children, but with at least three high-level members of the government who were very familiar with his claim of otherworldly revelation and with his works. He spoke openly and at length with those assembled there on the subject of his spiritual experiences.

The conversation he had hoped to start was underway.

Appendix 1

A Brief Summary of Swedenborg's Methods of Distribution

THE surviving evidence of the methods Swedenborg employed to make people aware of his works no doubt represents just a fraction of everything he actually did, said, and wrote to this purpose. Nevertheless, what does remain is enough to show that Swedenborg used a number of ways to promote and distribute his works.

As has been discussed in the introduction, we have no specific information about what he might have done with the fifty sets of the works of 1758 that he received permission to import. One tactic is clear, however, from the evidence of the way in which he distributed his later works: in addition to sending out individual copies, he would often send multiple copies to his correspondents, with the suggestion that they keep one and pass the rest on. Thus Swedenborg's Amsterdam acquaintance Johann Christian Cuno (1708–1796) became, apparently to his surprise, the recipient of ten copies of Swedenborg's book *Survey* in 1769.[III]

In cover letters that accompanied these distributions, Swedenborg would offer suggestions or make requests concerning the further dissemination of the extra copies. For example, he sent Beyer some individual volumes of *Secrets of Heaven* that Beyer lacked and included with them another unbound set of the entire work. In his cover letter he explained: "The unbound copies of Arcana Coelestia are sent as a present to the Bishop [i.e., Bishop Lamberg of Göteborg], to whom I send my respectful greetings" (Acton 1948–1955, 614). Sometimes Swedenborg specified some of the recipients and left some unspecified, as he does in the following letter to Beyer (here politely referred to in the third person as "the Herr Doctor") that accompanied *Revelation Unveiled:*

> I have now come to an end with the Revelation-book, and am sending to the Herr Doctor 8 copies thereof—2 stitched and 6 unstitched.

III. Acton 1948–1955, 648. Even when Swedenborg sent out individual copies he seems to have presumed that what he sent was likely to be shared and circulated among others, because at times he gave specific instructions to the contrary (Acton 1948–1955, 566, 693, 697).

> These the Herr Doctor will dispose of as follows: 1 for himself; 1 for the Bishop, 1 for the Dean, 1 for Dr. Rosen, 1 for the Burgomaster, Herr Petterson, 1 for the Library; the 2 remaining copies the Herr Doctor can hand out to his friends. (Acton 1948–1955, 610)

Likewise Friedrich Christoph Oetinger (1702–1782) reports that Swedenborg sent him several copies of *Marriage Love,* intending one for Oetinger himself and giving the other copies, says Oetinger, "with the request that I bring it to the attention of any illustrious duke I might know" (Acton 1948, 356). (Oetinger in fact did so.)

The known targets of Swedenborg's distribution fall across a wide range of individuals and institutions, including monarchs and members of the royal family, the royal court, members of the Privy Council, secretaries of state, senators, ambassadors, a duke, noblemen, and a burgomaster; a cardinal, bishops, a dean, university theologians and lectors, "clergymen qualified for a more than ordinary station" (Acton 1948–1955, 611), "preachers and priests of all sects" including Roman Catholics (Acton 1948–1955, 651), all the priests and professors in the Netherlands, and the foremost priests in Germany (Acton 1948–1955, 659); merchants, businessmen, and bankers; universities and academies, royal and learned societies, and libraries. And these people and institutions were scattered over a broad area of western Europe: we have evidence of his distributing to Sweden, Denmark, Poland, Germany, the Netherlands, Britain, France, Spain, and Russia.

Swedenborg did not supply copies for all potential recipients of a given status, sometimes because he did not have enough stock, and sometimes because he did not respect all members of a class equally. For example, in one case he is reported to have said that he was sending copies of *Secrets of Heaven* "only to those [bishops] who are *sapientes* [wise] and *intelligentes* [intelligent]" (Acton 1948–1955, 599). Likewise, Swedenborg suggested to Ludwig IX, landgrave of Hesse-Darmstadt (1719–1790), that he share copies of Swedenborg's theological works with "learned men among the clergy" in his duchy, and further recommended that "such learned men among your clergy be chosen as love truths and take delight in them because they are truths" (Acton 1948–1955, 751). At one point when he was banned from importing his theological works, and specifically *True Christianity,* into Sweden, Swedenborg wrote:

> If the prohibition should be removed, I will send copies as a gift to the libraries and also to those members of the most Reverend House of the

Clergy who are desirous of truth and, if they find it there, see light in themselves. (Acton 1948–1955, 748)

On one occasion Swedenborg singled out his nephew, Bishop Lars Benzelstierna, as the sole recipient of a book, because "in my opinion, Benzelstierna is a rational man even in theology" (Acton 1948–1955, 697). This sort of expressed preference, when communicated directly or indirectly to the recipients, may well have been intended to encourage their reading of the work in question.

Despite this occasional giving of preference to certain individuals in some groups, overall we see him sending his works to friend and foe alike. In both his choice of recipients and explicitly in the cover letters that accompanied his distribution, Swedenborg showed remarkable respect for the freedom of opinion of others. He might gently suggest that his recipients do things such as (a) express their opinion of the work in some group or committee of which they were a part, and/or (b) request that third parties who also received a copy express their opinions. For example, Swedenborg sends twelve copies of *Survey* to Beyer, requesting that one copy be given to the dean of Göteborg, and adds: "After the little work has been read by the Herr Dean, may it please the Herr Doctor [Beyer] to request him to express his opinion of it in the Consistory" (Acton 1948–1955, 659). When urging the landgrave of Hesse-Darmstadt to pass his theological works on to clergy in the landgrave's duchy, as just noted, Swedenborg adds, "If it be pleasing to you, you may perhaps order that some learned men among the clergy in your Duchy, present and lay open their judgments concerning it" (Acton 1948–1955, 751).

Another of his techniques was to tell people in these cover letters the names of others who were being sent copies. For example, he sent the Swedish ambassador to France twenty copies of *Revelation Unveiled* and then added:

> Of this work, I have sent 2 copies to Cardinal de Rohan, 2 to the Royal Society of Sciences, 2 to our Secretary of State, and 1 for the Royal Library. (Acton 1948–1955, 611)

Sometimes he also described what kind of response the book had received from other people or even in other nations generally. Of *True Christianity* Swedenborg told Bishop Mennander, "This work is already being bought by many persons, and in a short time the printed copies will likely be sold out" (Acton 1948–1955, 748). When he sent *Marriage Love* to Beyer, he said:

> This book is in great demand in Paris and in many places in Germany.... This little treatise has been sent to all the professors and clergymen in the whole of Holland, and has already reached the foremost universities in Germany. Moreover, it will be turned into English in London, and will also be published in Paris." (Acton 1948–1955, 672)

When copies of *Marriage Love* were confiscated as they were being imported into Sweden, Swedenborg requested that the impounded copies be released, adding, "I will mention here, that the above-mentioned book has been permitted entrance into Holland, England, Germany, Denmark, and also into France and Spain, and has been well received" (Acton 1948–1955, 689); he adds that if and when the copies are released they "will be sent abroad where they are much desired" (Acton 1948–1955, 691).

As we have seen above on pages 44–45, from early on in this effort Swedenborg knew that convincing others, especially those in positions of power, to read and consider his works would be an uphill battle. Yet he had also seen from the beginning that there were at least a few who felt inspired by these works. He seems to have tried every method he could think of to reach more such people—people who would be interested and become engaged, or as the angels put it, people who were "living by their faith." And in time he found not many, but enough.

Appendix 2

Analysis of References to Secrets of Heaven *in Swedenborg's Works between 1758 and 1763*

As discussed on pages 51 and 77–78 of the introduction, the number of Swedenborg's references from his later works to *Secrets of Heaven* declined markedly in the books he wrote during the years immediately prior to 1763 when he was refraining from publication.

For the purpose of demonstrating this decline, we utilize an edition in which both Swedenborg's published works and his drafts are apportioned into pages of standard length: the Redesigned Standard Edition (RSE) of Swedenborg's works in English.[112] We divide these works into four bodies of text in their chronological order (as well as that can be determined):[113]

1. The five works of 1758: *Other Planets, Heaven and Hell, Last Judgment, New Jerusalem,* and *White Horse*[114] (965 RSE pages)
2. The huge but unfinished manuscript of 1758–1759: *Revelation Explained* (3,822 RSE pages)
3. The other, smaller manuscripts written between 1759 and 1763, namely, *Draft of "The Lord"* (traditionally titled *De Domino*), *Commentary on the Athanasian Creed*, *Draft on the Inner Meaning of Prophets and Psalms*, *Draft of "Sacred Scripture"* (traditionally titled *De Verbo* or *Word of the Lord from Experience*), *Draft of "Supplements"* (traditionally titled *Last Judgment [Posthumous]*), *Draft of "Life"* (traditionally titled *De Praeceptis*), *Draft on Divine Love,* and *Draft on Divine Wisdom* (629 RSE pages)

---

112. Published by the Swedenborg Foundation, West Chester, Pa., 1994–1998.

113. For discussion of the drafts listed here, see Rose 2005a, 117–148.

114. On the order of composition of these works, see the editors' preface to *The Shorter Works of 1758* (= Rose and Shotwell 2018), 29–33.

4. The five shorter works of 1763: *The Lord, Sacred Scripture, Life, Faith,* and *Supplements* (351 RSE pages)

The references to *Secrets of Heaven* in these works appear in "bursts" of references on a particular topic. The term for these units here will be "indexlike statements." Each such statement gives a brief summary of some doctrinal point, usually in the form of a sentence but at times as a mere phrase, followed by one or more references to *Secrets of Heaven* (at times scores or even hundreds of them). Most commonly, these references point to specific section numbers in *Secrets of Heaven,* but occasionally they point to a topic or a portion of the Bible covered. The following is a typical example:

> All our evils cling to us: 2116. Evils cannot be removed from us; we can only be held back from them and be kept focused on doing what is good: 865, 868, 887, 894, 1581, 4564, 8206, 8393, 9014, 9333, 9446, 9447, 9448, 9451, 10057, 10109. (*New Jerusalem* 170:2)

Because an indexlike statement consists of both text and references, this example would count as two indexlike statements, even though the first is more succinct and refers to only one section in *Secrets of Heaven,* while the second is lengthier and refers to sixteen sections.

To provide a constant proportion, we take the average number of indexlike statements per one hundred pages throughout each body of work. (The average is rounded to the nearest whole number to avoid fractions.) And to show the change from one end to another within a given body of text, each of the bodies of text is evenly divided into thirds. Figure 2 shows the results in both graph and tabular form.

It can be seen that, as described on pages 77–78 of the introduction, in the works of 1758 the number of indexlike statements pointing to *Secrets of Heaven* starts at a high level and more than triples by the end. In the next body of text, which consists entirely of *Revelation Explained,* the number of indexlike statements per hundred pages starts at a robust eighty-four, drops in the middle to twenty-five, and ends up at just six, a more than thirteenfold decrease from one end of the work to the other. And the decline continues. In the manuscripts written between 1759 and 1763 there is a low of one and a high of just eleven indexlike statements per hundred pages, and in the shorter works of 1763, that number starts at three, decreases in the middle to two, and eventually drops to zero.

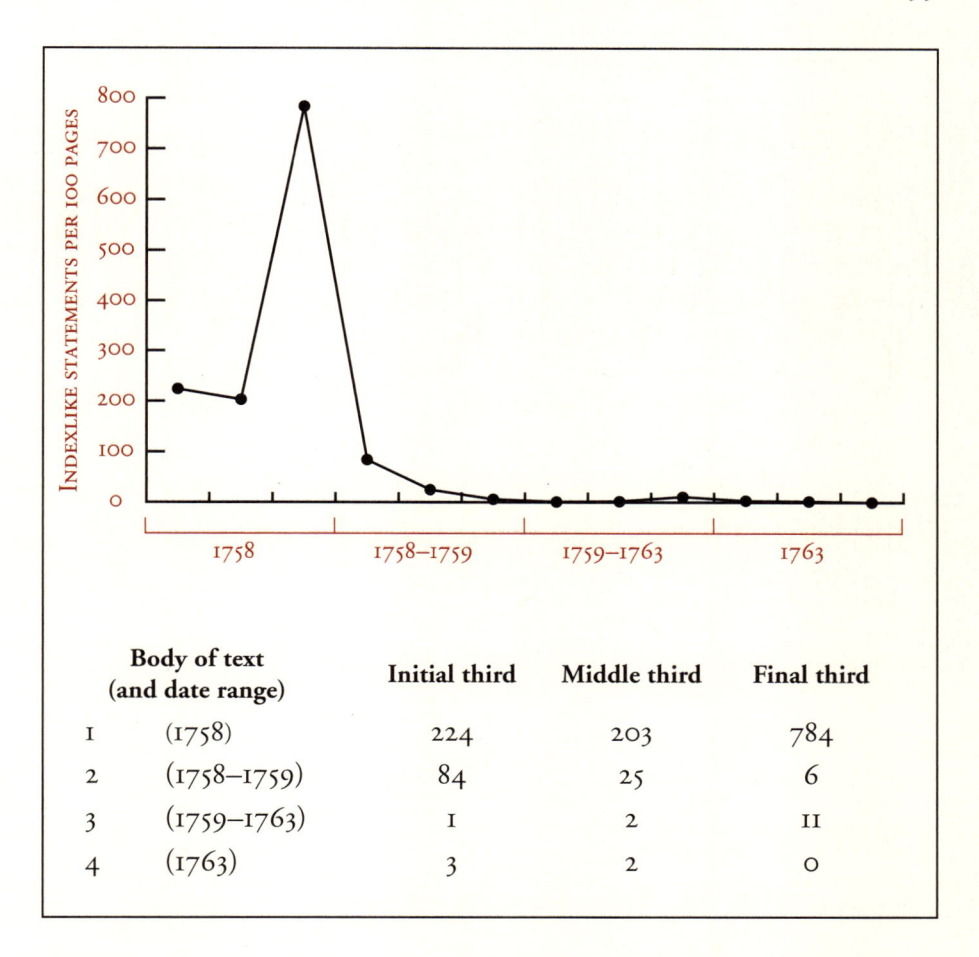

Body of text (and date range)	Initial third	Middle third	Final third
1 (1758)	224	203	784
2 (1758–1759)	84	25	6
3 (1759–1763)	1	2	11
4 (1763)	3	2	0

Figure 2. Indexlike statements per one hundred pages of Swedenborg's texts, 1758–1763

For greater detail on the second body of work, *Revelation Explained,* we can graph the average number of indexlike statements per hundred pages within each chapter. The result, shown in figure 3 on the next page, indicates the definite downward trend from beginning to end.

An additional point about *Revelation Explained* is worth adducing. Swedenborg apparently felt the need to insert a notification[115] in the rough draft of the work that reads as follows:

---

115. It is clear that the notification was an afterthought; it is inserted vertically in the margin of the rough draft.

> Please note: The many cross-references in the exegesis that now follows are to *Secrets of Heaven*. (*Revelation Explained* [= Swedenborg 1994–1997a] §3; JSR's translation)

Obviously Swedenborg added this because without such notice the reader might have been baffled by the abundance of otherwise unlabeled numbers in the text. This statement, occurring as it does in the author's prefatory material to *Revelation Explained* before the exegesis begins, would lead the reader to expect that the entire work would contain an abundance of such references, but in fact it does not.

These facts suggest that Swedenborg's publishing plan was changing even while he was in the act of writing *Revelation Explained*.

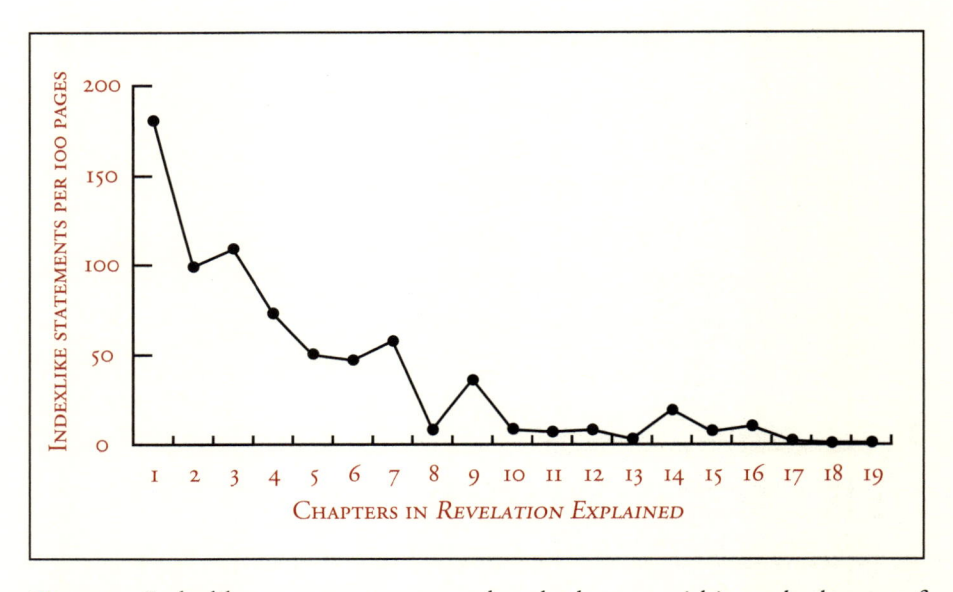

Figure 3. Indexlike statements per one hundred pages within each chapter of *Revelation Explained*

Appendix 3

Internal Evidence for the Publication and Presentation Order of the Shorter Works of 1763

IN general, cross-references from one work of Swedenborg's to another fall into two categories, about which we can make inferences as follows:

1. *References that use past- or present-tense verbs in the Latin, and may include specific section numbers, especially when the present tense is used.* Such references indicate that the other work referred to was already in print at the time of publication, and will here be referred to as a reference that "looks back to" the other work.
2. *References that use future-tense verbs in the Latin and do not include specific section numbers.* Such references indicate that the other work referred to was not yet in print at the time of publication, and will here be referred to as a reference that "looks forward to" the other work.

The Latin is the soundest basis for research into these references because the tenses involved are not always rendered literally in English translations.

If these assumptions are correct, then all the following evidence suggests that *The Lord, Sacred Scripture, Life, Faith,* and *Supplements* is the order in which the author both published and presented these works.

- The preface to *The Lord* lists *The Lord, Sacred Scripture, Life, Faith,* and *Supplements* in that order.
- *The Lord* 65 at the end somewhat obliquely mentions *Sacred Scripture, Life,* and *Faith* in that order, and refers to them as "forthcoming works" (Latin *sequentibus*).
- *Supplements* 76 refers to *The Lord, Sacred Scripture,* and *Life* all in the past tense, in that order.
- The individual references from one work to another are uniformly consistent with this sequence of publication. See figure 4 on the next page.

Not a single reference disrupts this pattern.

Work containing reference	Type of reference	Work referred to	Section containing reference Bold = Includes specific section references
The Lord	looks forward to	*Sacred Scripture*	future tense: 3, 7, 14:12
Sacred Scripture	looks back to	*The Lord*	past tense: **2:2, 10**, 32, **35:1**, **43**, 62, **89**
			present tense: **88, 98**
Life	looks back to	*The Lord*	present tense: **79:3**
	looks back to	*Sacred Scripture*	past tense: **14, 15, 62, 87**
			present tense: **66:2**
	looks forward to	*Faith*	future tense: 64
Faith	looks back to	*The Lord*	past tense: 37, 40
	looks back to	*Sacred Scripture*	past tense: **65**
	looks back to	*Life*	present tense: **12, 16, 22, 23**
	looks forward to	*Supplements*	future tense: 64:2
Supplements	looks back to	*The Lord*	present tense: **12**
	looks back to	*Sacred Scripture*	past tense: **48:1**
			present tense: **14, 81, 82:1**

Figure 4. Cross-references between the shorter works of 1763

Appendix 4

Swedish Bishops, 1760–1772

THE Swedish bishops in office in 1760, the year in which Swedenborg began making these bishops a target of distribution of his theological works, were as follows:

Archbishop of Uppsala: Samuel Troilius (1706–1764)
Bishop of Linköping: Andreas Olai Rhyzelius
Bishop of Skara: Engelbert Halenius
Bishop of Strängnäs: Eric Alstrin
Bishop of Västerås: Lars Larsson Benzelstierna
Bishop of Växjö: Olof Petri Osander (1700–1787)
Bishop of Lund: Johan Engeström (1699–1777)
Bishop of Göteborg (Gothenburg): Erik Lamberg (1719–1780)
Bishop of Karlstad: Nils Lagerlöf (1688–1769)
Bishop of Härnösand: Olof Kiörning (1704–1778)
Bishop of Visby (in Gotland): Gabriel Timoteus Lütkeman (1723–1795)
Bishop of Kalmar: Magnus Beronius (1692–1775)
Bishop of Åbo: Carl Fredrik Mennander

Between 1760 and the time of Swedenborg's death in 1772, only a handful of changes occurred in this group: In 1761 Bishop Rhyzelius died and was replaced by Petrus Filenius. In 1763, Jacob Serenius became bishop of Strängnäs after Bishop Alstrin passed away; in 1764 Archbishop Troilius died, Bishop Beronius then became archbishop of Uppsala, and Karl Gustaf Schröder (1717–1789) became bishop of Kalmar in his place; when Bishop Halenius passed away in 1767, Anders Forssenius (1706–1788) became bishop of Skara; and two years after Bishop Lagerlöf died in 1769, Göran Claes Schröder (1713–1773) became bishop of Karlstad. In the autobiographical statement that Swedenborg wrote at Hartley's request, he puts the number of Swedish bishops of his day at ten and adds that they all loved him (Acton 1948–1955, 678).

Works Cited in the Introduction

Academy Documents (Academy Collection of Swedenborg Documents). Swedenborg Library, Bryn Athyn College. Bryn Athyn, Pa.

Acton, Alfred. 1948. "Some New Swedenborg Documents." *New Church Life* 68:353–368, 393–405.

———. 1948–1955. *The Letters and Memorials of Emanuel Swedenborg.* 2 vols. Bryn Athyn, Pa.: Swedenborg Scientific Association.

Alnander, Samuel Johansson. [1763] 1772. *Anvisning til et Utvaldt Theologiskt Bibliothek: Andra Afdelningen.* Stockholm: Peter Hesselberg.

Bergianska Avskriftssamlingen, or "Bergius Collection," in the Royal Swedish Academy of Sciences. Stockholm.

Bergquist, Lars. 2005. *Swedenborg's Secret: The Meaning and Significance of the Word of God, the Life of the Angels, and Service to God: A Biography.* London: Swedenborg Society. Translation of *Swedenborgs hemlighet,* Stockholm: Natur och Kultur, 1999.

Bibliothèque des sciences et des beaux arts (The Hague). 1763. Review of *The Lord, Sacred Scripture, Life, Faith,* and *Supplements,* [by Emanuel Swedenborg]. Tome 20, part 2 (October–December):550–554.

———. 1764. Notice of *Divine Love and Wisdom* and *Divine Providence,* [by Emanuel Swedenborg]. Tome 22, part 1 (July–September):292.

The British Magazine (London). 1749. Notice of *Secrets of Heaven* vol. 1, [by Emanuel Swedenborg]. Vol. 4 (September):404.

Chadwick, John, and Jonathan S. Rose, eds. 2008. *A Lexicon to the Latin Text of the Theological Writings of Emanuel Swedenborg (1688–1772).* London: Swedenborg Society.

Daily Advertiser (London). February 5, 1750. Notice of *Secrets of Heaven* Genesis 16, [by Emanuel Swedenborg]. Page 4.

———. February 12, 1750. Notice of *Secrets of Heaven* Genesis 16, [by Emanuel Swedenborg]. Page 4.

Edvinsson, Rodney. 2010. "Foreign Exchange Rates in Sweden, 1658–1803." In *Exchange Rates, Prices, and Wages, 1277–2008,* edited by Rodney Edvinsson, Tor Jacobson, and Daniel Waldenström. Stockholm: Sveriges Riksbank.

Ernesti, Johann August. 1760. Review of *Secrets of Heaven,* [by Emanuel Swedenborg]. *Neue theologische Bibliothek* 1:515–527.

———. 1763. Review of *The Lord, Sacred Scripture, Life, Faith,* and *Supplements,* [by Emanuel Swedenborg]. *Neue theologische Bibliothek* 4:725–733.

———. 1766. Review of *Revelation Unveiled,* [by Emanuel Swedenborg]. *Neue theologische Bibliothek* 7:685–692.

Frängsmyr, Tore. 1975. "Christian Wolff's Mathematical Method and Its Impact on the Eighteenth Century." *Journal of the History of Ideas* 36:653–668.

General Advertiser (London). April 20, 1750. Notice of *Secrets of Heaven* Genesis 17, [by Emanuel Swedenborg]. Page 3.

———. June 18, 1750. Notice of *Secrets of Heaven* Genesis 18, [by Emanuel Swedenborg]. Page 3.

———. June 19, 1750. Notice of *Secrets of Heaven* Genesis 18, [by Emanuel Swedenborg]. Page 4.

Gjörwell, Carl Christoffer. 1764a. Review of *Anvisning til et Utvaldt Theologiskt Bibliothek: Andra Afdelningen*, by Samuel Johansson Alnander. *Svenska Mercurius* (January):68–76.

———. 1764b. Notice of *The Lord, Sacred Scripture, Life, Faith, Supplements, Divine Love and Wisdom,* and *Divine Providence,* by Emanuel Swedenborg. *Svenska Mercurius* (August):651.

———. 1765. Review of *The Lord, Sacred Scripture, Life, Faith,* and *Supplements,* by Emanuel Swedenborg. *Svenska Mercurius* (February):167–169.

———, ed. [1782]. *Anmärkningar i swenska historien, samlade af et sälskap. Första bandet, första afdelning.* Stockholm: A. J. Nordström.

Holberg, Ludvig. 1741. *Nicolai Klimii Iter Subterraneum: Novam Telluris Theoriam ac Historiam Quintae Monarchiae adhuc Nobis Incognitae Exhibens.* Copenhagen and Leipzig: Jacob Preuss.

Janssens, Guus. 2010. Personal communication with author, June 2010.

Journal des sçavans, avec des extraits des meilleurs journaux de France et d'Angleterre. Suite des CLXX. volumes du journal des sçavans, et des LXXIX. volumes du même journal combiné avec les mémoires de Trévoux (Amsterdam). 1764. Review of *The Lord, Sacred Scripture, Life, Faith,* and *Supplements,* [by Emanuel Swedenborg]. Vol. 1, tome 6, no. 11 (October):527–533.

Lewis, John. 1750. Pamphlet advertising *Secrets of Heaven,* [by Emanuel Swedenborg]. London: J. Lewis.

Lewis, John, and Stephen Penny. December 25, 1749. Letter and notice concerning *Secrets of Heaven* vol. 1, [by Emanuel Swedenborg]. *Daily Advertiser* (London), page 1.

Lindh, F. G. 1921. "Swedenborg som Söderbo." *Nya Kyrkans tidning* 46:137–140, 145–146, 161–163, 169–172.

Lloyd's Evening Post, and British Chronicle (London). April 5–7, 1758. Notice of *Heaven and Hell, Last Judgment, New Jerusalem, White Horse, Other Planets,* and *Secrets of Heaven* vols. 1–8, [by Emanuel Swedenborg]. 2:336.

———. April 10–12, 1758. Notice of *Heaven and Hell, Last Judgment, New Jerusalem, White Horse, Other Planets,* and *Secrets of Heaven* vols. 1–8, [by Emanuel Swedenborg]. 2:349.

The London Magazine or Gentleman's Monthly Intelligencer. 1749. Notice of *Secrets of Heaven* vol. 1, [by Emanuel Swedenborg]. Vol. 18 (September):436.

Luther, Martin. [1520] 1897. "Mar. Lutheri Tractatus de Libertate Christiana." In *Abteilung* 1, vol. 7 of *D. Martin Luthers Werke: Kritische Gesammtausgabe.* Weimar: Hermann Böhlau.

———. [1520] 1957. "The Freedom of a Christian, 1520." Translated by W. A. Lambert and revised by Harold J. Grimm. In vol. 31 of *Luther's Works,* American Edition, edited by Jaroslav Pelikan and Helmut T. Lehman. Philadelphia: Muhlenberg.

———. [1520] 2016. *The Freedom of a Christian, 1520.* Edited by Timothy J. Wengert. Minneapolis: Fortress Press.

Metcalf, Michael F., ed. 1987. *The Riksdag: A History of the Swedish Parliament.* New York: St. Martin's Press.
Monthly Review, or Literary Journal (London). 1764. Review of *The Lord, Sacred Scripture, Life, Faith,* and *Supplements,* [by Emanuel Swedenborg]. 30:573–575.
Neue Zeitungen von gelehrten Sachen (Leipzig). 1750. Review of *Secrets of Heaven,* [by Emanuel Swedenborg]. Part 1, no. 36 (May 4):313–316.
Nordencrantz, Anders. 1759. *Til Riksens höglofl. ständer församlade wid Riksdagen år 1760: en wördsam föreställning uti et omständeligit swar på de oförgripeliga påminnelser; som uti Stockholms Post-Tidningar, den 25 september 1758, kungjorde blifwit, wara af trycket utkomne, wid de under sidstledne Riksdag til Riksens höglofliga ständer aflemnade trenne skrifter om rättegångers förminskning, lag, domare och folk, samt en rättskaffens fri-och säkerhet.* Stockholm: Lorents Ludv. Grefing.
Nyrén, Carl. 1836. *Charakters Skildringar och Minnen af Sig Sjelf, Föräldrar och Syskon, m. fl. egenhändigt antecknade utaf Carl Nyrén.* Linköping: Petré.
Odhner, Carl Th. 1912. "Swedenborg and Ernesti." *New Church Life* 32:133–151, 197–209, and plates facing pages 133 and 197.
Public Advertiser (London). April 10, 1758. Notice of *Heaven and Hell, Last Judgment, New Jerusalem, White Horse, Other Planets,* and *Secrets of Heaven* vols. 1–8, [by Emanuel Swedenborg]. Page 4.
Rivers, Isabel. 2018. *Vanity Fair and the Celestial City: Dissenting, Methodist, and Evangelical Literary Culture in England, 1720–1800.* New York: Oxford University Press.
Rose, Frank S. 2005a. "Swedenborg's Manuscripts." In *Emanuel Swedenborg: Essays for the New Century Edition on His Life, Work, and Impact,* edited by Jonathan S. Rose and others. West Chester, Pa.: Swedenborg Foundation.
Rose, Jonathan S. 2005b. "Annotated Bibliography of Swedenborg's Writings." In *Emanuel Swedenborg: Essays for the New Century Edition on His Life, Work, and Impact,* edited by Jonathan S. Rose and others. West Chester, Pa.: Swedenborg Foundation.
———. 2006. Translator's preface to *True Christianity,* by Emanuel Swedenborg. Vol. 1. West Chester, Pa.: Swedenborg Foundation.
———. 2013. "Differences in Content, Terminology, and Approach within Swedenborg's Theological Latin Corpus." In *Emanuel Swedenborg—Exploring a "World Memory": Context, Content, Contribution,* edited by Karl Grandin. Stockholm: The Center for History of Science.
Rose, Jonathan S., and Stuart Shotwell. 2018. Editors' preface to *The Shorter Works of 1758,* by Emanuel Swedenborg. West Chester, Pa.: Swedenborg Foundation.
Sigstedt, Cyriel Odhner. 1981. *The Swedenborg Epic: The Life and Works of Emanuel Swedenborg.* London: Swedenborg Society. First edition: 1952, New York: Bookman Associates.
Smoley, Richard. 2005. "The Inner Journey of Emanuel Swedenborg." In *Emanuel Swedenborg: Essays for the New Century Edition on His Life, Work, and Impact,* edited by Jonathan S. Rose and others. West Chester, Pa.: Swedenborg Foundation.
———. 2018. "Glimpses of a Larger Vision: Swedenborg's Shorter Works of 1758." In *The Shorter Works of 1758,* by Emanuel Swedenborg. West Chester, Pa.: Swedenborg Foundation.

Swedenborg, Emanuel. 1722. *Miscellanea Observata circa Res Naturales.* Vol. 1. Leipzig.

———. 1744. *Regnum Animale, Anatomice, Physice, et Philosophice Perlustratum.* Vol. 1. The Hague: Adrian Blyvenburg.

———. 1768. *Delitiae Sapientiae de Amore Conjugiali: Post Quas Sequuntur Voluptates Insaniae de Amore Scortatorio.* Amsterdam.

———. 1927–1951. *The Word of the Old Testament Explained.* Translated and edited by Alfred Acton. 10 vols. Bryn Athyn, Pa.: Academy of the New Church.

———. 1994–1997a. *Apocalypse Explained.* Translated by John C. Ager, revised by John Whitehead, and edited by William Ross Woofenden. 6 vols. West Chester, Pa.: Swedenborg Foundation.

———. 1994–1997b. *The Athanasian Creed.* Translated by Samuel Worcester and revised by John C. Ager. In vol. 6 of *Apocalypse Explained,* edited by William Ross Woofenden. West Chester, Pa.: Swedenborg Foundation.

———. 1994–1997c. *Concerning the Lord and Concerning the Holy Spirit.* Translated by Samuel Worcester and revised by John C. Ager. In vol. 6 of *Apocalypse Explained,* edited by William Ross Woofenden. West Chester, Pa.: Swedenborg Foundation.

———. 1996. *The Doctrine of Charity.* In vol. 1 of *Posthumous Theological Works,* translated by John Whitehead and edited by William Ross Woofenden. West Chester, Pa.: Swedenborg Foundation.

———. 1998–2013. *Emanuel Swedenborg's Diary, Recounting Spiritual Experiences during the Years 1745 to 1765.* Vols. 1–3 translated by J. Durban Odhner; vol. 4 translated by Kurt P. Nemitz. Bryn Athyn, Pa.: General Church of the New Jerusalem.

Szabo, Franz A. J. 2013. *The Seven Years War in Europe, 1756–1763.* 3rd ed. London and New York: Routledge.

Tafel, R. L. 1875. *Documents Concerning the Life and Character of Emanuel Swedenborg.* Vol. 1. London: Swedenborg Society.

———. 1877. *Documents Concerning the Life and Character of Emanuel Swedenborg.* Vol. 2, parts 1 and 2. London: Swedenborg Society.

Tessin, Carl Gustaf. 1819. *Tessin och Tessiniana: biographie med anecdoter och reflexioner, samlade utur framledne riks rådet, m. m. grefve C. G. Tessins egenhändige manuscripter.* Edited by Fredrik Wilhelm von Ehrenheim. Stockholm: Johan Imnelius.

Voltaire. [1734] 2003. *Philosophical Letters: Letters Concerning the English Nation.* Translated by Ernest Dilworth. Mineola, N.Y.: Dover.

Whitehall Evening Post, Or London Intelligencer. November 10, 1750. Notice of *Secrets of Heaven* vols. 1 and 2, [by Emanuel Swedenborg]. Page 2.

———. March 28, 1758. Notice of *Heaven and Hell, Last Judgment, New Jerusalem, White Horse, Other Planets,* and *Secrets of Heaven* vols. 1–8, [by Emanuel Swedenborg]. Page 4.

———. March 30, 1758. Notice of *Heaven and Hell, Last Judgment, New Jerusalem, White Horse, Other Planets,* and *Secrets of Heaven* vols. 1–8, [by Emanuel Swedenborg]. Page 4.

Woofenden, William Ross, and Jonathan S. Rose. 2008. "A Reader's Guide to *Secrets of Heaven.*" In vol. 1 of *Secrets of Heaven,* by Emanuel Swedenborg. West Chester, Pa.: Swedenborg Foundation.

Short Titles and Other Conventions Used in This Work

THE following summaries of scholarly conventions common to Swedenborgian studies are offered as an aid to readers unfamiliar with Swedenborg's works. For a brief biography of Swedenborg, an overview of his theology, discussion of the content of his published and unpublished theological corpus, essays on his impact on international culture, and extensive bibliographies, the reader is referred to the companion volume to the New Century Edition series, *Emanuel Swedenborg: Essays for the New Century Edition on His Life, Work, and Impact* (2005, West Chester, Pennsylvania: Swedenborg Foundation).

Volume contents The five titles in this volume, *The Lord, Sacred Scripture, Life, Faith,* and *Supplements,* were originally published as separate works. Annotations and indexes for the titles have been combined here for ease of use, and annotations are numbered continuously throughout the volume.

Section numbers Following a practice common in his time, Swedenborg divided his published theological works into sections numbered in sequence from beginning to end. His original section numbers have been preserved in this edition; they appear in red boxes in the outside margins. Traditionally, these sections have been referred to as "numbers" and designated by the abbreviation "n." In this edition, however, the more common section symbol (§) is used to designate the section numbers, and the sections are referred to as such.

Subsection numbers Because many sections throughout Swedenborg's works are too long for precise cross-referencing, Swedenborgian scholar John Faulkner Potts (1838–1923) further divided them into subsections; these have since become standard, though minor variations occur from one edition to another. These subsections are indicated by bracketed arabic numbers that appear in the text itself: [2], [3], and so on. Because the beginning of the first *subsection* coincides with the beginning of the *section* proper, it is not labeled in the text.

Citations of Swedenborg's text Citations of Swedenborg's works refer not to page numbers but to section numbers, which are uniform in most editions. In citations the section symbol (§) is generally omitted after the title of a work by Swedenborg. Thus "*Heaven and Hell* 239" refers to section 239 (§239) of Swedenborg's *Heaven and Hell*, not to page 239 of any edition. Subsection numbers are given after a colon; a reference such as "239:2" indicates subsection 2 of section 239. The reference "239:1" would indicate the first subsection of section 239, though that subsection is not in fact labeled in the text. Where section numbers stand alone without titles, their function is indicated by the prefixed section symbol; for example, "§239:2".

Citations of the Bible Biblical citations in this edition follow the accepted standard: a semicolon is used between book references and between chapter references, and a comma between verse references. Therefore "Matthew 5:11, 12; 6:1; 10:41, 42; Luke 6:23, 35" refers to Matthew chapter 5, verses 11 and 12; Matthew chapter 6, verse 1; Matthew chapter 10, verses 41 and 42; and Luke chapter 6, verses 23 and 35. Swedenborg often incorporated the numbers of verses not actually represented in his text when listing verse numbers for a passage he quoted; these apparently constitute a kind of "see also" reference to other material he felt was relevant, and are generally retained in this edition. This edition also follows Swedenborg where he cites contiguous verses individually (for example, John 14:8, 9, 10, 11), rather than as a range (John 14:8–11). Occasionally this edition supplies a full, conventional Bible reference where Swedenborg omits one after a quotation.

Quotations in Swedenborg's works Some features of the original Latin texts have been modernized in this edition. For example, Swedenborg's first editions rely on context or italics rather than on quotation marks to indicate passages taken from the Bible or from other works. The manner in which these conventions are used in the original suggests that Swedenborg did not belabor the distinction between direct quotation and paraphrase; neither did he mark his omissions from or changes to material he quoted, whether biblical, creedal, or his own. In this edition, passages quoted more or less directly by Swedenborg from his sources are indicated by either block quotations or quotation marks, but passages that he only paraphrased are not specially marked. His practice of not indicating omissions or changes in quotations has been followed here. One exception consists of instances in which Swedenborg did not include a complete sentence in a Bible quotation. The omission in such cases has been marked in this edition with added points of ellipsis.

Italicized terms Any words in indented scriptural extracts that are here set in italics reflect a similar emphasis in the first editions.

Swedenborg's footnotes Referenced in each case by a superscript letter *a* in the main body of the text, the author's footnotes to *The Lord* 64:1, *Sacred Scripture* 6, and *Life* 101 include references to three of his previously published works: *Secrets of Heaven* (1749–1756), *Heaven and Hell* (1758), and *New Jerusalem* (1758).

Changes to and insertions in the text This translation is based on the first Latin editions, published by Swedenborg himself. It incorporates the silent emendation of minor errors, not only in the text proper but in Bible verse references and in section references to Swedenborg's other published theological works. The text has also been changed without notice where the verse numbering of the Latin Bible cited by Swedenborg differs from that of modern English Bibles. Throughout the translation, references or cross-references that were implied but not stated have been inserted in square brackets; for example, [John 3:27]. By contrast, references that occur in parentheses reflect references that appear in the first editions. In general, brackets represent an insertion of material that was not present in the first editions.

Endnotes Comments on the text are printed as endnotes, which are referenced by superscript numbers appearing in the main text. A reverse reference is given in the endnote itself. To find the location of the text treated in endnote 113, for example, the reader would turn back to the indicated section, §37 of *The Lord,* and the indicated subsection, [2]. The initials of the writer or writers (listed on the title page) are given in square brackets at the end of each note. Translations of material quoted in the endnotes are those of the indicated writer, except where otherwise specified or in cases in which the cited source is a translated text.

Chapter numbering Swedenborg did not number the chapters of the works in this volume. His decision not to do so seems to have been deliberate, and in accord with it chapter numbers are not included in the text. However, because some studies of this work make reference to chapter numbers, the table of contents provides them.

Titles of Swedenborg's works References to Swedenborg's writings in this edition accord with the short titles listed below, except where he gives his own version of a title in the text of the translation, or where other translations are cited by the annotators. In this list, the short title is followed by the traditional translation of the title; by the original Latin title, with its full translation; and finally by the place and date of original publication if Swedenborg published it himself, or the approximate date of writing if he did not. The list is chronological within each of the two groups shown—the published theological works, and the nontheological and posthumously published works. The titles given below as theological works published by Swedenborg are generally not further referenced in lists of works cited in the preface, introduction, and endnotes.

Biblical titles Swedenborg refers to the Hebrew Scriptures as the Old Testament and to the Greek Scriptures as the New Testament; his terminology has been adopted in this edition. As was the custom in his day, he refers to the Pentateuch (Genesis, Exodus, Leviticus, Numbers, and Deuteronomy) as the books of Moses, or simply as "Moses"; for example, in *Sacred Scripture* 44:2 he writes "This is what we read in Moses," and then cites a passage from Exodus 28; and in *Sacred Scripture* 101:3 he speaks of "what it says in Moses" and then cites Deuteronomy 32. Similarly, in sentences or phrases introducing quotations he sometimes refers to the Psalms as "David"; for example, in *The Lord* 33:5 he writes "There is also this in David," and then cites a passage from Psalm 24; and in *Sacred Scripture* 98 he refers to the Book of Revelation as "the Revelation of John." Conventional references supplied in parentheses after such quotations specify their sources more precisely.

Problematic content Occasionally Swedenborg makes statements that, although mild by the standards of eighteenth-century theological discourse, now read as harsh, dismissive, or insensitive. The most problematic are assertions about or criticisms of various religious traditions and their adherents—including Judaism, ancient or contemporary; Roman Catholicism; Islam; and the Protestantism in which Swedenborg himself grew up. As off-putting as such statements are today, it seems nonetheless necessary to retain them in these translations. The other option—to omit them—would obscure some aspects of Swedenborg's presentation and in any case compromise its historicity. These statements are far outweighed in size and importance by other passages in Swedenborg's works earnestly maintaining the value of every individual and of all religions.

Theological Works Published by Swedenborg

Secrets of Heaven
Traditional title: *Arcana Coelestia*
Original title: *Arcana Coelestia, Quae in Scriptura Sacra, seu Verbo Domini Sunt, Detecta: . . . Una cum Mirabilibus Quae Visa Sunt in Mundo Spirituum, et in Coelo Angelorum* [A Disclosure of Secrets of Heaven Contained in Sacred Scripture, or the Word of the Lord, . . . Together with Amazing

Things Seen in the World of Spirits and in the Heaven of Angels]. London: 1749–1756.

Heaven and Hell
Traditional title: *Heaven and Hell*
Original title: *De Coelo et Ejus Mirabilibus, et de Inferno, ex Auditis et Visis* [Heaven and Its Wonders and Hell: Drawn from Things Heard and Seen]. London: 1758.

New Jerusalem
Traditional title: *New Jerusalem and Its Heavenly Doctrine*
Original title: *De Nova Hierosolyma et Ejus Doctrina Coelesti: Ex Auditis e Coelo: Quibus Praemittitur Aliquid de Novo Coelo et Nova Terra* [The New Jerusalem and Its Heavenly Teachings: Drawn from Things Heard from Heaven: Preceded by a Discussion of the New Heaven and the New Earth]. London: 1758.

Last Judgment
Traditional title: *The Last Judgment*
Original title: *De Ultimo Judicio, et de Babylonia Destructa: Ita Quod Omnia, Quae in Apocalypsi Praedicta Sunt, Hodie Impleta Sint: Ex Auditis et Visis* [The Last Judgment and Babylon Destroyed, Showing That at This Day All the Predictions of the Book of Revelation Have Been Fulfilled: Drawn from Things Heard and Seen]. London: 1758.

White Horse
Traditional title: *The White Horse*
Original title: *De Equo Albo, de Quo in Apocalypsi, Cap. XIX: Et Dein de Verbo et Ejus Sensu Spirituali seu Interno, ex Arcanis Coelestibus* [The White Horse in Revelation Chapter 19, and the Word and Its Spiritual or Inner Sense (from *Secrets of Heaven*)]. London: 1758.

Other Planets
Traditional title: *Earths in the Universe*
Original title: *De Telluribus in Mundo Nostro Solari, Quae Vocantur Planetae, et de Telluribus in Coelo Astrifero, deque Illarum Incolis, Tum de Spiritibus et Angelis Ibi: Ex Auditis et Visis* [The Earthlike Bodies Called Planets in Our Solar System and in Deep Space, Their Inhabitants, and the Spirits and Angels There: Drawn from Things Heard and Seen]. London: 1758.

The Lord
Traditional title: *Doctrine of the Lord*
Original title: *Doctrina Novae Hierosolymae de Domino* [Teachings for the New Jerusalem on the Lord]. Amsterdam: 1763.

Sacred Scripture
Traditional title: *Doctrine of the Sacred Scripture*
Original title: *Doctrina Novae Hierosolymae de Scriptura Sacra* [Teachings for the New Jerusalem on Sacred Scripture]. Amsterdam: 1763.

Life
Traditional title: *Doctrine of Life*
Original title: *Doctrina Vitae pro Nova Hierosolyma ex Praeceptis Decalogi* [Teachings about Life for the New Jerusalem: Drawn from the Ten Commandments]. Amsterdam: 1763.

Faith
Traditional title: *Doctrine of Faith*
Original title: *Doctrina Novae Hierosolymae de Fide* [Teachings for the New Jerusalem on Faith]. Amsterdam: 1763.

Supplements
Traditional title: *Continuation Concerning the Last Judgment*
Original title: *Continuatio de Ultimo Judicio: Et de Mundo Spirituali* [Supplements on the Last Judgment and the Spiritual World]. Amsterdam: 1763.

Divine Love and Wisdom
Traditional title: *Divine Love and Wisdom*
Original title: *Sapientia Angelica de Divino Amore et de Divina Sapientia* [Angelic Wisdom about Divine Love and Wisdom]. Amsterdam: 1763.

Divine Providence
Traditional title: *Divine Providence*
Original title: *Sapientia Angelica de Divina Providentia* [Angelic Wisdom about Divine Providence]. Amsterdam: 1764.

Revelation Unveiled
Traditional title: *Apocalypse Revealed*
Original title: *Apocalypsis Revelata, in Qua Deteguntur Arcana Quae Ibi Praedicta Sunt, et Hactenus Recondita Latuerunt* [The Book of Revelation Unveiled, Uncovering the Secrets That Were Foretold There and Have Lain Hidden until Now]. Amsterdam: 1766.

Marriage Love
Traditional title: *Conjugial Love*
Original title: *Delitiae Sapientiae de Amore Conjugiali: Post Quas Sequuntur Voluptates Insaniae de Amore Scortatorio* [Wisdom's Delight in Marriage

Love: Followed by Insanity's Pleasure in Promiscuous Love]. Amsterdam: 1768.

Survey
Traditional title: *Brief Exposition*
Original title: *Summaria Expositio Doctrinae Novae Ecclesiae, Quae per Novam Hierosolymam in Apocalypsi Intelligitur* [Survey of Teachings of the New Church Meant by the New Jerusalem in the Book of Revelation]. Amsterdam: 1769.

Soul-Body Interaction
Traditional title: *Intercourse between the Soul and Body*
Original title: *De Commercio Animae et Corporis, Quod Creditur Fieri vel per Influxum Physicum, vel per Influxum Spiritualem, vel per Harmoniam Praestabilitam* [Soul-Body Interaction, Believed to Occur either by a Physical Inflow, or by a Spiritual Inflow, or by a Preestablished Harmony]. London: 1769.

True Christianity
Traditional title: *True Christian Religion*
Original title: *Vera Christiana Religio, Continens Universam Theologiam Novae Ecclesiae a Domino apud Danielem Cap. VII:13–14, et in Apocalypsi Cap. XXI:1, 2 Praedictae* [True Christianity: Containing a Comprehensive Theology of the New Church That Was Predicted by the Lord in Daniel 7:13–14 and Revelation 21:1, 2]. Amsterdam: 1771.

Nontheological and Posthumously Published Works by Swedenborg Cited in This Volume

Basic Principles of Nature
Traditional title: *Principia*
Original title: *Principia Rerum Naturalium sive Novorum Tentaminum Phaenomena Mundi Elementaris Philosophice Explicandi* [Basic Principles of Nature or of New Attempts to Explain Philosophically the Phenomena of the Elemental World]. Dresden and Leipzig: 1734.

First Draft of Three Transactions on the Brain
Traditional title: *The Cerebrum*
Original title: [Untitled]. Written before or during August 1738.

Dynamics of the Soul's Domain
Traditional title: *Economy of the Animal Kingdom*
Original title: *Oeconomia Regni Animalis in Transactiones Divisa* [Dynamics of the Soul's Domain, Divided into Treatises]. 2 vols. Amsterdam: 1740–1741.

Draft Introduction to a Rational Psychology
Traditional title: *Introduction to Rational Psychology*
Original title: [Untitled]. Written around 1741.

Draft on the Soul's Fluid
Traditional title: *Animal Spirit(s)*
Original title: *De Spiritu Animali* [The Soul's Fluid]. Written before or during 1742.

Draft on the Fiber
Traditional title: *The Fiber*
Original title: [Untitled]. Written around 1742.

The Soul's Domain, Volume 2
Traditional title: *The Animal Kingdom*
Original title: *Regnum Animale, Anatomice, Physice, et Philosophice Perlustratum. Cujus Pars Secunda, de Visceribus Thoracis seu de Organis Regionis Superioris Agit* [The Soul's Domain Thoroughly Examined by Means of Anatomy, Physics, and Philosophy. Part 2: The Viscera of the Thorax or Organs of the Higher Region]. The Hague: 1744.

The Old Testament Explained
Traditional title: *The Word Explained*
Original title: *Explicatio in Verbum Historicum Veteris Testamenti* [The Historical Word of the Old Testament Explained]. Written from November 1745 to February 1747.

Concordance of Proper Nouns in the Bible
Traditional title: *Bible Indexes*
Original title: *Nomina Virorum, Terrarum, Regnorum, Urbium* [Names of People, Lands, Realms, and Cities]. Compiled during 1746 to 1748.

Spiritual Experiences
Traditional title: *The Spiritual Diary*
Original title: *Experientiae Spirituales* [Spiritual Experiences]. Written from 1747 to 1765.

Isaiah and Jeremiah Explained
Traditional title: *Isaiah and Jeremiah Explained*
Original title: [Untitled]. Written around February 1747.

First Draft Concordance of Prophetic Material in the Bible
Traditional title: *Bible Indexes*
Original title: [Untitled]. Compiled during 1747.

Second Draft Concordance of Prophetic Material in the Bible
Traditional title: *Bible Indexes*
Original title: [Untitled]. Compiled during 1747 and early 1748.

Rough Copy of "Secrets of Heaven"
Traditional title: *Arcana Caelestia*
Original title: [Untitled]. Written around 1748 to 1756.

Revelation Explained
Traditional title: *Apocalypse Explained*
Original title: *Apocalypsis Explicata secundum Sensum Spiritualem, Ubi Revelantur Arcana, Quae Ibi Praedicta, et Hactenus Recondita Fuerunt* [The Book of Revelation Explained as to Its Spiritual Meaning, Which Reveals Secret Wonders That Were Predicted There and Have Been Hidden until Now]. Written from 1758 to 1759.

Draft of "The Lord"
Traditional title: *De Domino*
Reported original title: *De Domino* [On the Lord]. Written between 1759 and 1760.

Commentary on the Athanasian Creed
Traditional title: *Athanasian Creed*
Original title: *De Athanasii Symbolo* [On the Athanasian Creed]. Written before or during early 1760.

Draft on the Inner Meaning of Prophets and Psalms
Traditional title: *Prophets and Psalms*
Original title: [Untitled]. Written around 1761.

Draft of "Sacred Scripture"
Traditional title: *De Verbo*
Original title: *De Scriptura Sacra seu Verbo Domini ab Experientia* [On Sacred Scripture, or the Word of the Lord, from Experience]. Written around 1762.

Draft of "Supplements"
Traditional title: *Last Judgment (Posthumous)*
Original title: *De Ultimo Judicio* [On the Last Judgment]. Written around 1762.

Draft of "Life"
Traditional title: *De Praeceptis*
Original title: *De Praeceptis Decalogi* [On the Precepts of the Decalog]. Written around 1762.

Draft on Divine Love
Traditional title: *On Divine Love*
Original title: *De Divino Amore* [On Divine Love]. Written around late 1762 to early 1763.

Draft on Divine Wisdom
Traditional title: *On Divine Wisdom*
Original title: *De Divina Sapientia* [On Divine Wisdom]. Written in early 1763.

Second Sketch for "Marriage Love"
Traditional title: *De Conjugio II*
Reported original title: *De Conjugio* [On Marriage]. Written around 1766.

Sketch on Goodwill
Traditional title: *Charity*
Original title: *De Charitate* [On Charity]. Written between April and September 1766.

Draft of Five Memorable Occurrences
Traditional title: *Five Memorable Relations*
Reported original title: *Memorabilia* [Memorable Occurrences]. Written around 1766.

Sketch for "True Christianity"
Traditional title: *Canons of the New Church*
Reported original title: *Canones Novae Ecclesiae, seu Integra Theologia Novae Ecclesiae . . .* [Canons of the New Church, or the Entire Theology of the New Church . . .]. Written around 1769.

Draft Supplement to "White Horse"
Traditional title: *Appendix to White Horse*
Original title: *Appendix ad Codicillum "De Equo Albo"* [Appendix to the Little Work "The White Horse"]. Written in 1769.

Answers to Nine Questions
Traditional title: *Nine Questions*
Reported original title: *Quaestiones Novem de Trinitate, etc. ad Emanuelem Swedenborg Propositae a Thoma Hartley; Tum Illius Responsa* [Nine Questions on the Trinity and So On, Proposed to Emanuel Swedenborg by Thomas Hartley, and His Answers]. Written around 1771.

Sketch for "Coda to True Christianity"
Traditional title: *Sketch of the Coronis*
Original title: *Coronis seu Appendix ad Veram Christianam Religionem . . .* [Coda or Appendix to "True Christianity" . . .]. Written around 1771.

Draft for "Coda to True Christianity"
Traditional title: *Coronis*
Original title: *Coronis seu Appendix ad Veram Christianam Religionem . . .* [Coda or Appendix to "True Christianity" . . .]. Written around 1771.

Draft Invitation to the New Church
Traditional title: *Invitation to the New Church*
Original title: [Untitled]. Written around 1771.

Teachings for the New Jerusalem on the Lord

Preface

SOME years ago, I published five small works:[1]

1. *Heaven and Hell*
2. *The New Jerusalem and Its Heavenly Teachings*
3. *Last Judgment*
4. *White Horse*
5. *Planets, or Earthlike Bodies, in the Universe*

Many things were presented in these works that had previously been unknown. Now the following works are to be offered to the public at the command of the Lord,[2] who has been revealed to me.[3]

Teachings for the New Jerusalem on the Lord
Teachings for the New Jerusalem on Sacred Scripture
Teachings about Life for the New Jerusalem: Drawn from the Ten Commandments
Teachings for the New Jerusalem on Faith
Supplements on the Last Judgment [and the Spiritual World]
Angelic Wisdom about Divine Providence
Angelic Wisdom about Divine Omnipotence, Omnipresence, Omniscience, Infinity, and Eternity
Angelic Wisdom about Divine Love and Wisdom
Angelic Wisdom about Life[4]

"Teachings for the New Jerusalem" means teachings for the new church[5] now to be established by the Lord. The fact is that the old church has come to its end, as can be seen from what is said in §§33–39 of the booklet *Last Judgment* and from more that will be said in the forthcoming booklets just listed.

The twenty-first chapter of Revelation tells us that after the judgment the New Jerusalem will come. As you will see under the last heading below [§§62–65], this New Jerusalem means a new church.

Teachings for the New Jerusalem on the Lord

The Entire Sacred Scripture Is about the Lord, and the Lord Is the Word

We read in John,

> In the beginning was the Word, and the Word was with God, and the Word was God. He was in the beginning with God. All things were made through him, and nothing that was made came about without him. In him there was life, and that life was the light for humankind. And the light shines in the darkness, but the darkness did not grasp it. And the Word became flesh and lived among us; and we saw his glory, glory like that of the only-begotten child of the Father. He was full of grace and truth. (John 1:1, 2, 3, 4, 5, 14)

In the same Gospel,

> Light has come into the world, but people loved darkness rather than light, because their deeds were evil. (John 3:19)

And elsewhere in the same Gospel,

> While you have the light, believe in the light, so that you may become children of the light. I have come into the world as a light so that anyone who believes in me will not remain in darkness. (John 12:36, 46)

We can see from this that the Lord is God from eternity and that he himself is that Lord who was born into the world. It actually says that the Word was with God and that the Word was God, as well as that nothing that was made came about without him, and then that the Word became flesh and that they saw him.

There is little understanding in the church[6] of what it means to call the Lord "the Word." He is called the Word because the Word means divine truth or divine wisdom and the Lord is divine truth itself or divine wisdom itself. That is why he is also called the light that is said to have come into the world.

Since divine wisdom and divine love are one with each other and have been one in the Lord from eternity, it also says "in him there was life, and that life was the light for humankind." The life is divine love, and the light is divine wisdom.[7]

This oneness is what is meant by saying both that "in the beginning the Word was with God" and that "the Word was God." "With God" is in God, since wisdom is in love and love is in wisdom. This is like the statement elsewhere in John, "Glorify[8] me, Father, together with yourself, with the glory I had with you before the world existed" (John 17:5). "With yourself" is "in yourself." This is why it adds "and the Word was God." It says elsewhere that the Lord is in the Father and the Father is in him [John 14:10], and that the Father and he are one [John 10:30].

Since the Word is the divine wisdom of the divine love, it follows that it is Jehovah[9] himself and therefore the Lord, the one by whom all things were made that were made, since everything was created out of divine love by means of divine wisdom.[10]

2 We can see clearly that the specific Word[11] meant here is the Word made known through Moses, the prophets, and the evangelists,[12] since this is the actual divine truth from which angels[13] get all their wisdom and from which we get our spiritual intelligence. In fact, angels in the heavens have the very same Word that we have in the world, though for us in the world it is earthly, while in the heavens it is spiritual.[14] Further, since it is divine truth, the Word is also something divine that is emanating, and this is not only from the Lord but is the Lord himself.[15]

Since it is the Lord himself, absolutely everything written in the Word is about the Lord alone. From Isaiah to Malachi every detail has to do with the Lord,[16] either directly or in an opposite, negative sense.

No one has seen this before, but anyone who knows this and thinks of it can see it while reading, especially given the knowledge that in the Word there is not only an earthly meaning but a spiritual one as well;[17] and that in this latter meaning the names of persons and places are used to mean something about the Lord and therefore something about heaven and the church that come from him—or something opposed to the Lord.

Since absolutely everything in the Word is about the Lord, and since the Word is the Lord because it is divine truth, we can see why it says "The Word became flesh and lived among us; and we saw his glory" [John 1:14]. We can also see why it says "While you have the light, believe in the light, so that you may become children of the light. I have come into the world as a light; anyone who believes in me will not remain in darkness" [John 12:36, 46]. "Light" is divine truth and therefore the Word.

For this reason, even nowadays[18] anyone who turns to the Lord alone while reading the Word and who prays to him will find enlightenment in it.

3

I need at this point to say briefly what all the prophets of the Old Testament from Isaiah to Malachi have to say about the Lord, in general and in some detail.

1. The Lord came into the world in the fullness of time [Galatians 4:4], which was when he was no longer recognized by Jews and when for this reason there was no longer anything left of the church;[19] and unless the Lord had come into the world and revealed himself at that time, humankind would have suffered eternal death. He says in John, "If you do not believe that I am, you will die in your sins" (John 8:24).
2. The Lord came into the world to carry out a last judgment,[20] thereby subduing the hells that were then in control,[21] and doing so by means of battles or trials that were permitted to attack the human nature he had received from his mother,[22] and by a constant succession of victories. If the hells had not been subdued, no one could have been saved.
3. The Lord came into the world to glorify his human nature—that is, to unite it to the divine nature that he had from conception.
4. The Lord came into the world to found a new church that would recognize him as Redeemer and Savior and that would be redeemed and saved through its love for and faith in him.

5. At the same time he was reorganizing heaven and uniting it with the church.[23]
6. The suffering on the cross was the final battle or trial by means of which he completely subdued the hells and completely glorified his human nature.

In my forthcoming booklet on Sacred Scripture[24] it will become evident that these are the sole subjects of the Word.

4 In support of this, I would like in this first chapter simply to cite passages from the Word where it says "that day," "on that day," or "at that time," passages where "day" and "time" mean the Lord's Coming. From Isaiah:

> In *the days to come* it will happen that the mountain of Jehovah will be established as the highest of the mountains. On *that day* Jehovah alone will be exalted. *The day of Jehovah Sabaoth*[25] is majestic and high above all. On *that day* people will throw away their idols of silver and gold. (Isaiah 2:2, 11, 12, 20)

> On *that day* the Lord Jehovih[26] will take away adornments. (Isaiah 3:18)

> On *that day* the branch of Jehovah will be beautiful and glorious. (Isaiah 4:2)

> [Their enemy] will roar against the people on *that day* and look down on the earth. Behold, there is darkness and anxiety, and the light will be growing darker among their ruins. (Isaiah 5:30)

> It will happen on *that day* that Jehovah will whistle to the fly at the very end of the rivers of Egypt. On *that day* the Lord will shave [Judah] at the crossings of the river. On *that day* [a man] will bring [a young cow and two sheep] to life. On *that day* every place will become brambles and thorns. (Isaiah 7:18, 20, 21, 23)

> What will you do on *the day* of visitation? Who will come? On *that day* Israel will rely on Jehovah, the Holy One of Israel, in truth. (Isaiah 10:3, 20)

> It will happen on *that day* that the nations will seek out the root of Jesse, the one who stands as a sign for the peoples, and glory will be his rest. Above all, on *that day* the Lord will seek out the remnant of his people. (Isaiah 11:10, 11)

You will say on *that day,* "I will praise you, Jehovah." You will say on *that day,* "Praise Jehovah! Call upon his name!" (Isaiah 12:1, 4)

The day of Jehovah is near; it will come from Shaddai[27] like destruction. Behold, *the cruel day of Jehovah* is coming—a day of resentment, blazing wrath, and anger. I will violently move heaven, and the earth will be shaken out of its place, on *the day* of his blazing anger. Its *time* is at hand and it will come, and the days will not be prolonged. (Isaiah 13:6, 9, 13, 22)

It will happen on *that day* that the glory of Jacob will be worn away. On *that day,* people will look back to their Maker, and their eyes [will look] toward the Holy One of Israel. On *that day* there will be cities of refuge in the forsaken parts of the forest. (Isaiah 17:4, 7, 9)

Those who dwell on [this] island will say on *that day,* "Look at what has happened to our hope!" (Isaiah 20:6)

On *that day* there will be five cities in the land of Egypt speaking the languages of Canaan. On *that day* there will be an altar to Jehovah in the center of Egypt. On *that day* there will be a highway from Egypt to Assyria, and Israel will be at the center of the land. (Isaiah 19:18, 19, 23, 24)

A day of tumult, trampling, and confusion from the Lord Jehovih Sabaoth . . . (Isaiah 22:5)

On *that day* Jehovah will punish the army of the high place and the monarchs of the earth. After a great many *days* they will be punished. Then the moon will blush and the sun will be ashamed. (Isaiah 24:21, 23)

It will be said[28] on *that day,* "Behold, this is our God; we have waited for him to set us free." (Isaiah 25:9)

On *that day* this song will be sung in the land of Jehovah:[29] "We have a strong city." (Isaiah 26:1)

On *that day* Jehovah will bring punishment with his sword. On *that day* answer him by saying, "A vineyard whose wine is pure." (Isaiah 27:1, 2, 12, 13)

On *that day* Jehovah Sabaoth will become an ornate crown and a diadem. (Isaiah 28:5)

Then on *that day* the deaf will hear the words of the book, and the eyes of the blind will see out of the darkness. (Isaiah 29:18)

On *the day* of the great slaughter, when the towers fall, there will be a channel of waters. The light of the moon will be like the light of the sun on *the day* when Jehovah binds up the breach of his people. (Isaiah 30:25, 26)

On *that day* they will each throw away their idols of silver and gold. (Isaiah 31:7)

The day of Jehovah's vengeance, *the year* of his recompense . . . (Isaiah 34:8)

These two things will come to you in one *day:* the loss of your children, and widowhood. (Isaiah 47:9)

My people will know my name, and on *that day* [they will know that] I am the one saying "Here I am!" (Isaiah 52:6)

Jehovah has anointed me to proclaim *the year* of Jehovah's good pleasure and *the day* of vengeance for our God, to comfort all who are mourning. (Isaiah 61:1, 2)

The day of vengeance is in my heart and *the year* of my redeemed has arrived. (Isaiah 63:4)

From Jeremiah:

In *those days* you will no longer say, "The ark of the covenant of Jehovah." At that *time* they will call Jerusalem the throne of Jehovah. In *those days* the house of Judah will go to the house of Israel. (Jeremiah 3:16, 17, 18)

In *that day* the heart of the monarch will perish, and the heart of the royal family, and the priests and the prophets will be stunned. (Jeremiah 4:9)

Behold, *the days are coming* in which the earth will turn into a wasteland. (Jeremiah 7:32, 34)

They will fall among those who fall on *the day* of their visitation. (Jeremiah 8:12)

Behold, *the days are coming* in which I will execute judgment upon everyone whose foreskin has been circumcised. (Jeremiah 9:25)

In *the time* of their visitation they will perish. (Jeremiah 10:15)

There will be no remnant of them; I will bring evil upon them in *the year* of their visitation. (Jeremiah 11:23)

Behold, the *days are coming* in which it will no longer be said . . . (Jeremiah 16:14)

I will look at them in the back of the neck and not in the face on *the day* of their destruction. (Jeremiah 18:17)

Behold, *the days are coming* in which I will make this place a devastation. (Jeremiah 19:6)

Behold, *the days are coming* in which I will raise up for David a righteous branch who will rule as king. In *those days* Judah will be saved and Israel will dwell in safety. Therefore behold, *the days are coming* in which it will no longer be said . . . I will bring evil upon them in *the year* of their visitation. At the *very last of days* you will fully understand. (Jeremiah 23:5, 6, 7, 12, 20)

Behold, *the days are coming* in which I will turn back [the captivity of my people]. Alas, *that day* will be great, and there will be none like it. It will happen on *that day* that I will break the yoke and tear off the fetters. (Jeremiah 30:3, 7, 8)

The day will come when the guards cry out on Mount Ephraim, "Arise, let us climb Zion to Jehovah our God." Behold, *the days are coming* in which I will make a new covenant. *The days are coming* in which the city of Jehovah will be built. (Jeremiah 31:6, 27, 31, 38)

The days are coming in which I will perform the good word [that I promised]. In *those days* and at *that time* I will cause a righteous branch to grow for David. In *those days* Judah will be saved. (Jeremiah 33:14, 15, 16)

On *that day* I will bring words against this city for evil. You, though, I will rescue on *that day*. (Jeremiah 39:16, 17)

That day will be a *day* of vengeance for the Lord Jehovih Sabaoth; he will take vengeance on his enemies. *The day* of destruction has come upon them, *the time* of their visitation. (Jeremiah 46:10, 21)

Because of *the day that is coming* for devastation . . . (Jeremiah 47:4)

> I will bring upon [Moab] *the year* of visitation. Nevertheless I will bring back its captives at *the very last of days*. (Jeremiah 48:44, 47)

> I will bring destruction upon them at *the time* of their visitation. Their youths will fall in the streets and all their men of war will be cut down on *that day*. At *the very last of days* I will bring back their captives. (Jeremiah 49:8, 26, 39)

> In *those days* and at *that time* the children of Israel and the children of Judah will come together and seek Jehovah their God. In *those days* and at *that time* the iniquity of Israel will be sought, but there will be none. Woe to [the Babylonians], because their *day* has come, the *time* of their visitation. (Jeremiah 50:4, 20, 27, 31)

> They are vanity, a work of errors; they will perish at the *time* of their visitation. (Jeremiah 51:18)

From Ezekiel:

> The end has come; the end has come. It has come upon you like the morning. The *time* has come; the *day* of tumult is near. Behold *the day*; see, it has come. The trunk has blossomed; violence has sprouted. *The day* has arrived; *the time* has come upon their whole multitude. Their silver and gold will not rescue them on *the day* of *Jehovah's* wrath. (Ezekiel 7:6, 7, 10, 12, 19)

> People were saying of the prophet,[30] "The vision that he is seeing will not happen for many days; his prophecy concerns *distant times.*" (Ezekiel 12:27)

> They will not be able to stand up in the war on *the day* of Jehovah's wrath. (Ezekiel 13:5)

> You pierced, godless prince of Israel, whose *day* has come, in *the time* of iniquity of the end . . . (Ezekiel 21:25, 29)

> O city shedding blood in your own midst so that its *time* will come, you have made *the days* approach so that you will come to your years. (Ezekiel 22:3, 4)

> Surely on *the day* that I take their strength from them, on *that day* someone who has been rescued will come to you with information for you to hear. On *that day* your mouth will be opened to speak with the one who has been rescued. (Ezekiel 24:25, 26, 27)

On *that day* I will cause the horn of the house of Israel to grow. (Ezekiel 29:21)

Wail "Alas for *the day*," because *the day of Jehovah* is near, *the day of Jehovah* is near. It will be a *day* of cloud, *a time* for the nations. On *that day* messengers from me will go forth. (Ezekiel 30:2, 3, 9)

On *the day* you go down into hell . . . (Ezekiel 31:15)

I myself will search for my flock, [as] on *a day* when [a shepherd] is in the midst of [his] flock, and I will rescue them from all the places where they have been scattered on a cloudy and dark *day*. (Ezekiel 34:11, 12)

On *the day* when I cleanse you from all your iniquities . . . (Ezekiel 36:33)

Prophesy and say, "Will you not know it on *that day* when my people Israel settle safely? In *the days to come* I will bring you against my land. [This will happen] on *that day,* on *the day* when Gog comes upon the land [of Israel]. In my zeal, in *the day* of my indignation, surely on *this day* there will be a great earthquake upon the land of Israel." (Ezekiel 38:14, 16, 18, 19)

Behold, it is coming; *this* is *the day* of which I have spoken. It will happen on *that day* that I will give Gog a burial place in the land of Israel, so that the house of Israel will know that I, Jehovah, am their God from *that day* on. (Ezekiel 39:8, 11, 22)

From Daniel:

God in the heavens has revealed mysteries concerning what will happen in *the days to come.* (Daniel 2:28)

The time came for the saints to establish the kingdom. (Daniel 7:22)

"Understand that the vision concerns *the time of the end.*" [Gabriel] said, "Behold, I am making known to you what will happen at *the end* of the wrath, because at the appointed *time the end* will come." The vision of evenings and mornings is the truth. Hide the vision, because it is for *many days.* (Daniel 8:17, 19, 26)

I have come to make you understand what will happen to your people at *the very last of days,* because the vision applies to days yet to come. (Daniel 10:14)

> Those who understand will be tested in order to be purified and cleansed, until *the time of the end,* since it is yet for an appointed *time.* (Daniel 11:35)
>
> At *that time* Michael will rise up, the great leader who stands up for the children of your people. There will be *a time* of distress such as there has not been since the nation [began]. At *this time,* however, your people will be rescued—everyone who is found written in the book. (Daniel 12:1)
>
> You, Daniel, close up the words and seal the book until *the time of the end.* But from *the time* when the daily offering is taken away and the abomination that causes devastation is set up, there will be one thousand two hundred and ninety days. You will arise into your inheritance at *the end of days.* (Daniel 12:4, 9, 11, 13)

From Hosea:

> I will make *an end* of the kingdom of the house of Israel. On *that day* I will break the bow of Israel. Great will be *the day* of Jezreel.[31] (Hosea 1:4, 5, 11)
>
> On *that day* you will call [me] "my husband." On *that day* I will make them a covenant. On *that day* I will respond. (Hosea 2:16, 18, 21)
>
> The children of Israel will turn back and seek Jehovah their God and David their king at *the very last of days.* (Hosea 3:5)[32]
>
> Come, let us return to Jehovah. After two days he will revive us; on *the third day* he will raise us up, and we will live in his presence. (Hosea 6:1, 2)
>
> *The days* of visitation have come; *the days* of retribution have come. (Hosea 9:7)

From Joel:

> Alas for *the day,* because *the day* of Jehovah is at hand; it will come as destruction from Shaddai. (Joel 1:15)
>
> *The day of Jehovah* is coming, *a day* of darkness and gloom, *a day* of clouds and thick darkness. Great is *the day of Jehovah* and extremely terrifying; who can endure it? (Joel 2:1, 2, 11)

Upon my male and female servants I will pour out my spirit in *those days*. The sun will be turned into darkness and the moon into blood before the great and terrifying *day of Jehovah* comes. (Joel 2:29, 31)

In *those days* and at *that time* I will gather all nations together. The *day of Jehovah* is at hand. On *that day* it will happen that the mountains will drip with new wine. (Joel 3:1, 2, 14, 18)

From Amos:

The strong of heart will flee naked on *that day*. (Amos 2:16)

On *the day* that I punish Israel for its sins . . . (Amos 3:14)

Woe to you who long for *the day of Jehovah*. What is *the day of Jehovah* to you? It will be a day of darkness and not of light. Surely *the day of Jehovah* will be a day of darkness and not of light, a day of thick darkness with no light at all. (Amos 5:18, 20)

The songs of the Temple will be howls on *that day*. On *that day* I will make the sun set at noon, and will darken the earth on a day of light. On *that day* beautiful young women and also young men will faint from thirst. (Amos 8:3, 9, 13)

On *that day* I will raise up the fallen tent of David. Behold, *the days are coming* when the mountains will drip with new wine. (Amos 9:11, 13)

From Obadiah:[33]

On *that day* will I not destroy the wise of Edom? Do not rejoice over them on *the day* of their destruction, on *the day* of their distress. *The day* of Jehovah over all nations is at hand. (Obadiah verses 8, 12, 13, 14, 15)

From Micah:

On *that day* the lament will be "We have been utterly destroyed." (Micah 2:4)

At *the very last of days* the mountain of the house of Jehovah will be established on the top of the mountains. On *that day* I will gather the lame. (Micah 4:1, 6)

On *that day* I will cut off your horses and your chariots. (Micah 5:10)

> *The day* of your watchmen, your visitation, has come. *The day* for building the walls is here. This is the *day* in which he will come to you. (Micah 7:4, 11, 12)

From Habakkuk:

> The vision is still set for an appointed *time* and speaks concerning the end. If it delays, wait for it, because it will surely come and will not be postponed. (Habakkuk 2:3)

> Jehovah, do your work in *the midst of the years;* in *the midst of the years* you will make it known. God will come. (Habakkuk 3:2)

From Zephaniah:

> The *day of Jehovah* is at hand. On *the day* of the sacrifice of Jehovah I will execute judgment upon the royal family and upon the children of the monarch. On *that day* there will be the sound of shouting. At *that time* I will examine Jerusalem with lamps. The great *day of Jehovah* is at hand. *This day* is *a day* of blazing wrath; *a day* of distress and repression; *a day* of destruction and devastation; *a day* of darkness and gloom; *a day* of clouds and thick darkness; *a day* of trumpets and shouting. On *the day* of the blazing wrath of Jehovah the whole earth will be devoured and he will make a prompt end to all those who dwell in the land. (Zephaniah 1:7, 8, 10, 12, 14, 15, 16, 18)

> . . . when *the day* of the wrath of Jehovah has not yet come upon us. Perhaps you may be hidden on *the day* of the wrath of Jehovah. (Zephaniah 2:2, 3)

> Wait for me until *the day* I rise up for plunder, because that will be my judgment. On *that day* you will not be ashamed of your deeds. On *that day* it will be said to Jerusalem, "Do not be afraid." I will deal with your oppressors at *that time.* At *that time* I will bring you back. At *that time* I will gather you together to give you a name and praise. (Zephaniah 3:8, 11, 16, 19, 20)

From Zechariah:

> I will remove the iniquity of that land in *one day.* On *that day* each of you will invite your neighbor under a vine and under a fig tree. (Zechariah 3:9, 10)

> Then many nations will be joined to Jehovah on *that day.* (Zechariah 2:11)

> In *those days* ten men will take hold of the hem of a man of Judah. (Zechariah 8:23)
>
> Jehovah their God will save them on *that day,* as the flock of his people. (Zechariah 9:16)
>
> My covenant was broken on *that day.* (Zechariah 11:11)
>
> On *that day* I will make Jerusalem a heavy stone for all peoples. On *that day* I will strike every horse with confusion. On *that day* I will make the leaders of Judah like a fiery furnace surrounded by logs. On *that day* Jehovah will protect the inhabitants of Jerusalem. On *that day* I will seek to destroy all the nations [that are coming against Jerusalem]. On *that day* the mourning in Jerusalem will increase. (Zechariah 12:3, 4, 6, 8, 9, 11)
>
> On *that day* a fountain will be opened for the house of David and for the inhabitants of Jerusalem. It will happen on *that day* that I will cut off the names of idols from the land. On *that day* the prophets will be ashamed. (Zechariah 13:1, 2, 4)
>
> Behold, *the day of Jehovah* is coming. On *that day* his feet will stand on the Mount of Olives. On *that day* there will be no light or radiance. *One day* that will be known to Jehovah, not day or night, there will be light around the time of evening. On *that day* living waters will go forth from Jerusalem. On *that day* Jehovah will be one, and his name one. On *that day* there will be a great panic from Jehovah. On *that day* "Holiness belongs to Jehovah" will be engraved on the bells of the horses. There will no longer be a Canaanite in the house of Jehovah on *that day.* (Zechariah 14:1, 4, 6, 7, 8, 9, 13, 20, 21)

From Malachi:

> Who can bear *the day* of his coming? Who will stand when he appears? They will be mine on *the day* that I make them my treasure. Behold, *the day* is coming, burning like an oven. Behold, I will send you Elijah the prophet before the great and terrifying *day of Jehovah* comes. (Malachi 3:2, 17; 4:1, 5)

From David:[34]

> In *his days* the righteous will flourish and there will be much peace, and he will reign from sea to sea, and from the river all the way to the ends of the earth. (Psalms 72:7, 8)

There are other instances elsewhere.

5 In these passages, *day* and *time* mean the Lord's Coming. *A day* or *time* of darkness, gloom, thick darkness, no light, devastation, the iniquity of the end, or destruction means the Lord's Coming, when he is no longer recognized and therefore when there is nothing left of the church.35

A day that is cruel or terrifying, a *day* of blazing anger, wrath, panic, visitation, sacrifice, retribution, distress, war, or shouting means a coming of the Lord for judgment.36

A day when Jehovah alone will be exalted, when he will be one and his name one, when the branch of Jehovah will be beautiful and glorious, when the righteous will flourish, when he will bring [a young cow and two sheep] to life, when he will search for his flock, when he will make a new covenant, when the mountains will drip with new wine, when living waters will go forth from Jerusalem, and when people will look back to the God of Israel (and many similar expressions) mean the Coming of the Lord to set up a new church that will recognize him as Redeemer and Savior.37

6 Here I may add some passages that speak openly of the Lord's Coming, as follows:

> The Lord himself is giving you a sign. Behold, a virgin will conceive and bear a son, and she will call his name "*God with us.*"38 (Isaiah 7:14; Matthew 1:22, 23)

> A Child has been born to us; a Son has been given to us. Leadership will be upon his shoulder; and his name will be called Wonderful, Counselor, God, Hero, Father of Eternity, Prince of Peace. There will be no end of the increase of his leadership and peace, upon the throne of David and over his kingdom, to establish it in judgment and in justice from now on, even to eternity. (Isaiah 9:6, 7)

> A shoot will go forth from the trunk of Jesse, and a sprout from its roots will bear fruit. The spirit of Jehovah will rest upon him, a spirit of wisdom and intelligence, a spirit of counsel and strength. Justice will be a belt around his waist and truth a belt around his hips. Therefore it will happen on that day that the nations will seek the root of Jesse, the one who stands as a sign for the peoples, and glory will be his rest. (Isaiah 11:1, 2, 5, 10)

> Send the Lamb of the ruler of the earth from the rock by the wilderness to the mountain of the daughter of Zion. The throne has been

established through mercy; he sits upon it in truth in the tabernacle of David, judging and seeking a judgment, and hastening justice. (Isaiah 16:1, 5)

It will be said on that day, "Behold, this is our God; we have waited for him to set us free. *This is Jehovah;* we have waited for him. Let us rejoice and be glad in his salvation." (Isaiah 25:9)

A voice of someone in the wilderness crying out, "Prepare a pathway for *Jehovah;* make level in the desert a highway for *our God.* The glory of *Jehovah* will be revealed, and all flesh will see it together." Behold, *the Lord Jehovih* is coming in strength, and his arm will rule for him. Behold, his reward is with him. Like a shepherd he will feed his flock. (Isaiah 40:3, 5, 10, 11)

My chosen one, in whom my soul has pleasure: I, *Jehovah,* have called you in righteousness. I will make you a covenant for the people, a light for the nations, to open blind eyes, and to lead the captives out of prison and those who are sitting in darkness out of the house of confinement. I am *Jehovah.* This is my name; I will not give my glory to another. (Isaiah 42:1, 6, 7, 8)

Who has believed our word and to whom has the arm of Jehovah been revealed? He has no form: we have seen him, but he has no beauty. He bore our diseases and carried our sorrows. (Isaiah 53:1–12)

"Who is this who is coming from Edom, with spattered garments from Bozrah, approaching in the immensity of his strength?" "I who speak justice and have the power to save, because the day of vengeance is in my heart and the year of my redeemed has arrived." Therefore he became their Savior. (Isaiah 63:1, 4, 8)

Behold, the days are coming in which I will raise up for David a righteous branch who will rule as king, and prosper, and bring about judgment and justice on earth. And this is his name: they will call him "*Jehovah our Righteousness.*" (Jeremiah 23:5, 6; 33:15, 16)

Rejoice greatly, O daughter of Zion! Sound the trumpet, O daughter of Jerusalem! Behold, your king is coming to you. He is righteous and brings salvation. He will speak peace to the nations. His dominion will extend from sea to sea and from the river even to the ends of the earth. (Zechariah 9:9, 10)

Rejoice and be glad, O daughter of Zion! Behold, I am coming to dwell in your midst. Then many nations will be joined to *Jehovah* on that day and will become my people. (Zechariah 2:10, 11)

As for you, Bethlehem Ephrata, as little as you are among the thousands of Judah, one will come forth from you for me who will become the ruler in Israel; his coming forth is from ancient times, from the days of eternity. He will stand firm and feed [his flock] in the strength of *Jehovah*. (Micah 5:2, 4)

Behold, I am sending my angel, who will prepare the way before me; and *the Lord*, whom you seek, will suddenly come to his Temple, the angel of the covenant whom you desire. Behold, he is coming. But who can bear the day of his coming? Behold, I will send you Elijah the prophet before the great and terrifying day of Jehovah comes. (Malachi 3:1, 2; 4:5)

I was watching, and behold, someone like the Son of Humanity[39] was coming with the clouds of the heavens. To him was given dominion and glory and a kingdom; and all peoples, nations, and tongues will worship him. His dominion is an everlasting dominion, one that will not pass away, and his kingdom is one that will not perish. All dominions will worship and obey him. (Daniel 7:13, 14, 27)

Seventy weeks have been allotted for your people and your holy city to put an end to sinning, to seal the vision and the prophet, and to anoint the Most Holy. Know then and understand: from [the time] the word goes forth that Jerusalem must be restored and built until [the time of] Messiah the Leader will be seven weeks. (Daniel 9:24, 25)

I will place his hand on the sea and his right hand on the rivers. He will cry out to me, "You are my Father, my God, and the Rock of my salvation." I will also make him the firstborn, high above the monarchs of the earth. I will make his seed endure to eternity and his throne as the days of the heavens. (Psalms 89:25, 26, 27, 29)

Jehovah said to my *Lord:* "Sit at my right until I make your enemies a stool for your feet. *Jehovah* will send the scepter of your strength from Zion, to rule in the midst of your enemies. You are a priest forever after the manner of Melchizedek." (Psalms 110:1, 2, 4; Matthew 22:44; Luke 20:42, 43)

"I have anointed [him as] my king over Zion, which is my holy mountain." "I will proclaim concerning the statute, '*Jehovah* has said to me, "You are my Son; today I have begotten you. I will make the nations your inheritance, the ends of the earth your possession."'" Kiss the Son or he will become angry and you will perish on the way. Blessed are all who trust in him. (Psalms 2:6, 7, 8, 12)

You have indeed made him lack little in comparison with angels, and have crowned him with glory and honor. You have given him dominion over the works of your hands; you have placed all things under his feet. (Psalms 8:5, 6)

O *Jehovah,* be mindful of David, who swore to *Jehovah,* who vowed to the Mighty One of Jacob, "[God forbid]⁴⁰ that I enter the tent of my home, go up to my bed, and grant sleep to my eyes, until I have found a place for *Jehovah,* a dwelling for the Mighty One of Jacob. Behold, we have heard of him in Ephrata; we have found him in the fields of the forest. We will enter his dwelling and bow down at the stool for his feet. Let your priests be clothed with justice, and let your saints rejoice." (Psalms 132:1–9)

But the passages cited here are only a few.

7 There will be ample demonstration that the whole Sacred Scripture is written about the Lord alone later, especially in what will be presented in the booklet on Sacred Scripture.⁴¹ This and this alone is why the Word is holy. It is also what is meant by the statement in Revelation that "The testimony of Jesus is the spirit of prophecy" (Revelation 19:10).

To Say That the Lord Fulfilled All of the Law Is to Say That He Fulfilled All of the Word

8 MANY people nowadays believe that when it says of the Lord that he fulfilled the law [Matthew 5:17] it means that he fulfilled all of the Ten Commandments and that by doing so he became justice and justifies⁴² people in the world who believe this.

That is not what it means, though. It means rather that he fulfilled everything that was written about him in the Law and the Prophets—that is, in the whole Sacred Scripture[43]—because those writings, as stated under the preceding heading, are about him alone. The reason so many people believe something else is that they have not studied the Scriptures and seen what "the law" means in them.

In a strict sense "the law" does mean the Ten Commandments. In a broader sense it means everything Moses wrote[44] in his five books; and in the broadest sense it means the whole Word.

It is common knowledge that *in a strict sense "the law" does mean the Ten Commandments.*

9 *In a broader sense "the Law" means everything Moses wrote in his five books,* as we can see from the following passages. In Luke,

> Abraham said to the rich man in hell, "They have *Moses and the prophets;* let them hear them. If they do not hear *Moses and the prophets,* they will not be persuaded even if someone rises from the dead." (Luke 16:29, 31)

In John,

> Philip said to Nathanael, "We have found the one of whom *Moses in the Law,* and also *the prophets,* wrote." (John 1:45)

In Matthew,

> Do not think that I have come to destroy *the Law and the Prophets:* I have come not to destroy but to fulfill. (Matthew 5:17, 18)

Or again,

> All *the Prophets and the Law* prophesied until John. (Matthew 11:13)

In Luke,

> *The Law and the Prophets* extended to [the time of] John; since then, the kingdom of God has been proclaimed. (Luke 16:16)

In Matthew,

> Whatever you want people to do for you, you do the same for them. This is *the Law and the Prophets.* (Matthew 7:12)

Or again,

> Jesus said, "You are to love the Lord your God with all your heart and with all your soul, and you are to love your neighbor as yourself. On these two commandments hang all *the Law and the Prophets."* (Matthew 22:37, 39, 40)

In these passages "the Law and the Prophets" and "Moses and the prophets" mean everything written in the books of Moses and in the books of the prophets.

The following passages also show that "the Law" means specifically everything written by Moses. In Luke,

> When the days of their purification according to *the Law of Moses* were completed, they brought Jesus to Jerusalem to present him to the Lord—as it is written in *the Law of the Lord,* "Every male who opens the womb is to be called holy to the Lord,"—and to offer a sacrifice according to what is said in *the Law of the Lord,* "a pair of turtledoves or two young pigeons." And the parents brought Jesus into the Temple to do for him according to the custom of *the Law.* When they had completed all things according to *the Law of the Lord . . .* (Luke 2:22, 23, 24, 27, 39)

In John,

> *The Law of Moses* commanded that people like this should be stoned. (John 8:5)

Or again,

> *The Law* was given through Moses. (John 1:17)

We can see from these passages that sometimes it says "the Law" and sometimes "Moses" when it is talking about whatever is written in his books. See also Matthew 8:4; Mark 10:2, 3, 4; 12:19; Luke 20:28, 37; John 3:14; 7:19, 51; 8:17; 19:7.

Then too, many things that are commanded are called *the law* by Moses—for example, commandments about burnt offerings (Leviticus 6:9; 7:37), sacrifices (Leviticus 6:25; 7:1–11), the meal offering (Leviticus 6:14), leprosy (Leviticus 14:2), jealousy (Numbers 5:29, 30), and Naziritehood (Numbers 6:13, 21).

In fact, Moses himself called his books *the Law:*

> Moses wrote *this Law* and gave it to the priests, the sons of Levi, who carried the ark of the covenant of Jehovah, and said to them, "Take *the book* of this *Law* and put it beside the ark of the covenant of Jehovah." (Deuteronomy 31:9, 25, 26)

It was placed beside [the ark]: within the ark were the stone tablets that are "the law" in a strict sense.

Later, the books of Moses are called "the Book of the Law":

> Hilkiah the high priest said to Shaphan the scribe, "I have found *the Book of the Law* in the house of Jehovah." When the king heard the words of *the Book of the Law,* he tore his clothes. (2 Kings 22:8, 11; 23:24)

10 *In the broadest sense, "the law" means everything in the Word,* as we can see from the following passages,

> Jesus said, "Is it not written in *your law,* 'I said, "You are gods"?'" (John 10:34, in reference to Psalms 82:6)

> The crowd replied, "We have heard from *the law* that the Christ will abide forever." (John 12:34, in reference to Psalms 89:29; 110:4; Daniel 7:14)

> To fulfill the word written in *their law:* "They hated me for no reason." (John 15:25, in reference to Psalms 35:19)

> The Pharisees said, "Have any of the leaders believed in him? Only this crowd, that does not know *the law."* (John 7:48, 49)

> It is easier for heaven and earth to pass away than for the tip of one letter of *the law* to fall. (Luke 16:17)

"The law" in these passages means the entire Sacred Scripture.

11 To say that the Lord fulfilled all of the law is to say that he fulfilled all of the Word, as we can see from passages where it says that the Scriptures were fulfilled by him and that everything was brought to completion. See, for example, the following.

> Jesus went into the synagogue and stood up to read. He was handed the book of the prophet Isaiah. He unrolled the scroll and found the passage where it was written, "The spirit of the Lord is upon me, because he has anointed me to preach the gospel to the poor, to heal the brokenhearted, to proclaim release for the bound and sight for the blind, to preach the welcomed year of the Lord."[45] Then he rolled up the scroll and said, *"Today this Scripture has been fulfilled* in your hearing." (Luke 4:16–21)

> You search *the Scriptures,* and yet they testify of me. (John 5:39)

> . . . that *the Scripture may be fulfilled,* "The one who eats bread with me has lifted up his heel against me."[46] (John 13:18)

> None of them is lost except the son of perdition, so that *the Scripture may be fulfilled.*[47] (John 17:12)

§11   FULFILLING THE LAW   145

> . . . *so that the word that he said would be fulfilled:* "Of those whom you gave me I have lost none."[48] (John 18:9)

> Jesus said to Peter, "Put your sword in its place. How then *could the Scriptures be fulfilled,* that it must happen in this way?[49] All this was done so that *the Scriptures of the prophets would be fulfilled."*[50] (Matthew 26:52, 54, 56)

> The Son of Humanity is going, as it has been written of him, so that *the Scriptures will be fulfilled.*[51] (Mark 14:21, 49)

> In this way *the Scripture was fulfilled* that said, "He was numbered with the transgressors."[52] (Mark 15:28; Luke 22:37)

> . . . so that *the Scripture would be fulfilled,* "They divided my garments among them, and for my tunic they cast lots."[53] (John 19:24)

> After this, Jesus, knowing that all things were now accomplished, so that *the Scriptures would be fulfilled . . .*[54] (John 19:28)

> When Jesus had received the vinegar, he said, *"It is finished,"* [that is, *fulfilled*].[55] (John 19:30)

> These things were done so that *the Scripture would be fulfilled,* "Not one of his bones will be broken."[56] And again, *another Scripture says,* "They will look on the one whom they pierced."[57] (John 19:36, 37)

There are also other places where passages from the prophets are cited and it does not also say that the law or the Scripture has been fulfilled.[58]

As for the whole Word having been written about him and his having come into the world to fulfill it, this is what he taught the disciples before he departed:

> Jesus said to the disciples, "You are foolish, and you are slow of heart to believe everything the prophets said. Was it not necessary for the Christ to suffer this and enter into his glory?" Then beginning from *Moses and all the prophets,* he explained to them in *all the Scriptures the things concerning about himself.* (Luke 24:25, 26, 27)

Further,

> Jesus said to the disciples, "These are the words that I spoke to you while I was still with you, that *all things must be fulfilled that were written in the Law of Moses and the Prophets and the Psalms concerning me."* (Luke 24:44, 45)

From these words of the Lord we can see that in the world he fulfilled all of the Word down to the smallest details:

> Truly, I tell you—until heaven and earth pass away, *not one little letter or the tip of one letter*[59] *will pass from the law until all of it is fulfilled.* (Matthew 5:18)

From this we can now see clearly that to say that the Lord fulfilled all things of the law does not mean that he fulfilled all of the Ten Commandments but that he fulfilled all things of the Word.

The Lord Came into the World to Subdue the Hells and to Glorify His Human Nature; the Suffering on the Cross Was the Last Battle by Which He Completely Defeated the Hells and Completely Glorified His Human Nature

12 It is common knowledge in the church that the Lord conquered death, which means hell, and that afterward he ascended into heaven in glory.[60] What the church does not know, though, is that the Lord conquered death or hell by means of battles that are tests, and in so doing also glorified his human nature; and that his suffering on the cross was the last battle or trial by which he effected the conquest and glorification.

This is treated of in many passages in the prophets and David,[61] but not so frequently in the Gospels. In the Gospels the trials that he was subject to from his childhood are summed up in his trials in the wilderness, with their concluding temptations by the Devil,[62] and the final trials he suffered in Gethsemane and on the cross.

On his trials in the wilderness, which concluded with temptations by the Devil, see Matthew 4:1–11, Mark 1:12, 13, and Luke 4:1–13. By these, however, are meant all his trials, even to the last. He did not disclose anything more about them to his disciples, for it says in Isaiah,

> He was oppressed, but did not open his mouth, like a lamb being led to slaughter. Like a sheep before its shearers he kept silence and did not open his mouth. (Isaiah 53:7)

On his trials in Gethsemane, see Matthew 26:36–44, Mark 14:32–41, and Luke 22:39–46; and on his trials on the cross, see Matthew 27:33–56, Mark 15:22–38, Luke 23:33–49, and John 19:17–37. Trials are nothing more nor less than battles against the hells. On the trials or battles of the Lord, see the booklet *The New Jerusalem and Its Heavenly Teachings* (published in London) §§201, 302; and on trials in general, see §§189–200 of the same work.

The Lord himself tells us in John that he completely defeated the hells by his suffering on the cross:

> Now is the judgment of this world; *now the ruler of this world will be cast out.* (John 12:31)

The Lord said this when his suffering on the cross was at hand. And again,

> *The ruler of this world* is judged. (John 16:11)

And again,

> Take heart! *I have overcome the world.* (John 16:33)

And in Luke,

> Jesus said, "I saw *Satan fall like lightning from heaven.*" (Luke 10:18)

The world, the ruler of this world, Satan, and the Devil mean hell.

The Lord tells us in John that he also completely glorified his human nature by his suffering on the cross:

> After Judas went out, Jesus said, "Now *the Son of Humanity is glorified, and God is glorified* in him. If God is *glorified* in him, God will also *glorify* him in himself and glorify him immediately." (John 13:31, 32)

Again,

> Father, the hour has come. *Glorify* your Son, so that your Son may also *glorify* you. (John 17:1, 5)

And again,

> "Now my soul is troubled." And he said, "Father, *glorify* your name." And a voice came from heaven, saying, "I both have *glorified* it and will *glorify* it again." (John 12:27, 28)

In Luke,

> Was it not necessary for Christ to suffer this and enter into his *glory*? (Luke 24:26)

These sayings were about his suffering. Glorification is the complete union of the divine nature and the human nature, so it says "God will also glorify him in himself."63

14 There are many passages in the prophets where it is foretold that the Lord would come into the world to bring everything in the heavens and on earth back into order, that he would accomplish this by battles against the hells that were then attacking everyone coming into the world and leaving the world, and that in this way he would become justice and save people who could not be saved otherwise. I will cite only a few. [2] In Isaiah:

> "Who is this who is coming from Edom, with spattered garments from Bozrah, noble in his clothing, and approaching in the immensity of his strength?" "I who speak justice and have the power to save." "Why are your garments red? Why are your garments like those of someone who is treading a winepress?" "I have trodden the winepress alone, and there has been no man of the people with me. Therefore I have trodden them in my wrath and trampled them in my blazing anger. Victory over them is spattered on my garments, because the day of vengeance is in my heart and the year of my redeemed has arrived. My own arm brought about salvation for me; I have driven their victory down into the earth." He said, "Behold, these are my people, my children." Therefore he became their Savior. Because of his love and his mercy he has redeemed them. (Isaiah 63:1–9)

This is about the Lord's battles against the hells. The clothing in which he was noble and which was red means the Word, which had suffered violence at the hands of the Jewish people.64 The actual battles against the hells and victory over them is described by his treading them in his wrath and trampling them in his blazing anger. His having fought alone and from his own power is described by "There has been no man of the people with me; my own arm has brought about salvation for me; I have driven their victory down into the earth." His having brought about salvation and redemption by this is described by "Therefore he became their Savior; because of his love and his mercy he redeemed them." The fact that this was the reason for his Coming is described by "The day of vengeance is in my heart and the year of my redeemed has arrived." [3] In Isaiah,

> He saw that there was no one and was amazed that no one was interceding. Therefore his own arm brought about salvation for him and his own justice sustained him. Therefore he put on justice like a breastplate and put a helmet of salvation on his head. He also put on garments of vengeance and wrapped himself in zeal like a cloak. Then he came to Zion as the Redeemer. (Isaiah 59:16, 17, 20)

This too is about the Lord's battles with the hells while he was in the world. His fighting against them alone, with his own strength, is meant by "He saw that there was no one. Therefore his own arm brought about salvation"; his thereby becoming justice is meant by "his own justice sustained him. Therefore he put on justice like a breastplate"; and his bringing about redemption in this way is meant by "Then he came to Zion as the Redeemer." [4] In Jeremiah,

> They were terrified. Their mighty ones were beaten down. They fled in flight and did not look back. That day is a day of vengeance for the Lord Jehovih Sabaoth, to take vengeance on his enemies. The sword will devour and be satisfied. (Jeremiah 46:5, 10)

The Lord's battle with the hells and victory over them are described by "They were terrified. They fled in flight and did not look back." Their mighty ones and the enemies are the hells, because everyone in hell harbors hatred toward the Lord. His coming into the world for this reason is meant by "That day is a day of vengeance for the Lord Jehovih Sabaoth, to take vengeance on his enemies." [5] In Jeremiah,

> Their youths will fall in the streets and all their men of war will be cut down on that day. (Jeremiah 49:26)

In Joel,

> Jehovah puts forth his voice before his army. Great is the day of Jehovah, and extremely terrifying; who can endure it? (Joel 2:11)

In Zephaniah,

> On the day of Jehovah's sacrifice I will execute judgment upon the royal family, upon the children of the monarch, and upon all who dress themselves in foreign clothing. This day is a day of distress, a day of trumpets and shouting. (Zephaniah 1:8, 15, 16)

In Zechariah,

> Jehovah will go forth and fight against the nations like the day that he fought on the day of battle. On that day his feet will stand on the Mount of Olives, which faces Jerusalem. Then you will flee into the valley of my mountains. On that day there will be no light or radiance. Jehovah, though, will become king over all the earth. On that day Jehovah will be one, and his name one. (Zechariah 14:3, 4, 5, 6, 9)

In these passages too we are dealing with the Lord's battles. "That day" means his Coming; "the Mount of Olives, which faces Jerusalem" was where the Lord stayed by himself—see Mark 13:3, 4; 14:26; Luke 21:37; 22:39; John 8:1; and elsewhere. [6] In David,

> The cords of death surrounded me; the cords of hell surrounded me; the snares of death confronted me. Therefore he sent forth arrows and many bolts of lightning, and confounded them. I will pursue my enemies and seize them, and I will not turn back until I have devoured them. I will strike them down so that they cannot rise up again. You will gird me with strength for war and put my enemies to flight. I will crush them like dust before the face of the wind; I will empty them out like the mire of the streets. (Psalms 18:4, 14, 37, 39, 40, 42)

The cords and snares of death that surrounded and confronted him mean trials that are also called cords of hell because they come from hell. These verses and the rest of the whole psalm are about the Lord's battles and victories, which is why it also says, "You will make me the head of the nations; people I have not known will serve me" (verse 43). [7] In David,

> Gird a sword on your thigh, mighty one. Your arrows are sharp; peoples will fall beneath you, those who are the king's enemies at heart. Your throne is for the ages and forever. You have loved justice; therefore God has anointed you. (Psalms 45:3, 5, 6, 7)

This too is about battling with the hells and bringing them under control, since the whole psalm is talking about the Lord—specifically, his battles, his glorification, and his salvation of the faithful. In David,

> Fire will go forth before him; it will burn up his enemies round about; the earth will see and fear. The mountains will melt like wax before the Lord of the whole earth. The heavens will proclaim his justice, and all the peoples will see his glory. (Psalms 97:3, 4, 5, 6)

This psalm similarly is dealing with the Lord and with the same issues. [8] In David,

> Jehovah said to my Lord, "Sit at my right until I make your enemies a stool for your feet, to rule in the midst of your enemies." The Lord is on your right; on the day of his wrath he has struck down monarchs. He has filled [the nations] with corpses; he has struck the head of a great land. (Psalms 110:1, 5, 6)

Some words of the Lord himself show that these things were spoken about the Lord: see Matthew 22:44, Mark 12:36, and Luke 20:42.[65] Sitting at the right means omnipotence, the enemies mean the hells, monarchs mean people there who have evil lives and false beliefs. Making them a stool for his feet, striking them down on the day of wrath, and filling [the nations] with corpses mean destroying their power; and striking the head of a great land means destroying all of their power.

[9] Since the Lord alone overcame the hells with no help from any angel,[66] he is called *Hero and Man of War* (Isaiah 42:13), *King of Glory, Jehovah the Mighty, Hero of War* (Psalms 24:8, 10), *the Mighty One of Jacob* (Psalms 132:2, 5), and in many passages *Jehovah Sabaoth*, that is, Jehovah of Armies of War.

Then too, his Coming is called *the day of Jehovah*—terrifying, cruel, a day of resentment, blazing anger, wrath, vengeance, destruction, war, trumpet, shouting, and panic, as we can see from the passages cited in §4 above.

[10] Since a last judgment was carried out by the Lord when he was in the world, by battling with the hells and bringing them under control, in many passages it speaks of a *judgment* that is going to be executed. See David, for example—"Jehovah is coming to judge the earth; he will judge the world with justice and the peoples with truth" (Psalms 96:13)—and frequently elsewhere.

These citations are from the prophetic books of the Word.[67]

[11] In the historical books of the Word, though, matters of the same sort are represented as wars between the children of Israel and various nations.[68] This is because everything in the Word, whether prophetical or historical, is written about the Lord. So the Word is divine when it tells of the rituals of the Israelite church; for example, there are many secrets concerning the Lord's glorification contained in the descriptions of burnt offerings and sacrifices, in the Sabbaths and festivals, and in the priesthood of Aaron and the Levites. The same holds true for other parts of the books of Moses, the material called laws, judgments, and statutes. This is also the intent of what the Lord said to the disciples—that it was fitting for him to fulfill everything written about him in the Law of Moses (Luke 24:44); and what he said to the Jews—that Moses had written about him (John 5:46).

[12] We can now see from this that the Lord came into the world to subdue the hells and to glorify his human nature, and that the suffering on the cross was the last battle, by which he completely defeated the hells and completely glorified his human nature.

You may find more on this subject, though, in the forthcoming booklet *Sacred Scripture* [§103], where there is a complete collection in one place of all the passages in the prophetic Word that deal with the Lord's battles against the hells and victories over them, or (which amounts to the same thing) with the last judgment that he executed when he was in the world, together with the passages about his suffering and the glorification of his human nature. Of these latter there are so many that if they were fully quoted, they would fill volumes.

The Lord Did Not Take Away Our Sins by His Suffering on the Cross, but He Did Carry Them

15 THERE are people in the church who believe that through his suffering on the cross the Lord took away our sins and made satisfaction to the Father, and by so doing brought about redemption. Others believe

that he transferred to himself the sins of those who have faith in him, carried those sins, and cast them into the depths of the sea—that is, into hell.[69] They support this among themselves by what John says of Jesus,

> Behold the Lamb of God, who is taking up[70] the sins of the world. (John 1:29)

and by the Lord's words in Isaiah,

> He bore our diseases and carried our sorrows. He was pierced because of our transgressions and bruised because of our iniquities. Chastisement was upon him for the sake of our peace; with his wound, healing was given to us. Jehovah made the iniquities of us all fall upon him. He was oppressed and afflicted, but did not open his mouth, like a lamb being led to slaughter. He was cut off from the land of the living. He suffered a blow because of the transgression of my people, to send the ungodly to their grave and the rich to their deaths. As a result of the labor of his soul, he will see and be satisfied. By means of his knowledge he will justify many, because he himself carried their iniquities. He emptied out his own soul even to death and was counted among transgressors. He bore the sins of many and interceded for transgressors. (Isaiah 53:3–end)

Both of these passages are talking about the Lord's trials and suffering; his taking up our sins, [bearing] our diseases, and having the iniquities of us all fall upon him mean something similar to his carrying our sorrows and our iniquities.

[2] So I need to say first of all what his carrying iniquities means and then what his taking them up means. The true meaning of his carrying iniquities is that he was subjected to severe trials and endured being treated by the Jews the way the Word was treated by them; and they dealt with him in that way precisely because he was the Word. The church among the Jews was in utter shambles at that time; it had been brought to ruin by their perversion of everything in the Word to the point that there was nothing true left. As a result, they did not recognize the Lord.[71] That is in fact the intent and meaning behind each detail of the Lord's suffering.

The prophets suffered in much the same way because they represented the Lord's Word and therefore his church, and the Lord was the quintessential prophet.

[3] We can tell that the Lord was the quintessential prophet from the following passages:

Jesus said, "*A prophet* is not without honor except in his own country and in his own house." (Matthew 13:57; Mark 6:4; Luke 4:24)

Jesus said, "It is not fitting for *a prophet* to die outside of Jerusalem." (Luke 13:33)

They said of Jesus, "He is *a prophet* from Nazareth." (Matthew 21:11; John 7:40, 41)

Fear came upon all, and they glorified God, saying that *a great prophet* had been raised up among them. (Luke 7:16)

A prophet will be raised up from among his people; they will obey his words. (Deuteronomy 18:15–19)

[4] We can tell from the following passages that much the same was done to the prophets.

The prophet Isaiah was commanded to represent the state of the church by taking the sackcloth off his waist and the sandals off his feet and going naked and barefoot for three years as a sign and a wonder (Isaiah 20:2, 3).

The prophet Jeremiah was commanded to represent the state of the church by buying a belt and putting it around his waist without putting it in water, then hiding it in a crevice in the rocks near the Euphrates; after some days he found it ruined (Jeremiah 13:1–7).

The same prophet represented the state of the church by not taking a wife for himself in that place or entering the house of mourning or going out to grieve or going into the banquet house (Jeremiah 16:2, 5, 8).

[5] The prophet Ezekiel was commanded to represent the state of the church by taking a barber's razor to his head and his beard and then dividing the hair, burning a third of it in the middle of the city, striking a third with a sword, and scattering a third to the wind; also, he was told to bind a few hairs in his hems and eventually to throw a few into the midst of a fire and burn them (Ezekiel 5:1–4).

The same prophet was commanded to represent the state of the church by packing his belongings to take into exile and traveling to another place in the sight of the children of Israel. In a while he was to take out his belongings and leave in the evening through a hole dug through the wall, covering his face so that he could not see the ground. And this was to be a sign to the house of Israel. The prophet was also to say, "Behold,

I am a sign for you: what I have done, [your leaders] will do" (Ezekiel 12:3–7, 11).

[6] The prophet Hosea was commanded to represent the state of the church by taking a whore as his wife. He did so, and she bore him three children, the first of whom he named Jezreel, the second No Mercy, and the third Not My People[72] (Hosea 1:2–9).

Another time he was commanded to go love a woman who had a lover but was also committing adultery; he bought her for fifteen pieces of silver (Hosea 3:1, 2).

[7] The prophet Ezekiel was commanded to represent the state of the church by taking a clay tablet, carving Jerusalem on it, laying siege to it, building a siege wall and a mound against it, putting an iron plate between himself and the city, and lying on his left side for three hundred ninety days and then on his right side [for forty days]. He was also told to take wheat, barley, lentils, millet, and spelt and make himself bread from them, which he was then to weigh and eat. He was also told to bake a cake of barley over human dung; and because he begged not to do this, he was commanded to bake it over cow dung instead (Ezekiel 4:1–15).

Further, prophets also represented other things—Zedekiah with the horns of iron that he made, for example (1 Kings 22:11). Then there was another prophet who was struck and wounded and who put ashes over his eyes (1 Kings 20:37, 38).

[8] In general, prophets used a robe of coarse hair (Zechariah 13:4) to represent the Word in its outermost meaning, which is the literal meaning;[73] so Elijah wore that kind of robe and had a leather belt around his waist (2 Kings 1:8). Much the same is true of John the Baptist, who had clothing of camels' hair and a leather belt around his waist, and who ate locusts and wild honey (Matthew 3:4).

We can see from this that the prophets represented the state of the church and the Word. In fact, anyone who represents one represents the other as well because the church is from the Word, and its life and faith depend on its acceptance of the Word. So too, wherever prophets are mentioned in both Testaments it means the body of teaching the church draws from the Word, while the Lord as the supreme prophet means the church itself and the Word itself.

The state of the church in relation to the Word, as represented by the prophets, was the meaning of their "carrying the iniquities and sins of the people." This we can see from what is said about the prophet Isaiah, that he went naked and barefoot for three years as a sign and a wonder

(Isaiah 20:3). It says of Ezekiel that he was to take out his belongings to go into exile and cover his face so that he could not see the ground, and that this was to be a sign to the house of Israel; and he was also to say, "I am a sign for you" (Ezekiel 12:6, 11).

[2] It is abundantly clear from Ezekiel that this was carrying the people's iniquities, when Ezekiel was commanded to lie on his left side for three hundred ninety days and on his right side for forty days against Jerusalem and to eat a cake of barley baked over cow dung. We read there,

> Lie on your left side and place *the iniquity of the house of Israel* on it. According to the number of days that you lie on it *you will carry* their *iniquity*. I will give you years of their iniquity matching the number of days, three hundred ninety days, so that *you carry the iniquity of the house of Israel*. When you have finished them, you will lie a second time, but on your right side for forty days *to carry the iniquity of the house of Judah*. (Ezekiel 4:4, 5, 6)

[3] By carrying the iniquities of the house of Israel and the house of Judah in this way, the prophet did not take them away and thus atone for them, but simply represented them and made them clear. This we can see from what follows:

> Thus says Jehovah: "The children of Israel will eat their bread defiled among the nations where I am going to send them. Behold, I am breaking the staff of bread in Jerusalem so that they will lack bread and water. They will all become desolate and waste away because of their iniquity." (Ezekiel 4:13, 16, 17)

[4] Similarly, when Ezekiel appeared in public and said, "Behold, I am a sign for you," he also said, "What I have done, [your leaders] will do" (Ezekiel 12:6, 11).

Much the same is meant, then, when it says of the Lord, "He bore our diseases and carried our sorrows. Jehovah made the iniquities of us all fall upon him. By means of his knowledge he justified many, because he himself carried their iniquities." This is from Isaiah 53:[4, 6, 11], where the whole chapter is about the Lord's suffering.

[5] We can see from the details of the narrative of his suffering that he, as the greatest prophet, represented the state of the church in its relationship to the Word. For example, he was betrayed by Judas; he was seized and condemned by the chief priests and elders; they struck him with their fists; they struck his head with a stick; they put a crown of thorns on him; they divided his garments and cast lots on his tunic; they

crucified him; they gave him vinegar to drink; they pierced his side; he was entombed; and on the third day he rose again [Matthew 26:14–16, 47–68; 27:1–61; 28:1–10; Mark 14:43–65; 15:15–37; 16:1–8; Luke 22:47–71; 23:26–56; 24:1–35; John 18:1–14; 19:1–30; 20:1–18].

[6] His being betrayed by Judas meant that this was being done by the Jewish people, who at that time were custodians of the Word, since Judas represented them.74 His being seized and condemned by the chief priests and elders meant that this was being done by the whole church. Their whipping him, spitting in his face, striking him with their fists, and striking his head with a stick meant that they were doing this kind of thing to the Word in regard to its divine truths, all of which are about the Lord. Their putting a crown of thorns on him meant that they falsified and contaminated these truths. Their dividing his garments and casting lots on his tunic meant that they destroyed the connectedness of all the truths of the Word—though not its spiritual meaning,75 which is symbolized by the tunic. Their crucifying him meant that they destroyed and profaned the whole Word. Their giving him vinegar to drink meant offering nothing but things that were distorted and false, which is why he did not drink it and then said, "It is finished." Their piercing his side meant that they completely stifled everything true in the Word and everything good in it. His entombment meant his putting off any residual human nature from his mother.76 His rising again on the third day meant his glorification. Much the same is meant by the passages in the prophets and David where these events were foretold.

[7] That is why, after he had been whipped and led out wearing the crown of thorns and the purple robe the soldiers had put on him, he said, "Behold the man"77 (John 19:1–5). This was said because a human being means a church, since "the Son of Humanity" means what is true in the church, therefore the Word.

We can see from all this that his "carrying iniquities" means that he represented and offered an image of the sins that were being committed against the divine truths of the Word. And we will see in the following pages [§§19–29] that the Lord endured and suffered these torments as the Son of Humanity and not as the Son of God. "The Son of Humanity" means the Lord as the Word.

I need now to say something about the meaning of the Lord's "taking up sins" [John 1:29]. His "taking up sins" means much the same as his redeeming us and saving us, since the Lord came into the world so that we could be saved; if he had not come no one could have been reformed and reborn and therefore saved. This could happen, though, after the Lord had taken all power away from the Devil—that is, from hell—and had glorified his human nature—that is, united it to the divine nature of his Father. If these things had not happened, no human beings could have accepted anything divinely true that dwelt within them, let alone anything divinely good, because the Devil, who had had the greater power before these events,[78] would have snatched it from their hearts.

[2] We can see from all this that the Lord did not take away sins by his suffering on the cross, but that he does take away sins—that is, lay them aside—in those who believe in him and live by his commandments. This is what the Lord is telling us in Matthew:

> Do not think that I have come to destroy the Law and the Prophets. Whoever breaks the least of these commandments and teaches others to do the same will be called the least in the kingdom of the heavens; but whoever does and teaches [these commandments] will be called great in the kingdom of the heavens. (Matthew 5:17, 19)

[3] Reason alone should convince anyone who is the least bit enlightened that sins can be taken away from us only by active repentance—that is, by our seeing our sins, begging the Lord for help, and desisting from them.[79] To see and believe and teach anything else does not come from the Word or from sound reason but from the desire and ill intent that come from our own sense of self-importance—an attitude that corrupts our understanding.

The Imputation of the Lord's Merit Is Nothing More nor Less Than the Forgiveness of Sins That Follows upon Repentance

18 IT is believed in the church that the Lord was sent by the Father to make atonement for the human race, and that this was accomplished by his fulfilling the law and by his suffering on the cross, that in this way he bore our damnation and made satisfaction, and that if it were not for this atonement, satisfaction, and propitiation, the human race would have died an eternal death.[80] This is believed to have been a matter of justice, and some even refer to it as retributive.

It is quite true that we would all have perished if the Lord had not come into the world, but how we should understand the Lord's fulfilling everything in the law has been explained in its own chapter above [§§8–11]. An explanation of why he suffered the cross has also been given in its own treatment [§§12–14, 15–17], enabling us to see that this was not a matter of retributive justice, since that is not a divine attribute. Justice, love, mercy, and goodness are divine attributes, and God is justice itself, love itself, mercy itself, and goodness itself. Further, where we find these we find no vindictiveness and therefore no retributive justice.

[2] Until now, many people have understood "the fulfilling of the law" and "the suffering on the cross" as the two means by which the Lord made satisfaction for the human race and delivered it from the predicted or fated damnation. If we believe that these two actions—which constituted the Lord's merit—made satisfaction for us, and we put this together with the principle that we are saved simply by believing that they happened, what follows is the dogma that the Lord's merit is imputed to us. However, this dogma collapses in the light of what has been said about the Lord's fulfillment of the law and his suffering on the cross. At the same time we can see that "the imputation of merit"[81] is a phrase without substance unless we take it to mean the forgiveness of sins that follows repentance. You see, nothing that belongs to the Lord can be credited to us, but salvation can be transferred to us by the Lord after we practice repentance—that is, after we see and acknowledge our sins and then desist from them, doing this because of the Lord. Then there is a way in which salvation is transferred to us: we are saved not on the basis of our own worth and our own righteousness but by the Lord, the only one who has fought and overcome the hells and who alone thereafter fights for us and overcomes the hells for us. [3] These accomplishments are the Lord's merit and righteousness, and they can never be credited to our account—because if they were, the Lord's merit and righteousness would be attributed to us as though they were our own. This is something that never happens and that cannot happen. If imputation were possible, we could claim the Lord's merit when we were impenitent and irreverent and think ourselves justified by doing so. Yet this would be polluting what is holy with profane things and profaning the Lord's name, because it

would be focusing our thoughts on the Lord but our will on hell, when in fact all we are is what our will intends.[82]

There is a faith that is God's and a faith that is our own. People who practice repentance have the faith that is God's. People who do not practice repentance but think in terms of imputation have a faith that is their own. God's faith is a living faith; our own faith is a dead faith.

[4] The following passages show that both the Lord himself and his disciples taught repentance and the forgiveness of sins.

> Jesus began to preach and to say, "*Repent,* because the kingdom of the heavens is at hand." (Matthew 4:17)

> Jesus said,[83] "Bear fruit that is consistent with *repentance.* The axe is already lying against the root of the trees. Every tree that does not bear good fruit is cut down and thrown into the fire." (Luke 3:8, 9)

> Jesus said, "Unless you *repent,* you will all perish." (Luke 13:3, 5)

> Jesus came preaching the gospel of the kingdom of God, saying, "The time is fulfilled, and the kingdom of God is at hand. *Repent,* and believe in the gospel." (Mark 1:14, 15)

> Jesus sent out his disciples, and they went out and preached that people should *repent.* (Mark 6:12)

> Jesus said to the apostles that it was necessary for them to preach *repentance and the forgiveness of sins* in his name to all nations, beginning at Jerusalem. (Luke 24:47)

> John preached a baptism of *repentance for the forgiveness of sins.* (Luke 3:3; Mark 1:4)

"Baptism" means a spiritual washing, which is a washing from sins and is called "rebirth."

[5] This is how the Lord describes repentance and the forgiveness of sins in John:

> He came to what was his own, and yet his own people did not accept him. But as many as did accept him, he gave them power to become children of God and believe in his name, who were born, not of blood, and not of the will of the flesh, and not of the will of a man, but of God. (John 1:11, 12, 13)

"His own people" means people of the church at that time, the church where the Word was;[84] "children of God" and "believing in his name" mean people who believe in the Lord and who believe in the Word; blood means distortions of the Word and justifying what is false by that means; the will of the flesh means the will belonging to our own [lower] self, which is essentially evil; the will of a man means the understanding belonging to our own [lower] self, which is essentially false; and "those born of God" means people who have been reborn by the Lord.

We can see from this that we are saved if we are focused on good and loving actions that come from the Lord and on truths of our faith that come from the Lord; we are not saved if we are wrapped up in ourselves.

The Lord as the Divine-Human One Is Called "The Son of God" and as the Word Is Called "The Son of Humanity"

THE church is convinced that the Son of God is the second person of the Godhead, distinct from the person of the Father, which results in a belief in a Son of God born from eternity.[85] Since this is everywhere accepted and is about God, there is neither ability nor permission to think about this matter at all intelligently, not even about what it means to be "born from eternity." This is because people who think about it intelligently inevitably find themselves saying, "This is completely beyond me. Still, I say it because everybody else says it, and I believe it because everybody else believes it." They should realize, though, that there is no Son from eternity; rather, the Lord is from eternity. Only when they realize what "the Lord" means and what "the Son" means can they think intelligently about a triune God.

[2] As for the fact that the Lord's human side—conceived by Jehovah the Father and born of the Virgin Mary—was the Son of God, this is obvious from the following in Luke:

> The angel Gabriel was sent by God to a city in Galilee named Nazareth, to a virgin betrothed to a man whose name was Joseph, from the

house of David. The virgin's name was Mary. Having come in, the angel said to her, "Greetings, you who have attained grace. The Lord is with you; you are blessed among women." When she saw him, she was troubled by what he said and considered what kind of salutation this was. The angel said to her, "Do not be afraid, Mary: you have found favor with God. Behold, you will conceive and bear a Son, and you will call his name Jesus. He will be great and will be called *the Son of the Highest.*" But Mary said to the angel, "How will this take place, since I have not had intercourse?" The angel replied and said to her, "*The Holy Spirit will descend upon you,* and *the power of the Highest will cover you;* therefore the *Holy One* that is born from you will be called *the Son of God.*" (Luke 1:26–35)

This passage says "you will conceive and bear a Son. He will be great and will be called the Son of the Highest," and again, "The Holy One that is born from you will be called the Son of God." We can see from this that it is the human nature conceived by God and born of the Virgin Mary that is called "the Son of God." [3] In Isaiah,

> The Lord himself is giving you a sign. Behold, a virgin will conceive and bear a *son,* and she will call his name "*God with us.*" (Isaiah 7:14)

We can see that the Son born of the Virgin and conceived by God is the one who will be called "God with us" and is therefore the one who is the Son of God. There is further support for this in Matthew 1:22, 23.[86] [4] In Isaiah:

> A *Child* has been born to us; a *Son* has been given to us. Leadership is upon his shoulder; and his name will be called Wonderful, Counselor, God, Hero, *Father of Eternity,* Prince of Peace. (Isaiah 9:6)

It is the same here, since it says "A Child has been born to us; a Son has been given to us," who is not a Son from eternity but a Son born into the world. We can see this also from what the prophet says in verse 6 there and from the words of the angel Gabriel to Mary (Luke 1:32, 33), which are similar. [5] In David:

> "I will proclaim concerning the statute, 'Jehovah has said, "*You are my Son;* today I have begotten you."'" Kiss *the Son* or he will become angry and you will perish on the way. (Psalms 2:7, 12)

It does not mean a Son from eternity here either, but a Son born in the world, because this is a prophecy about the Lord who is going to come.

So it is called a statute about which Jehovah was making a proclamation to David. "Today" is not "from eternity" but is in time. [6] In David:

> I will place his hand on the sea. He will cry out to me, "You are my Father." I will make him the *firstborn.* (Psalms 89:25, 26, 27)

This whole psalm is about the Lord who is going to come, which is why it means the one who will call Jehovah his Father and who will be the firstborn—therefore the one who is the Son of God. [7] The same holds true elsewhere, when he is called "a shoot from the trunk of Jesse" (Isaiah 11:1), "the branch of David" (Jeremiah 23:5), "the seed of the woman" (Genesis 3:15), "the only-begotten" (John 1:18), "a priest forever" and "the Lord" (Psalms 110:4, 5).

[8] The Jewish church understood "the Son of God" to mean the Messiah whom they were awaiting, knowing that he would be born in Bethlehem. We can see from the following passages that they understood "the Son of God" to be the Messiah. In John:

> Peter said, "We believe and know that you are *the Christ, the Son of* the living *God."* (John 6:69)

In the same:

> You are *the Christ, the Son of God,* who is going to come into the world. (John 11:27)

In Matthew:

> The high priest asked Jesus whether he was *the Christ, the Son of God.* Jesus said, "I am." (Matthew 26:63, 64; Mark 14:62)

In John:

> These things have been written so that you may believe that Jesus is *the Christ, the Son of God.* (John 20:31; also Mark 1:1)

"Christ" is a Greek word and means "anointed," which is what "messiah" means in Hebrew.[87] This is why it says in John, "We have found the Messiah (which is translated, the Christ)" (John 1:41). And in another passage, "The woman said, 'I know that *the Messiah* is coming, who is called *the Christ'"* (John 4:25).

[9] I pointed out in the first chapter [§§1–7] that the Law and the Prophets (or the whole Word of the Old Testament) are about the Lord, so the Son of God who is going to come cannot mean anything but the human nature that the Lord took upon himself in the world. [10] It follows, then,

that this is the meaning of the Son mentioned by Jehovah from heaven when Jesus was being baptized: "This is *my beloved Son,* in whom I am well pleased" (Matthew 3:17; Mark 1:11; Luke 3:22), since his human nature was being baptized. Likewise when he was transfigured: "This is *my beloved Son,* in whom I am well pleased. Hear him" (Matthew 17:5; Mark 9:7; Luke 9:35).

Then there are other passages as well, such as Matthew 8:29; 14:33; 27:43, 54; Mark 3:11; 15:39; John 1:18, 34, 49; 3:18; 5:25; 10:36; 11:4.

20 Since "the Son of God" means the Lord in the human nature that he assumed in the world, which is a divine-human nature, we can see what was meant by the Lord's frequently saying that he was sent into the world by the Father and that he had gone forth from the Father.[88] His being sent into the world by the Father means that he was conceived by Jehovah the Father. This and nothing else is the meaning of "being sent" and "sent by the Father," as we can tell from all the places where it also says that he was doing the will of the Father and doing his works,[89] which were overcoming the hells, glorifying his human nature, teaching the Word, and establishing a new church. The only way these things could have been done was by means of a human nature conceived by Jehovah and born of a virgin—that is, by God becoming human. Open up the passages where it says "being sent" and "sent," and you will see: Matthew 10:40, for example, and Matthew 15:24; Mark 9:37; Luke 4:43; 9:48; 10:16; John 3:17, 34; 4:34; 5:23, 24, 36, 37, 38; 6:29, 39, 40, 44, 57; 7:16, 18, 28, 29; 8:16, 18, 29, 42; 9:4; 11:41, 42; 12:44, 45, 49; 13:20; 14:24; 15:21; 16:5; 17:3, 8, 21, 23, 25; 20:21. There are also the places where the Lord calls Jehovah "Father."[90]

21 Many people these days think of the Lord only as an ordinary person like themselves because they think only of his human nature and not at the same time of his divine nature, when in fact his human and divine natures cannot be separated. "The Lord is both God and a human being; and God and a human being in the Lord are not two but one person. He is one altogether, as the soul and the body are one human being"—this is according to what is taught throughout the Christian world, a teaching that has been ratified by councils and is called the Athanasian statement of faith.[91] So that people will not keep thinking of the divine nature and human nature in the Lord as separate, I would ask them to read the passages from Luke cited above, and also this from Matthew:

> The birth of Jesus Christ was like this. His mother, having been betrothed to Joseph, before they came together was found to be carrying

a child from *the Holy Spirit;* and Joseph her husband, being an upright man and not wanting to disgrace her, decided to divorce her secretly. But while he was considering this, an angel of the Lord suddenly appeared to him in a dream, saying, "Joseph, son of David, do not be afraid to take Mary as your wife, because what is being born in her is from *the Holy Spirit;* and she will give birth to a son, and you will call his name 'Jesus.' He will save his people from their sins." And Joseph woke from his dream and did as the angel of the Lord had commanded, and took [Mary] as his wife. *But he did not have intercourse with her* until she had given birth to her firstborn son. And he called his name "Jesus." (Matthew 1:18–25)

We are assured by this passage and by what Luke says about the circumstances of the Lord's birth, as well as by the passages cited earlier, that the Son of God is the Jesus who was conceived by Jehovah the Father and born of the Virgin Mary, the one of whom all the Prophets and the Law prophesied until John [Matthew 11:13; Luke 16:16].

Anyone who knows what it is about the Lord that "the Son of God" means and what it is about him that "the Son of Humanity" means can see many hidden wonders in the Word, since the Lord calls himself sometimes the Son, sometimes the Son of God, and sometimes the Son of Humanity, in each case depending on the subject of the discourse.

When the subject is his divinity, or his being one with the Father, or his divine power, or faith in him, or life from him, then he calls himself "the Son" and "the Son of God," as in John 5:16–26 and elsewhere. When the subject is his suffering, though, or his judging, or his Coming, or more generally his redeeming, saving, reforming, or regenerating us, then he calls himself the Son of Humanity. This is because it then means himself as the Word.

The Lord is identified by various names in the Word of the Old Testament. There he is called Jehovah, Jah, the Lord, God, the Lord Jehovih, Jehovah Sabaoth, the God of Israel, the Holy One of Israel, the Mighty One of Jacob, Shaddai, the Rock, as well as Creator, Maker, Savior, Redeemer—always depending on the subject of the discourse. This is the case in the Word of the New Testament, too, where he is called Jesus, the Christ, the Lord, God, the Son of God, the Son of Humanity, the Prophet, and the Lamb, among other names, again always depending on the subject of the discourse.

23 So far we have been talking about why the Lord is called the Son of God. Now we must turn to why he is called the Son of Humanity.

He is called the Son of Humanity when the subject is his suffering, his judging, his Coming, or more generally his redeeming, saving, reforming, or regenerating us. This is because the Son of Humanity is the Lord as the Word; and it is as the Word that he suffered, judges, comes into the world, redeems, saves, reforms, and regenerates. What follows may serve to demonstrate that this is the case.

24 *The Lord is called the Son of Humanity when the subject is his suffering.* This we can tell from the following passages.

> Jesus said to his disciples, "Behold, we are going up to Jerusalem, and *the Son of Humanity* will be betrayed to the chief priests and to the scribes; and they will condemn him to death and hand him over to the Gentiles, and they will whip him, and spit on him, and kill him. On the third day, though, he will rise again." (Mark 10:33, 34)

Likewise elsewhere, where it foretells his suffering, as in Matthew 20:18, 19; Mark 8:31; Luke 9:22:

> Jesus said to his disciples, "Behold, the hour is at hand, and *the Son of Humanity* is being betrayed into the hands of sinners." (Matthew 26:45)

> The angel said to the women who came to the tomb, "Remember what he said to you: '*The Son of Humanity* must be betrayed into the hands of sinful people and be crucified and rise again on the third day.'" (Luke 24:6, 7)

The reason the Lord then called himself the Son of Humanity is that he allowed people to treat him the way they were treating the Word, as has already been explained more than once [§§14–16, 22–23].

25 *The Lord is called the Son of Humanity when the subject is judgment.* This we can tell from the following passages:

> When *the Son of Humanity* comes in his glory, then he will sit on the throne of his glory and set the sheep on his right and the goats on the left. (Matthew 25:31, 33)

> When *the Son of Humanity* sits on the throne of his glory, he will judge[92] the twelve tribes of Israel. (Matthew 19:28)

> *The Son of Humanity* is going to come in the glory of his Father, and then he will repay all people according to their deeds. (Matthew 16:27)

> Be wakeful at every moment, so that you may be found worthy to stand before *the Son of Humanity*. (Luke 21:36)

> *The Son of Humanity* is coming at an hour you do not expect. (Matthew 24:44; Luke 12:40)

> The Father does not judge anyone; he has given all judgment to the Son, because he is the *Son of Humanity*. (John 5:22, 27)

The reason the Lord calls himself the Son of Humanity when the subject is judgment is that all judgment is executed according to the divine truth that is in the Word. He himself says in John that this is what judges everyone:

> If people hear my words[93] but do not believe, I do not judge them. I have not come to judge the world. *The Word that I have spoken* will judge them on the last day. (John 12:47, 48)

And in another passage,

> *The Son of Humanity* came not to condemn the world but so that the world would be saved through him. Those who believe in him are not condemned; but those who do not believe have already been condemned because they have not believed in the name of the only-begotten Son of God. (John 3:17, 18)

See *Heaven and Hell* 545–550 and 574 on the fact that the Lord never condemns anyone to hell or casts anyone into hell. Rather, evil spirits cast themselves in. The *name* of Jehovah, the Lord, or the Son of God means divine truth and therefore the Word as well, since this is from him and about him and therefore is he himself.

The Lord is called the Son of Humanity when the subject is his Coming, as we can see from the following: the disciples said to Jesus, "What will be the sign of your Coming and of the close of the age?"; and then the Lord foretold the states of the church in succession all the way to the end, saying this about its end: "Then the sign of *the Son of Humanity* will appear, and they will see *the Son of Humanity* coming in the clouds of heaven with power and glory" (Matthew 24:3, 30; Mark 13:26; Luke 21:27). The close of the age means the last time of the church; coming in the clouds of heaven with glory means opening the Word and making it clear that it was written about him alone. In Daniel:

> I was watching, and behold, *the Son of Humanity* was coming in the clouds of the heavens! (Daniel 7:13)

In Revelation:

> Behold, he is coming with clouds, and every eye will see him. (Revelation 1:7)

This too is about *the Son of Humanity,* as we can see from verse 13 in the same chapter. Again in Revelation:

> I looked, and behold, a white cloud, and on the cloud sat someone like *the Son of Humanity.* (Revelation 14:14)

[2] In his own mind, the Lord understood "the Son of God" and "the Son of Humanity" to mean different things, as we can see from his response to the high priest:

> The high priest said to Jesus, "I put you under oath by the living God: tell us whether you are the Christ, *the Son of God."* Jesus said to him, "It is as you said. I am. Nevertheless, I say to you, hereafter you will see *the Son of Humanity* sitting at the right hand of power and coming in the clouds of heaven." (Matthew 26:63, 64; [Mark 14:61, 62])

Here he first declares that he is the Son of God, and then says that they are going to see the Son of Humanity sitting at the right hand of power and coming in the clouds of heaven. This means that after suffering on the cross he would have access to the divine power to open the Word and establish a church, things that he could not do before because he had not yet overcome the hells and glorified his human nature.

The meaning of coming[94] in the clouds of heaven and coming with glory has been explained in §1 of *Heaven and Hell.*

27 *The Lord is called the Son of Humanity when the subject is redemption, salvation, reformation, and regeneration,* as we can tell from the following:

> *The Son of Humanity* came to give his life as a redemption for many. (Matthew 20:28; Mark 10:45)

> *The Son of Humanity* has come to save and not to destroy. (Matthew 18:11; Luke 9:56)

> *The Son of Humanity* has come to seek and to save that which was lost. (Luke 19:10)

> *The Son of Humanity* came so that the world would be saved through him. (John 3:17)

> The one who sows good seed is *the Son of Humanity.* (Matthew 13:37)

Here the subject is redemption and salvation; and since they are effected by the Lord through the Word, he refers to himself as *the Son of Humanity*.

The Lord said that *the Son of Humanity* has power to forgive sins (Mark 2:10; Luke 5:24)—that is, power to save. He also said that he was Lord of the Sabbath because he was *the Son of Humanity* (Matthew 12:8; Mark 2:28; Luke 6:5)—because he himself is the very Word that he is then teaching.

He also says in John,

> Do not work for the food that perishes, but for the food that endures to eternal life, which *the Son of Humanity* will give you. (John 6:27)

Food means everything true and good in the teaching drawn from the Word and therefore from the Lord. This is also the meaning of the manna and of the bread that comes down from heaven, as well as the meaning of these words in the same chapter:

> Unless you eat the flesh of *the Son of Humanity* and drink his blood, you will not have life within you. (John 6:53)

The flesh or bread is good actions done from love as a result of the Word, and the blood or wine is good actions done from faith as a result of the Word, both of which come from the Lord.

[2] *"The Son of Humanity" means much the same in various other passages where it is found,* such as the following:

> Foxes have dens and birds have nests, but *the Son of Humanity* has nowhere to lay his head. (Matthew 8:20; Luke 9:58)

This means that the Word had no place among the Jews, as the Lord also says in John 8:37, and that the Word was not abiding in them, because they did not acknowledge him (John 5:38).[95]

The Son of Humanity means the Lord as the Word in Revelation as well:

> In the midst of seven lampstands I saw one like *the Son of Humanity,* clothed with a garment down to the feet and girded about the chest with a golden band. (Revelation 1:13 and following)

In this passage various images are used to represent the Lord as the Word, so he is also called "the Son of Humanity." In David:

> Let your hand be with the man of your right hand, with *the Son of Humanity* whom you have strengthened for yourself. Then we will not turn back from you. Bring us to life. (Psalms 80:17, 18, 19)

The man of your right hand in this passage is also the Lord as the Word, and so is the Son of Humanity. He is called "the man of your right hand" because the Lord has power from divine truth, which is also the Word; and he gained divine power when he fulfilled the whole Word. That is why he also said that they would see *the Son of Humanity* sitting at the right hand of the Father with power (Mark 14:62).

28 *The reason "the Son of Humanity" means the Lord as the Word was that the prophets were also called "children of humanity."* The reason they were called this is that they represented the Lord as the Word and therefore meant the teaching of the church drawn from the Word. This is exactly how it is understood in heaven when "prophets" are mentioned in the Word. The spiritual meaning of "prophet" and also of "son of humanity" is *the teaching of the church drawn from the Word,* and when it is said of the Lord, it means *the Word itself.*

For the prophet Daniel being called a son of humanity, see Daniel 8:17.

For the prophet Ezekiel being called a son of humanity, see Ezekiel 2:1, 3, 6, 8; 3:1, 3, 4, 10, 17, 25; 4:1, 16; 5:1; 6:2; 7:2; 8:5, 6, 8, 12, 15; 11:2, 4, 15; 12:2, 3, 9, 18, 27; 13:2, 17; 14:3, 13; 15:2; 16:2; 17:2; 20:3, 4, 27, 46; 21:2, 6, 9, 12, 14, 19, 28; 22:18, 24; 23:2, 36; 24:2, 16, 25; 25:2; 26:2; 27:2; 28:2, 12, 21; 29:2, 18; 30:2, 21; 31:2; 32:2, 18; 33:2, 7, 10, 12, 24, 30; 34:2; 35:2; 36:1, 17; 37:3, 9, 11, 16; 38:2, 14; 39:1, 17; 40:4; 43:7, 10, 18; 44:5.

We can see from this that the Lord as the Divine-Human One is called "the Son of God," and as the Word is called "the Son of Humanity."

The Lord Made His Human Nature Divine out of the Divine Nature within Himself, and in This Way Became One with the Father

29 ACCORDING to *the church's doctrinal statement*[96] accepted throughout the Christian world,

> Our Lord Jesus Christ, the Son of God, is both God and a human being. Although he is God and a human being, yet he is not two, but

one Christ. He is one because the divine nature took the human nature to itself. Indeed, he is one altogether, because he is one person. Therefore as the soul and the body make one human being, so God and a human being is one Christ.

These words are quoted from the Athanasian statement of faith, which is accepted throughout the Christian world. These are that statement's essential points concerning the oneness of what is divine and what is human in the Lord. Other points concerning the Lord in that statement will be explained in their proper places [§§35, 55–61].

This shows us very clearly that according to *the statement of faith of the Christian church,* the divine and human natures in the Lord are not two but one, just as the soul and the body is one human being, and that the divine nature took the human nature to itself.

[2] It follows from this that the divine nature cannot be separated from the human or the human from the divine, because separating them would be like separating soul and body. Everyone will acknowledge this who reads the passages about the Lord's birth cited above (see §§19 and 21) from two Gospels (Luke 1:26–35 and Matthew 1:18–25). It is obvious from these passages that Jesus was conceived by Jehovah God and born of the Virgin Mary. This means that there was something divine within him, and that this was his soul.[97]

Now, since his soul was the actual divine nature of the Father, it follows that his body or human side was made divine as well, for where the one is, the other must also be. In this way and in no other way the Father and the Son are one, the Father in the Son and the Son in the Father, and all that is the Son's is the Father's, and all that is the Father's is the Son's, as the Lord himself tells us in the Word [John 17:10].

[3] But how this union was brought about I need to explain in the following sequence:

1. The Lord from eternity is Jehovah.
2. The Lord from eternity, or Jehovah, took on a human nature for the purpose of saving us.
3. He made the human nature divine from the divine nature within himself.
4. He made the human nature divine by the trials to which he made himself vulnerable.
5. The complete union of the divine nature and the human nature in him was accomplished by the suffering on the cross, which was his last trial.

6. Step by step he took off the human nature he had taken on from his mother and put on a human nature from what was divine within him, which is the divine-human nature and the Son of God.
7. In this way, God became human on both the first [or innermost] level and the last [or outermost] level.[98]

30 1. *The Lord from eternity is Jehovah.* This we know from the Word, since the Lord said to the Jews,

> Truly I say to you, before Abraham was, I am. (John 8:58)

And again,

> Glorify me, Father, with the glory I had with you before the world existed. (John 17:5)

This means the Lord from eternity and not the Son from eternity, because the Son is his human nature conceived by Jehovah the Father and born of the Virgin Mary in time, as explained above [§§19–20].

[2] We are assured by many passages in the Word that the Lord from eternity is Jehovah himself, a few of which passages may be cited now.

> It will be said on that day, "*This is our God;* we have waited for him to free us. [This is] *Jehovah;* we have waited for him. Let us rejoice and be glad in his salvation." (Isaiah 25:9)

We can see from this that the speakers were waiting for Jehovah God himself.

> A voice of someone in the wilderness crying out, "Prepare a pathway for *Jehovah;* make level in the desert a highway for *our God.* The glory of *Jehovah* will be revealed, and all flesh will see it together. Behold, *the Lord Jehovih* is coming in strength." (Isaiah 40:3, 5, 10; Matthew 3:3; Mark 1:3; Luke 3:4)

Here too, the Lord, who is to come, is called Jehovah.

> [3] I am Jehovah. I will make you a covenant for the people, a light for the nations. *I am Jehovah. This is my name, and I will not give my glory to another.* (Isaiah 42:6, 7, 8)

A covenant for the people and a light for the nations is the Lord in his human nature. Because this is from Jehovah and was made one with

Jehovah, it says "I am Jehovah. This is my name, and I will not give my glory to another"—that is, to no one other than himself. To give glory is to glorify, or to unite with himself.

[4] *The Lord,* whom you seek, will suddenly come to his Temple. (Malachi 3:1)

The Temple means the temple of his body, as he says in John 2:19, 21.

The Dayspring from on high has visited us. (Luke 1:78)

The Dayspring from on high is Jehovah, or the Lord from eternity.

We can see from these passages that "the Lord from eternity" means his divine nature as the source, which is called Jehovah in the Word. We will see from passages to be cited below that after his human nature had been glorified, both "the Lord" and "Jehovah" mean the divine nature and the human nature together as one, and that "the Son" by itself means the divine-human nature.

2. *The Lord from eternity, or Jehovah, took on a human nature for the purpose of saving us.* There is support for this from the Word in the preceding parts of this book. It will be said elsewhere that otherwise we could not have been saved.⁹⁹

There are many passages in the Word that show that he took on a human nature, places where it says that he came forth from God, came down from heaven, and was sent into the world. See the following, for example:

I came forth from the Father and *have come* into the world. (John 16:28)

I proceeded forth and came from *God.* I have not come of myself; *he sent me.* (John 8:42)

The Father loves you because you have believed that *I came forth from God.* (John 16:27)

No one has ascended to heaven except the one who *came down from heaven.* (John 3:13)

The bread of God is the one who *comes down from heaven* and gives life to the world. (John 6:33, 35, 41, 50, 51)

The one who *comes down from above* is above all. The one who *comes down from heaven* is above all. (John 3:31)

I know the Father because *I am from him* and *he sent me*. (John 7:29)

You may see in §20 above that being sent into the world by the Father means taking on a human nature.

32 3. *The Lord made the human nature divine from the divine nature within himself.* There is support for this in many passages in the Word. Here we select passages that support the following points.

(a) *This happened step by step:*

Jesus grew and became strong in spirit and in wisdom, and the grace of God was upon him. (Luke 2:40)

Jesus increased in wisdom and age, and in favor with God and humankind. (Luke 2:52)

[2] (b) *The divine nature worked through the human nature the way a soul works through its body:*

The Son cannot do anything on his own unless he sees the Father doing it. (John 5:19)

I do nothing of myself; as my Father taught me I say these things. The one who sent me is with me; he has not left me alone. (John 8:28, 29; 5:30)

I have not spoken on my own authority; the Father who sent me has given me a commandment regarding what I should say and what I should speak. (John 12:49, 50)

The words that I speak to you I do not speak on my own authority; the Father who dwells in me does these works. (John 14:10)

I am not alone, because the Father is with me. (John 16:32)

[3] (c) *The divine nature and the human nature worked in complete accord:*

Whatever the Father does, the Son also does in the same way. (John 5:19)

Just as the Father raises the dead and brings them to life, so also the Son brings to life those whom he wishes to. (John 5:21)

Just as the Father has life in himself, so he has also granted the Son to have life in himself. (John 5:26)

Now they know that all things you have given me are from you. (John 17:7)

[4] (d) *The divine nature was united to the human nature and the human nature to the divine:*

"If you have known me you have also known my Father and have seen him." When Philip wanted to see the Father, Jesus said, "Have I been with you for so long, and yet you have not known me, Philip? Those who have seen me have seen the Father. Do you not believe that I am in the Father and the Father is in me? Believe me that I am in the Father and the Father is in me." (John 14:7–11)

If I am not doing the works of my Father, do not believe me. If I am doing them, believe the works, so that you may know and believe that the Father is in me and I am in the Father. (John 10:37, 38)

. . . so that they all may be one, as you, Father, are in me and I am in you. (John 17:21)

On that day you will know that I am in my Father. (John 14:20)

No one will snatch the sheep from my Father's hand. I and the Father are one. (John 10:29, 30)

The Father loves the Son and has given all things into his hand. (John 3:35)

All things that the Father has are mine. (John 16:15)

All that is mine is yours, and all that is yours is mine. (John 17:10)

You have given the Son power over all flesh. (John 17:2)

All power has been given to me in heaven and on earth. (Matthew 28:18)

[5] (e) *We should turn to the Divine-Human One,* as we can see from the following passages:

. . . so that all people will honor the Son just as they honor the Father. (John 5:23)

If you had known me, you would also have known my Father. (John 8:19)

Those who see me see the one who sent me. (John 12:45)

If you have known me you have also known my Father, and from now on you know him and have seen him. (John 14:7)

> Those who accept me accept the one who sent me. (John 13:20)

This is because no one can see the divinity itself that is called "the Father"; only the Divine-Human One can be seen. The Lord in fact said,

> No one has ever seen God. The only-begotten Son, who is close to the Father's heart, has made him visible. (John 1:18)

> No one has seen the Father except the one who is with the Father. He has seen the Father. (John 6:46)

> You have never heard the Father's voice or seen what he looks like. (John 5:37)

[6] (f) *Since the Lord made his human nature divine from the divine nature within himself, and since we should turn to him and he is the Son of God, we are therefore to believe in the Lord who is both Father and Son,* as we can see from the following passages.

> Jesus said that as many as accepted him, he gave them power to become children of God and *believe in his name.* (John 1:12)

> . . . so that all who *believe in him* will not perish but will have eternal life. (John 3:15)

> God loved the world so much that he gave his only-begotten Son so that everyone who *believes in him* would have eternal life. (John 3:16)

> Those who *believe in the Son* are not condemned; but those who *do not believe* have already been condemned because *they have not believed in the name of the only-begotten Son of God.* (John 3:18)

> Those who *believe in the Son* have eternal life. Those who *do not believe in the Son* will not see life; instead, the wrath of God abides on them. (John 3:36)

> The bread of God is the one who comes down from heaven and gives life to the world. Those who come to me will not hunger, and those who *believe in me* will never thirst. (John 6:33, 35)

> This is the will of the one who sent me, that all those who see the Son and *believe in him* will have eternal life, and I will raise them up on the last day. (John 6:40)

> They said to Jesus, "What should we do in order to perform the works of God?" Jesus answered, "This is the work of God, that you *believe in the one whom he has sent."* (John 6:28, 29)

Truly I say to you, those who *believe in me* have eternal life. (John 6:47)

Jesus cried out, saying, "If any are thirsty, they must come to me and drink. As the Scripture has said, from the bellies of those who *believe in me* will flow rivers of living water." (John 7:37, 38)

If you do not believe that I am, you will die in your sins. (John 8:24)

Jesus said, "I am the resurrection and the life. Even if they die, those who *believe in me* will live; and anyone who lives and *believes in me* will never die." (John 11:25, 26)

Jesus said, "I have come into the world as a light so that anyone who *believes in me* will not remain in darkness." (John 12:46; 8:12)

While you have the light, *believe in the light,* so that you may become children of the light. (John 12:36)

I tell you truly, the dead will hear the voice of the Son of God, and those who hear will live. (John 5:25)

Abide in me, and I [will abide] in you. I am the vine; you are the branches. Those who abide in me and in whom I abide bear much fruit, because without me you cannot do anything. (John 15:1–5)

They were to abide in the Lord, and the Lord in them. (John 14:20; 17:23)

I am the way, the truth, and the life. No one comes to the Father except through me. (John 14:6)

[7] In these passages and all others, when it mentions "the Father" it means the divine nature that was in the Lord from his conception, which—according to the teaching embraced by the Christian world regarding faith—was like the soul within the body in human beings. The human nature that came from this divine nature is the Son of God.

Now, since this was also made divine, in order to prevent people from turning to the Father alone and thereby separating the Father from the Lord (in whom the Father dwells) in their thought, faith, and worship, the Lord went on to teach that the Father and he are one and that the Father is in him and he is in the Father, and that we are to abide in him; also that no one comes to the Father except through him. He also tells us that we are to believe in him and that we are saved by a faith focused directly on him.

[8] For many Christians, it is impossible to grasp the concept that in the Lord a human nature was made divine, primarily because they think

of "human" only in terms of the physical body and not in terms of anything spiritual. Yet all angels, who are spiritual beings, also have a completely human form, and everything divine that emanates from Jehovah God, everything from its first [or innermost] level in heaven to its last [or outermost] level on earth, tends to take on a human form.

On angels as human forms and on everything divine tending toward the human form, see *Heaven and Hell* 73–77 and 453–460. There will also be more on this subject in forthcoming works that will draw on angelic wisdom about the Lord.[100]

33 4. *The Lord made his human nature divine by the trials to which he made himself vulnerable and by then constantly being victorious.* This was discussed in §§12–14 above. I need add only the following.

Trials are battles against what is evil and false, and since what is evil and false comes from hell, they are also battles against hell. For us too, when we are subjected to spiritual trials, it is evil spirits from hell who are inflicting them. We are not aware that evil spirits are behind the trials, but an abundance of experience has taught me that they are.[101]

[2] This is why we are rescued from hell and raised into heaven when the Lord enables us to be victorious in our trials. This is how we become spiritual individuals by means of our trials or battles against our evils—how we therefore become angels.

The Lord, though, fought against all the hells with his own power and completely tamed and subdued them; and by doing so, since at the same time he glorified his human nature, he keeps them tamed and subdued to eternity.

[3] Before the Lord's Coming the hells had risen so far that they were beginning to trouble even angels of heaven, and with them, everyone who was entering the world and leaving the world. The reason for this rise of the hells was that the church was in utter ruins, and the people of our world were wholly devoted to evil and falsity because of their idolatrous practices; and it is people from earth who make up hell.[102] That is why no one could have been saved if the Lord had not come into the world.

There is a great deal in the Psalms of David and the prophets about these battles of the Lord, but little in the Gospels. These battles are what we refer to as the trials that the Lord underwent, the last being his suffering on the cross. [4] This is why the Lord is called the Savior and Redeemer. The church is sufficiently aware of this to say that the Lord conquered death or the Devil (that is, hell) and that he rose from death victorious, as well as that there is no salvation apart from the

Lord. We shall see shortly that he also glorified his human nature and in this way became the Savior, Redeemer, Reformer, and Regenerator to eternity.

[5] We can see from the ample supply of passages cited in §§12–14 above that the Lord became our Savior by means of battles or trials; and there is also this from Isaiah:

> "The day of vengeance is in my heart and *the year of* my *redeemed* has arrived. I have trodden them in my wrath; I have driven their victory down into the earth." *Therefore he became their Savior.* (Isaiah 63:4, 6, 8)

This chapter is about the Lord's battles. There is also this in David:

> Lift your heads, gates! Be raised up, doors of the world, so that *the King of Glory* may come in! Who is this *King of Glory? Jehovah, strong and heroic, Jehovah, a hero in war.* (Psalms 24:7, 8)

This too is about the Lord.

5. *The complete union of the divine nature and the human nature in him was effected by the suffering on the cross, which was his last trial.*

Support for this proposition was provided above [§§12–14], in the chapter explaining that the Lord came into the world to subdue the hells and to glorify his human nature, and that the suffering on the cross was the last battle, by which he gained complete victory over the hells and completely glorified his human nature. Since, then, by suffering on the cross the Lord completely glorified his human nature—that is, united it to the divine nature—and thereby made his human nature divine as well, it follows that he is Jehovah and God in respect to both natures. [2] That is why in so many passages in the Word Jehovah, God, or the Holy One of Israel is called the Redeemer, the Savior, or the Maker, as in the following:

> Mary said, "My soul magnifies *the Lord,* and my spirit has rejoiced in *God, my Savior.*" (Luke 1:46, 47)

> The angel said to the shepherds, "Behold, I am bringing you good news, a great joy, which will be for all people. There is born this day in the city of David a *Savior,* who is *Christ the Lord.*" (Luke 2:10, 11)

> They said, "This is truly *the Savior of the world, the Christ.*" (John 4:42)

> I, Jehovah God, am helping you; your *Redeemer* is *the Holy One of Israel.* (Isaiah 41:14)

Thus says *Jehovah, who is your Creator,* O Jacob, and *your Maker,* O Israel: *"I have redeemed you.* I am *Jehovah your God, the Holy One of Israel, your Savior."* (Isaiah 43:1, 3)

Thus says Jehovah your *Redeemer, the Holy One of Israel,* "I am Jehovah, *your Holy One,* the Creator of Israel, *your King."* (Isaiah 43:14, 15)

Thus says *Jehovah, the Holy One of Israel,* and Israel's *Maker.* (Isaiah 45:11, 15)

Thus says *Jehovah* your *Redeemer, the Holy One of Israel.* (Isaiah 48:17)

. . . so that all flesh may know that I, *Jehovah,* am your *Savior,* and *your Redeemer, the Mighty One of Jacob.* (Isaiah 49:26)

Then he will come to Zion as *the Redeemer.* (Isaiah 59:20)

. . . so that you may know that I, *Jehovah,* am *your Savior* and *your Redeemer, the Powerful One of Jacob.* (Isaiah 60:16)

Jehovah, the one who formed [me] from the womb. (Isaiah 49:5)

. . . *Jehovah,* my Rock and *my Redeemer.* (Psalms 19:14)

They remembered that God was their Rock, and *God on High their Redeemer.* (Psalms 78:35)

Thus says *Jehovah your Redeemer,* and the *one who formed* you from the womb. (Isaiah 44:24)

As for *our Redeemer, Jehovah Sabaoth* is his name, the Holy One of Israel. (Isaiah 47:4)

"With everlasting compassion I will have mercy on you," says *Jehovah, your Redeemer.* (Isaiah 54:8)

Their Redeemer is strong; Jehovah is his *name.* (Jeremiah 50:34)

Let Israel hope in *Jehovah,* because *with Jehovah* there is mercy; with him there is abundant *redemption. He will redeem* Israel from all his iniquities. (Psalms 130:7, 8)

Jehovah God is my rock, my fortress, the horn of my salvation, *my Savior.* (2 Samuel 22:2, 3)

Thus says *Jehovah, the Redeemer* of Israel, *Israel's Holy One:* "Monarchs will see and abide, because of Jehovah, who is faithful, the Holy One of Israel, who has chosen you." (Isaiah 49:7)

God is only among you, and *there is no other God*. Surely you are a hidden God, O *God of Israel, the Savior*. (Isaiah 45:14, 15)

Thus says Jehovah the King of Israel, and *Israel's Redeemer, Jehovah Sabaoth: "There is no God other than me."* (Isaiah 44:6)

I am Jehovah, and there is no Savior other than me. (Isaiah 43:11)

Am I not Jehovah? And there is no [God] other than me; and there is no Savior other than me. (Isaiah 45:21)

I am *Jehovah your God.* You are to acknowledge no God other than me; *there is no Savior other than me.* (Hosea 13:4)

Am *I* not *Jehovah?* And there is no God other than me. I am a just *God,* and *there is no Savior other than me.* Look to me so that you may *be saved,* all you ends of the earth, because *I am God and there is no other.* (Isaiah 45:21, 22)

Jehovah Sabaoth is his name, and your Redeemer, the Holy One of Israel. He will be called the God of the whole earth. (Isaiah 54:5)

[3] We can see from these passages that the Lord's divine nature called "the Father" (and here called "Jehovah" and "God") and his divine-human nature called "the Son" (and here "the Redeemer" and "the Savior" as well as "the Maker," meaning the Reformer[103] and Regenerator) are one, not two, for it not only says "Jehovah is God" and "the Holy One of Israel is the Redeemer and Savior," it also says "Jehovah is the Redeemer and Savior." Not only that, it even calls Jehovah "the Savior" and says, "there is no Savior other than me." This clearly shows that the divine nature and the human nature in the Lord are one person and that the human nature is divine as well, since the Redeemer and Savior of the world is no other than the Lord in his divine-human nature, which is called "the Son." Redemption and salvation are properly credited to his human nature, and are called "merit and righteousness," since his human nature bore the trials and the suffering on the cross, which means that he accomplished redemption and salvation by means of his human nature.

[4] Since, then, after the union of his human nature with his inner divine nature, which was like that of soul and body in us, they were no longer two but were one person (according to the teaching of the Christian world), the Lord was Jehovah and God in both respects. This is why some passages speak of "Jehovah and the Holy One of Israel, the Redeemer and

Savior," and others say "Jehovah, the Redeemer and Savior," as you can see from the citations above.

[The Word] also speaks of *Christ, the Savior;* see Luke 2:10, 11 and John 4:42. On *God* and *the God of Israel* being *the Savior and Redeemer,* see Luke 1:47; Isaiah 45:14; 54:5; Psalms 78:35. On *Jehovah, the Holy One of Israel* being *the Savior and Redeemer,* see Isaiah 41:14; 43:3, 11, 14, 15; 48:17; 49:7; 54:5. On *Jehovah* being *the Savior, Redeemer, and Maker,* see Isaiah 44:6; 47:4; 49:26; 54:8; 63:8; Jeremiah 50:34; Psalms 19:14; 130:7, 8; 2 Samuel 22:2, 3; [Isaiah 43:1, 3; 44:24; 45:11; 49:5]. On *Jehovah God* being *the Redeemer and Savior, "and there is no Savior other than me,"* see Isaiah 43:11; 44:6; 45:14, 18, 21, 22; Hosea 13:4.

35   6. *Step by step he took off the human nature he had taken on from his mother and put on a human nature from what was divine within him, which is the divine-human nature and the Son of God.*

It is generally known that the Lord was divine and human, divine because of Jehovah the Father and human because of the Virgin Mary. That is why he was God and a human being and therefore had a divine essence and a human outward nature, the divine essence from his Father and the human nature from his mother. This meant that he was equal to the Father with respect to his divinity, but less than the Father with respect to his humanity.[104] It also meant that, as we are taught by the so-called *Athanasian statement of faith,* this human nature from his mother was not changed into or mixed with a divine essence, since a human nature cannot be changed into or mixed with a divine essence. [2] All the same, this very statement of faith we have accepted says that the divine nature took on a human nature—that is, united itself with it as a soul with its body, so much so that they were not two but one person. It follows from this that he took off the human nature received from his mother, which was essentially like that of anyone else and therefore material, and put on a human nature from his Father, which was essentially like his divine nature and therefore substantial,[105] thus making his human nature divine.

That is why the Lord is even called "Jehovah" and "God" in the prophetic books of the Word, and in the Word of the Gospels is called "Lord," "God," "Messiah" or "Christ," and "the Son of God," the one in whom we are to believe and by whom we are to be saved.

[3] Now, since from the beginning the Lord had a human nature from his mother and took this off step by step, while he was in this world he therefore experienced two states, one called the state of being brought low or being emptied out[106] and one called the state of being glorified or united with the Divine called "the Father." The state of being brought

low occurred when and to the extent that he was primarily conscious of the human nature received from his mother, and the state of being glorified occurred when and to the extent that he was primarily conscious of the human nature received from his Father. In his state of being brought low he prayed to the Father as someone other than himself; while in his state of being glorified he talked with the Father as if talking with himself. In this latter state he said that the Father was in him and he in the Father and that the Father and he were one; while in his state of being brought low he bore trials, suffered on the cross, and prayed that the Father would not forsake him.[107] This is because his divine nature could not be subject to any trial, let alone suffer on the cross.

These passages then show us that by means of his trials and the subsequent constant victories, and by means of his suffering on the cross, which was the final trial, he completely subdued the hells and completely glorified his human nature, as has been explained above.

[4] As for his taking off the human nature received from his mother and putting on the human nature received from what was divine within him called "the Father," this we can see from the fact that whenever the Lord spoke directly to his mother he did not call her "mother" but "woman." We find only three places in the Gospels where he speaks directly to his mother or about her, and in two of these he called her "woman," while in one he did not acknowledge her as his mother. As for the two in which he called her "woman," we read in John,

> Jesus' mother said to him, "They have no wine." Jesus said to her, "What have I to do with you, *woman?* My hour has not yet come." (John 2:4)

And also

> When Jesus from the cross saw his mother, and the disciple whom he loved standing by her, he said to his mother, "*Woman,* behold your son!" Then he said to the disciple, "Behold your mother!" (John 19:25, 26, 27)

The one occasion on which he did not acknowledge her is in Luke:

> They announced to Jesus, "Your mother and your brothers are standing outside and want to see you." Jesus answered and said to them, "My mother and my brothers are these who hear the Word of God and do it." (Luke 8:20, 21; Matthew 12:46–49; Mark 3:31–35)

In other passages Mary is called his mother, but never from his own mouth.

[5] There is further support for this in the fact that he did not acknowledge himself to be the son of David. In fact, we read in the Gospels,

> Jesus asked the Pharisees, saying, "What is your view of the Christ? Whose son is he?" They said to him, "David's." He said to them, "So how is it that David, in the spirit, calls him his Lord when he says, 'The Lord said to my Lord, "Sit at my right until I make your enemies a stool for your feet"'? So if David calls him 'Lord,' how is he his son?" And no one could answer him a word. (Matthew 22:41–46; Mark 12:35, 36, 37; Luke 20:41–44; Psalms 110:1)

We can see from all this that as far as his glorified human nature was concerned, the Lord was neither the son of Mary nor the son of David.

[6] He showed Peter, James, and John what his glorified human nature was like when he was transfigured before their eyes:

> His face shone like the sun and his clothing was like light. And then a voice from a cloud said, "This is my beloved Son, in whom I am well pleased. Hear him." (Matthew 17:1–8; Mark 9:2–8; Luke 9:28–36)

The Lord also looked to John "like the sun shining in its strength" (Revelation 1:16).

[7] We are assured that the Lord's human nature was glorified by what it says about his glorification in the Gospels, such as the following from John:

> The hour has come for the Son of Humanity to be glorified. He said, "Father, glorify your name." A voice came from heaven, saying, "I both have glorified it and will glorify it again." (John 12:23, 28)

It says "I both have glorified it and will glorify it again" because the Lord was glorified step by step. Again,

> After Judas went out, Jesus said, "Now the Son of Humanity is glorified, and God is glorified in him. God will also glorify him in himself and glorify him immediately." (John 13:31, 32)

Again,

> Jesus said, "Father, the hour has come. Glorify your Son, so that your Son may also glorify you." (John 17:1, 5)

And in Luke,

> Was it not necessary for Christ to suffer this and enter into his glory? (Luke 24:26)

These things were said about his human nature.

[8] The Lord said, "God is glorified in him" and also "God will glorify him in himself" and "Glorify your Son, so that your Son may also glorify you." The Lord said these things because the union was reciprocal, the divine nature with the human nature and the human nature with the divine. That is why he also said, "I am in the Father and the Father is in me" (John 14:10, 11) and "All that is mine is yours, and all that is yours is mine" (John 17:10); so the union was full.

It is the same with any union. Unless it is reciprocal, it is not full. This is what the union of the Lord with us and of us with the Lord must be like,[108] as he tells us in this passage in John:

> On that day you will know that you are in me and I am in you. (John 14:20)

And in this passage:

> Abide in me, and I [will abide] in you. Those who abide in me and in whom I abide bear much fruit. (John 15:4, 5)

[9] Because the Lord's human nature was glorified—that is, made divine—on the third day after his death he rose again with his whole body, which is not true of any human being, since we rise again with our spirit only and not with our body.

So that we should know this, and so that no one should doubt that the Lord rose again with his whole body, he not only said so through the angels who were in the tomb but also showed himself to the disciples in his human form with his body, saying to them when they thought they were seeing a spirit,

> "See my hands and my feet—that it is I myself. Touch me and see, because a spirit does not have flesh and bones as you see I have." And when he had said this, he showed them his hands and his feet. (Luke 24:39, 40; John 20:20)

And again,

> Jesus said to Thomas, "Reach your finger here, and look at my hands; and reach out your hand and put it into my side; and do not be

unbelieving, but believing." Then Thomas said, "My Lord and my God." (John 20:27, 28)

[10] To make it even clearer that he was not a spirit but a person, he said to the disciples,

"Have you any food here?" They gave him a piece of broiled fish and some honeycomb, and he took it and ate in their presence. (Luke 24:41, 42, 43)

Since his body was no longer material but had become divine substance, he came to the disciples when the doors were closed (John 20:19, 26) and disappeared after they had seen him (Luke 24:31).

Once the Lord was in this state, he was carried up and sat down at the right hand of God, for it says in Luke,

It happened that, while Jesus blessed his disciples, he was parted from them and carried up into heaven. (Luke 24:51)

and in Mark,

After he had spoken to them, he was carried up into heaven and sat down at the right hand of God. (Mark 16:19)

Sitting down at the right hand of God means gaining divine omnipotence.

[11] Since the Lord rose into heaven with his divine and human natures united into one and sat at the right hand of God (which means gaining omnipotence), it follows that his human substance or essence is now just like his divine substance or essence.

To think otherwise would be like thinking that his divine nature was raised into heaven and sits at the right hand of God, but not together with his human nature. This is contrary to Scripture and also contrary to the Christian teaching that in Christ God and a human being are like the soul and the body. To separate them is also contrary to sound reason.

It is this union of the Father with the Son, or of the divine nature with the human nature, that is meant in the following passages:

I came forth from the Father and have come into the world. Again, I leave the world and go to the Father. (John 16:28)

I go (or come) to the one who sent me. (John 7:33; 16:5, 16; 17:11, 13; 20:17)

> What then if you were to see the Son of Humanity ascend where he was before? (John 6:62)
>
> No one has ascended to heaven except the one who came down from heaven. (John 3:13)

Every one of us who is saved ascends to heaven, though not on our own, but rather through the Lord's power. Only the Lord ascended on his own.

7. In this way, God became human on both the first [or innermost] level and the last [or outermost] level.

It is explained at some length in *Heaven and Hell* that God is human and that because of God all angels and spirits are human,[109] and there will be more on this topic in the books about angelic wisdom.[110]

While from the beginning God was human on the first [or innermost] level, he was not yet human on the last [or outermost] level. After he took on a human nature in the world, though, he also became human on the last [or outermost] level. This follows from what has been shown above [§§29–35], namely, that the Lord united his human nature with his divine nature and in this way made his human nature divine as well. [2] That is why the Lord is called the Beginning and the End, the First and the Last, and the Alpha and the Omega. This is in the Book of Revelation:

> "I am the Alpha and the Omega, the Beginning and the End," says the Lord, "who is and who was and who is to come, the Almighty." (Revelation 1:8, 11)

When John saw the Son of Humanity in the midst of the seven lampstands,

> [John] fell at his feet as dead, but [the Son of Humanity] laid his right hand on him, saying, "I am the First and the Last." (Revelation 1:13, 17; 2:8; 21:6)

> Behold, I am coming quickly, to give to all according to what they have done. I am the Alpha and the Omega, the Beginning and the End, the First and the Last. (Revelation 22:12, 13)

And in Isaiah,

> Thus says Jehovah the King of Israel, and Israel's Redeemer, Jehovah Sabaoth: "I am the First and the Last." (Isaiah 44:6; 48:12)

The Lord Is God Himself, the Source and Subject of the Word

37 IN the first chapter [§§1–7] I undertook to show that the whole of Sacred Scripture is about the Lord and that the Lord is the Word. At this point I need to set this forth further with passages from the Word where the Lord is called Jehovah, the God of Israel and Jacob, the Holy One of Israel, Lord, and God, as well as King, Jehovah's Anointed, and David.

By way of preface I may observe that I have been granted the opportunity to read through all the prophets and the Psalms, to reflect on the individual verses and see what they were about; and it became clear that they were about nothing but the church that had been established and was to be established by the Lord, about the Lord's Coming, his battles, glorification, redemption, and salvation and about the heaven that comes from him, together with their opposites.[111] Since these are all works of the Lord, I could see that the whole of Sacred Scripture is about the Lord and that therefore the Lord is the Word.

[2] The only people who can see this, though, are the ones who enjoy enlightenment from the Lord and who are also acquainted with the Word's spiritual meaning. All the angels in heaven are aware of this meaning, so when one of us is reading the Word, that and that alone is what they grasp.[112] There are always angels and spirits with us, and since they are spiritual beings, they understand spiritually what we understand in earthly terms.

From the passages cited earlier, in the first chapter (§§1–7), we can see only dimly, as though through a screen,[113] that the whole of Sacred Scripture is about the Lord. The passages about the Lord now to be cited show that he is often called "Lord" and "God." It may be very clear from this that he is the one who spoke through the prophets, in whose books it says again and again, "Jehovah spoke," "Jehovah said," and "the saying of Jehovah."

[3] We can see *that the Lord existed before his coming into the world* from the following passages:

> John the Baptist said of the Lord, "This is the one who is to come after me, who was before me; I am not worthy to undo the strap of his

sandal." And "This is the one of whom I said, 'One is coming after me, who was before me and was greater than me.'" (John 1:27, 30)

In the Book of Revelation:

> [The elders] fell down before the throne on which the Lord was, saying, "We give you thanks, O Lord God Almighty, who is and who was and who is to come." (Revelation 11:16, 17)

In Micah:

> As for you, Bethlehem Ephrata, as little as you are among the thousands of Judah, one will come forth from you for me who will become the ruler in Israel; his coming forth is from ancient times, from the days of eternity. (Micah 5:2)

We can also see from the Lord's words in the Gospels that he existed before Abraham [John 8:58], that he had glory with the Father before the foundation of the world [John 17:5, 24], that he came forth from the Father [John 16:28], that the Word was with God from the beginning and that the Word was God [John 1:1], and that the Word became flesh [John 1:14]. The passages that follow will serve to show that the Lord is called Jehovah, the God of Israel and of Jacob, the Holy One of Israel, God, and the Lord, as well as King, Jehovah's Anointed, and David.

We can see from the following passages that the Lord is called "Jehovah":

> Thus says *Jehovah,* who is your Creator, O Jacob, and your Maker, O Israel: "*I have redeemed* you. I am *Jehovah* your God, the Holy One of Israel, your *Savior."* (Isaiah 43:1, 3)

> I am *Jehovah,* your Holy One, *the Creator of Israel,* [your King. (Isaiah 43:15)]

> [Thus says *Jehovah,* the Holy One of Israel,] and Israel's *Maker,* [*the Savior*] . . .[114] (Isaiah 45:11, 15)

> . . . so that all flesh may know that *I, Jehovah,* am your *Savior,* and your *Redeemer,* the Mighty One of Jacob. (Isaiah 49:26)

> . . . so that you may know that I, *Jehovah,* am your *Savior* and your *Redeemer,* the Powerful One of Jacob. (Isaiah 60:16)

> . . . *Jehovah,* the one who formed [me] from the womb. (Isaiah 49:5)

> . . . *Jehovah,* my rock and my *Redeemer.* (Psalms 19:14)

> Thus says *Jehovah* your Maker and the *one who formed* you from the womb. Thus says *Jehovah,* the King of Israel, and Israel's *Redeemer, Jehovah Sabaoth.* (Isaiah 44:2, 6)
>
> As for our *Redeemer, Jehovah Sabaoth is his name,* the Holy One of Israel. (Isaiah 47:4)
>
> "With everlasting compassion I will have mercy [on you]," says Jehovah, your *Redeemer.* (Isaiah 54:8)
>
> *Their Redeemer is strong; Jehovah is his name.* (Jeremiah 50:34)
>
> *Jehovah* God is my rock, my fortress, the horn of my salvation, my *Savior.* (2 Samuel 22:2, 3)
>
> Thus says *Jehovah* your *Redeemer, the Holy One of Israel.* (Isaiah 43:14; 48:17)
>
> Thus says *Jehovah, the Redeemer* of Israel, Israel's Holy One: "Monarchs will see . . ." (Isaiah 49:7)
>
> I am *Jehovah,* and there is no *Savior* other than me. (Isaiah 43:11)
>
> Am I not *Jehovah?* And there is no [God] other than me; and there is no *Savior* other than me. Look to me so that you may *be saved,* all you ends of the earth. (Isaiah 45:21, 22)
>
> I am *Jehovah* your God; there is no *Savior* other than me. (Hosea 13:4)
>
> *You have redeemed* me, O *Jehovah* of truth. (Psalms 31:5)
>
> Let Israel hope in *Jehovah,* for with *Jehovah* there is mercy; with him there is abundant *redemption. He will redeem* Israel from all his iniquities. (Psalms 130:7, 8)
>
> *Jehovah Sabaoth* is his name, and your *Redeemer,* the Holy One of Israel. He will be called the God of the whole earth. (Isaiah 54:5)

In these passages, Jehovah is called Redeemer and Savior; and since the Lord alone is Redeemer and Savior, it is he who is meant by "Jehovah."

We can also see that the Lord is Jehovah—that is, that Jehovah is the Lord—from the following passages.

> A shoot [will go forth] from the trunk of Jesse, and a sprout from its roots will bear fruit. *The spirit of Jehovah* will rest upon him. (Isaiah 11:1, 2)

It will be said on that day, "Behold, this is our God; we have waited for him to set us free. [This is] *Jehovah;* we have waited for him. Let us rejoice and be glad in his salvation." (Isaiah 25:9)

A voice of someone in the wilderness crying out, "Prepare a pathway for *Jehovah;* make level in the desert a highway for our God." *The glory of Jehovah* will be revealed, and all flesh will see it. Behold, *the Lord Jehovih* is coming in strength, and his arm will rule for him. (Isaiah 40:3, 5, 10)

I am *Jehovah.* I will make you a covenant for the people, a light for the nations. I am *Jehovah.* This is my name, and *I will not give my glory to another.* (Isaiah 42:6, 7, 8)

Behold, the days [are coming] when I will raise up for David a righteous branch who will rule as king, and prosper, and bring about judgment and justice on earth. And this is his name: they will call him "*Jehovah our Righteousness.*" (Jeremiah 23:5, 6; 33:15, 16)

As for you, Bethlehem Ephrata, one will come forth from you for me who will become the ruler in Israel. He will stand firm and feed [his flock] in *the strength of Jehovah.* (Micah 5:2, 4)

A Child has been born to us; a Son has been given to us. Leadership is upon his shoulder; and his name will be called God, Hero, *Father of Eternity,* on the throne of David, to establish and found it in judgment and in justice, from now on, even to eternity. (Isaiah 9:6, 7)

Jehovah will go forth and fight against the nations, and his feet will stand on the Mount of Olives, which faces Jerusalem. (Zechariah 14:3, 4)

Lift your heads, gates, and be raised up, doors of the world, so that the King of Glory may come in! Who is this King of Glory? *Jehovah,* strong and heroic, *Jehovah,* a hero in war. (Psalms 24:7–10)

On that day *Jehovah Sabaoth* will become an ornate crown and a beautiful diadem for the remnant of his people. (Isaiah 28:5)

I will send you Elijah the prophet before the great *day of Jehovah* comes. (Malachi 4:5)

There are other passages as well where it says that *the day of Jehovah* is great and near, like Ezekiel 30:3; Joel 2:11; Amos 5:18, 20; and Zephaniah 1:7, 14, 15, 18.

39 *We can see that the Lord is called "the God of Israel" and "the God of Jacob" from the following passages:*

Moses took the blood and sprinkled it on the people and said, "This is the blood of the covenant that Jehovah has made with you." And they saw *the God of Israel,* under whose feet there was something like a work of sapphire stone and like the substance of heaven. (Exodus 24:8, 9, 10)

The crowds were amazed when they saw the mute speaking, the lame walking, and the blind seeing; and they glorified *the God of Israel.* (Matthew 15:31)

Blessed is *the Lord God of Israel,* because he has visited and freed his people Israel, when he raised up the horn of our salvation in the house of David. (Luke 1:68, 69)

I will give you treasures of darkness and the hidden wealth of secret places so that you may recognize that I, Jehovah, who have called you by your name, am *the God of Israel.* (Isaiah 45:3)

. . . the house of Jacob, people who swear by the name of Jehovah and of the God of Israel, for they are called by the name of the holy city and rely on *the God of Israel:* Jehovah Sabaoth is his name. (Isaiah 48:1, 2)

Jacob will see his descendants in his midst. They will sanctify my name and will sanctify the Holy One of Jacob; and they will fear *the God of Israel.* (Isaiah 29:23)

In the very last of days many people will come and say, "Come, and let us go up to the mountain of Jehovah, to the house of *the God of Jacob,* who will teach us about his ways so that we may walk in his paths." (Isaiah 2:3; Micah 4:2)

. . . so that all flesh may know that I, Jehovah, am your Savior, and your *Redeemer, the Mighty One of Jacob.* (Isaiah 49:26)

I, Jehovah, am your Savior and your Redeemer, the *Powerful One of Jacob.* (Isaiah 60:16)

In the presence of the Lord you give birth, O earth, in the presence of *the God of Jacob.* (Psalms 114:7)

David swore to Jehovah and made a vow to *the Mighty One of Jacob,* "[God forbid] that I enter the tent of my home until I have found a place for Jehovah, a dwelling for the *Mighty One of Jacob."* We have heard of him in Ephrata [that is, Bethlehem].[115] (Psalms 132:2, 3, 5, 6)

Blessed be *the God of Israel;* the whole earth will be full of his glory. (Psalms 72:18, 19)

There are also many other passages where the Lord is called "God of Israel," "Redeemer," and "Savior," such as Luke 1:47; Isaiah 45:15; 54:5; Psalms 78:35; and many other places where we find only "the God of Israel," as in Isaiah 17:6; 21:10, 17; 24:15; 29:23; Jeremiah 7:3; 9:15; 11:3; 13:12; 16:9; 19:3, 15; 23:2; 24:5; 25:15, 27; 29:4, 8, 21, 25; 30:2; 31:23; 32:14, 15, 36; 33:4; 34:2, 13; 35:13, 17, 18, 19; 37:7; 38:17; 39:16; 42:9, 15, 18; 43:10; 44:2, 7, 11, 25; 48:1; 50:18; 51:33; Ezekiel 8:4; 9:3; 10:19, 20; 11:22; 43:2; 44:2; Zephaniah 2:9; Psalms 41:13; 59:5; 68:8.

We can see that the Lord is called the Holy One of Israel from the following passages.

The angel said to Mary, "The *Holy One* that is born from you will be called the Son of God." (Luke 1:35)

I saw in visions, and behold, a Watcher, a *Holy One,* coming down from heaven. (Daniel 4:13, 23)

God will come from Teman and the *Holy One* from Mount Paran. (Habakkuk 3:3)

I am Jehovah, your *Holy One,* the Creator of Israel, [your King]. (Isaiah 43:15)

[Thus says Jehovah, *the Holy One of Israel,*] and Israel's Maker, [the Savior]. (Isaiah 45:11, 15)

Thus says Jehovah, the Redeemer of Israel, Israel's *Holy One.* (Isaiah 49:7)

I am Jehovah your God, the *Holy One of Israel,* your Savior. (Isaiah 43:1, 3)

As for our Redeemer, Jehovah Sabaoth is his name, the *Holy One of Israel.* (Isaiah 47:4)

Thus says Jehovah your Redeemer, the *Holy One of Israel.* (Isaiah 43:14; 48:17)

Jehovah Sabaoth is his name, and your Redeemer, the *Holy One of Israel.* (Isaiah 54:5)

They tested God and the *Holy One of Israel.* (Psalms 78:41)

> They have abandoned Jehovah and have angered the *Holy One of Israel*. (Isaiah 1:4)
>
> They said, "Make the *Holy One of Israel* cease from our presence."[116] Therefore thus said the *Holy One of Israel* ... (Isaiah 30:11, 12)
>
> ... those who say, "Let him hasten his work so that we may see; let the counsel of the *Holy One of Israel* draw near and arrive." (Isaiah 5:19)
>
> On that day they will rely on Jehovah, the *Holy One of Israel,* in truth. (Isaiah 10:20)
>
> Shout and rejoice, daughter[117] of Zion, because the *Holy One of Israel* is great in your midst. (Isaiah 12:6)
>
> The God of Israel has said, "On that day people will look back to their Maker, and their eyes will look toward the *Holy One of Israel.*" (Isaiah 17:7)
>
> The meek will increase their joy in Jehovah, and the poor of the people will rejoice in the *Holy One of Israel.* (Isaiah 29:19; 41:16)
>
> Nations will run to you because of Jehovah your God and because of the *Holy One of Israel.* (Isaiah 55:5)
>
> The islands will trust in me to bring your children from afar for the name of Jehovah Sabaoth and the *Holy One of Israel.* (Isaiah 60:9)
>
> Their land is full of sin against the *Holy One of Israel.* (Jeremiah 51:5)

There are many other instances elsewhere.

The Holy One of Israel means the Lord in his divine-human nature, since the angel Gabriel said to Mary, "The *Holy One* that is born from you will be called the Son of God" (Luke 1:35). As for Jehovah and the Holy One of Israel being one and the same even though they are given different names, this is quite clear from the passages just cited where it says that Jehovah is the Holy One of Israel.

41 We can see *that the Lord is called Lord and God* from many passages, so many that to cite them all would fill pages. These few may suffice. In John:

> When Thomas at the Lord's bidding looked at his hands and touched his side, he said, *"My Lord and my God."* (John 20:27, 28)

In David,

> They remembered that *God* was their Rock, and *God on High* their *Redeemer*. (Psalms 78:35)

And in Isaiah,

> Jehovah Sabaoth is his name, and your *Redeemer*, the Holy One of Israel. *He will be called the God of the whole earth.* (Isaiah 54:5)

We can see this also from the fact that they worshiped him and fell on their faces before him—Matthew 9:18; 14:33; 15:25; 28:9; Mark 1:40; 5:22; 7:25; 10:17; Luke 17:15, 16; John 9:38. And in David,

> We heard of him in Ephrata; let us enter his dwelling and *bow down at the stool for his feet.* (Psalms 132:6, 7)

It is much the same in heaven, as described in the Book of Revelation:

> I was in the spirit; and behold, a throne set in heaven, and one sat on the throne. He was like a jasper and a sardius stone, and there was a rainbow around the throne, in appearance like an emerald. And the twenty-four elders *fell down* before the one who sits on the throne and *worshiped the one who lives forever and ever, and cast their crowns before the throne.* (Revelation 4:2, 3, 10)

And again,

> I saw in the right hand of the one who sat on the throne a scroll, written inside and on the back, sealed with seven seals. And no one was able to open the scroll. Then one of the elders said, "Behold, the Lion of the tribe of Judah, the Root of David, has prevailed to open the scroll and to loose its seven seals." And I saw in the midst of the throne a Lamb standing. He came and took the scroll, and *[the twenty-four elders] fell down before the Lamb and worshiped the one who lives forever and ever.* (Revelation 5:1, 3, 5, 6, 7, 8, 14)

The reason *the Lord is called King and [Jehovah's] Anointed* is that he was the Messiah or Christ, and "Messiah" or "Christ" means "King" and "Anointed One." That is also why "King" in the Word means the Lord. *Much the same was meant by David,* who was king over Judah and over Israel.

We can see from many passages in the Word that the Lord was called "King" and "Jehovah's Anointed." That is why it says in Revelation, "The Lamb will overcome them, because he is *Lord of Lords and King of Kings*" (Revelation 17:14); and again, the one who sat on the white horse "had on his robe a name written—*King of Kings and Lord of Lords*" (Revelation 19:16).

It is because the Lord is called "King" that heaven and the church are called *his kingdom* and his coming into the world is called *the gospel of the kingdom.*

On heaven and the church being called his kingdom, see Matthew 12:28; 16:28; Mark 1:14, 15; 9:1; 15:43; Luke 1:33; 4:43; 8:1, 10; 9:2, 11, 60; 10:11; 16:16; 19:11; 21:31; 22:18; 23:51; and in Daniel:

> God will raise up a *kingdom* that will never be destroyed. It will crush and devour all these other kingdoms, and it will stand forever. (Daniel 2:44)

In the same,

> I was watching in the night visions, and behold, someone like the Son of Humanity was coming with the clouds of the heavens. To him was given *dominion* and glory and a *kingdom,* so that all peoples, nations, and tongues would worship him. His *dominion* is an everlasting *dominion,* and his *kingdom* is one that will not perish. (Daniel 7:13, 14, 27)

On his Coming being called "the gospel of the kingdom," see Matthew 4:23; 9:35; 24:14.

43 *We can see from the following passages that the Lord is called "David."*

> On that day they will serve Jehovah their God and David their king, whom I will raise up for them. (Jeremiah 30:9)

> Then the children of Israel will turn back and seek Jehovah their God and David their king; with fear they will come to Jehovah and his goodness at the very last of days. (Hosea 3:5)

> I will raise up one shepherd over them, who will feed them: my servant David. He will feed them and be their shepherd. I, Jehovah, will be their God, and David will be the leader in their midst. (Ezekiel 34:23, 24)

> So that they become my people, and I become their God, my servant David will be king over them; there will be one shepherd for them all. Then they will dwell in the land, they and their children and their children's children forever, and David will be their leader forever. And

I will make a covenant of peace with them, and it will be an everlasting covenant with them. (Ezekiel 37:23–26)

I will make an everlasting covenant with you, the sure mercies of David. Behold, I have made him a witness to the peoples, a prince and a lawmaker to the nations. (Isaiah 55:3, 4)

On that day I will raise up the fallen tent of David and patch its holes; I will restore its ruins and build it as it was in ancient days. (Amos 9:11)

The house of David will be like God, like the angel of Jehovah before them. (Zechariah 12:8)

On that day a fountain will be opened for the house of David. (Zechariah 13:1)

Once people realize that "David" means the Lord, they can know why David so often wrote about the Lord in his psalms when he was writing about himself. See Psalm 89, for example, where we find,

I have made a covenant with my chosen one, I have sworn to David my servant, "I will establish your seed even to eternity and build your throne for generation after generation. And the heavens will bear witness to your wondrous work, and to [your] truth, in the congregation of the saints." Then you spoke to your holy one in a vision and said, "I have put [ability to] help in a mighty one; I have raised up a chosen one from among the people. I have found David, my servant; I have anointed him with my holy oil. With him my hand will be strong; my arm will strengthen him also. My truth and my mercy will be with him, and his horn will be exalted in my name. And I will place his hand on the sea and his right hand on the rivers. He will cry out to me, 'You are my Father, my God, and the Rock of my salvation.' I will also make him the firstborn, high above the monarchs of the earth. My covenant will be established with him. I will make his seed endure to eternity and his throne as the days of the heavens. I have sworn once by my holiness; I will not lie to David. His seed will endure forever and his throne will be like the sun before me; it will be as established as the moon to eternity and a faithful witness in the clouds." (Psalms 89:3, 4, 5, 19, 20, 21, 24, 25, 26, 27, 28, 29, 35, 36, 37)

There is similar material in other psalms, such as Psalm 45:2–17, Psalm 122:4, 5, and Psalm 132:8–18.

God Is One, and the Lord Is God

45 ON the basis of the quite ample number of passages from the Word presented in the preceding chapter, we can determine that the Lord is called Jehovah, the God of Israel and of Jacob, the Holy One of Israel, Lord and God, as well as King, [Jehovah's] Anointed, and David, all of which enables us to see (though as yet through a kind of veil) that the Lord is God himself, the source and subject of the Word.

All the same, it is generally acknowledged everywhere in the whole world that God is one, and no one of sound reason denies this. What now remains to be done, then, is to support this from the Word and further, to show that the Lord is God.

[2] 1. *The following passages from the Word show that God is one.*

Jesus said, "The first of all the commandments is 'Hear, O Israel, *the Lord our God, the Lord is one;* therefore you are to love the Lord your God with all your heart and with all your soul.'" (Mark 12:29, 30)

Hear, O Israel, *Jehovah our God is one Jehovah;* you are to love Jehovah your God with all your heart and with all your soul. (Deuteronomy 6:4, 5)

Someone came to Jesus and said, "Good Teacher, what good thing should I do in order to have eternal life?" Jesus said to him, "Why do you call me good? *No one is good except the one God."* (Matthew 19:16, 17)

. . . so that all the kingdoms of the earth may acknowledge that *you alone are Jehovah.* (Isaiah 37:20)

I am Jehovah and there is no other. There is no God other than me. [I have prepared you] so that people will know from the rising of the sun to its setting that there is no God other than me. I am Jehovah and there is no other. (Isaiah 45:5, 6)

Jehovah Sabaoth, God of Israel, dwelling between the angel guardians,[118] *you alone are God* over all the kingdoms of the earth. (Isaiah 37:16)

Is there any God other than me? Or any other Rock? I do not know of one. (Isaiah 44:8)

Who is God, except Jehovah? Who is the Rock, if it is not our God? (Psalms 18:31)

[3] 2. *The following passages from the Word show that the Lord is God.*

God is only among you, *and there is no God except him.* Surely you are a hidden God, O God of Israel, *the Savior.* (Isaiah 45:14, 15)

Am I not Jehovah? And *there is no God other than me.* I am a just God, and *there is no Savior other than me.* Look to me so that you may *be saved,* all you ends of the earth, because *I am God and there is no other.* (Isaiah 45:21, 22)

I am Jehovah, and *there is no Savior other than me.* (Isaiah 43:11)

I am Jehovah your God. You are to acknowledge no God other than me; *there is no Savior other than me.* (Hosea 13:4)

Thus says Jehovah the King of Israel, and Israel's *Redeemer,* Jehovah Sabaoth: "I am the First and the Last, and *there is no God other than me."* (Isaiah 44:6)

Jehovah Sabaoth is his name, and the *Redeemer,* the Holy One of Israel. He will be called the God of the whole earth. (Isaiah 54:5)

On that day Jehovah will become king over all the earth. On that day Jehovah will be one, and his name one. (Zechariah 14:9)

Since the Lord alone is Savior and Redeemer, and since it says that Jehovah and no one else is that one, it follows that the one God is no other than the Lord.

The Holy Spirit Is the Divine Nature That Emanates from the Lord and Is the Lord Himself

JESUS said in Matthew,

All power has been given to me in heaven and on earth. Go forth, therefore, and make disciples of all the nations, baptizing them in the name of the Father, the Son, and the Holy Spirit, teaching them to observe all things that I have commanded you; and behold, I am with you all the days, even to the close of the age. (Matthew 28:18, 19, 20)

Up to this point I have shown that the divine nature called the Father and the divine nature called the Son are one in the Lord. I therefore need now to show that the Holy Spirit is the same as the Lord.

[2] The reason the Lord said that they were to baptize in the name of the Father, the Son, and the Holy Spirit is that there is a threeness or trinity in the Lord.[119] There is the divine nature that is called the Father, the divine-human nature that is called the Son, and the emanating divine nature that is called the Holy Spirit. The divine nature that is the Father and the divine nature that is the Son is the divine nature as the source, while the emanating divine nature that is the Holy Spirit is the divine nature as means.[120]

In the booklets *Divine Providence* and *Omnipotence, Omnipresence, and Omniscience*,[121] you will see more on the point that the only divine nature that emanates from the Lord is the divine nature that is he himself—it is a matter that takes more than a few words to explain.

[3] We can illustrate this threeness in the Lord by comparison with angels. They have souls and bodies and also emanations that radiate from them, emanations that are their own selves extending beyond themselves. I have been granted an abundance of knowledge about this emanation, but this is not the place to present it.[122]

[4] After death, everyone who turns to God is first taught by angels that the Holy Spirit is none other than the Lord and that "going forth" and "emanating" is nothing but enlightening and teaching by means of presence, a presence that depends on our acceptance of the Lord. So after death, many people leave behind the concept of the Holy Spirit that they had formed in the world and accept the idea that it is the Lord's presence with us through angels and spirits, a presence from and by means of which people are enlightened and taught.

[5] Then too, it is common practice in the Word to name two divine beings, sometimes three, who are nevertheless one, such as Jehovah and God, Jehovah and the Holy One of Israel, Jehovah and the Mighty One of Jacob, as well as God and the Lamb; and because they are one it says elsewhere that Jehovah alone is God, Jehovah alone is the Holy One and is the Holy One of Israel, and there is no God other than him. Sometimes God is called the Lamb and sometimes the Lamb is called God, the latter in the Book of Revelation and the former in the prophets.

[6] We can see that it is the Lord alone who is meant by "the Father, the Son, and the Holy Spirit" in Matthew 28:19 from what precedes and follows that verse. In the preceding verse the Lord says, "All power has been given to me in heaven and on earth," and in the next verse the Lord

says, "Behold, I am with you all the days, even to the close of the age." So he is talking about himself alone, saying this so that they would know that the trinity was in him.

[7] To make it known that the Holy Spirit is no divine thing other than the Lord himself, I need to show what "spirit" means in the Word.

1. "Spirit," in a broad sense, refers to an individual's life.
2. Since our life varies depending on our state, "spirit" means the variable attitude we take toward life.
3. It also means the life of those who have been regenerated, which is called spiritual life.
4. Where "spirit" is used in speaking of the Lord, though, it means his divine life and therefore the Lord himself.
5. Specifically, it means the life of his wisdom, which is called divine truth.
6. Jehovah himself—that is, the Lord—spoke the Word through prophets.

1. *"Spirit" refers to an individual's life.* This is clear from the fact that we commonly speak of "yielding up the spirit" when someone dies. In this sense, then, "spirit" means the life of our breathing. In fact, the word "spirit" is derived from [a word for] breathing, which is why in Hebrew the word that means "spirit" also means "wind."[123]

We have two inner springs of life. One is the motion of the heart, and the other is the breathing of the lungs. The life that depends on the breathing of the lungs is the one properly meant by "spirit" and also by "soul." In the appropriate place there will be a description of the way this is coordinated with our cognitive thinking, while the life dependent on the motion of the heart is coordinated with the love associated with our will.[124]

[2] It is clear from the following passages that "spirit" in the Word refers to an individual's life.

> You gather in their *spirit;* they breathe their last and return to dust. (Psalms 104:29)

> He remembered that they were flesh, a *spirit* that departs and does not return. (Psalms 78:39)

> When their *spirit* leaves, they will return to the earth. (Psalms 146:4)

> Hezekiah expressed grief that *"the life of his spirit"* was departing. (Isaiah 38:16)

The spirit of Jacob came back to life. (Genesis 45:27)

A molded image is a lie, and there is no *spirit* within it. (Jeremiah 51:17)

The Lord Jehovih said to the dry bones, "I will put *spirit* into you so that you will live. Come from the four winds, *O spirit, and breathe on these people who have been killed,* and they will live"; and *the spirit* came into them, and they came back to life. (Ezekiel 37:5, 6, 9, 10)

When Jesus took the daughter's hand, her *spirit* returned, and she arose immediately. (Luke 8:54, 55)

48 2. *Since our life varies depending on our state, "spirit" means the variable attitude we take toward life.* For example:
(a) *Living wisely.*

Bezalel was filled with *the spirit of wisdom,* intelligence, and knowledge. (Exodus 31:3)

You shall speak to all who are wise at heart, everyone whom I have filled with *the spirit of wisdom.* (Exodus 28:3)

Joshua was filled with *the spirit of wisdom.* (Deuteronomy 34:9)

Nebuchadnezzar said of Daniel that [*the spirit of the holy gods* was in him]. (Daniel 4:8)

[Belshazzar's queen said of Daniel that] there was an *excellent spirit* of knowledge, intelligence, and *wisdom* in him. (Daniel 5:11–12, 14)[125]

Those who go astray *in spirit* will know intelligence. (Isaiah 29:24)

[2] (b) *Living [under the influence of some particular] inspiration.*

Jehovah *has stirred up the spirit* of the kings of the Medes. (Jeremiah 51:11)

Jehovah *stirred up the spirit* of Zerubbabel and the *spirit* of all the remnant of the people. (Haggai 1:14)

I am putting the spirit into the king of Assyria [to cause him] to hear a rumor and return to his own land. (Isaiah 37:7)

Jehovah *hardened the spirit* of King Sihon. (Deuteronomy 2:30)

What *is rising up in* your *spirit* will never happen. (Ezekiel 20:32)

[3] (c) *Living in a state of freedom.*

The four beasts seen by the prophet, which were angel guardians, went wherever *the spirit* wanted to go. (Ezekiel 1:12, 20)

[4] (d) *Living in fear, sorrow, or anger.*

... so that every heart will melt, all hands will slacken, and *every spirit will recoil.* (Ezekiel 21:7)

My *spirit has fainted* within me; my heart is stupefied inside me. (Psalms 142:3; 143:4)

My *spirit is wasting away.* (Psalms 143:7)

I, Daniel, *was grieved in* my *spirit.* (Daniel 7:15)

The spirit of Pharaoh was disturbed. (Genesis 41:8)

Nebuchadnezzar said, "*My spirit is troubled.*" (Daniel 2:3)

I went in bitterness, *in the heat of* my *spirit.* (Ezekiel 3:14)

[5] (e) *Living in subjection to various evil mental states.*

... who has *no guile in his spirit.* (Psalms 32:2)

Jehovah has mixed together in their midst *a spirit of perversities.* (Isaiah 19:14)

[The Lord Jehovih] says, "[Woe] to the *foolish* prophets, who follow their own *spirit.*" (Ezekiel 13:3)

The prophet is foolish; *the man of the spirit is insane.* (Hosea 9:7)

Keep watch over *your spirit,* and do not act treacherously. (Malachi 2:16)

A spirit of whoredom has led them astray. (Hosea 4:12)

There is *a spirit of whoredom* in their midst. (Hosea 5:4)

When a *spirit of jealousy* has come over him ... (Numbers 5:14)

A man who is a wanderer *in spirit* and speaks lies ... (Micah 2:11)

... a generation whose *spirit was not constant with God* ... (Psalms 78:8)

He has poured *a spirit of sleepiness* over them. (Isaiah 29:10)

Conceive chaff and give birth to stubble. *As for your spirit,* fire will devour you. (Isaiah 33:11)

[6] (f) *Living in subjection to hell.*

I will make *the unclean spirit* depart from the land. (Zechariah 13:2)

When *an unclean spirit* goes out of someone, it wanders through dry places, and then recruits seven *spirits worse* than itself, and they come in and live there. (Matthew 12:43, 44, 45)

Babylon has become a refuge for every *unclean spirit.* (Revelation 18:2)

[7] (g) Then there are the hellish spirits by whom we are tormented: Matthew 8:16; 10:1; 12:43, 44, 45; Mark 1:23–28; 9:17–29; Luke 4:33, 36; 6:17, 18; 7:21; 8:2, 29; 9:39, 42, 55; 11:24, 25, 26; 13:11; Revelation 13:15; 16:13, 14.

3. *"Spirit" means the life of those who have been regenerated, which is called spiritual life.*

Jesus said, "Unless you have been born of water and *the spirit* you cannot enter the kingdom of God." (John 3:5)

I will give you a new heart and *a new spirit.* I will put *my spirit* within you and cause you to walk in my statutes. (Ezekiel 36:26, 27)

God will give a new heart and *a new spirit.* (Ezekiel 11:19)

Create a clean heart in me, O God, and renew *a strong spirit* within me. Bring back to me the joy of your salvation, and let *a willing spirit* uphold me. (Psalms 51:10, 11, 12)

Make yourselves a new heart and a new *spirit.* Why will you die, O house of Israel? (Ezekiel 18:31)

You send out your *spirit,* and they are created; you renew the face of the earth. (Psalms 104:30)

The hour is coming, and is now here, when true worshipers will worship the Father in *spirit* and in truth. (John 4:23)

Jehovah God gives soul to the people and *spirit* to those who are walking on [the earth]. (Isaiah 42:5)

Jehovah forms *the human spirit* within us. (Zechariah 12:1)

With my soul I have awaited you in the night; *with my spirit* within me I have awaited you in the morning. (Isaiah 26:9)

> On that day Jehovah will become *a spirit of judgment* to the one who sits in judgment. (Isaiah 28:6)
>
> *My spirit* has rejoiced in God my Savior. (Luke 1:47)
>
> They have given rest to *my spirit* in the land of the north. (Zechariah 6:8)
>
> Into your hand I commit *my spirit;* you have redeemed me. (Psalms 31:5)
>
> There was not one, even among the remnant who had *spirit.* (Malachi 2:15)
>
> After three and a half days the *spirit of life* from God entered the two witnesses who had been killed by the beast. (Revelation 11:11)
>
> I, Jehovah, form the mountains and create *the spirit.* (Amos 4:13)
>
> O God, the God of *the spirits* for all flesh . . . (Numbers 16:22; 27:18)[126]
>
> I will pour *a spirit from on high* upon the house of David and upon the inhabitants of Jerusalem. (Zechariah 12:10)
>
> . . . even until he has poured out upon us *a spirit from on high.* (Isaiah 32:15)
>
> I will pour out waters upon those who are thirsty and streams upon the dry land; *I will pour out my spirit* upon your seed. (Isaiah 44:3)
>
> I will pour out *my spirit* upon all flesh; also upon my male and female servants *I will pour out spirit* in those days. (Joel 2:28, 29)

To pour out *the spirit* means to regenerate, as does to give a new heart and a new spirit.

[2] *"Spirit"* refers to the spiritual life of people who have been genuinely humbled.

> I dwell in a crushed and *humble spirit,* to bring to life the *spirit of the humble* and to bring to life the heart of the crushed. (Isaiah 57:15)
>
> The sacrifices of God are *a broken spirit;* God will not scorn a crushed and broken heart. (Psalms 51:17)
>
> He will give the oil of joy in place of mourning, and a garment of praise in place of a confined *spirit.* (Isaiah 61:3)
>
> . . . a woman abandoned and *afflicted in spirit.* (Isaiah 54:6)
>
> Blessed are the *poor in spirit,* because theirs is the kingdom of the heavens. (Matthew 5:3)

50   4. *Where "spirit" is used in speaking of the Lord, it means his divine life and therefore the Lord himself.*

The one whom the Father sent speaks the words of God; without limit God has given him *the spirit*. The Father loves the Son and has given all things into his hand. (John 3:34, 35)

A shoot will go forth from the trunk of Jesse; *the spirit of Jehovah* will rest upon him, *the spirit of wisdom* and intelligence, *the spirit of counsel* and strength. (Isaiah 11:1, 2)

I have put *my spirit* upon him; he will bring forth judgment to the nations. (Isaiah 42:1)

He will come [to us] as a narrow river; in him *the spirit of Jehovah* will bring [us] a sign. Then he will come to Zion as the Redeemer. (Isaiah 59:19, 20)

The spirit of the Lord Jehovih is upon me; Jehovah has anointed me to bring good news to the poor. (Isaiah 61:1; Luke 4:18)

Jesus perceived *in his spirit* that they were having these thoughts within themselves. (Mark 2:8)

Jesus rejoiced *in his spirit* and said . . . (Luke 10:21)

Jesus was troubled *in his spirit*. (John 13:21)

Jesus sighed deeply *in his spirit*. (Mark 8:12)

[2] *"Spirit"* [stands] *for Jehovah himself or the Lord.*

God is *a spirit*. (John 4:24)

Who directed *the spirit* of Jehovah, or who was the man of his counsel? (Isaiah 40:13)

The spirit of Jehovah led them by means of the hand of Moses. (Isaiah 63:11, 12, 14)

Where shall I go from *your spirit,* and where shall I flee? (Psalms 139:7)

Jehovah said, "[Zerubbabel] will accomplish this not by might but by *my spirit."* (Zechariah 4:6)

They angered the *spirit of* his *holiness;* therefore he turned into an enemy for them. ([Isaiah 63:10]; Psalms 106:33)

> *My spirit* will not contend with humankind forever, because humankind is flesh. (Genesis 6:3)

> I will not dispute forever, because *the spirit* would fail in my presence. (Isaiah 57:16)[127]

> Blasphemy against the *Holy Spirit* will not be forgiven, but someone who says a word against the Son of Humanity will be forgiven. (Matthew 12:31, 32; Mark 3:28, 29, 30; Luke 12:10)

Blasphemy against the Holy Spirit is blasphemy against the Lord's divine nature. Blasphemy against the Son of Humanity is something contrary to the Word, understanding its meaning differently.[128] The Son of Humanity is the Lord as the Word, as already explained [§§23–28].

5. *When "spirit" is used in speaking of the Lord, it means specifically the life of his wisdom, which is divine truth.*

> I tell you *the truth*. It is to your advantage that I go away. If I do not go away, *the Comforter* will not come to you; but if I go away, I will send him to you. (John 16:7)

> When he, *the Spirit of Truth,* has come, he will guide you into all *truth*. He will not speak on his own authority, but will say whatever he has heard. (John 16:13)

> He will glorify me, because he will take *of what is mine* and declare it to you. All things that the Father has are mine. That is why I said that he will take *of what is mine* and declare it to you. (John 16:14, 15)

> I will ask the Father to give you another *Comforter, the Spirit of Truth*. The world cannot receive him, because it does not see him or know him; but you know him, because he dwells among you and will be in you. I will not leave you orphans; I am coming to you. You will see me. (John 14:16, 17, 18, 19)

> When *the Comforter* comes, whom I will send to you from the Father, *the Spirit of Truth,* he will testify concerning me. (John 15:26)

> Jesus cried out, saying, "If any are thirsty, they must come to me and drink. As the Scripture says, from the bellies of those who believe in me will flow rivers of living water." He said this concerning *the Spirit* that those who believed in him would receive. *There was not the Holy Spirit yet because Jesus was not yet glorified.* (John 7:37, 38, 39)

> Jesus breathed on the disciples and said, "Receive *the Holy Spirit.*" (John 20:22)

[2] We can see that the Lord meant himself by the Comforter, the Spirit of Truth, and the Holy Spirit from these words of the Lord, *that the world did not yet know him*—that is, they did not yet know the Lord. Further, when he said that he would send him, he added,

> I will not leave you orphans; I am coming to you, and you will see me. (John 14:16–19, 26, 28)

And in another passage,

> *Behold, I am with you all the days, even to the close of the age.* (Matthew 28:20)

And when Thomas said, "We do not know where you are going," Jesus said, "*I am the way and the truth*" (John 14:5, 6).

[3] Because the Spirit of Truth or the Holy Spirit is the same as the Lord, who is the truth itself, it also says "*There was not the Holy Spirit yet because Jesus was not yet glorified*" (John 7:39). This is because after his glorification or full union with the Father, which was accomplished by his suffering on the cross, the Lord was then divine wisdom itself and divine truth—therefore the Holy Spirit.[129]

The reason the Lord breathed on the disciples and said "Receive the Holy Spirit" was that all of heaven's breathing originates with the Lord. Angels breathe just as we do, and their hearts beat. Their breathing depends on their acceptance of divine wisdom from the Lord and their heartbeat or pulse depends on their acceptance of divine love from the Lord. This will be explained in its proper place.[130]

[4] From the following passages we can clearly see that the Holy Spirit is divine truth that comes from the Lord:

> When they hand you over to the synagogues, do not worry about what you are going to say. *The Holy Spirit* will teach you in that very hour what you should say. (Luke 12:11, 12; 21:14; Mark 13:11)

> Jehovah said, "*My spirit,* which is upon you, and my words, which I have placed in your mouth, shall not depart from your mouth." (Isaiah 59:21)

> A shoot will go forth from the trunk of Jesse. He will strike the earth with the rod of his mouth, and *with the spirit of his lips* he will slay the ungodly. *Truth* will be a belt around his hips. (Isaiah 11:1, 4, 5)

> Now he has commanded with his mouth and *his spirit* has gathered them. (Isaiah 34:16)
>
> Those who worship God must worship *in spirit and in truth*. (John 4:24)
>
> It is the spirit that gives life—the flesh is of no benefit. The words that I speak to you *are spirit and are life*. (John 6:63)
>
> John said, "I am baptizing you with water into repentance, but the one who is to come after me will baptize you with *the Holy Spirit and with fire.*" (Matthew 3:11; Mark 1:8; Luke 3:16)

To baptize with the Holy Spirit and with fire is to regenerate by means of the divine truth that produces faith and the divine goodness that produces love [within us].

> When Jesus was being baptized, the heavens were opened and he saw *the Holy Spirit* coming down like a dove. (Matthew 3:16; Mark 1:10; Luke 3:21; John 1:32, 33)

A dove represents purification and regeneration by means of divine truth.

[5] When "the Holy Spirit" is used in speaking of the Lord it means his divine life and therefore himself, and specifically it means the life of his wisdom, which is called divine truth; therefore the spirit of the prophets, which is also called the Holy Spirit, means divine truth that comes from the Lord. This is the case in the following passages:

> . . . what *the Spirit* says to the churches. (Revelation 2:7, 11, 29; 3:1, 6, 13, 22)
>
> The seven lamps of fire burning before the throne are *the seven spirits of God.* (Revelation 4:5)
>
> In the midst of the elders stood a Lamb, having seven eyes, which are *the seven spirits of God* sent out into all the earth. (Revelation 5:6)

The lamps of fire and the eyes of the Lord mean divine truths, and seven means what is holy.

> . . . says *the Spirit,* "so that they may rest from their labors." (Revelation 14:13)
>
> *The Spirit* and the bride say, "Come." (Revelation 22:17)

> They made their hearts diamond-hard so that they would not hear the law or the words that *Jehovah* sent *by his spirit* through the hand of the prophets. (Zechariah 7:12)

> *The spirit* of Elijah came upon Elisha. (2 Kings 2:15)

> John went before [the Lord] *in the spirit* and power of Elijah. (Luke 1:17)

> Elizabeth was filled *with the Holy Spirit* and prophesied. (Luke 1:41)

> Zechariah was filled *with the Holy Spirit* and prophesied. (Luke 1:67)

> David said by *the Holy Spirit,* "The Lord said to my Lord, 'Sit at my right hand.'" (Mark 12:36)

> *The testimony of Jesus is the spirit of prophecy.* (Revelation 19:10)

Since, then, the Holy Spirit means specifically the Lord's divine wisdom and therefore his divine truth, we can see why it is that people say of the Holy Spirit that it *enlightens, teaches,* and *inspires.*

52. 6. *Jehovah himself—that is, the Lord—spoke the Word through prophets.*

We read of the prophets that they had *visions* and that *Jehovah talked with them.* When they had visions, they were not focused on their bodies but on the spirit, in which state they saw things of a heavenly nature. When Jehovah talked with them, though, they were conscious of their bodies and heard Jehovah speaking.

We need to draw a clear distinction between these two states. In a *visionary* state, the eyes of their spirit were open and the eyes of their body were closed; and at such times they seemed to themselves to be taken from place to place while their bodies stayed where they were. Ezekiel, Zechariah, and Daniel were in this state at times, and so was John when he wrote the Book of Revelation. They were then said to be in *a vision* or in *the spirit.* In fact, Ezekiel says,

> The spirit lifted me up and brought me back into Chaldea, to the captivity, in *a vision from God,* in *the spirit of God.* In this way *the vision* that I saw came over me. (Ezekiel 11:1, 24)

He says that the spirit lifted him up and that he heard an earthquake and other things behind him (Ezekiel 3:12, 14). He also said that the spirit lifted him up between earth and heaven and took him off into Jerusalem in *visions from God,* and he saw abominations (Ezekiel 8:3 and following).

That is why (again in a vision of God or in the spirit) Ezekiel saw the four beasts that were angel guardians (chapters 1 and 10), and he saw a new earth and a new temple with the angel measuring them, as we are told in chapters 40–48. He says in chapter 40, verse 2, that he was then in visions from God; and in chapter 43, verse 5, he says that the spirit lifted him up at that time.

The same thing happened with *Zechariah.* There was an angel inwardly present with him when he saw a man riding among myrtle trees (Zechariah 1:8 and following); when he saw four horns and then a man with a measuring line in his hand (Zechariah 1:18; 2:1); when he saw Joshua the high priest (Zechariah 3:1 and following); when he saw a lampstand and two olive trees (Zechariah 4:1 and following); when he saw a flying scroll and a measuring basket (Zechariah 5:1, 6); and when he saw four chariots coming from between two mountains, along with horses (Zechariah 6:1 and following).

Daniel was in the same kind of state when he saw four beasts come up from the sea (Daniel 7:3) and when he saw battles between a ram and a goat (Daniel 8:1 and following).

We read in Daniel 7:1, 2, 7, 13; 8:2; 10:1, 7, 8 that he saw these things in visions. We read in Daniel 9:21 that he saw the angel Gabriel in a vision and talked with him.

Much the same happened with John when he wrote the Book of Revelation. He says that he was *in the spirit* on the Lord's day (Revelation 1:10), that he was carried away *in the spirit* into the wilderness (17:3), to a high mountain *in the spirit* (21:10), that he saw horses *in a vision* (9:17), and elsewhere that *he saw* what he described, being therefore in the spirit or in a vision (1:2; 4:1; 5:1; 6:1; and in the particular chapters that follow).

As for the Word itself, it does not say in the prophets that they spoke it from the Holy Spirit but that they spoke it from Jehovah, Jehovah Sabaoth, or the Lord Jehovih, since it says that *the Word of Jehovah came to me,* that *Jehovah spoke to me,* and very often, *Jehovah said* and *the saying of Jehovah.* Since the Lord is Jehovah, then (as already explained [§§38, 45]), the whole Word was spoken by him.

So that no one will doubt that this is the case, I want to list the places in Jeremiah alone where it says *the Word of Jehovah came to me, Jehovah spoke to me, Jehovah said,* and *the saying of Jehovah,* which are the following: Jeremiah 1:4, 11, 12, 13, 14, 19; 2:1, 2, 3, 4, 5, 9, 19, 22, 29, 31; 3:1, 6, 10, 12, 14, 16; 4:1, 3, 9, 17, 27; 5:11, 14, 18, 22, 29; 6:6, 9, 12, 15, 16, 21, 22; 7:1, 3, 11, 13, 19, 20, 21; 8:1, 3, 12, 13; 9:3, 6, 7, 9, 13, 15, 17, 22, 23, 24, 25; 10:1, 2, 18; 11:1, 6, 9, 11; 12:14, 17; 13:1, 6, 9, 11, 12, 13, 14, 15, 25; 14:1, 10, 14, 15; 15:1, 2, 3, 6, 11, 19, 20; 16:1, 3, 5, 9, 14, 16; 17:5, 19, 20, 21, 24; 18:1, 5, 6, 11, 13; 19:1, 3, 6, 12, 15; 20:4; 21:1, 4, 7, 8, 11, 12; 22:2, 5, 6, 11, 16, 18, 24, 29,

30; 23:2, 5, 7, 12, 15, 24, 29, 31, 38; 24:3, 5, 8; 25:1, 3, 7, 8, 9, 15, 27, 29, 32; 26:1, 2, 18; 27:1, 2, 4, 8, 11, 16, 19, 21, 22; 28:2, 12, 14, 16; 29:4, 8, 9, 19, 20, 21, 25, 30, 31, 32; 30:1, 2, 3, 4, 5, 8, 10, 11, 12, 17, 18; 31:1, 2, 7, 10, 15, 16, 17, 23, 27, 28, 31, 32, 33, 34, 35, 36, 37, 38; 32:1, 6, 14, 15, 25, 26, 28, 30, 36, 42; 33:1, 2, 4, 10, 11, 12, 13, 17, 19, 20, 23, 25; 34:1, 2, 4, 8, 12, 13, 17, 22; 35:1, 13, 17, 18, 19; 36:1, 6, 27, 29, 30; 37:6, 7, 9; 38:2, 3, 17; 39:15, 16, 17, 18; 40:1; 42:7, 9, 15, 18, 19; 43:8, 10; 44:1, 2, 7, 11, 24, 25, 26, 30; 45:1, 2, 5; 46:1, 23, 25, 28; 47:1; 48:1, 8, 12, 30, 35, 38, 40, 43, 44, 47; 49:2, 5, 6, 7, 12, 13, 16, 18, 26, 28, 30, 32, 35, 37, 38, 39; 50:1, 4, 10, 18, 20, 21, 30, 31, 33, 35, 40; 51:25, 33, 36, 39, 52, 58.

These are from Jeremiah alone. It says things like this in all the other prophets and does not say that the Holy Spirit spoke or that Jehovah spoke to them through the Holy Spirit.

54 We can now see from this that *Jehovah, who is the Lord from eternity,* spoke through the prophets and that where it speaks of *the Holy Spirit,* it is he himself.

Therefore, *God is one in person and in essence, and he is the Lord.*

The Athanasian Statement of Faith Agrees with the Truth, Provided That We Understand It to Be Referring Not to "a Trinity of Persons" but to "a Trinity within One Person," Who Is the Lord

55 THE reason Christians have acknowledged three divine persons and therefore something like three gods is that there is a trinity within the Lord; one element is called the Father, the second the Son, and the third the Holy Spirit. Further, these three are distinguished from each other in the Word, just as the soul and the body and what comes forth from them are distinguished from each other, even though they are one.

It is the nature of the Word in its literal meaning to distinguish things that are one as though they were not one. That is why Jehovah, who is the Lord from eternity, is sometimes called Jehovah, sometimes Jehovah Sabaoth, sometimes God, sometimes the Lord, as well as Creator, Savior, Redeemer, and Maker, and even Shaddai. Then too, the human nature that he took on in the world is called Jesus, Christ, Messiah, Son of God, Son of Humanity; and in the Word of the Old Testament it is called God, the Holy One of Israel, Jehovah's Anointed, King, Prince, Counselor, Angel, and David.

[2] Now, since it is typical of the Word in its literal meaning to name many when in fact they are one, Christians—the first of whom were simple individuals who took everything that was said literally—divided Divinity into three persons. This was tolerated because they were simple people. However, they took this in such a way that they also believed *the Son* to be infinite, uncreate, almighty, God, and Lord, completely equal to the Father; and they also believed that in essence, majesty, and glory, and therefore in divinity they were not two or three but one.

[3] If people believe this in a simple way, because this is what they were taught, and do not convince themselves of three gods but make the three into one, after death they are taught by the Lord through angels that he is that very One and that Trinity, a belief accepted by everyone who comes into heaven. This is because no one can be allowed into heaven who thinks in terms of three gods, no matter how much she or he verbally professes one God. The life of all heaven and the wisdom of all angels is based on the acknowledgment and consequent confession of one God, on a faith that this one God is also human, and on a belief that he is himself the Lord, who is at once God and a human being.

[4] We can see, then, that God allowed[131] the first Christians to accept a teaching regarding three persons provided they also accepted at the same time a belief that the Lord is the infinite, almighty God and Jehovah. This was because if they had not accepted this as well, it would have been all over with the church, since the church is the church because of the Lord, and the eternal life of all comes from the Lord and from no one else.

[5] We can be quite sure that the church is the church because of the Lord simply from the fact that the whole Word, from beginning to end, is about the Lord alone (as already explained [§§1–7]), that we are to believe in him, and that those who do not believe in him do not have eternal life; instead, the wrath of God abides on them (John 3:36).

[6] Now, since we can all see within ourselves that if God is one, he is *one both in person and in essence* (really, no one thinks anything else or can think anything else when thinking that God is one), I should like at this point to bring in the whole doctrinal statement named for Athanasius[132] and then show that everything it says is true, provided that we understand it to be referring to "a trinity within one person" rather than "a trinity of persons."

56 *The doctrinal statement* is this:

For all who want to be saved, it is necessary that they hold the catholic [other versions of the statement read "Christian"][133] faith. Unless they keep that faith whole and undefiled, without doubt they will perish everlastingly. And the catholic [or "Christian"] faith is this: That we worship one God in trinity, and trinity in unity, neither confounding the persons nor dividing the substance [or "essence"]. For there is one person of the Father, another of the Son, and another of the Holy Spirit. But the divinity of the Father, of the Son, and of the Holy Spirit is all one, the glory equal, the majesty coeternal. Such as the Father is, such is the Son, and such is the Holy Spirit. The Father is uncreate, the Son is uncreate, and the Holy Spirit is uncreate. The Father is infinite, the Son is infinite, and the Holy Spirit is infinite. The Father is eternal, the Son is eternal, and the Holy Spirit is eternal. And yet there are not three eternal beings but one eternal Being, as also there are not three infinite or three uncreated beings, but one uncreated and one infinite Being. So likewise the Father is almighty, the Son is almighty, and the Holy Spirit is almighty; and yet there are not three almighty beings, but one almighty Being. So the Father is God, the Son is God, and the Holy Spirit is God; and yet there are not three gods, but one God. So likewise the Father is Lord, the Son is Lord, and the Holy Spirit is Lord; and yet there are not three lords, but one Lord. For just as we are compelled by Christian truth to acknowledge each person by himself to be both God and Lord, so are we forbidden by the catholic religion to say that there are three gods or three lords [or "so in the Christian faith we cannot mention three gods or three lords"]. The Father is made by none, neither created nor begotten. The Son is from the Father alone, not made, nor created, but begotten. The Holy Spirit is from the Father and from the Son, neither made, nor created, nor begotten, but proceeding. So there is one Father, not three Fathers; one Son, not three Sons; one Holy Spirit, not three Holy Spirits. And in this trinity none is first or last; none is greatest or least; but all three persons are coeternal together, and coequal. So in all things, as said above, the unity in trinity and the trinity in unity is to be worshiped [or "three persons in one Divinity and one God in three persons is to be worshiped"]. So this is how we must think of the trinity if we want to be saved.

Furthermore, it is necessary to salvation that we also believe rightly in the Incarnation of our Lord Jesus Christ [or "that we firmly believe that our Lord is truly human"]. For the true faith is that we believe and confess that our Lord Jesus Christ, the Son of God, is God and a human being, God from the substance [or "essence"; others read "nature"] of the Father, begotten before the world; and human from the substance [or "nature"] of his mother, born in the world; perfect God and perfect human being, consisting of a rational soul and a human body; equal to the Father with respect to his divinity, and inferior to [or "less than"] the Father with respect to his humanity. Although he is God and a human being, yet he is not two, but one Christ; one, not by conversion of divinity into flesh, but by taking humanity into God [or "he is one, not because the divine nature was changed into the human nature but because the divine nature took the human nature into itself"]. One altogether; not by confusion [or "mixing"] of substance, but by unity of person [or "he is one altogether; not because the two natures were mixed but because he is one person"]. Therefore as the rational soul and the body is one human being, so God and a human being is one Christ; who suffered for our salvation, descended into hell, and rose again the third day from the dead. He ascended into heaven, and sits at the right hand of the Father Almighty. From there he will come to judge the living and the dead; at his Coming all will rise again with their bodies; and those who have done good will go into everlasting life and those who have done evil will go into everlasting fire.[134]

We can see that this whole doctrinal statement is true right down to the individual words, provided that rather than "a trinity of persons" we understand it to be referring to "a trinity within one person," by rewriting it and substituting this latter trinity. The "trinity within one person" is this: *the divine nature of the Lord is the Father, the divine-human nature is the Son, and the emanating divine nature is the Holy Spirit.*

When we have this trinity in mind, then we can think of one God and also say "one God"; otherwise, we cannot help but think in terms of three gods. Can anyone fail to see this? Athanasius saw it, which is why these words were inserted into his doctrinal statement:

> For just as we are compelled by Christian truth to acknowledge each person by himself to be both God and Lord, so by the catholic religion or the Christian faith we cannot say or mention three gods or three lords.

This is like saying that even though Christian truth allows us to acknowledge or think in terms of three gods or three lords, the Christian faith allows us to say or mention only one God or one Lord. Yet it is acknowledgment and thought that unite us to the Lord and to heaven, not speech alone.[135]

Further, no one understands how a divine nature that is one can be divided into three persons, each of which is God. That is, the divine nature is not divisible, and making the three one because of their essence or substance does not get rid of the idea of three gods. All it does is give the impression that they agree with each other.

58 If this whole doctrinal statement is rewritten as follows, [the point just made] becomes clear, that it is true right down to the individual words, provided that rather than a "trinity of persons" we understand it to be referring to a "trinity within one person":

> For all who want to be saved, it is necessary that they hold the Christian faith. And the Christian faith is this: That we worship one God in trinity, and trinity in unity, neither confounding the three aspects within his person nor dividing his essence. The three aspects within him as one person are what are referred to as the Father, the Son, and the Holy Spirit. The divinity of the Father, of the Son, and of the Holy Spirit is all one, the glory and majesty equal. Such as the Father is, such is the Son, and such is the Holy Spirit. The Father is uncreate, the Son is uncreate, and the Holy Spirit is uncreate. The Father is infinite, the Son is infinite, and the Holy Spirit is infinite. And yet there are not three infinite or three uncreated beings, but one uncreated and one infinite Being. So likewise the Father is almighty, the Son is almighty, and the Holy Spirit is almighty; and yet there are not three almighty beings, but one almighty Being. So the Father is God, the Son is God, and the Holy Spirit is God; and yet there are not three gods, but one God. So likewise the Father is Lord, the Son is Lord, and the Holy Spirit is Lord; and yet there are not three lords, but one Lord. Now, as in Christian truth we acknowledge three aspects in one person who is

God and Lord, so in Christian faith we can say one God and one Lord. The Father is made by none, neither created nor begotten. The Son is from the Father alone, not made, nor created, but begotten. The Holy Spirit is from the Father and from the Son, neither made, nor created, nor begotten, but proceeding. So there is one Father, not three Fathers; one Son, not three Sons; one Holy Spirit, not three Holy Spirits. And in this trinity none is greatest or least; they are absolutely equal. So in all things, as said above, the unity in trinity and the trinity in unity is to be worshiped.

This deals with what this doctrinal statement has to say about the trinity and unity of God. There then follow points about the Lord's taking on of a human nature in the world, which is called incarnation. These too are true in every way, provided we clearly differentiate between the human nature from the mother that the Lord was conscious of when he was in states of being brought low or being emptied out[136] and suffered trials and the cross, and the human nature from the Father that he was conscious of when he was in states of being glorified or united [to the divine nature]. That is, in the world the Lord took on a human nature that was conceived by Jehovah, who is the Lord from eternity, and was born of the Virgin Mary. This means he had a divine nature and a human nature—the divine from his own divine nature from eternity, and the human from his mother Mary in time. He put off this latter nature, though, and put on the divine-human nature. It is this human nature that is called "the divine-human nature" and in the Word is meant by "the Son of God." So when the points that come next in the statement about the Incarnation are understood to refer to the maternal human nature that he was conscious of in his states of being brought low, and the statements that follow those [are understood to be] about the divine-human nature that he was conscious of in his states of being glorified, then everything fits together.

The following things that come next in the statement are accurate in regard to the maternal human nature he was conscious of in his states of being brought low.

Jesus Christ is God and a human being, God from the substance of the Father, and human from the substance of his mother, born in the world; perfect God and perfect human being, consisting of a rational soul and a human body; equal to the Father with respect to his divinity, and less than the Father with respect to his humanity.

And this,

> That human nature was not converted into a divine nature or mixed with it but was put off, and a divine-human nature was put on in its place.

The things that follow those in the statement are accurate in regard to the human-divine nature that he was conscious of in his states of being glorified and in which he is now and will be to eternity.

> Although our Lord Jesus Christ, the Son of God, is God and a human being, yet he is not two, but one Christ. He is one altogether, because he is one person. Therefore as the soul and the body make one human being, so God and a human being is one Christ.

60 The assertions in this doctrinal statement that God and a human being in the Lord are not two but one person, and are one altogether the way the soul and the body are one, show through clearly in many of the things that the Lord himself said; for example, that the Father and he are one [John 10:30], that all that is the Father's is his, and all that is his is the Father's [John 17:10], that he is in the Father and the Father is in him [John 14:10], that all things have been given into his hand [John 13:3], that he has all power [Matthew 28:18], that he is the God of heaven and earth [Matthew 28:18], that those who believe in him have eternal life [John 6:47], and so on; also that both the divine nature and the human nature were raised into heaven and that in both respects he sits at the right hand of God [Mark 16:19] (that is, that he is almighty), and more passages from the Word concerning his divine-human nature that have been cited above [§§29–36] in ample number, all of which testify that *God is one both in person and in essence, in whom there is a trinity, and that that God is the Lord.*

61 The reason these facts about the Lord are now being made known for the first time is that in Revelation 21 and 22 it was foretold that a new church would be established by the Lord at the close of the former one, a church in which this teaching would be first and foremost. This church is what is meant in Revelation by the New Jerusalem [Revelation 3:12; 21:2] into which only those who recognize the Lord alone as God of heaven and earth can enter. This I can proclaim: that the whole heaven acknowledges the Lord alone, and anyone who does not share in this acknowledgment is not allowed into heaven. The fact of the matter

is that heaven is heaven because of the Lord. That very acknowledgment, made in the spirit of love and faith, causes the people there to be in the Lord and the Lord to be in them. This is what the Lord himself is telling us in John:

> On that day you will know that I am in my Father, and you are in me, and I am in you. (John 14:20)

And again,

> Abide in me, and I [will abide] in you. I am the vine; you are the branches. Those who abide in me and in whom I abide bear much fruit, because without me you cannot do anything. If any do not abide in me, they are cast out. (John 15:4, 5, 6; and 17:22, 23)

[2] The reason this has not been seen in the Word before is that if it had been seen too early it would not have been accepted. That is, the Last Judgment had not been carried out yet, and before that happened the power of hell was stronger than the power of heaven. We are in between heaven and hell, so if this had been seen too early, the Devil (that is, hell) would have snatched it out of our hearts and then proceeded to profane it. This state of hell's power was decisively broken by the Last Judgment that has now been carried out.[137] Since then—now, that is—anyone who wants to be enlightened and wise can be: see what is written about this in *Heaven and Hell* 589–596 and 597–603 as well as the booklet *Last Judgment* 65–72 and 73–74.

The New Jerusalem in the Book of Revelation Means a New Church

IN the Book of Revelation we find a description of the state of the Christian church as it would be at its close and as it now is. We are told that those people from that church who were meant by the false prophet, the dragon, the whore, and the beasts were cast into hell.[138] After this—after the completion of the Last Judgment, that is—it says the following:

> I saw a new heaven and a new earth, because the first heaven and the first earth had passed away. Then I, John, saw the holy city Jerusalem, coming down from God out of heaven. And I heard a loud voice from heaven saying, "Behold, the tabernacle of God is among people, and he will dwell with them, and they will be his people. And God himself will be with them and be their God." The one who sat on the throne said, "Behold, I am making all things new." And he said to me, "Write, because these words are true and faithful." (Revelation 21:1, 2, 3, 5)

The new heaven and the new earth that John saw after the first heaven and the first earth had passed away do not mean a new sky like the one we can see with our eyes, full of air and stars,[139] or a new earth for us to live on, but a new kind of church in the spiritual world and a new kind of church in this earthly world.

[2] Because the Lord, when he was in this world, made a new kind of church in both the spiritual and the earthly worlds, it says similar things in the prophets, namely, that a new heaven and a new earth were going to come into being at that time, as we find in Isaiah 65:17; 66:22; and elsewhere[140]—which cannot therefore be understood to refer to the sky that we can see with our eyes and the earth that we live on.

"The spiritual world"[141] means the world where angels and spirits live, and "the earthly world" means the world where we are living. On the recent founding of a new kind of church in the spiritual world and the eventual founding of a new kind of church in the earthly world, there is some information in the booklet *Last Judgment* [§§1–5] and more in the supplement[142] to that work.

63 The holy city Jerusalem means that new church in regard to its teachings. That is why it was seen coming down from God out of heaven, because the only source of genuinely true teaching is through heaven from the Lord.

It is because the city New Jerusalem means the church in regard to its teachings that it says "prepared as a bride adorned for her husband" (Revelation 21:2) and then,

> One of the seven angels came to me and talked with me, saying, "Come, I will show you the bride, the wife of the Lamb." And he carried me away in the spirit to a high mountain, and showed me the great city, the holy Jerusalem, coming down out of heaven from God. (Revelation 21:9, 10)

It is common knowledge that the bride and wife mean the church and the Bridegroom and Husband mean the Lord.[143] The church is the bride when it is willing to receive the Lord and is the wife when it does receive him. We can see that the Husband means the Lord in this passage because it says "the bride, the wife of the Lamb."

The reason Jerusalem in the Word means the church in regard to its teachings is that that was the only place in the land of Canaan[144] where the Temple was, where the altar was, where sacrifices were performed, and therefore where there was actual worship of God. That was also why the three annual feasts were celebrated there[145] and why every male in the whole land was commanded to go there. This is why Jerusalem means the church in regard to worship and therefore also the church in regard to its teachings, since worship is defined by teachings and carried out in accord with them. It is also because the Lord was in Jerusalem and taught in its Temple and afterward glorified his human nature there.

Moreover, in the Word as spiritually understood a city means a body of teaching, so a holy city means a body of teaching based on divine truth that comes from the Lord.[a]

[2] We can also see that Jerusalem means a church in regard to its teachings from other passages in the Word, such as this in *Isaiah*:

> For Zion's sake I will not be silent and for Jerusalem's sake I will not rest until her justice goes forth like radiance and her salvation burns like a lamp. Then the nations will see your justice and all monarchs will see your glory, and a new name will be given you that the mouth of Jehovah will utter. And you will be a crown of beauty in the hand of Jehovah and a diadem of the kingdom in the hand of your God. Jehovah will be well pleased with you and your land will be married. Behold, your salvation will come. See, his reward is with him. And they will call them a holy people, the redeemed of Jehovah; and you will be called a city sought out, not deserted. (Isaiah 62:1, 2, 3, 4, 11, 12)

This whole chapter is about the Lord's Coming and about the new church that he is about to establish. This is the new church meant by the Jerusalem that will be given a new name that the mouth of Jehovah will utter

---

a. A city in the Word means the teachings of a church and of a religion: see *Secrets of Heaven* 402, 2712, 2943, 3216, 4492, 4493. The gate of a city means the teachings through which we come into the church: 2943, 4477. That is why the elders sat in the gate of the city and gave judgment: 2943. Going out of the gate means departing from the teachings: 4492, 4493. Representations of cities and palaces appear in heaven when angels are discussing specific teachings: 3216.

and that will be a crown of beauty in the hand of Jehovah and a diadem of the kingdom in the hand of God, with which Jehovah will be well pleased, and which will be called a city sought out, not deserted. This cannot mean the Jerusalem inhabited by the Jewish people at the time the Lord came into the world, because this was the opposite in all respects,[146] and might more properly be called "Sodom," as it is in Revelation 11:8, Isaiah 3:9, Jeremiah 23:14, Ezekiel 16:46, 48. [3] Another passage from *Isaiah:*

> Behold, I am creating a new heaven and a new earth; the former ones will not be remembered. Be glad and rejoice forever in what I am creating. Behold, I am going to create Jerusalem as a rejoicing and her people as a gladness, so that I may rejoice over Jerusalem and be glad about my people. Then the wolf and the lamb will feed together; they will do no evil in all my holy mountain. (Isaiah 65:17, 18, 19, 25)

This chapter too is about the Lord's Coming and the church that he is going to establish—a church that was not established among people in Jerusalem but among people who were outside it. This church, then, is meant by the Jerusalem that would be a rejoicing for the Lord and whose people will be a gladness for him, and where the wolf and the lamb will feed together, and where they will do no evil.

Here it is also saying, as it does in the Book of Revelation, that the Lord is going to create a new heaven and a new earth, meaning much the same thing; and it also says that he is going to create Jerusalem. [4] Another passage from *Isaiah:*

> Wake up! Wake up! Put on your strength, O Zion. Put on your beautiful garments, O Jerusalem, holy city. No more will the uncircumcised or the unclean come into you. Shake yourself from the dust, rise up, and sit,[147] Jerusalem. The people will acknowledge my name on that day, because I am the one saying "Here I am!" Jehovah has comforted his people; he has redeemed Jerusalem. (Isaiah 52:1, 2, 6, 9)

This chapter too is about the Lord's Coming and the church that he is going to establish. So the Jerusalem into which the uncircumcised or the unclean will no longer come, and which the Lord will redeem, means the church; and Jerusalem the holy city means the church's teachings that come from the Lord. [5] In Zephaniah:

> Rejoice, O daughter of Zion! Be glad with all your heart, O daughter of Jerusalem! The King of Israel is in your midst. Do not fear evil

anymore. He will be glad over you with joy; he will rest in your love; he will rejoice over you with singing. I will give you a name and praise among all the peoples of the earth. (Zephaniah 3:14, 15, 16, 17, 20)

Again, this is about the Lord and the church from him, the church over which the King of Israel (who is the Lord) will rejoice with singing and be glad with joy, in whose love he will be at rest, and to whom he will give a name and praise among all the peoples of the earth. [6] In Isaiah:

> Thus says Jehovah your Redeemer and your Maker, who says to Jerusalem, "You will be inhabited," and to the cities of Judah, "You will be built." (Isaiah 44:24, 26)

And in Daniel:

> Know and understand: from [the time] the word goes forth that Jerusalem must be restored and built until [the time of] Messiah the Leader will be seven weeks. (Daniel 9:25)

We can see that here too Jerusalem means the church because this latter was restored and built up by the Lord, but Jerusalem, the capital city of the Jewish people, was not.

[7] Jerusalem means the church that comes from the Lord also in the following passages. In Zechariah:

> Thus says Jehovah: "I will return to Zion and dwell in the midst of Jerusalem. Jerusalem will be called the city of truth, and the mountain of Jehovah Sabaoth will be called the holy mountain." (Zechariah 8:3; see also 8:20–23)

In Joel:

> Then you will know that I am Jehovah your God, dwelling on Zion, my holy mountain. Jerusalem will be holy. And on that day it will happen that the mountains will drip with new wine and the hills will flow with milk; and Jerusalem will abide from generation to generation. (Joel 3:17–21)

In Isaiah:

> On that day the branch of Jehovah will be beautiful and glorious. And it will happen that those remaining in Zion and those left in Jerusalem will be called holy—all who are written as alive in Jerusalem. (Isaiah 4:2, 3)

In Micah:

> At the very last of days the mountain of the house of Jehovah will be established on the top of the mountains. Teaching will go forth from Zion and the word of Jehovah from Jerusalem. To you the former kingdom will come, the kingdom of the daughter of Jerusalem. (Micah 4:1, 2, 8)

In Jeremiah:

> At that time they will call Jerusalem the throne of Jehovah, and all nations will gather at Jerusalem because of the name of Jehovah. They will no longer follow the stubbornness of their own evil heart. (Jeremiah 3:17)

In Isaiah:

> Look upon Zion, the city of our appointed feasts! Your eyes will see Jerusalem as a peaceful abode and as a tabernacle that will not be taken down; its tent pegs will never be removed and not one of its cords will be torn away. (Isaiah 33:20)

There are other passages elsewhere, such as Isaiah 24:23; 37:32; 66:10–14; Zechariah 12:3, 6, 9, 10; 14:8, 11, 12, 21; Malachi 3:2, 4; Psalms 122:1–7; 137:4, 5, 6.

[8] As for Jerusalem in these passages meaning the church that the Lord was going to establish and that has in fact been established, and not the Jerusalem in the land of Canaan that was inhabited by Jews, this too we can tell from the places in the Word where this latter city is described as totally lost and as destined for destruction, passages such as Jeremiah 5:1; 6:6, 7; 7:17, 18, and following; 8:6, 7, 8, and following; 9:10, 11, 13, and following; 13:9, 10, 14; 14:16; Lamentations 1:8, 9, 17; Ezekiel 4:1 to the end; 5:9 to the end; 12:18, 19; 15:6, 7, 8; 16:1–63; 23:1–49; Matthew 23:37, 39; Luke 19:41–44; 21:20, 21, 22; 23:28, 29, 30; and in many other places.

65. It says in the Book of Revelation, *a new heaven and a new earth* [Revelation 21:1], and after that, *Behold, I am making all things new* [Revelation 21:5]. This means simply that in the church that is now about to be established by the Lord, *there will be a new body of teaching* that did not exist in the former church. The reason it did not exist is that if it had existed it would not have been accepted. The Last Judgment had not yet been carried out, and until that happened the power of hell was stronger than the power of heaven. Consequently, if the Lord had given the new body of teaching too early, it would not have lasted with us; and even today it does not last except with people who turn to the Lord alone and acknowledge him as the God of heaven and earth (see §61 above).

This same teaching had in fact already been given in the Word, but since the church changed into Babylon not long after its establishment—and then, among some, into Philistia[148]—this teaching could not be seen in the Word. This is because a church sees the Word only through the lens of its own religious principles and teachings.

The new principles that are in this booklet are, in general terms, the following:

1. God is one in person and in essence, and is the Lord.
2. The whole Sacred Scripture is about him alone.
3. He came into the world to subdue the hells and to glorify his human nature. He accomplished these two goals by allowing himself to undergo trials; he accomplished them fully by the last of these trials, which was the suffering on the cross. By this means he became Redeemer and Savior, and by this means he alone has merit and justice.
4. He fulfilled all of the law, meaning that he fulfilled all of the Word.
5. He did not take away our sins by his suffering on the cross, but he did carry them like a prophet—that is, he suffered in order to be a representation of how the church had abused the Word.
6. The imputation of merit is nothing unless we understand it to be the forgiveness of sins after repentance.

These principles have been presented in this booklet. In forthcoming works—on Sacred Scripture, on teachings about life, on faith, and on divine love and wisdom[149]—there will be more that is new.

Teachings
for the
New Jerusalem
on
Sacred Scripture

Teachings for the New Jerusalem on Sacred Scripture

Sacred Scripture, or the Word, Is Divine Truth Itself

EVERYONE *says* that the Word[150] that comes from God is divinely inspired, and is therefore holy, but thus far no one knows where in the Word this divine element is. This is because in the letter,[151] the Word seems pedestrian, stylistically strange, not sublime or brilliant the way some literature of the present century is.[152] That is why people who worship nature as God or who elevate nature over God[153] and whose thinking therefore comes from themselves and their own interests rather than from heaven and the Lord[154] can so readily slip into error concerning the Word and into contempt for it. When they read it they say to themselves, "What's this? What's that? Is *this* divine? Can a God of infinite wisdom say things like this? Where is its holiness, and where does its holiness come from except people's religious bias and consequent credulity?"[155]

People who think like this, though, are not taking into account the fact that Jehovah[156] himself, who is the God of heaven and earth, spoke the Word through Moses and the prophets,[157] so the Word can be nothing but divine truth itself, because what Jehovah himself says is exactly that. They are also not taking into account the fact that the Lord (who is the same as Jehovah) spoke the Word with the authors of the Gospels—much of it with his own mouth and the rest by means of the spirit of his mouth,[158] which is the Holy Spirit. That is why he said that there was life in his words [John 6:63], that he was the light that enlightens [John 1:9], and that he was the truth [John 14:6]. [2] It is shown in *Teachings for the New Jerusalem on the Lord*[159] 52–53 that Jehovah himself spoke the Word by means of the prophets.

See the Gospel of John for the fact that the words the Lord spoke with the authors of the Gospels are life:

> The words that I speak to you are spirit and are life. (John 6:63)

Again,

> Jesus said to the woman at Jacob's well, "If you knew the gift of God and who it is that is saying to you, 'Give me something to drink,' you would ask of him and he would give you living water. Those who drink of the water that I will give will not thirst to eternity; the water that I will give them will become a fountain of water within them, springing up into eternal life." (John 4:7, 10, 13, 14)

Jacob's well means[160] the Word here, as it does also in Deuteronomy 33:28, so that is why the Lord sat there and spoke with the woman; and its water means the truth of the Word. [3] Again,

> Jesus said, "If any are thirsty, they must come to me and drink. As the Scripture says, from the bellies of those who believe in me will flow rivers of living water." (John 7:37, 38)

Again,

> Peter said to Jesus, "You have the words of eternal life." (John 6:68)

So in Mark the Lord says,

> Heaven and earth will pass away, but my words will not pass away. (Mark 13:31)

The reason the Lord's words are life is that he himself is life and truth, as he tells us in John:

> I am the way, the truth, and the life. (John 14:6)

And

> In the beginning was the Word, and the Word was with God, and the Word was God. In him there was life, and that life was the light for humankind. (John 1:1, 2, 3)

In this passage "the Word" means the Lord as divine truth, in which alone there is life and light.

[4] That is why the Word, which comes from the Lord and which is the Lord, is called "a fountain of living waters" (Jeremiah 2:13; 17:13; 31:9); "a fountain of salvation" (Isaiah 12:3); "a fountain" (Zechariah 13:1); and "a river of water of life" (Revelation 22:1). It is also why it says that "the Lamb who is in the midst of the throne will shepherd them and lead them to living fountains of waters" (Revelation 7:17).

There are passages as well where the Word is called a sanctuary and a tabernacle where the Lord dwells with us.[161]

Earthly-minded people, though, are still not convinced by all this that the Word is divine truth itself, containing both divine wisdom and divine life. They evaluate it by its style, where they do not see wisdom or life.

However, the style of the Word is the divine style itself, and no other style, however sublime and excellent it may appear to be, can be compared with it; that would be like comparing darkness to light.[162]

It is characteristic of the Word's style that there is something holy in every statement, even in every word, even at times in the letters themselves;[163] so the Word unites us to the Lord and opens heaven.[164]

[2] There are two things that emanate from the Lord, divine love and divine wisdom, or (which amounts to the same thing) divine goodness and divine truth, since any divine goodness comes from his divine love, and any divine truth comes from his divine wisdom. In its essence, the Word is both, and since, as already stated, it unites us with the Lord and opens heaven, the Word fills us with good desires that come from love and truths that lead to wisdom, provided we read it with the help of the Lord and not just on our own. It fills our will with good desires that come from love and fills our understanding with truths that lead to wisdom. As a result, we gain life by means of the Word.

To free people from any doubt that this is the nature of the Word, the Lord has revealed to me an inner meaning of the Word, a meaning that is essentially spiritual and that dwells within the outer meaning, which is earthly, the way a soul dwells within a body. This meaning is the spirit that gives life to the letter;[165] therefore this meaning can bear witness to the divinity and holiness of the Word and be convincing even to earthly-minded people—if they are willing to be convinced.

There Is a Spiritual Meaning in the Word, Which Has Been Unknown until Now

THIS will be presented in the following sequence.

1. What the spiritual meaning is.
2. This spiritual meaning is throughout the Word and in all its details.
3. The spiritual meaning is what makes the Word divinely inspired and makes every word in it holy.
4. This meaning has not been recognized before.
5. From now on it can be given only to people who are focused on genuine truths that come from the Lord.

5   1. *What the spiritual meaning is.* The spiritual meaning is not the meaning that shines forth from the Word's literal meaning when we study and interpret the Word in order to confirm some dogma of the church.[166] That meaning is the literal meaning of the Word.

We cannot see the spiritual meaning in the literal meaning; it is within the literal meaning the same way the soul is within the body, thought is within the eyes, or a feeling is within a facial expression—the two act together as cause and effect.

It is primarily this meaning that makes the Word spiritual not only for us but for angels as well; so by means of this meaning the Word is in communication with the heavens.[167]

6   There emanate from the Lord what is *heavenly,* what is *spiritual,* and what is *earthly,* in that order. What emanates from his divine love is called *heavenly* and is divine goodness. What emanates from his divine wisdom

is called *spiritual,* and is divine truth. What is *earthly* is a product of the two; it is a combining of them on the outermost level.

Angels of the Lord's heavenly kingdom, the ones who make up the third or highest heaven, are focused on the divine quality emanating from the Lord that is called heavenly, since they are focused on good desires that come from love, which they receive from the Lord. Angels of the Lord's spiritual kingdom, the ones who make up the second or middle heaven, are focused on the divine quality emanating from the Lord that is called spiritual, since they are focused on the truths that lead to wisdom, which they receive from the Lord.[a] We of the church in the world, though, are focused on a divine-earthly quality, which also emanates from the Lord.

[2] It follows from all this that as what is divine emanates from the Lord to its outermost limits, it comes down through three levels, and that they are called heavenly, spiritual, and earthly. The divine emanation that comes down to us from the Lord comes down through these three levels, and when it has come down it has these three levels within itself. Everything divine is like this, so when it is on its outermost level, it is full [of the inner levels].

That is what the Word is like.

In its outermost meaning it is earthly, in its inner meaning it is spiritual, and in its inmost meaning it is heavenly; and on every level of meaning it is divine.

It is not obvious from the literal meaning (which is earthly) that the Word is like this, because we here on earth have not known anything about the heavens before.[168] This means that we have not known that spiritual quality or that heavenly quality; so we have not known the difference between them and what is earthly.

Then too, we cannot know what the difference between these qualities is unless we know about correspondence,[169] since these three qualities are absolutely distinguishable from each other, like a goal, the means to it, and its result;[170] or like the first, the intermediate, and the last. However, they coalesce by means of their correspondence, since what is earthly corresponds to what is spiritual and also to what is heavenly.

---

a. On the two kingdoms that make up the heavens, one called "the heavenly kingdom" and one called "the spiritual kingdom," see *Heaven and Hell* 20–28.

You may see what correspondence is, though, in *Heaven and Hell*,[171] under the headings "The Correspondence of Everything in Heaven with Everything in the Human Being" (§§87–102) and "The Correspondence of Heaven with Everything Earthly" (§§103–115). There will be more to see in the examples from the Word cited below [§§9–17, 29, 35, 40:2–49, 79].

8 Since the Word is inwardly spiritual and heavenly, it was composed using nothing but correspondences; and when something is written by means of nothing but correspondences, its outermost written sense takes on the kind of style we find in the prophets and in the Gospels, a style that has divine wisdom and everything angelic hidden within it even though it seems to be commonplace.

9 2. *There is a spiritual meaning throughout the Word and in all its details.* There is no better way to make this clear than by using examples, such as the following. In the Book of Revelation, John says,

> I saw heaven opened, and behold, a white horse. And the one who sat on it was called faithful and true, and with justice he judges and makes war. His eyes were a flame of fire, and on his head were many gems. He had a name written that no one knew except him. He was clothed with a robe dipped in blood, and his name is called *the Word of God.* His armies in heaven, clothed in fine linen, white and clean, followed him on white horses. He has on his robe and on his thigh a name written: *King of Kings and Lord of Lords.* Then I saw an angel standing in the sun; and he cried with a loud voice, "Come and gather together for the great supper, so that you may eat the flesh of monarchs and the flesh of commanders, the flesh of the mighty, the flesh of horses and of those who ride on them, and the flesh of all people, free and slaves, both small and great." (Revelation 19:11–18)

No one can tell what this means except on the basis of the spiritual meaning of the Word; and no one can see the spiritual meaning except on the basis of a knowledge of correspondences, because all the expressions are correspondential, and there is not a word there that does not matter.

A knowledge of correspondences tells us the meaning of the white horse and of the one who sat on it, of the eyes that were like a flame of fire, of the gems that were on his head, of the robe dipped in blood, of the white linen worn by the people of his army in heaven, of the angel standing in the sun, of the great supper to which they were coming and gathering, also of the flesh of monarchs and commanders and the many others that they were to eat.

You may find what these particular expressions mean when spiritually understood in the booklet *White Horse* [§1], where these expressions are interpreted, so there is no need to give further interpretation here. That booklet shows that this is a description of the Lord as the Word, that his eyes like a flame of fire, the gems on his head, and the name written that no one knew except him mean the spiritual meaning of the Word and that no one knows it except him and those to whom he wills to reveal it [Matthew 11:27]; and the robe dipped in blood means the earthly meaning of the Word, its literal meaning, which has suffered violence.[172] It is obvious that the Word is what is being described because it says "His name is called the Word of God"; and it is equally obvious that it means the Lord because it says that the name of the one who sat on the horse was written, "King of Kings and Lord of Lords."

The message that the spiritual meaning of the Word was to be opened at the close of the church[173] is conveyed not only by what I have just said about the white horse and the one who sat on it but also by the great supper to which all were invited by the angel standing in the sun, so that they might come and eat the flesh of monarchs and commanders, of the mighty, of horses, of those who ride on them, and of all people, both free and slaves. All these expressions would be meaningless words, with neither life nor spirit, if there were nothing spiritual within them like a soul within a body.

In the twenty-first chapter of Revelation we find the following description of the holy Jerusalem:

10

> Its light was like a most precious stone, like a jasper stone, clear as crystal. It had a great and high wall with twelve gates, and on the gates were twelve angels and the names written of the twelve tribes of the children of Israel. Its wall measured one hundred and forty-four cubits,[174] which is the measure of a human being, that is, of an angel. The construction of its wall was of jasper, and its foundations were made of precious stones of every kind—jasper, sapphire, chalcedony, emerald, onyx, sardius, chrysolite, beryl, topaz, chrysoprase, jacinth, and amethyst. The twelve gates were twelve pearls. The city was pure gold, like clear glass, and was square—its length, breadth, and height were equal at twelve thousand stadia each.[175] [Revelation 21:11–12, 16–21]

And so on.

We can tell that all these features are to be understood spiritually from the fact that the holy Jerusalem means a new church[176] that the Lord is going to establish, as explained in §§62–65 of *Teachings on the Lord.* Further, since Jerusalem here means the church, it follows that everything said about it—about the city, its gates, its wall, the foundations of the wall, and its dimensions—has spiritual meaning in it, since what goes to make up the church is spiritual.

As for the meaning of the details, though, these have been explained in §1 of *The New Jerusalem and Its Heavenly Teachings*[177] (published in London in 1758), so I forego further explanation.

Suffice it to say that we know from these examples that there is spiritual meaning in the details of the description of the city, like a soul within a body, and that if it were not for this meaning we would find nothing relevant to the church in what is written there—the city being of pure gold, the gates of pearls, the wall of jasper, the foundations of the wall of precious stones; the wall measuring a hundred and forty-four cubits by the measure of a human being, that is, of an angel; the city itself being twelve thousand stadia in length, breadth, and height; and so on.

Yet people who are familiar with the spiritual meaning because of their knowledge of correspondences understand that the wall and its foundations mean a body of teaching drawn from the literal meaning of the Word, and that the numbers twelve, a hundred and forty-four, and twelve thousand all mean much the same, namely, all the good and true features of the church viewed in one combined form.

11 It says in Revelation 7:[4–8] that one hundred and forty-four thousand were sealed, twelve thousand from each tribe of Israel: Judah, Reuben, Gad, Asher, Naphtali, Manasseh, Simeon, Levi, Issachar, Zebulun, Joseph, and Benjamin. The spiritual meaning of this is that everyone is saved who has accepted the church from the Lord. Being marked or sealed on the forehead, spiritually understood, means being recognized by the Lord and saved. The twelve tribes of Israel mean everyone from that church: twelve, twelve thousand, and one hundred and forty-four thousand mean all; Israel means the church; and each tribe means some particular aspect of the church. Anyone who does not know the spiritual content of these words may think that only that many people are going to be saved and that these will come only from the Israelite and Jewish people.[178]

12 It says in chapter 6 of Revelation:

> When the Lamb opened the first seal of the scroll a white horse came forth, and the one who sat on it had a bow and was given a crown. When he opened the second seal a red horse came forth, and the one

who sat on it was given a great sword. When he opened the third seal a black horse came forth, and the one who sat on it had a pair of scales in his hand. When he opened the fourth seal a pale horse came forth, and the name of the one who sat on it was Death. [Revelation 6:1–8]

The only way to decipher this is by means of its spiritual meaning, and it is fully deciphered when we know the meaning of the opening of seals, a horse, and so on. These serve to describe successive states of the church from beginning to end with reference to its understanding of the Word.

The opening of the seals of the book by the Lamb means the Lord's bringing those states of the church out into the open.

A horse means the understanding of the Word.

The white horse means an understanding of the truth of the Word during the first state of the church.

The bow of the one who sat on the horse means the teachings about caring and faith that fight against false beliefs.

The crown means eternal life as the reward of victory.

[2] *The red horse* means the understanding of the Word during the second state of the church: in ruins with respect to what is good.

The great sword means false principles fighting against what is true.

The black horse means the understanding of the Word during the third state of the church: in ruins with respect to what is true.

The pair of scales means thinking truth has so little value that it is virtually worthless.

The pale horse means the absence of any understanding of the Word in the fourth or final state of the church, because of evil lives and consequent false beliefs.

Death means eternal damnation.

It is not obvious in the literal or earthly meaning that this is what is intended in the spiritual meaning; so unless that spiritual meaning is opened at last, the Word will remain closed in regard to this passage and the rest of the Book of Revelation—so tightly closed that no one will know where in that book anything holy or divine is hidden.

This is equally true of the meaning of the four horses and the four chariots coming out from between the two mountains of bronze in Zechariah 6:1–8.

In chapter 9 of Revelation we read,

The fifth angel sounded. And I saw a star fallen from heaven to the earth. To him was given the key to the bottomless pit. And he opened the bottomless pit, and smoke arose out of the pit like the smoke of a great furnace; and the sun and the air were darkened because of the smoke of the pit. And out of the smoke locusts came onto the earth. And to them was given power, as the scorpions of the earth have power. The shapes of the locusts were like horses prepared for battle. On their heads were what seemed to be golden crowns, and their faces were like human faces. They had hair like women's hair, and their teeth were like those of lions. They had breastplates of iron, and the sound of their wings was like the sound of chariots with many horses running into battle. And they had tails like scorpions, and there were stingers in their tails. Their power was to hurt people for five months. And they had as king over them the angel of the bottomless pit, whose name in Hebrew is Abaddon, but in Greek he has the name Apollyon. [Revelation 9:1–3, 7–11]

Readers will not understand this either unless the spiritual meaning has been unveiled to them, because nothing in it is an empty statement. Everything, every detail, has meaning. It is about the state of the church when all the truth it has recognized in the Word lies in ruins, and when those who have become limited to their physical senses[179] therefore convince themselves that falsities are truths.

[2] *The star fallen from heaven* means the ruined state of the truth that was once recognized.

The darkened sun and air mean the light of truth turned into darkness.

The locusts that came out of the smoke of the pit mean false beliefs built on the outward kind of thinking characteristic of people who have become limited to their physical senses and see and evaluate everything on the basis of deceptive appearances.

Scorpions mean the force of their rhetoric.

The locusts looking like horses prepared for battle means their rationalizing as though they understood what was true.

The locusts having what seemed to be golden crowns on their heads and having faces that looked human means that it seemed to them that they were triumphant and wise.

Their having hair like women's hair means that it seemed to them that they were genuinely devoted to truth.

Their having teeth like those of lions means that their sensory impressions (which are the most superficial aspects of the earthly self)[180] seemed to them to have power over everything.

[3] *Their having breastplates like breastplates of iron* means the arguments from deceptive appearances that they use in order to fight and prevail.

The sound of their wings being like the sound of chariots with many horses running into battle means their rationalizations, based on supposedly true teachings from the Word, for which they feel compelled to fight.

Their having tails like scorpions means their persuasive ability.

Their having stingers in their tails means their skills in using this ability to deceive.

Their having power to hurt people for five months means that they induce a kind of stupor in people who are devoted to understanding what is true and perceiving what is good.

Their having as king over them the angel of the abyss whose name is Abaddon and Apollyon means that their false principles come from hell, where all the people are totally materialistic and in love with their own intelligence.

[4] This is the spiritual meaning of these words, none of which is obvious in the literal meaning. It is the same throughout the Book of Revelation.

Bear in mind that, when spiritually understood, everything is bound together in an ongoing connection, and every single word in the literal or earthly meaning contributes to its elegant construction. So if one little word were taken away, a connection would be broken and a link would be lost.[181] To prevent this from happening, the command not to take away a word is appended to the end of this prophetic book (Revelation 22:19). It is the same with the prophetic books of the Old Testament:[182] so that nothing would be lost, the Lord's divine providence arranged that their details were counted right down to the letters, which was done by the Masoretes.[183]

When the Lord speaks to his disciples about the close of the age, which is the last time of the church, at the end of his predictions about the sequence of changes of state he says,

> Immediately after the affliction of those days the sun will be darkened, the moon will not give its light, the stars will fall from heaven, and the powers of the heavens will be shaken. Then the sign of the Son of Humanity will appear in heaven, and then all the tribes of the earth will wail; and they will see the Son of Humanity coming in the clouds of heaven with power and great glory. And he will send out his angels

with a trumpet and a loud voice, and they will gather his chosen people from the four winds, from one end of the heavens to the other. (Matthew 24:29, 30, 31)

[2] Spiritually understood, this does not mean that the sun and moon will be darkened, that the stars will fall from heaven, and that a sign of the Lord will appear in heaven and he will be seen in the clouds accompanied by angels with trumpets. Rather, the particular words are here used to mean spiritual events that have to do with the church, spiritual events about its state at its end. The underlying reason is that in the spiritual meaning the sun that will be darkened is the Lord as an object of love; the moon that will not give its light is the Lord as an object of faith; the stars that will fall from heaven are the knowledge of what is good and what is true that will come to an end; the sign of the Son of Humanity in heaven is the manifestation of divine truth; the tribes of the earth that will wail are a complete lack of true belief and of good actions that come from love; the coming of the Son of Humanity in the clouds of heaven with power and glory is the Lord's presence in the Word, and a revelation—the clouds being the literal meaning of the Word and the glory being the spiritual meaning of the Word. The angels with a trumpet and a loud voice mean heaven as our source of divine truth;[184] and the gathering of the chosen people from the four winds, from one end of the heavens to the other, means a new kind of church, specifically its love and faith.

[3] It is obvious from the prophets that this does not mean the darkening of the sun and the moon and the falling of the stars to earth, because things like this are said there about the state of the church when the Lord will come into the world. It says in Isaiah, for example:

> Behold, the fierce day of Jehovah is coming, a day of blazing wrath. The stars of the heavens and their constellations will not shine their light. The sun will be darkened in its rising, and the moon will not make its light shine. I will execute judgment upon the world for its malice. (Isaiah 13:9–11; 24:23)

In Joel,

> The day of Jehovah is coming, a day of darkness and gloom; the sun and the moon will be darkened and the stars will withhold their light. (Joel 2:1, 2, 10; 3:15)

In Ezekiel,

> I will cover the heavens and darken the stars. I will cover the sun with a cloud, and the moon will not give its light. I will darken all the bright lights and bring darkness upon the land. (Ezekiel 32:7, 8)

The day of Jehovah means the Coming of the Lord, which happened when there was no longer anything good or true left in the church, and there was no knowledge of the Lord.

To show that many passages in the prophetic books of the Word of the Old Testament are not understood if we lack their spiritual meaning, I should like to cite just a few. This from Isaiah, for example:

> Then Jehovah will rouse up a whip against Assyria, like the blow against Midian on the rock Oreb; his staff will be stretched out over the sea, and he will lift it against the way of Egypt. And it will happen on that day that his burden will depart from your shoulder and his yoke from your neck. He will come against Aiath; he will cross over into Migron. He will command his weapons against Michmash; they will cross Mabara. Gibeah will be a place of lodging for us; Ramah will tremble with fear; Gibeah of Saul will flee. Wail with your voice, daughter of Gallim! Listen to Laishah, unfortunate Anathoth! Madmenah will wander; the inhabitants of Gebim will gather together. In Nob is it still a day for standing firm? The mountain of the daughter of Zion, the hill of Jerusalem, will move its hand. Jehovah will cut down the tangled places in the forest with iron, and Lebanon will fall by means of the Mighty One. (Isaiah 10:24–34)

All we find here are names from which we learn nothing[185] without the aid of the spiritual meaning, in which all the names in the Word point to matters of heaven and the church. We gather from this meaning that this passage refers to the ruin of the whole church by information that corrupted every true teaching and supported every false teaching.

[2] In another passage from the same prophet,

> On that day the rivalry of Ephraim will wane and the enemies of Judah will be cut off. Ephraim will not compete with Judah, and Judah will not trouble Ephraim, but they will swoop down upon the shoulder of the Philistines toward the sea. Together they will plunder the children of the east. Edom and Moab will be [subject to] the stretching out of

> their hand. Jehovah will curse the tongue of the sea of Egypt and will shake his hand over the river with the vehemence of his spirit; and he will strike it into seven streams, to make a pathway [that can be trodden] with sandals. Then there will be a highway for the rest of his people, the remnant from Assyria. (Isaiah 11:11, 13–16)

Here too, only those who know what these particular names mean will see anything divine, when in fact this is about the Lord's Coming and what will happen then, as is perfectly obvious from the first ten verses of the chapter.[186] So without the aid of the spiritual meaning, who would see what these statements in this sequence mean, namely, that if people are caught up in false beliefs because of ignorance but have not let themselves be led astray by evil tendencies, they will find their way to the Lord, and that the church will then understand the Word, so that their false beliefs will no longer harm them?

[3] It is much the same in other passages where there are no names, as in Ezekiel:

> Thus says the Lord Jehovih: "Son of Humanity, say to every winged bird and to every beast of the field, 'Gather and come. Gather yourselves from all around for my sacrifice, which I am sacrificing for you, a great sacrifice on the mountains of Israel, so that you may eat flesh and drink blood. You will eat the flesh of the mighty and drink the blood of the rulers of the earth. You will eat fat until you are full and drink blood until you are drunk, from my sacrifice, which I am sacrificing for you. At my table you will eat your fill of horses and chariots and the mighty and every man of war. This is how I will establish my glory among the nations.'" (Ezekiel 39:17–21)

If readers do not know from the spiritual sense the meaning of a sacrifice, of flesh and blood, of horses, chariots, the mighty, and men of war, all they can conclude is that they are going to eat and drink things like this. The spiritual meaning, though, tells us that eating flesh and drinking blood from a sacrifice that the Lord Jehovih offers on the mountains of Israel means taking divine goodness and divine truth into ourselves from the Word. This passage is about summoning everyone to the Lord's kingdom, specifically the Lord's establishment of a church among the nations. Can anyone fail to see that flesh does not mean flesh and that blood does not mean blood in this text? The same holds true for drinking blood until we are drunk and eating our fill of horses, chariots, the mighty, and every man of war.

There are passages like this in a thousand other places in the prophets.

16 Lacking a spiritual understanding, no one would know why the prophet Jeremiah was commanded to buy a belt and put it around his waist, not to put it in water, and to hide it in a crevice in the rocks near the Euphrates (Jeremiah 13:1–7). No one would know why the prophet Isaiah was commanded to take the sackcloth off his waist and the sandals off his feet and to go naked and barefoot for three years (Isaiah 20:2, 3). No one would know why the prophet Ezekiel was commanded to take a razor to his head and his beard and then to divide the hair, burning a third of it in the middle of the city, striking a third with a sword, and scattering a third to the wind; also, to bind a few hairs in his hems, and eventually to throw a few into the midst of a fire (Ezekiel 5:1–4). The same prophet was commanded to lie on his left side for three hundred ninety days and on his right side for forty days and to make himself a cake out of wheat, barley, millet, and spelt and bake it over cow dung and eat it; and at another time to make a siege wall and a mound against [an image of] Jerusalem and besiege it (Ezekiel 4:1–15). No one would know why the prophet Hosea was twice commanded to take a whore as his wife (Hosea 1:2–9; 3:2, 3), and other things of the same sort.

Beyond that, without a spiritual understanding who would know the meaning of all the objects in the tabernacle—the ark, for example, the mercy seat, the angel guardians,[187] the lampstand, the altar of incense, the showbread on the table, its veils and curtains? Without a spiritual understanding, who would know the meaning of Aaron's sacred garments—his tunic, robe, ephod, the Urim and Thummim,[188] his turban, and so on? Without a spiritual understanding, who would know the meaning of all the commandments about burnt offerings, sacrifices, grain offerings, and drink offerings, about Sabbaths and festivals?[189] The truth is that every bit of what was commanded meant something about the Lord, heaven, and the church.

You can see clearly in these few examples that there is a spiritual meaning throughout the Word and in its details.

17 We can tell from the Lord's parables, which have a spiritual meaning in their very words, that when he was in the world he spoke in correspondences—that is, he was speaking in spiritual terms when he was naming earthly things. The parable of the ten young women may serve as an example. He said,

> The kingdom of the heavens is like ten young women who took their lamps and went out to meet a bridegroom. Five of them were prudent and five were foolish. The foolish women took their lamps but

brought no oil. The prudent women took oil in their lamps. When the bridegroom was delayed, they all became drowsy and fell asleep. In the middle of the night there was a shout: "Behold, the bridegroom is coming! Go out to meet him." At that, all the women woke up and trimmed their lamps. The foolish women said to the prudent ones, "Give us some of your oil, because our lamps are going out." The prudent women replied, "There might not be enough for us and for you. Go instead to the sellers and buy some for yourselves." But while they were away buying some, the bridegroom arrived, and the women who were prepared went in with him to the wedding, and the door was closed. Later the other women came along and said, "Lord, Lord, open up for us." But he answered and said, "I tell you truly, I do not know you." (Matthew 25:1–12)

[2] Only people who know that there is such a thing as a spiritual meaning and what it is like will see that there is a spiritual meaning, and therefore something holy and divine, in the details of this parable. Spiritually understood, the kingdom of God means heaven and the church; the bridegroom means the Lord, the wedding means the marriage of the Lord with heaven and the church[190] brought about by good actions that come from love and faith; the young women mean the people of the church, ten meaning all of them and five meaning some of them; the lamps mean truths we believe; the oil means a love for doing good; sleeping and waking mean our life in this world, which is earthly, and our life after death, which is spiritual; buying means gaining for ourselves; going to the sellers and buying oil means trying to gain from others after death a love for doing good. Since this could then no longer be done, even though they came to the door of the wedding room with their lamps and the oil they had bought they were told by the bridegroom, "I do not know you." This is because after our life in this world we are still the same kinds of people we were when we were living in this world.[191]

[3] We can see from this that the Lord spoke in pure correspondences; and this is because he was speaking from the divine nature that was within him and that was his own.

That the bridegroom means the Lord; the kingdom of the heavens means the church; the wedding means the marriage of the Lord with the church through good actions that come from love and faith; the young women mean the members of the church; ten means all and five means some; sleeping means an earthly state; buying means gaining for ourselves; the door means admission to heaven; and our not being known by the Lord means our not participating in his love—all this we can conclude on the basis of many passages from the prophetic Word, where these words have similar meanings.

It is because young women mean members of the church that it so often speaks of the virgin and daughter of Zion, of Jerusalem, and of Israel in the prophetic Word. It is because oil means good actions that are done out of love that all the holy utensils of the Israelite church were anointed with oil.[192]

[4] It is much the same in other parables and in all the words that the Lord spoke and that are written in the Gospels. That is why the Lord said that his words were spirit and were life (John 6:63).

It is much the same with all the Lord's miracles, which were divine acts, because they pointed to the various states of people in whom the church was to be established by the Lord.[193] For example, the blind receiving sight meant that people who had been in ignorance of what is true would be given understanding; the deaf being given hearing meant that people who had not listened to the Lord and the Word would hear and obey; the dead being revived meant that people who would otherwise perish spiritually would be brought to life, and so on. This is the meaning of the Lord's answer to the disciples of John when they asked whether he was the one who was to come:

> Tell John the things that you hear and see: the blind are seeing, and the lame are walking; lepers are being cleansed, and the deaf are hearing; the dead are rising again, and the poor are hearing the gospel. (Matthew 11:3, 4, 5)

All the miracles that are recounted in the Word have something in them that involves matters of the Lord, heaven, and the church. That is what makes them divine miracles and distinguishes them from wonders that are not divine.

These few examples are offered by way of illustrating what the spiritual meaning is and showing that it is present throughout the Word and in all its details.

3. *The spiritual meaning is what makes the Word divinely inspired and makes every word in it holy.* We hear it said in the church that the Word is holy, but this is because Jehovah God spoke it. However, because people do not see anything holy about it from the letter alone, once they begin to have doubts about its holiness for this reason, then when they read the Word, there is much they can find to justify this attitude. That is,

they think, "Is *this* holy? Is *this* divine?" To prevent this kind of thinking from spreading to more and more people and then gaining strength and so destroying the Lord's union with the church where the Word is, it has now pleased the Lord to unveil the spiritual meaning so that we may know where in the Word that "holy material" lies hidden.

[2] But let me illustrate this too with some examples.

Sometimes the Word talks about Egypt, sometimes about Assyria, sometimes about Edom, Moab, the Ammonites, Tyre and Sidon, and Gog. If we do not know that these names mean matters of heaven and the church, we may be misled and believe that the Word has a lot to say about nations and peoples and only a little about heaven and the church—a lot about earthly matters and not much about heavenly ones. However, if we know what is meant by these nations and peoples or by their names, we can come out of error into truth. [3] By the same token, when we see in the Word the frequent mention of gardens, groves, forests, and their trees, such as olive, grapevine, cedar, poplar, and oak; when we see mention of lambs, sheep, goats, calves, and cattle, as well as mountains, hills, valleys, and their springs, rivers, waters, and so on; if we know nothing about the spiritual meaning of the Word, we can only believe that these and nothing else are the things that they mean. We would not know that garden, grove, and forest mean wisdom, intelligence, and knowledge; that the olive, grapevine, cedar, poplar, and oak mean the heavenly, spiritual, rational, earthly, and sensory types of goodness and truth in the church; that lambs, sheep, goats, calves, and cattle mean innocence, caring, and earthly feelings;[194] that mountains, hills, and valleys mean the higher, lower, and lowest forms of the church; and that Egypt means knowledge, Assyria reasoning, Edom what is earthly, Moab the corruption of what is good, Ammonites the corruption of what is true, Tyre and Sidon the knowledge of what is true and good, and Gog outward worship with no inner content. Once we know this, though, we can think that the Word is about nothing but heavenly matters and that these earthly things are only the vessels that contain them.

[4] But let me illustrate this with another example from the Word. We read in David,[195]

> The voice of Jehovah is upon the waters; the God of glory thunders; Jehovah is upon great waters. The voice of Jehovah breaks the cedars. Jehovah shatters the cedars of Lebanon. He makes them leap like a calf, and Lebanon and Sirion like a young unicorn.[196] The voice of Jehovah

comes down like a flame of fire. The voice of Jehovah makes the wilderness quake; it makes the wilderness of Kadesh quake. The voice of Jehovah makes the deer give birth and strips the woodlands bare, but in his temple, everyone says, "Glory!" (Psalms 29:3–9)

Anyone who is strictly earthly-minded and does not realize that the details, including every single word here, are holy and divine may say, "What *is* all this—Jehovah sitting on waters, breaking cedars with his voice, making them leap like a calf and Lebanon like a young unicorn, making deer give birth, and so on?" Such people do not realize that spiritually understood, these statements serve as a description of the power of divine truth or the Word. [5] When understood in this way, the "voice of Jehovah" (which here speaks in thunder) means divine truth or the Word in its power. The great waters on which Jehovah sits mean its truths; both the cedars that it breaks and [the cedars of] Lebanon that it shatters mean distortions produced by human reasoning; the calf and the young unicorn mean distortions produced by the earthly and sense-centered self; the flame of fire means the urge to distort; the wilderness and the wilderness of Kadesh mean the church where there is nothing true and nothing good; the deer that the voice of Jehovah causes to give birth mean people who are engaged in doing good on an earthly level; and the woodlands that he strips bare mean the facts and concepts the Word makes accessible to them. That is why it goes on to say that everyone in his temple says, "Glory!" This means that there are divine truths in the details of the Word, since the temple means the Lord and therefore the Word, as well as heaven and the church, and glory means divine truth.

We can see from all this that there is not a single word in this passage that is not describing the divine power of the Word against all kinds of false beliefs and perceptions in earthly people, and the divine power to reform people.

There is a still deeper level of meaning in the Word, one called *heavenly,* mentioned briefly in §6 above. It is almost impossible to extricate this meaning, though, because it is suited not so much to the thinking of our intellect as to the feelings of our will.

The reason this still deeper meaning (the one called heavenly) is present in the Word is that divine goodness and divine truth emanate from the Lord, divine goodness from his divine love and divine truth from his divine wisdom. Both are present in the Word, since the Word is a divine emanation. And since both are present, the Word brings to life people who read it with reverence. This subject will be discussed, though, under its own heading [§§80–90], where it will be explained that there is a marriage of the Lord and the church in the details of the Word and therefore a marriage of what is good and what is true.

20

4. *The spiritual meaning of the Word has not been recognized before.* It was explained in *Heaven and Hell* 87–105 that absolutely everything in the physical world corresponds to something spiritual, as does absolutely everything in the human body. However, the nature of this correspondence has been unknown until the present time, even though it was common knowledge in ancient times.[197] For the people who lived in those times, the knowledge of how things correspond to each other was the very essence of knowledge. This knowledge was so universal that it governed the writing of all their scrolls and books. [2] The Book of Job, which is an ancient work, is full of correspondences. So were the Egyptian hieroglyphs[198] and the fables of the earliest peoples.[199] All the ancient churches[200] had practices that symbolized heavenly things. Their rituals, as well as the regulations underlying their worship, were made up entirely of correspondences. The same held true for everything about the church among the children of Jacob—their burnt offerings and sacrifices were correspondences even with respect to details. So were the tabernacle and everything in it. So were their feasts—the Feast of Unleavened Bread, the Feast of Tabernacles, the Feast of First Fruits.[201] So too was the priesthood of Aaron and the Levites as well as the sacred garments of Aaron and his sons. So also were all the laws and judgments that had to do with their worship and life. [3] And since divine things become manifest in this world by means of correspondences, the Word was written entirely by means of them. That is why the Lord, speaking as he did from his divine nature, spoke in correspondences, since in the physical world whatever comes from the divine nature clothes itself in things that correspond to divine realities and that therefore conceal in their embrace the divine realities that we call heavenly and spiritual.

21

I have been taught that the people of the earliest church, the one that existed before the Flood,[202] were so heavenly in nature that they talked with angels of heaven, and that they were able to talk with them in correspondences. This meant that their wisdom developed to the point that when they saw anything on earth, they not only thought of it in earthly terms but thought of it in spiritual terms at the same time, and therefore their thoughts joined those of angels.

I have also been taught that Enoch (mentioned in Genesis 5:21–24) and others who joined him collected correspondences from the mouth of these [sages] and passed their knowledge on to their descendants. As a result of this, the knowledge of correspondences was not only familiar but was devotedly practiced in many Middle Eastern countries, especially in the land of Canaan,[203] Egypt, Assyria, Chaldea, Syria, and Arabia; and in Tyre, Sidon, and Nineveh. From coastal locations it was transmitted to Greece. There, however, the knowledge was changed into fables, as we can tell from the writings of the earliest people there.

With the passage of time, though, the symbolic practices of the church, which were correspondences, were turned into idolatrous practices and even into magic. When this happened, the Lord's divine providence saw to it that this knowledge was gradually erased, and among the people of Israel and Judah it became utterly lost and extinct.

The worship of those people, though, was still composed entirely of correspondences, so it represented heavenly realities even though they did not know what they meant. They were in fact completely earthly people and therefore neither wanted to know nor could know anything about spiritual things or, consequently, about correspondences.[204]

The idolatrous practices of the peoples in ancient times arose from their knowledge of correspondences because everything we see on our planet corresponds to something spiritual—not only trees, but also all kinds of animals and birds as well as fish, and so on. The ancients who were devoted to a knowledge of these correspondences made themselves images that corresponded to heavenly realities, and they took pleasure in them because they signified what was happening in heaven and the church. That is why they placed them not only in their temples but in their homes as well—not to be worshiped but to remind them of the heavenly reality signified by these objects. So in Egypt and elsewhere their images looked like calves, oxen, and snakes as well as children, old people, and young women. This is because calves and oxen mean the feelings and drives of the earthly self, snakes the shrewdness of the sensory self, children innocence and caring, old people wisdom, and young women the desire for what is true, and so on.

Because the ancients had placed these images and statues in and around temples, their descendants, after the knowledge of these correspondences had been lost, began to worship the images and statues themselves as sacred, and eventually regarded them as demigods. [2] Much the same happened in other nations—with the Philistines' Dagon in Ashdod, for example (see 1 Samuel 5:1–12). The upper part of Dagon looked human and the lower part looked like a fish, an image devised because a human means intelligence, a fish means knowledge, and intelligence and knowledge become one.

This is also why the ancients' worship was in gardens and groves depending on the species of trees, and on mountains and hills. Gardens and groves meant wisdom and intelligence, and each tree meant some specific aspect of them. Olive trees, for example, meant good actions done out of love; grapevines meant true insights that arise from doing good; cedars meant a rational understanding of what is good and true; mountains meant the highest heaven; and hills meant the heaven below it.

[3] The survival of the knowledge of correspondences until the Coming of the Lord among the greater part of those in the East[205] is demonstrated in the account of the wise men from that region who came to the Lord when he was born—because in that story a star went before them and they bore gifts of gold, frankincense, and myrrh (Matthew 2:1, 2, 9, 10, 11). That is, the star that went before them meant a new insight from heaven; and gold meant what is good on the heavenly level, frankincense what is good on the spiritual level, and myrrh what is good on the earthly level; and these three are the basis of all worship.[206]

[4] There was no knowledge at all of correspondences among the people of Israel and Judah, however, even though correspondence was the sole basis of all their worship, all the judgments and statutes given them through Moses, and all the contents of the Word. This was because they were idolatrous at heart, so much so that they did not even want to know that any element of their worship had a heavenly or spiritual meaning. That is, they wanted all these things to be holy in and of themselves and just for them, so if they had noticed anything heavenly and spiritual, they not only would have rejected it but would have profaned it as well. For this reason heaven was closed to them, so closed that they were scarcely aware that there was such a thing as eternal life. The truth of this is obvious from the fact that they did not recognize the Lord even though the whole Sacred Scripture prophesied about him and predicted him. The sole reason they rejected him was that he taught people about a heavenly kingdom and not an earthly one. That is, they wanted a Messiah who would raise them to supremacy over all the nations in the whole world and not some Messiah who would be concerned with their eternal salvation.

Further, they assert that the Word contains in itself many secrets that they call mystical, but they do not want those secrets to be about the Lord. They do want to know them, though, when they are told that they are about gold.[207]

The reason the knowledge of correspondences that gives access to the spiritual meaning of the Word was not discerned in later times was that the people of the early Christian church were quite uneducated, so this knowledge could not be revealed to them. That is, if it had been revealed it would have been of no use to them and they would not have understood it.

After those times, darkness spread over the whole Christian world as a consequence of papal rule; and the people who relied on papal authority and convinced themselves of its falsities neither could nor wanted to accept anything spiritual, including the correspondence of earthly things with spiritual things in the Word. If they had, they would have realized that Peter does not mean Peter but the Lord as the Rock. They would also have realized that the Word is divine all the way to its very heart and that a papal decree is of no importance by comparison.

After the Reformation[208] heavenly truths were hidden away, because people began to differentiate between faith and caring and to worship God in three persons and therefore to worship three gods whom they thought were one; and if heavenly truths had been discovered, people would have distorted them and brought them down to the level of faith alone.[209] They would not have associated any of those truths with caring and love, so they would have shut themselves out of heaven.

The reason the spiritual meaning of the Word has now been unveiled by the Lord is that a body of teaching based on genuine truth has now been revealed, and this teaching and no other is in harmony with the spiritual meaning of the Word.[210]

That spiritual meaning is indicated by the appearing of the Lord in the clouds of heaven with glory and power in Matthew 24:30, the chapter dealing with the close of the age, which is to be understood as the last time of the church.

Then too, the opening of the Word with respect to its spiritual meaning was promised in the Book of Revelation. That is what is meant there by the white horse and the great supper to which all were invited (Revelation 19:11–18). Chapter 19 also tells us that the spiritual meaning would not be recognized for a long time, at least by people mired in false teachings (especially about the Lord) and therefore closed to truth. That is the meaning of the beast and the monarchs of the earth in Revelation who were going to make war with the one who sat on the white horse (Revelation 19:19). The beast means Roman Catholics (see Revelation 17:3), and the monarchs of the earth mean Protestants who are mired in false theological principles.[211]

26   5. *From now on the spiritual meaning of the Word can be given only to people who are focused on genuine truths that come from the Lord.* This is because we cannot see the spiritual meaning unless we are given it by the Lord alone and unless we focus on genuine truths from him. The spiritual meaning of the Word is all about the Lord and his kingdom, and is the meaning that engages his angels in heaven.[212] It is actually his divine truth there. We can do violence to it if we have some knowledge of correspondences and try to use that knowledge to explore the spiritual meaning of the Word with our own brain power. This is because we can distort that meaning with the few correspondences familiar to us and twist them to support what is actually false. This would be doing violence to both divine truth and heaven. So if our efforts to open that meaning come from ourselves and not from the Lord, heaven is closed to us;[213] and once it is closed, we either see nothing or lose our spiritual sanity.

[2] Another reason is that the Lord teaches everyone by means of the Word; and he teaches using the truths that we have and does not pour new truths directly in.[214] This means that if we are not focused on divine truths or if the few we have are tangled in distortions, we can use these few to distort truths. This, as is commonly known, is what happens with heretics in their use of the literal sense of the Word. So to keep anyone from gaining access to the spiritual meaning of the Word or from distorting the genuine truth of that meaning, the Lord has stationed the guards meant in the Word by the angel guardians.[215]

[3] This is how the stationing of those guardians was represented to me:[216]

> I was shown some big purses that looked like bags, in which an ample supply of silver was stored; and since they were open, it seemed as though anyone could take out the silver stored in them—could in fact steal it. However, there were two angels sitting near the purses, serving as guards. The place where the purses were stored looked like a manger in a stable. In a nearby room I could see some modest young women together with a chaste wife. There were two little children standing near the room. I was told that I was to play with them, but wisely, not childishly. After that a prostitute appeared, and then a horse lying dead.

[4] After I had seen all this, I was told that this scene represented the literal meaning of the Word in which spiritual meaning was contained. The big purses full of silver meant an abundant supply of knowledge about what is true. Their being open but guarded by angels meant that anyone could draw knowledge of truth from them but care had to be taken to prevent anyone from distorting the spiritual meaning, in which there was nothing but truths. The manger in the stable where the purses were meant spiritual teaching for the sake of our understanding. That is what a manger means because horses, which eat from mangers, mean an understanding. [5] The modest young women whom I saw in the nearby room meant desire for what is true, and the chaste wife meant the union of good actions and truth. The little children meant an innocence of wisdom within. They were angels from the third heaven, all of whom look like little children.[217] The prostitute with the dead horse meant the distortion of the Word by so many people nowadays, a distortion that leads to the death of all understanding of truth—the prostitute meaning the distortion and the dead horse the total absence of any understanding of truth.

The Literal Meaning of the Word Is the Foundation, the Container, and the Support of Its Spiritual and Heavenly Meanings

27 IN every work of God there is something first, something intermediate, and something last; and what is first works through what is intermediate to what is last and in this way becomes manifest and persists, so what is last is a *foundation*.[218] The first is also in the intermediate, and through the intermediate is in what is last, so what is last is a *container;* and since what is last is a container and a foundation, it is also a *support*.

28 The learned world understands that this *series of three* can be called a goal, the means to it, and its result, as well as being, becoming, and

achieving full manifestation.[219] Being is the goal, becoming is the means, and achieving full manifestation is the result. This means that there is a series of three in everything that is complete—a series called first, intermediate, and last; or goal, means, and result; or being, becoming, and achieving full manifestation.

Once this is understood we can also understand that every work of God is complete and perfect in its final stage and also that the whole, which is a series of three, is in the final stage, because the prior stages are together in it.

29 This is why *three* in the Word spiritually understood means complete, perfect, and all together; and since this is its meaning it is used in the Word whenever anything is so described, as in the following instances:

Isaiah went naked and barefoot *for three years* (Isaiah 20:3). Jehovah called Samuel *three times,* Samuel ran to Eli *three times,* and *the third time* Eli understood what was happening (1 Samuel 3:1–8). David told Jonathan[220] that he would hide in the field *for three days;* later Jonathan shot *three arrows* beside the rock; and after that David bowed down to Jonathan *three times* (1 Samuel 20:5, 12–41). Elijah stretched himself out on the widow's son *three times* (1 Kings 17:21). Elijah ordered people to pour water over a burnt offering *three times* (1 Kings 18:34). Jesus said that the kingdom of the heavens was like yeast, which a woman took and hid in *three measures* [of flour] until it was all leavened (Matthew 13:33). Jesus said to Peter that Peter would deny him *three times* (Matthew 26:34). The Lord said to Peter *three times,* "Do you love me?" (John 21:15, 16, 17). Jonah was in the belly of the whale *three days and three nights* (Jonah 1:17). Jesus said that they would destroy the Temple, and he would build it in *three days* (Matthew 26:61). Jesus prayed *three times* in Gethsemane (Matthew 26:39–44). Jesus rose *on the third day* (Matthew 28:1).

There are many other passages where threes are mentioned, and they are mentioned when it is a matter of something finished and completed, because that is what this number means.

30 This is by way of preface to what follows, so that the discussion there can readily be understood; the point being to demonstrate that the earthly meaning of the Word, which is its literal meaning, is the foundation, container, and support of its spiritual and heavenly meanings.

31 It was noted in §§6 and 19 above that there are three levels of meaning in the Word and that the heavenly meaning is its first level, the spiritual meaning its intermediate level, and the earthly meaning its last level. This

enables anyone who thinks rationally to conclude that the first level of the Word, the heavenly, works through its intermediate, which is the spiritual, to the last level, which is the earthly. We can also conclude that the last level is therefore a *foundation*. We can conclude further that the first level (the heavenly) is within the intermediate level (the spiritual), and through this in the last level (the earthly), which means that the last level (the earthly), which is the literal meaning of the Word, is a *container;* and since it is a container and a foundation, it is also a *support*.

However, there is no way to explain briefly how this happens. These are mysteries familiar to heaven's angels that will be unfolded—as far as possible—in the treatises listed in the preface to *Teachings on the Lord: Angelic Wisdom about Divine Providence; Angelic Wisdom about Omnipotence, Omnipresence, and Omniscience; Angelic Wisdom about Divine Love and Wisdom;* and *Angelic Wisdom about Life.*[221]

The Word is essentially a divine work for the salvation of the human race. For present purposes, it will suffice to conclude from what has been said above that the Word's last level of meaning (which is earthly and is called "the literal meaning") is a foundation, container, and support for its two deeper levels of meaning.

It follows from all this that without its literal meaning the Word would be like a palace without a foundation, like a castle in the air. The only thing on the ground would be its shadow, and shadows disappear. The Word without its literal meaning would be like a temple containing an abundance of holy objects, with a central inner sanctum, but without a roof or walls to contain them. If these were lacking or were taken away, its holy contents would be plundered by thieves or torn apart by the beasts of the earth and the birds of heaven, and would therefore be scattered far and wide.

By the same token, it would be like the tabernacle's inmost area, which housed the ark of the covenant, and its middle area, which housed the golden lampstand, the golden altar of incense, and the table with the showbread on it—all its holy contents—without the curtains and veils that surrounded them.

The Word without its literal meaning would be like a human body without the coverings called layers of skin and without the structural supports called bones. Lacking both of these, all the internal organs would spill out.

Then too, it would be like the heart and lungs in the chest without the covering called the pleura[222] and the framework called the rib cage, or like the brain without its specific covering called the dura mater[223] or its general covering, container, and support called the skull.

That is what the Word would be like without its literal meaning, which is why it says in Isaiah that Jehovah creates a covering over all glory (Isaiah 4:5).

34 It would be the same for the heavens where angels live if it were not for the world where we live. We, as human beings, are their foundation, container, and support, and we have the Word with us and in us.

Overall, the heavens are divided into two kingdoms, which are called the heavenly kingdom and the spiritual kingdom. These two kingdoms are founded upon the earthly kingdom where we live. A similar structure exists in the Word, which we have with us and in us.[224]

See *Heaven and Hell* 20–28 on the division of the angelic heavens into two kingdoms, a heavenly one and a spiritual one.

35 *Teachings on the Lord* 28 shows that the Old Testament prophets represented the Lord in respect to the Word and therefore meant the teaching of the church drawn from the Word, and that because of this they were addressed as "children of humanity." It follows from this that by the various things they suffered and endured they represented the violence done to the literal meaning of the Word by Jews. Isaiah, for example, took the sackcloth off his waist and the sandals off his feet and went naked and barefoot for three years (Isaiah 20:2, 3). Similarly, Ezekiel the prophet took a barber's razor to his head and his beard, burned a third of the hair in the middle of the city, struck a third with a sword, and scattered a third to the wind; also, he bound a few hairs in his hems and eventually threw a few into the midst of a fire and burned them (Ezekiel 5:1–4).

Since the prophets represented the Word and therefore meant the teaching of the church drawn from the Word (as just noted), and since the head means wisdom from the Word, the hair and the beard mean the outermost form of truth.[225] It is because of this meaning that inflicting *baldness* on yourself was a sign of immense grief and being discovered to be *bald* was an immense disgrace. This and this alone is why the prophet shaved off his hair and his beard—to represent the state of the Jewish church in regard to the Word. This and this alone is why two she-bears tore apart forty-two boys *who called Elisha bald* (2 Kings 2:23, 24, 25)—because as just noted the prophet represented the Word, and his baldness signified the Word without an outermost meaning.

We shall see in §49 below that the Nazirites represented the Lord's Word in its outermost forms, which is why they were commanded to let their hair grow and not to shave any of it. In Hebrew, "Nazirite" actually means "hair."[226] It was commanded also that the high priest was not to shave his head (Leviticus 21:10) and that the fathers of their families as well were not to do so (Leviticus 21:5).

That is why they regarded baldness as such an immense disgrace, as we can tell from the following passages:

> There will be baldness upon all heads, and every beard will be cut off. (Isaiah 15:2; Jeremiah 48:37)

> There will be shame upon all faces and baldness on all heads. (Ezekiel 7:18)

> Every head was made bald and every shoulder hairless. (Ezekiel 29:18)

> I will put sackcloth around all waists and baldness upon every head. (Amos 8:10)

> Make yourself bald and cut off your hair because of your precious children; make yourself still more bald, because they have left you and gone into exile. (Micah 1:16)

Here making yourself bald and making yourself still more bald means distorting truths of the Word in its outermost forms. Once they have been distorted, as was done by Jews, the whole Word is ruined, because the outermost forms of the Word are what it rests on and what holds it up. In fact, every word in it is a base and support for the Word's heavenly and spiritual truths.

Since a head of hair means truth in its outermost forms, in the spiritual world everyone who trivializes the Word and distorts its literal meaning looks bald; but those who respect and love it have good-looking hair. On this, see §49 below.

The Word in its outermost or earthly meaning, which is its literal meaning, is also meant by the wall of the holy Jerusalem, which was made of jasper, by the foundations of the wall, which were precious stones, as well as by the gates, which were pearls (Revelation 21:18–21). This is because Jerusalem means the church in regard to its teachings. There will be more on this, though, under the next heading [§43]. We may now conclude from what has been presented that the literal meaning of the

Word, which is earthly, is the foundation, container, and support of its inner meanings, which are a spiritual meaning and a heavenly meaning.

Divine Truth, in All Its Fullness, Holiness, and Power, Is Present in the Literal Meaning of the Word

37 THE reason the Word is in its fullness, holiness, and power in the literal meaning is that the two prior or deeper meanings that are called spiritual and heavenly are together in the earthly meaning, which is the literal meaning, as explained in §31 above. Now I need to state briefly how they are together.

38 In heaven and in the world we find sequential arrangement and simultaneous arrangement. In sequential arrangement, one thing replaces and follows another, from the highest to the lowest. In simultaneous arrangement, though, one thing adjoins another, from the innermost to the outermost. The sequential arrangement is like a column with steps from top to bottom, while the simultaneous arrangement is like a composite object that forms a series of concentric circles [that radiate] from its center to its outer surfaces.

Next I need to explain how the sequential arrangement comes to be a simultaneous arrangement on the outermost level. It comes about like this. The highest elements of the sequential arrangement become the innermost elements of the simultaneous arrangement, and the lowest elements of the sequential arrangement become the outermost elements of the simultaneous arrangement. It is as though the column of steps collapsed and became a tightly fitted body on one level.[227]

[2] That is how the sequential becomes the simultaneous; and this holds for absolutely everything in the earthly world and absolutely everything in the spiritual world, since there is something first, something

intermediate, and something last everywhere, and what is first stretches toward its final form, passing through what is intermediate to reach it.

Now for the Word. What is heavenly, what is spiritual, and what is earthly emanate from the Lord sequentially, and they exist on the last level in a simultaneous arrangement. This means that now the heavenly and spiritual meanings of the Word are together within its earthly meaning.

Once this is grasped, we can see how the earthly meaning of the Word, which is its literal meaning, is the foundation, container, and support of its spiritual and heavenly meanings, and how divine goodness and divine truth are present in their fullness, holiness, and power in the literal meaning of the Word.

We can tell from this that in its literal meaning the Word is really the Word. There is spirit and life within; the spiritual meaning is its spirit and the heavenly meaning is its life. This is what the Lord said: "The words that I speak to you are spirit and are life" (John 6:63). The Lord said his words to the world and said them in their earthly meaning.

Apart from the earthly meaning, which is the literal meaning, the spiritual and heavenly meanings are not the Word; [without it] they are like a spirit and life without a body—and as just noted in §33, like a palace that has no foundation to rest on.

To a considerable extent, the truths of the literal meaning of the Word are not bare truths but are semblances of truth; like similes and comparisons, they are drawn from the kinds of things that are in the physical world and are therefore adapted and fitted to the comprehension of uneducated people and children.[228] Since they are correspondences, though, they are receptacles and dwelling places for genuine truth, like containers that gather in and hold something the way a crystal goblet holds a fine wine, or a silver plate holds gourmet food. They are like garments that serve as clothing, whether swaddling clothes for babies or attractive dresses for young women. They are also like the information in the earthly mind that comprehends within itself the perceptions of the spiritual self and its affection for truth.

The actual bare truths that are gathered in, contained, clothed, and comprehended are in the Word's spiritual meaning; and the bare goodness is in its heavenly meaning.

[2] However, this needs illustrations from the Word. Jesus said,

> Woe to you, scribes and Pharisees, because you cleanse the outside of the cup and the plate, but inside they are full of extortion and excess.

> Blind Pharisee, cleanse the inside of the cup and the plate first, so that the outside of them may be clean as well. (Matthew 23:25, 26)

The Lord said this using terms from the outermost level, which serve as containers. He said "the cup and the plate"—the cup meaning wine and the wine meaning the truth contained in the Word, the plate meaning food and the food meaning the goodness contained in the Word. Cleansing the inside of the cup and the plate means purifying what lies within us, matters of our will and thought and therefore of our love and faith, by means of the Word. The outside becoming clean by cleansing the inside means the consequent purification of our outer selves—our actions and speech, that is, since these have their essence from what lies within.

[3] Again, Jesus said,

> There was a certain rich man who was clothed in purple and fine linen and indulged himself in glorious feasting every day; and there was a poor man named Lazarus, full of sores, who was laid on his doorstep. (Luke 16:19, 20)

Here too the Lord was speaking in earthly terms that were correspondences and that contained spiritual realities. The rich man means the Jewish people, who are called "rich" because they have the Word, in which there is spiritual wealth. The purple and fine linen of his clothing means what is good and true in the Word, the purple meaning what is good in it, and the fine linen what is true. Indulging in glorious feasting every day means a delight in owning and reading it. The poor man Lazarus means the Gentiles who did not have the Word. Their being scorned and rejected by the Jews is meant by Lazarus being full of sores and laid on the rich man's doorstep.

[4] The reason Lazarus means Gentiles is that the Lord loved Gentiles the way the Lord loved the Lazarus whom he raised from the dead (John 11:3, 5, 36), who was called his friend (John 11:11), and who reclined with him at meals (John 12:2).

We can see from these two passages that the true and good statements of the literal meaning of the Word are like containers and clothing for the bare truths and goodness that lie hidden in the spiritual and heavenly meaning of the Word.

41 Since that is what the Word is like in its literal meaning, it follows that readers who are seeking divine truths see divine truths in an earthly light when they are reading the Word in enlightenment from the Lord, provided their faith is that at heart the Word is divinely holy; and especially if they have a basic trust that this quality of the Word is the result of its spiritual and heavenly meaning. This is because heaven's light, the light that shows us the spiritual meaning of the Word, flows into the earthly light that shows us the literal meaning of the Word and enlightens that mental function that we call our reasoning powers, causing them to see and recognize where divine truths stand out and where they lie hidden. These insights flow in with heaven's light for some people, sometimes even when they are not aware of it.[229]

Since at the heart of its inmost level our Word is like a flame that ignites us because of its heavenly meaning, and since at the heart of its intermediate level it is like a light that enlightens us because of its spiritual meaning, at the heart of its outermost level it is like a ruby and a diamond because of its earthly meaning, which contains both of the deeper ones. It is like a ruby because of its heavenly flame and like a diamond because of its spiritual light.

Since that is the nature of the Word in its literal meaning because of the way light shines through it, the Word's literal meaning is meant by *the foundations of the wall of Jerusalem* [Revelation 21:14, 19], by *the Urim and Thummim* of Aaron's breastplate [Exodus 28:30; Leviticus 8:8], by the *Garden of Eden* where the king of Tyre lived [Ezekiel 28:12–13], as well as by *the curtains and veils of the tabernacle* [Exodus 26:1–13; 36:8–17] and the *decorated surfaces inside the Jerusalem temple* [1 Kings 6–7]; while the Word in its essential glory is meant by *the Lord when he was transfigured* [Matthew 17:2; Mark 9:2].

As for *the truths of the literal meaning of the Word being meant by the foundations of the wall of the New Jerusalem in Revelation 21*, this follows from the fact that the New Jerusalem means a new church in regard to its teachings, as demonstrated in *Teachings on the Lord* 63 and 64. So the wall and its foundations must mean the outer level of the Word, which is its literal meaning. This, in fact, is the source of each body of teaching, and through that body of teaching, the source of the church; and it is like a wall with its foundations, which encloses and protects the city.

This is what we read in Revelation about the wall of the New Jerusalem and its foundations:

> The angel measured the wall of the city Jerusalem: one hundred and forty-four cubits, which is the measure of a human being, that is, of an angel. And the wall had twelve foundations, adorned with precious stones of every kind. The first foundation was jasper, the second sapphire, the

third chalcedony, the fourth emerald, the fifth onyx, the sixth sardius, the seventh chrysolite, the eighth beryl, the ninth topaz, the tenth chrysoprase, the eleventh jacinth, and the twelfth amethyst. (Revelation 21:17, 18, 19, 20)

The number one hundred and forty-four means all the true and good elements of the church that arise from its teachings, which are drawn from the literal meaning of the Word. Twelve means much the same. A human being means understanding; an angel means divine truth as the source of understanding; the measure means the quality of that [understanding and truth]; the wall and its foundations mean the literal meaning of the Word; precious stones mean the elements of truth and goodness contained and carefully arranged in the Word, which are the source of a body of teaching and through that teaching, the source of the church.

44 *The good and true elements of the literal meaning of the Word are meant by the Urim and Thummim.*

The Urim and Thummim[230] were on the ephod of Aaron, whose priesthood represented the Lord's divine goodness and his work of salvation. The sacred garments of priesthood represented the divine truth that arises from divine goodness. The ephod represented divine truth in its outermost form and therefore the Word in its literal meaning because this, as noted above [§§1–4, 6:2, 27–36, 38:2], is divine truth in its outermost form. So the twelve precious stones with the names of the twelve tribes of Israel, which were the Urim and Thummim, mean the complete assemblage of divine truths arising from divine goodness. [2] This is what we read in Moses:

> They shall make an ephod of blue, purple, and double-dyed scarlet [thread], and fine woven linen. Then they shall make a breastplate of judgment matching the work of the ephod. And you shall put settings of stones in it, four rows of stones: carnelian, topaz, and emerald, the first row; chrysoprase, sapphire, and diamond, the second row; jacinth, agate, and amethyst, the third row; and beryl, sardius, and jasper, the fourth row. The stones shall have the names of the sons of Israel, [like] the engravings of a signet, each one with its own name; they shall be according to the twelve tribes. Aaron shall wear the Urim and Thummim on the breastplate of judgment, and they shall be over Aaron's heart when he goes in before Jehovah. (Exodus 28:6, 15–21, 30)

[3] I have explained in the appropriate chapter of *Secrets of Heaven*[231] [§§9819–9966] the meaning of Aaron's garments—the ephod, the robe, the tunic, the turban, and the belt. There it is shown that the ephod represented

divine truth in its outermost form; the precious stones represented truths from which light shines because they teach what is good; the twelve precious stones represented all the truths, in the right arrangement, that shine in their outermost form because good actions from love are what they teach; the twelve tribes of Israel represented all aspects of the church; the breastplate represented divine truth that comes from divine goodness; and the Urim and Thummim represented the radiance of divine truth that comes from divine goodness, in its outermost forms. In fact, in the language of angels, "Urim" means shining fire and "Thummim" means radiance. (In Hebrew the latter means "wholeness".) It is also shown there that oracular answers were given by variations in the light accompanied by silently projected ideas or even by words that resounded aloud, and other methods.

[4] We can conclude from this that the precious stones also meant truths in the outermost meaning of the Word that come from goodness; and this is the only way oracular answers are given from heaven, because that is the meaning in which the emanating divine is fully present. By seeing precious stones and diamonds among angels and spirits in the spiritual world, I have been able to see very clearly that precious stones and diamonds mean divine truths in their outermost forms, like the truths in the literal meaning of the Word. I have seen angels wearing them and have seen gems in their jewel boxes. I have also been granted to know that they correspond to truths in outermost form—in fact, this correspondence is what causes these precious stones and diamonds to exist and to look the way they do.[232]

Since this is what diamonds and precious stones mean, John also saw them on the head of the dragon (Revelation 12:3), on the horns of the beast (Revelation 13:1), and on the whore who was sitting on the scarlet beast (Revelation 17:4). He saw them on these creatures because they meant the people of the Christian church, who have the Word.

Truths of the literal meaning of the Word are meant by the precious stones in the Garden of Eden where the king of Tyre was said to live, according to Ezekiel.

We read in Ezekiel,

> O king of Tyre, you had sealed your full measure and were full of wisdom and perfect in beauty. You were in Eden, the garden of God. Every precious stone was your covering—ruby, topaz, and diamond; beryl, sardonyx, and jasper; sapphire, chrysoprase, and emerald; and gold. (Ezekiel 28:12, 13)

Tyre in the Word means knowledge of what is true and what is good; a king means what is true in the church; the Garden of Eden means wisdom and understanding from the Word; precious stones mean truths from which light shines because they teach what is good—the kind we have in the literal meaning of the Word—and since this is what these stones mean, they are called its covering. On the literal meaning as the covering of the deeper levels of the Word, see under the preceding heading [§33; see also §40].

46. *The literal meaning of the Word is symbolized by the veils and curtains of the tabernacle.*

The tabernacle represented heaven and the church, which is why its form was outlined by Jehovah on Mount Sinai. Because of this, everything in the tabernacle—the lampstands, the golden altar of incense, the table for the showbread—represented and therefore referred to holy matters of heaven and the church; and the most holy place, where the ark of the covenant was, represented and therefore referred to the very heart of heaven and the church. Further, the actual law[233] written on the two stone tablets and kept in the ark meant the Lord as the Word. Now, since outer things get their essence from inner things, and both outer and inner things get their essence from the very center, which in this instance was the law, everything in the tabernacle also represented and referred to the holy contents of the Word. It then follows that the outermost features of the tabernacle, the veils and curtains that were coverings and enclosures, meant the outermost features of the Word, which are the true and good elements of its literal meaning. Because this is what they meant, *all the curtains and veils were made of fine linen tightly woven, and of blue, purple, and double-dyed scarlet [thread], [and were embroidered] with angel guardians* (Exodus 26:1, 31, 36).

The general and specific symbolism and meaning of the tabernacle and everything in it has been explained in the treatment of this chapter in *Secrets of Heaven* [9593–9692]. It is explained there that the curtains and veils represented outward features of the church and therefore also outward features of the Word. The linen or fine linen meant truth of a spiritual origin, blue meant truth of a heavenly origin, purple meant heavenly goodness, double-dyed scarlet meant spiritual goodness, and angel guardians meant protection for the inner contents of the Word.

47. *The outer attributes of the Word, which are its literal meaning, are represented by the decorated surfaces inside the Jerusalem temple.*

This is because the Temple in Jerusalem represented the same things as the tabernacle did—heaven and the church, that is, and therefore also the Word.

The Lord himself tells us in John that the Temple in Jerusalem meant his divine-human nature:

> "Destroy this temple, and in three days I will raise it up." He was speaking of the temple of his body. (John 2:19, 21)

And when something means the Lord it also means the Word, because the Lord is the Word. Now, since the inner contents of the Temple represented the inner attributes of heaven and of the church and therefore of the Word as well, so too the decorated surfaces inside the Temple represented and referred to the outer attributes of heaven and of the church and therefore of the Word as well, which are the elements of its literal meaning.

We read of the Temple and its decorated surfaces inside that it was built of whole uncut stones and was paneled on the inside with cedar, and that all its interior walls were carved with angel guardians, palm trees, and open flowers, and its floor was overlaid with gold (1 Kings 6:7, 9, 29, 30), all referring to the outer attributes of the Word, which are the holy features of its literal meaning.

The Word in its glory was represented by the Lord when he was transfigured.
We read of the Lord, when he was transfigured in the presence of Peter, James, and John, that his face shone like the sun and his clothing became like light; that Moses and Elijah appeared, talking with him; that a bright cloud overshadowed the disciples; and that a voice was heard coming from the cloud, saying, "This is my beloved Son. Hear him" (Matthew 17:1–5).

I have been taught that at this time the Lord represented the Word. His face, which shone like the sun, represented his divine goodness; his clothing, which became like light, represented his divine truth; Moses and Elijah represented the historical and prophetic books of the Word—Moses, broadly, the books written by him and by extension the historical books, and Elijah the books of the prophets; the bright cloud that overshadowed the disciples meant the Word in its literal meaning. So it was from this that they heard the voice say, "This is my beloved Son. Hear him." This is because all proclamations and answers from heaven, without exception, come about by means of outermost forms, the kind we

49 Up to this point I have shown that in its earthly or literal meaning the Word is in its holiness and fullness. I now need to explain that in its literal meaning the Word is also in its *power.*

You can tell the amount and the nature of the power of divine truth both in the heavens and on earth from what has been said about the power of heaven's angels in *Heaven and Hell* 228–233. The power of divine truth is exercised primarily against whatever is false and evil and therefore against the hells.[234] These need to be resisted by the use of truths from the literal meaning of the Word. The Lord also has power to save us by means of whatever truth we have, because we are reformed and reborn by means of truths from the literal meaning of the Word; and we are then rescued from hell and brought into heaven. The Lord assumed this power in his divine-human nature as well after he fulfilled all things of the Word even to the last. [2] That is why the Lord said to the chief priest, when he was about to fulfill what remained by suffering on the cross, "Hereafter you will see the Son of Humanity sitting at the right hand of power and coming in the clouds of heaven" (Matthew 26:64; Mark 14:62). The Son of Humanity is the Lord as the Word; the clouds of heaven are the Word in its literal meaning; sitting at the right hand of God is omnipotence by means of the Word (see also Mark 16:19).[235]

In the Jewish church, the Lord's power through the outermost forms of truth was represented by the Nazirites and by Samson, who is described as a Nazirite from his mother's womb and whose power was associated with his hair. "Nazirite" and "Naziriteship" also mean hair.[236] [3] Samson made this clear when he said, "No razor has come upon my head, because I [have been] a Nazirite from my mother's womb. If I am shorn, then my strength will leave me and I will become weak, and will be like anyone else" (Judges 16:17). No one could know why Naziriteship with its reference to hair was instituted, and therefore why Samson got his strength from his hair, except by knowing the meaning a head has in the Word. Heads mean the heavenly wisdom angels and people receive from the Lord by means of divine truth. So the hair of the head means heavenly wisdom in its outermost forms and also divine truth in its outermost forms.

[4] Since this is the meaning of hair because of its correspondence with heavenly realities, the command to the Nazirites was that they should not shave the hair of their heads, because this was the Naziriteship of God upon their heads (Numbers 6:1–21); so there was also the command that the high

priest and his sons were not to shave their heads or they would die and wrath would fall upon the whole house of Israel (Leviticus 10:6).

[5] Since hair was holy because of this meaning (which comes from its correspondence), the Son of Humanity, the Lord as the Word, was described as having hair that "was white like wool, as white as snow" (Revelation 1:14), and something similar is said of the Ancient of Days[237] (Daniel 7:9). See also what is said on this subject in §35 above.

In short, divine truth or the Word has power in the literal meaning because that is where the Word is in its fullness and because that is where angels from both of the Lord's kingdoms come together with people in this world.

The Church's Body of Teaching Is to Be Drawn from the Literal Meaning of the Word and Is to Be Supported by It

THE preceding chapter was devoted to showing that in its literal meaning the Word is in its fullness, holiness, and power; and since the Lord is the Word (because he is everything in the Word), it follows that the Lord is most present in that meaning and that he teaches and enlightens us through it.

I need to present this, though, in the following sequence.

1. The Word is not understandable without a body of teaching.
2. A body of teaching must be drawn from the literal meaning of the Word.
3. However, the divine truth that a body of teaching should have can be seen only when we are being enlightened by the Lord.

1. *The Word is not understandable without a body of teaching.* This is because in its literal meaning the Word is entirely made up of correspondences,[238] to allow spiritual and heavenly matters to be gathered within it in such a way that each word can be their container and support. That is

why in many passages the literal meaning is not made up of bare truths but of clothed truths, which we may call semblances of truth. Many of them are adapted to the comprehension of ordinary people who do not raise their thoughts above what they can see with their eyes. There are other passages where there seem to be contradictions, though there are no contradictions in the Word when it is seen in its own light. Then too, there are places in the prophets where we find collections of personal names and place-names that make no sense to us—see the examples in §15 above.

Since that is what the literal meaning of the Word is like, it stands to reason that it cannot be understood without a body of teaching.

[2] Some examples may serve to illustrate this. It says that Jehovah repents (Exodus 32:12, 14; Jonah 3:9; 4:2). It also says that Jehovah does not repent (Numbers 23:19; 1 Samuel 15:29). Without a body of teaching, these statements do not agree.

It says that Jehovah visits the iniquities of the parents on the children to the third and fourth generation (Numbers 14:18), and it says that parents will not be put to death for their children and children will not be put to death for their parents, but each will die in his or her own sin (Deuteronomy 24:16). Seen in the light of a body of teaching, these statements do not disagree but agree.

[3] Jesus said,

> Ask, and it will be given to you; seek, and you will find; knock, and it will be opened to you. Everyone who asks receives, those who seek find, and to those who knock it will be opened. (Matthew 7:7, 8; 21:21, 22)

In the absence of a body of teaching, people would believe that everyone's request is granted, but a body of teaching yields the belief that we are given whatever we ask if we ask it not on our own behalf but on the Lord's. That is in fact what the Lord tells us:

> If you abide in me and my words abide in you, you will ask for whatever you want and it will be done for you. (John 15:7)

[4] The Lord says "Blessed are the poor, because theirs is the kingdom of God" (Luke 6:20). Without a body of teaching, we might think that heaven belongs to the poor and not to the rich. A body of teaching instructs us, though, that this means those who are poor *in spirit,* for the Lord said,

> Blessed are the poor in spirit, because theirs is the kingdom of the heavens. (Matthew 5:3)

[5] The Lord says,

> Do not judge, or you will be judged; with the same judgment you pass [on others] you yourself will be judged. (Matthew 7:1, 2; Luke 6:37)

In the absence of a body of teaching, this could be used to support the assertion that we should not say that an evil act is evil or judge that an evil person is evil. A body of teaching, though, tells us that it is permissible to pass judgment if we do so in an upright, righteous way. In fact, the Lord says,

> Judge with righteous judgment. (John 7:24)

[6] Jesus says,

> Do not be called teacher, because one is your Teacher: Christ. You should not call anyone on earth your father, because you have one Father, and he is in the heavens. You should not be called masters, because one is your Master: Christ. (Matthew 23:8, 9, 10)

In the absence of a body of teaching, it would turn out that it was wrong to call anyone a teacher or a father or a master; but from a body of teaching we come to know that this is permissible in an earthly sense but not in a spiritual sense.

[7] Jesus said to the disciples,

> When the Son of Humanity sits on the throne of his glory, you will also sit on twelve thrones, judging the twelve tribes of Israel. (Matthew 19:28)

These words could lead us to believe that the Lord's disciples will be passing judgment, when quite the contrary, they cannot judge anyone. So a body of teaching unveils this mystery by explaining that only the Lord, who is omniscient and knows the hearts of all, will judge and can judge, and that his twelve disciples mean the church in the sense of all the true and good principles that it has received from the Lord through the Word. A body of teaching leads us to the conclusion that these principles will judge everyone, which follows from what the Lord says in John 3:17, 18 and 12:47, 48.[239]

[8] People who read the Word without the aid of a body of teaching do not know how to make sense out of what it says in the prophets about the Jewish nation and Jerusalem, namely, that the church will abide in

that nation and that its seat will be in that city forever. Take the following statements, for example.

> Jehovah will visit his flock, the house of Judah, and transform them into a glorious war horse; from Judah will come the cornerstone, from Judah the tent peg, from Judah the battle bow. (Zechariah 10:3, 4)

> Behold, I am coming to dwell in your midst. Jehovah will make Judah his inheritance and will again choose Jerusalem. (Zechariah 2:10, 11, 12)

> On that day it will happen that the mountains will drip with new wine and the hills will flow with milk; and Judah will abide forever, and Jerusalem from generation to generation. (Joel 3:18, 20)

> Behold, the days are coming in which I will sow the house of Israel and the house of Judah with the seed of humankind, and in which I will make a new covenant with the house of Israel and with the house of Judah. This will be the covenant: I will put my law in their midst and I will write it on their heart, and I will become their God and they will become my people. (Jeremiah 31:27, 31, 33)

> On that day ten men from every language of the nations will take hold of the hem of a man of Judah and say, "We will go with you, because we have heard that God is with you." (Zechariah 8:23)

There are other passages of the same nature, such as Isaiah 44:24, 26; 49:22, 23; 65:18; 66:20, 22; Jeremiah 3:18; 23:5; 50:19, 20; Nahum 1:15; Malachi 3:4. In these passages the subject is the Lord's Coming and what will happen at that time.

[9] However, it says something very different in any number of other passages, of which I will cite only the following:

> I will hide my face from them. I will see what their posterity is, for they are a perverse generation, children in whom there is no faithfulness. I have said, "I will cast them into the most remote corners, I will make them cease from human memory," for they are a nation devoid of counsel, and they have no understanding. Their vine is from the vine of Sodom and the fields of Gomorrah. Their grapes are grapes of gall; their clusters are bitter. Their wine is the venom of dragons and the cruel gall of poisonous snakes. All this is hidden with me, locked away in my treasuries. Vengeance and retribution belong to me. (Deuteronomy 32:20–35)

These words were spoken about that nation, and there are similar statements elsewhere, as in Isaiah 3:1, 2, 8; 5:3–6; Deuteronomy 9:5, 6; Matthew

12:39; 23:27, 28; John 8:44; and all through Jeremiah and Ezekiel. All the same, these statements that seem to contradict each other turn out to be in agreement in the light of a body of teaching, which tells us that Israel and Judah in the Word do not mean Israel and Judah but the church in each of two senses—one in which it lies in ruins and the other in which it is to be restored by the Lord. There are other contrasts like this in the Word that enable us to see that the Word cannot be understood apart from a body of teaching.

We can tell from all this that people who read the Word without a body of teaching or who do not get themselves a body of teaching from the Word are in complete darkness about truth. Their minds are wandering and unstable, prone to error and liable to heresies. Such people will in fact embrace heresies if those heresies have gained any popularity or authority and their own reputation is therefore not in danger. For them the Word is like a lampstand without a lamp, and while they seem to be seeing a great many things in their darkness, they actually see practically nothing because a body of teaching is the only lamp. I have seen people like this examined by angels, and it was found that they can use the Word to justify whatever they choose; and the things they justify are those that appeal to their self-centeredness and their love for people who are on their side. I have also seen them stripped of their clothing, a sign of their lack of truths. In that world, truths are clothing.

2. *A body of teaching must be drawn from the literal meaning of the Word and supported by it.* This is because there and only there the Lord is present with us, enlightening us and teaching us the truths of the church. Further, the Lord never does anything in a way that is less than complete, and it is in its literal meaning that the Word is in its fullness, as explained above [§§37–49]. That is why a body of teaching must be drawn from the literal meaning.

The reason the Word is not only understood but also shines with the aid of a body of teaching is that the Word is not understandable apart from a body of teaching but is like a lampstand with no lamp, as just noted [§52]. So the Word understood by means of a body of teaching is like a lampstand with a burning lamp on it. We then see more than we had seen before and understand what we had not understood before. Things that are obscure and contradictory we either do not see and ignore or we see and explain in such a way that they harmonize with our body of teaching.

The experience of the Christian world bears witness to the fact that people see the Word through their body of teaching and explain it from that perspective. Obviously, all Protestants see the Word in the light of their teachings and explain it accordingly. Catholics too see it and explain it in the light of their teachings, and Jews see it and explain it in the light of theirs. A body of false teaching yields false beliefs, and a body of true teaching yields true beliefs. We can therefore see that a body of true teaching is like a light in the darkness and like signposts along the way.

However, our body of teaching must not only be drawn from the literal meaning of the Word, it must be supported by it as well, since if it is not supported by it, the truth of our body of teaching would seem to contain only our own intelligence and none of the Lord's divine wisdom. That would make our body of teaching a castle in the air and not on the ground, a castle with no foundation.

55. A body of teaching made up of genuine truth can actually be drawn entirely from the literal meaning of the Word because in that meaning the Word is like a clothed person whose hands and face are bare. Everything that has to do with how we live and therefore with our salvation is bare, while the rest is clothed; and in many places where the meaning is clothed it shows through like a face seen through a thin veil. As the truths of the Word are multiplied by being loved and in this way gain coherence, they shine through their clothing more and more clearly and become more visible. A body of teaching is the means to this too.

56. People may believe that a body of genuinely true teaching can be acquired by the use of the spiritual meaning of the Word, the meaning that comes through a knowledge of correspondences. This is not how we develop a body of teaching, though. It is only how we illustrate and reinforce it, since, as already noted in §26, no one gains access to spiritual meaning through correspondences without first being focused on genuine truths as a result of a body of teaching. People who are not first focused on genuine truths can distort the meaning of the Word by the use of a few familiar correspondences, connecting and interpreting them with a view to supporting whatever is lodged in their minds as a result of their preconceptions.

Not only that, the spiritual meaning is not granted to anyone unless it is granted by the Lord alone; and it is guarded by him the way he guards heaven, because heaven is within it. Priority, then, should be given to the study of the Word in its literal meaning. It is the only ground for a body of teaching.

57. 3. *The genuine truth*[240] *that a body of teaching should have can be seen in the literal meaning of the Word only when we are being enlightened by the*

Lord. Enlightenment comes only from the Lord and for people who love truths because they are true and who put them to use in their lives. For others, there is no enlightenment in the Word.

The reason enlightenment comes only from the Lord is that the Lord is present in every bit of the Word. The reason enlightenment happens for people who love truths because they are true and who put them to use in their lives is that they are in the Lord and the Lord is in them. In fact, the Lord is his divine truth. When divine truth is loved because it is divine truth (and it is loved when it is put to use), then the Lord is within it for us.

This is actually what the Lord is telling us in John:

> On that day you will know that you are in me and I am in you. The people who love me are those who have my commandments and do them; and I will love them and will manifest myself to them. I will come to them and make a home with them. (John 14:20, 21, 23)

And in Matthew:

> Blessed are the pure in heart, because they will see God. (Matthew 5:8)

These are the people who are in enlightenment when they read the Word, the people for whom the Word shines or glows.

The reason the Word shines or glows for them is that there is spiritual and heavenly meaning in the details of the Word, and these meanings are in heaven's light. So through these meanings and through their light the Lord flows into the earthly meaning and into its light for us. As a result, we recognize what is true because of an inner perception that enables us to see it in our thinking. This happens whenever we desire the truth because it is true. So this desire gives rise to perception and this perception gives rise to thought; the result is the acknowledgment we refer to as faith.

I need to say more about this, though, in the next chapter, on the Lord's union with us through the Word [§§62–69].

The first task [of those who seek enlightenment when they read the Word] is to put together a body of teaching for themselves from the literal meaning of the Word. That is how they light a lamp in order to go further. Once they have put together a body of teaching and lit the lamp, they see the Word in the light of that lamp.

However, people who have not put together a body of teaching for themselves first look to see whether the theological perspective offered by others and generally accepted does in fact agree with the Word; and they accept what agrees and dissent from what does not. That is how they form their body of teaching, and through their body of teaching, their faith.

This [enlightenment] happens, though, only for people who are able to contemplate things without being distracted by their professional responsibilities in this world. If they love truths because they are true and put them to use in their lives, they have enlightenment from the Lord, and other people whose lives are to any degree guided by truths can learn from them.

60 It is very different for us if we read the Word with a body of false religious teaching in our mind, and even more different if we use the Word to support those teachings and then focus on earthly wealth or our own glory. Then it is as though the truth of the Word were in the shadow of night and what is false were in the light of day. What we read is true, but we do not see it; and if we see even a shadow of the truth we distort it. We are then the people of whom the Lord said that they have eyes, but they do not see, and ears, but they do not understand (Matthew 13:14, 15). This is because nothing blinds us more completely than our self-importance and our convincing ourselves of what is false. Our self-importance is our infatuation with ourselves and our consequent pride in our intelligence; and our convincing ourselves of what is false is a darkness that pretends to be light. Our light in that case is entirely earthly, and our sight is like that of someone who sees ghosts in the dark.

61 I have been granted the opportunity to talk with any number of individuals after their death who had believed they were going to shine like stars in heaven[241] because, they said, they had revered the Word, had read it through time and again, and had gained much from their reading that served to support the dogmas of their faith. All this led to their being celebrated as scholars, which in turn led them to believe they would become Michaels and Raphaels.[242] [2] However, many of them were examined to find out what love had inspired their study of the Word, and it turned out that for some it was self-infatuation, a desire to look important in the eyes of the world and therefore be revered as leaders in the church, while for others it was worldliness and a desire for wealth. When they were asked what they had learned from the Word, it turned out that they knew nothing that was really true. All they knew was distorted truth, which is essentially false. They were told that this was because they themselves and the world were their goals—or were what they loved the most, which amounts to the same thing—and not the Lord and heaven. If ourselves and the world are our goals, then when we read the Word

our minds are stuck on ourselves and the world. This means that our thinking is constantly focused on our self-importance, which is in darkness with respect to everything that has to do with heaven. People in this state cannot be lifted out of their self-infatuation by the Lord and thus raised up into heaven's light, so they are not open to any inflow[243] from the Lord through heaven, either.

[3] I have seen them let into heaven, but when it was found that they were lacking in truths, they were expelled. Even so, they retained the prideful conviction that they were worthy.

It worked out otherwise for individuals who studied the Word from a desire to know what was true because it was true and because it could be put to use in their lives not only for their own benefit but for the benefit of their neighbor. I have seen them raised up into heaven and therefore into the light of divine truth there; and at the same time they have been lifted up into angelic wisdom and into its happiness, which is eternal life.

By Means of the Literal Meaning of the Word We Unite with the Lord and Form a Companionship with Angels

62 THE reason we have union with the Lord through the Word is that the Word is entirely about him; and it is because of this that the Lord is its entire content and is called "the Word" [John 1:14], as was explained in *Teachings on the Lord* [§§1–2]. The reason the union takes place in the literal meaning is that this is where the Word is in its fullness, holiness, and power, as was explained previously under the appropriate heading [§§37–49]. This union is not something we can see, but it lies within our longing for what is true and our higher perception of it, so it lies within our inner love for and faith in divine truth.

63 The reason we have companionship with angels of heaven through the literal meaning is that within the literal meaning there are spiritual

and heavenly levels of meaning, and those levels are the ones on which angels are focused. Angels of the spiritual kingdom focus on the spiritual meaning of the Word and angels of the heavenly kingdom focus on the heavenly meaning. These meanings unfold from the earthly meaning of the Word, which is the literal meaning, when anyone who has become truly human[244] is absorbed in it. The unfolding is instantaneous, so the companionship is as well.

64   Abundant experience has made it clear to me that spiritual angels are focused on the spiritual meaning of the Word and that heavenly angels are focused on its heavenly meaning. I have been made aware that when I was reading the Word in its literal meaning a communication was opened with one community or another of the heavens, and that spiritual angels were understanding in a spiritual way, and heavenly angels in a heavenly way, what I was understanding in an earthly way, and that this was happening instantaneously. I have been aware of this so many thousand times that I can no longer have any doubt about it.[245]

[2] There are also spirits who live underneath the heavens who misuse this communication. What they do is repeat some things that are said in the literal meaning of the Word and promptly identify and mark the community with which communication has been effected. This too I have often seen and heard.[246]

This kind of firsthand experience has taught me that the Word in its literal meaning is a divinely granted means of union with the Lord and with heaven. On this union by means of the Word, see also what is presented in *Heaven and Hell* 303–310.

65   I need to explain briefly how this unfolding of meanings happens, but in order to understand it, we need to go back to what was said earlier, in §§6 and 38, about sequential arrangement and simultaneous arrangement— namely, that what is heavenly, what is spiritual, and what is earthly follow each other in sequence from the highest things that are in heaven to those things most remote from them in this world, and that in a simultaneous arrangement the same realities are within the most remote, which is the earthly, side by side from the innermost to the outermost. It was also explained [§38] that by the same token, the sequential meanings of the Word—the heavenly and the spiritual—are simultaneously present in the earthly meaning.

Once we grasp this, we can begin to understand how the two meanings, the spiritual and the heavenly, are unfolded from the earthly meaning when we are reading the Word. A spiritual angel will call to mind something spiritual and a heavenly angel will call to mind something heavenly.

They cannot do otherwise: the meanings have qualities that are similar in type and are in harmony with the angels' nature and essence.

[66] First, though, let me illustrate this with comparisons from the three kingdoms of nature, which we refer to as the animal, plant, and mineral kingdoms.

From *the animal kingdom:* From food, once it has been digested, the blood vessels derive and call forth their blood, the nerve fibers their juice, and the substances that are the sources of the fibers the fine fluid of the soul.[247]

From *the plant kingdom:* A tree, with its trunk, branches, leaves, and fruit, is based on its roots, and through its roots draws and calls forth from the ground a coarser sap for the trunk, branches, and leaves, a finer sap for the flesh of its fruit, and the finest for the seeds within the fruit.[248]

From *the mineral kingdom:* At various locations deep within the earth there are deposits of ore pregnant with gold, silver, and iron. From the hidden gases exhaled by the earth, the gold, silver, and iron each draw their own basic substance.[249]

[67] Now I may offer some examples to make clear how spiritual angels draw their meaning, and heavenly angels their meaning, from the earthly meaning that the Word presents to us. We may take five of the Ten Commandments as examples.

The commandment *"Honor your father and your mother"* [Exodus 20:12; Deuteronomy 5:16]. We understand "father and mother" to mean our earthly fathers and mothers and any individuals who act as fathers and mothers for us. We understand honoring them to mean admiring them and being obedient to them. A spiritual angel, though, understands "father" to mean the Lord and "mother" to mean the church; and they understand honoring to mean loving. But a heavenly angel understands "father" to mean the Lord's divine love and "mother" the Lord's divine wisdom, and honoring to mean doing what is good because of him.

[2] The commandment *"You are not to steal"* [Exodus 20:15; Deuteronomy 5:19]. We understand stealing to mean theft, cheating, or depriving others of their assets by any means. A spiritual angel understands stealing to mean using false and evil devices to deprive people of the truths of their faith and their good, caring actions. A heavenly angel, though, understands stealing to mean giving ourselves credit for what belongs to the Lord and claiming his righteousness and worth as our own.

[3] The commandment *"You are not to commit adultery"* [Exodus 20:14; Deuteronomy 5:18]. We understand committing adultery to mean the act of adultery, as well as promiscuity, indecent behavior, filthy language, and

impure thoughts. A spiritual angel understands adultery to mean perverting what is good in the Word and falsifying its truths. A heavenly angel, though, understands adultery to mean denying the divine nature of the Lord and profaning the Word.

[4] The commandment *"You are not to kill"* [Exodus 20:13; Deuteronomy 5:17]. We understand killing to mean harboring hatred as well [Matthew 5:22] and seeking revenge even as far as killing. A spiritual angel understands killing to mean playing the role of a devil and killing someone's soul [Matthew 10:28; Luke 12:5]. A heavenly angel, though, understands killing to mean hating the Lord and hating anything that belongs to the Lord.

[5] The commandment *"You are not to bear false witness"* [Exodus 20:16; Deuteronomy 5:20]. We understand bearing false witness to mean lying and slandering people as well. A spiritual angel understands bearing false witness to mean saying and persuading others to believe that something false is true and that something evil is good, and the reverse. A heavenly angel, though, understands bearing false witness to mean blasphemy against the Lord and the Word.

[6] This enables us to see how spiritual and heavenly meanings are unfolded and drawn from the earthly meaning of the Word that contains them; and strange as it may seem, angels draw these meanings out without knowing what we are thinking. Nevertheless, angels' thinking and our thinking become one because of correspondences, just as a goal, its means, and its results become one. Functionally, the goals are in the heavenly kingdom, the means in the spiritual kingdom, and the results in the earthly kingdom. This kind of union by correspondence comes from creation, and this is how we now associate with angels through the Word.

68 Another reason our companionship with angels is established through the earthly or literal meaning of the Word is that by virtue of our creation each of us has three levels of life—heavenly, spiritual, and earthly. As long as we are in this world we are focused on the earthly level, then on the spiritual level to the extent that we are intent on genuine truths, and then on the heavenly level to the extent that we are devoted to living by these truths. We do not, however, gain full access to that spiritual or heavenly level until after death. But there is more on this elsewhere.[250]

69 Since it is through the Word that we unite with the Lord and form a companionship with angels, we may conclude that the Word alone contains spirit and life, just as the Lord said:

> The words that I speak to you are spirit and are life. (John 6:63)

The water that I will give you will become a fountain of water, springing up into eternal life. (John 4:14)

Humankind does not live from bread alone but from every word that proceeds from the mouth of God. (Matthew 4:4)

Work for the food that endures to eternal life, which the Son of Humanity will give you. (John 6:27)

The Word Is in All the Heavens and Is the Source of Angelic Wisdom

UNTIL the present time, people have not known that the Word exists in heaven, and they could not know this as long as the church did not realize that angels and spirits are people just as we are in this world—like us in every respect except for the fact that they are spiritual and that everything around them has a spiritual origin, while we are earthly and everything around us has an earthly origin.[251] As long as this lay hidden there was no way to know that there was a Word in heaven as well and that it was read both by angels there and by spirits who live underneath the heavens.

But to keep this from remaining hidden forever, I have been granted companionship with angels and spirits, to talk with them, to see what their circumstances are like, and then to report many things that I have heard and seen. This reporting was done in the book *Heaven and Hell* (published in London in 1758). That will enable you to see that angels and spirits are people and that they are abundantly supplied with everything we have in this world.

On angels and spirits being people, see §§73–77 and 453–456 of that work. On their circumstances being similar to ours in this world, see §§170–190. On their also having worship of God and preaching in churches, see §§221–227. On their having written materials and books, see §§258–264; and on the Word, see §259.

71 As for the Word in heaven, it is written in a spiritual style that is completely different from an earthly style. This spiritual style of writing consists entirely of letters that have individual meanings. There are also marks over the letters that heighten the meaning.

For angels of the spiritual kingdom the letters look like typeset letters in our world; and the letters for angels of the heavenly kingdom—each of which enfolds a whole meaning—are like the ancient Hebrew letters, variously curved, with marks over and within them.

[2] Since this is what their writing is like, there are no personal or place names in their Word as there are in ours. Instead of the names there are the realities that they mean. Instead of Moses, for example, the text reads "the historical books of the Word"; for Elijah, "the prophetic books"; for Abraham, Isaac, and Jacob, "the Lord in respect to his divine nature and his divine-human nature"; for Aaron, "priesthood" and for David, "monarchy," both in reference to the Lord; for the names of the twelve sons of Jacob or the tribes of Israel, various aspects of heaven and the church, and the same for the names of the Lord's twelve disciples; for Zion and Jerusalem, the church in respect to the Word and its body of teaching drawn from the Word; for the land of Canaan, the church itself; for the cities on either side of the Jordan, various elements of the church and its teachings; and so on and so forth.

It is the same with numbers. These are not found in the Word that is in heaven either, but instead there are the realities to which the numbers in our Word correspond.[252]

We can therefore conclude that the Word in heaven is a Word that corresponds to our Word and that because of this they are one, for correspondences make unity.

72 It is wondrous that the Word in the heavens is written in such a way that ordinary people understand it simply and wise people understand it wisely. There are many marks and points over the letters that heighten the meaning, as already noted. Ordinary people pay no attention to these and do not know what they mean. The wise do pay attention to them, depending on how wise they are, even to the very wisest.

In every major community in heaven there is a copy of the Word that is written by angels inspired by the Lord, kept in that community's repository so that not a single point in it will be altered anywhere.

Our own Word is actually written like the Word in heaven, so that ordinary people understand it simply and wise people wisely, but this is accomplished in a different way.

73 The angels themselves confess that they get all their wisdom through the Word, since the amount of light they enjoy depends on how focused they are on understanding the Word. Heaven's light is divine wisdom, which is light to their eyes.

In the repository where their copy of the Word is kept, the light is flaming and brilliant, surpassing every level of light found outside it in heaven. The reason is the one already stated [§§57, 62]—the Lord is in the Word.

74 The wisdom of heavenly angels surpasses that of spiritual angels by almost as much as the wisdom of spiritual angels surpasses ours. This is because heavenly angels are focused on good, loving actions that come from the Lord, while spiritual angels are focused on truths of wisdom that come from the Lord. Wherever we find good actions that come from love, wisdom is dwelling with them. There is wisdom wherever we find truths, too, but only in an amount proportional to the presence of good actions that come from love. This is why the Word in the heavenly kingdom is written differently from the Word in the spiritual kingdom. In the version of the Word in the heavenly kingdom the letters themselves express good actions from love and the marks around them convey emotions; in the version of the Word in the spiritual kingdom the letters express truths that lead to wisdom and the marks convey insights.

75 We can tell from this what kind of wisdom lies hidden in the Word we have in this world. Within it lies all angelic wisdom, which is inexpressible. It is in fact the container of that wisdom; and we become conscious of that wisdom after death if we have been made angels by the Lord through the Word.

The Existence of the Church Rests on the Word, and Its Quality Depends on the Quality of Its Understanding of the Word

76 THERE can be no doubt that the existence of the church rests on the Word, since the Word is divine truth itself (§§1–4), the teachings of the church come from the Word (§§50–61), and our union with the Lord comes through the Word (§§62–69). However, some may doubt that our understanding of the Word is what makes the church, if only because there are people who believe that they are part of the church solely by virtue of having the Word, reading it, or hearing it from the pulpit, and by thus having acquired some knowledge of its literal meaning. They do not know how to understand a single thing in the Word, though, and some of them do not even attach much importance to the Word at all. So at this point I need to show that it is not the Word that makes the church but the way the Word is understood, and that the quality of the church depends on the quality of the understanding of the Word among the people who are in the church. This is shown by the following.

77 Whether or not the Word is the Word depends on our comprehension of it—that is, on how we understand it. If we do not understand it, we may of course call it "the Word," but for us it is not the Word.

The Word is truth depending on how it is understood, for the Word can be nontruth—it can be distorted. The Word is spirit and life depending on how we understand it, for the letter is dead if it is not understood.[253]

Since we gain truth and life depending on how we understand the Word, we also gain faith and love depending on how we understand it, because faith has to do with truth and life has to do with love.

Since the church exists by means of its faith and love and is only as good as its faith and love, it follows that a church exists by means of its understanding of the Word and is only as good as its understanding of the Word. A church is worthy if it is focused on genuine truths, unworthy if it is not focused on genuine truths, and ruined if it is focused on distorted truths.

78 To continue, the Lord is present with us and united to us through the Word because the Lord is the Word and is virtually talking with us in it. There is also the fact that the Lord is divine truth itself, and that is what the Word is.

We can see from this that the extent to which we understand the Word determines the extent to which the Lord is present with us and at the same time united to us. This is because our understanding of the Word determines the truth we possess, as well as the faith that arises from that truth. Similarly, our understanding of the Word determines the love we have, as well as the way in which we live, which arises from that love. The Lord is present with us when we read the Word; but he is united to us only when we understand what is true from the Word and only in proportion to that understanding; and to the extent that the Lord is united to us the church is within us.

And the church is indeed something within us. The church that is outside us is the church of the many who have the church within them. This is the meaning of what the Lord said to the Pharisees when they asked him when the kingdom of God was coming—"The kingdom of God is within you" (Luke 17:21). Here the kingdom of God means the Lord, and the church from him.

There are many passages in the prophets about our understanding of the Word, passages about the church, where it tells us that the church exists only where the Word is properly understood, and that the quality of a church depends on the quality of the understanding of the Word among its members. There are also many passages in the prophets that describe the church among the Israelite and Jewish people, a church that was utterly destroyed and annihilated by the distortion of the Word's meaning or message, for this is exactly what destroys a church.

[2] The name Ephraim in the prophets, especially in Hosea, symbolizes both true and false understandings of the Word, because Ephraim in the Word means the understanding of the Word in the church.[254] It is because the understanding of the Word makes a church that Ephraim is called "a precious child, and one born of delights" (Jeremiah 31:20), "the firstborn" (Jeremiah 31:9), "the strength of Jehovah's head" (Psalms 60:7; 108:8), "powerful" (Zechariah 10:7), and "filling a bow"[255] (Zechariah 9:13); and the children of Ephraim are called "armed" and "bow shooters" (Psalms 78:9). The bow means a body of teaching from the Word fighting against what is false.

So too, Ephraim was transferred to the right of Israel and blessed, and accepted in place of Reuben (Genesis 48:5, 11, and following; [1 Chronicles 5:1]). And therefore Ephraim, together with his brother Manasseh, was exalted over all by Moses in his blessing of the children of Israel in the name of their father Joseph (Deuteronomy 33:13–17).

[3] The prophets, especially Hosea, also use "Ephraim" to describe what the church is like when its understanding of the Word has been lost, as we can see from the following:

> Israel and Ephraim will stumble. Ephraim will be desolate. Ephraim is oppressed and broken in judgment. I will be like a lion to Ephraim: I will tear them and leave; I will carry them off and no one will rescue them. (Hosea 5:5, 9, 11, 14)

> What shall I do to you, Ephraim? Your holiness goes away like a cloud at dawn and like the morning dew that falls. (Hosea 6:4)

> [4] They will not dwell in the land of Jehovah: Ephraim will go back to Egypt and will eat what is unclean in Assyria. (Hosea 9:3)

The land of Jehovah is the church, Egypt is the preoccupation of the earthly self with mere facts, and Assyria is rationalizing based on those facts; all of which lead to distortion of the Word in regard to the way it is understood. That is why it says that Ephraim will go back to Egypt and will eat what is unclean in Assyria.

> [5] Ephraim feeds on the wind and chases the east wind. Every day he increases lies and devastation. He makes a covenant with Assyria, and oil is carried down into Egypt. (Hosea 12:1)

To feed on the wind, chase the east wind, and increase lies and devastation is to distort what is true and in this way destroy the church.

[6] Much the same is also meant by Ephraim's whoredom, since whoredom means distortion of the way the Word is understood—that is, distortion of its genuine truth. See the following passages:

> I know Ephraim; he has committed whoredom in every way and Israel has been defiled. (Hosea 5:3)

> I have seen something foul in the house of Israel: Ephraim has committed whoredom there, and Israel has been defiled. (Hosea 6:10)

Israel is the church itself and Ephraim is the understanding of the Word that is the source of the church and that determines its quality, so it says that Ephraim has committed whoredom and Israel has been defiled.

[7] Since the church among Jews had been completely destroyed because of its distortions, it says of Ephraim,

> Am I to give you up, Ephraim? Am I to hand you over, Israel? Like Admah? Shall I make you like Zeboiim? (Hosea 11:8)

Since the book of the prophet Hosea, from the first chapter to the last, is about the distortion of the Word and the consequent destruction of the church, and since whoredom means the distortion of truth in the church, the prophet was commanded to represent that state of the church by taking a whore as his wife and fathering children by her (chapter 1); and also by forming a relationship with a woman who was committing adultery (chapter 3).

[8] These instances have been presented so that readers may know and be assured from the Word that the quality of a church depends on the quality of the understanding of the Word in it—outstanding and priceless if its understanding comes from genuine truths from the Word, but in ruins, actually filthy, if it comes from distortions.

For further evidence that Ephraim means the understanding of the Word, and in its opposite sense a distorted understanding leading to the destruction of the church, you may check some other passages that deal with Ephraim: Hosea 4:17, 18; 7:1, 11; 8:9, 11; 9:11, 12, 13, 16; 10:11; 11:3; 12:1, 8, 14; 13:1, 8, 14; Isaiah 17:3; 28:1; Jeremiah 4:15; 31:6, 18; 50:19; Ezekiel 37:16; 48:5; Obadiah verse 19; Zechariah 9:10.

There Is a Marriage of the Lord and the Church in the Details of the Word and a Consequent Marriage of Goodness and Truth

80

UNTIL the present time, no one has seen that there is a marriage of the Lord and the church in the details of the Word and a consequent marriage of goodness and truth, and no one could see it because the spiritual meaning of the Word had not been uncovered, and without this, the marriage cannot be seen.

There are two levels of meaning in the Word that are hidden within the literal meaning, namely, a spiritual level and a heavenly level. Spiritually understood, the contents of the Word refer for the most part to the church, while understood on a heavenly level they refer for the most part to the Lord. On a spiritual level they also refer to divine truth and on a heavenly level they refer to divine goodness. As a result, this marriage is found in the literal meaning of the Word.

However, this is not apparent to anyone who does not know the meanings of words and names on the basis of the spiritual and heavenly meanings of the Word, since some words and names focus attention on what is good and some on what is true, and some include both, so unless this is realized the marriage in the details of the Word cannot be seen. That is why this mystery has not been disclosed before.

81 Because this marriage is in the details of the Word, time and again there are paired expressions in the Word that seem to be saying the same thing twice. However, they are not mere repetitions. One focuses on what is good and the other on what is true, and their combination makes a union of the two and therefore a single thing. That is actually the basis of the divinity of the Word and of its holiness, since in every divine work goodness is united to truth and truth is united to goodness.

82 I have said that there is a marriage of the Lord and the church in the details of the Word and a *consequent* marriage of goodness and truth because wherever there is a marriage of the Lord and the church there is also a marriage of goodness and truth. The latter comes from the former because when the church or its membership is focused on what is true, the Lord flows into their truths with what is good and brings those truths to life. Or to put it another way, when the church or members of the church are intelligent because of truths, then the Lord flows into their intelligence through the good they do out of love and caring, and fills their intelligence with life.

83 Each of us has two faculties of life, called understanding and will. Our understanding receives what is true and therefore receives what is wise, and our will receives what is good and therefore receives love. These must become one if we are to be part of the church; and they do become one when we form our understanding from genuine truth, to all appearances doing this ourselves, and when our will is filled with a love for doing good, which is accomplished by the Lord. In this way we have a life of what is true and a life of what is good, the life of what is true in our understanding from our will and the life of what is good in our will by means of our understanding; and this is a marriage of truth and goodness for us and a marriage of the Lord and the church for us.

But there is more on this mutual union, here called a marriage, in *Angelic Wisdom about Divine Providence*,[256] *[Angelic Wisdom] about Divine Love and Wisdom*,[257] and *[Angelic Wisdom] about Life*.[258]

84 It can seem to readers who pay attention to such things that there are paired expressions in the Word that seem to be repetitions of the same thing—brother [and companion], for example, [poor] and needy, waste and desolation, emptiness and void, enemy and foe, sin and iniquity, wrath and rage, nation and people, joy and gladness, grief and tears, justice and

judgment, and the like. They do seem to be synonyms, but they are not, since brother, poor, waste, [emptiness,] enemy, sin, wrath, nation, joy, grief, and justice describe what is good (or in an opposite sense, what is evil), while companion, needy, desolation, void, foe, iniquity, rage, people, gladness, tears, and judgment describe what is true (or in an opposite sense, what is false). It seems to a reader who is unfamiliar with this mystery that poor and needy, waste and desolation, emptiness and void, enemy and foe are the same thing, as are sin and iniquity, wrath and rage, nation and people, joy and gladness, grief and tears, justice and judgment; yet they are not the same thing. Rather they become one thing by being brought together.

[2] Many other things are paired in the Word, like fire and flame, gold and silver, bronze and iron, wood and stone, bread and water, bread and wine, purple and linen, and so on, and this is because fire, gold, bronze, wood, bread, and purple mean something good, while flame, silver, iron, stone, water, wine, and linen mean something true. In the same vein, it says that we are to love God with our whole heart and our whole soul and that God is going to create in us a new heart and a new spirit, "heart" describing the good that comes from love and "soul" the truth that comes from that good.

There are also expressions that occur alone with nothing appended because they designate both goodness and truth. These and many other expressions, though, are evident only to angels and to people who are aware of the spiritual meaning even while they are focused on the earthly meaning.

It would be a waste of time to show from the Word that there are in the Word paired expressions like these that seem like repetitions of the same thing, because that would fill many pages. To banish doubt, though, I would like to cite some passages where *judgment* and *justice* occur together, then *nation* and *people,* and then *joy* and *gladness.*

The following are passages where *judgment* and *justice* are paired:

The city used to be full of [good] *judgment; justice* used to spend its nights there. (Isaiah 1:21)

Zion will be redeemed in *justice,* and those of her who are brought back, in *judgment.* (Isaiah 1:27)

Jehovah Sabaoth will be exalted in *judgment,* and God, the Holy One, will be hallowed in *justice.* (Isaiah 5:16)

He will sit upon the throne of David and over his kingdom, to establish it in *judgment* and in *justice*. (Isaiah 9:7)

Let Jehovah be exalted, because he dwells on high and has filled the earth with *judgment* and *justice*. (Isaiah 33:5)

Jehovah says, "Watch over *judgment* and perform *justice,* for my *salvation* is at hand so that my *justice* may be revealed." (Isaiah 56:1)

As though they were a nation that did *justice* and had not abandoned the *judgment* of their God, they would ask for *judgments of justice*. (Isaiah 58:2)

Swear by the living Jehovah in *judgment* and in *justice*. (Jeremiah 4:2)

The one who glories should glory in this, that Jehovah is bringing about *judgment* and *justice* on the earth. (Jeremiah 9:24)

Do *judgment* and *justice*. Woe to those who build their house without *justice* and their upper chambers without *judgment*. Has not your father done *judgment* and *justice?* Then it will be well for him. (Jeremiah 22:3, 13, 15)

I will raise up for David a righteous branch who will rule as king and bring about *judgment* and *justice* on earth. (Jeremiah 23:5; 33:15)

If a man is righteous and has practiced *judgment* and *justice* . . . (Ezekiel 18:5)

If the ungodly turn back and practice *judgment* and *justice,* [their former deeds] will not be remembered against them. They have practiced *judgment* and *justice;* they will surely live. (Ezekiel 33:14, 16)

I will betroth myself to you forever in *justice* and *judgment,* and in *mercy* and *compassion*. (Hosea 2:19)

Let *judgment* flow down like water, and *justice* like a mighty torrent. (Amos 5:24)

You have turned *judgment* into gall and the fruit of *justice* into wormwood. (Amos 6:12)

Jehovah will plead my case and bring about a *judgment* for me. He will lead me into the light, and I will see his *justice*. (Micah 7:9)

Jehovah, your *justice* is like the mountains of God; your *judgments* are a great deep. (Psalms 36:6)

> Jehovah will bring forth his *justice* like light and *judgment* like noonday. (Psalms 37:6)
>
> Jehovah will judge his people with *justice* and his needy ones with *judgment*. (Psalms 72:2)
>
> *Justice* and *judgment* are the foundation of your throne. (Psalms 89:14)
>
> ... when I will have learned the *judgments* of your *justice*. Seven times a day I praise you for the *judgments* of your *justice*. (Psalms 119:7, 164)
>
> Gad enacts the *justice* of Jehovah and his *judgment* with Israel. (Deuteronomy 33:21)
>
> The Spirit of Truth will convict the world concerning *justice* and *judgment*. (John 16:8, 10)

There are other such passages as well.

The reason judgment and justice are mentioned so often is that the Word says "judgment" in reference to what is true and "justice" in reference to what is good; so "doing judgment and justice" also means acting on the basis of what is true and on the basis of what is good.

The reason the Word says "judgment" in reference to what is true and "justice" in reference to what is good is that the Lord's government in the spiritual kingdom is called "judgment," while the Lord's government in the heavenly kingdom is called "justice" (see *Heaven and Hell* 214–215). Because the Word says "judgment" in reference to what is true, in some passages it speaks of *truth* and *justice,* as in Isaiah 11:5, Psalms 85:11,[259] and elsewhere.

We can see more clearly from passages where it says *nations and peoples* that there are in the Word repetitions of what seems to be the same thing for the sake of the marriage of goodness and truth. See, for example, the following passages:

> Woe to a sinful *nation,* to a *people* weighed down with iniquity. (Isaiah 1:4)
>
> The *peoples* walking in darkness have seen a great light; you have multiplied the *nation*. (Isaiah 9:2, 3)
>
> Assyria is the rod of my anger. I will send him against a hypocritical *nation;* I will appoint him against the *people* of my rage. (Isaiah 10:5, 6)
>
> It will happen on that day that the *nations* will seek the root of Jesse, the one who stands as a sign for the *peoples*. (Isaiah 11:10)

Jehovah is striking the *peoples* with a plague that cannot be healed and ruling the *nations* in anger. (Isaiah 14:6)

On that day a gift will be brought to Jehovah Sabaoth—a *people* scattered and shaven and a *nation* measured and trampled. (Isaiah 18:7)

A strong *people* will honor you; a city of powerful *nations* will fear you. (Isaiah 25:3)

Jehovah will swallow up the covering that is over all *peoples* and the veil that is over all *nations*. (Isaiah 25:7)

Come near, O *nations*, and listen, O *peoples*. (Isaiah 34:1)

I have called you to be a covenant for the *people*, a light for the *nations*. (Isaiah 42:6)

Let all the *nations* be gathered together, and let the *peoples* convene. (Isaiah 43:9)

Behold, I will lift up my hand toward the *nations*, and my sign toward the *peoples*. (Isaiah 49:22)

I have made him a witness to the *peoples*, a prince and a lawgiver to the *nations*. (Isaiah 55:4, 5)

Behold, a *people* is coming from the land of the north and a great *nation* from the farthest parts of the earth. (Jeremiah 6:22)

I will no longer let you hear the slander of the *nations*, and you will not bear the reproach of the *peoples* anymore. (Ezekiel 36:15)

All *peoples* and *nations* will worship him. (Daniel 7:14)

Do not allow the *nations* to turn [your heritage] into a joke or to say among the *peoples*, "Where is their God?" (Joel 2:17)

The remnant of my *people* will plunder them and the remainder of my *nation* will possess them. (Zephaniah 2:9)

Many *peoples* and vast *nations* will come to seek Jehovah Sabaoth in Jerusalem. (Zechariah 8:22)

My eyes have seen your salvation, which you have prepared before the face of all *peoples*, a light to bring revelation to the *nations*. (Luke 2:30, 31, 32)

You have redeemed us by your blood out of every *people* and *nation*. (Revelation 5:9)

You must prophesy again about *peoples* and *nations*. (Revelation 10:11)

You will make me the head of the *nations; people* I have not known will serve me. (Psalms 18:43)

Jehovah makes the counsel of the *nations* ineffective; he overturns the thoughts of the *peoples*. (Psalms 33:10)

You are making us a byword among the *nations,* a shaking of the head among the *peoples*. (Psalms 44:14)

Jehovah will subdue *peoples* under us and *nations* under our feet. Jehovah has ruled over the *nations;* those who are willing among the *peoples* have gathered. (Psalms 47:3, 8, 9)

The *peoples* will praise you, the *nations* will be glad and rejoice, because you are going to judge the *peoples* with righteousness and lead the *nations* in the land. (Psalms 67:3, 4)

Remember me, Jehovah, in the good pleasure of your *people,* so that I may be glad in the joy of your *nations*. (Psalms 106:4, 5)

There are other passages as well.

The reason it says both nations and peoples is that "nations" means people who are focused on what is good (and in an opposite sense, on what is evil) and "peoples" means those who are focused on what is true (and in an opposite sense, on what is false). That is why those who are in the Lord's spiritual kingdom are called peoples, while those in the Lord's heavenly kingdom are called nations. The underlying reason is that everyone in the spiritual kingdom is focused on what is true and therefore on wisdom, while everyone in the heavenly kingdom is focused on what is good and therefore on love.

It is much the same in the other instances—for example, where it says *joy* it also says *gladness,* as in the following examples.

Behold *joy* and *gladness,* [people] slaughtering an ox.[260] (Isaiah 22:13)

They will obtain *joy* and *gladness;* sadness and groaning will flee. (Isaiah 35:10; 51:11)

Gladness and *joy* have been cut off from the house of our God. (Joel 1:16)

There will be an end to the voice of *joy* and the voice of *gladness*. (Jeremiah 7:34; 25:10)

The fast of the tenth month will become *joy* and *gladness* for the house of Judah. (Zechariah 8:19)

So that we may *rejoice* all our days, make us *glad*. (Psalms 90:14, 15)

Be *glad* in Jerusalem; *rejoice* in her. (Isaiah 66:10)

Rejoice and be *glad,* O daughter of Edom. (Lamentations 4:21)

Let the heavens be *glad* and the earth *rejoice*. (Psalms 96:11)

They will make me hear *joy* and *gladness*. (Psalms 51:8)

Joy and *gladness* will be found in Zion, praise and the voice of song. (Isaiah 51:3)

You will have *gladness,* and many will *rejoice* over his birth. (Luke 1:14)

I will make the voice of *joy* and the voice of *gladness* cease, the voice of the bridegroom and the voice of the bride. (Jeremiah 7:34; 16:9; 25:10)

Once again the voice of *joy* and the voice of *gladness* will be heard in this place, and the voice of the bridegroom and the voice of the bride. (Jeremiah 33:10, 11)

There are other passages as well.

[2] The reason it says both "joy" and "gladness" is that joy has to do with what is good and gladness with what is true, or joy has to do with love and gladness with wisdom. The underlying cause is that joy is of the heart and gladness is of the spirit, or joy arises from our will and gladness from our understanding.

We can see that this also involves a marriage of the Lord and the church from the fact that it speaks of "the voice of joy and the voice of gladness, the voice of the bridegroom and the voice of the bride" (Jeremiah 7:34; 16:9; 25:10; 33:10, 11), and the Lord is the bridegroom and the church is the bride. On the Lord as the bridegroom, see Matthew 9:15; Mark 2:19, 20; Luke 5:34, 35; and on the church as the bride, see Revelation 21:2, 9; 22:17. That is why John the Baptist said, "The bridegroom is the one who has the bride" (John 3:29).

88 Because of the marriage of the Lord with the church in the details of the Word (or because of the marriage of divine goodness and divine truth, which is the same thing), in many passages it says "Jehovah" and

"God," and "Jehovah" and "the Holy One of Israel" as though they were two when in fact they are one.[261] In fact, "Jehovah" means the Lord with respect to his divine goodness and "God" [and "the Holy One of Israel"][262] mean the Lord with respect to his divine truth. See *Teachings on the Lord* 34, 38, and 46 for many occurrences in the Word of "Jehovah" and "God" and of "Jehovah" and "the Holy One of Israel" when the intent is to communicate that the two are one, who is the Lord.

Since there is a marriage of the Lord and the church throughout the Word, we can be quite sure that absolutely everything in the Word is about the Lord, as I undertook to show in §§1–7 of *Teachings on the Lord*. The church, which is also the subject, is the Lord as well, since the Lord teaches that members of the church are in him and that he is in them (John 6:56; 14:20, 21; 15:5, 7).

Since we are dealing here with the divinity and holiness of the Word, I may add an interesting story to what has just been said.

On one occasion a little sheet of paper was sent down to me from heaven. It was inscribed with Hebrew letters, but written in the way the ancients used to write. Letters that today are largely straight were curved then and had little tips that turned upward. Angels who were with me at the time said that they found complete meanings in the letters themselves. They derived these meanings especially from the curvature of the lines and of the tips of the letters. They went on to explain what the letters meant individually and in combination, saying the *h* that was added to the names of Abram and Sarai [Genesis 17:5, 15] meant what was infinite and eternal. They also explained to me the meaning of the Word in Psalms 32:2[263] on the basis of the letters alone. Taken all together, the meaning of the letters was that *the Lord is also compassionate to people who do evil.*

[2] The angels told me that the writing in the third heaven consists of letters that are bent and curved in various ways, each of which has a specific meaning. The vowels in that writing indicate sounds that correspond to the feelings expressed. Angels in that heaven cannot pronounce the vowel sounds of *i* and *e,* so instead they use *y* and *eu.* The vowel sounds of *a, o,* and *u* are in common use among them because these give a full sound.[264] They also said that they do not pronounce any consonants as hard, they only pronounce them as soft, which is why some Hebrew letters have dots in them to signal that they are to be pronounced [as hard, but no dots when they are to be pronounced] as soft.[265] The angels said that [pronouncing] these letters as hard was a practice in the spiritual

heaven because there they are focused on what is true, and truth is open to what is hard. The goodness that is the focus of angels of the heavenly kingdom, or the third heaven, is not open to what is hard.

The angels [with me] said that the written Word they have also has curved letters with little tips or strokes that add to the meaning.[266] I could see from this the meaning of the Lord's words,

> Not one little letter or the tip of one letter will pass from the law until all of it is fulfilled. (Matthew 5:18)

and

> It is easier for heaven and earth to pass away than for the tip of one letter of the law to fall. (Luke 16:17)

It Is Possible to Wrench Heretical Ideas from the Literal Meaning of the Word, but What Is Damning Is to Convince Ourselves [That They Are True]

91 I have already shown [§§51–52] that the Word cannot be understood apart from a body of teaching and that a body of teaching serves as a kind of lamp that enables us to see genuine truths. This is because the Word is composed entirely of correspondences, which is why there are so many semblances of truth in it that are not bare truths, as well as many things written for the comprehension of earthly, sense-oriented people. Even so, they have been written so that ordinary people can understand them simply, intelligent people intelligently, and wise people wisely.

Now, since that is what the Word is like, semblances of truth—clothed truths—can be seized on as bare truths, which become false if we convince ourselves of them. This is done by people who believe they are wiser than others, though in fact they are not wise at all. Wisdom is seeing whether something is true before convincing ourselves of it, not convincing ourselves of whatever happens to suit us. This latter is what people do when they are particularly good at proving things and have pride in their own intelligence. The former, though, is what people do who love truths and are moved by them because they are true and who put them to use in their lives. These people are enlightened by the Lord and see truths in the light of truths. The others are enlightened by themselves and see falsities in the light of what is false.

We can tell that semblances of truth, which are clothed truths, can be taken from the Word as bare truths and that they become false when we convince ourselves of them, if we think of the abundance of heresies that have existed and still exist in Christianity.[267]

The heretical ideas themselves do not hurt us. What hurts us is living evil lives, and also using the Word and the rationalizations of our earthly self to convince ourselves of the false notions inherent in the heretical ideas.

We are all born into the religion of our parents and are introduced into it in early childhood, and we remain in it afterward, unable to extricate ourselves from its falsities because we are preoccupied with our dealings with this world. Living evil lives, though, and convincing ourselves of false beliefs even to the point of destroying genuine truth—that does condemn us. If we stay with our religion and believe in God (and within the Christian faith that means we believe in the Lord and revere the Word) and we live by the principles of the Ten Commandments out of religious conviction, we will not swear allegiance to notions that are false. Therefore when we hear something true and perceive it in our own particular way, we are in a position to embrace it and be led out of our former false beliefs. However, this will not happen if we have thoroughly convinced ourselves of the falsities of our religion, because once we have convinced ourselves of something false, that belief is there to stay and cannot be uprooted. Once we have convinced ourselves of something false we have in effect sworn allegiance to it, especially if it appeals to our beloved self-importance and therefore to our pride in our own wisdom.

I have talked with individuals in the spiritual world who lived some centuries ago and who had convinced themselves of the falsities of their religion, and I have found them to be still firmly loyal to the same opinions. I have talked with some there who were of the same religion and who thought along the same lines but had not inwardly convinced themselves of those falsities, and I have found that when given angelic instruction they rejected their false beliefs and absorbed true ones. These latter were saved while the others were not.[268]

Everyone is given angelic instruction after death, and we are accepted if we see what is true and see what is false on the basis of what is true, because after death everyone is given the ability to see truths spiritually. The people who do see what is true are the ones who have not convinced themselves [of what is false]; but the ones who have convinced themselves [of what is false] do not want to see what is true. If they do see it they turn their backs to it and either ridicule it or distort it.

94 Let me offer an example by way of illustration. There are many passages in the Word where the Lord is described as wrathful, raging, vengeful, and is said to punish, cast into hell, tempt, and the like. People who believe this in simplicity and therefore fear God and take care not to sin against him are not condemned because of their simplistic faith. However, if people convince themselves that these descriptions of the Lord are true even to the point of actually believing that wrath, rage, vengefulness, and the like, which are evil, are real characteristics of the Lord and that he does punish us and does cast us into hell out of wrath, rage, and vengefulness, they are condemned because they have destroyed the real truth, which is that the Lord is love itself, mercy itself, and goodness itself, and anyone who is these qualities is incapable of wrath, rage, and vengeance. Attributing the other qualities to the Lord is based on the way things seem. The same principle applies in many other cases.

95 There is an example from the physical world that may serve to illustrate the fact that within the literal sense are many semblances of truth that have genuine truth hidden within them, and that it does us no harm to think and talk as though they were true but that it does do us harm to convince ourselves of them to the point of destroying the genuine truth hidden within. I offer this example because something down to earth is more clearly instructive and persuasive than something spiritual.

[2] To all appearances, the sun travels around the earth in a daily cycle and also a yearly cycle, so it says in the Word that the sun rises and sets, causing morning, noon, evening, and night and the seasons of spring, summer, fall, and winter—days and years, therefore. The sun, though, is actually immobile. It is an ocean of fire and the earth rotates every day and orbits the sun yearly. People who simply and ignorantly think that the sun is circling the earth do not destroy the physical truth that the earth is rotating on its axis once a day and is borne along its elliptical path every year. However, if they convince themselves that the apparent motion and course of the sun is its true motion, bringing in support from

the Word and the ability to rationalize that is inherent in the earthly self, they undermine the actual truth and even destroy it.

[3] The apparent motion of the sun is a semblance of truth; the immobility of the sun is a genuine truth. We may talk in terms of the semblance, and we do so, but thinking that way with conviction weakens and blinds our ability to think things through rationally.

It is the same with the stars of the nighttime sky. The semblance of truth is that they too circle us once a day, like the sun; so we say of the stars too that they rise and set. The real truth, though, is that they are fixed and that their heaven is immobile.[269] Still, it is allowable for us all to talk in terms of the way things seem to be.

The reason we are condemned if we convince ourselves of the Word's semblances of truth and thereby destroy the inner genuine truth is that everything in the Word's literal meaning is in communication with heaven and opens it (see the material in §§62–69 above). This means that when we use that meaning to justify worldly loves that conflict with heavenly loves, the inner content of the Word becomes false. As a result, when an outer (that is, literal) meaning whose inner content is false is communicated to heaven, then heaven is closed because the angels, who treasure the inner content of the Word, reject it. We can see from this that a false inner reading, or distorted truth, deprives us of communication with heaven and closes it. This is why we are condemned if we convince ourselves of some heretical falsity. **96a** [270]

The Word is like a garden that we should refer to as a heavenly paradise in which there are all kinds of delicacies and delights—delicacies in the form of fruits and delights in the form of flowers—with trees of life in the middle next to springs of living water. Surrounding this garden, though, are the trees of a forest. When our religious perspective is based on divine truths we are in the middle, where the trees of life are, and we actively enjoy their delicacies and delights. When our religious perspective is based not on truths but only on the [Word's] literal meaning, then we are on the circumference and all we see is forest. If we are devoted to the teachings of a false religion and convince ourselves that its teachings are true, we are not even in the forest; we are outside it, on sand flats where there is not even any grass. **96b**

At some other time I will show that people actually do experience conditions like this after death.[271]

Further still, we need to realize that the literal meaning of the Word serves to protect the real truths that lie hidden within it. Its protection consists of its being susceptible to being turned in different directions **97** and interpreted to agree with our own grasp of it, so that the inner content is not damaged or transgressed. It does no harm if different people understand the literal meaning of the Word differently. It does do harm, though, if the divine truths that lie hidden within are distorted. This in fact does violence to the Word.

To prevent this from happening, the literal meaning offers protection, and it offers protection for people who take for granted the false beliefs of their religion but do not convince themselves that those false beliefs are true. These people do no harm.

[2] This protection is the meaning of angel guardians in the Word, and its description of angel guardians is a depiction of this protection.

This protection is the meaning of the angel guardians stationed at the entrance after Adam and his wife were expelled from the Garden of Eden, of whom we read,

> When Jehovah God drove them out, he made angel guardians dwell to the east of the Garden of Eden, and the flame of a sword turning this way and that, to guard the way of the tree of life. (Genesis 3:24)

The angel guardians mean protection; the way of the tree of life means entrance to the Lord, which we have through the Word; the flame of a sword turning this way and that means divine truth at its very boundaries, which is like the Word in its literal meaning—it too can be turned this way and that.

[3] There is a similar meaning to *the angel guardians of gold placed on top of the two ends of the mercy seat that was on the ark in the tabernacle* (Exodus 25:18–21). Because this was what the angel guardians meant, the Lord talked with Moses between them (Exodus 25:22; 37:9; Numbers 7:89). As noted in §§37–49 above, the Lord does not say anything to us unless it is complete, and divine truth is in its fullness in the literal meaning of the Word; so that is why the Lord talked with Moses between the angel guardians.

The meaning of the *angel guardians on the curtains of the tabernacle and on its veils* (Exodus 26:31) is no different, since the curtains and veils represent the boundaries of heaven and the church and therefore of the Word as well (see §46 above). The meaning of the *angel guardians in the middle of the Jerusalem temple* (1 Kings 6:23–28) and the *angel guardians carved on the walls and gates of the Temple* (1 Kings 6:29, 32, 35) is no different either. The same holds for the *angel guardians in the new temple* (Ezekiel 41:18, 19, 20; again, see §47 above).

[4] Since the angel guardians mean protection that keeps us from going straight to the Lord, heaven, and the divine truth of the Word as it is inwardly, and makes us instead move indirectly through its outermost forms, we read of the King of Tyre,

> You had sealed your full measure and were full of wisdom and perfect in beauty. You were in the Garden of Eden. Every precious stone was your covering. You, angel guardian, were the spreading of a covering. I destroyed you, covering angel guardian, in the midst of stones of fire. (Ezekiel 28:12, 13, 14, 16)

Tyre means the church in respect to its concepts of what is true and good, so the king of Tyre means the Word where these concepts can be found and where they come from. We can see that Tyre and the protecting angel guardians here mean the Word in its outermost form, which is its literal meaning, because it says "you had sealed your full measure," "every precious stone was your covering," and "you, angel guardian, were the spreading of a covering," as well as mentioning a "covering angel guardian." The precious stones that are also mentioned mean truths of the literal meaning of the Word (see §45 above).

Since angel guardians mean the outermost form of divine truth as protection, it says in David,

> Jehovah bowed the heavens and came down, riding upon angel guardians. (Psalms 18:9, 10)

> O Shepherd of Israel, who sits upon the angel guardians, shine forth! (Psalms 80:1)

and

> . . . Jehovah who sits upon the angel guardians. (Psalms 99:1)

To ride and to sit upon angel guardians is [to rest] on the outermost meaning of the Word.

[5] The divine truth in the Word and its nature are described [through correspondences] as angel guardians in chapters 1, 9, and 10 of Ezekiel; but since no one can know what the details of the description mean except those for whom the spiritual meaning has been opened, the meaning of all the things it says about the angel guardians in the first chapter of Ezekiel has been disclosed to me in summary form, as follows:[272]

There is a depiction of the outward divine aura of the Word (verse 4); that aura is represented as a human being (verse 5); it is shown to be united to spiritual and heavenly realities (verse 6). There is a depiction of the nature of the earthly level of the Word (verse 7), and of the nature of the spiritual and heavenly levels of the Word that are united to its earthly level (verses 8, 9). There is a depiction of the divine love within the heavenly, spiritual, and earthly levels of goodness and truth in the Word, together as one and also distinct from one another (verses 10, 11), and an indication that they share a common goal (verse 12). There is a depiction of the aura of the Word that comes from the Lord's divine goodness and divine truth, which give life to the Word (verses 13, 14), of the teachings of what is good and true that are in the Word and from the Word (verses 15–21), and of the divine nature of the Lord that is above it and within it (verses 22, 23) and that comes from it (verses 24, 25). It is shown that the Lord is above the heavens (verse 26) and that to him belong divine love and divine wisdom (verses 27, 28).

These summary statements have been checked against the Word in heaven and are in accord with it.

The Lord Came into the World to Fulfill Everything in the Word and So to Become Divine Truth or the Word Even on the Outermost Level

98 ON the Lord's having come into the world to fulfill everything in the Word, see *Teachings on the Lord* 8–11. As for his having become divine truth or the Word even on the outermost level by this means, that is the meaning of the following statement in John:

> And the Word became flesh and lived among us; and we saw his glory, glory like that of the only-begotten child of the Father. He was full of grace and truth. (John 1:14)

To become flesh is to become the Word even on the outermost level. The disciples were shown his nature as the Word on the outermost level when he was transfigured (Matthew 17:2 and following; Mark 9:2 and following; Luke 9:28 and following). It says there that Moses and Elijah were seen in glory; Moses and Elijah mean the Word (see §48 above).

The Lord as the Word on the outermost level is also described in the first chapter of the Revelation of John, verses 13–16, where all the elements of his description mean the outermost forms of divine truth or the Word.

The Lord had of course been the Word before, but on the very first level, for it says,

> In the beginning was the Word, and the Word was with God, and the Word was God. It was in the beginning with God. (John 1:1, 2)

When the Word became flesh, though, then the Lord became the Word on the outermost level as well. That is why he is called the First and the Last (Revelation 1:8, 11, 17; 2:8; 21:6; 22:13).

The state of the church was completely changed by the Lord's becoming the Word even on the outermost level. All the churches before his Coming were symbolic churches,[273] churches that could see divine truth only in the dark. However, after the Lord's coming into the world, a church was started by him that saw divine truth in the light. The difference is like the difference between evening and morning. In fact, the state of the church before his Coming is called evening, and the state of the church after his Coming is called morning.[274]

Before his coming into the world, the Lord was of course present with the people of the church, but indirectly, through heaven;[275] whereas since his coming into the world he is directly present with the people of the church. This is because he put on a divine earthly form in the world, the form in which he is present with us. The Lord's "glorification" is the complete glorification of the human nature that he took on in the world, and the glorified human form of the Lord is the divine-earthly form.

There are not many people who understand how the Lord is the Word. Yes, they do think that the Lord can enlighten and teach us through the Word, but they do not think that this warrants calling him "the Word." Let them know, though, that each one of us is her or his own distinctive love and therefore that each of us is whatever we have that is good and that is true. That is all that makes us human, and nothing else in us is human.

Every human being is her or his own goodness and truth. That is the reason why angels and spirits, too, are human—because everything good and true that emanates from the Lord is in its proper form human.

The Lord, though, is divine goodness and divine truth itself, so he is the Human, the source of all our humanity.

See *Heaven and Hell* 460 on the human form of everything divinely good and divinely true. This will also be more clearly presented in forthcoming works that are to be about angelic wisdom.[276]

Before the Word That We Have in the World Today, There Was a Word That Has Been Lost

101 BEFORE the Word was given to the Israelite nation through Moses and the prophets, people were familiar with sacrificial worship, and there was prophecy at Jehovah's command. We can tell this from what it says in the books of Moses.

As for their *familiarity with sacrificial worship,* we read that the children of Israel were commanded to overthrow the altars of the nations, shatter their statues, and cut down their groves (Exodus 34:13; Deuteronomy 7:5; 12:3). We also read that at Acacia Grove Israel began to commit whoredom with the daughters of Moab; they summoned people to sacrifices to their gods and the people feasted and bowed down to their gods and especially became attached to the Baal of Peor; and Jehovah became angry with Israel because of this (Numbers 25:1, 2, 3). And Balaam, who was from Syria, had altars built and sacrificed cattle and sheep (Numbers 22:40; 23:1, 2, 14, 29, 30).

[2] As for *there also being prophecy at Jehovah's command,* this we can tell from the prophecies of Balaam (Numbers 23:7–10, 18–24; 24:3–9, 16–24). In fact, he prophesied about the Lord, saying that a star would rise out of Jacob and a scepter out of Israel (Numbers 24:17). As for his prophesying at Jehovah's command, see Numbers 22:13, 18; 23:3, 5, 8, 16, 26; 24:1, 13.

This shows that the nations had divine worship that resembled the worship instituted by Moses for the Israelite nation.

[3] We get a glimpse of the fact that *this was the case even before the time of Abram* from what it says in Moses (Deuteronomy 32:7, 8).[277] It is

clearer, though, in the case of Melchizedek, King of Salem, who brought out bread and wine and blessed Abram, and Abram gave him a tenth of everything he owned (Genesis 14:18–20). Melchizedek represented the Lord, for he is referred to as "a priest to God the Highest" (Genesis 14:18) and it says of the Lord in David, "You are a priest forever after the manner of Melchizedek" (Psalms 110:4). That was why Melchizedek brought out the bread and the wine as holy elements of the church, just as they are in the sacrament of the Holy Supper.²⁷⁸ It is also why Melchizedek blessed Abram and why Abram gave him a tenth of everything he owned.

Angels of heaven have informed me that the ancients had a Word written entirely in correspondences, but that it was later lost; and they have said that this Word is still preserved among them in heaven and is in use among ancients in the particular heaven where the people live who had that Word when they were living in this world.

Some of the ancients among whom that Word is still in use in heaven came from the land of Canaan and its adjoining regions—from Syria, for example; from Mesopotamia, Arabia, Chaldea, Assyria; from Egypt; from Sidon, Tyre, and Nineveh—all regions inhabited by people who were devoted to symbolic worship²⁷⁹ and therefore to the knowledge of correspondences. Their wisdom in those days was based on that knowledge, and by means of it they had an inner perception and communication with the heavens. The ones who were more deeply knowledgeable about the correspondences of that Word were called "the wise" and "the intelligent," though later they were called "diviners" and "magi."²⁸⁰

[2] However, since that Word was full of a kind of correspondence that pointed in a remote way to heavenly and spiritual realities and therefore began to be distorted by too many people, in the course of time, under the Lord's divine providence, it vanished and eventually was lost; and they were given another Word composed by means of less remote correspondences. This was done through the prophets among the children of Israel.²⁸¹

All the same, that Word kept many of the place-names in Canaan and in surrounding parts of the Middle East with meanings similar to the ones they had in the earlier Word. That is the reason Abram was ordered to go to that land and why his descendants from Jacob on were brought back into it.

We can tell from the books of Moses that there was a Word among the ancients because he mentioned it and excerpted from it (Numbers 21:14, 15, 27–30). We can tell that the narrative portions of that Word were called *The Wars of Jehovah,* and that the prophetic portions were called *Pronouncements.* Moses quoted the following from the historical narratives of that Word:

> Therefore it says in *The Book of the Wars of Jehovah,* "Waheb in Suphah and the rivers Arnon, a watercourse of rivers that goes down to [where] Ar is inhabited and rests along the border of Moab." (Numbers 21:14, 15)

In that Word as in ours, the wars of Jehovah were understood to be, and served to describe in detail, the Lord's battles against hell and his victories over it when he would come into the world. These same battles are meant and described time after time in the historical narratives of our Word—in Joshua's battles against the nations of the land of Canaan, for example, and in the wars of the judges and the kings of Israel.

[2] Moses quoted the following from the prophetic portions of that Word:

> Therefore *those who make pronouncements* say, "Come to Heshbon! The city of Sihon will be built up and fortified, because fire has gone out from Heshbon, flame from the city of Sihon. It has devoured Ar of Moab, those who occupy the heights of Arnon. Woe to you, Moab! You have perished, people of Chemosh; he has made his sons fugitives and sent his daughters into captivity to Sihon, king of the Amorites. With arrows we have dealt with them; Heshbon has perished as far as Dibon, and we have spread destruction as far as Nophah, which extends to Medeba." (Numbers 21:27, 28, 29, 30)

Translators change [the title of] this to *Composers of Proverbs,* but it should be called *Makers of Pronouncements* or *Prophetic Pronouncements,* as we can tell from the meaning of the word *moschalim* in Hebrew.[282] It means not only proverbs but also prophetic utterances, as in Numbers 23:7, 18 and 24:3, 15 where it says that Balaam gave forth *his pronouncement,* which was actually a prophetic utterance and was about the Lord. In these instances each of his pronouncements is called a *mashal* in the singular. There is also the fact that what Moses quoted from this source are not proverbs but prophecies.

[3] We can see that this Word was similarly divine or divinely inspired from a passage in Jeremiah where we find almost the same words:

> A fire has gone out from Heshbon and a flame from the midst of Sihon, which has devoured the corner of Moab and the top of the children of tumult. Woe to you, Moab! The people of Chemosh have perished, for

your sons have been carried off into captivity and your daughters into captivity. (Jeremiah 48:45, 46)

Further, both David and Joshua mention another prophetic book of the former Word, *The Book of Jasher* or *The Book of the Righteous One.* Here is where David mentions it:

David lamented over Saul and over Jonathan and wrote, "'To Teach the Children of Judah the Bow.' (You will find this written in *The Book of Jasher.*)" (2 Samuel 1:17, 18)

Here is where Joshua mentions it:

Joshua said, "'Come to rest, O sun, in Gibeon; and, O moon, in the valley of Aijalon.' Is this not written in *The Book of Jasher?*" (Joshua 10:12, 13)

Then too, I have been told that the first seven chapters of Genesis are right there in that ancient Word, so that not the slightest word is missing.[283]

By Means of the Word, There Is Light Even for People Who Are outside the Church and Do Not Have the Word

THERE can be no union with heaven unless somewhere on our planet there is a church where the Word is present and the Lord is known by means of it. This is because the Lord is the God of heaven and earth, and there is no salvation apart from the Lord.

It is adequate if there is simply a church where the Word is present even though that church may consist of relatively few people. Even so, by means of it the Lord is present everywhere in the whole world, because by means of it heaven is united with the human race. As for the union being by means of the Word, see §§62–69 above.

105 I need to explain, though, how the presence and union of the Lord and heaven happens in all lands by means of the Word.

In the Lord's sight, the whole heaven is like one human being, and so is the church (see *Heaven and Hell* 59–86 on the fact that they actually look like a human being to him). In that human being, the church (that is, the church where the Word is read and the Lord is therefore known) functions as the *heart* and as the *lungs*—the [church's] heavenly kingdom as the heart and the [church's] spiritual kingdom as the lungs.

[2] Just as all the other members and organs are maintained and live from these two founts of life in the human body, so too all the people in the various countries of the world who have any religion, worship one God, and live good lives are maintained and live from the union of the Lord and heaven with the church through the Word. By virtue of their faith and life, they are in that human being and reflect its members and organs that are outside the chest cavity where the heart and lungs are. This is because even though the Word in the church may be among relatively few, it gives life from the Lord through heaven to the rest [of the world], just as the heart and lungs give life to the members and organs of the whole body. In fact the sharing is similar.

[3] This is why Christians who read the Word[284] form the chest of that human being. They are at the center, with the Catholics around them; the Muslims who recognize the Lord as the greatest prophet and as the Son of God[285] are around them. Next come the Africans. And the outermost circle is made up of nations and peoples in Asia and in India. There is some further information about this arrangement in §48 of *Last Judgment*.[286]

All the people in that human being face toward the central area where the Christians are.

106 The light is greatest in the central area where the Christians who have the Word are. The explanation is that in the heavens, light is the divine truth that radiates from the Lord as heaven's sun;[287] and since the Word is that truth, we find the most light where we find the people who have the Word.

From there, the light spreads outward from its center, so to speak, to all the surrounding areas, all the way to the boundary, so there is also enlightenment from the Word for nations and peoples outside the church.

On the light in the heavens being the divine truth that radiates from the Lord, and on that light being what gives enlightenment not only to angels but also to us, see *Heaven and Hell* 126–140.

107 We can conclude that this is characteristic of the whole heaven on the basis of a similar phenomenon in each community there. This is because every community of heaven is a heaven in smaller form and is also like a human being (on this, see *Heaven and Hell* 41–86).

In every community of heaven, the people in the middle similarly serve as heart and lungs and are the ones who have the most light. From that middle, that same light and consequent perception of what is true spread in all directions to the boundaries and therefore to everyone in the community. This is what makes their spiritual life.

I have been shown that when the people in the middle went away—the ones who made up the province of the heart and lungs and who had the most light—the people around them were in darkness and had a perception of what was true that was so slight as to be nearly nonexistent. As soon as the others came back, though, the light reappeared and they had their former perception of what was true.

108 Another experience may serve to illustrate the same thing. There were some African spirits with me, from Abyssinia. At one point their ears were opened so that they heard one of the Psalms of David being sung in a house of worship on earth. This moved them with such pleasure that they joined in the singing. Before long, though, their ears were closed so that they could not hear anything from that house of worship; but when that happened they were moved by a pleasure that was even greater because it was spiritual, and were flooded with understanding at the same time because the psalm was about the Lord and redemption. The reason they felt more pleasure was that they were granted communication with the community in heaven that was united with the people who were singing the psalm in this world. It has become clear to me from this and from many other experiences that there is communication with the whole heaven through the Word.

For this reason, there is, by the Lord's divine providence, a universal interaction between the countries of Europe (especially those where the Word is read) and the nations outside the church.

109 We can draw a comparison with the warmth and light of earth's sun, which nurtures the growth of trees and shrubs even if they stand in the shadows or under a cloud, as long as the sun rises and appears in the world. Likewise, heaven's light and warmth is from the Lord as its sun. That light is the divine truth that is the source of all our intelligence and wisdom, whether we are angels or people [still in this world]. That is why it says of the *Word* that it "was with God and was God" and that it "enlightens everyone who comes into the world" (John 1:1, 9), and that "that light" even "shines in the darkness" (John 1:5).

110 We can tell from this that the Word that is found in the Protestant church enlightens all nations and peoples by means of a spiritual communication, and that the Lord provides that there should always be a church on earth where the Word is read and the Lord is known through it.

So when the Word was virtually cast out by Catholics,[288] divine providence brought about the Reformation, and this meant that the Word was accepted again. Providence also ensured that the Word is regarded as holy by one noble Catholic nation.[289]

111 Because without the Word there is no recognition of the Lord and therefore no salvation, when the Word was utterly distorted and corrupted by the Jewish nation[290] and therefore made virtually null and void, it pleased the Lord to come down from heaven, come into the world, fulfill the Word, and thereby make it whole again, restore it, and give light again to us who live on earth. That is the intent of the Lord's words:

> The people who were sitting in darkness have seen a great light; the light has risen for those who were sitting in the region and shadow of death. (Matthew 4:16; Isaiah 9:2)

112 It was foretold that at the end of the present church[291] darkness would rear up out of the lack of recognition and acknowledgment of the fact that the Lord is the God of heaven and earth and out of the separation of faith from caring. Therefore, to prevent this from leading to the death of any real understanding of the Word, it has now pleased the Lord to unveil the spiritual meaning of the Word and to make it clear that in that meaning—and thereby in the earthly meaning—the Word is all about the Lord and the church. In fact, it is about those subjects alone. He has also unveiled many other things that may serve to restore a light of truth from the Word—a light that has almost been snuffed out.

[2] There are many passages in the Book of Revelation where it predicts that the light of truth would be almost snuffed out at the end of this church.[292] This is also the meaning of these words of the Lord in Matthew:

> Immediately after the affliction of those days the sun will be darkened, the moon will not give its light, the stars will fall from heaven, and the powers of the heavens will be shaken. Then they will see the Son of Humanity coming in the clouds of heaven with glory and power. (Matthew 24:29, 30)

The sun here means love for the Lord; the moon means faith in the Lord; the stars mean concepts from the Lord regarding what is good and true; the Son of Humanity means the Lord as the Word; the clouds mean the Word's literal meaning, and the glory means its spiritual meaning and the way it shines through in the literal meaning.

113 I have been granted an abundance of experience that has taught me that there is a communication with heaven for us through the Word. When I was reading through the Word from the first chapter of Isaiah to the last of Malachi and the Psalms of David, I was given a clear sense that every verse communicated with a specific community of heaven, and that in this way the whole Word communicated with the entire heaven.

If There Were No Word, No One Would Know about God, Heaven and Hell, Life after Death, and Least of All, about the Lord

114 THIS follows as a general conclusion from everything that has been said and explained up to this point—that the Word is divine truth itself (§§1–4); the Word is a means of union with heaven's angels (§§62–69); everywhere in the Word there is a marriage of the Lord and the church and therefore a marriage of goodness and truth (§§80–89); the quality of a church depends on the quality of its understanding of the Word (§§76–79); the Word exists in the heavens as well, and it is the source of angels' wisdom (§§70–75); there is spiritual light through the Word for nations and peoples outside the church as well (§§104–113); and more. From this we may conclude that if it were not for the Word, no one would have a spiritual understanding. That is, no one would know about God, heaven and hell, and life after death; and there would be absolutely no knowledge about the Lord and about faith in him and love for him. This means there would be no knowledge of redemption, though this is the means to salvation.

The Lord said to his disciples, "Without me you cannot do anything" (John 15:5), and John [the Baptist] said, "People cannot receive anything unless it has been given to them from heaven" (John 3:27).

115 But then there are people who propose and then prove to themselves that without the Word we could know about the existence of God, about heaven and hell, too, and something about other things that the Word teaches.[293] They then use this assumption to undermine the authority and holiness of the Word, if not out loud, then in their hearts. There is no dealing with them on the basis of the Word. We must appeal to the light of reason because they do not believe the Word, only themselves.

If you look into it with the light of reason you will discover that human beings possess two faculties of life, called will and understanding, and that our understanding is subject to our will, while our will is not subject to our understanding. All our understanding does is teach and show us the way.

Look further, and you will discover that our will involves a sense of our own self-importance; that in and of itself, this self-importance is nothing but evil; and that it gives rise to falsity in our understanding.

[2] Once you have discovered this, you will see that on our own we do not *want* to understand anything except what follows from our will, and that we would not *be able* to understand anything else if there were no external basis of our knowing. On the basis of the self-importance associated with our will, we do not want to understand anything that does not focus on ourselves and the world. Anything higher is in darkness for us. When we see the sun, the moon, and the stars, for example, and we happen to think about their origin, can we come up with any thought but that they brought themselves into being? Can we raise our thoughts higher than those of many of this world's scholars, who believe that nature created itself[294] even though they know from the Word that God created everything? What would they think, then, if they knew nothing from the Word?

[3] Do you think that the ancient sages, including Aristotle, Cicero, Seneca, and others who wrote about God and the immortality of the soul, picked this up first from themselves? No, it was from others, who had it handed down to them from still others who first learned it from the Word.[295]

Writers of natural theology,[296] too, do not get anything like this from themselves. They are only using rational means to support what they have learned from the church, where the Word is found—and there may be some among them who vocally support it but nevertheless do not believe.

116 I have been allowed to see people born on [remote] islands who were rational in civic matters but knew absolutely nothing about God. In the spiritual world they look like apes and lead an almost apelike life; but since they were born human and have the ability to accept spiritual life, they are taught by angels and brought to life by recognizing that the Lord is human.

What we are like left to our own devices is obvious from people in hell. This includes some of the eminent and learned who are unwilling to hear anything about God and therefore cannot pronounce the word "God." I have seen them and talked with them, and have also talked with some who burst into flaming wrath and rage when they hear anyone talking about God.

[2] Stop and think, then, what people would be like who had never heard about God, when there are people like this who have heard about God, who have written about God, and who have preached about God. Many people of this sort are Jesuits.[297]

The basic cause of this kind of nature is a will that is evil; and this, as already noted [§115], leads our understanding and takes away any truth it has from the Word. If it is possible for us to know on our own that God exists and that we go on living after death, why then do some people not know that we remain human beings after death? Why do some believe that the soul or spirit is like the wind or the ether,[298] and does not see with its own eyes or hear with its own ears or speak with its own mouth before it is [once again] united and merged with its body, even though that is now a cadaver or even a skeleton?[299]

[3] So imagine a theory of worship concocted solely in the light of reason. Would it not teach that we ourselves are to be worshiped, as has been done for ages and still is by people, despite the fact that they know from the Word that we should worship God alone? No other kind of worship can come from our own self-aggrandizement, not even the worship of the sun and the moon.

117 As for the fact that there has been religion from the earliest times and that people all over the world have known about God and have known something about life after death, this did not come from the people themselves and from their own mental acuity, but from that former Word discussed in §§101–103 above, and later from the Israelite Word.[300] Religious principles spread from these sources into southeast Asia, including

its islands; through Egypt and Ethiopia into Africa; and from the coast of Asia Minor into Greece and from there into Italy.

But since there was no way the Word could be composed except in the language of representative imagery, in images of things characteristic of this world that corresponded to and therefore signified heavenly realities, the religions of many nations were turned into idolatries—in Greece into fables—and divine attributes and characteristics were turned into individual gods led by one highest God whom people called Jove, from "Jehovah."[301] It is common knowledge that [ancient people] were familiar with paradise, the Flood, sacred fire, and the four ages—from the first Golden Age to the last Iron Age[302]—which serve in the Word to mean the four states of the church,[303] as in Daniel 2:31–35.

It is also common knowledge that Islam, which came later and wiped out the preceding religious cultures of many nations, was drawn from the Word of both Testaments.[304]

118 Let me say in closing what people are like after death if they have attributed everything to their own intelligence and little if anything to the Word. At first they seem to be drunk, then foolish, and finally brainless; and they sit in darkness. So beware of this kind of insanity in yourselves.

Teachings about Life for the New Jerusalem Drawn from the Ten Commandments

Teachings about Life for the New Jerusalem

Religion Is All about How We Live, and the Religious Way to Live Is to Do Good

EVERYONE who has any religion knows and acknowledges that people who lead a good life are saved and people who lead an evil life are damned. That is, they know and acknowledge that if we lead a good life we think good things not only about God but also about our neighbor, which is not the case if we lead an evil life.

What we love constitutes our life, and whatever we love we not only do freely but also think freely. So we say that life is doing good things because doing good things is inseparable from thinking good things. If this doing and this thinking are not working together in us, then they are not part of our life. This, though, needs to be explained in what follows.

As for the fact that religion is about how we live and that the [religious] way to live is to do good, everyone who reads the Word[305] sees this and acknowledges it on reading it. We find the following in the Word:

> Whoever breaks the least of these commandments and teaches others to do the same will be called the least in the kingdom of the heavens, but whoever *does and teaches* [these commandments] will be called great in

the kingdom of the heavens. I tell you, unless your *righteousness* exceeds that of the scribes and Pharisees, you will not enter the kingdom of the heavens. (Matthew 5:19, 20)

Every tree that does not *bear good fruit* is cut down and thrown into the fire; therefore *by their fruits* you will know them. (Matthew 7:19, 20)

Not everyone who says to me, "Lord, Lord," will enter the kingdom of the heavens, but *those who do the will* of my Father who is in the heavens. (Matthew 7:21)

On that day many will say to me, "Lord, Lord, haven't we prophesied in your name and done many great things in your name?" But then I will declare to them, "I do not know you. Depart from me, *you workers of iniquity."* (Matthew 7:22, 23)

Everyone who hears my words and *does them* I will liken to a wise man who built his house on the rock; but everyone who hears my words and *does not do them* will be likened to a foolish man who built his house on the sand. (Matthew 7:24, 26)

Jesus said, "A sower went out to sow. Some seed fell on a hard-packed path, some on stony ground, some among thorns, and some into good ground. The people who received seed in good ground are those who hear and understand the Word, and as a result *bear fruit and become productive,* some a hundredfold, some sixtyfold, and some thirtyfold." When he had said these things, Jesus cried out and said, "Those who have ears to hear must hear this." (Matthew 13:3–9, 23)

The Son of Humanity is going to come in the glory of his Father, and then *he will repay all people according to their deeds.* (Matthew 16:27)

The kingdom of God will be taken from you and given to *a nation that bears its fruits.* (Matthew 21:43)

When the Son of Humanity comes in his glory, then he will sit on the throne of his glory and will say to the sheep on his right, "Come, you who are blessed, and possess as your inheritance the kingdom prepared for you since the founding of the world; *because I was hungry and you gave me something to eat. I was thirsty and you gave me something to drink. I was a stranger and you took me in. I was naked and you clothed me. I was sick and you visited me. I was in prison and you came to me."* Then the righteous will answer him, "When did we see you like this?" But the king will answer and say, "I tell you truly, as much as you did this to one of the least of my people, you did it to me." And the king will say similar things to the goats on the left, but since they had not done things like these, he will say, "Depart from me, you who are cursed, into the everlasting fire prepared for the Devil and his angels." (Matthew 25:31–46)

Bear fruit that is consistent with repentance. The axe is already lying against the root of the trees. Every tree *that does not bear good fruit* is cut down and thrown into the fire. (Luke 3:8, 9)

Jesus said, "Why do you call me 'Lord, Lord,' and *not do what I say?* Everyone who comes to me and hears what I am saying and *does it* is like someone building a house who laid its foundation on the rock; but anyone who hears and does nothing is like someone building a house on the ground without a foundation." (Luke 6:46–49)

Jesus said, "My mother and my brothers are these who hear the Word of God and *do it.*" (Luke 8:21)

Then you begin to stand outside and knock on the door, saying, "Lord, open the door for us!" But he will say in reply, "I do not know where you are from. *Depart from me, all you workers of iniquity.*" (Luke 13:25–27)

This is the condemnation, that light has come into the world, but people loved darkness rather than light, because *their deeds were evil.* All *who do evil* hate the light, because *their deeds* would be exposed; but those who do the truth come to the light so that *their deeds* may be clearly seen, because *their deeds were done in God.* (John 3:19–21)

Those who have done what is good will go forth into [the resurrection of life, but *those who have done what is evil* will go forth into][306] the resurrection of condemnation. (John 5:29)

We know that God does not hear sinners; but he does hear people who worship God and *do his will.* (John 9:31)

If you know these things, *you are blessed if you do them.* (John 13:17)

The people who love me are those who have my commandments and *do them;* and I will love them and will manifest myself to them. I will come to them and make a home with them. Those who do not love me *do not keep my words.* (John 14:15, 21–24)

Jesus said, "I am the vine, and my Father is the vinedresser. Every branch in me *that does not bear fruit* he takes away; and every branch *that bears fruit* he prunes, so that *it will bear more fruit.*" (John 15:1, 2)

> My Father is glorified *by your bearing much fruit* and becoming my disciples. (John 15:8)

> You are my friends if you do whatever I command you. I have chosen you *so that you will bear fruit* and *your fruit will remain*. (John 15:14, 16)

> The Lord said to John, "To the angel of the church of Ephesus write, '*I know your works.* I have this against you, that you have left your first *love*. Repent and *do the first works,* or else I will remove your lampstand from its place.'" (Revelation 2:1, 2, 4, 5)

> To the angel of the church in Smyrna write, "*I know your works.*" (Revelation 2:8, 9)

> To the angel of the church in Pergamum write, "*I know your works. Repent!*" (Revelation 2:12, 13, 16)

> To the angel of the church in Thyatira write, "*I know your works and your love; your* last *works* are more than the first." (Revelation 2:18, 19)

> To the angel of the church in Sardis write, "*I know your works,* that you have a name that you are alive, but you are dead. *I have not found your works perfect before God. Repent!*" (Revelation 3:1, 2, 3)

> To the angel of the church in Philadelphia write, "*I know your works.*" (Revelation 3:7, 8)

> To the angel of the church in Laodicea write, "*I know your works. Repent!*" (Revelation 3:14, 15, 19)

> I heard a voice from heaven saying, "Write: 'Blessed are the dead who die in the Lord from now on.'" "[Yes,]" says the spirit, "so that they may rest from their labors, and *their works follow them.*" (Revelation 14:13)

> A book was opened, which is the book of life. And the dead were judged by the things that were written in the book; *all* were judged *according to their works.* (Revelation 20:12, 13)

> Behold, I am coming quickly, and my reward is with me, *to give to all according to what they have done.* (Revelation 22:12)

In the Old Testament, too:

> Repay them *according to their work and according to the deeds of their hands.* (Jeremiah 25:14)

Jehovah,[307] whose eyes are open to all the ways of humankind, *to give to all according to their ways and according to the fruit of their deeds . . .* (Jeremiah 32:19)

I will punish them *according to their ways* and repay them *according to their deeds.* (Hosea 4:9)

Jehovah deals with us *according to our ways* and *according to our deeds.* (Zechariah 1:6)

There are also many passages where it says that we are to *do* the statutes, commandments, and laws, such as the following:

Keep my statutes and my judgments. *Anyone who does so will live by means of them.* (Leviticus 18:5)

You shall observe all my statutes and my judgments *by doing them.* (Leviticus 19:37; 20:8; 22:31)

The children of Israel were promised blessings *if they did the precepts* and curses *if they did not do them* (Leviticus 26:3–46). They were commanded to make for themselves a fringe on the hems of their garments to remind them of all the precepts of Jehovah *so that they would do them* (Numbers 15:38, 39)—and there are thousands more passages.

Then too, the Lord teaches in parables that works are what make us part of the church[308] and that our salvation depends on them. Many of his parables are about those who do good being accepted and those who do evil being rejected. See, for example, the parable of the workers in the vineyard (Matthew 21:33–44), the parable of the fig tree that bore no fruit (Luke 13:6 and following), the parable of the talents and the minas[309] which those [in the parable] were to use in business (Matthew 25:14–31; Luke 19:12–25), the parable of the Samaritan who bound up the wounds of the man beaten by robbers (Luke 10:30–37), the parable of the rich man and Lazarus (Luke 16:19–31), and the parable of the ten young women (Matthew 25:1–12).

Everyone who has any religion knows and acknowledges that those who lead a good life are saved and those who lead an evil life are damned. They know this because heaven is united with people who know from the Word that there is a God, that there is a heaven and a hell, and that there is a life after death. This [connection with heaven] gives rise to this widespread perception.

For this reason in the Athanasian statement of faith[310] concerning the Trinity, which is accepted throughout the whole Christian world, what it says at the end is also accepted everywhere, namely,

> Jesus Christ, who suffered for our salvation, ascended into heaven, and sits at the right hand of the Father Almighty. From there he will come to judge the living and the dead; and *then those who have done good will go into everlasting life and those who have done evil will go into everlasting fire.*

4. Even so, there are many people in Christian churches who teach that it is faith alone that saves, and living a good life or doing what is good has nothing to do with it. They even go so far as to teach that living an evil life or doing what is evil does not damn those who have been justified by faith alone, because they are in God and in grace. Strange as it may seem, though, despite the fact that this is what they teach, they still have an acknowledgment (which comes from that widespread perception bestowed by heaven) that people are saved if they live a good life and damned if they live an evil life. We can see this acknowledgment in the *prayer* that is read to people who are taking the Holy Supper[311] in churches in Britain and in Germany, Sweden, and Denmark. It is common knowledge that there are people in these countries who teach faith alone.[312] The prayer that is read in Britain to people taking the sacrament of the Supper is the following.

5 & 6 [313]
> The way and means to be received as worthy partakers of that Holy Table [the Holy Supper] is, first, to examine your lives and conversations [dealings with others] by the rule of God's commandments, and wherever you shall perceive yourselves to have offended either by will, word, or deed, there to bewail your own sinfulness, and to confess yourselves to Almighty God, with full purpose of amendment of life; and if you shall perceive your offenses to be such as are not only against God, but also against your neighbors, then you shall reconcile yourselves to them, being ready to make restitution and satisfaction according to the utmost of your power, for all injuries and wrongs done by you to any other, and being likewise ready to forgive others that have offended you, as you would have forgiveness of your offenses from God's hand; for otherwise the receiving of the Holy Communion does nothing else but increase your damnation. Therefore if any of you be a blasphemer of God, or a hinderer or slanderer of his Word, or an adulterer, or be in malice or envy or in any other grievous crime, repent of your sins, or else do not come to the Holy Table; lest after the taking of that Holy Sacrament the Devil enter into you, as he entered into

Judas, and fill you full of all iniquities, and bring you to destruction of both body and soul.

I was granted the opportunity in the spiritual world[314] to question some elders from Britain who believed in and preached faith alone. I asked them whether when they were in church and read this prayer—which does not mention faith—they really believed that if people did evil things and did not repent, the Devil would enter into them as he had into Judas and would destroy both body and soul. They said that when they were in the state they were in when they read the prayer, they simply knew and thought that this was the essence of their religion, but when they were composing and polishing their own speeches or sermons they did not think along the same lines. This was because they were focusing on faith as the sole means of salvation and of living a good life as a moral side effect useful for the public welfare.

All the same, they held the conviction, which was also a matter of common sense for them, that people who live a good life are saved and that people who live an evil life are damned; and they felt this way whenever they were not wrapped up in themselves.

The reason religion is all about how we live is that after death we all are our own life. It remains the same for us as it was in the world and does not change. An evil life cannot be altered into a good one or a good life into an evil one, because they are opposites, and alteration into something opposite is extinction. So because they are opposites, a good life is called life and an evil life is called death.

That is why religion is all about how we live and why the way to live is to do good. On our nature after death being determined by our life in the world see *Heaven and Hell*[315] 470–484.

No One Can Do Anything Genuinely Good on His or Her Own

THE reason hardly any of us has known whether our good actions were coming from ourselves or from God is that the church has divorced faith from caring,[316] and doing good comes from caring. We give to the poor; help those in need; endow churches and hostels; are considerate of our church, our country, and our fellow citizens; attend church regularly and worship and pray devoutly when we do; read the Word and religious literature; and think about our salvation—all without knowing whether our actions come from ourselves or from God. These same actions can come from ourselves or from God. If these actions come from God, they are good; if they come from ourselves, they are not good. In fact, there are acts that in and of themselves resemble good ones and yet are obviously evil—hypocritical good deeds, for example, that are deceptive and deliberately misleading.

10   Good deeds that come from God and good deeds that come from ourselves could be compared to gold. Gold that is nothing but gold and is called unalloyed gold is good gold. Gold that is alloyed with silver is gold, too, but its value depends on the alloy, while gold alloyed with copper is less valuable.

Artificial gold, though, and things given the color of gold, are not good; there is no real gold in them.

There is also gilding. There is gilt silver, copper, iron, tin, and lead, and also gilt wood and gilt stone. They may look like gold superficially, but since they are not gold they are valued according to their artistry or the cost of the gilding or the cost of the gold that can be stripped from them. This value is as different from that of gold as the value of clothes is from the value of the one who is wearing them.

For that matter, you can cover rotten wood or slag or even excrement with gold. This is "gold" that could be compared to pharisaical "good works."

11   We can tell by science whether gold is substantially good, whether it is alloyed or fake, or whether it is just gilding; but science cannot tell us whether the good we are doing is essentially good. All we know is that good actions that come from God are good and good actions that come from ourselves are not good; so since it is important for our salvation to know whether the good things we are doing come from God or not, this needs to be revealed. Before it is revealed, though, something needs to be said about good works.

12   There are good works that are civic, good works that are moral, and good works that are spiritual. Good works that are civic are things we do because of civic law. To the extent that we practice civic goodness, we

are citizens of this earthly world. Good works that are moral are things we do because of rational law. To the extent that we practice moral goodness, we are human. Good works that are spiritual are things we do because of spiritual law. To the extent that we practice spiritual goodness, we are citizens of the spiritual world.

These types of goodness follow in this sequence: spiritual goodness is highest, moral goodness is intermediate, and civic goodness is lowest.[317]

13 If we have spiritual goodness we are moral and civic individuals as well; but if we do not have spiritual goodness we may seem to be moral and civic individuals but in fact we are not.

The reason we are moral and civic if we have spiritual goodness is that spiritual goodness contains within itself the essence of what is good and is the source of moral and civic goodness. The only possible source of the real essence of goodness is the one who is goodness itself. Cast the net of your thinking as wide as you will, concentrate, and ask what makes good good, and you will see that it is its essence; a good deed is good if it has the essence of goodness within it. This means that a deed is good if it originates in goodness itself—in God. So if some good deed originates not in God but in ourselves, it is not good.[318]

14 You can see from what it says in §§27, 28, and 38 of *Teachings on Sacred Scripture*[319] that what is first, what is intermediate, and what is last make a single entity like a goal, the means to it, and its result;[320] and because they do make a single entity, the goal itself is called the primary goal, the means is an intermediate goal, and the result is the final goal. So you must see that for us, if we have spiritual goodness, our moral goodness is spiritual on the intermediate level, and our civic goodness is spiritual on the lowest level.

That is why, as already noted, if we have spiritual goodness we are moral and civic individuals as well; but if we do not have spiritual goodness we are neither moral nor civic but only seem to be. We seem to be to ourselves and to others as well.

15 The reason we can still think and therefore talk rationally, like spiritual people, even when we ourselves are not spiritual is that our understanding can be raised into heaven's light,[321] which is truth, and can see things on that basis. However, our will cannot in the same way be lifted into heaven's warmth, which is love, and act on that basis.

That is why truth and love are not united in us unless we are spiritual. It is also why we possess the power of speech. This actually is what differentiates us from animals. It is because our understanding can be raised into heaven when our will has not yet been raised that we can be reformed and can become spiritual. We are not reformed and do not become spiritual, though, until our will has been raised.

Because at first our understanding has more of this ability than our will does, we are able to think and therefore talk rationally like spiritual people no matter what our nature, even if we are evil. However, the reason we are not rational is that our understanding does not lead our will. Rather, our will leads our understanding, as noted in §115 of *Teachings on Sacred Scripture.* All understanding does is teach us and show us the way; and as long as our will is not one with our understanding in heaven, we are not spiritual and therefore are not rational. You see, when we are left to our will or love, then we toss out our rational thinking about God, heaven, and eternal life and instead pick up whatever agrees with our will or love and call this "rational." But this will be given further attention in the works on angelic wisdom.[322]

16 In what follows, people who do good actions that come from themselves will be called "earthly people," since their moral and civic behavior is earthly in essence; while people who do good actions that come from the Lord will be called "spiritual people," because their moral and civic behavior is spiritual in essence.

17 The Lord tells us in John that no one can do anything that is genuinely good on his or her own:

> People cannot receive anything unless it has been given to them from heaven. (John 3:27)

And again,

> Those who abide in me and in whom I abide bear much fruit, because without me you cannot do anything. (John 15:5)

"Those who abide in me and in whom I abide bear much fruit" means that everything good comes from the Lord—"fruit" meaning what is good. "Without me you cannot do anything" means that none of us can do good on our own.

People who believe in the Lord and who do what is good from him are called "children of the light" (John 12:36; Luke 16:8), "children of the wedding" (Mark 2:19), "children of the resurrection" (Luke 20:36), "children of God" (Luke 20:36; John 1:12), and those "born of God"

(John 1:13). It says that "they will see God" (Matthew 5:8), that "the Lord will make a home with them" (John 14:23), that they "have the faith of God" (Mark 11:22), and that "their deeds have been done in God" (John 3:21).

These statements are summed up in the following words:

> As many as received Jesus, he gave them power to become children of God and believe in his name, who were born not of blood, and not of the will of the flesh, and not of the will of a man, but of God. (John 1:12, 13)

Believing in the name of the Son of God is believing the Word and living by it. The will of the flesh is our own will, which in and of itself is evil; and the will of a man is our own understanding, which in and of itself is false as a result of the evil. Those who are born of these are people who derive what they intend and act and think and speak from their own selves. Those born of God are people who derive what they intend and act and think and speak from the Lord.

In brief, what comes from us is not good. What comes from the Lord is good.

To the Extent That We Turn Our Backs on Evil Deeds Because They Are Sins, the Good Deeds We Do Come Not from Ourselves but from the Lord

IS there anyone who does not and cannot know that our evils stand in the way of the Lord's ability to come in to us?[323] Evil is hell and the Lord is heaven, and hell and heaven are opposites; so to the extent that we are in one we cannot be in the other. One acts against the other and cancels it.

19 As long as we are in this world we are in between hell and heaven—hell is below us and heaven above us—and during this time we are kept in a freedom to turn toward hell or toward heaven. If we turn toward hell we are turning away from heaven, while if we turn toward heaven we are turning away from hell.[324]

In other words, as long as we are in this world we are placed in between the Lord and the Devil[325] and are kept in a freedom to turn toward the one or the other. If we turn toward the Devil we turn our backs on the Lord, while if we turn toward the Lord we turn our backs on the Devil.

Or to put it yet another way, as long as we are in this world we are in between what is evil and what is good and are kept in a freedom to turn toward the one or the other. If we turn toward what is evil we turn our backs on what is good, while if we turn toward what is good we turn our backs on what is evil.

20 I have stated that we are kept in a freedom of turning either way. This freedom never comes from us; it comes from the Lord, which is why I just said that we are kept in it.

On the balance between heaven and hell, our being in that balance, and our therefore being in freedom, see *Heaven and Hell* 589–596 and 597–603. As for everyone being kept in freedom and no one being deprived of it, that will come up in its own place [§§101–102].

21 This makes it very clear that to the extent that we turn our backs on evil deeds we are with the Lord and in the Lord; and to the extent that we are in the Lord the good deeds we do come not from ourselves but from the Lord. This yields the following general law: *To the extent that we turn our backs on evil deeds, we do good deeds.*

22 Two things are required, though. First, we need to turn our backs on evil deeds because they are sins—that is, because they are hellish and diabolical and therefore contrary to the Lord and to divine laws. Second, we need to turn our backs on evil deeds because they are sins as if we were doing it on our own, but we need to know and believe that it comes from the Lord. Both of these requirements will be discussed under other headings [§§62–66 and 101–107].

23 There are three corollaries to this.

1. If we intend and do good deeds before we turn our backs on evil deeds because they are sins, our good deeds are not good.
2. If we think and speak devoutly but do not turn our backs on evil deeds because they are sins, our devout thoughts and words are not devout.

3. Even if we are well informed and insightful, if we do not turn our backs on evil deeds because they are sins, we are not wise.

1. *If we intend and do good deeds before we turn our backs on evil deeds because they are sins, our good deeds are not good.* This is because we are not in the Lord yet, as just noted [§21]. For example, if we give to the poor, help the needy, endow churches and hospices, support the church, our country, and our fellow citizens, teach the gospel, make converts, practice justice in judgment, honesty in business, and righteousness in our behavior, but still think nothing of evil like fraud, adultery, hatred, blasphemy, and such things, which are sins, then the only good deeds we can do are inwardly evil. We are doing them on our own behalf, that is, and not on behalf of the Lord. This means that we are inside them and the Lord is not; and any good deeds that have ourselves within them are all polluted by our evils and are focused on ourselves and the world.

However, the same deeds just listed are inwardly good if we are turning from evils because they are sins, evils like fraud, adultery, hatred, blasphemy, and the like. That is, the actions we are doing come from the Lord, and are called *deeds done in God* (John 3:19, 20, 21).

2. *If we think and speak devoutly but do not turn our backs on evil deeds because they are sins, our devout thoughts and words are not devout.* This is because we are not in the Lord. For example, if we attend church regularly, listen reverently to the sermons, read the Word and religious literature, take the Holy Supper, offer our prayers every day, and give a great deal of thought to God and salvation, if we think nothing of evils that are sins—fraud, for example, or adultery, hatred, blasphemy, and the like—then the only devout thought and speech we are capable of is thought and speech that inwardly are not devout at all, because we ourselves with all our evils are within them. We are not aware of this when these acts are happening, but our evils are still in there and are hiding from our sight. It is like a spring whose waters are impure from their source.

At those times our devotional practices are nothing but a routine that has become habitual; or we are thinking highly of ourselves; or we are hypocritical. They do rise up toward heaven, yes, but along the way they turn back and come down the way smoke does in the atmosphere.

I have been granted the opportunity to see and hear many people after their deaths listing their good works and their devotional practices along the lines of those just mentioned in §§24 and 25, along with some others as well. I also saw that some of them had lamps but no oil,[326] and when they were asked whether they had turned their backs on evil deeds because they are sins it turned out that they had not. So they were told that they were evil, and later I saw them going into caves where there were other evil people like themselves.

27   3. *Even if we are well informed and insightful, if we do not turn our backs on evil deeds because they are sins, we are not wise.* This too is for the reason just given [§§21, 24, 25], that our wisdom comes from ourselves and not from the Lord. For example, if we know the theology of our church right down to the last detail and know how to support it on the basis of the Word and of reason; if we know the theologies of all the churches through the ages, along with the edicts of all the councils; in fact, if we know truths and see and understand them as well—if, for example, we know what faith is, what caring is, what piety is, what repentance and the forgiveness of sins are, what regeneration is, what baptism and the Holy Supper are, what the Lord is and what redemption and salvation are—we still are not wise unless we turn our backs on evils because they are sins. These are lifeless pieces of information, because they involve only our power of understanding and not at the same time our power of willing. Things like this perish in the course of time for the reasons given in §15 above. After death we ourselves actually discard them because they do not agree with the love that belongs to our will.

All the same, these pieces of information are absolutely necessary because they tell us how we are to behave; and when we do them they come to life for us, but not before.

28   Everything said so far can be found in many places in the Word. I may cite only the following few.

The Word tells us that no one can be focused on doing good and doing evil at the same time, or—which amounts to the same thing—with respect to our souls we cannot be in heaven and in hell at the same time. It tells us this by saying,

> No one can serve two masters; for you will either hate the one and love the other or hold to the one and despise the other. You cannot serve God and Mammon. (Matthew 6:24)

> How can the things you say be good when you are evil? Out of the abundance of the heart the mouth speaks. Good people out of the good treasure of their hearts bring forth good things, and evil people out of the evil treasure bring forth evil things. (Matthew 12:34, 35)

> A good tree does not bear bad fruit, and a bad tree does not bear good fruit. Every tree is known by its own fruit. People do not gather figs from thorns or harvest grapes from a bramble bush. (Luke 6:43, 44)

29 The Word tells us that none of us can do what is good on our own; our actions are good only if they come from the Lord.

> Jesus said, "I am the vine, and my Father is the vinedresser. Every branch in me that does not bear fruit he takes away; and every branch that bears fruit he prunes, so that it will bear more fruit. Abide in me, and I [will abide] in you. As a branch cannot bear fruit on its own unless it abides in the vine, the same goes for you unless you abide in me. I am the vine; you are the branches. Those who abide in me and in whom I abide bear much fruit, because without me you cannot do anything. If any do not abide in me they are cast out as branches and wither; people gather them and throw them into the fire, and they are burned." (John 15:1–6)

30 The Word tells us in the following passage that to the extent that we are *not* purified from our evils, any good things we do are not good, any devout deeds are not devout, and we are not wise; but the reverse is the case if we *are* purified.

> Woe to you, scribes and Pharisees, hypocrites, because you make yourselves like whitewashed tombs that look beautiful outwardly, but are inwardly full of dead people's bones and filth of every kind. Even so, you look righteous outwardly, but are inwardly full of hypocrisy and iniquity. Woe to you, because you cleanse the outside of the cup and the plate, but inside they are full of extortion and excess. Blind Pharisee, cleanse the inside of the cup and the plate first, so that the outside of them may be clean as well. (Matthew 23:25–28)

Then there are these words of Isaiah:

> Hear the word of Jehovah, you princes of Sodom! Hear the law of our God, you people of Gomorrah! What use to me are your abundant sacrifices? Do not keep bringing worthless offerings! Your incense is an abomination to me, your celebrations of the new moon and Sabbaths. I cannot abide iniquity. My soul hates your new moon celebrations and prescribed feasts, so when you spread forth your hands I hide my eyes from you. Even though you multiply your prayers, I am not

listening—your hands are full of blood. Wash yourselves! Purify yourselves! Take away the evil of your deeds from before my eyes! Stop doing evil! Even if your sins have been like scarlet, they will become white like snow; even if they have been red, they will be like wool. (Isaiah 1:10–18)

Put briefly, this is saying that unless we turn our backs on evil deeds, none of our worship is any good. The same holds true for everything we do, since it says "I cannot abide iniquity; purify yourselves; take away the evil of your deeds; stop doing evil." In Jeremiah,

Turn back, all of you, from your evil way, and make your works good. (Jeremiah 35:15)

[2] These people are not wise, either. See the following from Isaiah:

Woe to those who are wise in their own eyes and intelligent in their own estimation. (Isaiah 5:21)

Again,

The wisdom of the wise will perish, as will the intelligence of the intelligent. Woe to those whose wisdom is profound and whose deeds are done in darkness. (Isaiah 29:14, 15)

And yet again,

Woe to those who go down to Egypt for help and who rely on horses, who trust in an abundance of chariots and in the strength of riders, but do not look to the Holy One of Israel and do not seek Jehovah. He will rise up against the house of the malicious and against the aid of those who work iniquity, because Egypt is not God, and its horses are flesh, and not spirit. (Isaiah 31:1, 2, 3)

That is how our own intelligence is described. Egypt is mere facts; a horse is our understanding of those facts; chariots are religious teachings based on those facts; and riders are the intelligence we develop as a result. Of these qualities we read, "Woe to those who do not look to the Holy One of Israel and do not seek Jehovah." "He will rise up against the house of the malicious and against the aid of those who work iniquity" means the destruction of these qualities by evils. "Egypt is human, not God, and her horses are flesh, and not spirit" means that this understanding comes from our own sense of self-importance and that therefore there is no life in it. "Human" and "flesh" are our own sense of self, and "God" and "spirit" are life that comes from the Lord. The horses of Egypt are the intelligence that we claim as our own.[327]

There are many similar passages in the Word whose focus on self-derived intelligence and intelligence that comes from the Lord can be seen only through their spiritual meaning.

[3] We can see from the following passages that none of us can be saved by means of good works done by ourselves, because they are not good.

> Not everyone who says to me, "Lord, Lord," will enter the kingdom of the heavens, but those who do the will of my Father. On that day many will say to me, "Lord, Lord, haven't we prophesied in your name, cast out demons in your name, and done many great things in your name?" But then I will declare to them, "I do not know you. Depart from me, *you workers of iniquity.*" (Matthew 7:21, 22, 23)

And in another passage,

> Then you begin to stand outside and knock on the door, saying, "Lord, open the door for us!" Then you will begin to say, "We ate and drank in your presence, and you taught in our streets." But he will say, "I tell you, I do not know where you are from. Depart from me, all you *workers of iniquity.*" (Luke 13:25, 26, 27)

They are in fact like the Pharisee who prayed, standing in the Temple, saying that he was not greedy, unjust, or adulterous like other people, but fasted twice a week and gave tithes of all he possessed (Luke 18:11–14). They are also the ones called "worthless servants" (Luke 17:10).

The truth is that none of us can on our own do anything good that is really good; but it is outrageous to use this principle to nullify all the good and caring actions done by people who turn away from evils because they are sins.[328] Using this principle in this way is in fact diametrically opposed to the Word, which mandates what we are to do; it is contrary to the commandments of love for the Lord and love for our neighbor on which depend all the Law and the Prophets[329] [Matthew 22:40]; and it is to demean and subvert everything that has to do with religion. Everyone knows that religion means doing what is good and that we are all going to be judged according to our deeds.

We are all by nature capable of turning away from evils with apparent autonomy because of the Lord's power, if we pray for that power; and what we then do is good that comes from the Lord.

To the Extent That We Turn Our Backs on Evils Because They Are Sins, We Love What Is True

32 THERE are two absolutes that emanate from the Lord: divine goodness and divine truth. Divine goodness comes from his divine love, and divine truth comes from his divine wisdom. In the Lord, these two are one and therefore they emanate from him as one. However, they are not received as one by angels in the heavens[330] or by us on earth. There are some angels and people who receive more of divine truth than of divine goodness, and there are others who receive more of divine goodness than of divine truth. That is why the heavens are divided into two kingdoms, one called the heavenly kingdom and the other called the spiritual kingdom. The heavens that receive more of divine goodness form the heavenly kingdom, and the ones that receive more of divine truth form the spiritual kingdom. On these two kingdoms into which the heavens are divided, see §§20–28 of *Heaven and Hell*.

[2] Still, the angels of all the heavens enjoy wisdom and intelligence only to the extent that the goodness they practice is united to truth. Any good action of theirs that is not united to truth is for them not actually good; and conversely any truth they possess that is not united to good actions is for them not actually true. We can see from this that goodness united to truth makes love and wisdom for an angel and for us; and since angels are angels because of their love and wisdom, and since the same holds true for us, we can see that goodness united to truth is what makes an angel an angel of heaven and a person a true member of the church.[331]

33 Since what is good and what is true are one in the Lord and emanate from him as one, it follows that goodness loves truth, truth loves goodness, and they want to be one. The same holds true for their opposites. What is evil loves what is false and what is false loves what is evil, and they want to be one. In the following pages the union of goodness and truth will be called "the heavenly marriage" and the union of evil and falsity "the hellish marriage."[332]

34 One consequence of this is that to the extent that we turn our backs on evils because they are sins, we love what is true. That is, we are to that extent focused on what is good, as explained under the previous heading [§§18–31]. Conversely, to the extent that we do not turn our backs on evils because they are sins, we do not love what is true, because to that same extent we are not focused on what is good.

Actually, people who do not turn their backs on evils because they are sins can love what is true. However, they do not love it because it is true but because it enhances their reputation as a means to rank or profit. So if the truth does not enhance their reputation, they do not love it.

Goodness shapes our will, and truth shapes our understanding. From a love for what is good in our will comes a love for what is true in our understanding. From the love for what is true comes a perception of what is true; from a perception of what is true comes thought about what is true; from these comes the recognition of what is true that is faith in its proper definition. It will be shown in the work *Divine Love and Wisdom* that this is how we progress to faith from a love for what is good.[333]

Since goodness is not genuinely good unless it is united to what is true, as noted [§32], it follows that goodness does not become actual prior to that union, and yet it is constantly trying to become so. In order to become actual, it longs for and acquires truths for itself. These are the means of its nourishment and its formation. This is why we love what is true to the extent that we are focused on what is good, and accordingly to the same extent that we turn our backs on evils because they are sins; because that determines the extent to which we are focused on what is good.

To the extent that we are focused on what is good and love what is true for the sake of what is good, we are loving the Lord, because the Lord is goodness itself and truth itself. So the Lord is with us in what is good and in what is true. If we love truth for the sake of goodness, then and only then do we love the Lord. This the Lord tells us in John:

> The people who love me are those who have my commandments and do them. Those who do not love me do not keep my words. (John 14:21, 24)

And again,

> If you keep my commandments, you will abide in my love. (John 15:10)

The Lord's words and commandments are truths.

We can illustrate the fact that goodness loves what is true by taking priests, soldiers, merchants, and artisans as examples. With respect to *priests,* if they are focused on the good that a priest can do, which is looking out for the salvation of souls, teaching the way to heaven, and leading the people they teach, then because they are focused on this goodness, because they love and long for it, they acquire the truths that they teach and that enable them to lead.

On the other hand, priests who are not focused on the good that priests can do but rather on the rewards of the office[334]—and who are this way because of love for themselves and for the world, which is all they regard as good—then because of that love and longing they too acquire as much truth as the reward that is their "goodness" inspires them to acquire.

As for *soldiers,* if they have a love for military service and see some good in it, whether in providing protection or in seeking their own glory, then because of the goodness they seek and in keeping with it they acquire the necessary knowledge and, if they are officers, understanding. These are the truths by which the pleasure of their love, which is their "goodness," is nourished and given form.

As for *merchants,* if they commit themselves to being in business because they love it, they gladly take in everything that serves as a means of putting together and building what they love. These means, too, are like truths, when doing business is the goodness these people love.[335]

As for *artisans,* if they apply themselves to their work diligently and love it as what makes their life worthwhile, they buy their tools and improve themselves by learning what they need to know. This is what makes their work good.

We can see from all this that truths are the means by which the good that we do out of love becomes manifest, becomes something; so goodness loves what is true in order to become manifest.

So in the Word, "doing the truth" means acting in such a way that some good will be done. This is the meaning of "doing the truth" in John 3:21, "doing what the Lord says" in Luke 6:46, "doing his commandments" in John 14:21, "doing his words" in Matthew 7:24, "doing the Word of God" in Luke 8:21, and "doing the statutes and judgments" in Leviticus 18:5.

This is also the meaning of "doing good" and "bearing fruit," because what is done is something "good," some "fruit."

40 We can illustrate the fact that what is good loves what is true and wants to be united to it if we think of food and water or bread and wine. We need both. Food or bread alone does nothing for the nourishment of the body without water or wine, so each seeks for and calls for the other. In fact, in the Word as spiritually understood, food and bread mean what is good, while water and wine mean what is true.[336]

[41] We may conclude from what has been said that if we turn our backs on evils because they are sins, then we love truths and long for them. The more resolutely we turn our backs, the more we love and long for truths, because we are that much more focused on what is good. This is how we attain the heavenly marriage that is the marriage of goodness and truth, the marriage in which heaven is and the church should be.

To the Extent That We Turn Our Backs on Evils Because They Are Sins, We Have Faith and Are Spiritual

[42] OUR faith and our life are distinct from each other in the same way that our thought and our actions are distinct. Since our thinking comes from our understanding and our actions come from our will, it follows that our faith and our life are also distinct from each other in the same way that our understanding and our will are distinct. And therefore someone who knows how our understanding and our will are distinct also knows how our faith and our life are distinct; and someone who knows how our understanding and our will become one also knows how our faith and our life become one. That is why I need to start with something about understanding and will.

[43] We have two abilities, one called *will* and the other *understanding*. They can be distinguished from each other, but they were so created as to be one, and when they are one they are called *the mind*. This means that they are the human mind; they are the home of all that is alive in us. Just as all things in the universe (those that agree with the divine design)337 trace their origin back to goodness and truth, so everything in us traces its origin back to our will and our understanding. This is because whatever is good in us resides in our will and whatever is true in us resides in our understanding. These two faculties receive and are acted upon by what is good and true: our will is what receives and is acted upon by anything

that is good, and our understanding is what receives and is acted upon by anything that is true. Further, since what is good and what is true in us are not to be found anywhere else, neither are love and faith, since love and goodness are mutually dependent, and so are faith and truth.

[2] There is no knowledge more relevant than knowing how our will and understanding make one mind. They make one mind the way goodness and truth make a single reality. There is the same kind of marriage between will and understanding as there is between what is good and what is true. You can catch a glimpse of what that marriage is like from what has just been presented under the previous heading [§§32–41]; to which I should add that just as everything has goodness as its underlying reality and truth as its consequent manifestation, so our will is the underlying reality of our life and our understanding is its consequent manifestation. This is because any instance of goodness that comes from our will takes form in our understanding and makes itself visible[338] to us there in some specific way.

44 I explained in §§27–28 above that we can know a great deal, can think and understand, and still not be wise; and since faith involves knowing and thinking and especially understanding that something is so, we can believe that we have faith although in fact we do not. The reason we do not have faith is that we are leading an evil life, and there is no way that an evil life and the truth we believe can act in unison. The evil we practice destroys the truth we believe. This is because the evil we practice resides in our will, but the truth we believe resides in our understanding; and will leads understanding and makes it act in unison with itself. So if there is anything in our understanding that does not agree with our will, when we are left to ourselves and are thinking on the basis of our evil and its love, then we either discard the truth that is in our understanding or make it cooperate by distorting it.

It is different if we are leading a good life. Then when we are left to ourselves we think on the basis of what is good, and love the truth that is in our understanding because it agrees. So there is a union of faith and life like the union of what is true and what is good, and both the former and the latter are like the union between understanding and will.

45 It then follows that as we turn our backs on evils because they are sins we have faith, because as explained just above this means that we are focused on what is good. There is support for this in the contrasting fact that if we do not turn our backs on evils because they are sins we do not have faith, because we are focused on what is evil, and evil has an intrinsic hatred for truth. Outwardly, yes, we can befriend truth and put up with it and even love having it in our understanding; but when we shed that outwardness, as happens after death, we first discard the truth we befriended in the world, then we deny that it is true, and finally we turn away from it.

When we are evil, our faith is an intellectual faith that has nothing good in it from our will. As a result, it is a dead faith[339] that is like breathing with our lungs but without any life from our heart (our understanding corresponds to our lungs and our will corresponds to our heart).[340] It is also like an alluring whore, decked out with rouge and jewels, who has a virulent disease within. In fact, whores correspond to the distortion of what is true and therefore have that meaning in the Word.

It is also like a tree with lush foliage that does not bear fruit, a tree that the gardener cuts down. A tree stands for a person, too, its flowers and leaves meaning the truths we believe and its fruit meaning our love for doing good.[341]

But the faith residing in our understanding is different if it has within itself a goodness that comes from our will. It is alive and is like the breathing of our lungs that has its life from our heart. It is also like an attractive wife who is loved by her husband because of her chastity, and like a tree that is fruitful.

There are many things that seem to require faith only, such as the existence of God, the Lord who is God being our Redeemer and Savior, the reality of heaven and hell, life after death, and any number of other issues. We describe them not as things to be done but as things to be believed. Yet even these matters of faith are dead if we are focused on what is evil, but alive if we are focused on what is good.

This is because when we are focused on what is good we not only behave well because of our will but also think well because of our understanding; this not only in front of others, in public, but also in our own sight, when we are alone. It is different when we are focused on what is evil.

As just mentioned, these beliefs seem to require faith only. But the thinking in our understanding is a manifestation of the love that belongs to our will; that love is the underlying reality of the thinking in our understanding (see §43 above). That is, if we will to do something because of love, we want to do it—we want to think it, we want to understand it, and we want to say it. Or in other words, whatever we love because of intent we love to do, we love to think, we love to understand, and we love to say.

Then too, when we turn our backs on evils because they are sins we are in the Lord, as explained above [§§18–31], and the Lord is doing everything. That is why the Lord said to those who were asking him what they should do in order to work the works of God, "This is the work of God, that you believe in the one whom he has sent" (John 6:29). Believing in the Lord is not simply thinking that he exists but is also doing what he says, as he tells us elsewhere.[342]

49 People who are caught up in evil do not have any faith even though they believe that they do, as I have been shown by seeing some people of this sort in the spiritual world. They were brought into a heavenly community, which caused the spiritual quality of the angels' faith to enter into the deeper levels of the faith of the visitors. This made the visitors aware of the fact that all they had was an earthly or outward faith and not its spiritual or inner reality. So they themselves admitted that they had no faith whatever and that in the world they had convinced themselves that if they thought something was true for any reason at all, that was "believing" or "having faith."

The faith of people who have not been devoted to evil, though, looks very different.

50 This shows us what a spiritual faith is and what a nonspiritual faith is. Spiritual faith is characteristic of people who do not commit sins, because the good actions of people who do not[343] commit sins come from the Lord and not from themselves (see §§18–31 above); and through their faith they become spiritual. For them, faith is truth.

This is how the Lord says it in John:

> This is the condemnation, that light has come into the world, but people loved darkness rather than light, because their deeds were evil. All who do evil hate the light and do not come to the light, or else their deeds would be exposed; but those who do the truth come to the light so that their deeds may be clearly seen, because their deeds were done in God. (John 3:19, 20, 21)

51 The following passages support what has been said thus far:

> Good people out of the good treasure of their hearts bring forth what is good; evil people out of the evil treasure of their hearts bring forth what is evil. Out of the abundance of the heart the mouth speaks. (Luke 6:45; Matthew 12:35)

In the Word, the heart means our will, and since this is the source of our thinking and speaking, it says that "out of the abundance of the heart the mouth speaks."

> It is not what goes into the mouth that makes people unclean but what comes out of the heart;³⁴⁴ this is what makes people unclean. (Matthew 15:11)

Again, the heart means our will. And Jesus said of the woman who had washed his feet with anointing oil that her sins were forgiven because she loved greatly; and later added, "Your faith is saving you" (Luke 7:46–50).

We can see from these words that when our sins are forgiven—that is, when they are no longer there—our faith saves us.

In John 1:12, 13 the Lord tells us that people are called "children of God" and "born of God" when their will is not full of a sense of self-importance and their understanding is therefore not clouded by that same sense of self-importance—that is, when they are not focused on what is evil and therefore on what is false. He also teaches us there that such people are the ones who believe in the Lord. For an explanation of these verses, see the end of §17 above.

The conclusion follows from this that there is not the slightest bit more of truth in us than there is of what is good, so there is not the slightest bit more of faith than there is of life. The knowledge that something is so may exist in our understanding, but unless our will agrees, that knowledge is not the acknowledgment that constitutes faith. So faith and life walk side by side.

This now allows us to see that to the extent we turn our backs on evils because they are sins, we have faith and are spiritual.

The Ten Commandments Tell Us Which Evils Are Sins

IS there any society anywhere on the globe that does not know that it is evil to steal, commit adultery, murder, and bear false witness? If they did not know this, and if they were not prevented by laws from doing these things, it would be all over for them, because any community or republic or kingdom would collapse if it did not have these laws. Could anyone presume that the Israelite nation was so much more stupid than everyone else that they did not know these things were evil? So we might wonder why these laws, so well known over the whole face of the earth, were made public by Jehovah himself from Mount Sinai in such miraculous fashion.

But the truth is that they were made public in such miraculous fashion to let Israel know that these laws are not merely civil and moral laws but are spiritual laws as well, and that breaking them is not only harmful to our fellow citizens and communities but is also a sin against God. So the proclamation of these laws from Mount Sinai by Jehovah made them laws of religion. It is obvious that if Jehovah God commands something, he does so in order to make it a part of our religion, as something that needs to be done for his sake and for the sake of our own salvation.

54 Because these laws were the very beginnings of the Word and therefore of the church[345] that the Lord was establishing with the Israelite people, and because they brought together in a brief summary all the elements of religion that make possible the Lord's union with us and our union with the Lord, they were so holy that nothing is holier.

55 We can tell how supremely holy they were from the fact that Jehovah himself—the Lord, that is—came down upon Mount Sinai in fire, with angels, and proclaimed them from there with his own voice, and that the people spent three days preparing themselves for seeing and hearing all this. The mountain was also fenced off so that no one would approach it and die. Not even priests or elders were allowed near; Moses alone was allowed. The laws were written on two stone tablets by the finger of God. When Moses brought the tablets down from the mountain the second time, his face shone. Later they were placed in an ark, which was set in the very heart of the tabernacle and had a mercy seat on it, with angel guardians made of gold above that. There was nothing holier in their church, and it was called "the most holy place." Outside the veil that surrounded it they brought together things that represented holy elements of heaven and the church—the lampstand with its seven golden lamps, the golden altar of incense, and the gilded table for the showbread, all surrounded by curtains of fine linen and purple and scarlet thread. The sole reason for the holiness of this whole tabernacle was the law that was in the ark.

[2] Because of the holiness of the tabernacle, which resulted from the presence of the law in the ark, the whole Israelite population camped around it, in a set arrangement tribe by tribe, and traveled behind it in a set sequence. There was also a cloud above it in the daytime then, and

fire above it at night. Because of the holiness of the law and the Lord's presence in it, it was upon the mercy seat between the angel guardians that the Lord spoke to Moses, and the ark was called "Jehovah" there. In fact Aaron was not allowed to go behind the veil without sacrifices and incense.

Because the law was the essential holiness of the church, David brought the ark into Zion, and it was later placed at the center of the Jerusalem temple where [Solomon] had made an inner sanctuary for it.

[3] Because of the Lord's presence in and around the law, miracles were performed by means of the ark in which the law lay. For example, the waters of the Jordan were cut off, and as long as the ark rested in its midst, the people crossed over on dry ground. The walls of Jericho fell because the ark was carried around them. Dagon, the god of the Philistines, fell before the ark and later lay on the threshold of the shrine with its head broken off. Tens of thousands of the people of Beth-shemesh were struck down because of the ark, and so on. All these things happened simply because of the Lord's presence in his "Ten Words," which are the Ten Commandments.[346]

Another reason for the power and holiness of that law is that it is a summary of everything that constitutes religion. That is, it consisted of two tablets, one briefly containing everything that has to do with God and the other everything that has to do with us.[347] That is why the commandments of that law are called "the Ten Words"—so called because "ten" means "all."

How that law summarizes everything that constitutes religion, though, will be explained under the next heading [§64].

Because that law is the means of the Lord's union with us and our union with the Lord, it is called a *covenant* and a *testimony*—a covenant because it unites and a testimony because it bears witness.

That is why there were two tablets, one for the Lord and one for us. The union is effected by the Lord, but it is effected when we do what is written on our tablet. That is, the Lord is constantly present and active and wanting to come in, but because of the freedom he gives us, it is up to us to open [the door], for he says,

> Behold, I stand at the door and knock. If any hear my voice and open the door, I will come in to them and dine with them and they with me. (Revelation 3:20)

In the second tablet, which is for us, it does not say that we must do some specific good thing but that we must not do some specific evil thing—for example, "You are not to kill, you are not to commit adultery, you are not to steal, you are not to bear false witness, you are not to covet." This is because we cannot do anything good on our own, but when we do not do evil things, the good things we do come not from ourselves but from the Lord.

We shall see in what follows [§§101–107] that we can turn our backs on evil—seemingly on our own, but actually with the Lord's power—if we ask for this humbly.

59 The statements made in §55 above about the proclamation, holiness, and power of the law may be found in the following passages in the Word: Jehovah came down in fire upon Mount Sinai and the mountain smoked and shook; and there was thunder, lightning, thick clouds, and the sound of a trumpet (Exodus 19:16, 18; Deuteronomy 4:11; 5:22–23). Before Jehovah came down, the people spent three days preparing and sanctifying themselves (Exodus 19:10, 11, 15). The mountain was fenced off so that no one would approach and come near its base and die; not even priests were allowed near; Moses alone was allowed (Exodus 19:12, 13, 20–23; 24:1, 2). The law was proclaimed from Mount Sinai (Exodus 20:2–17; Deuteronomy 5:6–21). The law was written on two stone tablets by the finger of God (Exodus 31:18; 32:15, 16; Deuteronomy 9:10). When Moses brought the tablets down from the mountain the second time, his face shone (Exodus 34:29–35). The tablets were placed in an ark (Exodus 25:16; 40:20; Deuteronomy 10:5; 1 Kings 8:9). On top of the ark there was a mercy seat, and on the mercy seat were placed angel guardians made of gold (Exodus 25:17–21). The ark, with the mercy seat and the angel guardians, formed the very heart of the tabernacle, while the golden lampstand, the golden altar of incense, and the gilded table for the showbread were placed just outside [the veil], and all these objects were surrounded in turn by the ten curtains of fine linen and purple and scarlet [thread] (Exodus 25:1 to the end; 26:1 to the end; 40:17–28). The area set aside for the ark was called "the most holy place" (Exodus 26:33). The whole Israelite population camped around the dwelling, in a set arrangement tribe by tribe, and traveled behind it in a set sequence (Numbers 2:1 to the end). There was a cloud above the tabernacle in the daytime then, and fire above it at night (Exodus 40:38; Numbers 9:15, 16 to the end; 14:14; Deuteronomy 1:33). The Lord spoke with Moses from above the ark, between the angel guardians (Exodus 25:22; Numbers 7:89). Because it contained the law, the ark was called "Jehovah" there: when the ark would set out, Moses would say, "Rise up, Jehovah," and when it would come to rest he would say, "Return, Jehovah" (Numbers 10:35, 36; see also 2 Samuel 6:2 and Psalms 132:7, 8). Because of the holiness of the law, Aaron was not allowed to go behind the veil without sacrifices and incense (Leviticus 16:2–14 and following). David brought the ark into Zion with sacrifices and rejoicing (2 Samuel 6:1–19). At that time Uzzah died because he touched the ark (2 Samuel 6:6, 7). [Solomon] placed the ark at the center of the Jerusalem temple, where he had made an inner sanctuary for it (1 Kings 6:19 and following; 8:3–9). Because of the Lord's presence and power in the law that was in the ark, the waters of the Jordan were cut off; and as long as the ark rested in its midst, the people crossed over on dry ground (Joshua 3:1–17; 4:5–20). The walls of Jericho fell because the ark was carried around them (Joshua 6:1–20). Dagon, the god of the Philistines, fell to the earth before the ark and later lay on the threshold of the shrine with its head broken off (1 Samuel 5:1–4). Tens of thousands of the people of Beth-shemesh were struck down because of the ark (1 Samuel 6:19).

60 The stone tablets on which the law was written were called "the tablets of the covenant," and because of them the ark was called "the ark of the covenant" and the law itself was called "the covenant" (Numbers 10:33; Deuteronomy 4:13, 23; 5:2, 3; 9:9; Joshua 3:11; 1 Kings 8:21; Revelation 11:19; and often elsewhere).

The reason the law was called the covenant is that "covenant" means union. That is why it says of the Lord that he will be "a covenant for the people" (Isaiah 42:6; 49:8); why he is called "the angel of the covenant" (Malachi 3:1); and why his blood is called "the blood of the covenant" (Matthew 26:28; Zechariah 9:11; Exodus 24:4–10). That is why the Word is called "the Old Covenant" and "the New Covenant."[348]

Covenants are made for the sake of love, friendship, and companionship, and therefore for the sake of union.

61 The commandments of the law were called "the ten words" (Exodus 34:28; Deuteronomy 4:13; 10:4). This is because "ten" means all and "words" means truths. After all, there were more than ten.

Because "ten" means all, there were ten curtains of the tabernacle (Exodus 26:1). That is why the Lord said that the one who was going to receive a kingdom called ten servants and gave them ten minas for doing business (Luke 19:13). It is why the Lord compared the kingdom of the heavens to ten young women (Matthew 25:1), and why the dragon is described as having ten horns, and ten diadems on his horns (Revelation 12:3).[349] The same holds true for the beast rising up out of the sea (Revelation 13:1), and the other beast (Revelation 17:3, 7), as well as the beast in Daniel (Daniel 7:7, 20, 24). "Ten" means the same in Leviticus 26:26, Zechariah 8:23, and elsewhere.

Similarly, "tithes"[350] mean a portion of all.

All Kinds of Murder, Adultery, Theft, and False Witness, Together with Urges toward Them, Are Evils on Which We Must Turn Our Backs Because They Are Sins

62 IT is common knowledge that the law of Sinai was written on two tablets and that the first tablet contains matters concerning God and the second, matters concerning us.[351] It is not obvious in the literal text that the first tablet contains everything to do with God and that the second contains everything to do with us, but it is all in there. It is actually why they are called "the ten words," meaning all truths in summary (see §61 just above). However, there is no way to explain briefly how everything is there, though it can be grasped by reference to what is presented in §67 of *Teachings on Sacred Scripture,* which the reader may consult.

This is the reason for mentioning "*all kinds* of murder, adultery, theft, and false witness."

63 The prevailing religious belief holds that no one can fulfill the law. And [yet] the law demands that we must not kill, commit adultery, steal, or bear false witness. Any civic and moral individual can fulfill these elements of the law by living a good civic and moral life; but this religious belief denies that we can do so by living a good spiritual life. This leads to the conclusion that our reason for not committing these crimes is simply to avoid punishment and loss in this world, but not to avoid punishment and loss after we leave this world. The result is that people who hold this conviction think that immoral actions are permissible in the eyes of God but not in the eyes of the world.

[2] Because of the kind of thinking that is based on this religious principle, people have cravings to commit all these evils; for worldly reasons only, they forgo doing them. So even if they have not committed murder, adultery, theft, or false witness, after death people like this still feel the urge to commit such sins; and they actually do when they lose the outer facade they had in the world.352 All our cravings await us after death. This is why people like this act in concert with hell and cannot help suffering the same fate as people in hell.

[3] Things turn out differently, though, if we do not want to murder, commit adultery, steal, or bear false witness, because such behavior is contrary to God. Once we have fought against them to some extent we do not intend them, so we feel no urge to do them. We say in our hearts that they are sins, essentially hellish and diabolic. Then after death, when we lose any facade we maintained for worldly reasons, we act in concert with heaven; and because we are focused on the Lord, we also enter heaven.

Every religion has the general principle that we are to examine ourselves, practice repentance, and refrain from sins, and if we do not do this, we suffer damnation. (See above, §§1–8, on this being a common feature of all religion.)

The whole Christian world also has the common practice of teaching the Ten Commandments as a way of introducing little children to the Christian religion. These commandments are in every little child's hand.353 Their parents and teachers tell them that doing such things is sinning against God. In fact, when they talk with children they have no other thought in their heads but this. It is little short of amazing that these same people, and the children when they grow up, think that they are not subject to the law and that they are incapable of doing what the law requires. Can there be any reason why they learn to think like this other than that they love evils and therefore love the false notions that support them? These are the individuals, then, who do not regard the Ten Commandments as matters of religion. See *Teachings on Faith*354 on the fact that there is no religion in the lives of such people.

Every society on the face of the whole earth that has any religion has laws like the Ten Commandments, and all the individuals who live by them as a matter of religion are saved, while all who do not live by them as a matter of religion are damned. After death, the ones who have lived by them as a matter of religion are taught by angels, accept truths, and acknowledge the Lord. This is because they have turned their backs on evils because they are sins and have therefore been devoted to doing what is good, and their resulting goodness loves truth and eagerly drinks it in (see §§32–41 above).

This is the meaning of the Lord's words to the Jews:

> The kingdom of God will be taken from you and given to a nation that bears fruit. (Matthew 21:43)

And also these words:

> When the lord of the vineyard comes, he will destroy those evil people and lease his vineyard to other farmers who will give him its fruits in their season. (Matthew 21:40, 41)

And these:

> I tell you that many will come from the east and the west, and from the north and the south, and will sit down in the kingdom of God, but the children of the kingdom will be cast out into outer darkness. (Matthew 8:11, 12; Luke 13:29)

66 We read in Mark that a certain rich man came to Jesus and asked him what he needed to do in order to inherit eternal life. Jesus said, "You know the commandments: you are not to commit adultery; you are not to kill; you are not to steal; you are not to bear false witness; you are not to commit fraud; honor your father and mother." He replied, "Since my youth I have kept all these things." Jesus looked at him and loved him, but said, "One thing you lack: Go, sell whatever you have and give to the poor, and you will have treasure in the heavens; and come, take up the cross, and follow me" (Mark 10:17–22).

[2] It says that Jesus loved him, and this was because he had kept the commandments since his youth. Because he lacked three things, though—he had not detached his heart from wealth, he had not fought against his cravings, and he had not yet acknowledged the Lord as God—the Lord told him that he was to sell everything he had, meaning that he was to detach his heart from wealth; that he was to take up the cross, meaning that he was to fight against his cravings; and that he was to follow him, meaning that he was to acknowledge the Lord as God. The Lord said these things the way he said everything else—in correspondences (see *Teachings on Sacred Scripture* 17). The fact is that we—and this means everyone—cannot turn our backs on evils because they are sins unless we acknowledge the Lord and turn to him, and unless we fight against evils, and in this way distance ourselves from our cravings.

More on this, though, under the heading concerning doing battle against evils [§§92–100].

To the Extent That We Turn Our Backs on All Kinds of Killing Because They Are Sins, We Have Love for Our Neighbor

ALL kinds of killing means all kinds of hostility, hatred, and vengefulness, which yearn for murder. Killing lies hidden within such attitudes like fire that smolders beneath the ashes. That is exactly what hellfire is.[355] It is why we say that people are on fire with hatred and burning for vengeance. These are types of killing in an earthly sense; but in a spiritual sense "killing" means all the many and varied ways of killing and destroying people's souls. Then in the highest sense it means harboring hatred for the Lord.

These three kinds of killing align and are united, since anyone who intends the physical murder of someone in this world intends the murder of that individual's soul after death and intends the murder of the Lord, actually burning with hatred against him and wanting to eradicate his name.

These kinds of killing lie hidden within us from birth, but from early childhood we learn to veil them with the civility and morality we need when we are with others in this world; and to the extent that we yearn for rank or money, we take care not to let them become visible. This latter character becomes our outside, while the former is our inside and is what we are like in and of ourselves; so you can see how demonic we will be after death, when we put off that outside along with our bodies, unless we have been reformed.

Since the kinds of killing just mentioned lie hidden within us from birth, as noted, along with all kinds of theft and all kinds of false witness and the urges to commit them (which will be described shortly [§§80–86,

87–91]), we can see that if the Lord had not provided means of reformation, we would inevitably perish forever.

The means of reformation that the Lord has provided are the following: we are born into utter ignorance; as newborns we are kept in a state of outward innocence; soon thereafter we are kept in a state of outward caring and then in a state of outward friendship. But as we become capable of thinking with our own intellect, we are kept in some freedom to act rationally. This is the state described in §19 above, and I need to turn back to it at this point for the sake of what will follow.

> As long as we are in this world we are in between hell and heaven—hell is below us and heaven above us—and during this time we are kept in a freedom to turn toward hell or toward heaven. If we turn toward hell we are turning away from heaven, while if we turn toward heaven we are turning away from hell.
>
> In other words, as long as we are in this world we are placed in between the Lord and the Devil and are kept in a freedom to turn toward the one or the other. If we turn toward the Devil we turn our backs on the Lord, while if we turn toward the Lord we turn our backs on the Devil.
>
> Or to put it yet another way, as long as we are in this world we are in between what is evil and what is good and are kept in a freedom to turn toward the one or the other. If we turn toward what is evil we turn our backs on what is good, while if we turn toward what is good we turn our backs on what is evil.

This you will find in §19; see also §§20, 21, and 22, which follow it.

70 Now, since what is evil and what is good are two opposite things, like hell and heaven or like the Devil and the Lord, it follows that if we turn our backs on something evil as a sin we come into something good that is the opposite of that evil. The goodness that is opposite to the evil meant by killing is loving our neighbor.

71 Since this goodness and that evil are opposites, it follows that the latter is repelled by the former. Two opposites cannot be one, as heaven and hell cannot be one. If they did, it would be like that lukewarm state described in the Book of Revelation as follows:

> I know that you are neither cold nor hot. It would have been better if you were cold or hot; but since you are lukewarm and neither cold nor hot, I am about to vomit you out of my mouth. (Revelation 3:15, 16)

72 When we are no longer caught up in the evil of killing but are moved by the good we do out of love for our neighbor, then whatever we do is something good that results from that love, so it is a good work. Priests who are engaged in this goodness are doing a good work whenever they teach and lead because it comes from a love for saving souls. People in administrative roles who are engaged in this goodness are doing a good work whenever they make arrangements and decisions because it comes from a love for serving the country, the community, and their fellow citizens. By the same token, if merchants are engaged in this goodness all their business is a good work. There is love for their neighbor within it, and their neighbor is the country, the community, their fellow citizens, and their own households as well, whose well-being concerns them as much as their own does. Laborers who are devoted to this goodness do their work faithfully because of it, acting as much for others as for themselves, and being as fearful of harming others as of harming themselves.

The reason their actions are good deeds is that to the extent that we turn our backs on anything evil we do something good, in keeping with the general principle presented above in §21; and anyone who turns away from something evil as a sin is doing what is good not because of his or her self but because of the Lord (see §§18–31).

On the contrary, if we do not regard all kinds of killing—hostility, hatred, vengeance, and the like—as sins, then whether we are priests, administrators, merchants, or laborers, no matter what we do it is not a good deed, because everything we do shares in the evil that is within it. It is in fact what is inside that is producing it. The outside may be good, but only for others, not for ourselves.

The Lord teaches good and loving actions in many passages in the Word. He teaches such actions in Matthew when he instructs us to be reconciled with our neighbor:

> If you bring your gift to the altar and in doing so remember that your brother or sister has something against you, leave your gift there in front of the altar. First be reconciled with your brother or sister, and then come and offer your gift. And be kind and generous to your adversary when you are both on the way [to court], to keep your adversary from turning you over to a judge, keep the judge from turning you over to an officer, and keep you from being thrown in prison. I tell you in truth, you will not be released until you have paid the last penny. (Matthew 5:23–26)

Being reconciled with our brother or sister is turning our backs on hostility, hatred, and vengefulness. We can see that this is turning our backs on these evils because they are sins.

The Lord also tells us in Matthew,

> Whatever you want people to do for you, you do the same for them. This is the Law and the Prophets. (Matthew 7:12)

[We should do] nothing evil, then; and [this is said] quite often elsewhere. Then too, the Lord tells us that killing is also being angry with our sister or brother or neighbor for no good reason and harboring hatred against them (see Matthew 5:21, 22).

To the Extent That We Turn Our Backs on All Kinds of Adultery Because They Are Sins, We Love Chastity

74 UNDERSTOOD on an earthly level, the adultery named in the sixth commandment means not only illicit sexual acts but also lecherous behavior, lewd conversation, and filthy thoughts. Understood on a spiritual level, though, adultery means polluting what is good in the Word and distorting what is true in it, while understood on the highest level it means denying the divine nature of the Lord and profaning the Word. These are "all kinds of adultery."

On the basis of rational light, earthly-minded people can know that "adultery" also means lecherous behavior, lewd conversation, and filthy thoughts, but not that adultery means polluting what is good in the Word and distorting what is true in it, and certainly not that it means denying the divine nature of the Lord and profaning the Word. So they do not know that adultery is so evil that it can be called the height of wickedness. This is because anyone who is intent on earthly adultery is also intent on spiritual adultery, and the reverse. This will be shown in a separate booklet on marriage.[356] But in fact, people whose faith and way of life do not lead them to regard adultery as a sin are engaged in the totality of adultery at every moment.

75 The reason people love marriage to the extent that they turn their backs on adultery—or to be more precise, love the chastity of marriage[357] to the extent that they turn their backs on the lechery of adultery—is that the lechery of adultery and the chastity of marriage are two opposite things. This means that to the extent that we are not intent on the one we are intent on the other. This is exactly like what has been said in §70 above.

76 We cannot know the true nature of the chastity of marriage if we do not turn our backs on the lechery of adultery as a sin. We can know something we have experienced, but not something that we have not experienced. If we know about something we have not experienced, know it on the basis of a description or by thinking about it, we know it only in the shadows, and doubt clings to it. So we see it in the light and without doubt only when we have experienced it. This is knowing, then; the other is knowing and yet not knowing.

The truth of the matter is that the lechery of adultery and the chastity of marriage are as different from each other as hell and heaven are from each other, and that the lechery of adultery makes hell for us and the chastity of marriage makes heaven for us.

However, there is no chastity of marriage for anyone but those who turn their backs on adultery as a sin—see §111 below.

77 This enables us to conclude and see beyond doubt whether someone is a Christian or not, in fact whether or not someone has any religion at all. People who do not regard adultery as a sin in their faith and their way of life are not Christians and have no religion. On the other hand, people who turn their backs on adultery as a sin, and more so people who steer clear of it altogether for that reason, and even more so people who detest it for that reason, do have a religion, and if they are in the Christian church, they are Christians.

There will be more on this in the booklet on marriage,[358] though; and in the meanwhile those interested may consult what it says on this subject in *Heaven and Hell* 366–386.

78 We can tell from what the Lord says in Matthew that adultery also means lecherous behavior, lewd conversation, and filthy thoughts:

> You have heard that it was said by the ancients, "You are not to commit adultery"; but I tell you that anyone who has looked at someone else's wife in order to desire her has already committed adultery with her in his heart. (Matthew 5:27, 28)

79 The following passages show that spiritually understood, "adultery" means polluting what is good in the Word and distorting what is true in it:

> Babylon has made all nations drink of the wine of her fornication. (Revelation 14:8)

> An angel said, "I will show you the judgment of the great whore who sits on many waters, with whom the kings of the earth committed fornication." (Revelation 17:1, 2)

> Babylon has made all nations drink of the wine of the wrath of her fornication, and the kings of the earth have committed fornication with her. (Revelation 18:3)

> God has judged the great whore who corrupted the earth with her fornication. (Revelation 19:2)

Fornication is associated with Babylon because Babylon means people who claim the Lord's divine power for themselves and profane the Word by polluting and distorting it.[359] That is why Babylon is called "the Mother of Fornications and of the Abominations of the Earth" in Revelation 17:5.

[2] Fornication means much the same in the prophets—in Jeremiah, for example:

> In the prophets of Jerusalem I have seen appalling obstinacy; they commit adultery and walk in a lie. (Jeremiah 23:14)

In Ezekiel:

> Two women, daughters of one mother, played the whore in Egypt; in their youth they behaved wantonly. The first was unfaithful to me and took delight in lovers from neighboring Assyria. Upon them, too, she bestowed her acts of whoredom, but without giving up her wantonness in Egypt. The second became more corrupt in her love than the first, and her acts of whoredom were worse than her sister's. She increased her whoredom and made love to Chaldeans; sons of Babel came to her, into the bed of love, and defiled her with their debauchery. (Ezekiel 23:2–17)

This is about the church of Israel and Judah, who are the "daughters of one mother" in this passage. Their acts of whoredom mean their pollutions and distortions of the Word, and since in the Word Egypt means factual knowledge, Assyria reasoning, Chaldea the profanation of what is true, and Babel the profanation of what is good, it says that they committed acts of whoredom with those countries.[360]

[3] Much the same is said in Ezekiel of Jerusalem, meaning the church in respect to its teachings:

> Jerusalem, you trusted in your own beauty, and played the whore because of your fame, even to the point that you poured out your whoredom on everyone who passed by. You played the whore with the Egyptians, your very fleshly neighbors, and increased your acts of whoredom. You played the whore with the Assyrians, because you were insatiable; indeed you played the whore with them. You multiplied your acts of whoredom as far as the land of the trader, Chaldea. An adulterous wife takes strangers instead of her husband. All make payment to their whores, but you made payments to all your lovers to come to you from all around for your whoredom. Now then, O whore, hear the Word of Jehovah. (Ezekiel 16:15, 26, 28, 29, 32, 33, 35, and following)

On Jerusalem meaning the church, see *Teachings on the Lord*[361] 62, 63. Fornication means much the same in Isaiah 23:17, 18; 57:3; Jeremiah 3:2, 6, 8, 9; 5:7; 13:27; 29:23; Micah 1:7; Nahum 3:4; Hosea 4:7, 10, 11; also Leviticus 20:5; Numbers 14:33; 15:39; and elsewhere.

That is why the Lord called the Jewish nation "an adulterous generation" (Matthew 12:39; 16:4; Mark 8:38).

To the Extent That We Turn Our Backs on All Kinds of Theft Because They Are Sins, We Love Honesty

IN earthly terms, "theft" means not only theft and robbery but also cheating and taking other people's assets by some pretext. Spiritually understood, though, "theft" means depriving others of the truths of their faith and good actions motivated by their caring, while in the highest sense it means taking from the Lord what is properly his and claiming it for ourselves—that is, claiming righteousness and worth for ourselves. These are "all kinds of theft," and like "all kinds of adultery" and "all kinds of killing," as just described [§§74–79 and §§67–73], they too are united. They are united because one is within the other.

81. The evil of theft infects us more deeply than some other evils because it is united with guile and trickery, and guile and trickery work their way into our spiritual mind where our thinking with understanding takes place. We shall see below that we have a spiritual mind and an earthly mind [§86].

82. The reason we love honesty to the extent that we turn our backs on theft as a sin is that theft is also deception, and deception and honesty are two opposite things. This means that to the extent that we are not devoted to deception, we are devoted to honesty.

83. "Honesty" also means integrity, fairness, faithfulness, and morality. On our own, we cannot be devoted to these so as to love them for what they are, for their own sakes, but if we turn our backs on deception, guile, and trickery as sins, we have a devotion to these virtues that comes not from ourselves but from the Lord, as explained in §§18–31 above. This applies to priests, administrators, judges, merchants, and laborers—to all of us then, in our various roles and tasks.

84. There are many passages in the Word that say this, the following being a few of them:

> Those who walk in righteousness and say what is upright, who loathe oppression for the sake of profit, who shake bribes from their hands in order not to accept them, who block their ears so as not to hear bloodshed, who close their eyes so as not to see evil—they will dwell on high. (Isaiah 33:15, 16)

> Jehovah, who will dwell in your tabernacle? Who will live on your holy mountain? Those who walk uprightly and do what is fair, who do not disparage others with their tongues, and who do no evil to their companions. (Psalms 15:1, 2, 3, and following)

> My eyes are toward the faithful of the earth so that they may sit down with me. Anyone who walks the path of integrity will serve me. No one who practices deceit will sit in the midst of my house; no one who speaks lies will stand in my presence. At dawn I will cut off all the

ungodly of the earth, to cut off from the city all those who work iniquity. (Psalms 101:6, 7, 8)

[2] In the following words, the Lord tells us that we are not truly honest, fair, faithful, or upright until we are inwardly honest, fair, faithful, and upright:

> Unless your righteousness exceeds that of the scribes and Pharisees, you will not enter the kingdom of the heavens. (Matthew 5:20)

Righteousness that exceeds that of the scribes and Pharisees means the more inward righteousness that is ours when we are in the Lord. As for our being "in the Lord," he also teaches this in John:

> The glory that you gave me I have given them, so that they may be one just as we are one—I in them and you in me—so that they may be made perfect in one, and so that the love with which you loved me may be in them, and I may be in them. (John 17:22, 23, 26)

This shows that people become complete when the Lord is in them. These are the people who are called "pure in heart," the ones who "will see God," and the ones who are "perfect, like their Father in the heavens" (Matthew 5:8, 48).

I noted in §81 above that the evil of theft infects us more deeply than some other evils because it is united with guile and trickery, and guile and trickery work their way into our spiritual mind where our thinking with understanding takes place; so now I need to say something about the human *mind*. On the human mind being our understanding together with our will, see §43 above.

We have an earthly mind and a spiritual mind, the earthly mind below and the spiritual mind above. The earthly mind is our mind for this world and the spiritual mind is our mind for heaven. The earthly mind can be called the animal mind, while the spiritual mind can be called the human mind. We are differentiated from animals by our having a spiritual mind that makes it possible for us to be in heaven while we are in this world. It is also what makes it possible for us to live after death.

[2] We can use our faculty of understanding to be in the spiritual side of our mind, and thus to be in heaven, but we cannot use our faculty of willing to be so unless we turn our backs on evils because they are sins;

and if our will is not in heaven as well [as our understanding], we ourselves are still not there, because our will drags our understanding back down and makes it just as earthly and animal as itself.

[3] We can be compared to a garden, our understanding to light, and our will to warmth. A garden has light in winter but no warmth, while it has both light and warmth in summer. So when all we have is the light of our understanding, we are like a garden in winter, but when we have both light in our understanding and warmth in our will we are like a garden in summer.

In fact, the wisdom in our understanding comes from spiritual light and the love in our will comes from spiritual warmth, for spiritual light is divine wisdom and spiritual warmth is divine love.

[4] If we fail to turn our backs on evils because they are sins, the cravings of our evils clog the deeper levels of our earthly mind on the side where our will resides and are like a thick veil, like black clouds beneath the spiritual mind, preventing it from opening. However, as soon as we turn our backs on evils because they are sins, the Lord flows in from heaven, takes the veil away, dispels the cloud, and opens the spiritual mind, thereby admitting us to heaven.

[5] As already noted, as long as cravings for evil behavior clog the deeper levels of the earthly mind, we are in hell, but as soon as those cravings are dispelled by the Lord, we are in heaven. Again, as long as cravings for evil behavior clog the deeper levels of the earthly mind we are earthly people, but as soon as those cravings are dispelled by the Lord, we are spiritual people. Again, as long as cravings for evil behavior clog the deeper levels of the earthly mind we are animals, differing from them only in that we are capable of thinking and talking, even about things we cannot see with our eyes (we can do this because of the ability of our understanding to be lifted up into heaven's light). As soon as those cravings have been dispelled by the Lord, though, we are human because we are thinking what is true in our understanding because of what is good in our will. And yet again, as long as cravings for evil behavior clog the deeper levels of the earthly mind we are like a garden in winter, but as soon as those cravings are dispelled by the Lord, we are like a garden in summer.

[6] In the Word, the union of our will and understanding is meant by "heart and soul" and by "heart and spirit," as when it says that we are to love God with all our heart and with all our soul (Matthew 22:37) and that God will give a new heart and a new spirit (Ezekiel 11:19; 36:26, 27).

Our "heart" means our will and its love, while our "soul" or "spirit" means our understanding and its wisdom.

To the Extent That We Turn Our Backs on All Kinds of False Witness Because They Are Sins, We Love Truth

UNDERSTOOD on an earthly level, bearing false witness means not only committing legal perjury but also telling lies and slandering others. Understood on a spiritual level, bearing false witness means saying and convincing ourselves that something false is true and that something evil is good, and the reverse. Understood on the highest level, though, bearing false witness means blaspheming the Lord and the Word. These are the three meanings of false witness.

The information about the threefold meaning of everything in the Word presented in *Teachings on Sacred Scripture* 5, 6, 7, and following may show that these three are united in people who commit perjury, tell lies, and slander.

Since lying and truth are two opposite things, it follows that to the extent that we turn our backs on lying because it is a sin, we love truth.

To the extent that we love truth we want to know it and we find our hearts moved when we find it. That is the only way to arrive at wisdom; and to the extent that we love to do the truth, we take pleasure in the light that contains it.[362]

This is the same as in the case of the commandments already discussed, such as honesty and fairness in those who turn their backs on all kinds of theft, chastity and purity in those who turn their backs on all kinds of adultery, love and caring in those who turn their backs on all kinds of killing, and so on.

People who are caught up in the opposite attitudes, though, know nothing about all this, even though it involves everything that is actually anything.

90 "Truth" is meant by the seed in the field, which the Lord described as follows:

> A sower went out to sow seed. As he was sowing, some seed fell on a much trodden path, and the birds of heaven devoured it. Some seed fell on stony places, but as soon as it grew up it withered, because it had no root. Some seed fell among thorns, and the thorns grew up with it and choked it. And some seed fell on good ground, and when it grew up it bore abundant fruit. (Luke 8:5–8; Matthew 13:3–8; Mark 4:3–8)[363]

In this parable the sower is the Lord and the seed is his Word and therefore the truth. The seed on the path refers to the way the Word is viewed by people who do not[364] care about truth. The seed in stony places refers to the way the Word is viewed by people who do care about truth, but not for its own sake, and therefore not deeply. The seed among thorns refers to the way the Word is viewed by people who are caught up in cravings for evil behavior, while the seed in good ground is the way the Word is viewed by people who love the truths that come from the Lord and are found in the Word, the people who bear fruit because their doing of those truths comes from him. We are assured of these meanings by the Lord's explanation (Matthew 13:19–23, 37; Mark 4:14–20; Luke 8:11–15).

We can see from this that the truth of the Word cannot take root in people who do not care about truth or in people who love truth superficially but not deeply or in people who are caught up in cravings for evil behavior. However, it can take root in people whose cravings for evil behavior have been dispelled by the Lord. In these the seed can take root—that is, the truth can take root in their spiritual minds (see the close of §86 above).[365]

91 It is generally thought nowadays that being saved is a matter of believing one thing or another that the church teaches, and that being saved is not a matter of obeying the Ten Commandments in particular—not killing, not committing adultery, not stealing, not bearing false witness; and it is said in a wider sense that the focus should not be on deeds but on faith that comes from God. However, to the extent that we are caught up in evils we do not have faith (see §§42–52 above). Consult your reason and you will clearly see that no killer, adulterer, thief, or false witness can have faith while he or she is caught up in such cravings. You will also clearly see that we cannot dispel these cravings in any other way than by our being unwilling to act on them because they are sins—that is, because they are hellish and diabolical. So if people think that being saved is a matter of believing one thing or another that the church teaches, while at the same time they remain people of this kind, they cannot help being foolish. This is according to what the Lord says in Matthew 7:26.[366]

This is how Jeremiah describes this kind of church:

> Stand in the gate of the house of Jehovah and proclaim this word there: "Thus says Jehovah Sabaoth, the God of Israel: 'Make your ways and your deeds good. Do not put your trust in lying words, saying, "The temple of Jehovah, the temple of Jehovah, the temple of Jehovah are these." Are you going to steal, kill, commit adultery, and tell lies under oath, and then come and stand before me in this house that bears my name and say, "We are delivered" when you are doing these abominations? Has this house become a robbers' cave? Indeed, behold, I have seen it,' says Jehovah." (Jeremiah 7:2, 3, 4, 9, 10, 11)

The Only Way to Abstain from Sinful Evils So Thoroughly That We Develop an Inner Aversion to Them Is to Do Battle against Them

[92] EVERYONE knows on the basis of the Word and teachings drawn from it that from the time we are born our self-centeredness is evil and that this is why we have an inborn compulsion to love evil behavior and to be drawn into it.[367] We are deliberately vengeful, for example; we deliberately cheat, disparage others, and commit adultery; and if we do not think that these behaviors are sins and resist them for that reason, we do them whenever the opportunity presents itself, as long as our reputation or our wealth is not affected.

Then too, we really enjoy doing such things if we have no religion.

[93] Since this self-centeredness is the taproot of the life we lead, we can see what kind of trees we would be if this root were not pulled up and a

new root planted. We would be rotten trees that needed to be cut down and thrown into the fire (see Matthew 3:10; 7:19).

This root is not removed and a new one put in its place unless we see that the evils that constitute it are harmful to our souls, and therefore we want to banish them. However, since they are part of our self-centeredness and therefore give us pleasure, we can do this only reluctantly and in the face of opposition, and therefore by doing battle.

94
Everyone undertakes this battle who believes that heaven and hell are real and that heaven is eternal happiness and hell eternal misery, and who believes that we come into hell if we do evil and into heaven if we do good. Whenever we do battle in this way, we are acting from our inner selves and against the compulsions that constitute the root of evil, because when we are fighting against something we are not intending it, and compulsions are intentions.

We can see from this that the only way to dig out the root of evil is by doing battle against it.

95
The more we do battle and thereby set evils to one side, the more what is good replaces them and we look what is evil in the face from the perspective of what is good and see that the evil is hellish and hideous. Since this is how we see it then, we not only abstain from it but develop an aversion to it and eventually loathe it.

96
When we battle against what is evil, we cannot help but fight using what seems to be our own strength, because if we are not using what seems to be our own strength, we are not doing battle. We are standing there like an automaton,[368] seeing nothing and doing nothing, while constantly thinking on the basis of evil and in favor of it, not against it.

However, we need to be quite clear about the fact that it is the Lord alone who is fighting within us against the evils, that it only seems as though we are using our own strength for the battle, and that the Lord wants it to seem like that because if it does not, no battle occurs, so there is no reformation either.

97
This battle is hard only if we have given free rein to our cravings and indulged in them deliberately, or if we have stubbornly rejected the holy principles of the Word and the church. Otherwise, it is not hard. We need only resist evils in our intentions once a week or twice a month and we will notice a change.

98
The Christian church is called "the church militant."[369] It is called that because it fights against the Devil and therefore against evils that come from hell. ("The Devil" is hell.) The inner trials that church people endure are that fight.

99

There are many passages in the Word about battles against evils, or trials. That is what these words of the Lord are about:

> I say to you, unless a grain of wheat falls into the ground and dies, it remains alone; but if it dies, it produces much fruit. (John 12:24)

Then there is this:

> Those who wish to come with me must deny themselves and take up their cross and follow me. Those who try to save their own life will lose it, but those who lose their life for my sake and the gospel's will save it. (Mark 8:34, 35)

The "cross" means these trials, as it does also in Matthew 10:38; 16:24; Mark 10:21; and Luke 14:27. "Life" means the life we claim as our own, as it does also in Matthew 10:39; 16:25; Luke 9:24; and especially John 12:25. It is also the life of "the flesh," which "is of no benefit at all" (John 6:63). In the Book of Revelation, the Lord spoke to all the churches about battles against evils and victories over them:

> To *the church in Ephesus:* To those who overcome I will give [food] to eat from the tree of life, which is in the midst of the paradise of God. (Revelation 2:7)

> To *the church in Smyrna:* Those who overcome will not be hurt by the second death. (Revelation 2:11)

> To *the church in Pergamum:* To those who overcome I will give the hidden manna to eat; and I will give them a white stone, and on the stone a new name written that no one knows except the one who receives it. (Revelation 2:17)

> To *the church in Thyatira:* To those who overcome and keep my works to the end I will give power over the nations, and give the morning star. (Revelation 2:26, 28)

> To *the church in Sardis:* [Those who overcome will be clothed in white garments, and I will not blot their names from the book of life; I will confess their names before my Father and before his angels. (Revelation 3:5)

> To *the church in Philadelphia:*] Those who overcome I will make pillars in the temple of my God, and will write upon them the name of God, the name of the city of God, the New Jerusalem, which is coming down out of heaven from God, and my new name. (Revelation 3:12)[370]

To the church in Laodicea: To those who overcome I will grant to sit with me on my throne. (Revelation 3:21)

100. You may find material specifically about these battles or trials in *The New Jerusalem and Its Heavenly Teachings*³⁷¹ (published in London in 1758) §§187–201; on their source and nature, see §§196 and 197; on how and when they happen, §198; on the good they accomplish, §199; on the Lord fighting for us, §200; and on the Lord's battles or trials, §201.

We Need to Abstain from Sinful Evils and Fight against Them As Though We Were Doing So on Our Own

101. It is part of the divine design that we act in freedom and according to reason, because acting in freedom according to reason is acting on our own.

However, these two powers, freedom and reason, are not our own. They are the Lord's within us; and since we are human they are not taken from us, because we cannot be reformed without them. That is, we cannot practice repentance, we cannot fight against evils and as a result bear fruit that is consistent with repentance [Matthew 3:8; Luke 3:8].

So since we are given freedom and reason by the Lord and we act from them, it follows that we are not acting on our own but as though we were on our own.ᵃ

102. The Lord loves us and wants to dwell with us but cannot love and dwell with us unless he is received and loved in return. This is the one and only means to union. This is why the Lord gives us freedom and the power to reason—the freedom of thinking and intending with seeming autonomy,

---

a. On our being given freedom by the Lord, see §§19 and 20 above and §§589–596 and 597–603 in *Heaven and Hell*. On what freedom is, see *The New Jerusalem and Its Heavenly Teachings* (published in London in 1758) §§141–149.

and the power of reason that serves as our guide. It is impossible to love and be united with someone who is unresponsive, impossible to come in and abide with someone who is unreceptive. It is because our own receptiveness and responsiveness are given by the Lord that the Lord said,

> Abide in me, and I [will abide] in you. (John 15:4)

> Those who abide in me and in whom I abide bear much fruit. (John 15:5)

> On that day you will know that you are in me and I am in you. (John 14:20)

The Lord also tells us that he is present in whatever is true and good that we have received and that is within us:

> If you abide in me and my words abide in you . . . If you keep my commandments, you will abide in my love. (John 15:7, 10)

> The people who love me are those who have my commandments and do them; and I will love them and dwell with them. (John 14:21, 23)

So the Lord dwells with us in what is his own, and we dwell in what the Lord is giving us and are therefore in the Lord.

103

Since the Lord gives us this ability to respond in turn—and therefore a mutual relationship [with him]—he says that we are to repent, and no one can repent without a sense of autonomy.

> Jesus said, "Unless you repent, you will all perish." (Luke 13:3, 5)

> Jesus said, "The kingdom of God is at hand. Repent, and believe in the gospel." (Mark 1:14, 15)

> Jesus said, "I have come to call sinners to repentance." (Luke 5:32)

> Jesus said to the churches, "Repent!" (Revelation 2:5, 16, 21, 22; 3:3)

> They did not repent of their deeds. (Revelation 16:11)

104

Since the Lord gives us this ability to respond in turn—and therefore a mutual relationship [with him]—the Lord says that we are to do his commandments and bear fruit:

> Why do you call me, "Lord, Lord," and not do what I say? (Luke 6:46–49)

> If you know these things, you are blessed if you do them. (John 13:17)

> You are my friends if you do what I command you. (John 15:14)

> Whoever does and teaches [the commandments] will be called great in the kingdom of the heavens. (Matthew 5:19)
>
> Everyone who hears my words and does them I will liken to a wise man. (Matthew 7:24)
>
> Bear fruit that is consistent with repentance. (Matthew 3:8)
>
> Make the tree good and its fruit good. (Matthew 12:33)
>
> The kingdom will be given to a nation that bears its fruits. (Matthew 21:43)
>
> Every tree that does not bear fruit is cut down and thrown into the fire. (Matthew 7:19)

and often elsewhere.

We can see from these passages that we are to act on our own, but through the power of the Lord, which we must pray for; and that this is acting as if we were on our own.

105 Since the Lord gives us this ability to respond in turn—and therefore a mutual relationship [with him]—we must therefore give an account of our deeds and be recompensed accordingly, for the Lord says:

> The Son of Humanity is going to come, and he will repay all people according to their deeds. (Matthew 16:27)
>
> Those who have done what is good will go forth into the resurrection of life, and those who have done what is evil will go forth into the resurrection of condemnation. (John 5:29)
>
> Their works follow them. (Revelation 14:13)
>
> All were judged according to their works. (Revelation 20:13)
>
> Behold, I am coming, and my reward is with me, to give to all according to what they have done. (Revelation 22:12)

If we had no ability to respond, we could not be held accountable.

106 Since it is up to us to be receptive and to respond in turn, the church teaches that we are to examine ourselves, confess our sins in the presence of God, stop committing them, and lead a new life. Every church in the Christian world teaches this, as stated in §§3–8.

107 If we did not have the power to be receptive and therefore had no apparent ability to think independently, faith could not have even entered the discussion, since faith does not come from us either. If it were not for that ability to be receptive, we would be like straw blowing in the wind, and would stand around lifelessly, with our mouths gaping and our hands hanging limp, waiting for something to flow in, neither thinking nor doing anything about what matters for our salvation. We are in no way the active force in these matters, true, but we do react seemingly on our own.

These matters will be presented in still clearer light, though, in the works on angelic wisdom.[372]

If We Turn Our Backs on Evils for Any Other Reason Than That They Are Sins, We Are Not Turning Our Backs on Them but Are Simply Making Sure They Are Not Visible in the Eyes of the World

108 THERE are moral individuals who keep the commandments of the second tablet of the Ten Commandments, who do not cheat, blaspheme, take vengeance, or commit adultery, and who are convinced that such behavior is evil because it is harmful to the state and therefore contrary to the laws of humanity. They also practice caring, honesty, fairness, and chastity.

If they are doing these good things and turning their backs on evil things only because the latter are evil, though, and not because they are sins as well, these people are merely earthly, and in merely earthly individuals the root of the evil remains in place and is not removed. So the good things they do are not good, because they arise from the doers themselves.

109 Moral earthly individuals can look just like moral spiritual individuals to people on earth, but not to angels in heaven. To angels in heaven they look like lifeless wooden statues if the individuals are focused on goodness, and like lifeless marble statues if they are focused on truth.[373] It is different for moral spiritual individuals because a moral earthly person is moral on the outside, while a moral spiritual person is moral on the inside, and the outside has no life apart from the inside. Technically speaking, the outside is alive, of course, but it has no life worthy of the name.

110 The compulsions to evil that constitute our deeper nature from birth can be set aside only by the Lord, because the Lord flows from what is spiritual into what is earthly, but of ourselves we flow from what is earthly into what is spiritual.374 This latter flow goes against the divine design and does not operate on our compulsions and set them aside but envelops them more and more tightly as we reinforce them. So since this means that our inherited evil remains hidden and enclosed within us, when we become spirits after death it bursts the coverings that veiled it on earth and breaks out like pus from an ulcer that has been healed only superficially.

111 The reasons we may be moral in outward form are many and varied, but if we are not inwardly moral as well, we are not really moral at all. For example, we may refrain from adultery and fornication out of fear of civil law and its penalties, fear of loss of our good name and therefore our rank, fear of associated diseases, fear of being berated by a wife at home and a consequent loss of tranquillity, fear of vengeance by a husband or relatives. We may refrain because of poverty or greed, because of incompetence caused by disease, abuse, age, or impotence—in fact, if we refrain from them because of any earthly or moral law and not because of spiritual law as well, we are adulterers and lechers all the same. That is, we believe that they are not sins and in our spirits regard them as not illegal in the sight of God. This means that in spirit we are committing them even though we are not doing so in the flesh in this world; so when we become spirits after death, we speak openly in favor of them.

We can see from this that irreligious people can turn their backs on evils as harmful, but only Christians can turn their backs on evils because they are sins.375

112 It is much the same with all kinds of theft and cheating, all kinds of killing and vengeance, all kinds of false witness and lying. None of us can be cleansed and purified from them by our own strength. There are infinite complexities hidden within a compulsion that we see as a single, simple thing, but the Lord sees the tiniest details in complete sequence.

In a word, we cannot regenerate ourselves. That is, we cannot form a new heart and a new spirit within ourselves [Ezekiel 11:19; 36:26]. Only the Lord, who is the true Reformer and Regenerator, can do this; so if we try to make ourselves new with our own plans and our own intelligence, this is like putting rouge on a disfigured face or smearing cleansing cream over an area that is inwardly infected.

That is why the Lord says in Matthew,

> Blind Pharisee, cleanse the inside of the cup and the plate first, so that the outside of them may be clean as well. (Matthew 23:26)

and in Isaiah,

> Wash yourselves! Purify yourselves! Take away the evil of your deeds from *before my eyes!* Stop doing evil! And then, even if your sins have been like scarlet, they will become white like snow; even if they have been as red as purple-dyed cloth, they will be like wool. (Isaiah 1:16, 18)

❋ ❋ ❋ ❋ ❋ ❋

The following should be appended to what has now been said: first, for us all, Christian charity is actually a matter of faithfully performing a useful occupation.[376] *If we turn our backs on evils because they are sins, we are daily doing what is good, and are ourselves the useful functions we should be in the body politic. This means that the larger body is being cared for, and so is each member in particular. Second, all the other things we do [outside of our occupation] are not works of charity, strictly speaking, but are either further reflections of our charity, or else simply good deeds or things we are properly obligated to do.*[377]

Teachings
for the
New Jerusalem
on
Faith

Teachings for the New Jerusalem on Faith

Faith Is an Inner Recognition of Truth

NOWADAYS, people understand "faith" to mean nothing more than thinking that something is true because the church[378] teaches it and because it is not obvious to the intellect. In fact, the common saying is, "Believe, and don't doubt."[379] If someone replies, "I don't understand it," people say, "That's why you have to believe it." The result is that today's faith is faith in the unknown and can be called "blind faith"; and since it involves a decree from one person to another, it is faith handed down from the past.

It will become clear in the following pages that this is not a spiritual faith.

Real faith is simply recognizing that something is so because it is true. This means that people who are devoted to real faith both think and say, "This is true, and that's why I believe it." That is, faith is dependent on truth, and what is true is the object of faith. So if we do not understand that something is true, we say, "I don't know whether this is true or not, so I don't believe it yet. How can I believe something that doesn't make sense to me? It may be false."

All the same, the widely shared opinion is that no one can understand things that are spiritual or theological because they are supernatural.

However, spiritual truths can be grasped just as earthly ones are[380]—perhaps not as clearly, but still, when we hear them we do get a sense as to whether they are true or not. This is especially so in the case of people who have a longing for truth.

I have been taught this by an abundance of experience. I have been granted the opportunity to talk with people who lacked education, people who lacked common sense, and people who lacked intelligence, and with people who, despite having been born in the church and having therefore heard something about the Lord, faith, and caring, were convinced of false ideas or were immersed in evil. I have been granted the opportunity to tell them secrets of wisdom, and they understood and acknowledged everything. At such times, of course, they were in that light of understanding that is common to us all, and also in a state of glory because they were in a condition of understanding. This happened during my interactions with spirits.[381]

These experiences convinced many who were with me that spiritual matters are just as comprehensible as earthly matters—at least when people hear or read them—but hard to understand when people are left on their own to think for themselves. The reason we can understand spiritual matters is that we can be lifted mentally into heaven's light, the light in which all the things we see are spiritual—all the truths that belong to the faith. The light of heaven is spiritual light.[382]

[4] This is why the people who have an inner recognition of what is true are those who have a spiritual love for truth. Since angels have this love, they flatly reject the dogma that our intellect must be subject to faith. On the contrary, they say, "Is there any such thing as believing something without first seeing whether it is true?" And if someone says that we must nevertheless believe, they reply, "Do you think you are God, that I should believe you, or that I am so crazy that I will believe some statement in which I see nothing true? Make me see it." Then the adherent of dogmatism slinks away.

The angels' wisdom consists entirely in seeing and understanding the things they are thinking about.

[5] There is a spiritual perspective, of which few people know anything at all, a perspective that inflows in the case of people who have a longing for truth and tells them inwardly whether what they are hearing or reading is true or not. When we are reading the Word[383] with enlightenment from the Lord, we have this perspective. Having enlightenment is nothing more nor less than having a perception and therefore an inner acknowledgment that this or that statement is true. Isaiah calls such people "taught by Jehovah" (Isaiah 54:13; see also John 6:45); and Jeremiah says of them,

> Behold, the days are coming in which I will make a new covenant. This will be the covenant: I will put my law in their midst and I will write it on their heart. No longer will people teach their friends or their family, saying, "Know Jehovah," for they will all know me. (Jeremiah 31:31, 33, 34)

[6] We can see from all this that faith and truth are one and the same; and this is why the ancients, who thought more about truths than we do because they had a longing for them, talked about "truth" rather than "faith." This is also why in Hebrew the same word—for example, *emuna,* and also *amen*—can mean both "truth" and "faith."[384]

[7] The reason the Lord talked about faith in the Gospels and Revelation was that the Jews did not believe it was true that he was the Messiah foretold by the prophets; and wherever the truth is not believed, faith enters the discussion. Nevertheless, it is one thing to have faith and believe in the Lord and something else to have faith and believe someone else. We will get to that difference shortly.[385]

[8] With the regime of the papacy, faith apart from truth entered—even invaded—the church, because the primary bulwark of that religion was ignorance of the truth. That is why the reading of the Word was forbidden—otherwise people could not have been worshiped as having divine authority, there could have been no invocation of saints, and religious practices could not have become so idolatrous that the cadavers and bones and tombs of their saints were regarded as holy and used to generate revenue.[386] We can see from this what monstrous misconceptions blind faith can produce.

[9] Blind faith also lived on among many Protestants because they separated faith from caring; and if people separate these two things, then they cannot help but be ignorant of what is true, and they define faith as thinking that something is true apart from any inner recognition that it is true. For such people, ignorance is the defender of dogmatism, because as long as ignorance holds sway, accompanied by the conviction that theological matters are beyond reach, they can say anything and not be contradicted. They can believe that what they say is true and that they understand it.

[10] The Lord said to Thomas,

> Because you have seen me, Thomas, you have believed. Blessed are those who do not see, and yet they believe. (John 20:29)

This does not mean faith apart from an inner recognition of truth, but that people are blessed who do not see the Lord with their eyes as Thomas did and who still believe that he exists, because this recognition occurs in the light of truth from the Word.

11 Since faith is an inner recognition that something is true, and since faith and truth are one and the same (as noted in §§2, 4, 5, and 6 above), it follows that an outward recognition without an inner one is not faith, and that being convinced of something false is not faith.

An outer recognition apart from an inner one is faith in the unknown, and faith in the unknown is nothing but information held in our memory that becomes a conviction if there are arguments to support it. People who hold to such convictions think something is true because someone else has said so, or believe it is true because they have convinced themselves; yet it is as easy to convince ourselves of something false as it is of something true, and sometimes such a conviction is even stronger.

Thinking something is true because we have convinced ourselves of it means thinking what someone else has said is true and looking for support for it without first examining it for ourselves.

12 Some may think to themselves or say to someone else, "Who is capable of having the inner recognition of truth that is faith? Not I." I will tell them how they can: Turn your back on evils because they are sins and turn to the Lord, and you will have as much of that inner recognition as you wish.

You may see in *Teachings about Life for the New Jerusalem*[387] 18–31 that if we turn our backs on evils because they are sins we are in the Lord; in §§32–41 that we then love what is true and see it; and in §§42–52 that we then have faith.

The "Inner Recognition of Truth" That Is Faith Is Found Only in People Who Are Devoted to Caring

13 HAVING just said what faith is, I need now to say what caring is. Caring originates in a desire to do something good. Since what is

good loves what is true, this desire leads to a desire for truth and therefore to the recognition of what is true, which is faith. By these steps, in proper sequence, a desire to do something good[388] takes form and turns into caring. This is how caring develops from its origin, which is a desire to do something good, through faith, which is a recognition of what is true, to its goal, which is caring. The goal is the doing of something.

We can see from this how love, which is a desire to do something good, brings forth faith, which is the same as recognizing what is true, and by this means brings forth caring, which is the same as love acting through faith.

[14] To put it more clearly, a thing that is good must be of use, so the origin of caring is wanting to be of use; and since usefulness loves the means [of being of use], it prompts a desire for those means and leads to a recognition of them. So by the steps in this sequence, wanting to be of use takes visible form and becomes caring.

[15] This sequence is like the sequence of everything that starts in our will and moves through our understanding into the actions of our bodies. Our will accomplishes nothing on its own apart from our understanding, nor does our understanding on its own apart from our will. They need to act together for anything to happen.

That is to say, a motivating feeling, which comes from our will, has no effect on its own except by means of thought, which is an activity of our faculty of understanding; and the converse holds true as well. They must act together for anything to happen.

Think it through. If you empty thinking of any feeling that comes from some love, can you think? Or by the same token, if you deprive a motivating feeling of its thought, can you accomplish anything? Or again, if you empty thought of its motivating feeling, can you talk, or if you deprive a motivating feeling of its thinking or understanding, can you do anything?

That is how it is with caring and faith.

[16] Comparison with a tree may serve to illustrate this. In its first origin, a tree is a seed in which there is a drive to produce fruit. Stimulated by warmth, this drive first produces roots, and then from the roots a shoot or stem with branches, leaves, and finally fruit. That is how the drive to produce fruit manifests itself. We can see from this that the drive to produce fruit is constant throughout the whole process until it becomes manifest, since if it were to fail, the power to grow would promptly die.

This is how the illustration works: The tree is the person. Our drive to produce the means to an end comes from our will and passes into our understanding. Our shoot or stem and its branches and leaves are the means we use, means called the truths that belong to religious faith. The fruits, which in the case of the tree are the final effects of its drive to be fruitful, are in our case the useful acts in which our will becomes manifest.

We can see from this that our will to be of service by using our understanding is constant throughout the whole process until finally it becomes manifest.

On will and understanding and their union, see *Teachings about Life for the New Jerusalem* 43.

17. We can see from what has now been said that caring, to the extent that it is a prompting to do something good, something of use, brings forth faith as its means, through which it becomes manifest. This means that to bring forth something of use, caring and faith must act together.

It also means that faith does not accomplish anything good or useful by itself, but only from caring as its source. Faith, in fact, is just caring in its middle phase, so it is a fallacy to think that faith brings forth what is good the way a tree brings forth fruit. The tree is not faith; the tree is the person.

18. It is important to know that caring and faith are united in the same way that our will and our understanding are united, since our will is the part of us that cares and our understanding is the part of us that has faith. It is also important to know that caring and faith are united in the same way our desiring and our thinking are united, since our will is the part of us that feels desire and our understanding is the part of us that thinks. And again, caring and faith are united in the same way that goodness and truth are united, since what is good is the object of the desire in our will and what is true is the object of the thinking in our understanding.

[2] In short, caring and faith are united in the same way that essence and form are united,[389] because the essence of faith is caring and the form of caring is faith. So we can see that faith without caring is like a form with no essence, which is nothing, and that caring without faith is like an essence with no form, which also is nothing.

19. Our caring and faith work exactly the same way as the motion of the heart that we call systole and diastole and the motion of the lungs that we call breathing. There is also a complete correspondence between

these two motions and our will and understanding and therefore also our caring and faith, which is why will and its motivating feelings are meant by "the heart" in the Word, and understanding and its thinking by "the breath" in the Word and also by "the spirit." So "breathing one's last" is no longer living and "giving up the ghost" is no longer breathing.[390]

[2] It follows, then, that there can be no faith without caring or caring without faith, and that faith without caring is like the breathing of the lungs without a heart. This is impossible for any living creature; only an automaton could do it.[391] Caring without faith is like having a heart but no lungs, in which case we would have no awareness that we were alive. So caring does useful things by means of faith the way the heart accomplishes action by means of the lungs.

The likeness between "heart" and caring on the one hand and "lungs" and faith on the other is so strong that in the spiritual world[392] everyone can tell simply from people's breathing what their faith is like and from their heartbeat what their caring is like. Angels and spirits[393] live by heartbeat and breathing just as we do, which is why they feel, think, act, and talk as we do in the world.

20 Since caring is love for our neighbor, I need to say what "our neighbor" is. In an earthly sense, our neighbor is humankind both collectively and individually. Humankind collectively understood is the church, the country, and the community; humankind individually understood is the fellow citizen who in the Word is called our brother or sister or companion.[394]

In a spiritual sense, though, our neighbor is whatever is good, and since useful service is good, useful service is our neighbor in a spiritual sense.

It is important for everyone to realize that spiritually speaking, useful service is our neighbor. Who actually loves someone simply as "someone"? No, we love people because of what is within them, what makes them the kind of people they are. That is, we love them for their nature, because that is what each human being is. The quality we love is their usefulness and is what we call "good"; so this is our neighbor.[395]

Since the Word is spiritual at heart, this is the spiritual meaning of "loving our neighbor."

21 It is one thing, though, when we love our neighbors for the benefit or service they offer us and another thing to love them for the benefit or service we offer them. Even when we are evil we can love our neighbors for the benefit or service they offer us, but only when we are good can we love our neighbors for the benefit or service we offer them. Then we are loving to do good because it is good—loving useful service because we have a desire to be of use. The difference between the two attitudes is described by the Lord in Matthew 5:43–47.[396]

People often say, "I love such and such a person because that person loves me and does me good," but loving others for this reason alone is not loving them deeply, unless we ourselves are intent on what is good and love the good things that they do for that reason. That is being devoted to caring: the other is being focused on a kind of friendship that is not the same as caring.

When we love others because we care about them, we unite with the good they do and not with their personality, except insofar and as long as they are engaged in doing what is good. Then we are spiritual and are loving our neighbor spiritually. If we love others merely out of friendship, though, we unite ourselves with their personality, including the evil that belongs to them. In that case it is hard for us to separate ourselves after death from a personality that is devoted to evil, though in the former case, we can.

Caring makes this distinction by means of faith because faith is truth, and when through truth we are truly caring we look carefully and see what we should love; and when we are loving and benefiting others, we focus on the quality of usefulness in what we are doing.

22 Love for the Lord is what "love" really means, and love for our neighbor is caring. There can be no love for the Lord in us except when we are caring: it is in this that the Lord unites with us.

Since faith in its essence is caring, it follows that no one can have faith in the Lord except while caring. Union comes from caring, through faith—a union of the Lord with us through caring and a union of us with the Lord through faith. On the reciprocal nature of this union, see *Teachings about Life for the New Jerusalem* 102–107.

23 To summarize, to the extent that we turn our backs on evils because they are sins and turn to the Lord, we are engaged in caring, and therefore in faith to the same extent.

On our being engaged in caring to the extent that we turn our backs on evils because they are sins and turn toward the Lord, see *Teachings about Life for the New Jerusalem* 67–73 and 74–91, and on our having faith to the same extent, see §§42–52. On the true meaning of the word "caring," see §114 of that work.

[24] We may conclude from all this that a saving faith, the faith that is an inner recognition of what is true, can be found only in people who are caring.

Our Knowledge of What Is True and Good Does Not Become Faith until We Are Engaged in Caring. Once We Have a Faith That Is Born of Caring, Though, That Knowledge Becomes a Resource That Gives Form to Our Faith

[25] RIGHT from earliest childhood we are eager to know things. Because of this we learn a great many things, some of which will be useful to us and some of which will not. When we grow up, we get involved in some occupation and absorb information about it; and as we do, the occupation becomes a way for us to be useful, and we begin to love it. This is how our love of being useful begins; and this love leads us to also love the means that allow us to do our occupation and make it effective.

This process applies to everyone in this world because we all have some occupation to which we progress, beginning from the service we envision as a goal, through the means, to the actual service that is the result. However, since this service and its means have to do with life in this world, loving it is an earthly type of love.

[26] Since we all not only look toward what is useful for our lives in this world but should also look toward what is useful for our lives in heaven (after all, we will get there after life in this world, and that is where we will go on living forever), from our childhood we acquire some familiarity with what is good and true from the Word, from the teachings of the church, or from sermons, and this knowledge is relevant to our eternal life. We store this away in our earthly memory,[397] in greater or lesser abundance

depending on our own desire to know, a desire that is both inborn and reinforced by various stimuli.

27 All this knowledge, though, no matter how much or how valuable, is nothing more than a resource out of which a caring faith can be formed; and this kind of faith is formed only as we turn our backs on evils because they are sins.

If we turn our backs on evils because they are sins, then this knowledge becomes part of our faith, which has some spiritual life in it; but if we do not turn our backs on evils because they are sins, then our knowledge is nothing but knowledge, and does not become part of a faith that has spiritual life within it.

28 This resource is of critical importance because without it no faith can take form. Our knowledge of what is true and good becomes part of our faith and strengthens it. If we have no such knowledge, faith does not happen. There is no such thing as an empty faith, a faith without content. If we have only a little of such knowledge, our faith is weak and needy. If we have an abundance of such knowledge, our faith becomes rich and full in proportion to that abundance.

29 It is important to know, though, that faith is supported by knowledge of what is *genuinely* true and good; this is definitely not the case with knowledge of what is false. Faith is truth (see §§5–11 above), and since falsity contradicts truth, it destroys faith. Caring, too, cannot occur where there are nothing but falsities, since as noted in §18 above, caring and faith are united the way goodness and truth are united.

It also follows from all this that a total absence of knowledge of what is true and good makes for no faith; slight knowledge makes for some faith; and an abundance of knowledge makes for a faith that is enlightened in proportion to its fullness.

The quality of faith we have as a result of caring determines the quality of our intelligence.

30 There are many people, too, who do not have an inner recognition of what is true but still have a faith that comes from caring. These are people who have turned toward the Lord in their lives and who have refrained from evil behavior for religious reasons, but who have been hindered from thinking about truths by worldly concerns and by their professional responsibilities as well as by a lack of truth on the part of their teachers. More deeply, or in spirit, though, they are able to recognize what is true, because they are drawn to it; so after they die, become spirits, and are taught by angels, they recognize what is true and are overjoyed to receive it.

However, it is different for people who have not turned toward the Lord in their lives and have failed to refrain from evil behavior in accord with their religion. Inwardly or in spirit they do not feel drawn to truth and therefore have no ability to recognize it. So when they become spirits after death and are taught by angels, they are unwilling to acknowledge what is true and therefore do not accept it. Inside an evil life there is a hatred of truth, while inside a good life there is a love for truth.

The knowledge of what is true and good that we have before we have faith might be seen by some people as constituting faith, but in actuality it is not faith. Our thinking and saying we believe does not mean that we actually do believe, or that we have faith—it is just that we think we do. The things we know do not spring from an inner recognition that they are truths; and a faith that things are true when we do not actually know whether they are or not is a kind of bias quite remote from any inner acknowledgment. However, as soon as caring takes root, this knowledge becomes part of our faith—though only to the extent that there is caring within it.

In the first stage, before there is a sense of caring, it seems to us that faith is primary and caring secondary. In the second stage, though, when there is a sense of caring, faith becomes secondary and caring primary. The first stage is called "reformation" and the second is called "regeneration." When we are in this latter stage, day by day our wisdom grows, and day by day goodness causes our truths to multiply and bear fruit. Then we are like a tree that is bearing fruit and developing seeds in the fruit that will yield new trees and eventually an orchard.

Then we become truly human, and after death we will be angels, whose life is an embodiment of caring and whose form is an embodiment of faith.[398] That form will be as beautiful as our faith. But our faith will no longer be called faith: it will be called an understanding.

This shows us that every bit of faith comes from caring and nothing from faith itself. It also shows us that caring produces faith, but faith does not produce caring. The knowledge of truth that comes first is like grain stored in a cellar, which does not nourish us at all until we want to make some food with it and we take some out.

I need to tell also how faith is formed out of caring. Each of us has an earthly mind and a spiritual mind, the earthly mind for this world and the spiritual mind for heaven. We have access to both with respect to our intellect but not with respect to our will, until we turn our backs on evils and reject them because they are sins. When we do this, our spiritual mind is opened with respect to our will as well, and a spiritual warmth from heaven flows into our earthly mind. Essentially, this warmth is caring, and it brings to life our knowledge of what is true and good, a knowledge that is in our earthly mind, and forms a faith out of it. Again, this is like a tree that does not get any vegetative life until warmth from the sun flows into it and unites itself with light, as happens in spring.

There is actually a complete parallel between humans coming to life and the sprouting of a tree. The parallel rests on the fact that earthly warmth causes the latter and heavenly warmth causes the former. That is why the Lord so often compared people to trees.[399]

[33] These few thoughts may suffice to show that our knowledge of what is true and good does not constitute faith until we are committed to caring, but that it is a resource from which a caring faith can be formed.

When we have been reborn, our knowledge of what is true turns into truth. A similar thing happens to our knowledge of what is good, since our learning about what is good takes place in our understanding, but a desire to do what is good develops in our will. So we call something true if it is in our understanding and call it good if it is in our will.

The [True] Christian Faith in One All-Encompassing View

[34] THE following is the [true] Christian faith in one all-encompassing view:[400]

The Lord from eternity, who is Jehovah, came into the world to gain control over the hells[401] and to glorify his human nature. Without this no human being could have been saved; and those are saved who believe in him.

[35] I refer to this belief as the faith in one all-encompassing view because it is inherent in the faith, and what is inherent in the faith must be present throughout it and in every detail of it.

Inherent in this faith is the belief that God, in whom there is a trinity, is one in person and in essence, and that the Lord is God.

Inherent in this faith is the belief that no human being could have been saved if the Lord had not come into the world.

Inherent in this faith is the belief that the Lord came into the world to move hell away from us and that he moved it away by means of battles against it and victories over it. That is how he gained control over it, brought it back into order, and made it obey him.

Also inherent in this faith is the belief that the Lord came into the world to glorify the human nature that he took on in the world—that is, to unite it to the divine nature that was its source. Once he had gained control over hell, this allowed him to keep it in order and obedient to him forever. Since neither of these goals could have been achieved without trials, even to the absolute extreme, and since the absolute extreme was his suffering on the cross, he underwent this.

These are beliefs concerning the Lord that are central to the [true] Christian faith.

Central to the [true] Christian faith as it applies to us is that we believe in the Lord, since believing in him is the union with him that gives us salvation. Believing in him is trusting that he saves people; and since we can have this trust only if we live good lives, believing in him also means leading a good life.

I have elsewhere dealt specifically with these two central elements of the [true] Christian faith: with the *first,* the one about the Lord, in *Teachings for the New Jerusalem on the Lord,*[402] and with the *second,* the one that focuses on us, in *Teachings about Life for the New Jerusalem;* so there is no need to expand them further here.

The Present-Day Faith in One All-Encompassing View

THE following is the present-day faith in one all-encompassing view:

God the Father sent his Son to make satisfaction for the human race;[403] because of this merit on the part of the Son, the Father feels compassion and saves those who believe this. (Others would say, "Who believe this and also do what is good.")

39 To make the nature of this faith clearer, I would like to add a list of things that it claims to be the case.

1. The present-day faith claims that God the Father and God the Son are two, both of whom have existed from eternity.
2. It claims that God the Son came into the world, as a result of the will of the Father, to make satisfaction for the human race, which otherwise would have perished in eternal death because of divine justice, which [those who hold to these beliefs] also call retributive justice.
3. It claims that the Son made satisfaction by his fulfillment of the law and by his suffering on the cross.
4. It claims that the Father gave mercy because the Son did these things.
5. It claims that the Son's merit is credited to those who believe this.
6. It claims that this crediting of merit happens instantaneously and therefore, if it has not happened before, it can happen at the last hour of death.
7. It claims that [when it happens], some element of trial occurs, followed by a liberation by means of this faith.
8. It claims that those [who have this faith] gain a special assurance and confidence.
9. It claims that justification[404] is granted especially to these individuals, with the full grace of the Father for the sake of the Son, as well as forgiveness of all their sins, and therefore salvation.
10. The more learned claim that there is an impulse toward goodness in these people that works in the background and does not openly direct their will. Others claim that this impulse works openly. In either case, the impulse comes from the Holy Spirit.
11. Most people, though, who have convinced themselves that we are incapable of doing anything that is genuinely good on our own without claiming credit for it and that we are not under the yoke of the law, leave all this out and give no thought to whether the life they are living is good or evil. They say to themselves that doing good does not save and doing evil does not damn, because faith alone[405] does everything.
12. For the most part, they claim that their understanding must be subordinated to this faith. For them, "faith" means anything they do not understand.

40 I will forego a detailed examination and evaluation of whether their claims are the truth. The truth is quite clear from what has already been said, and especially from the material from the Word presented and supported with reasoning in *Teachings for the New Jerusalem on the Lord* and *Teachings about Life for the New Jerusalem.*

All the same, to show the nature of a faith divorced from caring and a faith not divorced from it, I would like to share something I heard from one of heaven's angels. This angel described having talked with many Protestants to learn about their faith, and told of a conversation with one devoted to a faith divorced from caring and a conversation with one devoted to a faith not divorced from caring. The angel told me what questions had been posed and what the responses had been; and since they can shed light on the subject, I would now like to present these conversations.

The angel told me of the following conversation with the individual who was devoted to a faith divorced from caring.

"Friend, who are you?"

"I am a Protestant Christian."

"What is your theology, and what religious practice does it lead to?"

"Faith."

"What is your faith?"

"My faith is that *God the Father sent his Son to make satisfaction for the human race, and that those who believe this are saved.*"

"What else do you know about salvation?"

"Salvation is granted through this faith alone."

"What do you know about redemption?"

"Redemption was effected through the suffering on the cross; the merit of the Son is credited to us through this faith."

"What do you know about regeneration?"

"Regeneration happens by means of this faith."

"What do you know about repentance and the forgiveness of sins?"

"They happen by means of this faith."

"Tell me what you know about love and caring."

"They are this faith."

"Tell me what you know about good works."

"They are this faith."

"Tell me what you think of all the commandments in the Word."

"They are in this faith."

"So you do not do anything?"

"What should I do? On my own, I cannot do anything good that is really good."

"Can you have faith on your own?"

"I cannot."

"Then how can you have faith?"

"I don't ask questions about this; I just have to have faith."

Finally, "Do you know anything else, anything at all, about salvation?"

"What else is there to know, when salvation is granted through this faith alone?"

But then the angel said, "You sound like someone who keeps playing the same note on a flute. All I hear is 'faith.' If that is all you know, and nothing else, then you don't know anything. Go see your companions." So the Protestant Christian went and met others in a wilderness where there was no grass. When they were asked why there was not even grass there, they said it was because they had not a shred of the church within themselves.[406]

43 The following is the conversation of the angel with the individual who was devoted to a faith not divorced from caring.

"Friend, who are you?"

"I am a Protestant Christian."

"What is your theology, and what religious practice does it lead to?"

"Faith and caring."

"That is two things."

"They cannot be separated."

"What is faith?"

"Believing what the Word teaches us."

"What is caring?"

"Doing what the Word teaches."

"Do you just believe this, or do you also do it?"

"I do it as well."

The angel from heaven then looked at this individual and said, "My friend, come with me and live with us."

The Nature of a Faith Divorced from Caring

44 TO show what faith divorced from caring is really like, I need to present it stark naked. This is how it looks.

God the Father, outraged by the human race, rejected it from himself and for reasons of justice decided to get even by damning it forever.

Then he said to the Son, "Go down, fulfill the law, and take upon yourself the damnation assigned to them. Then perhaps I will have mercy." So the Son went down, fulfilled the law, and allowed himself to be hung on the cross and brutally murdered. Once this had happened, he went back to the Father and said, interceding for them, "I have taken upon myself the damnation of the human race; now be merciful to them." The Father answered, though, "I cannot do it for their sakes, but since I saw you on the cross and then saw your blood, I have become merciful. Still, I will not pardon them, but I will credit them with your merit, but only for the people who acknowledge what you have done. This must be the faith through which they can be saved."

This is that faith in stark naked form. Can anyone whose reason is at all enlightened fail to see in it absurd notions that run counter to the divine essence itself? For example, there is the notion that a God who is love itself and mercy itself could be moved by rage and vengefulness to damn us and consign us to hell. There is the notion that God chose to be moved to mercy by transferring the damnation to his Son and by gazing at his suffering on the cross and his blood.

Can anyone whose reason is at all enlightened fail to see that no God worthy of the name could say, "I do not pardon them, but I am transferring your merit to them"? Or even, "Now let them live as they wish and they will be saved as long as they believe this"? And so on.

The reason this has not been seen, though, is that they have persuaded people that faith is blind and have used this notion to close people's eyes and plug their ears.

Close people's eyes and plug their ears—that is, prevent them from thinking with any understanding—and people who have some notion of eternal life will believe anything you say, even if you say that God can be angry and breathe vengeance, that God can inflict eternal damnation on anyone, that God chooses to be moved to mercy by the blood of his Son and transfer this as credit to our accounts as though it were ours and save us simply by what we think. People will believe, for example, that one God could make a deal with another God (of the same essence) and lay down requirements, and things of that sort.

Open your own eyes, though, and unplug your ears—that is, think intelligently about these matters—and you will see how they clash with the actual truth.

Close people's eyes and plug their ears—that is, prevent them from thinking with any understanding—and can't you then induce a belief that God has given all his power to some person to act as God on earth? Can't you induce a belief that we are to pray to dead people, that we are to bare our heads and bend our knees to their images, to regard their corpses, their bones, and their tombs as holy and worthy of reverence?[407]

But if you open your own eyes and unplug your ears, that is, if you think about these matters with some understanding, will you not see these beliefs as monstrous things that are appalling to human reason?

48 When people whose understanding has been closed because of their religion accept these and similar beliefs, can't we compare the church in which they worship to a cave or underground grotto where they do not know what they are seeing?[408] And can't we compare their religion to living in a house without windows and the voice of their worship to noise rather than speech?

Heaven's angels cannot talk with people like this because neither side understands the language of the other.

The Philistines Mentioned in the Word Represent People Devoted to a Faith Divorced from Caring

49 IN the Word all the names of nations and peoples as well as of persons and places are used to stand for matters of the church.[409] The church itself is meant by Israel and Judah because that is where it was established; and various other religious perspectives are meant by the surrounding nations and peoples—compatible perspectives by the good nations and incompatible ones by the evil nations.

There are two evil versions of religion into which all churches degenerate with the passage of time. One is the corruption of what a given church has that is good and the other is the distortion of what that church has that is true. The origin of the version that pollutes the good qualities of the church is the love of having complete control [over others], and the origin of the second version, which distorts the true ideas of the church, is pride in our own intelligence.

The version that comes from a love of having complete control is the one meant in the Word by Babylon, and the version that comes from pride in our own intelligence is the one meant in the Word by Philistia.

Everyone knows who the Babylonians are in our own times,[410] but not who the Philistines are. The Philistines are people who are devoted to faith but not to caring.

[50] From various things that the Word, when spiritually understood, tells us about the Philistines, we can determine that they are those who are devoted to faith but not to caring. This we can tell both from their arguments with the servants of Abraham and Isaac in Genesis 21 and 26 and from their wars with the children of Israel in Judges, Samuel, and Kings. In fact, all the wars described in the Word have a spiritual meaning; they reflect and symbolize spiritual wars.[411] And since this form of religion, which is one of faith divorced from caring, is constantly trying to invade the church, the Philistines remained in the land of Canaan[412] and often attacked the children of Israel.

[51] Since the Philistines represented people devoted to a faith divorced from caring, they were called "uncircumcised," and "uncircumcised" means lacking in spiritual love and therefore having only earthly love.[413] Spiritual love is caring.

The reason they were called uncircumcised is that "the circumcised" means those who are devoted to spiritual love. On the Philistines being called "the uncircumcised," see 1 Samuel 17:26, 36; 2 Samuel 1:20; and elsewhere.

[52] We can determine that people devoted to a faith divorced from caring were represented by the Philistines not only from their wars with the children of Israel but also from a number of other things we are told about them in the Word. For example, there is what it says about their idol, Dagon; about the hemorrhoids they were afflicted with and the rats they were invaded by because they had put the ark in their idol's shrine; and about what happened after that (see chapters 5 and 6 of 1 Samuel). There is also Goliath, the Philistine killed by David (see 1 Samuel 17).

As for their idol Dagon, it looked human from the waist up but looked like a fish from the waist down. This was an image of their religion, which seemed to be spiritual because of its faith but was merely earthly because of its lack of caring. The hemorrhoids that afflicted them symbolized their unclean loves; the rats that invaded them symbolized the destruction of the church through its distortions of truth; and Goliath, [the Philistine] killed by David, represented their pride in their own intelligence.[414]

53. We can also see from what the Word's prophets say about the Philistines that they represented people devoted to a faith divorced from caring. There is the following passage from Jeremiah, for example:

> Against the Philistines: Behold, waters are rising up from the north that will become an overflowing river and will flood the earth and all that is in it, the city and all those who live in it. People will cry out and everyone who lives on the earth will wail. Jehovah will devastate the Philistines. (Jeremiah 47:1, 2, 4)

The waters rising up from the north are falsities from hell; their becoming an overflowing river and flooding the earth and all that is in it means the consequent destruction of everything in the church; their flooding the city and all those who live in it means the complete destruction of its teachings; people crying out and everyone who lives on earth wailing means the loss of everything true and good in the church; and Jehovah devastating the Philistines means their demise.[415] From Isaiah:

> All Philistia, do not rejoice because the rod that was striking you has been broken, for out of the root of the serpent will come a basilisk,[416] and its fruit will be a flying fiery serpent.[417] (Isaiah 14:29)

The command to all Philistia not to rejoice means that people devoted to faith divorced from caring should not rejoice in the fact that they are surviving; "for out of the root of the serpent will come a basilisk" means the destruction of everything true they have because of their pride in their own intelligence; "its fruit will be a flying fiery serpent" means rationalizations based on malevolent distortions that oppose what is true and good in the church.[418]

54. We can see from the following passages that circumcision represented purification from evils that are caused by strictly earthly love:

> Circumcise your heart and take away the foreskin of your heart, so that my wrath will not break forth because of the ill will of your deeds. (Jeremiah 4:4)

> Circumcise the foreskin of your heart and no longer stiffen your neck. (Deuteronomy 10:16)

To circumcise the heart or the foreskin of the heart is to purify ourselves from evils.

Conversely, then, being uncircumcised or having a foreskin refers to people who have not been purified from evils caused by strictly earthly love and who are therefore not devoted to caring, and since having a foreskin means being unclean at heart, it says that no one who is uncircumcised at heart or uncircumcised in the flesh is to enter the sanctuary (Ezekiel 44:9); that no uncircumcised person is to eat the Passover meal (Exodus 12:48); and that the uncircumcised are damned (Ezekiel 28:10; 31:18; 32:19).

The Dragon Mentioned in the Book of Revelation Symbolizes People Devoted to a Faith Divorced from Caring

I noted earlier [§49] that in the course of time every church degenerates into two common evil versions of religion, one that comes from a love of having control and one that comes from intellectual pride. I noted that in the Word the first kind of religion is identified and depicted as *Babylon* and the second as *Philistia*.

Now, since the Book of Revelation deals with the state of the Christian church, especially at its close, it deals in general and in particular with these two evil versions of religion. The kind of religion meant by Babylon is described in chapters 17, 18, and 19 as the whore who sat on the scarlet beast, and the kind of religion meant by Philistia is described in chapters 12 and 13 as the dragon, and also as the beast rising up out of the sea and the beast rising up out of the earth.

Until now there has been no way to know that this kind of religion was meant by the dragon and his two beasts. This is because the spiritual meaning of the Word had not yet been opened, so the Book of Revelation had not been understood, and particularly because in the Christian world a form of religion based on faith divorced from caring had become so strong that no one was able to see this. Every evil kind of religion blinds the eyes.

As for the fact that a religion of faith divorced from caring is meant and described in the Book of Revelation by the dragon and his two beasts, this is something I have not only been told by a heavenly source but have also been shown in the world of spirits that is below heaven.[419] I have seen people devoted to faith alone gathered into a crowd that looked like a great dragon whose tail was stretched out toward heaven;[420] and I have seen separate individuals of this type who looked like dragons. In that world we see things like this because of the way spiritual and earthly phenomena correspond to each other.[421] That is also why heaven's angels call these people dragons.

There are many kinds of these people, though—some who form the head of the dragon, some who form the body, and some who form the tail. The ones who form the tail are the ones who distort everything that is true in the Word, which is why in the Book of Revelation it says of the dragon that its tail drew down a third of the stars of heaven [Revelation 12:4]. "The stars of heaven" means knowledge concerning what is true, and "a third" means all.

[57] Now, since in the Book of Revelation the dragon means people devoted to a faith divorced from caring, and since this has not been known before and has been hidden because the spiritual meaning of the Word has not been recognized, I need to offer at this point an overview of the meaning of what is said about the dragon in the twelfth chapter [of Revelation].

[58] This is what the twelfth chapter of Revelation says about the dragon:[422]

> And a great sign appeared in heaven: a woman clothed with the sun, with the moon under her feet, and on her head a crown of twelve stars. And being pregnant, she cried out in labor and in pain to give birth. And another sign appeared in heaven: behold, a great red dragon having seven heads and ten[423] horns, and seven gems on his heads. His tail drew a third of the stars of heaven and threw them to the earth. And the dragon stood before the woman who was about to give birth, to devour her child as soon as it was born. She bore a male child who was to rule all nations with a rod of iron. And her child was caught up to God and his throne. And the woman fled into the wilderness, where she has a place prepared by God, so that they would feed her there for one thousand two hundred and sixty days. And war broke out in heaven: Michael and his angels fought with the dragon; and the dragon and his angels fought, but they did not prevail, and no place was found for them in heaven any longer. And when the dragon saw that he had been cast to the earth, he persecuted the woman who had given birth to the male child. But the woman was given two wings of a great eagle, so

that she could fly into the wilderness to her place, where she would be nourished for a time and times and half a time, away from the presence of the serpent. So the serpent spewed water out of his mouth like a flood after the woman, to cause her to be carried away by the flood. But the earth helped the woman, and the earth opened its mouth and swallowed up the flood that the dragon had spewed out of his mouth. And the dragon was enraged with the woman, and he went away to make war with the rest of her offspring, who keep the commandments of God and have the testimony of Jesus Christ. (Revelation 12:1–8, 13–17)

The meaning of these verses is as follows:[424]

A great sign appeared in heaven means a revelation by the Lord concerning a church that is to be, and concerning how its teachings will be received and who will attack it.

A woman clothed with the sun, with the moon under her feet means a church that has love and faith from the Lord.

And on her head a crown of twelve stars means that the people [of that church] will have wisdom and intelligence arising from divine truths.

And being pregnant means the new teachings being born.

She cried out in labor and in pain to give birth means resistance by those people who were devoted to a faith divorced from caring.

And another sign appeared in heaven means a further revelation.

Behold, a great red dragon means a faith divorced from caring, which is called "red" because of its strictly earthly love.

Having seven heads means a distorted understanding of the Word.

And ten horns means the power they have because many people adopt [their point of view].

And seven gems on his heads means distorted truths of the Word.

His tail drew a third of the stars of heaven and threw them to the earth means the destruction of all recognition of what is true.

And the dragon stood before the woman who was about to give birth, to devour her child as soon as it was born means their hatred of and intent to destroy the teachings of the church at its very beginning.

She bore a male child means new teachings.

Who was to rule all nations with a rod of iron means teachings that will carry conviction because of the power of earthly truth derived from spiritual truth.

And her child was caught up to God and his throne means that those teachings will be kept safe by the Lord and heaven.

And the woman fled into the wilderness means the church among few people.

Where she has a place prepared by God means that its state is such that in the meantime it may be made available to many.

So that they would feed her there for one thousand two hundred and sixty days means until it grows to its appointed size.

And war broke out in heaven: Michael and his angels fought with the dragon, and the dragon and his angels fought means the disagreement and battle of those devoted to a faith divorced from caring against those devoted to the teachings of the church with respect to the Lord and a life of caring.

But they did not prevail means that [those devoted to faith alone] yielded.

And no place was found for them in heaven any longer means their being cast down.

And when the dragon saw that he had been cast to the earth, he persecuted the woman who had given birth to the male child means an attack on the church on account of its teachings by those devoted to a faith divorced from caring.

But the woman was given two wings of a great eagle, so that she could fly into the wilderness to her place means caution while it was still among few.

Where she would be nourished for a time and times and half a time, away from the presence of the serpent means until the church would grow to its appointed size.

So the serpent spewed water out of his mouth like a flood after the woman, to cause her to be carried away by the flood means their rationalizations based on abundant distortions aimed at the destruction of the church.

But the earth helped the woman, and the earth opened its mouth and swallowed up the flood that the dragon had spewed out of his mouth means that because the rationalizations were based on distortions, they collapsed on their own.

And the dragon was enraged with the woman, and he went away to make war with the rest of her offspring means their abiding hatred.

Who keep the commandments of God and have the testimony of Jesus Christ means against those who live caring lives and believe in the Lord.

60   In the next chapter of Revelation, chapter 13, the subject is the dragon's two beasts, the one that was seen rising up out of the sea and the one that was seen rising up out of the earth. Verses 1–10 are about the

first and verses 11–18 about the second. We can see from verses 2, 4, and 11 that these are the dragon's beasts. The first beast means faith divorced from caring with respect to the confirmations it draws from the earthly self, and the second means faith divorced from caring with respect to the confirmations it draws from the Word, which are in fact distortions of the truth. I will forgo an explanation of all this, though, since these verses reflect the lines of reasoning [of those devoted to faith divorced from caring], and require a great deal of verbiage to expound.[425] I will limit myself to the last one: "Let those who understand calculate the number of the beast. It is the number of a human being; its number is six hundred and sixty-six" (Revelation 13:18). "Let those who understand calculate the number of the beast" means that those who are enlightened should examine the nature of the confirmations of that faith that have been drawn from the Word. "It is the number of a human being" means that those confirmations are of the same nature as the self-centered understandings [of those who hold that faith]; and "its number is six hundred and sixty-six" means that it is a distortion of everything true in the Word.

The Goats Mentioned in Daniel and Matthew Symbolize People Devoted to a Faith Divorced from Caring

WE can tell that the goat in the eighth chapter of Daniel and the goats in the twenty-fifth chapter of Matthew mean people devoted to a faith divorced from caring, because in those passages they are set in contrast to a ram and sheep, and rams and sheep mean people who are devoted to caring. In the Word the Lord is called the Shepherd, the church is called the fold, the people of the church in general are called the flock, and the individuals are called sheep; and since sheep mean people devoted to caring, in these passages goats mean people who are not devoted to caring.

62 Reference to the following is needed to show that goats mean people who are devoted to a faith divorced from caring:

1. Experience in the spiritual world
2. Those on whom the Last Judgment was carried out
3. The description of the battle between the ram and the goat in Daniel
4. Lastly, the failure of caring in the people described in Matthew

63 1. *Experience in the spiritual world shows that in the Word, goats mean people who are devoted to a faith divorced from caring.* In the spiritual world we can see everything we see in this earthly world. We can see houses and mansions, parks and gardens with all kinds of trees in them. We can see fields and farmland, plains and meadows, as well as herds and flocks, all looking much as they do in our world. In fact, the only difference is that those in our world come from an earthly origin, while those in the spiritual world come from a spiritual origin. Since angels are spiritual, they see things that are from a spiritual origin just the way we see things that are from an earthly origin.

[2] Everything visible in the spiritual world is a correspondence. That is, everything corresponds to something the angels and spirits are feeling. That is why people who are moved by what is good and true and who therefore enjoy wisdom and intelligence live in splendid mansions that are surrounded by gardens with an abundance of trees (all of which things are correspondences), and these in turn are surrounded by farmlands and fields where flocks lie at rest (all of which things are appearances).[426]

For people who are drawn to evil, the correspondences are quite the opposite. These people are either confined to windowless workhouses in the hells where the only light is like that of marsh gas, or live in shacks in the wilderness where everything around is barren, where there are snakes, lizards, owls, and many other things that correspond to their evils.

[3] There is an intermediate space between heaven and hell called the world of spirits. That is where we all arrive immediately after death. We interact with each other there much the way we do here on earth; and there as well, everything we see is a correspondence. We see gardens and groves there, forests with trees and bushes, and green, flowery meadows, along with all kinds of animals, tame and wild, all corresponding to what we are feeling.

[4] I have often seen sheep and goats there and fights between them like the one described in the eighth chapter of Daniel [Daniel 8:2–14]. I have seen goats with horns bent forward or backward and have seen them

angrily attacking sheep. I once saw goats with two horns using them to batter some sheep, and when I looked to see what was happening, I saw some people arguing about caring and faith. I could see from this that what looked like a goat was faith divorced from caring and that what looked like a sheep was a caring that gave rise to faith.[427]

Because I have seen this so often, I have been granted the opportunity to know for certain that in the Word, goats mean people devoted to a faith divorced from caring.

2. *Those on whom the Last Judgment was carried out show that goats in the Word mean people who are devoted to a faith divorced from caring.* The Last Judgment was carried out exclusively on people who were moral on the outside but not spiritual on the inside—or at best were only slightly spiritual within. Those who had been both outwardly and inwardly evil, though, had been consigned to hell long before the Last Judgment, and those who had been both outwardly and inwardly spiritual had been raised into heaven long before the Last Judgment. This is because the judgment was not carried out on people in heaven or people in hell but on people who were halfway between heaven and hell and were making what seemed to be heavens for themselves there.

[2] You can see in *Last Judgment* 59 and 70 that the Last Judgment was on these individuals and these only; and there is further relevant information in *Supplement on the Last Judgment*[428] [16–22] where it discusses Protestants. These passages show that people were consigned to hell if they were devoted both in theory and in practice to a faith divorced from caring, but that they were raised into heaven if they were committed to this same faith in theory only but were nevertheless devoted to leading caring lives. I could see from this that these were just what the Lord meant by the goats and the sheep in Matthew 25:[32–33], where it speaks of the Last Judgment.

3. *The description of the battle between the ram and the goat in Daniel shows that in the Word, goats mean people who are devoted to a faith divorced from caring.* Spiritually understood, everything in Daniel, like everything in Sacred Scripture as a whole (as noted in *Sacred Scripture* 5–26),[429] is about matters of heaven and the church. This then holds true for what it says in chapter 8 about the battle between the ram and the goat, as follows:

> In a vision I saw a ram that had two tall horns, the taller of which rose up behind [the other]. With its horn the ram pushed westward, northward, and southward and became enormous.

Then I saw a goat that came from the west across the surface of the whole earth; it had a horn between its eyes. It charged at the ram in the fury of its strength, broke the ram's two horns, and cast the ram to the ground and trampled it. The large horn of the goat was broken, and four horns sprang up in its place. A little horn came out of one of them, which grew tremendously toward the south, toward the dawn, and toward the beautiful [land],430 and even to the host of the heavens, and cast down to earth some of the host and some of the stars, and trampled them. The goat even exalted itself toward the Leader of the Host, and took the daily offerings away from him and cast down the dwelling place of his sanctuary, because it cast truth to the ground. And I heard a holy one saying, "How long will this vision last concerning the daily offerings and this destructive sinning, the trampling of the holy place and the host?" And he said, "Until the evening [and] the morning: then the holy place will be set right." (Daniel 8:2–14)

66 It is obvious that this vision is predicting future states of the church, since it says that the goat took the daily offerings away from the Leader of the Host, that it cast down the dwelling place of his sanctuary, and that it cast truth to the ground. It also says that a holy one said, "How long will this vision last concerning the daily offerings and this destructive sinning, the trampling of the holy place and the host?" and that this would continue until the evening and the morning: then the holy place will be set right. Evening serves to mean the end of a church when there must be a new one.

The kings of Media and Persia later in this chapter [Daniel 8:20] mean much the same as the ram, and the king of Greece means much the same as the goat, because in the Word the names of realms, nations, and peoples, as well as those of persons and places, mean matters of heaven and the church.

67 The interpretation is as follows:431

The ram that had two tall horns, the taller of which rose up behind [the other], means people devoted to a faith prompted by caring.

With its horn the ram pushed westward, northward, and southward means the scattering of what is evil and false.

Its becoming enormous means growth.

The goat that came from the west across the surface of the whole earth means people devoted to a faith divorced from caring and their invasion of the church (the west is the evil of the earthly self).

Its having a horn between its eyes means intellectual pride.

Its charging at the ram in the fury of its strength means a violent attack against caring and its faith.

Its breaking the ram's two horns and casting the ram to the ground and trampling it means its complete scattering of both caring and faith, since scattering either one is scattering the other—they make a single entity.

The large horn of the goat being broken means the end of the illusion of intellectual pride.

The four horns springing up in its place means using the literal meaning of the Word for support.

A little horn coming out of one of them means the claim that no one can fulfill the law or do any good on his or her own.

Its growing tremendously toward the south, toward the dawn, and toward the beautiful [land] means a consequent rebelliousness throughout the whole church.

Doing this even to the host of the heavens, and casting down some of the host and some of the stars and trampling them means in this way destroying all awareness of what is good and true, the very substance of caring and faith.

Even exalting itself toward the Leader of the Host, taking the daily offerings away from him and casting down the dwelling place of his sanctuary means that this entailed the ravaging of every aspect of the worship of the Lord and every aspect of his church.

Casting truth to the ground means the distortion of the truth of the Word.

Until the evening [and] the morning: then the holy place will be set right means the end of that church and the beginning of a new one.

4. *The failure of caring in the people described in Matthew shows that goats mean people who are devoted to a faith divorced from caring.* We can see that the goats and sheep in Matthew 25:31–46 have the same meaning as the goat and the ram in Daniel because deeds of caring are listed for the sheep and it says that they did them, and the same deeds of caring are listed for the goats but it says that they did not do them, and that this is why these latter are condemned. A neglect of deeds is characteristic of people who are devoted to a faith divorced from caring because of their refusal to believe that deeds have anything to do with salvation or the church. When people so set aside caring—which consists of deeds—then faith fails as well, because faith comes out of caring; and when there is neither caring nor faith, there is damnation.

If the goats in this passage had meant all evil people it would have listed all the evil things they did rather than all the deeds of caring they did not do.[432]

People like this are also meant by goats in Zechariah:

> My wrath blazes against the shepherds, and I will execute judgment upon the goats. (Zechariah 10:3)

And in Ezekiel:

> Behold, I am judging between sheep and sheep, between rams and goats. Is it too little for you to have eaten up the good pasture? Will you also trample what remains of the food with your feet? You attack all the weak sheep with your horns until you have scattered them. Therefore I will save my flock, so that it will no longer be prey. (Ezekiel 34:17, 18, 21, 22, and following)

A Faith Divorced from Caring Destroys the Church and Everything It Stands For

69 A faith divorced from caring is no faith at all, because caring is the life of faith, its soul, its essence; and where there is no faith because there is no caring, there is no church. That is why the Lord says,

> When the Son of Humanity comes, will he find faith on the earth? (Luke 18:8)

70 From time to time I have heard "goats" and "sheep" discussing whether people devoted to a faith divorced from caring have any truth; and since some said they have a great deal, the contested issue was put to a test. They were asked whether they knew what love is, what caring is, and what good is, and since these were things they had divorced themselves from, all they could reply was that they did not know.

They were asked what sin is, what repentance is, and what the forgiveness of sins is. They replied that people who are justified by their faith are forgiven their sins so that their sins will no longer be in evidence. They were told that this is not the truth.

They were asked what regeneration is. They replied that it is either baptism or the forgiveness of sins by means of faith. They were told that this is not the truth.

They were asked what constitutes a spiritual person. They replied that a spiritual person is someone who is "justified by the faith we profess"; but they were told that this is not the truth.

They were asked about redemption, about the union of the Father and the Lord, and about the oneness of God, and they gave answers that are not truths—and so it went.

After the questions and answers, the debate was submitted to judgment; and the decision was that people who had convinced themselves of a faith divorced from caring had no truth whatever.⁴³³

[71] In this world, we cannot believe that this is in fact the case, because when people are convinced of things that are false they cannot help but see those false things as true and find little point in knowing more than what their faith tells them. Further, their faith is divorced from their intellect. That is, it is a blind faith, so they ask no questions; and this subject can be explored only on the basis of the Word as understood through enlightenment. This means that the truths the Word contains are turned into falsities by their thinking "faith" when they see "love," "repentance," "the forgiveness of sins," and many other words that concern things that we need to do.

[72] Make no mistake, though. That is what people are like when they convince themselves of faith alone in both theory and practice. It does not apply to people who turn their backs on evils because they are sins even though they have heard and believed that faith alone saves.

Supplements
on
the Last Judgment
and
the Spiritual World

Supplement on the Last Judgment

The Last Judgment Has Taken Place

THE earlier booklet *Last Judgment*[434] dealt with the following subjects: **1**

"Judgment Day" Does Not Mean the End of the World	§§1–5
The Reproduction of Humankind Will Not Cease	6–13
Heaven and Hell Come from Humankind	14–22
All Humans without Exception Who Have Been Born and Have Died since the Beginning of Creation Are either in Heaven or in Hell	23–27
A Last Judgment Must Take Place Where Everyone Is Together, So It Must Take Place in the Spiritual World,[435] and Not in the Physical World	28–32
A Last Judgment Occurs When the Church[436] Is at Its End, and the Church Is at Its End When There Is No Faith Because There Is No Caring	33–39
Everything That Was Foretold in the Book of Revelation Has Been Fulfilled at the Present Time	40–44
The Last Judgment Has Taken Place	45–52
Babylon and Its Destruction	53–64

The First Heaven, and How It Was Done Away With	65–72
The State of the World and the Church from Now On	73–74

[2] The primary purpose of this supplement to *Last Judgment* is to make known what the state of the world and the church was like before the Last Judgment and how that state has changed after it, and also how the Last Judgment was carried out on Protestants.

[3] In the Christian world it is commonly thought that on the day of the Last Judgment the whole of the heavens that we see with our eyes[437] and the whole earth that we live on are going to come to an end, that new heavens and a new earth are going to come into being to replace them, and that our souls will then be reunited with our bodies, allowing us to live as human beings again.[438]

This particular belief has arisen because the Word[439] has been understood only in its literal meaning: in fact, there was no other way it could be understood before its spiritual meaning[440] was disclosed. There is also the fact that many people have come to believe that the soul is nothing more than a breath that we exhale and that spirits—and angels, too—are made of wind.[441] As long as that was all there was to their understanding of souls and spirits and angels,[442] there was no other way they could think about the Last Judgment.

In fact, though, we are completely human after death, just as human as we are in this world except that we are then clothed with spiritual bodies rather than our former earthly ones. And spiritual people see spiritual bodies just as earthly people see earthly bodies. Once we come to understand that this is the case, then we are in a position to realize that the Last Judgment is not going to happen in this earthly world but in the spiritual world. After all, that is where all the people who have ever lived and died are gathered together.

[4] When we realize this, then we can rid ourselves of absurd notions that would otherwise plague our thinking about the state of our souls after death, about a reunion of those souls with our rotted bodies, about a destruction of the created universe, and therefore about the Last Judgment.

Concerning the state of our souls after death, we would otherwise have the notion that they must be like a breath or a breeze or like ether, fluttering around in the air or else being no longer in space at all but instead in that "somewhere-or-other."[443] We will not be able to see anything because souls have no eyes, hear anything because they have no ears, or say anything because they have no mouths—we will be blind, deaf, and mute, and will be in a state of constant waiting, which cannot help but be profoundly depressing—waiting for the day of the Last Judgment when our souls will finally be given back the abilities that were the source of all our life's pleasures.444 Further, we would think that the soul of everyone from the first creation must be in this wretched state, that people who lived fifty or sixty centuries ago445 are still fluttering about in the air like this or existing in that "somewhere-or-other," waiting for the judgment. And other depressing things.

[5] Allow me to skip over the absurd notions we would have concerning the destruction of the universe if we did not know that we are just as human after death as before. These notions are all of the same nature, and there are a lot of them.

Once we know that we are not breaths or breezes after death but spirits—and if we have led good lives, angels in heaven—and that spirits and angels have a form that is human in every way, then we can think intelligently about our state after death and about the Last Judgment. We do not need to think about these matters on the basis of an unintelligible faith, a faith that spawns only idle beliefs that are handed down through the ages. We can instead use our intellect to conclude for certain that the Last Judgment foretold in the Word is not going to happen in this earthly world but in the spiritual world, where everyone is gathered together. We can recognize as well that when the Last Judgment happens, that fact will surely be revealed, for the sake of the credibility of the Word.

[6] Set aside for a moment the idea of the soul as a breath that we exhale and think instead about your own state or the state of your friends or your children after death. Don't you think that you are going to live as a person, and don't you think the same of them? And since they would have no life worthy of the name if they had no senses, surely you think they will be seeing and hearing and talking. Think also of how eulogies depict the deceased: they are in heaven with the angels, in white robes, in beautiful gardens.

Now go back to the idea of the soul as a breath that will live without sensations until after the Last Judgment. Couldn't you lose your mind wondering, "What kind of creature will I be? Where will I be all this while? Will I be flying around in the air or left in that 'somewhere-or-other'? But the preacher told me that if I had good beliefs and lived a good life I'd be joining the blessed after I die!"

Believe instead, because it is the truth, that you will be just as human after death as before, the only difference being the difference between

7   You can conclude from what has been said so far that the Last Judgment cannot take place in the physical world but can take place in the spiritual world. You can also see that the Last Judgment did in fact happen in that world, from the eyewitness accounts in the earlier booklet *Last Judgment* (§§45–72) and also from the eyewitness accounts of the judgment on Protestants, which follow below [§§14–31].

Anyone who gives it careful consideration might also be able to tell that this has happened from the fact that new information about heaven, the Word, and the church is now being revealed. Who could make all this up out of nothing?

The State of the World and the Church before and after the Last Judgment

8   WHAT has been said above shows that the Last Judgment has already taken place in the spiritual world; but if there is to be any knowledge about the state of the world and the church before and after that judgment, the following information is essential.

1. What is meant by the first heaven and the first earth that passed away (Revelation 21:1).
2. Who the people of the first heaven and the first earth were and what they were like.
3. Before the Last Judgment on these people was carried out, much of the communication between heaven and earth, and also therefore between the Lord and the church, was blocked.
4. Since the Last Judgment, that communication has been restored.
5. That is why revelations for the new church[446] were given after the Last Judgment and not before.

6. The state of the world and the church before the Last Judgment was like evening and nighttime; after it, the state is like morning and daytime.

9

1. *What is meant by the first heaven and the first earth that passed away, described in Revelation 21:1.* The first heaven and the first earth in this passage do not mean the heavens that we here on earth see with our eyes or the planet that we live on, nor do they mean the first heaven that is the abode of all the people since creation who have lived rightly. Rather, they mean gatherings of spirits who made pseudo-heavens[447] for themselves between heaven and hell; and since all spirits and angels live in lands just as we do, those lands are meant by the first heaven and the first earth.

I witnessed the passing away of that heaven and that earth; in the booklet *Last Judgment* (§§45–72) I describe what I saw.

10

2. *Who the people of the first heaven and the first earth were and what they were like.* This has also been described in the booklet *Last Judgment* [§§68–71], but since understanding what follows depends on a recognition of who they were and what they were like, I need to say more about them now.

All those people who gathered below heaven and made pseudo-heavens for themselves in various places (which they actually called "heavens") were closely connected with angels of the lowest heaven.[448] The connection, though, involved only outward matters, not inward ones. Many were "the goats" mentioned in Matthew 25:41–46 or members of their family. They were people who had not done evil things in the world and who had lived good moral lives, but who had not done what was good for good reasons; they had in fact separated faith from caring and had therefore not regarded evil deeds as sins. Since they had lived like Christians outwardly, they were closely connected with the angels of the lowest heaven, who resembled them outwardly, although not inwardly. These angels were in fact the sheep [mentioned in Matthew 25:31–40]. They were people of faith too, but in their case their faith was the result of their caring.

Because of this close connection, there was no way to avoid making allowances for the goats, since separating them before the Last Judgment would have been harmful to the people in the lowest heaven. These people would actually have been dragged down with the others into destruction. This is what the Lord foretold in Matthew:

> Jesus spoke a parable: "The kingdom of heaven is like a man who sowed good seed in his field, but while people slept, an enemy of his came and

sowed tares and went away. When the grain had sprouted and bore fruit, the tares also appeared. The servants of the owner came and said to him, 'Lord, didn't you sow good seed in your field? Do you want us to go and gather in the tares?' But he said, 'No, because while gathering in the tares, you might uproot the wheat with them. Let both grow together until the harvest, and at harvest time I will tell the reapers, "First gather the tares and bind them in bundles for burning; then gather the wheat into the barn."' The one who sowed good seed is the Son of Humanity; the field is the world; the good seeds are the children of the kingdom; the tares are the children of the evil one; the harvest is the close of the age. As the tares are gathered and burned, so it will be at the close of the age." (Matthew 13:24–30, 37–40)

The close of the age is the last time of the church; the tares are people who are inwardly evil; the wheat is people who are inwardly good; binding the former in bundles for burning is the Last Judgment on them; "because while gathering in the tares, you might uproot the wheat with them. Let both grow until the harvest" means that by separating them before the Last Judgment harm might have been done to good people.

[11] 3. *Before the Last Judgment on these people was carried out, much of the communication between heaven and earth, and therefore between the Lord and the church, was blocked.* Any enlightenment we have comes to us from the Lord through heaven and enters us by an inner route. As long as there were gatherings of people like this between heaven and the world, that is, between the Lord and the church, we could not be enlightened. It was like what happens when the brilliance of the sun is obscured by the interference of a black cloud or when the sun is eclipsed by the moon and its light is cut off. This means that if anything had been revealed by the Lord it would not have been understood, or if it were understood it would not have been accepted, or if it were accepted, over time it would have been smothered.

Since all the gatherings that were causing obstructions have now been dispersed by the Last Judgment, we can see that:

4. *Communication has been restored between heaven and the world, that is, between the Lord and the church.*

[12] 5. *That is why revelations for the new church were given after the Last Judgment had taken place and not before.*[449] This is because once communication is restored by the Last Judgment we can be enlightened and reformed. That is, we can understand the divine truth of the Word, accept it as

something we understand, and retain it as something we have accepted. The obstacles have in fact been removed. So John says that after the first heaven and the first earth passed away, he saw a new heaven and a new earth, and then saw the holy city Jerusalem coming down from God out of heaven, prepared as a bride adorned for her husband; and he heard the one who sat on the throne say, "Behold, I am making all things new" (Revelation 21:1, 2, 5).

On Jerusalem as meaning a church, see *Teachings on the Lord*[450] 62–64, and for new principles taught by that church, see §65 there.

6. *The state of the world and the church before the Last Judgment was like evening and nighttime; after it, the state is like morning and daytime.* When the light of truth cannot be seen and truth is not accepted, the state of the church in the world is like evening and nighttime. We can see that this was the state of the church before the Last Judgment from what was said above in §11. When the light of truth becomes visible, though, and truth is accepted, the state of the church in the world is like morning and daytime.

This is why in the Word these two states of the church are called evening and morning or night and day, as in the following passages:

> The holy one said to me, "Until two thousand three hundred evenings and mornings: then the holy place will be set right." (Daniel 8:14)

> The vision of evenings and mornings is the truth. (Daniel 8:26)

> One day that is known to Jehovah will not be day or night, because there will be light around the time of evening. (Zechariah 14:7)

> Someone crying out to me from Seir, "Watchman, what of the night?" The watchman said, "Morning is coming, but so is night." (Isaiah 21:11, 12)

The following sayings of Jesus concern the last time of the church:

> Stay awake, because you do not know when the master of the house is coming—in the evening, at midnight, at the rooster's crow, or in the morning. (Mark 13:35)

> Jesus said, "I must work while it is day. The night is coming, when no one can work." (John 9:4)

For other examples, see also Isaiah 17:14; Jeremiah 6:4, 5; Psalms 30:5; 65:8; 90:6.

Since this is the meaning of evening and morning, in order to fulfill the Word the Lord was entombed in the evening and then rose in the morning.

The Last Judgment on Protestants

14 IN my earlier booklet *Last Judgment* [§§53–64], I dealt with the judgment on the people meant by Babylon[451] and also gave some information about the judgment on Muslims [§§50–51] and people of other religions. I did not deal with the judgment on Protestants, though. I noted only that they were in the center, arranged there by nationality [§48], with the Catholics around their circumference, the Muslims around the Catholics, and various other non-Christians around the Muslims.

The reason Protestants occupied the center or central area was that they read the Word and worship the Lord. This means that they have the most light; and the spiritual light that radiates from the Lord as the sun[452] (the Lord in essence being divine love) reaches out in all directions and enlightens even the people who are at the outermost circumference, opening them to understand as many truths as their religion can accept.

In its essence, spiritual light is divine wisdom; it enters our understanding to the extent that the knowledge we have gained in the past gives us an ability to perceive it. It does not travel through space like the light of this world but travels through our desire for and perception of what is true, so it comes to the farthest reaches of heaven in an instant. These workings are what give rise to apparent distances in that world.[453]

For more on this subject, see *Teachings on Sacred Scripture*[454] 104–113.

15 I need to describe the judgment on Protestants in the following sequence:

1. The Protestants on whom the Last Judgment was carried out
2. The signs and the reckoning that preceded the Last Judgment
3. An outline of what happened during the judgment
4. The salvation of the sheep[455]

1. *The Protestants on whom the Last Judgment was carried out.* The only Protestants on whom the Last Judgment was carried out were individuals who in this world had acknowledged God, read the Word, listened to sermons, observed the sacrament of the Supper, and had not neglected the church's holy days of worship, but who had seen nothing wrong with adultery and various kinds of theft, deceit, vengefulness, hatred, and the like. Even though they acknowledged God, they thought nothing of sins against him; they read the Word but thought nothing of its precepts for life; they heard sermons but paid no attention to them; they took the sacrament of the Supper but did not desist from the evils of their prior life; they observed the holy days of worship, but did nothing to amend their lives. So outwardly they lived as though they were religious, but inwardly they had no religion whatsoever.

[2] These were the people meant by the dragon in Revelation 12, for it says there that the dragon appeared in heaven, fought with Michael in heaven, and drew down a third of the stars of heaven. It says these things because people like this communicated with heaven by virtue of their acknowledgment of God, their reading of the Word, and their outward worship.

They are also meant by the goats in Matthew 25:[41–46], who are not told that they have done evil things but that they have failed to do good things. All such people fail to do good things that are genuinely good, because they do not turn their backs on evil deeds as sinful; even though they do not do them, they see nothing wrong with them. This means that they are doing them in spirit, and even do them physically when they can get away with it.

The Last Judgment was carried out on all these Protestants. It did not involve Protestants who had no belief in God, felt contempt for the Word, and threw the holy principles of the church out of their hearts, since all such Protestants had been cast into hell when they came from the earthly world into the spiritual world.

All the people who had lived like Christians outwardly and yet saw no intrinsic value in living a Christian life made common cause with the heavens outwardly but with the hells inwardly. Since their connection with heaven could not be abruptly cut off, they were kept in the world of spirits,[456] which is halfway between heaven and hell, and were allowed to form communities there and to live together just as they had in this world. They were also allowed to use arts unknown in our world to make everything look wonderful there and so to convince themselves and others that they were indeed in heaven; so on the basis of these appearances they called their communities "heavens." These "heavens" and "earths" where they lived are the ones meant in Revelation 21:1 by the first heaven and the first earth that passed away.

19 As long as they stayed there, the deeper levels of their minds[457] were closed and the outward levels were open, so the evils that united them to the hells did not show. Once the Last Judgment started, though, their deeper levels were revealed; and then everyone could see what they were really like. Since they were in full cooperation with the hells, they could no longer pretend to live a Christian life but instead rushed enthusiastically into all kinds of evil and wicked practices. They turned into devils[458] and even looked like devils—some black, some fiery, some as gray as corpses. The ones who were full of pride in their own intelligence looked black;[459] the ones obsessed with gaining power over everyone looked fiery; and the ones who totally disregarded and had contempt for the truth looked as gray as corpses.

That is how the scenes of their drama changed.

20 In the world of spirits, which is halfway between heaven and hell, Protestants make up the core, or form a central area, and are arranged there by nationality. In that central area, the British are in the middle, the Dutch to the south and east, the Germans to the north, the Swedes to the west and north, and the Danes to the west; but of these nationalities, only those people live in that central area whose earthly lives were governed by caring and by the faith that comes from caring. There are many communities there. Around them are Protestants who did not lead lives of faith and caring. These are the ones who made pseudo-heavens for themselves.

Heaven, though, is arranged differently than this, and so is hell.

The reason Protestants occupy the central area there is that the Word is read among them and the Lord is worshiped as well, which means that this is where the greatest light is—a light that spreads from there as from its center to the whole circumference, and brings enlightenment. The light in which spirits and angels live comes from the Lord as the sun. That sun, in its essence, is divine love, and the light that radiates from it is, in its essence, divine wisdom. This is the source of everything spiritual in that world.

On the Lord as the sun in the spiritual world, and on the light and warmth that come from it, see *Heaven and Hell*[460] 116–140.

[21] The whole arrangement of communities in that world is an arrangement based on differences among various kinds of love. This is because love is our very life; and the Lord, who is divine love itself, arranges these differences according to the way that that love is received. Further, the various kinds of love are beyond counting and are known to the Lord alone.

The Lord joins the communities together in such a way that they all, in effect, lead one human life—the communities of the heavens leading one life of heavenly and spiritual love, and the communities of the hells, one life of demonic and hellish love. He also joins the heavens and the hells in mutual opposition.

Because there is this kind of arrangement, after death we all go to the community of our own love. We cannot go anywhere else, because our love strongly resists our doing so.

This is why people who are devoted to spiritual love are in heaven and people who are devoted only to earthly love are in hell. Spiritual love is given us solely through a life of caring. If we neglect a life of caring, our earthly love remains earthly; and earthly love that is not subservient to spiritual love actually opposes it.[461]

[22] With this in mind we can tell which Protestants were subject to the judgment. It was not the ones who were in the central area but those around them, who, as noted, seemed to be Christians because of their outward morality but who were not Christians inwardly, because they had no spiritual life.

[23] *2. The signs and the reckoning that preceded the Last Judgment.* Above the people who had made pseudo-heavens for themselves something like storm clouds appeared as a result of the Lord's presence in the angelic heavens that were overhead,[462] especially his presence in the lowest heaven. His presence increased there in order to prevent any of that heaven's inhabitants from being carried off to destruction at the same time because of the closeness of their connection [with the pseudo-heavens].

The higher heavens also came down closer to them, which revealed the deeper levels of the people on whom the judgment was about to come. Once this happened these people no longer bore any resemblance to moral Christians as they had before, but became instead like demons. They rioted and squabbled with each other about God, the Lord, the Word, faith, and the church; and since their compulsions to evil had been given free rein as well, they rejected all these things with contempt and ridicule, and plunged into wickedness of every kind.

That is how the state of these supposed heaven-dwellers changed.

At the same time, all the wonderful things they had made for themselves by arts unknown in the world vanished. Their mansions turned into wretched huts, their gardens into swamps, their churches into rubble, and even the hills they lived on into piles of rocks and other such things that corresponded to their lawless dispositions and compulsions. This is because everything we see in the spiritual world corresponds to the feelings that are prevalent among spirits and angels.[463]

These were *signs* of the coming judgment.

24 As the revealing of their deeper natures increased, the hierarchy among these inhabitants changed and was reversed. The ones who made the strongest arguments against the holy principles of the church invaded the center and took control, while the rest, whose arguments were less forceful, retreated to the circumference and hailed the ones in the middle as their guardian angels.

In this way they bound themselves into bundles for hell.[464]

25 In connection with these changes of their state, there were various disturbances of the dwellings and lands around them, followed by earthquakes, which were massive because their [spiritual] upheavals were massive. Here and there, too, gaps opened up toward the hells that were underneath them, and in this way communication with those hells was opened. Then I could see great exhalations that looked like smoke with sparks of fire rising up.

These were also signs that came in advance. They were the ones meant by what the Lord said in the Gospels about the close of the age and then the Last Judgment:

> Nation will rise against nation. There will be great earthquakes in various places. There will be fearful sights and great signs from heaven. And there will be distress of nations, the sea and the waves roaring. [Luke 21:10, 11, 25]

26 *The reckoning* was carried out by angels. Before any community that is bound together by evil comes to an end, there is always a reckoning first. During the reckoning the angels kept urging the people to change their ways and threatening them with destruction if they did not.

During that time the angels also explored whether there were any good people among them, and removed these from the community; but the crowds were so stirred up by their leaders that they hurled insults at the angels and charged at them, trying to drag them into the public square and torment them in all kinds of unspeakable ways. What happened there was like what happened in Sodom [Genesis 19:1–29].

Many of them came from a faith separated from caring; and there were a few as well who claimed to believe that caring was important but still lived wicked lives.

3. *An outline of what happened during the judgment.* The reckoning and the signs foretelling the coming judgment could not make them give up their criminal behavior. Nothing could deter them from their plots to overthrow everyone who acknowledged the Lord as God of heaven and earth, held the Word to be holy, and lived a caring life. As a result, the Last Judgment came upon them; it happened in the following way.

The Lord appeared in a bright cloud, surrounded by angels, and out of the cloud came a sound like trumpets. This was a sign representing the Lord's protection of heaven's angels and his gathering of good people from all sides.

The Lord does not bring destruction on anyone.[465] All he does is protect his own and withdraw them from their communication with the evil. Once the good people have been withdrawn, the evil become fully engaged in their own obsessions and therefore plunge into all kinds of reprehensible behavior.

At that stage all the people who were about to perish gathered together, looking like a great dragon whose tail was stretched out in a curve and raised toward the sky, thrashing back and forth on high as though it wanted to destroy heaven and drag it down. This effort proved fruitless, though, because the tail was thrown back down, and the body of the dragon, which also looked as though it had risen up, sank down again.

I was allowed to see this representation so that I would know, and could make known, which people are meant by the dragon in Revelation. Specifically, the dragon means all those who read the Word, listen to sermons, and observe the rites of the church, but see nothing whatever wrong with the cravings for evil behavior with which they are saturated. Inwardly, they think about acts of theft and cheating, adultery and obscenity, hatred and vengeance, lying and blasphemy, and are therefore living like devils in spirit, although in their outward lives they are like angels. These are the people who made up the body of the dragon. The ones who made up the tail were like these others in regard to their thoughts and intentions, but had been particularly dedicated in the world to faith as something separate from caring.

29 Then I saw what happened to the rocks people were living on: some of them sank to the deepest depths, some were carried far away, some split open in the middle so that the people living on them were cast down into a cave, and some were submerged as if by a flood. I saw the many people on them gathered into groups like bundles, sorted by types and subtypes of evil, and cast far and wide into whirlpools, swamps, marshes, and deserts, all of which were hells.

The rest, who did not live on those rocks but on either side of them (even though they were given to the same kinds of evil), fled thunderstruck to the Catholics, Muslims, and people of other religions and professed those religions. They could do this without even changing their minds because they actually had no religion. To prevent them from leading the others in those religions astray, though, they were driven off and forced down to live with their true companions in the hells.

This provides a general outline of their fate. The details of what I saw are more than can be described here.[466]

30 4. *The salvation of the sheep*.[467] After the Last Judgment was accomplished, joy broke out in heaven and a greater light than ever broke forth in the world of spirits. The nature of the joy in heaven after the dragon was cast down is described in Revelation 12:10, 11, 12. Light broke forth in the world of spirits because those hellish communities had been in the way like clouds that were darkening the earth. A similar light then arose on us in this world, too, bringing us a new enlightenment.

31 Then I saw angelic spirits rising from the lower regions in great numbers and being lifted up into heaven. These were the sheep, individuals from previous centuries who had been held there and protected by the Lord so that they would not be overcome by the malignant aura that flowed out from the dragon and so that their caring would not be suffocated by it.

These are the people meant in the Word by the ones who woke up and came out of their graves, by the souls of those who had been killed because of their testimony for Jesus, and by those who were part of the first resurrection.[468]

Supplement on the Spiritual World

The Spiritual World

THE spiritual world was the topic of the book *Heaven and Hell,* which offers a description of many of the features of that world; and because we all enter that world after death, it also describes what our state will then be like.

Surely everyone knows that we will go on living after death, because we are born human, created in the image of God [Genesis 1:27], and because the Lord tells us this in his Word. Until now, though, there has been no knowledge of what life will be like for us then. People believe that we will then be souls, but their concept of a soul is that it is something airy or ethereal,[469] which retains some capacity for thought, but has no eyesight, no hearing, and no ability to speak. Yet the fact is that we are still human beings after death—so much so that we do not realize we are not still in the physical world. As we used to in the world, we see, hear, and talk. As we used to in the world, we walk, run, and sit. As we used to in the world, we eat and drink. As we used to in the world, we sleep and wake up. As we used to in the world, we enjoy making love to our spouse. Briefly put, we are still human in every way.

This makes it clear that our death is simply a continuation of our life. Death is just a transition.

33 There are many reasons for our not knowing that this is the state we will be in after death. One of them is that we have been unable to be enlightened because we have had so little belief in the immortality of the soul. This is clear from the many people, including scholars, who believe that we are the same as animals, our only advantage over them being that we are capable of speech.[470] So even though such people's words affirm life after death, at heart they deny it. This type of thinking has made them so oriented to their physical senses that they cannot believe we continue to be human after death; after all, they do not see [the souls of the dead] with their eyes. So they say, "How can a soul be human?"

It is different for people who believe they are going to go on living after death. Inwardly, they believe that they are going to arrive in heaven, enjoy themselves in the company of angels, see heavenly paradises, stand before the Lord in white garments [Revelation 3:4–5], and so on. No matter how their outer thinking may stray from this when they think about the soul on the basis of scholarly theories, these remain their inner thoughts.

34 It is clear that people are still human after death—even though they are not visible to our physical eyes—from the angels seen by Abraham, Gideon, Daniel, and other prophets; from the angels seen at the Lord's tomb and later from those seen a number of times by John in Revelation; and above all from the Lord himself, who showed the disciples that he was human by being touched and by eating and yet he also vanished from their sight.[471] The reason they could see him was that the eyes of their spirits were opened, and when these are opened we can see things in the spiritual world just as clearly as we see things in this earthly world.

35 Because it has pleased the Lord to open the eyes of my spirit and to keep them open for nineteen years now,[472] I have been granted the opportunity to see what is in the spiritual world and also to describe it.

I swear to you that these things are not mere visions but are things I have *seen* when I was wide awake.[473]

36 The difference between a person in the earthly world and one in the spiritual world is that the latter is clothed with a spiritual body and the former with an earthly body. A spiritual person sees another spiritual person just as clearly as an earthly person sees another earthly person, but an earthly person cannot see a spiritual one and a spiritual person cannot see an earthly one. This is because of the difference between what is earthly and what is spiritual. (The difference between these could be described, but the description would not be brief.)

37 On the basis of my own eyewitness experience of many years, I can testify to the following. Just as in the physical world, in the spiritual world there are landmasses, hills and mountains, plains and valleys, springs and rivers, lakes and oceans. There are parks and gardens, groves and forests. There are mansions and houses. There are manuscripts and books. There are jobs and business transactions. There are precious stones, gold, and silver. To put it briefly, that world contains absolutely everything that exists in the physical world, although in heaven, these things are infinitely more perfect.

38 In general, the difference is this. Everything in the spiritual world comes from a spiritual source and is therefore spiritual in its essence. The source of everything there is a sun[474] that is pure love. Everything in this earthly world comes from an earthly source and is therefore earthly in its essence. The source of everything here is a sun that is pure fire.[475]

As a result, spiritual people need to be nourished by food that is spiritual in origin, just as earthly people need to be nourished by food that is earthly in origin.

There is more on this topic in *Heaven and Hell* [§§111, 116–125, 340, 582].

The British in the Spiritual World

39 WE have two levels of thought, outer and inner. In our outer thinking we are in this earthly world, but in our inner thinking we are in the spiritual world. In good people these levels are in harmony with each other, but in evil people they are not. In this earthly world it is rarely clear what someone is like inwardly, because from early childhood we have tried to be moral and have learned to seem so; but in the spiritual world our nature is plain to see. Spiritual light uncovers this. And we are then spirits, and the spirit *is* the inner self.

Since I have been granted the opportunity to be in that light and to see by that light what the inner selves of people from various nations are like—this through associating with angels and spirits for many years—I have a duty to reveal this information; it is important.

I will first say something about that excellent nation, the British.

40 The better individuals among the British people are at the center of all Christians (see §20 above on the Christians being at the center [of the world of spirits]). This is because they have a profound intellectual light. This trait of theirs is not noticeable to anyone in the earthly world but it is obvious in the spiritual world. They owe this light to their freedom of thought and consequent freedom of speech and writing. (Among other peoples who have no such freedoms, the intellectual light is smothered because it has no outlet.)476

This light is not automatically activated in them, however; it is stimulated by others, especially by those who are famous or powerful among them. As soon as people hear statements from these authorities or read something they have recommended, then this light blazes forth; it rarely happens before [such stimulation].

Because of this the British in the spiritual world are assigned governors and are given preachers renowned for their scholarship and brilliance. The people willingly obey edicts and advice from them because to do so is in their nature.

41 They seldom leave their own community in the spiritual world because they love it the way they loved their country in the physical world. They all have similar dispositions, too, which lead them to associate closely with friends from their own country, and rarely with others. They also help each other out and love honesty.

42 There are actually two major cities just like London in the spiritual world.477 Most British people come into one or the other of them after they die. I have been granted the opportunity to see these and to walk around in them.

The center of one of them is [like] the part of London, England, where the merchants are concentrated, which is called the Exchange.478 That is where their governors live. Above that city center is the eastern quarter; below it is the western quarter; on its right side is the southern quarter, and on its left is the northern quarter.

[2] In the eastern quarter reside individuals who were more devoted than others to leading a life of caring. The mansions there are magnificent. The wise live in the southern quarter; they have an abundance of glorious possessions. In the northern quarter live people who more than others had loved freedom of speech and of writing. In the western quarter

live individuals who profess faith [alone]. There is an entrance to the city toward the right in this last area, and there is also an exit from the city there. Individuals who live evil lives are sent away through that exit.

The priests who live in the west—who, as just noted, profess faith [alone]—do not dare come into the city [center] by its main streets, but enter instead by rather narrow alleys, because no one is allowed to live in the city [proper] except those who are devoted to a faith that comes from caring.

[3] I have heard complaints raised about the preachers from the west—that they compose their sermons with such skill and eloquence, weaving in a concept of justification by faith that is foreign to their listeners, that the listeners cannot tell whether one is supposed to do what is good or not. They preach a goodness within that they distinguish from outer goodness, sometimes calling the latter "credit seeking" and therefore unacceptable to God—though they still call it good because it is useful. However, when people from the eastern and southern quarters of the city hear sermons on these mystical topics they walk out of the building; and later those preachers are stripped of their priesthood.

43 The other major city that is like London is not in the Christian central area described in §20 but lies outside it, to the north. British people who have been inwardly evil come into this London after they die. In the center of it there is open access to hell. Hell swallows these people up from time to time.

44 I once heard some priests from Britain talking to each other about faith alone and saw a kind of statue they had made to represent how they saw faith alone.[479] In the dim light they had, it looked like a huge giant, and to their eyes it had a beautiful human form; but when light from heaven was let in, the upper part looked like a monster and the lower like a serpent, not unlike the description of the Philistines' idol, Dagon [Judges 16:23; 1 Samuel 5]. When they saw this, they backed away, and some bystanders threw the statue into a pond.

45 From people from Britain in the spiritual world I have gathered that they have two different religious perspectives: one is focused on teachings about faith, and the other on teachings about the way to live. Individuals who have been ordained into the priesthood are focused on teachings about faith, while individuals who have not been ordained (commonly known as the laity) are focused on teachings about how to live. This focus on how to live is manifestly present in the prayer read in churches on Sundays to people who are about to take the Holy Supper,[480] in which it is clearly stated that if they are not turning their backs on evil deeds because they are sins, they are casting themselves into eternal damnation, and that if they come to take Holy Communion on any other terms, the Devil will enter into them as he entered into Judas [Luke 22:3; John 13:27].[481]

I have occasionally talked with British clergy about the discrepancy between this teaching of the importance of how we live and the teachings about faith. They gave no response, but were having thoughts that they did not dare express.

You may find this prayer in §§5, 6, and 7 of *Teachings about Life for the New Jerusalem*.

46. I have often seen a particular British man[482] who became famous because of a book he had published some years before, a book in which he labored to prove a union of faith and caring through the inflow and inner working of the Holy Spirit, proposing that this inflow affects us in an indescribable way and without our awareness of it. However, it does not touch, let alone move, our will or arouse our thinking to do anything (in what would be apparent independence). It only allows our will to act. The thinking behind this is that otherwise we would be playing a role in divine providence, and also that our evils would then appear before God. This rules out outward works of caring as being of any benefit to our salvation but nevertheless advocates them for the public good. Because his arguments were ingenious and no one saw the snake in the grass, this book was accepted as the height of orthodoxy.

[2] After his departure from the world this author held to the same dogma and was unable to retreat from it because he had thoroughly convinced himself. Some angels talked with him and told him that his dogma was not the truth but only an eloquent presentation of something clever, and that the truth was that we should abstain from doing evil and do good as though we were doing it on our own, but with a recognition that it was being done by the Lord. They said that until we do that, there is no faith at all, and certainly not the complex thing that he was imagining and calling "faith." Since this conflicted with his dogma, he was encouraged to use his astute intellect to inquire further and see whether this kind of unrecognized inflow and inner working actually did occur, without any outward effort on the individual's part. He seemed then to focus his mind and to follow wandering paths in his thought,[483] always with the conviction that this was the only way we could be restored to wholeness and be saved. Every time he reached the end of a path, though, his

eyes were opened and he saw that he had gone astray. He actually admitted it to some who were present.

[3] For a couple of years I saw him wandering like this; and at the end of his journey, he admitted that there was no such inflow unless the evil in the outer self was removed, which was accomplished by turning one's back on evil because it is sinful, in apparent autonomy. Eventually I heard him say that all the people who convinced themselves of this heresy had been driven insane by their pride in their own intelligence.

I talked with *Melanchthon*[484] and asked him about his situation. He did not want to answer, so I was told about his situation by others. They said that he was sometimes in a stone-vaulted room and sometimes in hell, and that because it was so cold in the room, he seemed to be wearing a bearskin. They said that because of the uncleanness of his room he did not admit newcomers from the world who came to him as visitors, drawn by his reputation and fame.

He still talked about faith alone, something he had done more to establish than anyone else in the world.

The Dutch in the Spiritual World

I stated in §20 above that Christians among whom the Word is read and the Lord is worshiped are at the center of the nations and peoples of the whole world of spirits because they are in the greatest spiritual light; and the light radiates from them as from a center into the entire surroundings, even the most remote, and brings enlightenment (see what is presented in *Teachings for the New Jerusalem on Sacred Scripture* 104–113).

Within this Christian central region, Protestants are assigned particular places according to how receptive they are to spiritual light from the Lord. Since the British have that light hidden away in the intellectual part of themselves, they are in the inmost region of that central area. The Dutch, though, keep that spiritual light more closely connected to earthly light, which means that the light they see is not as snowy white. Instead, they see something that is not completely clear, but is receptive to a rationality that comes from both spiritual light and spiritual warmth; so they have been given homes in the eastern and southern parts of that central Christian area. They have homes in the east because they are receptive to spiritual warmth, which is their caring, and homes in the south because they are receptive to spiritual light, which is their faith.

[2] See *Heaven and Hell* 141–153 on these facts: that geographical regions in the spiritual world are not like geographical regions in the earthly world; that the particular region people live in depends on how receptive they are to faith and love; and that the people in the east are the ones who excel in love and caring, while the people in the south are the ones who excel in intelligence and faith.

[3] Another reason they are in the central area of the Christian region is that for them, business is what they love most and money is loved as a means; and this is a spiritual love; but when money is what is loved most and business is loved as a means, that is an earthly love that comes from greed.

The Dutch are more devoted than anyone else to the spiritual love just mentioned. That love truly equates to the common good, and this includes and subsumes the good of the nation.

49 The Dutch hold more firmly to their religious principles than others do. They will not be moved. If someone proves to them that this or that teaching is out of step with the other things they believe, they still will not accept it. They turn away and remain fixed in the position they had held before. They also avoid undertaking any investigation of inner truth; on spiritual matters they keep their rational faculty strictly obedient [to what they already believe].

Since this is their nature, when they come into the world of spirits after death they are brought to accept spiritual teachings from heaven, which are divine truths, in a completely different way than others are. They are not taught them, since they are not receptive. Instead, this is what they go through: They are offered descriptions of what heaven is like, and then are granted the opportunity to go up to heaven and see it for themselves. Then anything [there] that is in harmony with their own disposition is instilled into them and they are brought back down to their own people, full of a longing for heaven.

[2] For example, suppose that they do not accept the truth that God is one in person and in essence, that that God is the Lord, and that the Trinity is within him. Suppose, too, that they do not accept the truth

that faith and caring, even if they are acknowledged and made the subject of conversation, do not accomplish anything unless people actually live them, and that faith and caring are given by the Lord when we turn our backs on evil deeds because they are sins. If they do not accept these truths when they are taught them and persist instead in thinking of God as three persons and thinking no more of religious practice than that some such thing exists, they are reduced to misery and deprived of their business until they see that they are completely out of options.

Then they are brought to some people who have everything, whose businesses are flourishing. At the same time, under heaven's influence it occurs to them to think about why these people have this success, and to reflect on what these people believe about the Lord and how they live. They notice in particular that these people turn their backs on evil deeds because they are sins. They even make a few inquiries about it, and what they learn confirms their thinking and reflection.

They then go back and forth, back and forth like this [between their own lives and those of the successful people]. Eventually, they decide of their own accord that if they want to get free of their misery they need to believe and live as these others do. Then they accept this faith and lead this life of caring, and as they do so, they are given wealth and an enjoyable life.

Therefore although they are not open to being corrected by others, in this way the ones who had lived any kind of life of caring in the world can correct themselves and become prepared for heaven.

[3] Thereafter they are more steadfast than other people are, to the point that they could be called embodiments of constancy; they do not allow themselves to be swayed by any faulty rationale, any fallacy, any confusion created by subtly deceptive reasoning, or any misleading insight, no matter how many supporting arguments it might have.

50. It is easy to identify the Dutch in the spiritual world because they dress as they did in the earthly world, except that the clothes of the ones who have accepted the spiritual faith and way of life just mentioned are neater and more elegant.

The reason they still dress the same is that they remain steadfastly loyal to their religious principles, and in the spiritual world everyone is clothed according to those principles. This is why people in the spiritual world who are devoted to divine truths wear clothes of white linen.[485]

51. The cities where the Dutch live are protected in a unique way. All their streets are covered and gated to prevent the Dutch from being seen

by anyone on the surrounding cliffs and hills. They structure things in this way because of their deep-seated concern to keep their negotiations confidential and not make their intentions public, since in the spiritual world observers can see your plans just by looking at you.

Curious visitors sometimes come there to find out what life is like in those cities. When they are about to leave the Dutch take them to gateways [at the ends] of their streets that are locked, then take them by other routes to more gateways that are locked, until the visitors become thoroughly frustrated, at which point they are finally released. This is done to ensure that they never come back.

[2] Wives who seek to control their husbands live on one side of the city and are allowed to get together [with their husbands] only when the husbands have sent them an invitation, which is done with some formality. Then those couples are taken to homes occupied by married partners, neither of whom is trying to dominate the other. They are shown how well-decorated and clean these homes are and how enjoyable their lives are, and they see that this is because mutual love is part of the couple's marriage. The wives who are attentive to this, and are moved by it, stop trying to control their husbands and instead share life together with them. These couples are then given homes nearer to the center and are called angels.

This is because marriage love is a heavenly love; it has nothing to do with domineering.

53 [486] During the days of the Last Judgment I saw many thousands of people from that nation cast out of those cities and out of the surrounding towns and regions, people who in this world had not performed any good action for the sake of its connection with religion or conscience, but had done so solely for the sake of their own reputation, in order to be regarded as honest so that they could make a profit. When people like this lose their concern for their reputation or profit, which happens in the spiritual world, they plunge into all kinds of criminal behavior, robbing everyone they run into when they are in the fields and outside the cities.

I saw them cast down, some into a burning chasm that extended beneath the eastern quarter and others into a dark cave that extended beneath the southern quarter. I witnessed this on January 9, 1757.

The ones who lived by their religion, though, and had a conscience as a result, were allowed to stay.

54 I have spoken with *Calvin*,[487] but only once. He was in a community of heaven that can be seen toward the front, above the head. He said that he did not agree with Luther[488] and Melanchthon[489] about faith alone, because so often the Word speaks of works and commands us to act, and therefore faith and works are to be united.

I heard from a governor of that community that Calvin was welcome there because he was honest and caused no trouble.

Elsewhere I will discuss what happened to *Luther;*[490] I have seen and heard him a number of times. Here I will say only that he has often tried to let go of his belief about faith alone, but without success, and that therefore he is still in the world of spirits, which is halfway between heaven and hell, and sometimes life is hard for him there.

Roman Catholics in the Spiritual World

IN §§53–64 of the booklet *Last Judgment* I wrote about the Roman Catholics and the Last Judgment on them.[491] In the spiritual world Catholics surround the area where the Protestants are, but they are separated from them by an intervening space that they are not allowed to cross. Some from the Order of the Jesuits, though, use devious means to set up channels of communication with Protestants. They also send their agents along uncharted paths with the intent of luring Protestants away from Protestantism. These agents are found out, however, and after they have been punished they are either sent back to their people or cast into hell.

After the Last Judgment circumstances in the spiritual world changed. Newly arrived people are no longer allowed to congregate in large groups as they had been doing. Now instead there are pathways assigned for every type of love, whether good or evil. People who arrive from this world immediately take these pathways, which lead them to a community that corresponds to what they love. Evil people are drawn to a community that is closely connected with the hells, and good people to a community that is closely connected with the heavens. This new arrangement prevents people from forming pseudo-heavens the way others did in the past.

In the world of spirits, which is halfway between heaven and hell, there are countless communities like this. There are as many communities as there are general and specific kinds of good and evil loves; and in the interim before these communities are either taken up into heaven or cast down into hell, they have a close connection with us in this world, because we too are halfway between heaven and hell.

58. All Catholics who have not been outright idolaters, who have done good things with sincerity of heart because of the teachings of their religion, and who have also focused on the Lord are brought to communities that have been established near the border with the Protestants. There they are given instruction: they hear readings from the Word and sermons about the Lord, and the ones who accept these truths and apply them to their lives are taken up into heaven and become angels.

There are many communities of these kinds of Catholics in each region, and they are thoroughly protected against the cunning, deceitful schemes of monks and against the leaven of Babylon.[492]

All Catholic children as well are in heaven. They have no knowledge of the false teachings of their parents' religion, because they have been raised by angels under the watchful care of the Lord.

59. All people who come into the spiritual world from our earth, including Catholics, are kept at first in the confession of faith and the religion of their homeland. Therefore the Catholics there always have someone set over them to represent the papacy, someone to whom they give the same ritual adoration they gave the pope in the world. It is rare for anyone who has actually been a pope in the world to play the role of pope there. One exception, though, is the person who had been pope of Rome twenty years previously.[493] He was given this position in the spiritual world because at heart he had treasured a conviction that the Word was holier than people believed and that the Lord was to be the focus of worship. After he had served as a pope there for a few years, he stepped down and went over to join the Protestant Christians. He is still with them, and is leading a blessed life.

I was granted an opportunity to talk with him. He said that he reveres the Lord alone, because the Lord is God and has power over heaven and earth. He also said that prayers to the saints are of no value and that the same holds true for masses in their honor. He said that in the world he had tried to reform the church but had been unable to for various reasons, which he told me.

When a great northern city where Catholics lived was destroyed on the day of the Last Judgment, I saw him being carried away on a sedan chair and set down in a place of safety. Something quite different happened to his successor.[494]

60 I may add to this an account of a memorable occurrence. I was granted an opportunity to talk with Louis XIV,[495] the great-grandfather of the present king of France,[496] who during his earthly life had worshiped the Lord, read the Word, and recognized the pope as no more than the head of the church. In the spiritual world he therefore has a highly honored position, governing the best community of people from France.

I saw him once apparently going down a flight of stairs, and after he had done so I heard him say that it seemed to him as though he were at Versailles. Then there was silence for a couple of hours, after which he said that he had just talked with his great-grandson, the king of France, about the Bull *Unigenitus*,[497] saying that he himself no longer held his former position on it; he now did not accept the bull, because it was detrimental to the French nation. He said that he had impressed this thought very deeply upon the current king's mind.

This happened at about 8 P.M. on December 13, 1759.

The Catholic Saints in the Spiritual World

61 IT is common knowledge that we all have innate, that is, inherited, evil from our parents, but few know what that evil is. It consists of a love of controlling others. The nature of this love is that the more its reins are let out, the more it breaks forth until it becomes a burning desire to control everyone; ultimately it wants to be called upon and worshiped as God.

This love is the serpent that deceived Eve and Adam. It said to the woman, "God knows that on the day when you eat of the fruit of the tree your eyes will be opened, *and then you will be like God*" (Genesis 3:4, 5). The more the reins are let out, then, and we plunge into this love, the more we turn away from God and toward ourselves and become atheists. Then the divine truths of the Word may indeed serve us as means; but since our goal is to have control over others, we take the means to heart only to the extent that is expedient for us.

This is why the people who have this love of controlling others, whether at an extreme level or only halfway, are all in hell. In fact, this demonic love is present wherever you encounter people who by nature cannot stand even a mention of God.

62. This love is characteristic of those Catholics who exerted control over others because of the irresistible itch of the pleasure involved, and who had no use for the Word and preferred the decrees of the pope. First they are deprived of all their outer knowledge so completely that they no longer know anything about the church; then they are cast into hell and become devils.

There is a particular separate hell for the ones who want to be called upon as gods. The people who live there are so deep in fantasy that they see not what is, but what is not. It is like the delirium of people with a severe fever who see little things in the air, in the room, and on their bedspread that are not there at all.

This worst of all evils is meant by the head of the serpent that was trampled by the seed of the woman, and that wounded his heel (Genesis 3:15). The heel of the Lord (who is the seed of the woman) is the emanating divine influence at the outermost level, which is the Word in its literal meaning.

63. Given the fact that we inherit this characteristic of wanting control [over some people]—and gradually, as the reins are let out, wanting control over more people and eventually over everyone—and since at its core this love is a desire to be called upon and worshiped as God, therefore all the people who have been canonized by papal bull are moved out of sight of others and hidden away, cut off from any contact with those who worship them. This is to prevent that worst root of their inner evils from being activated, which would lead them into the delirious fantasies of the hell mentioned just above. This kind of delirium obsesses people who during their earthly lives longed and worked to become saints after death so that people would pray to them.

64. When arriving in the spiritual world, many Catholics, particularly the monks, look for their saints, especially the patron saint of their order. They are bewildered when they cannot find them. Later, others inform them that their saints are living as ordinary people, among either those in the heavens or those in the hells, depending on how they lived their life in the

world; and in either case they are completely unaware that anyone is worshiping them or praying to them. (The ones who do know and who want to be prayed to are in that separate, delusional hell mentioned just above.)

The worship of saints is so distasteful in heaven that as soon as such worship is mentioned the angels shudder, because to the extent that worship is offered to any human, worship is diverted from the Lord. In this case, he is not the sole focus of worship, and if the Lord is not our sole focus, there is a division that robs us of our relationship with him and the happiness of life that flows from it.

65 To teach me what the Catholic saints are like so that I could make the information known, a hundred or so of them who knew they had been canonized were brought up from the lower earth.[498] Most of them rose up behind me—only a few in front of me.

I talked with one who was said to have been Xavier.[499] When he was talking with me he was behaving very foolishly. He did manage to tell me, though, that when he remained where he belonged he was not a fool, but became one whenever he thought of himself as a saint.

I heard a murmur to the same effect from the ones who were behind me.

66 It is different for the so-called saints who are in heaven. They know nothing whatever about what is happening on earth; and when I talked with them, no such idea ever came to their minds.

On just one occasion, Mary, the Lord's mother, passed by. I saw her overhead, dressed in white. She paused for a moment and said that she had been the Lord's mother and that he had indeed been born of her, but that when he became God he shed everything human that he had received from her. Now, therefore, she reveres him as her God and does not want anyone to think of him as her son, because everything in him is divine.

67 Here I may add another account of a memorable occurrence. To the Parisians who are together in a community in the spiritual world a woman sometimes appears in midair, wearing radiant clothes and having a saintly face. She says that she is Geneviève,[500] but when some begin to worship her, both her face and her clothing change so that she looks like a peasant. She criticizes people for wanting to worship a woman who is no more esteemed among her friends than a servant girl would be, and marvels at the fact that people in the world are taken in by this kind of nonsense.

Some angels said that the reason she appears in that community is to separate worshipers of mere human beings from worshipers of the Lord there.

Muslims and Muhammad in the Spiritual World

68 IN the spiritual world, Muslims appear beyond the Catholics in the west; they form a kind of perimeter around them. The main reason they appear there is that they recognize the Lord as the greatest prophet, the Son of God, and the wisest of all, who was sent into the world to teach us.[501]

In the spiritual world, the place where each person lives in relation to the central Christian region, inhabited by Protestants, is determined by that person's acknowledgment of the Lord and of the oneness of God. This is because such acknowledgment joins people's minds to heaven and determines their distance from the east, above which is the Lord.[502] People who lack that acknowledgment in their hearts because they have lived an evil life are in the hells underneath these communities.

69 Since our religion is absolutely central to our nature and everything else about us derives from that center, and since Muslims think of Muhammad whenever they think of their religion, there is always a Muhammad set visibly before Muslims in the spiritual world; and in order to turn their faces toward the east, above which is the Lord, he is placed next to the central Christian region.

This is not, however, Muhammad himself, the writer of the Qur'an, but someone else who plays that role. It is not always the same individual either; it changes. At one time it was a man originally from Saxony who had become a Muslim after being taken captive by some Algerians.[503] Because he had originally been a Christian, he was persuaded to talk to them about the Lord, saying that Jesus was not the son of Joseph, as they had believed in the world, but the son of God himself; he instilled in them a concept of the oneness of the Lord with the Father both in person and in essence.

This Muhammad was followed by others who were persuaded to say similar things, with the result that many Muslims have gained a belief concerning the Lord that could be called truly Christian. These Muslims are brought to a community nearer to the east where they are granted communication with heaven, and eventually are raised into heaven itself.

In the place where this Muhammad is to be found, the fire of a burning torch appears as a sign so that people will know where he is; but this fire is visible only to Muslims.

70 The real Muhammad, the writer of the Qur'an, is not seen in public these days. I was told that in the beginning he was the leader of the

Muslims in the spiritual world, but because he wanted to control all aspects of their religious life as if he himself were God, he was removed from where he was living, which was next to the Catholic region, and was sent down to the right near the southern quarter.

At one point malevolent individuals persuaded several Muslim communities to acknowledge Muhammad as God. To quell this uprising, Muhammad himself was brought up from the lower regions and shown to them. I, too, saw him at that time. He looked like those body-oriented spirits who have no deeper perception, with a face that was almost black.[504] I heard him say only these words: "I am your Muhammad." Shortly afterward he appeared to sink back down and return to his place.

As for their religion, this kind of belief was allowed because it suits the viewpoint of those in the Middle East. That is why it has been accepted in so many nations—this and the fact that in it the rules given in the Ten Commandments are made matters of religious practice, and there is material from the Word in it as well.[505] In particular, the Lord is recognized as the Son of God and as the wisest of all.[506] Islam also eliminated the idolatrous practices of many nations.

The reason an inward religion was not opened to them by Muhammad was their polygamy, which causes an unclean atmosphere to blow toward heaven. This is because the marriage of one husband and one wife corresponds to the marriage of the Lord and the church.

Many of them are very receptive to truth and are capable of seeing what is right on the basis of rational argumentation—something I have been able to observe in my conversations with them in the spiritual world. I talked with them about the one God, about resurrection, and also about marriage.

Concerning *the one God,* they said that they see no sense in what Christians say about the Trinity, namely, that there are three persons and that each one is God, and yet they maintain that there is nevertheless one God. I said in response that angels in the Christian heaven do *not* say things like that; they say that God is one person and has one essence, but there is a trinity that exists within him. I added that people on earth refer to this trinity as three "persons," but actually all three exist within the Lord. To support this I read to them the passages in Matthew and Luke about the Lord's conception by God the Father [Matthew 1:18–25; Luke 1:26–38], and then the passage where the Lord says that he and the Father are one [John 10:30]. When they heard this they perceived that it was so and said that the Lord's essence, then, is divine.

[2] As for *resurrection,* they said they see no sense in what Christians say about our state after death. Christians say the soul is something like air or a breeze and is incapable of experiencing any pleasure before being reunited with its body on the day of the Last Judgment. I replied that only a particular group of Christians says things like that; Christians who are not part of that denomination believe instead that they will go to heaven after they die, will talk with angels, and will enjoy heavenly delight, and although they do not specify what that delight is, they see it as being not unlike the pleasures they experience in the world. I added that many things about our state after death are just now being revealed to Christians, things they had not known about before.

[3] I have also had many conversations with them about *marriage,* saying among other things that marriage love is a heavenly love and is possible only between two individuals, and that a husband's partnering with many wives blocks access to the heavenliness of this love.[507] They heard the reasons and perceived the fairness in them. I added that polygamy was permitted them because they were Middle Easterners; if polygamy had not been allowed, they would have been even more vulnerable than Europeans to falling into flagrant adulteries of the filthiest kinds and would have destroyed themselves.[508]

Africans, and People of Other Religions, in the Spiritual World

73. THE people of other religions, who had had no knowledge of the Lord, appear farther from the center than the people who had had such knowledge. They are arranged in such a way that those who are at the farthest edge are all complete idolaters and worshipers of the sun or the moon.[509]

The ones who acknowledge one God, though, and who take precepts like those of the Ten Commandments to be religious principles that determine how they live, are situated in a higher region and therefore have more direct communication with the Christians who are in the central region. Their location keeps this communication from being blocked by Muslims and Catholics.

People of other religions are also sorted by disposition and by their ability to receive light through the heavens from the Lord. Some of them are shallow by nature and some are deep. How deep or shallow they are is attributable not to their native soil but to the religion they practice. The Africans are by nature deeper than the rest.[510]

74. All the people who acknowledge and worship one God as creator of the universe have a concept of God as a human being. They assert that no one can have any other mental image of God than this. When they hear that many actually think of God as a little cloud, they ask where these people are; and when they are told that they are among the Christians, they say that this cannot be. They are given the reply, though, that these people get this idea from the fact that God is called a spirit in the Word [John 4:24], and they think of a spirit only as a little wisp of cloud, not realizing that every spirit and every angel is a human being. Such people were examined to find out whether the spiritual concept they have now was like the earthly one they used to have, and it turned out that those who inwardly recognize the Lord as the God of heaven and earth have a different spiritual concept than they used to.

I heard a particular Christian elder stating that no one could have a concept of a divine-human being. I saw him taken to various people of other religions, going in sequence to people of greater and greater depth; these people took him to their heavens, and eventually to a Christian heaven. At every step, how they inwardly perceived God was communicated to him; he realized that they all conceived of God as a human being, which is the same as having a concept of a divine-human being.

75. There are many communities of people of other religions, especially Africans, who, when they have been taught about the Lord through angels, say that it makes perfect sense that God, the creator of the universe, became visible in the material world. After all, he created us and loves us; and how else could he become visible to our eyesight except in human form? When they are told that he did not become momentarily visible the way angels do but was instead born as a human and became visible in this way, they pause for a moment and ask whether he was born of a human father. When they hear that he was conceived by the God of the universe and born of a virgin, they say that this means he has a divine essence, and that

because this essence is infinite and is life itself, he was not the same kind of human as others are. Angels then tell them that he looked just like other people do, but that when he was in the world his divine essence, which is intrinsically infinite and is life itself, cast out the finite nature and life he had received from his mother. In this way he took his human nature, which had been conceived and born in the world, and made it divine.

Since Africans think more spiritually within themselves than others do, they understood and accepted this.

76. Because this is also what Africans in this world are like, a revelation is occurring among them at the present time, beginning in central [Africa] and spreading outward, though not all the way to the seacoasts. They acknowledge our Lord as the Lord of heaven and earth. When monks arrive there, the Africans laugh at them. They also laugh at Christians who talk about a threefold Divinity and about being saved by what you think. The Africans say that there are no worshipful people who do not put their religion into practice. If we do not live by our religion, they say, we cannot help but become stupid and evil, because we are not open to anything from heaven. Even malice that is ingenious the Africans call stupid, because within it there is not life but death.

I have heard the angels rejoicing over this revelation [in Africa], since it is opening up for them a communication with the human rational faculty that had previously been closed by a blindness in regard to matters of faith.

I have been informed by a heavenly source that angelic spirits are communicating to the inhabitants of that region what it says in *Teachings for the New Jerusalem on the Lord, [Teachings for the New Jerusalem] on the Word,* and *Teachings about Life for the New Jerusalem,* which have just been published.

77. The African men I have talked with in the spiritual world wore garments of striped linen. They told me that these clothes were correspondential, and that the women wore garments of striped silk.

They said of their children that they often ask the women who are their teachers for something to eat, saying that they are hungry, and yet when they are given some food they look at it, taste it to see whether it agrees with them, and eat only a little. Clearly then, the cause is a spiritual hunger, which is a longing for knowing genuine truths. This is an actual correspondence.

When the Africans in the spiritual world are unsure whether something they are perceiving and enjoying is the truth, they draw a sword. If the sword gleams, they know that the truths they are engaged with are genuine; they also know this from the way the sword gleams. This too is caused by a correspondence.[511]

On the subject of marriage, they said that by law they were actually allowed to have more than one wife, but that they still had only one because true marriage love cannot be divided. If it is divided, its essence, which is heavenly, perishes. It becomes superficial and therefore merely lustful. Before long, as its potency dwindles, that love becomes cheapened; and once its potency is completely lost, that love becomes tiresome. True marriage love, on the other hand, which is inward, derives nothing from lust. It lasts forever and grows in potency, and proportionally, in delight.

As for people who come their way from Europe, the Africans said that these are not allowed in. A few, though—most of them monks—do manage to get through. In these cases, the Africans ask them what they know; when the Europeans start speaking about their religious beliefs, the Africans call it nonsense that hurts their ears. They send them off to do work that is useful. If the Europeans refuse to do this work, the Africans sell them as slaves, and by law are allowed to punish them whenever they want. If the Europeans cannot be coerced into doing anything useful, they are eventually sold to social outcasts for next to nothing.

Jews in the Spiritual World

BEFORE the Last Judgment the Jews were in a valley on the left side of the central Christian area, but afterward they were transferred to the north and forbidden to interact with Christians unless those Christians were traveling outside of their own cities.[512]

In that [northern] region there are two large cities to which Jews are brought after death. Before the Last Judgment both of these were called Jerusalem, but afterward they were renamed, because now that the judgment has taken place "Jerusalem" means the church where the Lord alone is worshiped.

The residents of these cities are governed by converted Jews who caution them not to speak disparagingly of Christ and who punish any who do.

The streets of these cities are ankle-deep in muck and their houses are full of unclean things giving off such foul smells that no one else can come near.[513]

80   From time to time an angel with a rod in his hand appears in midair above them. He leads them to believe that he is Moses. He urges them to give up the folly of waiting for a messiah there, since Christ, who is ruling over them and over everyone, is the Messiah. He tells them that he himself knows this now, and that even when he was living in the world he knew something about Christ. After hearing this they go their way; most of them forget it but a few retain it. The ones who retain it are sent to synagogues of converted Jews, and are taught. The ones who accept this teaching are given new clothes instead of the ragged ones they had been wearing. They are also given a beautifully written copy of the Word and a nicer home in the city.

The ones who do not accept what they are taught are cast down into hells underneath that large region of theirs, many into forests and deserts, where they keep robbing each other.

81   In the spiritual world Jews trade in various commodities, just as they do in this world—especially in precious stones, which they get by clandestine routes from heaven, where precious stones are plentiful.

The reason why they deal in precious stones is that they read the Word in its original language and hold its literal meaning to be holy; and precious stones correspond to the literal meaning of the Word (on this correspondence, see *Teachings for the New Jerusalem on Sacred Scripture* 42–45). They sell them to people of other religions who live near them in the northern region.

They also possess the skill to manufacture similar stones and create the illusion that they are genuine, but individuals who do this are severely punished by the governors.

82   More than others, Jews are unaware that they are in the spiritual world; they think they are still in the physical world. This is because they are thoroughly external people and do not think about their religion in an inward way. Therefore they still speak about the Messiah as they had before, saying that he is going to come with David and, gleaming with jewels, go before them and lead them into the land of Canaan,[514] along the way raising up his rod and making the rivers dry so they can cross. The Christians (whom they refer to among themselves as "Gentiles") will then seize the hem of their garments, pleading to be allowed to go with them. They will accept the rich in proportion to their wealth and the rich will also serve them.[515] They are unwilling to know that in the Word, the land of Canaan means the church and Jerusalem means the church in respect to its teachings, so

"Jews" means all the people who will be part of the Lord's church. On this meaning of "Jews" in the Word, see *Teachings on Sacred Scripture* 51.

[2] When they are asked whether they truly believe that they are going to come into the land of Canaan, they say that they will indeed go down there when the time comes. When they are told that that land is not big enough for them all, they say that it will be enlarged.

When it is pointed out that they do not know where the Bethlehem [of prophecy] is[516] or who belongs to the lineage of David, they reply that the Messiah who is to come knows this.

When they are asked how the Messiah, the Son of Jehovah, could live among such evil people, they say that they are not evil. When they are reminded that in his song in Deuteronomy 32 Moses describes them and indicates that they are very wicked, they reply that at that point Moses was angry because he was not allowed to go with them;[517] but when they are told that Moses wrote this at Jehovah's command, they fall silent and withdraw to confer.

When they are told that they were originally descended from a Canaanite woman and also from Judah's whoring with his own daughter-in-law (Genesis 38:[2, 16]), they get angry and say that it is enough for them that they are descended from Abraham.

When they are told that there is a spiritual meaning within the Word that is about Christ alone, they say that this is not true; there is nothing within the Word except gold. And more along the same lines.

Quakers in the Spiritual World

THERE are fanatical spirits who are convinced they are divinely inspired. They are kept apart from all others and are so thickheaded[518] that they believe they are the Holy Spirit. When Quakerism was just beginning,[519] these spirits were drawn forth from the surrounding forests where they had been wandering. They infested many individuals [on earth], filling them with the conviction that they were being impelled by the Holy Spirit. And because those who were infested felt an inflow physically, this conviction took possession of them all to such an extent that they believed they were holier and more enlightened than other people. As a result, they could not be induced to give up their [new] religion.

People who have completely convinced themselves of this come after death into the same kind of fanaticism. They are separated from others and sent away to kindred spirits in the forests, where from a distance they look like wild boars. People who have convinced themselves less completely are first separated from others and then sent to a similar place in a wilderness in the far south, where caves serve as their places of worship.

84. After the fanatical spirits just mentioned have been distanced from them and the infestation of quaking that had taken over their bodies has ceased, they then just feel a motion on their left side.[520]

I have been shown that from very early on, Quakers started straying more and more into evil practices, and eventually into heinous acts, under the command of their "holy spirit"—practices they keep secret from everyone.[521] I have talked, though, with the founder of their religion[522] and with Penn,[523] both of whom said that they had had no part in anything like that.

After they die, individuals who have perpetrated such acts are sent away to a place of darkness and they sit in the corners there, looking like the dregs in a bottle of oil.

85. Because Quakers rejected the two sacraments, baptism and the Holy Supper, and yet still read the Word and preach about the Lord, and because when they speak they are possessed by fanatical spirits and therefore mix the holy teachings of the Word with truths that have been profaned, no community is formed from them in the spiritual world. Instead, their associations are broken up and they wander here and there, then disappear from view, and gather in the wilderness location mentioned above [§83].

Moravians in the Spiritual World

86. I have had many conversations with Moravians (also known as Herrnhuters).[524] At first they were to be found in a valley not far from the Jews. After they had undergone examination and had been revealed for what they were, they were taken off to some uninhabited areas.

The examination of them revealed that they were very knowledgeable and skillful in how to captivate people's minds, presenting themselves as a remnant of the apostolic church.⁵²⁵ For this reason they would call each other "brother"⁵²⁶ and use the term "mother" of women who were open to learning their deeper mysteries. They also said that they more than others stress faith and that they love the Lord because he suffered on the cross, calling him the Lamb and the Throne of Grace, and more in the same vein, in order to foster a belief that they are the true Christian church.⁵²⁷ People who are taken in by their smooth words are then examined by the Moravians to see whether they are the kind to whom they would dare disclose their mysteries. If those who are examined are not the right kind, the Moravians keep their mysteries to themselves; but if they find they can disclose their mysteries to them, they do so. They then give them warnings and even utter threats against any of them who would divulge their secret teachings about the Lord.

Since they continued to present themselves in this same manner in the spiritual world, and yet [the angels] perceived that their inward thoughts differed from what they were presenting outwardly, to uncover this discrepancy they were brought into the lowest heaven. They could not stand the atmosphere of caring and consequent faith among the angels there, so they hurried away.

Later, because in the world they had believed that they were the only people who were really alive and that after death they would enter the third heaven, they were actually taken up to that heaven. But when they sensed the atmosphere of love for the Lord there, they felt as though they were having a heart attack. They began to suffer intense inner pain and to have convulsions like people in the throes of death, so they hurled themselves headfirst out of there. This was the first method by which it was revealed that inwardly they attach no value whatever to caring for their neighbor or loving the Lord.

They were then sent to people charged with the task of exploring the deeper levels of their thinking. The report these people made of them was that they despise the Lord, reject the life of caring so completely that they loathe it, regard the Word of the Old Testament as useless, and look down on the Word of the Gospels. All they do with Scripture is take what they please from Paul in the passages where he talks about faith alone.⁵²⁸ Such are the mysteries that the Moravians keep hidden from the world.

So it became clear that the Lord is someone they regard as Arians do, that the Word of the prophets and of the Gospels is something they despise, and that the life of caring is something they hate,[529] when in fact these are the three pillars on which all heaven rests. Therefore the ones among them who knew and believed in these mysteries were judged to be antichrists who rejected the three essential beliefs of the Christian church—the divine nature of the Lord, the Word, and caring. They were cast out of the Christian world into a wilderness that is at the border of the southern region, near the Quakers.

89. I heard *Zinzendorf*[530] when he arrived in the spiritual world shortly after his death. He was allowed to talk just as he had previously in the world—arguing that he knew the mysteries of heaven and that no one would enter heaven except those who relied on his teaching.[531] He insisted that those who do good deeds for the sake of salvation are utterly damned, and that he would sooner accept atheists into his congregation than them.

He said that the Lord was adopted by God the Father as his son because of his suffering on the cross, but that he was nevertheless just an ordinary human being. When it was explained to him that the Lord was conceived by God the Father, he replied that he thought whatever he pleased about that but did not dare to talk the way Jews did.[532]

From his followers, too, I sensed multiple objections when I read the Gospels.

90. The Moravians said they had been given a sensation and had taken this as an inner confirmation of their teachings,[533] but they were shown that this sensation had come from delusional spirits who confirm for people whatever constitutes their religion, and that these spirits enter more fully into people who, like the Moravians, are passionate about their religion and are constantly thinking about it. There these spirits actually talked with them, and they recognized each other.

Notes & Indexes

Notes

A list of the works of Swedenborg that are mentioned in these notes can be found on pages 112–119. Quotations from the theological works published by Swedenborg are drawn from the translations of the New Century Edition.

Notes to *The Lord* Preface

1 (in *The Lord* preface). The five works listed here were all published by Swedenborg in London in 1758. In this edition *The New Jerusalem and Its Heavenly Teachings* is generally referred to by the short title *New Jerusalem,* and *Planets, or Earthlike Bodies, in the Universe* is generally referred to as *Other Planets.* For the full Latin titles of all five of these works, with their publication data and English equivalents, see the list on page 113. It is striking that Swedenborg refers to *Heaven and Hell* as a "small work," since it is longer (by word count) than the other four works combined. However, it is distinctly shorter than the volumes of *Secrets of Heaven* that preceded it. [SS]

2 (in *The Lord* preface). In Swedenborg's works, "the Lord" (Latin *Dominus*) generally refers to Jesus Christ as God, though sometimes to God previous to the Incarnation. A core concept in Swedenborg's theology is that there are not three persons in the Trinity; there is one person, whose soul is the unknowable Divine, whose human manifestation is Jesus Christ, and whose operative influence is the Holy Spirit. Of the many names and terms from philosophical and biblical backgrounds that Swedenborg uses to denote God (the Divine Being, the Divine, the Divine-Human One, the One, the Infinite, the First, the Creator, the Redeemer, the Savior, Jehovah, God Shaddai, and many more), "the Lord" is the most frequently met with. It is a title rather than a name, meaning "the one in charge," and referring to Jesus Christ as the manifestation of the one and only God. For Swedenborg's brief explanation of his reasons for using "the Lord," see *Secrets of Heaven* 14. See also chapter 2 of *True Christianity.* [JSR]

3 (in *The Lord* preface). In the years 1743–1745 Swedenborg underwent a profound spiritual awakening that, he claimed, enabled him to see and converse with spirits, angels, and devils. He also believed that the Lord Jesus Christ had appeared to him and told him that he had chosen Swedenborg to expound the hidden sense of Scripture—a labor that led in time to Swedenborg's compendious work *Secrets of Heaven.* For a brief account of Swedenborg's spiritual awakening, see Smoley 2005, especially 19–24. [RS]

4 (in *The Lord* preface). All the promised works were eventually published except *Angelic Wisdom about Life* and the work on omnipotence, omnipresence, omniscience, infinity, and eternity. As to the latter, in a letter of February 1767 to a follower, Gabriel Beyer (1720–1779), Swedenborg listed passages on these subjects that had been included in his works *Divine Providence, Divine Love and Wisdom,* and *Revelation Unveiled.* He noted that "to write a separate treatise on these Divine attributes, without the assistance of something to support them, would cause too great an elevation of the thoughts;

wherefore these subjects have been treated in a series with other things which fall within the understanding" (Tafel 1877, 261). The remaining works listed here are referred to in this edition by these short titles: *The Lord* (1763), *Sacred Scripture* (1763), *Life* (1763), *Faith* (1763), *Supplements* (1763), *Divine Providence* (1764), *Divine Love and Wisdom* (1763). For the full Latin titles of all the published theological works, with their publication data and English equivalents, see the list on pages 112–115. [GFD]

5 (in *The Lord* preface). The term "new church" here refers to a renewed Christianity that Swedenborg came to believe was in its beginning stages in his day. He took it as his mission to publish to the world the doctrines of that church, as communicated to him by the Lord while he was reading the Bible (see *True Christianity* 779–780). He called this renewed Christianity a "new church" in comparison to the "old church" that he mentions in the next sentence, which in this context refers to the preexisting Christian church in its various branches, together with their doctrines and practices. Swedenborg divided human spiritual history into five general eras, each of which he called a "church." Each church is associated with a particular segment of the Bible narrative. These five churches are: the "earliest church," represented by the Bible narrative from the initial creation story and the Garden of Eden to the time of the Flood; the "early church," covering the biblical narrative from the Flood to the time of Moses (but with a phase called the "Hebrew church," starting at the time of Eber); the "Israelite church" or "Jewish church," from Moses to the time of Christ; the "Christian church" represented in the four Gospels and coming to its end at the point indicated by the apocalyptic visions of the Book of Revelation; and a new church represented by the New Jerusalem in Revelation 21 and 22, seen as beginning in Swedenborg's own time and covering the rest of human spiritual history. For more on these churches, see *Secrets of Heaven* 1850, 10248:7, 10355; *Heaven and Hell* 115, 327 (which contain brief overviews); *Divine Providence* 328; *True Christianity* 760, 786; *Revelation Explained* (= Swedenborg 1994–1997a) §948:3. For an extensive series of references to sections in *Secrets of Heaven* on the churches in general, and on the first four churches in particular, see *New Jerusalem* 246–248. [LSW]

Notes to *The Lord* Chapter 1, §§1–7

6 (in *The Lord* 1). Swedenborg is here using the Latin term for "the church" to refer to Christianity in general, including all its branches and sects, a sense common in his day and culture. For a discussion of his broader use of the term "church," see note 5. [LSW]

7 (in *The Lord* 1). The usual statement in Swedenborg's theological writings is that divine love is spiritual warmth and divine wisdom is spiritual light. However, in *Divine Love and Wisdom* 1–6 and *True Christianity* 39–40 Swedenborg identifies life especially with divine love, and states that divine wisdom partakes of that life by its association with divine love. For more on life as divine love, see *Secrets of Heaven* 1803; *Divine Love and Wisdom* 363; *Draft on Divine Love* chapter 9:[1] = §§21–22 [Mongredien's numbering] (= Swedenborg 1994–1997c, 425). For more on light as divine wisdom, see *Heaven and Hell* 131; *Divine Providence* 166; *True Christianity* 242; *Spiritual Experiences* (= Swedenborg 1998–2013) §6086. Other statements on both of these together can be found in *Life* 86:3; *Divine Love and Wisdom* 358; *Divine Providence* 298:4; *Revelation Explained* (= Swedenborg 1994–1997a) §926:2. For a more general discussion on the subject of spiritual light and warmth, see the chapter in *Heaven and Hell* "Light and Warmth in Heaven" (§§126–132). [LSW]

8 (in *The Lord* 1). The term "glorify" here may be misunderstood by today's readers. The word has two essential meanings: to deem glorious or ascribe glory to, and to render glorious or actually transform. It is the latter meaning that Swedenborg generally intends by "glorify" and "glorification" in relation to Jesus' human nature (and thus this edition often uses the renderings "transform" and "transformation," respectively). Swedenborg makes explicit that glorification is a rendering divine or a uniting with the Divine (in addition to *The Lord* 12–14, see *True Christianity* 2:2, 97, 105, 110:4, 114, 126, 128, 130:3, 154:6). Swedenborg apparently derives this usage from passages such as this in the Gospel of John. Although generally in the Bible the word "glorify" means to praise or extol (the first meaning just given) and Swedenborg occasionally uses the word in this sense (see, for example, *True Christianity* 16:1, 117), the Gospel of John often uses "glorify" in the second sense just given. For example, to say that the Holy Spirit had not yet come into existence because Jesus was not glorified yet (John 7:39) clearly does not mean that Jesus was not praised yet; it means, in Swedenborg's view, that Jesus was not yet completely transformed, or rendered fully divine. (For Swedenborg's further discussion of John 7:39 specifically, see the references in note 129.) [JSR]

9 (in *The Lord* 1). Following a Christian practice of his time, Swedenborg used the name "Jehovah" as a rendering of the tetragrammaton, יהוה *(yhvh,* sometimes transliterated "YHVH" or "YHWH"), the four-letter name of God in the Hebrew Scriptures. A complex set of circumstances gave rise to the name "Jehovah." The Hebrew alphabet originally consisted only of consonants. It was not until the eighth century of the Common Era that a complete system of diacritical marks for Hebrew vowel notation was developed. When for any reason the consonantal text was held not to be suitable for reading as it stood, the vowels of an approved reading would be added to the consonants in the text, whether the number of syllables in the two words matched or not. Since the sanctity of the name of God, YHWH, was felt to preclude its being pronounced, under most circumstances the word אֲדֹנָי *('ădōnāy),* "Lord," was substituted, and to indicate this, vowels closely resembling those of the name Adonai were added to YHWH: YeHoWaH. This combination of consonants and vowels was transliterated into Latin as "Jehovah." (Some English Bibles since then have adopted the name "Jehovah," while others have rendered the term as "Lord," so capitalized.) When the Hebrew text used the expression "YHWH God" (יהוה אֱלֹהִים *[yhvh 'ĕlōhîm]*), however, this was read as "the Lord God," and the divine name was given the vowels of the word אֱלֹהִים *('ĕlōhîm),* "God." This gave rise to the relatively rare reading of the name as "Jehovih," which Swedenborg occasionally employs (see, for example, §§4, 6, 14:4, 22), although in English Bibles it is more commonly expressed as "the Lord God," so capitalized. The currently accepted scholarly reconstruction of the original pronunciation of the tetragrammaton is "Yahweh": see *Theological Dictionary of the Old Testament* 1986, under "YHWH." Swedenborg, like others, relates the meaning of the name to the concept of being or "is-ness" (see *True Christianity* 19:1). [GFD, JSR]

10 (in *The Lord* 1). For more detailed explanations of the creation of all that exists out of divine love by means of divine wisdom, see *Divine Love and Wisdom* 52–60, 282–295; *Divine Providence* 3; *True Christianity* 76. [LSW]

11 (in *The Lord* 2). By "the Word" Swedenborg generally means the Bible—a terminology that was prominent in the world of his Lutheran upbringing. However, though he does at times use the term in that general sense, especially in his later theological

works, his predominant use of it refers to a biblical canon that is a subset of the Protestant canon. His canon is defined and listed in three parallel passages in his earlier theological works: *Secrets of Heaven* 10325, *New Jerusalem* 266, and *White Horse* 16. In these passages Swedenborg defines "the Word" as those books of the Bible "that have an inner meaning" (more on this below), and provides a list of the books that qualify. In *New Jerusalem* 266 the relevant passage reads: "In the Old Testament, the books of the Word are the following: the five books of Moses, the Book of Joshua, the Book of Judges, the two books of Samuel, the two books of Kings, the Psalms of David, and the prophets— Isaiah, Jeremiah, Lamentations, Ezekiel, Daniel, Hosea, Joel, Amos, Obadiah, Jonah, Micah, Nahum, Habakkuk, Zephaniah, Haggai, Zechariah, and Malachi. In the New Testament: the four Gospels—Matthew, Mark, Luke, and John—and the Book of Revelation." The books in the Protestant and Catholic canons of the Bible that are not on this list—namely, Ruth, 1 and 2 Chronicles, Ezra, Nehemiah, Esther, Job, Proverbs, Ecclesiastes, and Song of Songs (Song of Solomon) in the Old Testament; all the books now included in the Apocrypha; and Acts and the Epistles in the New Testament—are not part of "the Word" as Swedenborg most commonly uses the term. However, in his last theological works and manuscripts, which seem to be addressed more specifically to a traditional Christian audience, he often uses the term "the Word" to refer to the more familiar Protestant canon of Scripture, including Acts and the Epistles; see, for example, *True Christianity* 158, 176, 601, 675:2, 730:1; *Draft for "Coda to True Christianity"* (= Swedenborg 1996c) §§2:3, 23:2; *Draft Invitation to the New Church* (= Swedenborg 1996f) §47. In one of these passages, for example, he cites a phrase that is "frequently mentioned in the Word of the New Testament, both in the Gospels and in the Acts of the Apostles and their Epistles" (*True Christianity* 158). In two other passages, he apparently refers to Acts and the Epistles as "the Apostolic Word" (*Draft for "Coda to True Christianity"* 1, 59:5; compare *True Christianity* 730:1). By contrast, he never overtly quotes or cites Acts or the Epistles in his earlier works, such as *Secrets of Heaven* and the works of 1758, although there are allusions to them. The first explicit reference to Acts or the Epistles in his published theological writings occurs in his 1764 work *Divine Providence*, §115, in which he quotes Romans 3:28 and Romans 3:31. However, in his earlier works there are scattered explicit references to several books in the Protestant canon of the Old Testament that are not included in Swedenborg's canon: 1 and 2 Chronicles, Ezra, Job, and Song of Songs. References to the Book of Job, in particular, are occasionally included in lists of references to passages from "the Word" (see, for example, *Secrets of Heaven* 46:2, 737:2, 3901:6, 9125:3, 9818), indicating that even in his earlier works Swedenborg sometimes uses that term in its more generally accepted meaning. Still, he is careful to point out that although Job and the Song of Songs, in particular, are ancient books containing deeper meanings, they do not have the same kind of inner meaning that is contained in the books he defines more specifically as "the Word" (see, for example, *Secrets of Heaven* 1756:2, 3540:4, 9942:5; *Sacred Scripture* 20). The inner meaning of the books he includes in his canon of Scripture, he says, is characterized by a "vertical" series of layers of meaning that extend inward and upward all the way to the Lord, and whose subject is the Lord, his kingdom, and the church, which is the Lord's kingdom on earth (see *Secrets of Heaven* 1–4, 4442:2, 5275:2, 7417; *Divine Love and Wisdom* 221). He also describes that inner meaning as being "horizontally" continuous in the sense of extending seamlessly from one word, verse, and chapter to the next, without break or interruption (see *Secrets of Heaven* 1659:1, 2102:2, 4987, 7933:3, 9022; and compare *Divine Love and Wisdom* 222–229, on vertical and horizontal levels). Without this type of "vertical" and "horizontal" series and continuity of deeper meaning, Swedenborg says, a book is not a book of "the Word" in the fullest and most proper sense of the term—which is the sense in which he most commonly uses that term in his theological writings. Compare note 43, on "the Law and the Prophets." [JSR, LSW]

12 (in *The Lord* 2). That is, the traditional authors of the four canonical Gospels: Matthew, Mark, Luke, and John. [RS]

13 (in *The Lord* 2). Although a belief in angels is common to many religious traditions, Swedenborg's view of them is unusual: he asserts that they were all once people in the physical universe (see *Last Judgment* 14–22), and that they remain human in every respect after death (see *Heaven and Hell* 75; *Marriage Love* 44:2). According to traditional Christian theology, by contrast, humans "can in no way be taken into the angelic orders" (*Summa Theologiae* 1:108:8 [= Aquinas 2012, 14:552]), and thus angels were created to "fill the gap" between humans and God (Adler 1982, 55–67), either at the time of the creation event described in Genesis 1 or in another, "separate" creation (see Aquinas *Summa Theologiae* 1:61:3 [= Aquinas 2012, 14:93–95]). On Swedenborg's rejection of the belief that devils and demons too are distinct from humans, see note 102. [JSR, SS]

14 (in *The Lord* 2). In the chapter in *Heaven and Hell* "Written Materials in Heaven" (§§258–264), Swedenborg says that the Word exists in heaven just as it does on earth, though without the literal meaning that relates to material-world people, places, and events. Like the Bible on earth, the Word in heaven serves as a source of the doctrinal principles of the angels and as a basis for their sermons. See also *Secrets of Heaven* 1767–1777, 1869–1879, 9396:3; *Sacred Scripture* 70–75; *True Christianity* 240–242. [LSW]

15 (in *The Lord* 2). "Something divine that is emanating" (Latin *Divinum Procedens*, traditionally translated "the Divine Proceeding") refers to the Lord's divine being (consisting of love and wisdom) as it flows out into creation generally and into human beings in particular. This emanating presence of God does not become separate from God as it flows out. Therefore it is God itself within the finite, created (and nondivine) entities that it flows into. In biblical and Christian terminology, it is called the Holy Spirit. For more on the emanating divine presence that is the Holy Spirit, see *The Lord* 46–54; *Divine Love and Wisdom* 146–150; *Commentary on the Athanasian Creed* (= Swedenborg 1994–1997b) §§174–178; *Sketch for "True Christianity"* 32–37 (= Swedenborg 1996b, 1:211–218). For an extensive discussion of the Holy Spirit, see *True Christianity* 138–158. [LSW]

16 (in *The Lord* 2). Swedenborg has just stated that absolutely everything in the Word (as he defines it; see note 11) is about the Lord; his further statement here that the same is true specifically of the prophets is preparatory to the discussion of these books that follows in the next section. For more on the spiritual meaning of the prophets, from Isaiah through Malachi, see Swedenborg's manuscript of 1761, *Draft on the Inner Meaning of Prophets and Psalms* (= Swedenborg 1996i, 2:21–234), where he recorded brief summaries of their spiritual meanings, as well as those of the Psalms, keying each range of verses to a table of subjects related to the Lord. In *Draft of "Sacred Scripture"* §§10, 18 [Rogers's numbering] = §§25, 45 [Whitehead's numbering] (= Swedenborg 1997c, 28, 44) Swedenborg mentions that angels perceived the spiritual meaning as he read through these books. [LSW]

17 (in *The Lord* 2). The "earthly meaning," "literal meaning," or "letter" of the Word as used in Swedenborg's theological writings refers to the plain meaning of the Bible consisting primarily of history, prophecy, poetry, and teachings relating to events and behavior in the material world. It stands in contrast to the "spiritual meaning," which comprises several deeper levels of meaning relating to spiritual and divine matters (on which see note 11 toward its end). For more on the literal meaning of the Bible and its relationship to the spiritual meaning, see *Secrets of Heaven* 1408, 3432, 9025, 9406–9407, 10453; *Sacred Scripture* 27–69, 91–97; *Revelation Explained* (= Swedenborg 1994–1997a) §§175:2, 597, 778:6; and the topical articles on the Word appended after each individual section of *Revelation Explained* 1065–1089. [LSW]

18 (in *The Lord* 2). Swedenborg saw himself as living in the final days of the Christian era that had existed up to his time; he believed the Christian church had ceased to be the Lord's church on earth because of a lack of faith and kindness in it, especially among its clergy. He therefore believed he was living in a time of great spiritual darkness. For more on the series of five "churches," or spiritual eras, into which Swedenborg divided human history, see note 5. [LSW]

19 (in *The Lord* 3). On Swedenborg's use of the term "church" to mean a particular spiritual era of humankind, together with its doctrines and religious practices—of which ancient Judaism as it existed up to the time of Christ was one example, and Christianity as it had existed up to Swedenborg's time was another—see note 5. On Swedenborg's references to Jews and Judaism, see note 204; on offensive material in Swedenborg's works generally, see the translator's preface, pages 4–6. [LSW]

20 (in *The Lord* 3). In §1 of his 1758 work *Last Judgment,* Swedenborg insists that the term "the Last Judgment" does not refer to the end of the world, but to events taking place primarily in the *spiritual* world, and in the spiritual life of people on earth. In §46 of that work he notes two previous "last judgments," one at the time of the Flood and one that occurred when the Lord was in this world. He takes the word "last" to refer to the end *of a religious era;* and the era he usually means by "the Last Judgment" proper is the one that began with the life and resurrection of Jesus Christ, and that by Swedenborg's account ended with a cataclysmic upheaval in the spiritual world in 1757. Here, however, he is speaking of a last judgment at the time of the Incarnation. Compare note 23, on the Last Judgment of 1757. [JSR, GFD, LSW]

21 (in *The Lord* 3). Although Swedenborg often speaks of "hell" in the singular, he also frequently uses the plural, "hells," by which he apparently means the many communities of hell, each of which is in effect a hell in smaller form (*Heaven and Hell* 542; see also §§584–588 in that work). On hell being "in control," see note 78. [JSR]

22 (in *The Lord* 3). One distinctive element of Swedenborg's theology of the Incarnation is the concept that though the Lord (Jesus) did indeed start out with both an infinite divine nature from the Father (God) and a finite human nature from his mother (Mary), during his life on earth he gradually put off everything that came from his human mother and replaced it with a divine-human nature from the Father. This process of substitution took place through spiritual trials and temptations brought about by constant attacks on him by the evil forces of hell, which gained access to him through the hereditary evil contained in the human nature that he derived from his mother. By means of his struggles against evil and hell, and his continual victories over them, he gradually dispersed the finite, fallible human nature that came from his human mother.

His suffering on the cross was the final trial he endured, through which he completed the process of putting off that finite humanity and putting on an infinite divine humanity from the Father. Any remnants of his finite human heredity were dispersed in the tomb, so that when he rose from death his humanity was fully divine. For more on the Lord's process of putting off the human nature from the mother, see *The Lord* 35, 59; *Secrets of Heaven* 2159, 2288, 2649; *True Christianity* 94, 102, 130; *Revelation Explained* (= Swedenborg 1994–1997a) §§205:6, 899:14; *Commentary on the Athanasian Creed* (= Swedenborg 1994–1997b) §§161–162; *Sketch for "True Christianity"* 22 (= Swedenborg 1996b, 1:199–200). On the spiritual trials to which people in general are subject, see note 101. [LSW]

23 (in *The Lord* 3). On the union of heaven with people on earth, and thus with the church, see the chapter in *Heaven and Hell* "The Union of Heaven with the Human Race" (§§291–302). For more on the Lord's reorganization of heaven, the world of spirits, and hell at the time of the Last Judgment, see *Secrets of Heaven* 4287:2, 9715; *True Christianity* 118–120, 123:2, 599. (For a definition of "the world of spirits," see note 141 below.) On the overall process of the Last Judgment, see the two small works *Last Judgment* and *Supplements,* as well as the posthumously published *Draft of "Supplements"* (= Swedenborg 1997a). Specifically, *Last Judgment* 65–72 describes how the previous pseudo-heavens were dispersed in order to prepare for the reorganization of the heavens. An overview of how heaven was reorganized is presented in *Draft for "Coda to True Christianity"* (= Swedenborg 1996c) §§14–17. And for the effects on the church of the reorganization of heaven, see *Last Judgment* 73–74; *Revelation Explained* (= Swedenborg 1994–1997a) §670:2. Compare note 20, on the general meaning of a "Last Judgment" in Swedenborg's theology. [LSW]

24 (in *The Lord* 3). This work, included in this volume under the title *Sacred Scripture,* was published by Swedenborg in 1763. Compare note 4, on various works promised by Swedenborg in the preface to *The Lord.* [Editors]

25 (in *The Lord* 4). *Sabaoth* is a Hebrew term (צְבָאוֹת [ṣəbā'ôt]) meaning "legions." *Jehovah Sabaoth* means "Jehovah of the Legions," the legions being the "heavenly host"—either the angels or, when viewed on a more concrete level, the sun, moon, and stars. [LHC, RS]

26 (in *The Lord* 4). On "Jehovih," an occasional variation of the divine name traditionally translated as "Jehovah," see note 9. [Editors]

27 (in *The Lord* 4). A Hebrew epithet of God of obscure origin, the word *Shaddai* (שַׁדַּי [šadday]) was already archaic by the time the Hebrew Scriptures were written. Its etymology and meaning are uncertain. The traditional translation is "the Almighty"; another possible rendition is "the Mountain One" (Cross 1973, 55). Swedenborg discusses the name at length in *Secrets of Heaven* 1992; in §1416:3 of that work he renders it as "the Thunderer" (Latin *Fulminator*). [GFD, LHC, RS]

28 (in *The Lord* 4). Where the translation here reads "It will be said" (Latin *Dicetur*) matching accepted biblical texts, Swedenborg's first edition reads "Jehovah will say" (Latin *Jehovah dicet*). Apparently this is simply a passing mistake, since the text takes its usual form in the three other passages in this work where it is quoted: *The Lord* 6, 30:2, 38. [JSR]

29 (in *The Lord* 4). Where the translation reads "the land of Jehovah" (for the first edition's *terra Jehovae*), most Bibles, including Swedenborg's preferred Latin Bible, Schmidt 1696, read "the land of Judah" (Latin *terra Judae*), as in fact do the other instances in which Swedenborg himself quotes this passage. It is possible that Swedenborg was

looking at a Hebrew Bible when he made this error: Jehovah (יְהֹוָה) and Judah (יְהוּדָה) look somewhat alike in Hebrew. [JSR]

30 (in *The Lord* 4). The clause "People were saying of the prophet" is Swedenborg's paraphrase. The Hebrew text has the equivalent of "the house of Israel is saying." [GFD]

31 (in *The Lord* 4). The first edition has *Israelis,* "of Israel," instead of *Jisreelis,* "of Jezreel." This error likely resulted from a simple misreading of the Latin translation of Hosea 1:4, 5, 11 in Schmidt 1696, which uses the word *Jisraëlis,* an alternate spelling of *Israelis,* and also the very similar word *Jisreelis.* [GFD, JSR, LSW]

32 (in *The Lord* 4). After this reference in the first edition, a partial sentence referenced as Hosea 4:1 appears. However, the material is actually from Joel 3:1, and most of it appears in the series of quotations from Joel just below in the text. This seems to have been an error that Swedenborg noticed while he was copying the references, but neglected to mark for deletion before the manuscript was typeset. [JSR, RS]

33 (in *The Lord* 4). The first edition lists the quotation from Obadiah before the quotations from Amos, which is out of the usual biblical order. The placement has been corrected here. [GFD]

34 (in *The Lord* 4). As was the custom in his day, Swedenborg refers to Psalms as a book of David. [Editors]

35 (in *The Lord* 5). For more on the meanings of these types of day or time in the Bible, see *Secrets of Heaven* 1837, 1839, 2441, 4060, 5360, 6000; *Sacred Scripture* 14; *Revelation Unveiled* 414, 476; *Revelation Explained* (= Swedenborg 1994–1997a) §§372, 401:15, 526, 781:16. [LSW]

36 (in *The Lord* 5). For more on the meanings of these types of day or time in the Bible, see *Secrets of Heaven* 5360, 6767, 8902, 8906:2–3; *Revelation Unveiled* 765; *Revelation Explained* (= Swedenborg 1994–1997a) §§304:4–6, 315:9, 401:12, 405:23, 413, 1004. [LSW]

37 (in *The Lord* 5). For more on the meanings of these types of day or time in the Bible, see *Secrets of Heaven* 5117:7; *Revelation Unveiled* 704; *True Christianity* 782, 786–791; *Revelation Explained* (= Swedenborg 1994–1997a) §401:9. [LSW]

38 (in *The Lord* 6). The Hebrew is עִמָּנוּאֵל (*'immānû'ēl*), most accurately transliterated as "Immanuel" or, under the influence of the Greek transcription of the word (see Matthew 1:23), "Emmanuel" or "Emanuel." But since the Hebrew expression, as is usual in that language, does not include any form of the verb "to be," Swedenborg renders it literally as "God with us," even though it would usually be translated as the full sentence "God is with us." In accord with the traditional naming practice seen elsewhere in the Bible (see, for example, Genesis 4:25; 29:32–33; 1 Samuel 1:20; 2 Samuel 12:25), this would be understood simply as the mother's acknowledgment of the favor of God demonstrated by the birth of a healthy child. But by not supplying the verb, Swedenborg conveys the assertion that this child is in fact God with us, a quite legitimate assertion under the then common principles of exegesis. [GFD]

39 (in *The Lord* 6). The Latin here translated "Son of Humanity" is *Filius hominis.* This term is traditionally translated "Son of man," but is rendered elsewhere in this edition with the less gender-specific terms "Son of Humankind," "Child of Humankind," and "Human-born One." The phrase is particularly frequent in Ezekiel, where it functions as a designation of the prophet himself, apparently with the limited intent of identifying him as a member in good standing of the human race. In the New Testament it is applied to Jesus. Despite the simplicity of the literal sense of the term, its

full meaning is sufficiently mysterious that scholars have generated a wide array of possible interpretations of the phrase in the course of a debate reaching back for centuries (see Borsch 1967; Colpe 1972, 400–477; Hare 1990). Given that the range of proposed meanings extends from humble humanity to incarnate divinity, any single rendering of it will leave something to be desired. It should be noted that the *spiritual* meaning of the term is explained unambiguously by Swedenborg as "the Lord as the Word" (*The Lord* 16, 23); see *The Lord* 23–28 for his summary of its uses in the Bible. [JSR, GFD]

40 (in *The Lord* 6). The Latin text reads simply "If I enter," strictly following the Hebrew, which leaves part of the oath unstated, as is idiomatic in biblical Hebrew. Thus the phrase "God forbid" has been supplied here. Another way of reading this is to assume that some result such as "may I suffer every kind of evil" is to be understood. [SS]

41 (in *The Lord* 7). The work *Sacred Scripture* does not offer any *explicit* ample demonstration that the whole Bible ("Sacred Scripture") is written about the Lord alone. This specific thesis is mentioned only once in that work, in §62. However, in *Divine Providence* 172:2 Swedenborg cites *Sacred Scripture* 62–69, 80–90, 98–100 as explaining this. The most extensive coverage of the Bible *in its deepest level of meaning* being written about the Lord alone occurs in *Secrets of Heaven,* where the bulk of Swedenborg's exegesis of Genesis chapters 12–47 relates the biblical text to the Lord's process of glorification (on which term, see note 8). See the chart in *Secrets of Heaven* volume 1 (= Swedenborg [1749–1756] 2008), page 98. Indeed, Swedenborg introduces this theme in §2 of that first-published volume of his theological works, where he writes, "Where, after all, does life come from if not from what is living? That is, if not from the fact that every single thing in the Word relates to the Lord, who is truly life itself? Whatever does not look to him at some deeper level, then, is without life; in fact, if a single expression in the Word does not embody or reflect him in its own way, it is not divine." [LSW]

Notes to *The Lord* Chapter 2, §§8–11

42 (in *The Lord* 8). On the special theological use of the term "justify" here, see the explanation of justification at note 404. [Editors]

43 (in *The Lord* 8). The equating of the Law and the Prophets with all of Sacred Scripture may require explanation. Generally, the phrase "the Law and the Prophets" refers to two of the three main divisions of the Hebrew Scriptures: the Law or Torah, comprising the five books of Moses: Genesis, Exodus, Leviticus, Numbers, and Deuteronomy; and the Prophets or *Nevi'im,* including the "Former Prophets," namely, Joshua, Judges, 1 and 2 Samuel, and 1 and 2 Kings, and the "Latter Prophets," namely, Isaiah, Jeremiah, Ezekiel, and the twelve minor prophets. The third division is the Writings or *Ketuvim,* comprising the remainder of the books of the Old Testament—not including the Apocrypha, which is not part of the Jewish canon of Scripture. Swedenborg's categorization is slightly different. He grouped the books traditionally designated as "Former Prophets" with the Law; see *Secrets of Heaven* 2606, 5922:8, 6752:3. Additionally, Swedenborg included Lamentations, Daniel, and the Psalms with the Prophets, though they are usually categorized with the Writings. Therefore those books are also included in his definition of the Law and the Prophets as "the whole Sacred Scripture" as of Jesus' time. Of the Christian scriptures written after Jesus' death, Swedenborg regarded the Book of Revelation as a prophetic book (see *Last Judgment* 60; *Revelation Explained* [= Swedenborg 1994–1997a] §§95, 224; *Draft for "Coda to True Christianity"* [= Swedenborg 1996c] §1); and a

statement in *Revelation Explained* 556:8 suggests that he viewed the four Gospels as the "Law" of the New Testament. For more on Swedenborg's definition of "the Word," or Sacred Scripture, see note 11. Compare note 67, on Swedenborg citing the Psalms as a prophetic book. [JSR, LSW, GFD]

44 (in *The Lord* 8). Throughout his theological works Swedenborg adopts the traditional view of Moses as the author of the first five books of the Bible (the Pentateuch). He accords the books no special authority because of this authorship. [GFD]

45 (in *The Lord* 11). The passage Jesus quotes here is Isaiah 61:1. [Editors]

46 (in *The Lord* 11). In John 13 there are several references to Judas Iscariot's betrayal of Jesus; this provides the context for the quotation here, which is from Psalms 41:9. [GFD, SS]

47 (in *The Lord* 11). The phrase "son of perdition" means essentially "the one destined to be lost" (and is so rendered by the New Revised Standard Version); it refers to Judas Iscariot. This reference to Scripture has generally been taken to point to Psalms 41:9 (for which see the preceding verse quoted by Swedenborg) and to Psalms 109:6–8, "Appoint a wicked man against him; let an accuser stand on his right. When he is tried, let him be found guilty; let his prayer be counted as sin. May his days be few; may another seize his position" (New Revised Standard Version). Compare Acts 1:16–20, which interprets Psalms 109:8 as a prophecy about Judas. [GFD, LSW, SS]

48 (in *The Lord* 11). This is evidently a reference to the passage just quoted by Swedenborg, John 17:12. It thus points directly to a previous saying of Jesus rather than to an Old Testament verse, unlike the other passages cited in this section. [GFD, SS]

49 (in *The Lord* 11). Because of the context, in which Jesus yields to a mob that "lays hands on" him (Matthew 26:50), this reference is traditionally taken to point specifically to Isaiah 53:10: "Yet it pleased the Lord to bruise him" (King James Version). [GFD]

50 (in *The Lord* 11). Because of the context, in which Jesus is taken captive, this reference to the prophets is traditionally taken to point specifically to Lamentations 4:20: "The Lord's anointed, the breath of our life, was taken in their pits" (New Revised Standard Version). [GFD, SS]

51 (in *The Lord* 11). It is not clear which Scripture passage is intended by this reference, if it is in fact a specific verse rather than the Scriptures in general. [GFD]

52 (in *The Lord* 11). The reference quoted is Isaiah 53:12. It is apt in Mark 15:28 because the preceding verse says, "And with him they crucified two bandits, one on his right and one on his left" (New Revised Standard Version). In the context of Luke 22:37, the verse in Isaiah seems to be being understood as a more general prophecy that Jesus, and by implication his followers, were to be outcasts. [GFD, SS]

53 (in *The Lord* 11). The passage quoted is Psalms 22:18. The context in John describes how the Roman soldiers who crucified Jesus then cast lots for his clothing. [GFD]

54 (in *The Lord* 11). The verse cited here, John 19:28, and the next verse cited, John 19:30, occur in the context of Jesus thirsting on the cross. They refer to Psalms 69:21, "They gave me poison for food, and for my thirst they gave me vinegar to drink" (New Revised Standard Version). [GFD, SS]

55 (in *The Lord* 11). The explanatory phrase here set in square brackets was added by Swedenborg. [Editors]

56 (in *The Lord* 11). The passage quoted here at John 19:36 is from Psalms 34:20: "He keeps all their bones; not one of them will be broken" (New Revised Standard Version).

The context in John describes how the Roman soldiers at Jesus' Crucifixion did not break his legs, as was customary at such executions to hasten death. See also Exodus 12:46 and Numbers 9:12, which forbid the breaking of the bones of the Passover lamb. [GFD, SS]

57 (in *The Lord* 11). The verse quoted here at John 19:37 is Zechariah 12:10. The context in John describes how a Roman soldier at Jesus' Crucifixion pierced his side with a spear. [GFD, SS]

58 (in *The Lord* 11). For a few examples, see Matthew 2:3–6; 3:3; 10:34–36; 13:11–15. [LSW]

59 (in *The Lord* 11). The Latin here translated "little letter" is *jotha* (sometimes spelled *iota*), a word that can refer to either the yodh (׳), the smallest letter of the Hebrew alphabet, or the iota (ι), the smallest letter of the Greek alphabet. The traditional translation is "jot." The Latin here translated "tip of one letter" is *corniculum;* it is used by Swedenborg to translate the word κεραία *(keraía)* in the Greek text. Both the Latin and Greek mean "hornlike projection," referring to the apical brush stroke of the "square" script used for Hebrew sacred texts after the fifth century B.C.E. The traditional translation for this is "tittle." The modern English equivalent of the biblical phrase would be "the dots on the i's and the crosses on the t's." [GFD]

Notes to *The Lord* Chapter 3, §§12–14

60 (in *The Lord* 12). The "common knowledge in the church" on these subjects is based on various Scripture passages. On the Lord conquering death, see, for example, Mark 10:33–34; Luke 18:31–33; Acts 2:22–24; Romans 6:8–9; 1 Corinthians 15:26, 54–55; Hebrews 2:14–15; Revelation 1:18; 20:14; 21:4. On the Lord ascending into heaven in glory, see Mark 16:19; Luke 24:50–51; John 3:13; 6:62; 20:17; Acts 1:9; Ephesians 4:8–10. [LSW]

61 (in *The Lord* 12). For listings of passages in the prophets and Psalms on the Lord's battles against and victory over death and hell, see *The Lord* 14, 33; *Secrets of Heaven* 9715; *True Christianity* 116; *Revelation Explained* (= Swedenborg 1994–1997a) §357. [LSW]

62 (in *The Lord* 12). Although Swedenborg here follows the general Christian practice in referring to "the Devil" as if it designated a single evil being opposite God, in fuller discussions elsewhere he asserts that there is no such thing: instead he uses "the Devil" as a collective term for hell (see *Secrets of Heaven* 251:2; *Heaven and Hell* 311, 544). Nor is there one supreme "Satan," or a "Lucifer," that is, an angel who was cast down and became the Devil, a concept based on Isaiah 14:12 and mentioned in *Last Judgment* 14; *Divine Providence* 27:1. Swedenborg does, however, speak of two classes of people in hell, one called "satans," and the other called "devils," or "demons." The distinction is outlined in *Divine Love and Wisdom* 273 and *Divine Providence* 310:3, and mentioned in *Heaven and Hell* 311:2 and *True Christianity* 281:12. In general, "satans" are associated with false thoughts, love for the world, and justification of obsessions with evil, whereas "devils" are associated with demonic loves, love for oneself, and acting out obsessions with evil. Swedenborg consistently describes "devils" or "demons" as more profoundly wicked than "satans." [JSR]

63 (in *The Lord* 13). For more on the Lord's process of glorification, see *The Lord* 35; *Secrets of Heaven* 3212, 5078, 5256, 10047, 10053, 10057, 10655; *True Christianity* 104–106, 126–128. [LSW]

64 (in *The Lord* 14:2). For more discussion by Swedenborg on his concept of the Word having suffered "violence at the hands of the Jewish people," see *The Lord* 15:2–8,

16:6; *Sacred Scripture* 35, 79. These passages give examples of Jesus and the prophets as representing, through their own actions and sufferings, the Word in its relationship to the Jewish "church," or religion, as it existed in their time periods. On Swedenborg's references to Jews and Judaism, see note 204; on offensive material in Swedenborg's works generally, see the translator's preface, pages 4–6. [LSW]

65 (in *The Lord* 14:8). These passages record a conversation in which Jesus quotes the opening verse of Psalm 110 to show that the Messiah is David's lord rather than David's son. [GFD]

66 (in *The Lord* 14:9). An integral part of Swedenborg's theology of the Incarnation is that the Lord needed to overcome the hells because the force of evil flowing out of hell had become so overwhelming that neither people on earth nor angels in heaven could withstand it. Therefore the Lord had to take on a human nature and personally conquer hell by his own power, without the aid of any human being or any angel. In doing so, the Lord freed both humans and angels from the power of evil and hell, and continues to do so for all who are willing to accept divine help in resisting and overcoming the evil within themselves. For more on the Lord overcoming the hells by his own power, see *The Lord* 33; *Secrets of Heaven* 1573, 1813, 1820, 1921, 2025, 4287, 8273, 9715, 9937; *Revelation Unveiled* 829; *True Christianity* 116, 121–123, 224:3; *Revelation Explained* (= Swedenborg 1994–1997a) §§359, 650:70. [LSW]

67 (in *The Lord* 14:10). The Book of Psalms has traditionally been regarded as one of "the Writings," on which see note 43. Swedenborg's inclusion of it in the prophetic works is surprising. Note, however, that in the story of Jesus speaking to his followers in Jerusalem after the Resurrection (Luke 24:36–49), Jesus refers to things written about him "in the Law of Moses, the Prophets, and the Psalms" (Luke 24:44), implying that the Psalms, too, have prophetic value. For more on Swedenborg's definition of "the Word," or Sacred Scripture, see note 11. [GFD]

68 (in *The Lord* 14:11). For the wars of Israel against various nations, see, for example, Exodus 17:8–16; Numbers 31:1–12; Joshua 6; 8:1–29; 10; 11; Judges 3:7–31; 4; 6:1–7:25; 11:1–12:6; 1 Samuel 13–14; 17; 30; 2 Samuel 5:5–25; 8:1–14; 10; 1 Kings 20; 22:1–40; 2 Kings 3; 18:9–19:36; 24:1–17. [RS]

Notes to *The Lord* Chapter 4, §§15–17

69 (in *The Lord* 15:1). Swedenborg refers here to the satisfaction theory of atonement, which is shared in various forms by the Roman Catholic Church and by most Protestant denominations. The first reference seems to be to the early form of the theory, in which Christ substituted himself for sinful humankind and averted the punishment of the Father; the second reference seems to be to the later exposition that is now called penal substitution, by which Christ substituted himself for us and actually suffered punishment on our behalf (Pugh 2014, 56–57). The satisfaction theory can be traced back to the theologian Anselm of Canterbury (around 1033–1109); it was developed by Peter Abelard (1079–1142) and Thomas Aquinas (1224 or 1225–1274) into the model currently accepted by the Catholic Church. The penal substitution model is associated primarily with Martin Luther (1483–1546) but also with John Calvin (1509–1564), though some scholars insist it did not entirely originate with them. For discussion of these two theories of atonement, see Pugh 2014, 45–82. [SS, RS, GFD]

70 (in *The Lord* 15:1). Most English translations of the Bible have "who takes away" here in John 1:29. However, the root meaning of the original Greek verb αἴρειν *(aírein)* is "to lift up," "raise," from which its meaning of "to carry," "take away" is derived. The same Greek verb is used in New Testament passages that speak of "taking up" the cross (for example, Matthew 16:24; Mark 8:34; Luke 9:23), "taking up" one's bed (for example, Matthew 9:6; Mark 2:11; Luke 5:24; John 5:8), and so on. Swedenborg here translates it with the Latin word *tollere,* which has a similar root meaning of "to lift or take up," "to raise." See further in *The Lord* 17 for his exposition of the phrase *tollere peccata* as "taking up sins," and how this relates to the taking away of sins. See also his commentary on John 1:29 and related verses in *Revelation Explained* (= Swedenborg 1994–1997a) §§778:7, 805:5. [JSR, LSW, SS]

71 (in *The Lord* 15:2). On Swedenborg's references to Jews and Judaism, see note 204; on offensive material in Swedenborg's works generally, see the translator's preface, pages 4–6. [Editors]

72 (in *The Lord* 15:6). Jezreel was the royal city of Ahab and his lineage; the implication may be that the horrific scenes of violence that played out in Jezreel and elsewhere against Ahab's successors (2 Kings 9:1–10:17) would be reenacted against the Jewish people as a whole. But the name, which means "God Will Scatter," is ominous even in its literal sense. The name "No Mercy" likewise indicates the extent of God's putative wrath against the Jewish people, just as "Not My People" indicates his supposed rejection of them. (On Swedenborg's insistence that God is never angry or rejecting, see note 465.) [SS]

73 (in *The Lord* 15:8). On the literal meaning of the Bible, see note 17. [Editors]

74 (in *The Lord* 16:6). On the long tradition of Judas Iscariot serving as a representative of Jews and their alleged betrayal of Jesus, see Maccoby 1992. Compare *Secrets of Heaven* 4751:3; *True Christianity* 130:3. [RS, LHC]

75 (in *The Lord* 16:6). For more on the kinds of meaning in the Bible, see note 17. "Spiritual meaning" here is used in a general sense that includes all the deeper levels of meaning in the Bible beyond the literal. In this schema, one of the functions of the literal meaning is to serve as a guard to protect the deeper levels of meaning from being corrupted, or "profaned," by those who would use spiritual and divine truth to achieve worldly and self-centered goals. For more on this protective function of the literal meaning, which is also represented by "cherubim" or "angel guardians" in the Bible, see *Sacred Scripture* 26, 56, 97; *Revelation Unveiled* 239; *Revelation Explained* (= Swedenborg 1994–1997a) §1088. For more discussion of profanation and how God guards against it, see *Divine Providence* 221–233. For more on angel guardians, see note 118. For more on the dividing of Jesus' tunic, see *Secrets of Heaven* 9942:13; *True Christianity* 130:2–3. [LSW]

76 (in *The Lord* 16:6). On the Lord's having received a human nature from his mother, see note 22. [Editors]

77 (in *The Lord* 16:7). The Latin here translated "Behold the man" is *ecce Homo,* reflecting the words Ἰδοὺ ὁ ἄνθρωπος *(Idoù ho ánthropos)* in the original Greek. This statement in John 19:5 is commonly attributed to Pilate and is so understood in most English translations. But Swedenborg's reading is grammatically plausible: the subject of the verb is unspecified in the original Greek, and the immediate antecedent is not "Pilate," but "Jesus," as reflected in the text here. *Secrets of Heaven* 9144:10–11 is the only other place in

Swedenborg's theological writings where he comments on this verse. In that passage, he similarly interprets it as a statement made by Jesus referring to his own position as the embodiment of divine truth, or the Word, and the various details of his mistreatment at the hands of his executioners as representing the mistreatment of the Word and its truth at the hands of the church of Jesus' day. Swedenborg there summarizes the inner meaning as "Look: divine truth as it exists in the church today." It should also be noted that the Latin *homo,* here translated "man," refers to a human being without specification of gender, as does the underlying Greek, and thus in Swedenborg's original Latin there is a verbal connection with the term "Son of Humanity" subsequently mentioned. (On "Son of Humanity," see note 39.) [LSW, RS, SS]

78 (in *The Lord* 17:1). On the mounting power of hell before the Lord's Coming as a result of more evil people than good coming to the spiritual world from the corrupted church on earth, see *The Lord* 33; *True Christianity* 3, 114–122; *Last Judgment* 33–34; *Revelation Explained* (= Swedenborg 1994–1997a) §702. On the Lord overcoming the power of hell, see note 66. [LSW]

79 (in *The Lord* 17:3). For a comprehensive discussion of "active repentance," see *True Christianity* 528–563. [Editors]

Notes to *The Lord* Chapter 5, §18

80 (in *The Lord* 18:1). On the satisfaction theory of atonement in Western Christian theology, see note 69. [Editors]

81 (in *The Lord* 18:2). The imputation of merit is a concept found in the doctrine of certain Protestant denominations, though Swedenborg traces its ultimate origin back to the Council of Nicaea in 325 (see *True Christianity* 632–635). According to this doctrine, the merit of Christ is imputed or assigned to those who believe in him. Without that imputed merit, all humans, even believers, are so deeply sinful that the justice of God would preclude their ever being saved. The doctrine has several variants, but Swedenborg takes exception to the basic idea; he holds instead that individuals are saved or damned as a result of their own actions and affinities. For an extensive discussion, see *True Christianity* 626–666; and for a shorter discussion, *Marriage Love* 524. [SS, RS]

82 (in *The Lord* 18:3). Fundamental to Swedenborg's psychology is the concept that our will constitutes the core of our being. Our will works through our understanding to form, drive, and direct our entire self. Another way of saying this is that "love is our life" (*Divine Love and Wisdom* 1). Specifically, our dominant love is what determines and directs everything that we are. For more on this concept, see *Secrets of Heaven* 4884:2, 10076:2–4, 10130, 10177:4; *Heaven and Hell* 474–477; *Divine Love and Wisdom* 1–2, 399, 403; *Divine Providence* 193–196; *True Christianity* 399; *Revelation Explained* (= Swedenborg 1994–1997a) §666:2. [LSW]

83 (in *The Lord* 18:4). Though Swedenborg attributes the words in Luke 3:8–9 to Jesus, the speaker is actually John the Baptist. This attribution is repeated in *Divine Providence* 114:2, and similar substitutions occur in other passages: the subject of Luke 1:80 is identified as Jesus instead of John the Baptist in *Secrets of Heaven* 1457, and a saying of Jesus in Mark 1:14, 15 is ascribed to John the Baptist in *True Christianity* 113:7. The likely cause is that Swedenborg sees John the Baptist as in some respects representing Jesus; see *Secrets of Heaven* 9372. [SS, LHC]

84 (in *The Lord* 18:5). According to Swedenborg, "The human race would perish if there were not a church in our world where the Word was found and the Lord was known" (*Heaven and Hell* 305 note b). He holds that the identity of this church has shifted over time (see note 5) as knowledge of the Word passed from one dominant spiritual movement to another, because "The Lord ensures that there is always a church on earth where the Word is being read and the Lord is becoming known through it" (*True Christianity* 270). In this passage in *The Lord* 18:5, the church referred to is the Jewish religion. [SS]

Notes to *The Lord* Chapter 6, §§19–28

85 (in *The Lord* 19:1). The expression "born from eternity" is used in traditional Christian doctrine as shorthand for the notion that the second person of the Trinity has existed forever as the only-begotten Son of the Father. It is found, for instance, in *Tractate on the Gospel of St. John* 46:3 by the church father Augustine (354–430), where it is given in a fuller form: *in aeternum ab aeterno genitus,* "born into eternity from eternity." One of Swedenborg's purposes in this chapter is to take exception to the common Christian belief that the Son has eternally existed as a second person of the Godhead, distinct from the person of the Father. Swedenborg's understanding of the Trinity can be found in *The Lord* 46–61, and is more extensively treated in *True Christianity* 163–184. [SS]

86 (in *The Lord* 19:3). Matthew 1:22–23 reads: "All this took place to fulfill what had been spoken by the Lord through the prophet: 'Look, the virgin shall conceive and bear a son, and they shall name him Emmanuel,' which means, 'God is with us'" (New Revised Standard Version). (On the name Emmanuel, see note 38.) [Editors]

87 (in *The Lord* 19:8). The Greek word is Χριστός *(Christós);* the Hebrew word is מָשִׁיחַ *(māšîaḥ)*. [GFD]

88 (in *The Lord* 20). For examples of Jesus saying that he was sent into the world by the Father (God), and that he had gone forth from the Father, see John 3:17; 8:42; 10:36; 16:28; 17:18. [RS]

89 (in *The Lord* 20). For examples of Jesus saying that he was doing the will, and the works, of the Father, see John 5:36; 10:25, 32; 14:10. [RS]

90 (in *The Lord* 20). For examples of Jesus calling Jehovah (God) "Father," see Matthew 11:25; Mark 14:36; Luke 23:34; John 11:41. [LSW]

91 (in *The Lord* 21). Swedenborg's claim that the statement in question, better known as the Athanasian Creed, "is taught throughout the Christian world" is not strictly speaking true: in general the Eastern church, including the Greek Orthodox church, never accepted it. The creed was, however, well known to the Western church, and was used in worship in varying degrees in the Roman Catholic Church and in different branches of the Protestant church. For the full text of the creed in English, see Swedenborg's own version in *The Lord* 56, or standard versions in Schaff 1931, 2:66–71, and Kolb and Wengert 2000, 23–25. Swedenborg wrote an outline for an entire work on the subject of this creed; see *Commentary on the Athanasian Creed* (= Swedenborg 1994–1997b, 6:571–634). For further details on Swedenborg's titling, translation, and use of the Athanasian Creed, see note 96; on the disputed authorship of the creed, see note 132. [JSR, SS]

92 (in *The Lord* 25). The original text of Matthew 19:28 would translate as "you will judge" (referring to Jesus' twelve disciples) rather than "he will judge." This is a change Swedenborg occasionally makes when quoting this verse. Other examples occur in *Revelation Unveiled* 273, 808:2. In *Revelation Unveiled* 284 he paraphrases that segment of the verse as "they with the Lord will judge the twelve tribes," suggesting that he reads this passage as meaning that it is ultimately the Lord doing the judging from his "throne of glory," while the twelve disciples on their thrones serve under him. In keeping with this shift of power away from the Lord's subordinates as individuals, Swedenborg elsewhere identifies the enthroned disciples in such passages as a symbol for all those who possess love and faith (see *Secrets of Heaven* 3857:7). [JSR]

93 (in *The Lord* 25). The first edition inserts the Latin word *non* ("do not") before *audiverit* ("hear"), which does not reflect the original Greek text of John 12:47. [Editors]

94 (in *The Lord* 26:2). The first edition here has *sedere,* "sitting," instead of the expected *venire,* "coming." The translation has been corrected to reflect the wording of Matthew 26:64, quoted at the beginning of subsection 2. [LSW]

95 (in *The Lord* 27:2). John 8:37 reads: "I know that you are descendants of Abraham; yet you look for an opportunity to kill me, because there is no place in you for my word"; John 5:38 reads: "And you do not have his word abiding in you, because you do not believe him whom he has sent" (New Revised Standard Version). On Swedenborg's references to Jews and Judaism, see note 204; on offensive material in Swedenborg's works generally, see the translator's preface, pages 4–6. [GFD]

Notes to *The Lord* Chapter 7, §§29–36

96 (in *The Lord* 29:1). In the original Latin, the words corresponding to those here set in italics, *"the church's doctrinal statement,"* appear in a format frequently used to indicate formal titles. The choice of the words is somewhat puzzling, since the expression is not one of several well-known titles of the Athanasian Creed. It was generally known by its first words, *Quicunque Vult* ("Whoever wants [to be saved]") and thus as the *Symbolum Quicunque* (literally, "the 'Whoever' Creed"); or it was called *Symbolum Athanasii* ("the creed of Athanasius"), *Symbolum Athanasianum* ("the Athanasian Creed"), or *Fides Athanasiana* (literally, "the Athanasian Faith"). Later in this section and in *The Lord* 35:1, Swedenborg does use something like this last term, when he refers to the creed as "the teaching known as the Athanasian [statement of] faith"; the second time he uses this expression, it is set in small caps as a title. But overall, he shows a surprising avoidance of the titles commonly used for the creed. A similar pattern of avoiding accepted practice appears with respect to the text of the creed itself: Before 1768, he seems to have quoted his own translation into Latin, apparently based on an English version that appeared in the prayer book of the Anglican Church, the Book of Common Prayer. (Swedenborg himself hints at this source in *Revelation Explained* [= Swedenborg 1994–1997a] §1091:1, and he is known to have owned a copy of the 1711 edition of the prayer book at the time of his death.) It is not surprising, then, that Swedenborg's translation is different from the standard Latin version in many respects; but a word-for-word comparison of the standard text with his version of the entire document in *The Lord* 56 shows that he in fact weaves phrases and paraphrases of the creed into striking new juxtapositions. Beginning in 1768, however, Swedenborg cites the approved Latin wording in his new works,

apparently taking it from the 1756 Leipzig edition of *The Book of Concord*. This shift in sources suggests that he acquired a personal copy of *The Book of Concord* for the first time in 1768. On the title and acceptance of the Athanasian Creed, and for references to standard versions, see note 91. On its authorship, see note 132. [JSR]

97 (in *The Lord* 29:2). Swedenborg returns now and then throughout his theological works to the theory that the soul of an individual comes from the father and the body from the mother, a theory that dates back at least to the time of Aristotle (384–322 B.C.E.); see, for example, *Generation of Animals* 738b25 (= Aristotle 1984, 1146). The theory is important to Swedenborg's theology because it accords with his exposition of Jesus as having a divine inner nature and yet a human outer nature. For discussion of apparent variations in Swedenborg's view of this theory, see *Secrets of Heaven* volume 2 (= Swedenborg [1749–1756] 2013), page 548 note 321; for the mechanics of the theory, see pages 568–569 note 529 in that volume. For a thorough study of seventeenth- and eighteenth-century understandings of conception, see Pinto-Correia 1997. [JSR, RS]

98 (in *The Lord* 29:3). The first or innermost level includes the highest heavenly and spiritual aspects of Jesus; the last or outermost level includes his earthly or physical aspects. These levels of the incarnated Lord parallel the levels of reality, which range in a continuum from the highest or innermost level, which is divine, to the lowest and outermost, which is lifeless physical matter. For more on the levels of reality in Swedenborg's cosmology, see note 105; for the parallels between these levels and the levels of a human being, see note 180. Compare also notes 218 and 374. The terms "first" and "last" here allude in passing to Revelation 1:17; 2:8; 22:13, in which the Lord is referred to as the First and the Last. Compare Isaiah 44:6; 48:12. See also *Sacred Scripture* 98. [SS]

99 (in *The Lord* 31). For biblical support for this proposition, see especially *The Lord* 12–14. For brief statements to the effect that we could not be saved if the Lord had not taken on a human nature, see *Faith* 35 and *Survey* 117. For a more extended treatment, published eight years after the present work, see *True Christianity* 118–120. [GFD, LSW]

100 (in *The Lord* 32:8). As Swedenborg had projected in the preface of *The Lord*, shortly after the publication of the present work he published two volumes whose full titles began with the words *Sapientia Angelica de . . .* , "Angelic Wisdom about . . ." These works are commonly known by their short titles, *Divine Love and Wisdom* and *Divine Providence*. While neither work contains a sustained treatment of the subject of the human form, the prevalence of the human form is noted in §§11, 63, and 400 of the former; and §§201–202 of the latter develop the striking proposition "By his divine providence the Lord is gathering the impulses of the whole human race into a single form, which is a human form." For more on the focus of Swedenborg's "books of angelic wisdom," see the introduction, pages 78–82. [GFD]

101 (in *The Lord* 33:1). Spiritual trial, as Swedenborg depicts it, is not a divine punishment for human sin, as it has been traditionally understood. As he notes here, beneath the individual's immediate experience of struggle, doubt, and despair during such trials, an internal battle rages between evil spirits attempting to draw the object of their attention down into evil, falsity, and hell, and God and angels attempting to lift the individual up to goodness, truth, and heaven. In the context of this severe testing of character, the individual makes the ultimate choices that will determine his or her eternal home in either heaven or hell. For a copious list of references to the subject

in Swedenborg's works, see the entry "Temptation" in Potts 1888–1902, 6:191–211. For brief topical discussions of spiritual trials, see *New Jerusalem* 187–201; *True Christianity* 596–600. [LSW]

102 (in *The Lord* 33:3). Swedenborg rejects the concept of the Devil and demons as distinct, nonhuman creations who were originally angels but rebelled against God and thus fell from heaven to form hell. He holds instead that all the demons in hell were once human beings who chose evil over good during the course of their lives in the material world, and that "the Devil" is a collective term for hell (see note 62). On Swedenborg's rejection of the nonhuman nature of angels, see notes 13 and 251. [LSW]

103 (in *The Lord* 34:3). Swedenborg here makes a verbal connection in the original Latin between *Formator* (here translated "the Maker") and *Reformator* (here translated "Reformer"), a connection that is difficult to convey in English translation. For more on this connection between "making" or "creating," and reforming or regenerating, including supporting references to the Bible, see *Secrets of Heaven* 16, 88, 472, 8043; *True Christianity* 573, 583. [LSW]

104 (in *The Lord* 35:1). This material that is "generally known" is a rephrasing of a segment of the Athanasian Creed, to which Swedenborg makes reference in the following sentence. See Kolb and Wengert 2000, 24.28–25.31. On the Athanasian Creed, see notes 91 and 96. [JSR]

105 (in *The Lord* 35:2). The term "substantial" here refers to a type of substance distinct from physical matter. In Swedenborg's cosmology everything that exists consists of some substance that is tangible on its own level. There are three major types of substance that form the grand levels of reality. These three are distinct from one another, yet the lower are derived from the higher. The highest type of substance is the Divine Being itself, which consists of divine love and is formed by divine wisdom. This level of substance is called "divine substance." The next major type of substance, which is created by and derived from divine substance, is "spiritual substance." The entire spiritual world, as well as the human mind, consists of spiritual substance, which is spiritual love formed by spiritual truth. The third major level of substance is the physical matter of which the entire material universe consists, in various physical structures and forms. This includes not only solid, liquid, and gaseous matter but also more subtle forms of matter and energy that were called the "aura" and the "ether" in Swedenborg's day. For more on divine substance, spiritual substance, and physical matter, their tangible reality, and their relationships with one another, see *Secrets of Heaven* 3726:3–4; *Divine Love and Wisdom* 40–43, 173–178, 300–306; *Divine Providence* 5–6, 157; *Marriage Love* 31, 207:5; *True Christianity* 20, 33–34. [LSW]

106 (in *The Lord* 35:3). For more on "emptying out" (Latin *exinanitio*) as one of two major states between which Jesus alternated during his time in this world, see *True Christianity* 104–106. In choosing this terminology, Swedenborg probably had in mind biblical passages such as Isaiah 53:12 (quoted in *The Lord* 15:1), in which it is said of the coming Messiah that he will "pour out" or "empty" his soul unto death. Though the term as it appears in Swedenborg's usage may have affinities with the traditional Christian concepts of *exinanition* and *kenosis* (from words for "emptying" in Latin and Greek, respectively), Swedenborg has put the existing terminology to a new purpose, as is often the case in his works. [JSR]

107 (in *The Lord* 35:3). The allusion is to Matthew 27:46 and Mark 15:34, in which Jesus cries out, shortly before his death, "My God, my God, why have you forsaken me?" quoting Psalm 22:1. [GFD]

108 (in *The Lord* 35:8). For more on this reciprocal union both within the Lord and between the Lord and human beings, see *Heaven and Hell* 380; *Divine Love and Wisdom* 35, 115–116; *Divine Providence* 92–95; *True Christianity* 97–100, 371–372; *Draft on Divine Wisdom* chapter 10 = §§115–127 [Mongredien's numbering] (= Swedenborg 1994–1997c, 495–505). [LSW]

109 (in *The Lord* 36:1). On God's humanity as the source of angels' and spirits' humanity, see especially *Heaven and Hell* 78–86. [GFD]

110 (in *The Lord* 36:1). In the preface of *The Lord,* Swedenborg projected four works whose full titles were to begin "Angelic Wisdom about . . ." (compare note 100). Of the two of these works that ultimately were published, the human nature of God is treated in one, *Divine Love and Wisdom* 11–13, and is touched on in the other, *Divine Providence* 64–65. [GFD]

Notes to *The Lord* Chapter 8, §§37–44

111 (in *The Lord* 37:1). The results of this reading and reflection may be found in *Draft on the Inner Meaning of Prophets and Psalms*. There is also an extensive commentary on Isaiah and a partial one on Jeremiah published in English translation in volume 8 of Swedenborg 1927–1951. (In the current edition, this material is titled *Isaiah and Jeremiah Explained.*) Less accessible are three phototype volumes (Swedenborg 1859–1873) of otherwise unpublished manuscripts containing indexes, traditionally referred to by the Latin title *Index Biblicus* (Bible Index). Volume 1 contains an index of much of Isaiah (current edition title: *First Draft Concordance of Prophetic Material in the Bible*), and volume 2 an index of the major and minor prophets (current edition title: *Second Draft Concordance of Prophetic Material in the Bible*). The third volume includes a section of biblical references under specific headings including damnation and hell, redemption, sin, and heaven and salvation (current edition title: *Concordance of Proper Nouns in the Bible*). [GFD]

112 (in *The Lord* 37:2). For more on angels perceiving the spiritual meaning of the Word while people on earth read its literal meaning, see *Secrets of Heaven* 1767–1771; *Heaven and Hell* 303–310; *Sacred Scripture* 62–69; *True Christianity* 234–239; *Draft of "Sacred Scripture"* §18 [Rogers's numbering] = §§45–48 [Whitehead's numbering] (= Swedenborg 1997c, 44–45). On angels reading their own version of the Word in heaven, see note 14. [LSW]

113 (in *The Lord* 37:2). This is likely an allusion to 1 Corinthians 13:12: "For now we see in a mirror, dimly, but then we will see face to face" (New Revised Standard Version). [LSW]

114 (in *The Lord* 38). It appears that in the first edition of *The Lord* the similarity between Isaiah 43:15 and Isaiah 45:11, 15, led to an error in which the two passages were combined into one, and the reference to Isaiah 43:15 was dropped. The material here added in square brackets restores missing text in both quotations to clarify the original state of this material. [LSW, JSR]

115 (in *The Lord* 39). This bracketed interpolation is Swedenborg's. Bethlehem Ephrata is the name given to the city of Bethlehem in Micah 5:2. See also Ruth 4:11; 1 Chronicles 2:50–51, 54; 4:4. [Editors]

116 (in *The Lord* 40). The Latin here translated "from our presence" is *a faciebus nostris,* "from our faces," a severely literal translation of a Hebrew idiom. The Hebrew word for "face," פָּנִים *(pānim),* while construed as singular, is plural in form. Swedenborg regularly translates it as such, as does his preferred Latin Bible, Schmidt 1696. [GFD]

117 (in *The Lord* 40). The Hebrew here, יוֹשֶׁבֶת *(yôšebet),* properly means "[female] inhabitant," but Swedenborg renders it *filia,* "daughter," perhaps to make it parallel the many other actual occurrences of the phrase "daughter of Zion" elsewhere in the Old Testament. [GFD, SS]

Notes to *The Lord* Chapter 9, §45

118 (in *The Lord* 45:2). The Latin word here translated "angel guardians" is a plural form of *cherub* (or *cherubus*). The Latin word is a transliteration of the Hebrew כְּרוּב *(kərûb),* traditionally translated "cherub," of which the plural is כְּרוּבִים *(kərûbîm)* or כְּרֻבִים *(kərubîm),* traditionally translated "cherubim." See *Sacred Scripture* 97 for an account of the occurrences of these guardians in the Hebrew Bible and for Swedenborg's interpretation of their meaning. One biblical account of a cherub occurring in the first chapter of Ezekiel (but not identified as a cherub until Ezekiel 10:15) describes it as a creature with the stature and hands of a man, the feet of a calf, and four wings, as well as four different faces: a lion's, an ox's, an eagle's, and a man's. This loosely parallels figures in ancient art that have the wings of an eagle, the head of a man, and the body of a bull combined with that of a lion. In the Bible, cherubs have interrelated functions such as guarding paradise (Genesis 3:22–24) and being the bearers of God's throne (Ezekiel 10:1, 20) and even of God himself (2 Samuel 22:11 = Psalms 18:10). It needs to be added that these figures have no resemblance to *putti,* the winged babies familiar from Renaissance art, though such "baby angels" are commonly called cherubs today. For further discussion, see Metzger and Coogan 1993, 107–108. [RS, GFD]

Notes to *The Lord* Chapter 10, §§46–54

119 (in *The Lord* 46:2). The traditional Christian doctrine of the Trinity of Persons took form during the early centuries of the Christian church, and was a matter of intense controversy. As to its scriptural basis, the only occurrence of the phrase "the Father, the Son, and the Holy Spirit" is in Matthew 28:19, where Jesus commands the disciples to baptize "in the name of the Father, the Son, and the Holy Spirit." The effort of the church fathers was to find philosophical and metaphysical terms that would do full justice to both this "threeness" and the "oneness" of God; and the task was complicated by the fact that the Latin terminology of the Western churches and the Greek terminology of the Eastern churches did not, and probably could not, exactly coincide. Swedenborg insists that the fourth-century Nicene Creed was in fact tritheistic; and in his critique of the later Athanasian Creed he highlights the irrationality of the statement that while we are to confess that individually each of the three persons is God and Lord, the Christian faith forbids us to say "three gods" or "three lords" (see, for example, *True Christianity* 172:2). Throughout the theological works, he uses the title *Dominus,* "the Lord," referring to the risen and glorified Christ, and insists that, in the words of Colossians 2:9, "in him [Christ] the whole fullness of deity dwells bodily" (New Revised Standard Version). When he presents the new theology in the format of a typical Lutheran systematic theology in *True Christianity,* he surprisingly devotes separate chapters to God the Creator,

the Lord the Redeemer, and the Holy Spirit and divine action; but he opens these chapters with an insistence on the oneness of God (§§5–15); and he concludes them with a scathing critique of the functional tritheism of the post-Nicene church (§§171–184). The statement about the nature of the trinity in the Lord that follows in the text here is a very brief synopsis of Swedenborg's theology of the Father, Son, and Holy Spirit as three "essential components" (Latin *essentialia*) existing in a *single* person of God (see *True Christianity* §§164–170). [GFD, LSW]

120 (in *The Lord* 46:2). The Latin here translated "the divine nature as the source" and "the divine nature as means" contrasts *Divinum ex Quo* and *Divinum per Quod*, literally, "the divine nature from which" and "the divine nature through which." [GFD]

121 (in *The Lord* 46:2). On the projected work on omnipotence, omnipresence, and omniscience, see note 4. [Editors]

122 (in *The Lord* 46:3). Swedenborg's term for the emanation that radiates from the Lord, from angels, from good and evil spirits, and from humans on earth is "aura" (Latin *sphaera*, traditionally translated "sphere"). This aura surrounds not only all living beings but inanimate objects as well. For some of his "abundance of knowledge" about this emanating and surrounding aura, see *Secrets of Heaven* 925, 1388–1399, 1504–1520, 4464, 5179, 7454, 10130, 10188; *Heaven and Hell* 17, 49, 538, 591; *Divine Love and Wisdom* 291–293; *Marriage Love* 171; *Revelation Explained* (= Swedenborg 1994–1997a) §392:2. [LSW]

123 (in *The Lord* 47:1). The Hebrew word רוּחַ (*rûaḥ*) can mean "breath," "spirit," and "wind" (Brown, Driver, and Briggs 1996, pages 924–926, Strong's 7307). The Latin *spiritus* can also have all three of these meanings. [RS]

124 (in *The Lord* 47:1). See the extended treatment of the heart and the lungs in *Divine Love and Wisdom* 371–431. [GFD]

125 (in *The Lord* 48:1). The first edition here references Daniel 4:5 (Daniel 4:8 in English Bibles) as saying, "Nebuchadnezzar [said] of Daniel that there was an excellent spirit of knowledge, intelligence, and wisdom in him." This seems to be a conflation of Daniel 4:8 and Daniel 5:11–12, 14, or perhaps the typesetter skipped a line of text. The translation here supplies in brackets missing material from the verses in the Book of Daniel that Swedenborg presumably had in mind. [LSW]

126 (in *The Lord* 49:1). The quotation given here is from Numbers 16:22. The other verse referred to, Numbers 27:18, is not actually quoted here by Swedenborg, although perhaps he intended it to be, as it shows in context that Joshua was divinely appointed to succeed Moses as leader of the Israelites because Joshua was "a man in whom is the spirit" (New Revised Standard Version). [JSR]

127 (in *The Lord* 50:2). In its own context, Isaiah 57:16 seems to be speaking of the human spirit rather than the divine spirit. However, in *Secrets of Heaven* 573 Swedenborg quotes this verse in the course of his explanation of part of Genesis 6:3: "Then the Lord said, 'My spirit shall not abide in mortals forever'" (New Revised Standard Version). His interpretation there suggests that he views the "spirit" mentioned in Isaiah 57:16 as being the presence of the Lord's spirit in human beings. This may explain his inclusion of the verse in this series of quotations on the spirit of the Lord. [LSW, JSR]

128 (in *The Lord* 50:2). For more on the meaning of "blasphemy against the Holy Spirit" and "blasphemy against the Son of Humanity" as understood by Swedenborg, see *Secrets of Heaven* 8882, 9013:6, 9818:27; *Divine Providence* 98:3, 231:6; *True Christianity* 299; *Revelation Explained* (= Swedenborg 1994–1997a) §§778, 960:15. In general,

"blasphemy against the Holy Spirit" involves people who present themselves as Christians denying the divinity of the Lord and the holiness of the Word not just theoretically, but by living an evil life based on that denial. "Blasphemy against the Son of Humanity" generally involves misunderstanding or misinterpreting the literal meaning of the Bible but still living a good life. [LSW]

129 (in *The Lord* 51:3). For additional commentary on this statement in John 7:39, see *Secrets of Heaven* 6993, 7499, 8724, 9199:4, 9818:14; *New Jerusalem* 292; *Revelation Unveiled* 962:10; *True Christianity* 140, 153, 158; *Revelation Explained* (= Swedenborg 1994–1997a) §§183:10, 748; *Answers to Nine Questions* (= Swedenborg 1997b) §5. [LSW]

130 (in *The Lord* 51:3). For an extended treatment of the heart and lungs and their connection with the divine love and divine wisdom of the Lord, see *Divine Love and Wisdom* 371–431. [GFD]

Notes to *The Lord* Chapter 11, §§55–61

131 (in *The Lord* 55:4). In *Divine Providence* 234–284, Swedenborg discusses at some length why God allows people to commit errors (a concept he treats under the general heading "laws of permission," which, he says, are also laws of divine providence). [GFD]

132 (in *The Lord* 55:6). Though the attribution of the Athanasian Creed to Athanasius (around 295–373 C.E.) had been effectively challenged by scholars by Swedenborg's day, references to the creed in Swedenborg's works of 1763 and 1764 (see *The Lord* 57; *Divine Providence* 262:1) suggest that at that time Swedenborg believed Athanasius had been the author, or at least accepted that identification of the author for the sake of convenience. By 1769–1771, however, when he was writing *True Christianity,* a speaker in an account of a memorable occurrence in the spiritual world in §110:3 refers in general terms to the *conceptores Symboli Athanasiani* ("the framers of the Athanasian Creed"), implying that Athanasius was not its author. On Swedenborg's encounter with Athanasius in the spiritual world, see *Spiritual Experiences* (= Swedenborg 1998–2013) §5959 and *Commentary on the Athanasian Creed* (= Swedenborg 1994–1997b) §43. On the title and translation of the creed used by Swedenborg, see note 96. [JSR, SS, RGE]

133 (in *The Lord* 56). The bracketed additions throughout this section are Swedenborg's. Presumably they echo alternate readings in German and Swedish translations of the Athanasian Creed (see note 96). Compare, for example, the version in Swedberg 1694, 486–490, a psalmbook compiled and published by Swedenborg's father, Jesper Swedberg (1653–1735). The specific alternate reading shown here, "Christian" for "catholic," likely arose from the fact that before the Reformation the term *catholic* was understood to mean "universal," whereas afterward it was increasingly taken to refer to the Roman Catholic Church. [JSR, GFD]

134 (in *The Lord* 56). To compare this translation of Swedenborg's version of the creed with the full text of the creed in English, see Schaff 1931, 2:66–71, or Kolb and Wengert 2000, 23–25. [Editors]

135 (in *The Lord* 57). For more on union with the Lord and heaven taking place not through speech alone, but through acknowledgment and thought, as well as love and action in harmony with them, see *Secrets of Heaven* 4126, 10205; *True Christianity* 457; *Revelation Explained* (= Swedenborg 1994–1997a) §§328:6, 649, 1096. [LSW]

136 (in *The Lord* 59). On the concept of Jesus' being "emptied out" (Latin *exinanitio*), see note 106. [Editors]

137 (in *The Lord* 61:2). Swedenborg describes this judgment as having happened in 1757. See *Last Judgment* in its entirety, and the far more detailed record of his experience of witnessing this judgment in *Spiritual Experiences* (= Swedenborg 1998–2013) intermittently between §§4925 and 6020. For excerpts that provide a running synopsis of the *Spiritual Experiences* material on this topic, see Potts 1888–1902, 4:129–166, under "Last Judgment." For more on the process and consequences of this judgment, see the references provided in note 23. [GFD, SS]

Notes to *The Lord* Chapter 12, §§62–65

138 (in *The Lord* 62:1). Descriptions of various evil figures being cast into hell, using metaphors such as being thrown into a lake of fire or being burned with fire, are found in Revelation 18:8–10, 15–19; 19:20; 20:10, 14–15. Elsewhere the figures Swedenborg names here as representing various segments of the then-existing Christian church are individually interpreted. On the false prophet, see *Revelation Unveiled* 701, 834, 864; *Revelation Explained* (= Swedenborg 1994–1997a) §999; on the dragon, see *Revelation Unveiled* 537; *Revelation Explained* 714; on the whore, see *Revelation Unveiled* 719, 729, 805; *Revelation Explained* 1032, 1076, 1200; on the beasts, see *Revelation Unveiled* 567, 594; *Revelation Explained* 774, 815. [LSW]

139 (in *The Lord* 62:1). The Latin word here translated "sky" is *caelum*. Like the Hebrew word שָׁמַיִם *(šāmayim)* and Greek οὐρανός *(ouranós),* this word can refer either to the sky or to heaven; so specifying here that it is a "sky like the one we can see with our eyes, full of air and stars" is necessary in order to prevent the reader of the Latin from thinking that the word *caelum* refers to heaven. [LSW, SS]

140 (in *The Lord* 62:2). The two passages here referenced, Isaiah 65:17 and 66:22, are the only places in the Hebrew Bible that specifically mention God creating a new heaven and a new earth. By "and elsewhere" here, Swedenborg presumably has in mind the numerous predictions in the books of the prophets of cosmic upheaval and renewal on "the day of the Lord." See, for example, Isaiah 2:6–21; Joel 2:1–11; Amos 5:18–27. For Swedenborg's compilation of references to "that day" in the Bible, see *The Lord* 4. [GFD, RS, LSW]

141 (in *The Lord* 62:2). In Swedenborg's theological works "the spiritual world" refers to an entire universe distinct from the material world in that it is composed of spiritual substance rather than physical matter. The overall regions of the spiritual world, he says, are heaven, hell, and the world of spirits. Heaven consists of countless communities of like-minded angels who were all once human beings living in the material world, and who have focused their lives on loving God and loving the neighbor. Correspondingly, hell consists of countless communities of like-minded evil spirits, called variously "devils," "satans," and "demons," who were all once human beings living in the material world, and who have focused their lives on loving themselves and material possessions and pleasures to the exclusion of love for God and the neighbor. The world of spirits is an intermediate region between heaven and hell where all people first come after the death of their physical bodies. This is where both good and evil people live as spirits until they move on to their permanent homes in heaven or hell. The world of spirits also consists of communities, which are generally arranged according to people's former religious, national, cultural, and social ties in the material world. For an extensive description of the spiritual world, see *Heaven and Hell* in its entirety. For more compact

descriptions of the spiritual world and its layout, see *Secrets of Heaven* 684–700, 1273–1278; *Heaven and Hell* 20–50, 421–431, 582–588; *New Jerusalem* 223–240; *Divine Love and Wisdom* 140–145; *Spiritual Experiences* (= Swedenborg 1998–2013) §§5162–5169. [LSW]

142 (in *The Lord* 62:2). The supplement to Swedenborg's work *Last Judgment* was published in Amsterdam in 1763 along with a supplement to his previous material on the spiritual world. The combination volume is referred to by the short title *Supplements* in this edition. *Supplements* does not actually provide any detail on the new church, which Swedenborg presents as having been founded in the spiritual world and on earth at the time of the Last Judgment. Sections 3 and 12 of that work do, however, contain references to the new heaven, the new earth, and the new church. [LSW]

143 (in *The Lord* 63). The use of the metaphor of bride and bridegroom to characterize the relationship between God and the community of Israel, and later between Christ and the church, goes back to the Bible itself. The source of this metaphor lies in the Old Testament, which portrays Israel as the bride of the Lord. See, for example, Isaiah 62:1–5, which depicts God as marrying the nation of Israel, and Hosea 1–3, which depicts Israel as a faithless wife. The Song of Songs (Song of Solomon) was from an early time regarded as an allegory of love between God and Israel (Schmithals 1997, 166–167). In the New Testament, Revelation describes "the holy city, the new Jerusalem, coming down from God out of the sky, prepared as a bride dressed up for her husband" (Revelation 21:2). The "bride" is said to be "the Lamb's wife" (Revelation 21:9). The union between Christ and the church is thus portrayed as a heavenly marriage. In Mark 2:18–20, Jesus likens himself to a bridegroom. See also Ephesians 5:23–27, which likens the relationship between a husband and wife to that of Christ and the church. [RS]

144 (in *The Lord* 64:1). The land of Canaan encompassed an area that included most of present-day Israel and Palestine, Lebanon, and parts of western Syria. In the biblical narrative it commonly refers to the territory in which the Israelites established their sovereign nation. For a fuller discussion of the land of Canaan, see the appendix on pages 529–530. [LSW]

145 (in *The Lord* 64:1). The three annual feasts Swedenborg is referring to here are the Feast of Unleavened Bread (more commonly known as Passover), the Feast of Weeks (which begins with the celebration of the harvest of first fruits), and the Feast of Tabernacles (also known as the Feast of Ingathering, the Feast of Booths, Sukkoth, Succoth, or Sukkot). Every male in the land is commanded to attend these three feasts in Exodus 23:14–17; 34:18, 22–24; and in Deuteronomy 16:16, where "the place that [the Lord your God] will choose" was subsequently specified as Jerusalem and the Temple there (see 1 Kings 8:29; 9:3; 14:21; 2 Chronicles 6:6; 7:16; 33:7). For biblical descriptions of and commandments concerning these feasts, see Exodus 12:1–28 (the original institution of the Feast of Unleavened Bread); Leviticus 23:4–21, 33–43; Deuteronomy 16:1–17. For some of Swedenborg's commentary on these three annual feasts, see *Secrets of Heaven* 7093, 9285–9301, 10654–10659, 10670–10672; *Revelation Explained* (= Swedenborg 1994–1997a) §911:18. [LSW, JSR]

146 (in *The Lord* 64:2). The morally degenerate condition of the leaders of Jerusalem around the time of Jesus is independently supported. Of Herod the Great (73–4 B.C.E.), who made the Jerusalem of his time into the most notable city of the eastern Mediterranean, one author observes, "Historians from the ancient world bitterly anatomise the nastiness of Herod's personality and record the lurid family politics and violence of his

reign. And lurid and nasty it was, with enough jealousies, sexual misdemeanours, poisonings, plots, and double-crossings to create for the historians a perfect image of the decadence of the East combined with the corruption of empire" (Goldhill 2005, 58). [RS]

147 (in *The Lord* 64:4). The imagery here in Isaiah 52:2 is that of rising up from lying prone and downtrodden on the ground, as depicted in Isaiah 51:23, and sitting in splendor on a seat or throne. Swedenborg is not alone in reading the passage in this way, but some understand the Hebrew differently, emending the word for "sit" to another that means "captive"; see, for example, the New Revised Standard Version, which reads: "Shake yourself from the dust, rise up, O captive Jerusalem." [LSW, SS]

148 (in *The Lord* 65). By "the church changing into Babylon," Swedenborg means that the early Christian church became what we today know as the Roman Catholic Church; by its "changing into Philistia," he refers to the rise of Protestantism from a schism within the Roman Catholic Church. The identification of Catholicism with the "Babylon" of the Book of Revelation was common in the Protestantism of Swedenborg's day; see note 410. In his own theology, Swedenborg justified this interpretation by charging that the Roman Catholic Church had been corrupted by a love of ruling driven by self-love; and in line with this view, his interpretation of "Babylon" as it occurs in the Bible is that it represents in general terms a love of ruling over others with self-love at its root. He similarly ties his identification of "Philistia" to the Protestant branch of Christianity because of its doctrinal insistence that faith alone can save the sinning human. With this tenet, Protestantism intended to exclude any attempt to secure salvation through one's "works," or actions. (For more on faith alone, see note 209.) Swedenborg, however, saw actions undertaken out of loving care for others to be an indispensable part of salvation. He thus condemned Protestantism for holding to what he called "faith without caring," or belief not accompanied by loving action. For his equations of "faith alone" and Philistia or Philistines, see, for example, *Faith* 49–54; *Survey* 81, 108; *True Christianity* 515; *Revelation Explained* (= Swedenborg 1994–1997a) §879:3. For general identifications of "Babylon" and "Philistia," see *Faith* 49, 55; *Divine Providence* 264:2–3; *Revelation Explained* 1029:18. For more discussion specifically on Swedenborg's interpretation of "Babel" or "Babylon," including his identification of it with the Roman Catholic Church, or allusions thereto, see *Secrets of Heaven* 1326, 4748:5, 10412; *Last Judgment* 53–64; *Revelation Unveiled* 717; *Revelation Explained* 1029. For more specifically on Swedenborg's interpretation of "Philistia," see *Secrets of Heaven* 1197–1198, 3412, 8313, 9340; *Faith* 49–54; *Revelation Explained* 817:6–11. [LSW, SS]

149 (in *The Lord* 65). Swedenborg is referring to the texts that immediately follow in this volume—*Sacred Scripture, Life,* and *Faith*—and to his work *Divine Love and Wisdom,* which was published in Amsterdam in the same year, 1763. [RS]

Notes to *Sacred Scripture* Chapter 1, §§1–4

150 (in *Sacred Scripture* 1). On Swedenborg's use of the term "the Word," see note 11. [Editors]

151 (in *Sacred Scripture* 1). On the "letter" or literal meaning of the Bible, see note 17. [Editors]

152 (in *Sacred Scripture* 1). In Swedenborg's times, readers of literature increasingly found sublimity and brilliance in directness; they would have seconded the criticism made by Voltaire (1694–1778) that the Bible was "full of repetition, confused, [and]

ridiculously metaphorical" (Voltaire 1994, 36:500–517; translated by Graham Gargett). The British philosopher Robert Boyle (1627–1691) summarized the complaints against it thus:

> Some . . . are pleased to say that Book is too obscure, others, that 'tis immethodical, others, that it is contradictory to itself, others, that the neighbouring parts of it are incoherent, others, that 'tis unadorned, others, that it is flat and unaffecting, others, that it abounds with things that are either trivial or impertinent [irrelevant], and also with useless Repetitions. (Boyle 1675, 4)

In *Secrets of Heaven* 8783, Swedenborg rejects the claim of the learned that they would accept the Bible if only it set forth spiritual and heavenly matters in direct terms. He quotes John 3:12 against them: "If I have told you about earthly things and you do not believe, how can you believe if I tell you about heavenly things?" (New Revised Standard Version). See also note 162. [SS, DNG]

153 (in *Sacred Scripture* 1). It was characteristic of a great deal of Enlightenment thinking to exalt "Nature" as the guide to truth and the guarantor of happiness. The work of the Roman poet Titus Lucretius Carus (around 94–51 B.C.E.)—rediscovered in the fifteenth century and much published thereafter—was highly influential in this regard: his Epicurean poem *De Rerum Natura* (On the Nature of Things) denied the existence of an afterlife and claimed that the gods had no influence on human affairs: "Nature is her own mistress and is exempt from the oppression of arrogant despots, accomplishing everything by herself spontaneously and independently and free from the jurisdiction of the gods" (Lucretius 2001, 63). Some of the key doctrines of ancient Epicureanism, including scientific atomism and ethical hedonism, enjoyed a great vogue during the seventeenth and eighteenth centuries. Christian thinkers like René Descartes (1596–1650) tried to reconcile the increasingly mechanistic understanding of the natural world with a traditional Judeo-Christian insistence on God's omnipotence by identifying natural laws with divine edicts. As Descartes said: "By Nature, I do not understand some Goddess, or some other imaginary power; I make use of this word to signify matter itself . . . under the condition that God continues to preserve it in the same way he created it" (quoted in Wilson 2008, 91–92). The Dutch Jewish philosopher Benedict de Spinoza (1632–1677) went much further, setting Nature in apposition to God (for example, in the phrase *Deus sive Natura,* "God, or Nature"). He defined God as "an absolutely infinite being, that is, substance consisting of infinite attributes" (Spinoza [1677] 2006, 4), but held that another name for this "substance" was nature. While his views were more nuanced than this recapitulation may suggest, this was how he was often understood. Hence Spinoza was frequently characterized as an atheist, and in Swedenborg's times, "Spinozism" was more or less synonymous with atheism (Edwards 1967, 7:533, 541). To view the matter in a larger context, Swedenborg lived in a time when the vanguard of philosophical thought was moving from Deism, which posited a rational order to the universe proceeding from God, to naturalism and materialistic monism, which held that physical reality—that is, nature—constituted the sole reality of the universe. Diverse thinkers held these materialistic views (one prominent example being the French-German philosopher Paul-Henri Dietrich, Baron d'Holbach [1723–1789]), and it is likely that Swedenborg had in mind such thinkers as a group, rather than any specific individuals. For a discussion of this issue, see Taylor 1989, 272,

283, 308. On the preeminence of "nature" as a concept in the eighteenth century, see Lovejoy 1960, 184. On natural religion, compare note 293. [RS, DNG]

154 (in *Sacred Scripture* 1). On Swedenborg's use of the term "the Lord," see note 2. [Editors]

155 (in *Sacred Scripture* 1). Though Swedenborg doubtless intended this as a fictional sketch of a typical skeptic's derogatory comments on the Bible, its plausibility is confirmed by a similar set of rhetorical questions protesting the validity of Christian belief that can be found in the work of an actual skeptic who lived during the Enlightenment, Jean Meslier (1664–1729). Though he made his living as a Catholic priest, Meslier wrote a secret memoir repudiating Christianity in its entirety; when the book was discovered after his death, no less famous a figure than Voltaire undertook to abridge and publish it. The abridgment includes such passages as: "What then are the worthless resources of these Christ-worshipers? . . . Their miracles? But what people do not have their own such things, and who among the wise do not scorn them as fables? Their prophecies? Has not their falsity been proven? . . . Their doctrine? But is that not the height of absurdity?" (Meslier 1830, 363–364; translated by Stuart Shotwell). [SS]

156 (in *Sacred Scripture* 2:1). On Swedenborg's use of "Jehovah" as a name of God, see note 9. [Editors]

157 (in *Sacred Scripture* 2:1). Throughout his theological works Swedenborg adopts, as was customary in his day, the traditional view that Moses was the author of the first five books of the Bible (the Pentateuch) and the various prophets were actually the authors of the books attributed to them. He similarly accepted the view that David was the author of the Psalms. Thus he sometimes cites the Pentateuch as "Moses" and the Psalms as "David." [Editors]

158 (in *Sacred Scripture* 2:1). "The authors of the Gospels" here means the historical people named Matthew, Mark, Luke, and John to whom the Gospels are traditionally attributed. John is also the traditionally recognized author of the Book of Revelation. "Much of it with his own mouth" refers to the words recorded in the Gospels as being spoken by the Lord (Jesus) himself. "The rest by means of the spirit of his mouth" refers to a divine inspiration of the biblical authors resulting in the books of the Word being not simply a human composition but a divine one. On the Word, see note 11. For more on this divine inspiration of the Word, see *Sacred Scripture* 18–19; *Secrets of Heaven* 1–2, 1886–1888, 4726; *The Lord* 52–54. [LSW]

159 (in *Sacred Scripture* 2:2). This work, referred to in this edition by the short title *The Lord*, was published by Swedenborg in Amsterdam in 1763. [Editors]

160 (in *Sacred Scripture* 2:2). On Swedenborg's concept of a deeper meaning existing within the literal meaning of the Bible, see *Sacred Scripture* 4–26, and also note 11 toward its end. [Editors]

161 (in *Sacred Scripture* 2:4). The Bible passage most likely to be included among those Swedenborg is referring to here is John 1:14: "And the Word became flesh and lived among us," where the Greek word ἐσκήνωσεν *(eskénosen)*, here translated "lived," literally means "made his tabernacle." Along the same lines, Swedenborg may also have in mind passages that mention "the tabernacle of the testimony" (or "the tabernacle of the covenant"), such as Exodus 38:21; Numbers 1:50, 53; Acts 7:44; Revelation 15:5. The Hebrew word מִשְׁכָּן *(miškān)*, commonly translated "tabernacle," means "a dwelling place," "a tent"— and the tabernacle was seen as God's dwelling place among the people (see 2 Samuel 7:6;

1 Chronicles 17:5). It was sometimes called "the tabernacle of the testimony" because in its central and most sacred place were kept the two tables of the Ten Commandments, which were regarded as the testimony, or covenant, between God and the people of Israel. Swedenborg sees the Ten Commandments as representing in brief form the entire Word of God. Drawing on all of this, he interprets the words of Revelation 15:5, "the temple of the tabernacle of the testimony," in this way: "In the highest sense, the *temple* means the Lord in his divine-human nature and therefore heaven and the church. Here it means the Christian heaven. The *tabernacle of the testimony* means the center of that heaven where the Lord is present in his holiness in the Word and in the law that is the Decalogue" (*Revelation Unveiled* 669; see also *Revelation Explained* [= Swedenborg 1994–1997a] §948.) Other relevant passages are Ezekiel 37:26–28 and Revelation 21:3, which speak of God's sanctuary or tabernacle as God's dwelling among the people. [LSW]

162 (in *Sacred Scripture* 3:1). This passage extends the rebuttal of common complaints about the literary style of the Bible just touched upon in *Sacred Scripture* 1, on which see note 152. The method Swedenborg uses in this rebuttal is to shift away from the usual definition of "style" as a function of prose attributes (in this case, for example, limited vocabulary, simple sentence structure, repetition) and toward a definition of "style" as a vehicle for expressing content (specifically, divine truths). When he says that critics of the Bible "evaluate it by its style, where they do not see wisdom or life," he means its prose attributes as compared to the attributes of prose valued in his day. When he goes on to say that "the style of the Word is the divine style," he is referring to style in the sense of the *symbolic function and content* of the prose. For example, if the style of a biblical parable such as that of the prodigal son were assessed purely in terms of its prose attributes, it would be considered eminently simple; but if its style were assessed in terms of symbolic function and content, it would be considered quite rich and complex—much more so than if its content were stated in abstract terms. We still use both definitions of style today in English. We might, for example, criticize Jane Austen's style (its prose attributes) as difficult for today's readers, while at the same time praising her style for its wit and irony (that is, its content). For more of Swedenborg's description of the "style of the Word," see *Secrets of Heaven* 66, 4442, 9086:3; *Heaven and Hell* 310; *Last Judgment* 40; *Revelation Explained* (= Swedenborg 1994–1997a) §§1, 71:4; *Draft of "Sacred Scripture"* §6 [Rogers's numbering] = §16 [Whitehead's numbering] (= Swedenborg 1997c, 16–18); Swedenborg's letter to Beyer dated April 15, 1766, published in English in Acton 1948–1955, 612–613. [SS, LSW]

163 (in *Sacred Scripture* 3:1). Swedenborg is more emphatic elsewhere about the Word being inspired right down to the letters. See, for example, *White Horse* 13, where he states that in the Word "there is something holy and divine in absolutely every bit of its literal meaning, right down to the smallest letter," and a more extended statement in *Secrets of Heaven* 1870: "I have been shown through amazing experiences that Sacred Scripture was inspired not only in its individual words but also in every tiny letter of each word. So it was literally inspired down to the smallest jot (as the idiom goes). Each jot contains a measure of emotion and vital energy, which affects the whole word it appears in and which therefore permeates the most minor details in a correspondential way." Compare note 59. [GFD]

164 (in *Sacred Scripture* 3:1). For more on the Bible uniting people to the Lord and opening heaven, see *Secrets of Heaven* 1775–1776, 3476, 3735, 4217, 9410, 10452,

10632–10634; *Heaven and Hell* 303–310; *Revelation Explained* (= Swedenborg 1994–1997a) §701:11; *Draft of "Sacred Scripture"* §18 [Rogers's numbering] = §45 [Whitehead's numbering] (= Swedenborg 1997c, 44–45). According to Swedenborg, this opening of heaven goes in both directions. For a person on earth it takes place through learning about God and heaven from the Bible so that these things can become part of the person's life. For the angels in heaven it takes place through the angels when a person understands the spiritual meaning of the Bible while reading its literal meaning. "Opening heaven" in this context does not refer to people on earth having their spiritual senses opened so that they can see and hear what takes place in heaven. Rather, it means having an inner connection with heaven, and through heaven with the Lord. For more on what opens heaven to people on earth generally, see *Secrets of Heaven* 2760:2, 2851:2, 9594, 10156; *Revelation Explained* 800:2, 954:2, 970:2–3. [LSW]

165 (in *Sacred Scripture* 4). This is an allusion to 2 Corinthians 3:5–6, "God . . . has made us competent to be ministers of a new covenant, not of letter but of spirit; for the letter kills, but the Spirit gives life" (New Revised Standard Version). [LSW]

Notes to *Sacred Scripture* Chapter 2, §§4–26

166 (in *Sacred Scripture* 5). Swedenborg is here using the term "the church" in a common meaning for his day and culture, as referring to Christianity in general, including all its branches and sects. For a discussion of his broader use of the term "church," see note 5. [LSW]

167 (in *Sacred Scripture* 5). On the multiplicity of heavens, see *Heaven and Hell* 20–40. For more on the relationship between the residents of heaven and earth through the Bible, see note 164. [GFD, LSW]

168 (in *Sacred Scripture* 6:2). The assertion that "we here on earth have not known anything about the heavens before" is an expression in absolute terms of an idea that Swedenborg states elsewhere with more nuance. For example, in the opening section of *Heaven and Hell* he writes: "*Church people these days* know *practically nothing* about heaven and hell or their life after death, *even though there are descriptions of everything available to them in the Word*. In fact, many who have been born in the church deny all this. In their hearts they are asking who has ever come back to tell us about it" (*Heaven and Hell* 1, emphasis added). This statement suggests that the ignorance is not absolute, and it confines itself to the Christian church as it exists in his day. Elsewhere he says that people in ancient times commonly had open communication with angels in heaven, but this communication was gradually closed off as people became less and less spiritual in their orientation. See, for example, *Sacred Scripture* 21; *Secrets of Heaven* 784, 920, 2179:3, 3482; *Heaven and Hell* 87. Compare note 197, on the lost knowledge of correspondences. [LSW]

169 (in *Sacred Scripture* 7). The concept of correspondence is briefly defined in *Divine Love and Wisdom* 71 as "the mutual relationship between spiritual and earthly things." In its full formulation, it holds that there are two separate "universes" or worlds, one spiritual and one material, that are related to each other through similarity but not through any shared matter or direct continuity. The material world is caused by God through the spiritual world and therefore reflects that constantly changing world; physical phenomena and events *offer images of*—that is, "answer to" or "correspond to"—spiritual phenomena and events. For an extended discussion of correspondence and the related

phenomenon of "representation," see *Secrets of Heaven* 2987–3002; for a brief and contextual overview, see the "universal principles" listed in *Heaven and Hell* 356:15. [JSR, SS, GFD]

170 (in *Sacred Scripture* 7). The Latin terms here translated "a goal, the means to it, and its result" are *finis, causa,* and *effectus,* traditionally translated "end," "cause," and "effect," respectively. Swedenborg is here using concepts his readers would have recognized as having been drawn from Aristotle's theory of causation; see, for example, Aristotle *Physics* 194b–195b (= Aristotle 1984, 332–334). [GFD, SS]

171 (in *Sacred Scripture* 7). Swedenborg here refers to his work *Heaven and Hell,* published in London in 1758. [Editors]

172 (in *Sacred Scripture* 9). For more on the Word suffering violence, which Swedenborg saw as happening through its being falsified and misused both in its literal meaning and in general, see *Sacred Scripture* 26, 35, 97; *Secrets of Heaven* 3454, 9127; *Divine Providence* 231:3; *Revelation Unveiled* 825, 829; *True Christianity* 260; *Revelation Explained* (= Swedenborg 1994–1997a) §§1048–1050. [LSW]

173 (in *Sacred Scripture* 9). Swedenborg saw human history as divided into five general "churches," or spiritual eras, on which see note 5. Each of these churches was, during its own era, the reigning spiritual institution or paradigm in the world. In this instance "the close of the church" refers to the end of the era associated with the Christian church that had existed from the time of Jesus to Swedenborg's own day. [LSW]

174 (in *Sacred Scripture* 10). A cubit was a varying ancient measurement based on the distance from the elbow to the tips of the fingers—about 18 to 22 inches, or 46 to 56 centimeters; therefore 144 cubits was roughly 240 feet, or 73 meters. [JSR]

175 (in *Sacred Scripture* 10). A stadium (plural: stadia) was an ancient Greek unit of distance equal to about 607 feet, or 185 meters. Twelve thousand stadia, then, would be around 1,380 miles, or 2,220 kilometers. [JSR]

176 (in *Sacred Scripture* 10). On the term "new church" as used here, see note 5. [Editors]

177 (in *Sacred Scripture* 10). This work, referred to in this edition by the short title *New Jerusalem,* was published by Swedenborg in London in 1758. [Editors]

178 (in *Sacred Scripture* 11). For a more detailed account of the spiritual meaning of Revelation 7:4–8, see *Revelation Unveiled* 348–362. [Editors]

179 (in *Sacred Scripture* 13:1). The Latin for the phrase here translated "have become limited to their physical senses" is *sensualis factus,* traditionally translated "having become sensuous" or "having become sensual." In Swedenborg's usage it refers to a state in which people are primarily focused on what is experienced through their physical senses, and base their thinking largely or entirely on information derived from that source. For more on this state, see *Secrets of Heaven* 191–210, 5079–5084, 5094, 5114, 5125–5128, 6844–6845, 10236; *Heaven and Hell* 267; *Divine Love and Wisdom* 254; *True Christianity* 402. [LSW]

180 (in *Sacred Scripture* 13:2). Central to Swedenborg's psychology is the view that a human being has multiple levels, especially levels of the mind, and that these levels can equally well be differentiated as being either "higher" or "lower" or as being either "inner" or "outer" (see *Divine Love and Wisdom* 205–206). The Latin word here translated "earthly" is *naturalis,* literally, "natural." Swedenborg uses this word very broadly both of material things (including all that is human-made) and of the "lower" or "outer" of three levels of the mind or spirit, which are the heavenly (sometimes translated "celestial"),

spiritual, and earthly levels. Within these general levels there are also sublevels. In *Marriage Love* 496 Swedenborg describes three levels of the earthly self: the worldly, the sense-centered, and the body-centered. It is in this context that Swedenborg here speaks of "the most superficial aspects of the earthly self"—although in this case he assigns that position to sensory impressions (that is, to the sense-centered aspects) rather than to the body-centered aspects. [JSR, LHC, LSW]

181 (in *Sacred Scripture* 13:4). For similar statements elsewhere about the importance to the spiritual meaning of every single word in the text of the Bible, see *Secrets of Heaven* 1870, 7933:3, 9349; *Last Judgment* 41; *Draft of "Sacred Scripture"* §4 [Rogers's numbering] = §14 [Whitehead's numbering] (= Swedenborg 1997c, 13). [LSW]

182 (in *Sacred Scripture* 13:4). The prophetic books of the Old Testament in Swedenborg's enumeration of them are: Psalms, Isaiah, Jeremiah, Lamentations, Ezekiel, Daniel, Hosea, Joel, Amos, Obadiah, Jonah, Micah, Nahum, Habakkuk, Zephaniah, Haggai, Zechariah, and Malachi. See note 11 on "the Word." [RS]

183 (in *Sacred Scripture* 13:4). The Masoretes were Jewish scribes and scholars of the seventh through eleventh century C.E. who undertook to determine and transmit the authentic text of the Hebrew Scriptures at a time when the only available means was copying by hand. To ensure accurate reproduction, they counted the verses, words, and letters of each book, and scribes were expected to test their final versions against these standards. A colophon at the close of the Book of Deuteronomy in the Torah, for example, lists the number of verses in Deuteronomy, as well as the number of verses, words, and letters in the Torah as a whole. (For a version of this colophon in a modern edition, see Kittel 1950, 320.) [GFD]

184 (in *Sacred Scripture* 14:2). The word "our" is supplied by the translator in recognition of repeated statements in Swedenborg's writings that the Lord himself, not heaven, is the ultimate source of all truth. "Heaven as our source of divine truth" refers to Swedenborg's schema of heaven as a plane of reality and abode of angels that by its nature receives divine truth from God and passes that divine truth on to the minds of humans on earth. According to Swedenborg, this takes place both by the direct inspiring of enlightenment from within and by the inspiring of written texts containing divine truth that readers can then assimilate from outside themselves. For more on this subject, see *Secrets of Heaven* 8805:2, 9503, 10330, 10608; *Heaven and Hell* 13, 126–140; *Revelation Unveiled* 754; *Revelation Explained* (= Swedenborg 1994–1997a) §§55, 502, 644, 1094. [LSW]

185 (in *Sacred Scripture* 15:1). Clarification that follows here and in *Sacred Scripture* 15:2 suggests that by "we learn nothing," Swedenborg means "we learn nothing divine"; that is, we learn nothing about God or our relationship with him. Though the Hebrew text of Isaiah 10:24–34 presents difficulties of interpretation, Swedenborg does not seem to be claiming that it lacks all literal sense. The likely literal meaning was appreciated by scholars even previous to Swedenborg's time: The named towns are known or conjectured to have been situated within about ten miles (sixteen kilometers) to the north of Jerusalem, and are given more or less in order of increasing proximity to that city. Since the theme of the Isaiah chapter is a promise that the Lord will free Israel from the Assyrians, the literal picture presented is thus that of the Assyrian army proceeding town by town toward Jerusalem, but being halted before it can complete its conquest. For examples of previous commentators who understood the passage in this way, see Calvin

[1559] 1854, 1:361–370; White 1709, 81–85; Henry [1708–1710] 1991, 4:55–56. For a map and brief discussion of the location of these towns, see *Archaeology Study Bible* 2017, 975–976. For further comment on the Isaiah passage itself, see Young 1965, 1:373–377; Beyer 2007, 88. [GFD, SS, JSR]

186 (in *Sacred Scripture* 15:2). The first ten verses of Isaiah 11 contain the well-known prophecy of a "peaceable kingdom," in which predatory and domestic animals will dwell together in amity—"the wolf shall live with the lamb" (Isaiah 11:6), for example. This passage is widely interpreted within Christianity as a prophecy of the Lord's Coming because of its opening lines: "A shoot shall come out from the stump of Jesse, and a branch shall grow out of his roots. The spirit of the Lord shall rest upon him . . . ." (New Revised Standard Version). Jesse was the father of David, the founder of the dynasty that was to culminate in the Messiah. See the genealogies of Jesus in Matthew 1:1–17 and Luke 3:23–38, which trace Jesus' lineage through Jesse and David. [LSW, GFD]

187 (in *Sacred Scripture* 16). On these angel guardians, see note 118. [Editors]

188 (in *Sacred Scripture* 16). "Urim" and "Thummim" are transliterations of two plural Hebrew words, אוּרִים *('ûrîm)* and תֻּמִּים *(tummîm),* meaning "the lights" and "the perfections," respectively. (Swedenborg says that Thummim means "radiance" in the language of angels; see *True Christianity* 218.) Their exact nature and function are unknown. They are commonly associated with the breastplate of the high priest of the Israelites (Exodus 28:30; Leviticus 8:8). Here Swedenborg seems at first (until he reaches the quotation in subsection 2) to associate them with the high priest's ephod, but in discussion elsewhere in his works he equates them with the stones in the breastplate or with the breastplate itself (see *Secrets of Heaven* 3858:9, 3862:6–7, 6335:2, 9905; *True Christianity* 218; *Revelation Explained* [= Swedenborg 1994–1997a] §431:3, 15). The Jewish historian Flavius Josephus (37 or 38–after 93 C.E.) states: "God declared beforehand, by those twelve stones which the high priest bare on his breast, and which were inserted into his breastplate, when [the Israelites] should be victorious in battle; for so great a splendor shone forth from [the stones] before the army began to march, that all the people were sensible of God's being present for their assistance" (Flavius Josephus *Antiquities of the Jews* 3:8:9 [= Josephus 1997, 105]). Hence the common view that the Urim and Thummim were themselves the twelve stones and grew bright or dimmed in response to questions. This view is reflected in Swedenborg's discussions of them, as seen in the references above, and in *Secrets of Heaven* 6640:2. A comprehensive recent study (Van Dam 1997) does conclude that "Urim and Thummim" should be translated as "perfect light" and that they were believed to authenticate inspired prophecy. According to Van Dam's reconstruction of Jewish belief about their usage, military or political questions with existential significance for the kingdom of Israel would be ritually posed to the high priest; the high priest would then respond in the form of an ecstatic or prophetic utterance, and the Urim and Thummim on his breastplate would shine with "perfect light" if his words had been sent by Jehovah. Nevertheless, 1 Samuel 14:41–42, the most specific description of their use, suggests that they were a kind of lot. Other references in the Hebrew Bible give little indication of what they were or how they were used: Numbers 27:21; Deuteronomy 33:8; 1 Samuel 28:6; Ezra 2:63; Nehemiah 7:65. [LHC, RS, JSR, DNG, LSW]

189 (in *Sacred Scripture* 16). For a description of the ark with its cherubim and mercy seat, as well as the table, lampstand, and incense altar, see Exodus 25:10–40; 30:1–10; 37. For the tent and tabernacle, see Exodus 26; 36:8–38. For Aaron's garments, see Exodus

28; 39:1–31. For grain and meat offerings, see Leviticus 1–7. For Sabbaths and appointed festivals, see Exodus 34:21–22; Leviticus 23; Numbers 28:9–10, 16–31; 29:12–39; Deuteronomy 16:1–17. Compare note 145, on the three major annual festivals (or feasts) that all Israelite males were commanded to attend. [RS, LSW]

190 (in *Sacred Scripture* 17:2). For the biblical origins of the concept of the marriage of the Lord with the church, also called "the heavenly marriage," see note 143. Swedenborg saw the kingdom of God, which is the Lord's metaphorical "bride," as comprising both heaven and the church, the latter (in Swedenborg's usage of the term) composed of everyone who has faith in the Lord and lives a good life. See, for example, *Secrets of Heaven* 29:2, 6823; *The Lord* 42; *True Christianity* 416. [LSW]

191 (in *Sacred Scripture* 17:2). For additional exegesis of Matthew 25:1–12, see *Secrets of Heaven* 4635–4638; *Revelation Explained* (= Swedenborg 1994–1997a) §§187:4, 252:8, 375:41. For more on Swedenborg's principle that in the afterlife people remain as they were inwardly while living in the world, see *Secrets of Heaven* 4588, 7186:3, 8991, 10596; *Heaven and Hell* 363, 470–484; *Divine Providence* 277b; *Spiritual Experiences* (= Swedenborg 1998–2013) §§2803–2805, 4645a–4646a; *Revelation Explained* 860; and the portion of *Rough Copy of "Secrets of Heaven"* extracted and published as *On Miracles* §2877 [Acton's numbering] = §8 [Johnson's numbering] (= Swedenborg 1942, 407–408). [LSW]

192 (in *Sacred Scripture* 17:3). For "daughters of Zion" and "daughters of Jerusalem," see Isaiah 3:16, 17; 4:4; Luke 23:28; for "daughters of Israel," see Deuteronomy 23:17; Judges 11:40; 2 Samuel 1:24. For the anointing of the Israelite church's sacred objects with oil, see Exodus 40:9–11; Numbers 7:1. [RS, JSR]

193 (in *Sacred Scripture* 17:4). For more on Jesus' miracles—as well as miracles in the historical and prophetic books of the Bible—pointing to states characteristic of the church as established by the Lord, see *Secrets of Heaven* 2916:4, 6988:3, 7337; *Revelation Explained* (= Swedenborg 1994–1997a) §376:29. [LSW]

194 (in *Sacred Scripture* 18:3). Swedenborg here assigns five animals just three meanings. From other passages it becomes clear that innocence is represented by lambs (*Secrets of Heaven* 10132); caring is represented by sheep (*Secrets of Heaven* 9263:4); and earthly feelings are represented by goats (*Revelation Explained* [= Swedenborg 1994–1997a] §730:43), calves (*True Christianity* 623:1), and oxen (*Secrets of Heaven* 9090). [JSR]

195 (in *Sacred Scripture* 18:4). As was the custom in his day, Swedenborg refers to Psalms as a book of David. [Editors]

196 (in *Sacred Scripture* 18:4). The original Hebrew of this phrase in Psalms 29:6 is בֶּן־רְאֵמִים (ben-rə'ēmîm). The Latin translation Swedenborg adopts here, *filium monoceratum*, accords with the Septuagint's υἱὸς μονοκερώτων (*huiòs monokeróton*), literally, "son of [creatures] having one horn." The Hebrew word is now thought to denote the aurochs, a species of wild cattle once common in Europe, Asia, and North Africa. It is now extinct. [GFD]

197 (in *Sacred Scripture* 20:1). On its face, this statement seems self-contradictory, but the meaning is clear from Swedenborg's treatment of this theme elsewhere: the knowledge of correspondence, widespread in ancient times, died out and was not revived until Swedenborg's day. This extinction is mentioned in *Sacred Scripture* 22. Compare note 168, on the lost knowledge about heaven. [SS]

198 (in *Sacred Scripture* 20:2). Swedenborg here echoes the prevailing view of his times that Egyptian hieroglyphics were a symbolic and pictorial language, a concept that

dated back to the Greek historian Diodorus Siculus of the first century B.C.E. and the Greek philosopher Plotinus (205–270). [JSR]

199 (in *Sacred Scripture* 20:2). By "fables" here, Swedenborg means specifically myths, typically about the doings of gods and heroes, rather than short moral tales like the "fables" of the legendary Greek writer Aesop. Swedenborg himself identifies these myths with those collected by the Roman poet Ovid (43 B.C.E.–17 C.E.) in the poem *Metamorphoses;* see *Draft of "Sacred Scripture"* §7:3 [Rogers's numbering] = §18 [Whitehead's numbering] (= Swedenborg 1997c, 20). A few specific mythic symbols Swedenborg cites as examples of correspondences lingering into ancient Greek times are the spring of Helicon, the winged horse Pegasus, and the nine Muses; in addition to the passage just cited, see *Marriage Love* 182:2; *True Christianity* 693:2. [SS]

200 (in *Sacred Scripture* 20:2). On Swedenborg's concept of various "churches," or spiritual eras on earth, see note 5. The term "ancient churches" here may refer to different strains of religion and culture within the period encompassed by the "earliest church" and the "early church" discussed in that note. Compare the opening sentences of *New Jerusalem* 9, which refer to many churches going into the making of one in ancient times. [LSW]

201 (in *Sacred Scripture* 20:2). On these three feasts, see note 145. [Editors]

202 (in *Sacred Scripture* 21). This is a reference to the biblical Flood described in Genesis 7–8. *Secrets of Heaven* 482 states that the first eleven chapters of Genesis do not contain "any history that is literally accurate." Instead these early stories, as Swedenborg interprets them, are metaphorical or "correspondential" accounts of the early spiritual development of humanity. He takes the story of the Flood itself to describe a kind of spiritual suffocation (see *Secrets of Heaven* 662) that happened at a particular time and marked a radical step in the development of human nature. On "the earliest church" in relation to the other four "churches" (that is, the spiritual eras Swedenborg identifies in world history), see note 5. [GFD, LSW]

203 (in *Sacred Scripture* 21). For a discussion of the meaning of the term *Canaan,* see the appendix on pages 529–530. [Editors]

204 (in *Sacred Scripture* 22). In eighteenth-century Europe, harsh and even virulent statements against other religions were very common. (For illustrative examples focusing on Sweden, see Helander 2004, 319–344.) In that context, Swedenborg's comments of this kind seem relatively mild, but he nonetheless includes in this volume some statements that modern readers may find offensive or distasteful. His opprobrium often concerns Jews of Old and New Testament times and is no doubt based largely on passages in the Bible, but it often has a more general application. Other examples in this volume include statements that Jews of Bible times were "idolatrous at heart" (*Sacred Scripture* 23:4), that they did violence to Jesus and the Word and even annihilated the latter (*The Lord* 15:2; *Sacred Scripture* 35, 79:1, 79:7), that they scorned and rejected other nations and religious groups (*Sacred Scripture* 40:3), and that they deserve to live in harsh conditions in the afterlife (*Supplements* 79–82). On offensive material in Swedenborg's works generally, see the translator's preface, pages 4–6. [JSR, SS]

205 (in *Sacred Scripture* 23:3). The term "the East" in the Matthew 2:1–12 account of the wise men, or Magi, visiting Jesus is a vague reference to lands east of the Jewish world. Here Swedenborg seems to be using the term to refer generally to the region now known as the Middle East. Compare *Sacred Scripture* 21. [LSW, SS]

206 (in *Sacred Scripture* 23:3). For more on the meaning of the star that went before the wise men, see *Secrets of Heaven* 1808, 4697; *Revelation Explained* (= Swedenborg 1994–1997a) §422:20. For more on the meanings of gold, frankincense, and myrrh and their relationship to worship, see *Secrets of Heaven* 10177; *Revelation Unveiled* 277; *Revelation Explained* 324, 491. [LSW]

207 (in *Sacred Scripture* 23:4). The shift to the present tense in this paragraph suggests that Swedenborg is referring to those in his own times who study the Bible to gain either cabalistic ("mystical") or alchemical wisdom—thus the reference to gold, which could supposedly be produced from base metals by alchemy. On the origin and progress of Jewish mysticism from the medieval period up to the eighteenth century, the classic text is Scholem 1946. There were numerous alchemical readings of Scripture in Swedenborg's times; see Principe and Newman 2001, 398; Matton 1988. [JSR, GFD]

208 (in *Sacred Scripture* 24). "The Reformation" refers to the Protestant Reformation in sixteenth-century Europe, led by such figures as Martin Luther (1483–1546), John Calvin (1509–1564), and Ulrich Zwingli (1484–1531). Swedenborg here identifies this era of change with the introduction of the two innovations he goes on to mention: the principle of differentiating between faith and caring, otherwise known as the Lutheran principle of salvation by faith alone (see note 209); and worshiping three gods as one, or understanding the Trinity as three divine persons existing from eternity (see note 85) instead of as one God who developed over time into three "components" (see *The Lord* 46–61; *True Christianity* 173–174). Generally, Swedenborg maintains that the erroneous doctrine of the Trinity as three divine persons originated in the First Council of Nicaea in 325 C.E., or in other words, with the Roman Catholic Church rather than with the arrival of Protestantism. For his discussion of the Council of Nicaea, see *True Christianity* 632–634. [SS, LSW]

209 (in *Sacred Scripture* 24). The expression "faith alone" refers to a teaching found in Protestantism, most notably in the Lutheran and Reformed (Calvinist) traditions. More fully known as "the doctrine of justification by grace through faith alone," it holds that one is judged to be just by God and therefore saved from damnation through a grace bestowed strictly on the grounds of one's faith in Jesus Christ, and not at all through good works, which are seen as *resulting* from saving faith, but not contributing to salvation. See, for discussion of the Lutheran teaching, the Solid Declaration of the Formula of Concord, article 4 (= Kolb and Wengert 2000, 574–581), and the Augsburg Confession, article 6 (= Kolb and Wengert 2000, 41). For more on Swedenborg's response to this teaching, see *Faith* 44–72, as well as note 148. [SS, LSW]

210 (in *Sacred Scripture* 25). Swedenborg is here referring to the biblical exegesis and Christian theology contained in his own theological writings, which he said were revealed to him by the Lord for the use of the new church, or new spiritual era, that he saw as beginning in his day. See *True Christianity* 779–780, and compare note 5 on the five major "churches" Swedenborg identified as succeeding one another throughout human spiritual history. On Swedenborg's spiritual experiences, see note 3. [LSW]

211 (in *Sacred Scripture* 25). For Swedenborg's more detailed interpretation of Revelation 19:11–19, see *White Horse* 1–5; *Revelation Unveiled* 820–833. For his more detailed interpretation of Revelation 17:3, see *Revelation Unveiled* 722–724; *Revelation Explained* (= Swedenborg 1994–1997a) §§1036–1041. [LSW]

212 (in *Sacred Scripture* 26:1). For more on the Bible in heaven and the engagement of angels in its spiritual meaning in contrast to the engagement of people on earth in the

Bible's literal meaning, see *Sacred Scripture* 64, 67, 70–75; *Secrets of Heaven* 9396; *Heaven and Hell* 259; *Spiritual Experiences* (= Swedenborg 1998–2013) §§5561–5563, 5964–5965; *Draft of "Sacred Scripture"* §14 [Rogers's numbering] = §§30–35 [Whitehead's numbering] (= Swedenborg 1997c, 34–37). For more on the relationship between heaven and earth through the Bible, see note 164. [LSW]

213 (in *Sacred Scripture* 26:1). For more on what closes heaven to people, see *Sacred Scripture* 96a; *Secrets of Heaven* 2750; *Heaven and Hell* 384; *Divine Providence* 208–209; *True Christianity* 719–720; *Revelation Explained* (= Swedenborg 1994–1997a) §§797–798, 812, 1111. The common thread running through Swedenborg's statements in these passages is that those who reject spiritual truth and live evil lives close heaven to themselves. For more on how heaven is opened to people both through the Bible and generally, see note 164. [LSW]

214 (in *Sacred Scripture* 26:2). In *Divine Providence* 154–174, Swedenborg states that rather than directly implanting truth into people's minds, which would take away their individuality and sense of self, the Lord provides people with means of learning truth for themselves (the Bible being primary among these). As people engage in the study and effort of learning for themselves, the Lord inwardly gives them light so that they can understand what they are learning and see how it applies to their lives. Thus in Swedenborg's account the learning process has been designed by the Lord so that people have a sense of learning for themselves, though in fact the Lord is teaching them from within. By operating in this way, says Swedenborg, the Lord makes it possible for people to feel that their minds and lives are their own, so that they can have a basis on which to have relationships with one another and with God. [LSW]

215 (in *Sacred Scripture* 26:2). On these angel guardians, see note 118. [Editors]

216 (in *Sacred Scripture* 26:3). In the first edition, the text from here to the end of §26 is marked off by double quotation marks in the left margin. This is a typographical device often used in the eighteenth century to highlight material or indicate that it came originally from another source. In this case Swedenborg is quoting material he has written down twice before, though he had not published it previously. He first recorded the experience with some different details in an October 1748 entry in his *Spiritual Experiences* (= Swedenborg 1998–2013) §3605$^{1}/_{2}$. In 1762, the year before the publication of the present work, he recounted the story in *Draft of "Sacred Scripture"* §1 [in both Rogers's numbering and Whitehead's numbering] (= Swedenborg 1997c, 5–6) in a form very similar to this instance of it. He later repeated the story almost verbatim in *Revelation Unveiled* 255 and *True Christianity* 277. [GFD, LSW]

217 (in *Sacred Scripture* 26:5). In the version of this story found in *True Christianity* 277 this sentence is expanded to read, "The angels of the highest heaven, who are the wisest angels, look like little children from a distance because of their innocence." For more on angels of the highest heaven looking like children from a distance but like adults at close range, see *Marriage Love* 75:4, 137; *True Christianity* 508:6; *Sketch for "Coda to True Christianity"* (= Swedenborg 1996h) §37:4. [LSW]

Notes to *Sacred Scripture* Chapter 3, §§27–36

218 (in *Sacred Scripture* 27). The statement that "what is last is a foundation" is in line with the discussion of creation in *Divine Love and Wisdom* 290–304. There Swedenborg describes how the universe was created from the top down, so to speak: an emanation

from God passed down through various levels and became, or "terminated in," material substance. Swedenborg frequently refers to this terminating level as the base or foundation of the higher levels, a terminology that runs counter to the assumption that a base or foundation is built first—before the building that is to rest on it, for instance. For further discussion of this concept of a base or foundation as the final element of a created series, see *Divine Love and Wisdom* 209–221, under the propositions "The final level is the composite, vessel, and foundation of the prior levels" and "The vertical levels find their full realization and power in their final form." The principle has wide applicability in Swedenborg's writings. In *Divine Love and Wisdom* 214, for example, he describes how human desires find their expression and their dwelling in the outward actions that flow from them. Though the desire comes first, motivates the act, and directs it through thought, the act provides the foundation in real existence for the desire, and also expresses the desire both generally and in detail. For more on this principle in the context of a discussion of the literal meaning of the Bible, see *True Christianity* 210–213. For references to *Secrets of Heaven* on this general subject, see *New Jerusalem* 47:10. [LSW]

219 (in *Sacred Scripture* 28). With his reference to "the learned world," Swedenborg seems to be implying merely that the terms he mentions here are part of common philosophical parlance, not that the learned world in general endorses his particular use of them in this context. On the series of a goal, the means to it, and its result (sometimes translated "end," "cause," and "effect," respectively), see note 170 and *Divine Love and Wisdom* 167–172. For discussion of the centrality of this series in Swedenborg's thought, see Sewall 1888, 3–92. The concepts of "being" (Latin *esse*), "becoming" *(fieri),* and "achieving full manifestation" *(existere)* are treated by many philosophical luminaries, from the pre-Socratics and Aristotle through the present day, often in relation to explorations of movement, change, and immutability. [SS]

220 (in *Sacred Scripture* 29). The first edition here in effect says that "Jonathan told David that he would hide in the field," but both the grammatical context of Swedenborg's paraphrase and the biblical statements that underlie it make clear that the two names should be reversed. [JSR]

221 (in *Sacred Scripture* 32). On these works, some of which were eventually written and published and some of which were not, see note 4. [Editors]

222 (in *Sacred Scripture* 33). The pleura is a membrane that envelops and cushions the lungs in mammals, providing lubrication and protection. Its benefits include the separation of one lung from another, which allows for continued respiration even if the thorax is breached and one lung collapses, and which prevents one lung from compressing the other when the body is turned on its side. Furthermore, by separating the lungs from the heart, it allows the heart to continue to move freely when the body is turned on its back. For Swedenborg's writings on the pleura, see *The Soul's Domain* volume 2, §§349–353 (= Swedenborg [1744–1745] 1960, §§411–415). [SS]

223 (in *Sacred Scripture* 33). Part of the dura mater, now generally referred to simply as the dura, lines the inside of the skull, surrounding and protecting the brain. It supports the two hemispheres of the brain and the various sinuses (liquid-filled spaces) within it. For Swedenborg's discussion of the dura, see *First Draft of Three Transactions on the Brain* (= Swedenborg 1976b) vol. 1, §§184–230. [SS]

224 (in *Sacred Scripture* 34). On the Bible having several deeper layers of meaning related to spiritual and divine matters, see note 11 toward its end. On the parallelism

between the structure of inner meanings in the Bible and the various kingdoms named here, see *Sacred Scripture* 6. On the corresponding levels within a human being, see note 180. [Editors]

225 (in *Sacred Scripture* 35). "The outermost form of truth" as found in the "outermost meaning" and "the Word in its outermost forms" mentioned later in this section is the same as the much more frequently mentioned "literal meaning" of the Bible. See *Secrets of Heaven* 9406; *Revelation Explained* (= Swedenborg 1994–1997a) §§419:20, 593, 768:3, 1066:4, 1087:2; *Draft of "Sacred Scripture"* §10 [Rogers's numbering] = §§25–26 [Whitehead's numbering] (= Swedenborg 1997c, 27–29). For more on the literal meaning of the Bible, see note 17. [LSW]

226 (in *Sacred Scripture* 35). A Nazirite was one who vowed herself or himself to live apart in holiness according to the specific discipline ("the law of the Nazirite") described in Numbers 6:1–21. One of the requirements of this discipline was that the Nazirite leave her or his hair uncut; this is most likely the basis of the connection Swedenborg makes between the Hebrew word and hair. (Compare his discussion of this term in the passage he references here, *Sacred Scripture* 49:2–4.) From the linguistic point of view, the Hebrew in question, נָזִיר *(nāzîr),* "Nazirite," is best regarded as a passive formation from the verb נָזַר *(nāzar),* "to set aside," "to devote." See, for example, Ezekiel 14:7, where the verb is used of Israelites who separate themselves from the Lord and practice idolatry. However, Swedenborg may also have in mind the closely related Hebrew word נֵזֶר *(nēzer),* whose basic meaning is "crown," but which is applied in Jeremiah 7:29 to the long, unshorn hair of a woman; see Brown, Driver, and Briggs 1996, 634, under נֵזֶר. [GFD, RS]

Notes to *Sacred Scripture* Chapter 4, §§37–49

227 (in *Sacred Scripture* 38:1). An example of such a "collapsed object" might be a hand telescope. If the large end of the telescope were placed lens down on a table top and the telescope were fully extended upward, it would illustrate elements in a sequential arrangement: starting at the upper end, the narrowest cylinder would be first, the middle-size cylinder would be next, and the widest of all would be last. If the small end were then pushed down, collapsing the telescope into its most compact form, it would illustrate the same elements, but now in a simultaneous arrangement. The cylinder that was first and at the top would now be in the center, and the "later" cylinders would now surround it. Swedenborg's frequent allusions to "inner" and "higher" as opposed to "outer" and "lower" elements suggest that for him this manner of visualizing the contrast between the simultaneous and the sequential (1) captures an important facet of the way spiritual reality is both above and within physical reality, and (2) helps to show how the stages that have led up to something are also present within it; see *Divine Providence* 12. [JSR]

228 (in *Sacred Scripture* 40:1). The Latin word here translated "adapted" is *accommodata,* which points to the technical term *accommodation,* employed in Christian theology since at least the time of the church fathers. Elsewhere in his theological writings Swedenborg states generally that accommodation involves expressing through the use of material images and events ideas that in themselves are divine or spiritual truth, and thus above the material level. In this way people on earth, whose minds are shaped by time, space, and the material objects and events that occur within time and space, can have some means of grasping ideas that in themselves do not partake of time, space, or

matter. For more on semblances of truth and the adaptation of truth to the comprehension of humans on earth, see *Secrets of Heaven* 3207, 3739, 7381, 8443, 8920; *New Jerusalem* 262; *True Christianity* 257; *Revelation Explained* (= Swedenborg 1994–1997a) §816:2. For the various senses of the term *accommodation* in Christian theology, see the *Oxford Dictionary of the Christian Church* 2005, under "accommodation"; Muller 1985, under "accommodation." For a survey of the concept in Jewish and Christian thought, see Benin 1993, and in Augustine's writings in particular, see Benin 1993, 94–112; Polman 1961, 57–58. [LSW, SS]

229 (in *Sacred Scripture* 41). For a concise discussion of heavenly light versus earthly light, see *Heaven and Hell* 126–140. In essence, Swedenborg says there that heavenly light comes from the Lord as the sun of heaven, as opposed to earthly light, which comes from the physical sun. Heavenly light is equated with truth: "To the extent to which angels are open to divine truth, . . . they have light" (*Heaven and Hell* 128). For more on the light of heaven in comparison to the light of the physical world, see *Secrets of Heaven* 1521–1534, 3195, 3223–3224, 3636, 4415; *New Jerusalem* 49. [RS]

230 (in *Sacred Scripture* 44:1). On the Urim and Thummim, see note 188. [Editors]

231 (in *Sacred Scripture* 44:3). *Secrets of Heaven* was published by Swedenborg in eight volumes between 1749 and 1756. [Editors]

232 (in *Sacred Scripture* 44:4). For some of these experiences of seeing precious stones and diamonds among angels and spirits in the spiritual world, see *Marriage Love* 15, 20, 42:3–4, 136, 315:3. On correspondence as the cause of precious stones and their appearance, see *Revelation Unveiled* 231; *Revelation Explained* (= Swedenborg 1994–1997a) §717. [LSW]

233 (in *Sacred Scripture* 46). In this context "the law" refers to the Ten Commandments as recorded in Exodus 20:1–17 and Deuteronomy 5:6–21, which were written on the two stone tablets and kept in the ark of the covenant. In other contexts "the Law" may mean the first five books of the Bible (Genesis, Exodus, Leviticus, Numbers, and Deuteronomy), which make up one of the three divisions of the Hebrew Scriptures, the other two being the "Prophets" and the "Writings" (see note 43). "The law" may also refer to the entire Bible. See *Secrets of Heaven* 6752, 8695, 9416, 10451; *The Lord* 8–10; *True Christianity* 288. [LSW]

234 (in *Sacred Scripture* 49:1). On Swedenborg's frequent use of "hells" in the plural, see note 21. [Editors]

235 (in *Sacred Scripture* 49:2). Mark 16:19 reads: "So then the Lord Jesus, after he had spoken to them, was taken up into heaven and sat down at the right hand of God" (New Revised Standard Version). [GFD]

236 (in *Sacred Scripture* 49:2). On Swedenborg's interpretation of "Nazirite" and "Naziriteship" as "hair," see note 226. [Editors]

237 (in *Sacred Scripture* 49:5). "The Ancient of Days" is a name applied to God. In the Bible it appears in only three verses: Daniel 7:9, 13, 22. All are in the segment of the Book of Daniel that is written in Aramaic rather than in Hebrew. [RS, LSW]

Notes to *Sacred Scripture* Chapter 5, §§50–61

238 (in *Sacred Scripture* 51:1). On correspondences, see note 169. [Editors]

239 (in *Sacred Scripture* 51:7). John 3:17–18 reads: "Indeed, God did not send the Son into the world to condemn the world, but in order that the world might be saved

through him. Those who believe in him are not condemned; but those who do not believe are condemned already, because they have not believed in the name of the only Son of God." John 12:47–48 reads: "I do not judge anyone who hears my words and does not keep them, for I came not to judge the world, but to save the world. The one who rejects me and does not receive my word has a judge; on the last day the word that I have spoken will serve as judge." (All verses cited from the New Revised Standard Version.) [GFD]

240 (in *Sacred Scripture* 57). Swedenborg here uses the term "genuine truth" (Latin *genuinum verum*) instead of the term "divine truth" (Latin *Divinum Verum*) used in the original proposition in §50. [Editors]

241 (in *Sacred Scripture* 61:1). The belief described here is derived by Christians from Bible passages such as Daniel 12:3: "Those who are wise shall shine like the brightness of the sky, and those who lead many to righteousness, like the stars forever and ever" (New Revised Standard Version). See also Matthew 13:43; Philippians 2:14–15. [GFD, LSW]

242 (in *Sacred Scripture* 61:1). Though Swedenborg's theology does not include archangels, this higher order of angels originating in postexilic Judaism was an accepted part of the Christian theology of his day. Among them Michael and Raphael were the most conspicuous. Michael is mentioned in the Protestant canon of the Bible (see Jude verse 9; Revelation 12:7). Raphael is not mentioned in the Protestant canon, but plays a prominent role in the apocryphal Book of Tobit. There Raphael says that he is one of seven angels who stand before the Lord (Tobit 12:15). On Swedenborg's view of angels, see note 13. [JSR, GFD]

243 (in *Sacred Scripture* 61:2). "Inflow" (Latin *influxus,* traditionally translated "influx") is a term derived from philosophy that denotes a one-way influence of one level or entity on another. In Swedenborg's time and before, a vigorous debate had been going on about how the soul or nonmaterial aspect of a human being and the body or material aspect affect each other. In this debate, Swedenborg took a firm stand in favor of "spiritual inflow," the position that what is spiritual acts upon and affects what is physical, but what is physical does not act upon or affect what is spiritual (see his 1769 work *Soul-Body Interaction;* see also *Divine Providence* 314:1; *Secrets of Heaven* 6322:2). The reverse position was known as physical inflow. In his theological works, Swedenborg uses the term *inflow* of several one-way influences: the influence of a higher/inner/spiritual part of a human being on a lower/outer/earthly part (see, for example, *Secrets of Heaven* 1707:2–4); the influence of the spiritual world on the physical world (see, for example, *Divine Love and Wisdom* 340); the influence of the will on the intellect (see *Divine Providence* 233:7; *True Christianity* 50, 395:3); and here, divine influence on human beings. [JSR]

Notes to *Sacred Scripture* Chapter 6, §§62–69

244 (in *Sacred Scripture* 63). The concept of "being truly human," as it appears in Swedenborg's theological writings, involves the opening up and constructive use of the higher levels of spiritual love and rationality that are unique to humans. True humanity, according to Swedenborg, does not reside in the physical body or the natural drives that humans have in common with animals, but in the ability to love the Lord and love the neighbor, and to choose to act on these loves intelligently and effectively in preference to mere animal drives and the desire for personal pleasure, power, and benefit. Ultimately, to be truly human is to be in the image and likeness of God, who is the

only *fully* human being in existence by virtue of his infinitely human love, wisdom, and power. For more on this subject, see *Secrets of Heaven* 1894, 2293, 3860, 7424, 8979, 9503; *New Jerusalem* 33; *True Christianity* 69, 328, 417. [LSW]

245 (in *Sacred Scripture* 64:1). In many places throughout his theological writings when Swedenborg is explaining the spiritual meaning of the Bible, he makes statements to the effect that a particular understanding of a passage is "how the angels in heaven understand it." See, for example, *Secrets of Heaven* 1025:2–3, 4373:2, 4976:2, 6226:2, 8906, 10568, 10604; *Revelation Unveiled* 194, 364, 882; *Revelation Explained* (= Swedenborg 1994–1997a) §§328:4, 710:25. For instances in which Swedenborg specifically mentions how angels in heaven understood the Bible spiritually while he himself was reading it, see *Secrets of Heaven* 64–65, 1769–1771, 2592. For more on the difference in the way the heavenly angels and the spiritual angels understand the Bible, in addition to the discussion in the immediately following sections of the current work, see *Secrets of Heaven* 2157, 2275; *Draft of "Sacred Scripture"* §§8:2–3, 14 [Rogers's numbering] = §§23, 30–35 [Whitehead's numbering] (= Swedenborg 1997c, 25–26, 34–37). For more on the connection between heaven and earth by means of the Bible, see note 164. [LSW]

246 (in *Sacred Scripture* 64:2). For one place in which Swedenborg speaks further on spirits abusing this connection between particular passages in the Bible and specific communities of heaven, see *Revelation Explained* (= Swedenborg 1994–1997a) §832:2. Compare *Revelation Explained* 816:3; *Draft of "Sacred Scripture"* §18 [Rogers's numbering] = §§45–48 [Whitehead's numbering] (= Swedenborg 1997c, 44–45) on particular passages in the Bible communicating with particular communities in heaven. [LSW]

247 (in *Sacred Scripture* 66). By the "juice" of the nerve fibers, Swedenborg likely means a thin fluid that he believed flowed through the nerves, which he thought were hollow in the center. By "the fine fluid of the soul" he means an even finer fluid that (as he believed) could be found in the origins of the fibers and gave rise to the "juice." This finer fluid was commonly called "the animal spirit" (the Latin here is *spiritum animalem*), where "animal" means "pertaining to the *anima,* or soul" and "spirit" means an extremely fine fluid. For Swedenborg's description of these substances, see *Draft on the Fiber* (= Swedenborg 1976a) §§201–202, where he refers to further discussion at *Dynamics of the Soul's Domain* (= Swedenborg [1740–1741] 1955) part 2, §§208–366, and *Draft on the Soul's Fluid* (= Swedenborg 1984a, 75–92). On the tubelike nature of nerve fibers, see *Draft on the Fiber* 117a: "Whether we say fiber, or vessel, or duct, they are all nevertheless little canals, because hollow and permeable." For a discussion of the term *animal spirits,* including references to its occurrences in Swedenborg's scientific works, see Odhner 1933; for a general history of the concept of animal spirit, see Smith and others 2012. [SS]

248 (in *Sacred Scripture* 66). The tripartite enumeration of the types of sap seems to have arisen from the analogy Swedenborg is drawing between human anatomy and that of plants: both are seen as circulating three vital fluids, the human in its blood vessels and nerve fibers, the tree in the tissues that reach from the roots to the seeds. Current biology separates sap into two broad categories: the xylem sap, which carries nutrients from the roots up the height of the plant, and the phloem sap, which carries nutrients from production or storage areas to the places the nutrients are required. [SS, GMC]

249 (in *Sacred Scripture* 66). This passage reflects a premodern belief about how minerals are formed within the earth. Many alchemical and mystical theories about

this process had been developed; they still persisted in Swedenborg's day, and as a government supervisor of Sweden's mining industry, Swedenborg would have been very familiar with them. In sum, the earth was thought to be a vast womb in which minerals form from raw mineral substances in underground veins. (The term still used to describe the surrounding rocky substance from which the ore is extracted is *matrix,* Latin for "womb.") The minerals listed here appear by rank according to the relative "nobility" they possessed in the premodern classification of metals. Thus the parallels in *Sacred Scripture* 65–66 line up in progressively finer order as: the earthly, spiritual, and heavenly meanings of the Word; the blood, nerve fluid, and the fine fluid of the soul (see note 247); the three types of plant sap (see note 248); and the hidden exhalations or gases that produce the three metals iron, silver, and gold. (Swedenborg inverts the order in this last example and gives the finest substance first.) For a more detailed version of the comparison, see *True Christianity* 237. On categories of metals, and early theories concerning their formation, see Collier 1934, 399–427; Emerton 1984, 201–205; Laudan 1987, 42–69; Oldroyd 1996, 17, 32, 34, 50. [GMC, JSR, SS]

250 (in *Sacred Scripture* 68). On these levels and the sequential process of their opening in us during our lifetime on earth, see part 3 of *Divine Love and Wisdom,* especially §§230–241. [GFD]

Notes to *Sacred Scripture* Chapter 7, §§70–75

251 (in *Sacred Scripture* 70). On Swedenborg's view that all angels are people who have gone on to live in heaven after death, see note 13. The spirits of the dead have to some extent been viewed as "people just as we are in this world" for thousands of years. See, for example, the story in 1 Samuel 28:3–25 of Saul consulting a medium to communicate with the spirit of Samuel. In Swedenborg's theology, spirits are humans who have lived on earth but are now residents of the world of spirits, an intermediate realm between heaven and hell (see *Heaven and Hell* 421–422), although "evil spirits" may also refer to humans who are now residing in hell. For a general description of the spiritual world and its inhabitants, see note 141. [RS, LSW]

252 (in *Sacred Scripture* 71:2). Swedenborg provides extensive commentary throughout his theological works on the spiritual meaning of various numbers used in the Bible. For a few of his more general statements on numbers having deeper meanings, and those meanings being perceived by angels in heaven in place of the numbers themselves, see *Secrets of Heaven* 487:2, 493, 813; *Heaven and Hell* 263; *Revelation Unveiled* 10. For the symbolism of specific numbers, as described in *Secrets of Heaven,* see the following: On the number one, see §§1013, 1285, 1316. Two: §§649, 720, 755:2, 900. Three: §§482, 720, 900, 901. Four: §1686. Five: §§649, 798, 1686. Six: §§62, 84–85. Seven: §§395, 433, 482:1. Eight: §2044. Nine: §§1988, 2075. Ten: §468:4. Eleven: §9616. Twelve: §§575, 577, 648:2. This is only a very small sampling of passages that deal with the meaning of these numbers. For other perspectives on the meaning of sacred numbers, see Schneider 1995 and Lawlor 1982. [LSW, LHC, RS]

Notes to *Sacred Scripture* Chapter 8, §§76–79

253 (in *Sacred Scripture* 77). Swedenborg is here alluding to John 6:63: "It is the spirit that gives life; the flesh is useless. The words that I have spoken to you are spirit and life"; to Romans 8:6: "To set the mind on the flesh is death, but to set the mind on the spirit

is life and peace"; and to 2 Corinthians 3:5–6: ". . . God, who has made us competent to be ministers of a new covenant, not of letter but of spirit; for the letter kills, but the spirit gives life." (All verses cited from the New Revised Standard Version.) [GFD, LSW]

254 (in *Sacred Scripture* 79:2). In the Bible, Ephraim is the younger son of the patriarch Joseph (Genesis 41:52; 46:20) and the eponymous ancestor of one of the tribes of Israel. In a story told in Genesis 48 (which is cited slightly further on in the translation), Jacob gives primacy to Ephraim over his older brother Manasseh. In the historical period of Israel, Ephraim (the tribe) came to occupy the central hill country of Canaan. In the monarchical period of Israel (from about 1000 to 586 B.C.E.), the importance of Ephraim as a tribe is indicated by the fact that in many biblical passages—such as those quoted here by Swedenborg—Ephraim is used as a synecdoche for the northern kingdom of Israel, though the latter included ten of the twelve tribes; see Metzger and Coogan 1993, 190, under "Ephraim." For some of Swedenborg's key statements on the spiritual meaning of Ephraim, see *Secrets of Heaven* 3325:10, 3969:8, 5354, 6296; *Revelation Explained* (= Swedenborg 1994–1997a) §§440, 624:11–12. [RS, LSW]

255 (in *Sacred Scripture* 79:2). "Filling a bow" (Latin *impletus arcu*) is a rendering of a Hebrew poetic turn of phrase in Zechariah 9:13 that is usually interpreted as painting a picture of Ephraim as an arrow "filling" a bow that will be wielded against Israel's enemies. Compare the New Revised Standard Version translation of this verse: "For I have bent Judah as my bow; I have made Ephraim its arrow. I will arouse your sons, O Zion, against your sons, O Greece, and wield you like a warrior's sword." (Note that the word for "arrow" does not appear in the original Hebrew.) [LSW, JSR]

Notes to *Sacred Scripture* Chapter 9, §§80–90

256 (in *Sacred Scripture* 83). Swedenborg refers here to his work issued in 1764, *Divine Providence,* in which §§2–26 are particularly relevant. [GFD]

257 (in *Sacred Scripture* 83). Swedenborg refers here to his work issued in 1763, *Divine Love and Wisdom*. Part 5 (§§358–432) of that work offers a detailed analysis of a process by which an individual's will (volition) and understanding (discernment) can become united, using imagery drawn from the relationship between heart and lungs, and from the marriage relationship. An overview of the marriage imagery is provided in §398 and is developed in subsequent sections. [GFD]

258 (in *Sacred Scripture* 83). This is one of the works promised in the preface to *The Lord* but never published. See note 4 above. [GFD]

259 (in *Sacred Scripture* 85). Because of the semantic ranges of the underlying Hebrew words, English translations of these biblical passages sometimes have "faithfulness" in place of "truth" and "righteousness" in place of "justice." See the New Revised Standard Version for examples of such translations in the case of Isaiah 11:5 and Psalms 85:11. [LSW, JSR]

260 (in *Sacred Scripture* 87:1). The reference is to the celebratory mood in anticipation of a sacrificial feast. [GFD]

261 (in *Sacred Scripture* 88). The distinction between "Jehovah" and "God" that Swedenborg refers to here is somewhat obscured in most English translations because instead of rendering the Hebrew divine name יהוה, "YHWH" or "YHVH," as a proper name (whether "Jehovah" or some other approximation), translators have often chosen to use the title "the Lord," sometimes set in small caps. On the name Jehovah as used by Swedenborg, see note 9. [GFD]

262 (in *Sacred Scripture* 88). The phrase inserted in brackets here is present in *True Christianity* 253, a passage closely parallel to this one. [JSR]

263 (in *Sacred Scripture* 90:1). Psalms 32:2 reads: "Happy are those to whom the Lord imputes no iniquity, and in whose spirit there is no deceit" (New Revised Standard Version). [GFD]

264 (in *Sacred Scripture* 90:2). Presumably Swedenborg is describing the sound of these angelic vowels in terms of the Neo-Latin with which he was familiar. Though Neo-Latin is commonly described as having been the European lingua franca until through Swedenborg's era, that is true primarily of its written form. There was wide variation in the pronunciation of Neo-Latin throughout Europe, to the point that scholars from different countries often had difficulty understanding one another when speaking together in the language (Sacré 2014, 161–170; Waquet 2001, 160–171). Given these variations, it would be pure conjecture to suggest equivalents in current English for the vowels discussed here. For a slightly different account of the use of vowels in heaven, see *Heaven and Hell* 241. [SS, RS]

265 (in *Sacred Scripture* 90:2). The words in brackets are taken from an earlier version of this statement found in *Spiritual Experiences* (= Swedenborg 1998–2013) §5620. Swedenborg apparently omitted them when he made the same statement in *Draft of "Sacred Scripture"* §4:2 [Rogers's numbering] = §14 [Whitehead's numbering] (= Swedenborg 1997c, 12–13) and that error was repeated in the present passage and the parallel passage in *True Christianity* 278. The six Hebrew letters transcribed as *b, d, g, k, p,* and *t* are aspirated when they do not have a dot (dagesh) in them and are either unaspirated or doubled when they do. An aspirated *t,* for example, is pronounced like *th,* a sound that can be maintained, while an unaspirated *t* requires a complete and abrupt stoppage of breath. The unaspirated or stopped pronunciation is referred to in the text here as a "hard" pronunciation while the aspirated pronunciation is referred to as a "soft" pronunciation. [GFD, LSW]

266 (in *Sacred Scripture* 90:2). See note 59 for an explanation of the meaning of the Latin word *corniculum,* used in the sense "tip [of a letter]." In the current passage, Swedenborg adds a second Latin word, *apex,* as a synonym. This combination of synonyms is the basis for the translation "little tips or strokes." [JSR]

Notes to *Sacred Scripture* Chapter 10, §§91–97

267 (in *Sacred Scripture* 92). Well-known movements in Christian history commonly referred to as heretical include Gnosticism, Docetism, Montanism, Arianism, Pelagianism, and Catharism, to name only a few of the most prominent. While these are heresies from the point of view of Western orthodoxy, including both Catholicism and Protestantism, the numerous errors that Swedenborg sees in the mainstream Christian churches make the churches themselves heretical as well, from his point of view. See *True Christianity* 378, where Swedenborg provides an extensive list of heretical movements and sects throughout Christian history—a list in which he includes both Roman Catholicism and Protestantism as a whole. [RS, LSW]

268 (in *Sacred Scripture* 93). For further clarification of these statements, see *Secrets of Heaven* 845; *Divine Love and Wisdom* 268; *Divine Providence* 318; *Revelation Unveiled* 421; *True Christianity* 798; *Spiritual Experiences* (= Swedenborg 1998–2013) §5150. In general, according to Swedenborg, those who have "inwardly convinced themselves" of falsities are those who have lived evil lives and justified their actions by means of

their confirmed falsities, whereas those who have not inwardly convinced themselves are those who have lived good and charitable lives even though they believed things that were false. For some accounts of people in the spiritual world continuing in the beliefs they had convinced themselves of in the world, but in some cases later rejecting those beliefs because they had not confirmed them inwardly, see *Secrets of Heaven* 4658; *Supplements* 47, 55; *Marriage Love* 151b–154b; *Soul-Body Interaction* 19; *True Christianity* 797; *Spiritual Experiences* 5911–5916, 5920–5923. [LSW]

269 (in *Sacred Scripture* 95:3). Compare Aristotle's statement in *On the Heavens* 270b (= Aristotle 1984, 451) on the unchanging nature of the "outermost heaven," that is, the firmament of stars: "In the whole range of time past, so far as our inherited records reach, no change appears to have taken place either in the whole scheme of the outermost heaven or in any of its proper parts." [SS]

270 (in *Sacred Scripture* 96a). In the first edition, this section and the following one are both numbered 96. [GFD]

271 (in *Sacred Scripture* 96b). In the parallel passage in *True Christianity* 259, Swedenborg refers the reader to his previously published work *Heaven and Hell,* where relevant statements can be found in §§176, 488:2, 489:4, 586. [GFD]

272 (in *Sacred Scripture* 97:5). The material in the following paragraph was drawn, with some editing, from Swedenborg's *Draft on the Inner Meaning of Prophets and Psalms* (= Swedenborg 1996i). [GFD]

Notes to *Sacred Scripture* Chapter 11, §§98–100

273 (in *Sacred Scripture* 99). The Latin here translated "symbolic churches" is *Ecclesiae Representativae,* elsewhere in this edition translated "representative churches." In *Secrets of Heaven* 1437 Swedenborg states that a symbolic, or representative, church is one "in which everything in general and particular represented the Lord and the heavenly and spiritual elements of his kingdom. It was not just their rituals that had a representative meaning but everything connected with ritual as well—the people who ministered, the tools of their ministry, and the places where they carried it out." See *Secrets of Heaven* 4288:2 for the contrast between this kind of church and a representation of a church in which the outward forms have been retained but have lost their connection with inner worship. Compare *Secrets of Heaven* 1003, which similarly speaks of the cessation of the symbolic meaning of outward religious rituals after the Lord's Coming. [GFD]

274 (in *Sacred Scripture* 99). This refers to the numerous passages in the Bible that mention evening and morning. Genesis 1 provides especially clear examples. At the end of each day of creation there is a repeated motif in the form "And there was evening and there was morning, the first day" (Genesis 1:5; New Revised Standard Version; see also Genesis 1:8, 13, 19, 23, 31). For more on the meaning of "evening" and "morning" and their symbolic relationship with the Lord's Coming, see *Secrets of Heaven* 22–23, 2405, 7844, 8426; *Revelation Unveiled* 151. Compare also *Supplements* 13. [LSW]

275 (in *Sacred Scripture* 99). As Swedenborg describes it, this presence of the Lord indirectly through heaven took place most specifically by means of the Lord filling an angel with his presence. The angel's own awareness was submerged so that the angel temporarily became an embodiment of the Lord, enabling the Lord to appear to people on earth and speak to them. For more on this phenomenon, including biblical examples cited by Swedenborg, see *Secrets of Heaven* 1925; *Revelation Unveiled* 465;

True Christianity 109; *Revelation Explained* (= Swedenborg 1994–1997a) §412:16; *Answers to Nine Questions* (= Swedenborg 1997b) §§2, 6. On the Lord's more general presence through the higher heavens prior to the Incarnation, see *Secrets of Heaven* §6371:2. [LSW]

276 (in *Sacred Scripture* 100). On these promised works, see the author's preface to *The Lord* and note 4 there. [Editors]

Notes to *Sacred Scripture* Chapter 12, §§101–103

277 (in *Sacred Scripture* 101:3). Deuteronomy 32:7–8 reads: "Remember the days of old, consider the years long past; ask your father, and he will inform you; your elders, and they will tell you. When the Most High apportioned the nations, when he divided humankind, he fixed the boundaries of the peoples according to the number of the Israelites" (adapted from the New Revised Standard Version). Swedenborg here states that these verses provide "a glimpse of the fact" that there was prophecy even before the time of Abram (who was later renamed Abraham). Elsewhere in his theological writings Swedenborg is a little more specific in his interpretation of these verses, stating that the phrase rendered "the days of old" refers to the earliest church, and that the phrase rendered "the years long past" refers to the early church. (On Swedenborg's equation of a "church" with a "religious era," and on these two churches specifically, see note 5.) Together these churches cover the period of the Bible narrative from the initial creation story to the exodus from Egypt. See *Secrets of Heaven* 477:3, 1259:6, 6239:4; *Revelation Explained* (= Swedenborg 1994–1997a) §431:10. In Swedenborg's view, then, Deuteronomy 32:7–8 speaks of God's relationship, presumably in part through "prophecy at Jehovah's command," with peoples and nations that existed before the time of Abram. [LSW]

278 (in *Sacred Scripture* 101:3). "Holy Supper" (Latin *Sancta Caena*) is Swedenborg's preferred term for Holy Communion or the Eucharist. For an extended discussion, see *True Christianity* 698–752. [JSR]

279 (in *Sacred Scripture* 102:1). On "symbolic worship" and the churches that practice it, see note 273. [Editors]

280 (in *Sacred Scripture* 102:1). "Diviners" and "magi" were individuals recognized for their skill in interpreting omens. Diviners are frequently mentioned in the Hebrew Bible, as in Deuteronomy 18:14; Joshua 13:22; 1 Samuel 6:2; Isaiah 3:2; usually in a pejorative context. In fact, divination is prohibited in Deuteronomy 18:10. "Magi" is derived from the Greek μάγος *(mágos)*, which originally referred to members of a particular tribe of Medes and later to practitioners of the magical arts. The most famous are the magi who present themselves to the newborn Jesus (Matthew 2:1–12). Like the magi Simon (Acts 8:9–24) and Bar-Jesus (Acts 13:6–12), they were presumably Jewish. [RS, GFD]

281 (in *Sacred Scripture* 102:2). The Word mentioned here as succeeding the Word that the ancients had is the Hebrew Bible as we know it. "The prophets of Israel" is used here in a generic sense that includes all the biblical authors, not just the ones specifically identified as prophets in present-day Bibles. The statement about this later Word using "less remote correspondences" is made only here and in the parallel passages in *Draft of "Sacred Scripture"* §15:1 [Rogers's numbering] = §36 [Whitehead's numbering] (= Swedenborg 1997c, 38) and *True Christianity* 279:1–2. However, some sense of its intended meaning can be gained from a passage in *Spiritual Experiences* (= Swedenborg 1971) §5716: "The correspondence is close and material, according to the ideas of the thoughts of [people]

in the world." This suggests that "less remote" means "closer to the material ideas and experiences of people on earth." In other words, the Word that the ancients had, which was "written entirely in correspondences," was not based on actual historical events, though it did utilize material-world imagery and place-names in the composition of its symbolic narrative. By contrast, the later Word has a narrative based for the most part on historical, material-world locations and events, such as the land of Palestine and the history of the Hebrew people, and it is this historical material that supplies the literal basis for its spiritual meaning. This contrast may be seen in the present Bible by comparing the first eleven chapters of Genesis with the later historical parts of the Word. On the opening chapters of Genesis being "fictional" and exhibiting the style of the Word that was used by the ancients, see note 202, as well as *Sacred Scripture* 103; *Secrets of Heaven* 2897; *True Christianity* 279:4; *Draft of "Sacred Scripture"* §15:4 [Rogers's numbering] = §37 [Whitehead's numbering] (= Swedenborg 1997c, 40). [LSW]

282 (in *Sacred Scripture* 103:2). The Hebrew word מָשָׁל (*māšāl*), of which the plural is מְשָׁלִים (*məšālîm*), here transliterated *moschalim*, comes from a root meaning "to be like," and can be applied to a wide variety of literary forms—proverbs, poetry, and prophecies, for example—whose common characteristic seems to be imagery. See Brown, Driver, and Briggs 1996, 605, under מָשָׁל. Swedenborg's assertion that translators change the title of the prophetic portion of the ancient Word to "Composers of Proverbs" is exemplified by the rendering *proverbiorum compositores* in the 1696 translation of Sebastian Schmidt, which Swedenborg owned and consulted. [GFD]

283 (in *Sacred Scripture* 103:3). Compare *Secrets of Heaven* 482, in which Swedenborg states that the first *eleven* chapters of Genesis are not historical. See also notes 202 and 281. For a brief overview of Swedenborgian efforts to find the ancient Word, see Acton 1983, 3–6. The Book of Jasher ("The Book of the Righteous") is one of several collections of ancient texts mentioned in the Bible that have not survived. Others include the Book of the Wars of Jehovah mentioned in Numbers 21:14. See Metzger and Coogan 1993, 342, under "Jashar, the Book of." [GFD, RS, JSR]

Notes to *Sacred Scripture* Chapter 13, §§104–113

284 (in *Sacred Scripture* 105:3). As becomes clear in the next sentence, in Swedenborg's mind these "Christians who read the Word" stand in contrast to Roman Catholics. A key historical basis of the accusation inherent in this passage is the medieval papacy's reluctance to translate the Bible out of the Latin Vulgate and into the new European vernaculars, in which it could be read by the laity. Martin Luther made lay readership of vernacular Bibles a central plank of the Reformation, and the Catholic Counter-Reformation responded by banning the reading of vernacular Bibles absent the formal permission of the Inquisition (see MacCulloch 2003, 393–394, 565–566; compare also the decrees of the Council of Toulouse [1229], canon 14 [Peters 1980, 195], and "Ten Rules on Prohibited Books," rules 3–4 [Janz 2008, 422–426], authorized by the Council of Trent in 1563, and approved in 1564 by Pope Pius IV [1499–1565]). The ban was never consistently applied, and in Swedenborg's day approved vernacular translations in all the major European languages were permitted to circulate among the Catholic faithful. Nevertheless, the accusation that the Roman Catholic Church discouraged its communicants from reading the Bible was still widely repeated, and Swedenborg clearly accepted its substance. For more on the history of vernacular

Bible translation in this period, see Hunter and others 1969, 2:338–490 (= chapter 9, "The Vernacular Scriptures"). [DNG, RS, JSR, SS]

285 (in *Sacred Scripture* 105:3). On the implication here that orthodox Muslims "recognize the Lord as the greatest prophet and as the Son of God," see note 501. For Swedenborg's report on the beliefs and status of Muslims in the spiritual world, see *Supplements* 68–72. [SS]

286 (in *Sacred Scripture* 105:3). *Supplements* was not published at the time Swedenborg wrote this passage directing readers to the material in *Last Judgment*. *Supplements* has much more extensive discussion of the placement and condition of different groups in the spiritual world. The theme appears in *Supplements* 14 and resurfaces periodically throughout the book, but it is covered in the most detail in §§39–90, the supplement on the spiritual world. [SS]

287 (in *Sacred Scripture* 106). For a substantial discussion of the sun in heaven, see *Heaven and Hell* 116–125. [RS]

288 (in *Sacred Scripture* 110). On the perception among Protestants that the Bible was "virtually cast out by Catholics," see note 284. [Editors]

289 (in *Sacred Scripture* 110). Swedenborg identifies this "one noble Catholic nation" as France in *Divine Providence* 257:4; *Revelation Unveiled* 740; *Revelation Explained* (= Swedenborg 1994–1997a) §§1070:2, 1071:1. [Editors]

290 (in *Sacred Scripture* 111). For passages offering more discussion by Swedenborg on the Word in its relationship to the Jewish nation, see note 64. On Swedenborg's references to Jews and Judaism, see note 204; on offensive material in Swedenborg's works generally, see the translator's preface, pages 4–6. [Editors]

291 (in *Sacred Scripture* 112:1). "The present church" here refers to historical Christianity in its various branches. Swedenborg saw this Christianity as representing the fourth of a series of five major church eras on earth. According to Swedenborg, that church, like its predecessors, came to an end as the reigning religious paradigm in the world when there was no faith because there was no caring (see *Secrets of Heaven* 931, 2910, 3353; *New Jerusalem* 8; *Last Judgment* 33–39)—something he believed had already happened by the middle of the eighteenth century, when he began writing and publishing his theological works. For more on Swedenborg's schema of five church eras, see note 5. [LSW]

292 (in *Sacred Scripture* 112:2). Though the Book of Revelation does not make this prediction in a literal sense, it does contain many passages predicting darkness at the time of a future great judgment, which Swedenborg interprets as a prediction that the light of truth would be snuffed out at the end of the then-existing Christian church (on which see note 291 just above). See, for example, Revelation 6:12, 8:12, 9:2, 16:10, and 18:23, and Swedenborg's explanations of these verses in *Revelation Unveiled* 332, 413–414, 423, 695, and 796, respectively. [GFD, LSW]

Notes to *Sacred Scripture* Chapter 14, §§114–118

293 (in *Sacred Scripture* 115:1). The position that Swedenborg mentions here is typical of so-called natural religion, which arose during the seventeenth and eighteenth centuries as a reaction to "revealed religion," especially mainstream Christianity, with its emphasis on the need for Scripture. Natural religion argued that reason without the aid of revelation was capable of arriving at certainty about the existence of God, and

even about an afterlife in which virtue is rewarded and vice is punished. It also held that morality could be derived on the basis of reason rather than revealed divine law. Its exponents included Richard Bentley (1662–1742), Samuel Clarke (1675–1729), and William Derham (1657–1735), who all lent their voices to the cause in the Boyle Lectures, a series (most celebrated in the years 1692–1713) established by the scientist Robert Boyle (1627–1691) to defend the Christian religion against atheism. For a brief sketch of the history of the idea, see Kors 2003, 3:142–150; for a general study, see Byrne 1989. Compare note 153, about eighteenth-century philosophical views on "nature." [JSR, SS]

294 (in *Sacred Scripture* 115:2). On the reference to scholars "who believe that nature created itself," compare note 153. These people are mentioned in similar terms elsewhere in Swedenborg's works; see, for example, *Secrets of Heaven* 4733:2, 4950, 8944; *Heaven and Hell* 353–354; *True Christianity* 79. [SS, LSW]

295 (in *Sacred Scripture* 115:3). From the parallel passage in *True Christianity* 273, it is clear that Swedenborg is here referring to the ancient Word (on which see *Sacred Scripture* 101–103). Aristotle (384–322 B.C.E.) was a Greek philosopher who conceived of God as an "unmoved mover." Marcus Tullius Cicero (106–43 B.C.E.) was a Roman statesman, orator, and philosopher; Lucius Annaeus Seneca (born between 4 B.C.E. and 1 C.E., died 65 C.E.) was a Roman philosopher, statesman, and dramatist. Cicero tended to accept Stoic doctrines of theology; Seneca was essentially a Stoic. Stoicism viewed God as the formative power that creates all things in the universe and harmonizes them. On these thinkers and their attitude toward religion, see Edwards 1967, 1:160; 2:114; 7:406; 8:21. It should also be noted that in general, the category of "ancient sages" includes early Greek writers such as the pre-Socratic philosophers and the poet Hesiod (flourished around 700 B.C.E.). Swedenborg may have had them in mind in addition to those whom he lists. [RS, LSW]

296 (in *Sacred Scripture* 115:3). On natural theology, or natural religion, see note 293. [JSR]

297 (in *Sacred Scripture* 116:2). The "Society of Jesus," also known as the Jesuits, is a Roman Catholic monastic order founded in 1540 by Ignatius Loyola (1491–1556). Its members were nicknamed "Jesuits" in the order's early years because of their allegedly overfrequent use of the name "Jesus"; the nickname was at first derogatory but was later accepted and interpreted in a more positive sense. The Jesuits were the chief agents of the Counter-Reformation of the sixteenth and seventeenth centuries, and were known for a skill in casuistry that was often seen as dishonest. It was the general European perception of the ill-dealings of Jesuits in economic and political matters, however, that led to their suppression by the pope in 1773. For the history and legends of the Jesuit order as seen from a Lutheran point of view, see Barthel 1984. On taunts leveled against the Jesuits in contemporary Protestant Sweden, see Helander 2004, 332–334. [RS, JSR, SS]

298 (in *Sacred Scripture* 116:2). Swedenborg shared the belief of his times that there is an atmosphere finer than air, called "ether," that is the medium of light the way air is the medium of sound (see *Secrets of Heaven* 4523:1, 6013, 6057:1; *True Christianity* 32:8, 79:2–6). This substance was also considered by some to be the stuff of which souls, angels, and spirits are made, for which reason some writers called them "ethers" (see *Marriage Love* 315:11). To give a single notable example, the French philosopher René Descartes says of his own early thoughts of the soul that he "imagined it to be something tenuous, like a wind or fire or ether" (Descartes *Meditations on First Philosophy*, second meditation = Descartes [1641] 1984, 17). Compare note 441. [JSR, SS]

299 (in *Sacred Scripture* 116:2). This mention of the spirit's rejoining its corpse and skeleton is a reference to a Christian belief, based on an interpretation of such passages as Revelation 20:12–13, that at the time of the Last Judgment people's souls will be reunited with their material bodies—an idea that Swedenborg criticizes as ludicrous (see, for example, *Marriage Love* 29). According to this theory, souls would not possess eyes, ears, or mouths previous to their reversion to the body, and so would be incapable of sight, hearing, or speech. Some believed that souls after death would enter a "soul sleep," but others believed they would still be capable of thought. See, for example, the speculations on this subject by the British theologian and hymn writer Isaac Watts (1674–1748): "When the human Body dies, the Soul exists and continues to think and act in a separate State . . . freed from all the Avocation of Sensations and sensible Things" (Watts 1733, 131). For more on the history of the concept of "soul sleeping" in Britain, see Burns 1972. [JSR, SS]

300 (in *Sacred Scripture* 117). "The Israelite Word" is another term for the Hebrew Bible, commonly referred to in Christianity as "the Old Testament." [LSW]

301 (in *Sacred Scripture* 117). On Swedenborg's use of the name "Jehovah" as a rendering of the sacred Hebrew name for God known as the tetragrammaton, see note 9. Modern philologists no longer support the long-held notion of a linguistic connection between the names "Jove" and "Jehovah." "Jove" is understood to come not from a Hebrew or Semitic root, as does Jehovah, but from a Proto-Indo-European root (Shipley 1984, 54–55). [JSR, SS]

302 (in *Sacred Scripture* 117). Swedenborg connects the classical myth of a Golden Age, as described by Ovid in *Metamorphoses* 1:89–112, with the biblical paradise of Genesis 1–3 in his pretheological work *Basic Principles of Nature,* part 3, chapter 12 (= Swedenborg [1734] 1988, 2:360–361). For one classical telling of the myth of a flood that overwhelmed the earth, see Ovid *Metamorphoses* 1:143–215, 244–312; for lost works by other ancient writers that mention the event, see Flavius Josephus *Antiquities of the Jews* 1:3:6 (= Josephus 1998, 38–39). One well-known instance of sacred fire of which Swedenborg may be thinking is the one that burned on the hearth in the temple of Vesta in ancient Rome. For a classical description of the "ages of humankind" denoted by the metals gold, silver, bronze, and iron, see Hesiod *Works and Days* 109–201; Vergil *Eclogues* 4; Ovid *Metamorphoses* 1:89–150. [SS]

303 (in *Sacred Scripture* 117). On Swedenborg's schema of five "churches," or spiritual eras of humankind, see note 5. Swedenborg often associates that series of churches with the classical "ages of humankind" denoted by the metals gold, silver, bronze, and iron (compare note 302). However, Swedenborg here goes even further, saying that each of these "churches" has a four-stage life cycle analogous to the four ages. This analogy parallels one he draws elsewhere between the stages of a particular church and the four seasons of the year; and another he draws between these stages and the four periods of day (morning, afternoon, evening, and night). For more on these four stages of a particular church, see *Secrets of Heaven* 2323; *True Christianity* 753–764. For the connection specifically between these four stages and the statue made of various metals described in Daniel 2:31–35, see *Secrets of Heaven* 1837; *Revelation Explained* (= Swedenborg 1994–1997a) §1029:5. [LSW]

304 (in *Sacred Scripture* 117). The Qur'an contains frequent references to the Torah (for example, Surah 5:43–44, 46) and the Gospels (for example, Surah 5:46–47), and

includes Jews and Christians under the description "the People of the Book" (for example, Surah 5:15, 19), a phrase that emphasizes the scriptures those groups hold in common with Islam. [GFD]

Notes to *Life* Chapter 1, §§1–8

305 (in *Life* 2). On Swedenborg's use of the term "the Word," see note 11. [Editors]

306 (in *Life* 2). The bracketed part of the verse is missing from the first edition. The typesetter's eye apparently skipped from the first occurrence of *resurrectionem* ("the resurrection") to the second. [GFD]

307 (in *Life* 2). On Swedenborg's use of the name "Jehovah" as a rendering of the sacred Hebrew name for God known as the tetragrammaton, see note 9. [Editors]

308 (in *Life* 2). Here Swedenborg is likely using the term "the church" in a common meaning for his day and culture, as referring to Christianity in general, including all its branches and sects; or he may be using it in a more general sense, as referring to all people who live a good life according to their own religion. Compare note 331. For a discussion of Swedenborg's general use of the term "the church," see note 5. [LSW]

309 (in *Life* 2). Talents and minas were units of weight and money used in ancient Greece, Rome, and the Middle East. At different times and places, a talent ranged from fifty-seven to eighty-eight pounds (twenty-six to forty kilograms) of gold, silver, or copper. A mina was a sixtieth of a talent. [JSR]

310 (in *Life* 3). On "the Athanasian statement of faith," usually referred to as the Athanasian Creed, see notes 91, 96, and 132. [Editors]

311 (in *Life* 4). "Holy Supper" (Latin *Sancta Caena*) is Swedenborg's preferred term for Holy Communion or the Eucharist. For an extended discussion, see *True Christianity* 698–752. [JSR]

312 (in *Life* 4). The doctrine of faith alone was taught in article 11 of the Thirty-Nine Articles of the Anglican church in Britain (Schaff 1931, 3:494). For the teaching of the doctrine in the Lutheran church then prominent in Germany, Sweden, and Denmark, see note 209. [SS]

313 (in *Life* 5 & 6). In the Latin first edition, Swedenborg prints the text of this Anglican exhortation in English in §5 and in his own Latin translation in §6. The latter section has been omitted as redundant in this translation, and only the English text has been included, with updated and Americanized spelling, punctuation, and, to a limited extent, word usage. Words in square brackets have been inserted by the editors. In the original text of *Life,* each line of the text is preceded by quotation marks, a typographical device used in the eighteenth century to indicate that a portion of the text was of a different nature than the preceding—in this instance, to indicate that this is quoted material. Swedenborg owned the 1711 edition of the Book of Common Prayer (see Altfelt 1969, 119); the version on page 30 of that text was likely his source for the exhortation. In that text the exhortation is specified to be read to the congregation on the Sunday or holy day immediately preceding Communion Sunday. For the biblical basis of the exhortation, see 1 Corinthians 11:17–34, as well as John 13:2; Acts 1:15–20. [SS, GFD]

314 (in *Life* 7). On "the spiritual world," see note 141. [Editors]

315 (in *Life* 8). Swedenborg here refers to his work *Heaven and Hell,* published in London in 1758. [Editors]

Notes to *Life* Chapter 2, §§9–17

316 (in *Life* 9). Although Swedenborg commonly uses the term "the church" to refer to Christianity as a whole (see note 308), he here seems to be referring primarily to the Reformed or Protestant branch of Christianity, and its doctrinal tenet of justification by faith alone; on which see note 209. [LSW]

317 (in *Life* 12). In *Secrets of Heaven* 4538:4 spiritual goodness is defined as "willing and doing good to others not for any selfish reason but because we like to and want to." In *Secrets of Heaven* 9812 moral goodness is described as involving "all the honorable virtues," and civic goodness as "treating one's fellow citizens fairly." In general, moral and civic goodness have to do with outward behavior that is honorable and just toward others, while spiritual goodness involves intending and behaving justly and honorably toward others from a genuine love for others and for God, and not for mere personal advancement or material gain. For more on these levels of goodness, in addition to *Sacred Scripture* 13–17 and the two *Secrets of Heaven* sections just cited, see *Secrets of Heaven* 2915; *Revelation Explained* (= Swedenborg 1994–1997a) §§741:4, 794:3, 831:5; *Sketch on Goodwill* (= Swedenborg 1996d) §§23, 55–61. [LSW]

318 (in *Life* 13). For more on the concept that a deed is good if it comes from God but not good if it comes from a person and not from God, see *Life* 9–11, 17; *Secrets of Heaven* 987, 8480, 9974–9984, 10299, 10330; *New Jerusalem* 150–158; *Revelation Explained* (= Swedenborg 1994–1997a) §802; *Draft on Divine Love* chapter 14 = §§41–42 [Mongredien's numbering] (= Swedenborg 1994–1997c, 435–437). [LSW]

319 (in *Life* 14). This work, referred to in this edition by the short title *Sacred Scripture,* was published by Swedenborg in Amsterdam in 1763. [Editors]

320 (in *Life* 14). On "a goal, the means to it, and its result," see note 170. [Editors]

321 (in *Life* 15). For references on the light of heaven, see note 229. [Editors]

322 (in *Life* 15). On Swedenborg's planned "works on angelic wisdom," see the author's preface to *The Lord,* and note 4 there. The subjects mentioned in this section are covered in detail in part 5 (§§358–432) of one of those promised works, *Divine Love and Wisdom.* There Swedenborg provides an extended treatment of the human will and understanding using the imagery of the heart and lungs. On the specific topics covered here, see especially *Divine Love and Wisdom* 413–425. Note that Swedenborg's statements in the current section are, as he says, applicable to our state when we are *not* spiritual. In *Divine Love and Wisdom* 426 he speaks of the nature of our love when it *has* become spiritual and heavenly: that it is then focused on loving the Lord and the neighbor rather than on loving the world and ourselves. Other statements on the ability of our understanding to be raised into heaven's light compared to our will's ability to be raised into heaven's warmth, and on the related subject of the differences between humans and animals, occur in *Divine Love and Wisdom* 39, 243–244, and 255. See also *Secrets of Heaven* 6–13, in which Swedenborg summarizes the process of spiritual rebirth, or regeneration, culminating in a state in which we act as much from love as from understanding; and *Secrets of Heaven* 81–88, in which he speaks of people who have reached the final stage of spiritual rebirth. In that state, he says, "love rather than faith begins to play the leading role" (*Secrets of Heaven* 83)—faith being associated with the understanding in Swedenborg's theology, and love with the will. [LSW]

Notes to *Life* Chapter 3, §§18–31

323 (in *Life* 18). This reference to "the Lord's ability to come in to us" is likely an allusion to Revelation 3:20: "Listen! I am standing at the door, knocking; if you hear my voice and open the door, I will come in to you and eat with you, and you with me" (New Revised Standard Version). [LSW]

324 (in *Life* 19). In the basic topography of the spiritual world as presented in Swedenborg's theological writings, heaven is above and hell is below an intermediate state called "the world of spirits." According to Swedenborg, the state of people on earth is most closely connected with the world of spirits; the result is that people on earth are also situated spiritually between heaven and hell. In this intermediate state there is a balance of forces between heaven and hell, leaving people on earth in an equilibrium that makes possible freedom of choice between heaven and hell. See *Secrets of Heaven* 5852; *Heaven and Hell* 421–422, 536–540, 582–583, 589–600. See also note 141 on the spiritual world. [LSW]

325 (in *Life* 19). On Swedenborg's use of the term "the Devil," see note 62. [Editors]

326 (in *Life* 26). The reference to having lamps but no oil is an allusion to the parable of the wise and foolish young women in Matthew 25:1–13. [RS]

327 (in *Life* 30:2). For further commentary on Isaiah 31:1–3, see *Secrets of Heaven* 574:2, 5321:10, 6125:3, 8409:2, 9818:12, 10283:10; *Revelation Unveiled* 298:4, 503:3; *Revelation Explained* (= Swedenborg 1994–1997a) §§355:36, 654:42; *Draft Supplement to "White Horse"* 3 (= Swedenborg 1996a, 421–422). [LSW]

328 (in *Life* 31). The arguments in this section are aimed squarely at adherents of the doctrine of justification by faith alone (see notes 148 and 209) discussed earlier in *Life* 4–7, who, Swedenborg charges, nullify good and caring actions by judging them to be irrelevant to our salvation. [LSW, SS]

329 (in *Life* 31). On the Law and the Prophets, see note 43. [Editors]

Notes to *Life* Chapter 4, §§32–41

330 (in *Life* 32:1). On Swedenborg's concept of multiple heavens, see *Heaven and Hell* 20–40. [Editors]

331 (in *Life* 32:2). Here Swedenborg may be referring to "the church" in the ordinary sense of Christianity in general, including all its branches and sects. However, in this context it is more likely that he is referring to the church in a broad sense as the Lord's kingdom on earth, which, he says, "consists of all who are intent on goodness. Even if they are scattered over the whole globe, they are still one and, like a person's limbs, make up a single body" (*Secrets of Heaven* 2853:2). [LSW]

332 (in *Life* 33). "The heavenly marriage" is touched on only in *Life* 41; "the hellish marriage" is not mentioned again in this work. For more on the heavenly marriage as the union of goodness and truth, the hellish marriage as the union of evil and falsity, and their relationship to human marriages, see *Secrets of Heaven* 2508, 3960, 5138, 8904:12, 9188, 9382:2, 10175; *Heaven and Hell* 377; *New Jerusalem* 13–15, 17. See also *Life* 76, on the contrast between marriage and adultery. [LSW, JSR]

333 (in *Life* 36). A series of propositions addressed in *Divine Love and Wisdom* 399–406 covers most of the process described here. See also *Draft of "Sacred Scripture"* §12

[Rogers's numbering] = §28 [Whitehead's numbering] (= Swedenborg 1997c, 31–32), which provides a somewhat expanded version of the progression described in the current section. [GFD, LSW]

334 (in *Life* 39). This was written in a time and place in which a career in the church could be quite lucrative. The subversion of religion for private advantage is a common theme in Swedenborg's theological writings. See, for example, *Secrets of Heaven* 2027:3, 2261:2, 2329:1, 2354:2; *Revelation Unveiled* 784, 799. [LHC]

335 (in *Life* 39). Compare *Supplements* 48:3, where Swedenborg draws a contrast between our loving business the most, in which case we love money only as a means to successful business, and our loving money the most, in which case we love business only as a means to acquiring money. [GFD]

336 (in *Life* 40). For more on these spiritual meanings of food and bread and of water and wine, and their relationship to the symbolism of the Holy Supper as practiced by Christians, see *Secrets of Heaven* 680, 1072, 2165, 4217, 6377; *New Jerusalem* 210–222; *True Christianity* 702–710; *Revelation Explained* (= Swedenborg 1994–1997a) §617. [LSW]

Notes to *Life* Chapter 5, §§42–52

337 (in *Life* 43:1). The Latin term *ordo* ("the divine design," traditionally translated "divine order") is used by Swedenborg to refer to the structure of the universe—divine, spiritual, and material. According to Swedenborg, the inner essence of the design is divine love or divine good, and its outward form is divine wisdom or divine truth. Since God is the creator and source of the universe, the divine design that has its fullest reality in God pervades the universe, defining and directing everything in it. In Swedenborg's theology, everything good and true in the universe is an expression of the divine design, while everything evil and false opposes the divine design even while it still operates subject to the laws of the divine design. See *Secrets of Heaven* 2447:1–3, 7256, 7995, 8700, 8988; *Heaven and Hell* 107; *Divine Providence* 331–332; *True Christianity* 65–70. [LSW]

338 (in *Life* 43:2). The Latin contains a mild pun that is untranslatable. Swedenborg is here explaining *existere* (contracted from *ex + sistere*), "to come into being," "to arise," here translated with the noun "manifestation," by linking it with a form of the verb *se sistere,* "to make itself visible." [GFD]

339 (in *Life* 46). This, and the similar expression in *Life* 47, is likely an allusion to James 2:17: "So faith by itself, if it has no works, is dead" (New Revised Standard Version). [RS]

340 (in *Life* 46). On the connection of understanding with the lungs and of will with the heart, see *Secrets of Heaven* 3883–3895; *Faith* 19; *Divine Love and Wisdom* 374–385; *True Christianity* 87; *Draft on Divine Wisdom* chapter 6 = §§87–93 [Mongredien's numbering] (= Swedenborg 1994–1997c, 475–478). On correspondence, see note 169. [LSW]

341 (in *Life* 46). This is an allusion to the parable of the fig tree in Luke 13:6–9. For more on the meaning of the items in the parable, see *Secrets of Heaven* 9337; *Revelation Explained* (= Swedenborg 1994–1997a) §403:20. [LSW]

342 (in *Life* 48). In *Secrets of Heaven* 10645:6, Swedenborg quotes two other passages from the Gospel of John as examples of Jesus teaching that *believing* in the Lord and *loving* him consists in keeping his commandments: "If you love me, you will keep my commandments. . . . They who have my commandments and keep them are those who love me. . . . Those who love me will keep my word, and my Father will love them, and we will come to them and make our home with them. Whoever does not love me

does not keep my words" (John 14:15, 21, 23–24); and: "Abide in my love. If you keep my commandments, you will abide in my love. . . . You are my friends if you do what I command you" (John 15:9–10, 14; New Revised Standard Version). These are therefore most likely the passages Swedenborg is referring to here. He may also have in mind the parable of the wise and foolish builders in Matthew 7:24–27 and Luke 6:46–49. The Luke version begins, "Why do you call me 'Lord, Lord,' and do not do what I tell you?" (Luke 6:46). [LSW, RS]

343 (in *Life* 50). The obviously necessary *non,* meaning "not," is missing in the first edition. [GFD]

344 (in *Life* 51). Though Swedenborg here references Matthew 15:11, the quotation includes wording from both that verse and Matthew 15:18, where Jesus is explaining his earlier words to his disciples. Matthew 15:11 says "what comes out of the mouth" rather than "what comes out of the heart." Matthew 15:18, however, says that what comes out of the mouth proceeds from the heart, and that this is what makes people unclean. [LSW, JSR]

Notes to *Life* Chapter 6, §§53–61

345 (in *Life* 54). The Ten Commandments, which first occur in Exodus 20, are not literally the very beginning of the Bible. Swedenborg expands on his statement here that "these laws [the Ten Commandments] were the very beginnings of the Word" in *Revelation Explained* (= Swedenborg 1994–1997a) §939:3:

> Because our evils have to be laid aside before the good things we do can become truly good, the first form the Word took was the Ten Commandments—they were given from Mount Sinai before the Word [of the Old Testament] was written by Moses and the prophets. And the things mentioned in the Ten Commandments are not good things we should do but evil actions we must avoid. (Translation by Jonathan S. Rose)

This idea that the Ten Commandments were the first segment of the Bible to be written is based on the traditional belief, common in Swedenborg's day, that Moses was the author of the first five books of the Bible. In that case, Moses would not have written those books until after the Lord had called him to lead the Israelites out of slavery in Egypt, and thus after the Ten Commandments had been written on two stone tablets by the finger of God (Exodus 31:18; Deuteronomy 9:10) and delivered to Moses. By extension, the Ten Commandments would also be the beginnings of the church, which is based on the Bible. [LSW]

346 (in *Life* 55:3). As Swedenborg indicates in *Life* 61, the Hebrew word דְּבָרִים (*dəḇārîm*), commonly translated "Commandments" where it appears in references to the Ten Commandments in Exodus 34:28; Deuteronomy 4:13; 10:4, literally means "words," among other things. [RS]

347 (in *Life* 56). On this statement about the two tablets of the Ten Commandments, see note 351. [Editors]

348 (in *Life* 60). The Latin here translated "'the Old Covenant' and 'the New Covenant'" is *Foedus vetus et Foedus novum.* This is an alternate wording for the traditional designation of the two parts of the canonical Christian Bible: the Old Testament (Latin *Vetus Testamentum*) and the New Testament (Latin *Novum Testamentum*). The Latin word *testamentum* does mean "covenant" when used in this context. However, Swedenborg

does not use that word here, perhaps because it can also mean "a will" (that is, a "last testament"). He avoids this ambiguity by using the Latin word *foedus* instead, which can mean only "covenant" or "pact." In doing so he is also referring no doubt to such passages as 2 Corinthians 3 and Hebrews 8, which describe God's new covenant with humankind. [GFD]

349 (in *Life* 61). Revelation 12:3 speaks of a dragon that has ten horns, but seven, rather than ten, diadems. However, Revelation 13:1, which Swedenborg references next, speaks of a beast that has ten horns and ten diadems. The remaining passages he references in Revelation and Daniel speak only of ten horns, and make no mention of diadems. [LSW]

350 (in *Life* 61). The Latin word here translated "tithes" is *decimae,* a noun formed from the Latin word for "tenth," on the model of the underlying Hebrew word מַעֲשֵׂר *(ma'ăśēr),* "tithe," which comes from the word עָשָׂר *('āśār),* "ten." In biblical usage, a tithe was a tenth of the produce of the land set aside for the use of the priesthood or kings. For biblical references to the practice, see Leviticus 27:30–32; Deuteronomy 14:22–23; 1 Samuel 8:15, 17. Given this connection between "tithes" and "ten," Swedenborg commonly takes the two words as having identical meanings. See, for example, *Secrets of Heaven* 576, 5291:1; *Revelation Unveiled* 101:3. [LSW, SS]

Notes to *Life* Chapter 7, §§62–66

351 (in *Life* 62). Christian tradition held that the commandments extending through the injunction about the Sabbath (Exodus 20:2–11; Deuteronomy 5:6–15) were written on the first tablet, and that the remaining commandments, beginning at the injunction to honor one's father and mother (Exodus 20:12–17; Deuteronomy 5:16–21) were written on the second tablet. For example, the church father Augustine (354–430) wrote, "The Ten Commandments were given on two tablets. Specifically, three are said to have been written on one tablet, and seven on the other: just as the three pertain to our love for God, the seven are given over to our love for our neighbor" (*Sermo* 33:2:2 [= Migne 1863, 38:208]; translated by Stuart Shotwell). (Note that Augustine's numerical division of the Ten Commandments, which is used in the Roman Catholic and Lutheran churches, differs from the numerical division used in most other churches.) Augustine's choice of wording suggests that this distinction antedates him. Both Catholic and Lutheran theologians followed Augustine in this division of the Ten Commandments into two groups: see *Catechism of the Catholic Church* 2000, §2066, which cites the passage from *Sermo* 33, and see the beginning of the explanation of the fourth commandment in Martin Luther's *Large Catechism* (= Kolb and Wengert 2000, 400). For similar statements elsewhere in Swedenborg's writings, see *Revelation Unveiled* 490:3; *True Christianity* 287, 456; *Revelation Explained* (= Swedenborg 1994–1997a) §§1026:3, 1179:3. Despite these repeated endorsements of the idea that the Commandments were divided between the tablets in this way, in one anomalous passage Swedenborg explicitly rejects it: "The two tablets were . . . separate from but in physical contact with each other, and the writing ran from one tablet onto the other, as if it had been inscribed on a single tablet. It was not that some of the commandments were on one tablet and others on the other, as popular opinion would have it" (*Secrets of Heaven* 9416:2). [SS, LSW, RS, LHC]

352 (in *Life* 63:2). According to Swedenborg, as described in *Heaven and Hell* 499–511, this loss of our outer facade occurs in our second stage after death, when we are still

living in "the world of spirits," an intermediate area between heaven and hell where we first arrive after death. On the overall arrangement of the spiritual world as presented in Swedenborg's theological writings, see note 141. [LSW]

353 (in *Life* 64). It has been traditional in the major Christian denominations to give children instruction in the Ten Commandments, the Lord's Prayer, and other basics in the form of stock questions and answers to be memorized. These are usually presented in a small volume called a "Catechism," from a Greek word for echoing back and forth, or an "Enchiridion," from the Greek word for a handbook. For a Lutheran example that has been in use for the past five centuries, see Luther's Small Catechism in *The Book of Concord* (Kolb and Wengert 2000, 347–375; McCain 2006, 313–348). [JSR]

354 (in *Life* 64). This work, referred to in this edition by the short title *Faith,* was published by Swedenborg in Amsterdam in 1763. [Editors]

Notes to *Life* Chapter 8, §§67–73

355 (in *Life* 67). For an extended essay on the nature and meaning of hellfire, see *Heaven and Hell* 566–574. [Editors]

Notes to *Life* Chapter 9, §§74–79

356 (in *Life* 74). The promised work, published in Amsterdam in 1768, bore the Latin title *Delitiae Sapientiae de Amore Conjugiali: Post Quas Sequuntur Voluptates Insaniae de Amore Scortatorio* (Wisdom's Delight in Marriage Love: Followed by Insanity's Pleasure in Promiscuous Love). This edition uses the short title *Marriage Love.* It is striking that here, writing when the work was still in prospect, Swedenborg refers to it as a "booklet"; at over 158,000 Latin words (328 pages) in the original, it turned out to be a far larger work. [GFD, SS]

357 (in *Life* 75). All major Christian traditions recognize chastity as a term applicable to faithful marriage, though some important Christian thinkers have judged such marital chastity inferior to a condition of complete sexual abstinence (see, for example, 1 Corinthians 7 in general; Augustine *On Virginity* 19; Aquinas *Summa Theologiae* 2:2:152:4). By contrast, Swedenborg defines chastity exclusively with respect to the faithful sexual relationship between husband and wife (*Marriage Love* 139), though in some places, such as *Marriage Love* 44:5, 55:2, and 150 (by implication), it is extended to include unmarried young men and women who have begun to experience sexual attraction but who remain virtuous in their thoughts about sex and marriage. Here Swedenborg follows his regular usage of the word "chastity" as applying to marital relationships. For more on his application of the terms *chaste* and *unchaste,* see *Marriage Love* 138–155a. [SS, LSW, FLS]

358 (in *Life* 77). For some passages in the promised "booklet on marriage" (see note 356) on the connection between faithful monogamous marriage and being religious and a Christian, see *Marriage Love* 70–72, 80, 336–339, 457–458. [LSW]

359 (in *Life* 79:1). On Swedenborg's explanation of the term "Babylon," see note 148. [Editors]

360 (in *Life* 79:2). For additional commentary on Ezekiel 23:2–17, see *Revelation Explained* (= Swedenborg 1994–1997a) §§555:7, 654:67–70. [LSW]

361 (in *Life* 79:3). This work, referred to in this edition by the short title *The Lord,* was published by Swedenborg in Amsterdam in 1763. [Editors]

Notes to *Life* Chapter 11, §§87–91

362 (in *Life* 89). The somewhat unusual turn of phrase "do the truth" indicates that this is an allusion to John 3:21; which, following Swedenborg's Latin rendering in *True Christianity* 377, would read: "Those who do the truth come to the light so their works will be revealed, since those works were done in God." [JSR]

363 (in *Life* 90). In the first edition the text of this passage is set in italics, which Swedenborg often uses to indicate direct quotations. It is not, however, a complete citation of any of the three versions of the parable. It most closely resembles that of Luke. [GFD]

364 (in *Life* 90). The obviously necessary *non*, meaning "not," is missing in the first edition. [GFD]

365 (in *Life* 90). For further commentary on the parable of the sower, see *Secrets of Heaven* 778, 1940:3, 3310:2, 5149:6, 5335, 9144:8; *Divine Providence* 278b:3; *Revelation Explained* (= Swedenborg 1994–1997a) §§401:35, 632:6, 740:6. [LSW]

366 (in *Life* 91). Matthew 7:26 reads: "And everyone who hears these words of mine and does not act on them will be like a foolish man who built his house on sand" (New Revised Standard Version). [Editors]

Notes to *Life* Chapter 12, §§92–100

367 (in *Life* 92). For examples of biblical passages with this purport, see Psalms 51:5, "Indeed, I was born guilty, a sinner when my mother conceived me," and Genesis 8:21, "The Lord said in his heart, 'I will never again curse the ground because of humankind, for the inclination of the human heart is evil from youth'" (New Revised Standard Version). [RS, JSR]

368 (in *Life* 96). Some readers may be surprised to find a mention of automata, or robots, in an eighteenth-century text; but they were a familiar concept in Swedenborg's day and even long before. Self-operating humanoid mechanisms are mentioned in the Western tradition at least as early as Homer's *Iliad* 18:417–420. For discussion of attitudes toward such automata in Swedenborg's time, including numerous examples, see Schaffer 1999, 126–165. [SS]

369 (in *Life* 98). The traditional term "church militant" (that is, the church combating for Christ against the Devil) refers to those members of the Christian church alive on earth. It stands in contrast with the "church triumphant," which refers to the souls in heaven. Roman Catholic teaching also includes a "church penitent" composed of the souls in Purgatory. [RS, SS]

370 (in *Life* 99). The first edition skips over Revelation 3:5, which describes the reward for victory promised to those in Sardis, jumping directly to Revelation 3:12, which describes the reward for victory promised to those in Philadelphia. This translation restores the missing material in brackets. [JSR]

371 (in *Life* 100). This work, referred to in this edition by the short title *New Jerusalem*, was published by Swedenborg in London in 1758. [Editors]

Notes to *Life* Chapter 13, §§101–107

372 (in *Life* 107). See especially *Divine Providence* 191–213. On the promised works on angelic wisdom, see the author's preface to *the Lord* and note 4 there. [GFD]

Notes to *Life* Chapter 14, §§108–114

373 (in *Life* 109). In Swedenborg's theology, this appearance of moral earthly individuals as wooden or marble statues stems from the "correspondential" nature of reality in the spiritual world, in which inner character is expressed visually by external imagery. The reason for the particular materials mentioned here is that in Swedenborg's symbology wood corresponds to what is good in its outward expression, or in outward act (see *Secrets of Heaven* 643, 2784; *Revelation Explained* [= Swedenborg 1994–1997a] §1145); while marble, as a variety of nonprecious stone, corresponds to what is true in its outward expression, or in outward act (*Secrets of Heaven* 1298, 9863; *Revelation Unveiled* 231, 775; *Revelation Explained* 1148). For more on correspondence, see note 169. [LSW]

374 (in *Life* 110). Swedenborg states consistently and emphatically in his theological writings that what is higher can flow into what is lower, but not the reverse. Specifically, what is spiritual can flow into what is earthly or material, but what is material cannot flow into what is spiritual. See, for example, *Secrets of Heaven* 3721, 5119, 5779, 6322, 9109–9110; *Soul-Body Interaction* 1. See also note 243 above, on inflow. His statement here that "of ourselves we flow from what is earthly into what is spiritual" is in contrast to that principle. More detailed statements of his views elsewhere in his writings suggest that when people attempt to reverse the flow and to force what is physical to flow into what is spiritual, what actually takes place is that their higher spiritual levels, where love for God and love for the neighbor reside, become closed. Meanwhile those parts of their spiritual self that are associated with the physical senses and with physical and social functioning in the material world descend of their own accord to a materialistic level so that they are in harmony with the various selfish and materialistic loves that drive such people. See *Secrets of Heaven* 4946–4948, 9726; *Heaven and Hell* 354; *New Jerusalem* 36–46, 59–61; *True Christianity* 14, 40, 77, 401–402, 565. [LSW]

375 (in *Life* 111). For more on turning one's back on evil actions as sins and the role it plays in the process of repentance and spiritual rebirth, see *New Jerusalem* 159–169; *Divine Providence* 100–123; *True Christianity* 528–531; *Revelation Explained* (= Swedenborg 1994–1997a) §§971–975 (where the discussion is continued serially in the later subsections of each section); and a passage in *Sketch on Goodwill* most conveniently found in the appendix of Swedenborg 1996d, §§199–208. Swedenborg's contrast here between irreligious people and Christians, rather than between irreligious people and religious people in general, likely reflects the perspective of the Europe of his times, in which religion was virtually synonymous with Christianity. He is elsewhere at pains to point out that people bearing the label "Christian" do not necessarily turn their backs on evil actions as sins, and that people of other faiths are able to do so effectively even though they are not Christians. See, for example, *Divine Providence* 330:5–7. [LSW]

376 (in *Life* 114). In the first edition this entire section is set in relatively large type, apparently for emphasis—which is represented here by the use of italics. [GFD]

377 (in *Life* 114). The "reflections," "good deeds," and "obligations" related to charity are defined and expanded upon in *Sketch on Goodwill* (= Swedenborg 1996d) §§173–188. The brief definitions provided in that work are as follows (as translated here by Jonathan S. Rose): "The reflections of charity are all things that pertain to worship" (§173). "The good deeds related to charity are all the good things that a person, who is charity, does

freely outside of his or her occupation" (§184). "The obligations related to charity are all the things that a person ought to do besides those above mentioned" (§187). See also *Divine Love and Wisdom* 431; *True Christianity* 425–432; *Spiritual Experiences* (= Swedenborg 1998–2013) §6105. [LSW]

Notes to *Faith* Chapter 1, §§1–12

378 (in *Faith* 1). Swedenborg is here using the term "the church" in a common meaning for his day and culture, as referring to Christianity in general, including all its branches and sects. For a discussion of his broader use of the term "church," see note 5. [LSW]

379 (in *Faith* 1). The still common saying "Believe and don't doubt" is based on Bible passages such as Matthew 21:21, Mark 11:23, John 20:27, and James 1:6. [SS, LSW]

380 (in *Faith* 3). On the relationship between earthly truth and spiritual truth, see *Secrets of Heaven* 3167, 8861:2; *Revelation Explained* (= Swedenborg 1994–1997a) §1088:2–4. [LSW]

381 (in *Faith* 3). On Swedenborg's spiritual experiences, see note 3. [Editors]

382 (in *Faith* 3). On "the light of heaven," see note 229. [Editors]

383 (in *Faith* 5). On "the Word," see note 11. [Editors]

384 (in *Faith* 6). The Hebrew words for "truth" (אֱמֶת [*ĕmet*]), "faith" (in the sense of faithfulness or fidelity, אֱמוּנָה [*ĕmûnā*]), and "amen" are all derived from the same root, אָמַן (*'āman*), meaning "to confirm" or "to support": see Brown, Driver, and Briggs 1996, page 52 right column, under אָמַן (*'āman*), Strong's 539; page 53 left column, under אָמֵן (*'āmēn*), Strong's 543; page 53 right column, under אֱמוּנָה (*ĕmûnā*), Strong's 530; and page 54 left column, under אֱמֶת (*ĕmet*), Strong's 571. This is the likely basis for Swedenborg's statement here that "the ancients . . . talked about 'truth' rather than 'faith.'" Swedenborg expands on this somewhat in *Revelation Explained* 813: "Faith is never mentioned in the Old Testament, which speaks instead of truth. In fact, those of the ancients who were part of the church had no notion that faith was anything but truth" (translation by Stuart Shotwell). See also *Secrets of Heaven* 4690; *Revelation Explained* 837:10, 895. [RS, LSW]

385 (in *Faith* 7). On this difference, see the discussion in *Faith* 11 of people who "think something is true because someone else has said so, or believe it is true because they have convinced themselves," and the fallacious faith that this easily leads to, in contrast with Swedenborg's advice in *Faith* 12 to those who want the inner recognition of truth that is real faith: "Turn your back on evils because they are sins and turn to the Lord, and you will have as much of that inner recognition as you wish." The sections that follow then take up this theme in more detail. [LSW]

386 (in *Faith* 8). Swedenborg here repeats various negative characterizations of Roman Catholic beliefs. On the charge that Catholics are forbidden to read the Bible, see note 284. The charge that Catholics worship mere "people" may refer to the church's doctrine that its hierarchy ultimately rests on divine sanction, and specifically, on the claim that the pope is the bearer of authority invested in Peter by Christ. The invocation of saints, or calling on them to offer intercessory prayers to God, was sanctioned in Session 25 of the Council of Trent, and Lutherans and other Protestants saw both that invocation and the veneration of the relics of saints, including body parts and tombs, as idolatry (see Kolb and Wengert 2000, 305.22–23, 399.91). [JSR, SS]

387 (in *Faith* 12). This work, referred to in this edition by the short title *Life*, was published by Swedenborg in Amsterdam in 1763. [Editors]

Notes to *Faith* Chapter 2, §§13–24

388 (in *Faith* 13). Where the translation reads "a desire to do something good," the first edition reads *affectio veri,* "a desire for truth," but context strongly suggests that *veri* ("truth") here should be *boni* ("goodness"), a reading found in the same section once above and twice below the phrase in question. The second Latin edition (Swedenborg [1763] 1859) suggests this emendation at this passage. [JSR]

389 (in *Faith* 18:2). "Essence," in Scholastic philosophy and its successors, refers to "the internal principle whereby a thing is *what* it is and has its specific perfections" (Wuellner 1956, 42); in the classic formation, the essence of a human being is that she or he is a rational animal. "Form" is the external shape (McCormick 1940, 127). [RS]

390 (in *Faith* 19:1). The Latin here translated "breathing one's last" is *emittere animam,* literally, "to send out the soul," or "to send out the breath." (The Latin word *anima* can mean either "breath" or "soul.") In a mild play on words, Swedenborg says here that "to send out the soul" is *non amplius animare,* literally, "no longer to draw breath." The Latin here translated "giving up the ghost" is *emittere spiritum,* literally, "to send out the spirit" or "to send out the breath." (The Latin word *spiritus* can mean either "breath" or "spirit.") This, he says, is *non amplius respirare,* to be "no longer breathing," the pun in this case turning on the repeated element *spir-*. [LSW]

391 (in *Faith* 19:2). On automata in Swedenborg's time and before, see note 368. [Editors]

392 (in *Faith* 19:2). On the term "the spiritual world" as used in Swedenborg's writings, see note 141. [Editors]

393 (in *Faith* 19:2). On Swedenborg's view that all angels and spirits are people who have gone on to live in the spiritual world after death, see notes 13 and 251. [Editors]

394 (in *Faith* 20). For more on the individual and collective levels of the neighbor, see *New Jerusalem* 91–96; *True Christianity* 412–416; *Sketch on Goodwill* (= Swedenborg 1996d) §§72–89. For examples of fellow citizens being called our brother or sister or companion in the Bible, see Genesis 19:7; Exodus 32:27; Psalms 122:8; 133:1; Matthew 12:48–50; 23:8; Acts 1:16; 1 Timothy 5:1–2; James 2:15; Revelation 1:9; 22:9. [LSW]

395 (in *Faith* 20). For more on the concept that good is the neighbor to be loved, see *Secrets of Heaven* 2425, 3768:2; *New Jerusalem* 84–90; *True Christianity* 417–419; *Sketch on Goodwill* (= Swedenborg 1996d) §§42–71. In these passages Swedenborg ties this concept in with the levels of the neighbor referred to earlier in this section by pointing out that since the Lord is the highest neighbor, and what is good and true is the Lord's presence in human beings, when people love what is good and true in others they are loving the Lord in them. [LSW]

396 (in *Faith* 21). The Latin first edition here erroneously reads *Cap V:32. 33. seq.* ("chapter 5:32, 33, and the verses following"), but it is clear which verses were actually intended. See especially Matthew 5:46: "For if you love those who love you, what reward do you have? Do not even the tax collectors do the same?" (New Revised Standard Version). [GFD]

Notes to *Faith* Chapter 3, §§25–33

397 (in *Faith* 26). "Earthly memory" here is the same as that referred to elsewhere by Swedenborg as the "outer memory," which is "the last of a series" (*Secrets of Heaven* 2492:2). This memory, or collecting area for facts, is frequently likened to the sea, which

is the last of the series of earth's bodies of water; all water flows to it and the gathered waters are stored there. (See, for example, *Secrets of Heaven* 991, 2850, 9340, 9755.) According to Swedenborg, what is gathered in this memory is simply raw facts and experiences. These remain superficial and not a real part of our character until we make use of them in our lives. At that point they become part of our "inner memory," to which, unlike the outer memory, we retain conscious access after death. For more on the outer and inner memories, see *Secrets of Heaven* 2469–2494, 9841:3; *Heaven and Hell* 463; *New Jerusalem* 52; *Divine Providence* 227; *Revelation Explained* (= Swedenborg 1994–1997a) §569:3. [LSW]

398 (in *Faith* 31). For more on the concept that as truly human beings, angels are expressions of caring, see *Secrets of Heaven* 553, 3484, 4735:2, 5133, 10153; *Heaven and Hell* 414; *Revelation Explained* (= Swedenborg 1994–1997a) §157:2; *Sketch on Goodwill* (= Swedenborg 1996d) §158. On faith as the form that caring takes in truly human beings, see *Faith* 18; *Secrets of Heaven* 668, 3868, 9783; *Revelation Unveiled* 875:3; *True Christianity* 367:1–3. [LSW]

399 (in *Faith* 32). For some examples of Jesus comparing people to trees, see Matthew 3:10; 7:15–20; 12:33; Luke 13:6–9. [LSW]

Notes to *Faith* Chapter 4, §§34–37

400 (in *Faith* 34). In the first edition, this chapter and the next (§§34–43) are set in noticeably larger type than the rest of the work, apparently for emphasis. In content as well, the two chapters are clearly juxtaposed and set in contrast to one another. This chapter is the first of four places in which Swedenborg published this brief summation of what he identified as true Christian faith, each time accompanied by nearly identical explanatory commentary. The others are in *Revelation Unveiled* 67; *Survey* 116; and *True Christianity* 2. [GFD, LSW, JSR]

401 (in *Faith* 34). On Swedenborg's use of "hell" in the plural, see note 21. [Editors]

402 (in *Faith* 37). This work, referred to in this edition by the short title *The Lord,* was published by Swedenborg in Amsterdam in 1763. [Editors]

Notes to *Faith* Chapter 5, §§38–43

403 (in *Faith* 38). On the satisfaction theory of atonement in Western Christian theology, see note 69. [Editors]

404 (in *Faith* 39). Here Swedenborg uses the Latin word *justificatio* ("justification") not in its simple, secular sense, but as a Christian theological term. Justification is the action or process by which a given individual is either deemed or actually made "just," meaning righteous and therefore worthy of salvation. [JSR]

405 (in *Faith* 39). On "faith alone," see note 209. [Editors]

406 (in *Faith* 42). The connection between the lack of vegetation around the clergyman's companions and the angels saying that they have no trace of a church is that, as Swedenborg asserts a number of times, in the spiritual world one's surroundings correspond to one's inner state (*Heaven and Hell* 109, 111; *True Christianity* 78:1–3). All vegetation, he says, relates to wisdom and intelligence; grass specifically corresponds to the least and lowest form of true faith (*Revelation Unveiled* 401). See also *Sacred Scripture* 96b. [JSR]

Notes to *Faith* Chapter 6, §§44–48

407 (in *Faith* 47). Giving "power to some person to act as God on earth" is Swedenborg's negative characterization of the authority invested in the pope by the Roman Catholic Church. In the ensuing list of attentions to "dead people," Swedenborg refers negatively to various forms of the veneration of saints in Roman Catholic practice. See note 386. [Editors]

408 (in *Faith* 48). This is probably an allusion to the famous metaphor of the cave offered by the Greek philosopher Plato (427–347 B.C.E.). In this symbolic account, people are chained and forced to watch nothing but shadows on the wall, which they then mistake for reality (Plato *Republic* 514a–517e [= Plato 1997, 1132–1135]). [RS]

Notes to *Faith* Chapter 7, §§49–54

409 (in *Faith* 49). On Swedenborg's concept of the Bible as having an inner meaning, see note 11. On his concept of "correspondence," the specific principle by which that inner meaning operates, see note 169. [Editors]

410 (in *Faith* 49). The identification of the Babylon of the Book of Revelation with the Roman Catholic Church, and specifically with its clerical element, is not unique to Swedenborg but extends as far back as medieval times, if not before. Many examples of others who made this equation could be given; one would be Dante Alighieri (1265–1321), who likens the corrupt ecclesiastics of his day to the whore of Babylon mentioned in Revelation 17:4–18 (*Inferno* 19:106–108). In the sixteenth century, the chief Protestant reformers almost unanimously agreed that biblical references to the whore of Babylon had been intended to point prophetically to the future Roman Catholic Church. In 1520 Martin Luther (1483–1546) published a treatise on the Catholic sacraments titled *On the Babylonian Captivity of the Church* (Luther [1520] 1955–1986, 36:3–126). A woodcut appearing in the first edition of Luther's German translation of the New Testament, the so-called *September-Testament* of 1522, shows the whore of Babylon wearing a papal tiara. The image was so explosive that George of Saxony (1471–1539), Luther's secular opponent, insisted that it be removed in a republication of the same material later in the same year, but a full-color reimagining of the scene was pointedly reinserted into the complete Bible published in 1534 (see Füssel and Taschen 2009, 22–25, 184–185). On Swedenborg's symbolic interpretation of Babylon and the Philistines, see note 148. On problematic material in general in Swedenborg's works, see the translator's preface, pages 4–6. [RS, LSW, DNG]

411 (in *Faith* 50). For more on the meaning of wars in the Bible as spiritual wars, see *Secrets of Heaven* 1659:3, 1664, 8273, 10455; *Revelation Unveiled* 52, 500, 586; *Revelation Explained* (= Swedenborg 1994–1997a) §357. On how this principle applies to present-day wars, and more on war in general, see *Divine Providence* 251. [LSW]

412 (in *Faith* 50). For a discussion of the meaning of the term *Canaan*, see the appendix on pages 529–530. [Editors]

413 (in *Faith* 51). In *Divine Love and Wisdom* 424 spiritual love is defined as "love for the Lord and love for our neighbor," and earthly love is defined as "love for ourselves and love for the world." According to Swedenborg, when earthly love fails to serve spiritual love and becomes dominant in a person, it then becomes corrupted into demonic and hellish love. For more on these loves, see *Secrets of Heaven* 9434, 10463;

New Jerusalem 54–107; *Divine Love and Wisdom* 416; *Divine Providence* 106–107. In some of these passages "heavenly love" is used as a synonym for "spiritual love." On circumcision as a symbol of purification from the hellish loves that hinder and corrupt heavenly loves, see *Faith* 54; *Secrets of Heaven* 2039, 4462; *True Christianity* 674. [LSW]

414 (in *Faith* 52). For more on these meanings of the story contained in 1 Samuel 5, 6, see *Divine Providence* 326:12; *True Christianity* 203. For more specifically on the meaning of Dagon, see *Sacred Scripture* 23:2; *Revelation Explained* (= Swedenborg 1994–1997a) §§700:22, 817:10. On the meanings of hemorrhoids and of rats (or, in some translations, mice), see *Secrets of Heaven* 7524:3; *Revelation Explained* 700:21, 700:23, 827:4. On Goliath, see *Revelation Explained* 781:12. [LSW]

415 (in *Faith* 53). For additional commentary on Jeremiah 47:1, 2, 4, see *Secrets of Heaven* 705, 1201, 6015:4, 6297, 9340:7; *Revelation Explained* (= Swedenborg 1994–1997a) §§406:13, 518:34; *Sketch for "Coda to True Christianity"* (= Swedenborg 1996h) §34:2. [LSW]

416 (in *Faith* 53). The Latin is *basiliscus*. The basilisk was a legendary serpent thought to be able to kill with a glance. The Hebrew is צֶפַע (*ṣepaʿ*), now thought to be a particular species of viper. [GFD]

417 (in *Faith* 53). The Hebrew underlying the Latin here translated "fiery serpent" is שָׂרָף (*śārāp*), which is closely associated with the verb שָׂרַף (*śārap*), "burn"; but it clearly means some kind of snake, as indicated in this passage in Isaiah 14:29. Compare Deuteronomy 8:15. [GFD]

418 (in *Faith* 53). For additional commentary on Isaiah 14:29, see *Secrets of Heaven* 251:2, 1197:3; *Divine Providence* 340; *True Christianity* 487:4; *Revelation Explained* (= Swedenborg 1994–1997a) §§581:8, 727:21. [LSW]

Notes to *Faith* Chapter 8, §§55–60

419 (in *Faith* 56). On the world of spirits and its place in Swedenborg's overall conception of the spiritual world, see note 141. [Editors]

420 (in *Faith* 56). For some of Swedenborg's accounts of seeing, in the spiritual world, the great dragon described in Revelation 12:3–4 as a visual representation of people who are devoted to faith alone, see *Supplements* 28; *Survey* 90; *Spiritual Experiences* (= Swedenborg 1998–2013) §§4872–4888, 5370–5376. [LSW]

421 (in *Faith* 56). On Swedenborg's concept of a correspondence between spiritual and material phenomena, see note 169. [Editors]

422 (in *Faith* 58). In the first edition, this entire section is set in noticeably larger type than the rest of the text, apparently for emphasis. [GFD]

423 (in *Faith* 58). The Latin of the first edition reads *cornua septem*, "seven horns," clearly an error; both the original Greek and Swedenborg's preferred Latin Bible, Schmidt 1696, indicate ten. Compare note 349. [GFD]

424 (in *Faith* 59). In the first edition, each line of this section begins with quotation marks, a typographical device used by Swedenborg and others to highlight material or to indicate that it came originally from another source. In *The Lord* 44, for example, an excerpt from Psalm 89 is so marked; in §56 of the same work, an extended excerpt from the Athanasian Creed; and then in §65, a list of six "new" creedal elements. The marking of the present example, together with a number of terminological similarities, suggests that this section may be a condensation of the summaries of the spiritual meaning of Revelation 12 given in *Revelation Explained* (= Swedenborg 1994–1997a) §§705, 712,

723, 729, 733, 756, 762, and 766. On a similarly marked passage in *Sacred Scripture,* see note 216. [GFD]

425 (in *Faith* 60). Swedenborg provides detailed verse-by-verse explanations of Revelation 13 in *Revelation Unveiled* 567–610 and *Revelation Explained* (= Swedenborg 1994–1997a) §§773–847. [LSW]

Notes to *Faith* Chapter 9, §§61–68

426 (in *Faith* 63:2). The Latin is *apparentiae*. Strictly speaking, according to *Secrets of Heaven* 3207, only God can see things as they actually are. We see only "what things look like"; and how accurately this represents "what is" depends on the state of our perception. In the present instance, the meaning is that the farmland, fields, and flocks are projections of the states of the angels according to the correspondences previously described. On correspondences, see note 169. On the "real appearances" that exist in heaven, see *Secrets of Heaven* 3485; *Heaven and Hell* 175. [GFD, SS, LSW]

427 (in *Faith* 63:4). For other descriptions of fights between sheep and goats, see *Survey* 82–86; *Draft of "Supplements"* §§180–181 [Rogers's numbering] = §§180–182 [Potts's numbering] (= Swedenborg 1997a, 125–126). Compare also with the account found in *Revelation Unveiled* 655 and *True Christianity* 388, and the account found in *Revelation Unveiled* 417 and *True Christianity* 506. [LSW]

428 (in *Faith* 64:2). The work here identified as *Supplement on the Last Judgment* is the first of two supplements to previous works issued by Swedenborg in Amsterdam in 1763. The combined titles were published in one volume and are referred to in this edition by the short title *Supplements*. [Editors]

429 (in *Faith* 65). *Sacred Scripture* was published by Swedenborg in Amsterdam in 1763. [Editors]

430 (in *Faith* 65). Swedenborg here uses the Latin word *decus,* "beauty," "glory," to translate the word הַצְּבִי (*haṣṣəḇî*), "the beauty," in the original Hebrew of Daniel 8:9. This is commonly read by biblical scholars as a short form of the phrase אֶרֶץ הַצְּבִי (*'ereṣ haṣṣəḇî*), "the beautiful land," which occurs in Daniel 11:16, 41, referring to the land of Israel; and it seems likely that Swedenborg too took that to be the meaning, given his explanation elsewhere that the word refers to "the church" (*Secrets of Heaven* 9642:6), a meaning he often assigns to the land of Israel. In addition, in his preferred Bible translation, Schmidt 1696, Swedenborg will have seen the word *decus* in this verse, followed by an editorial insertion in parentheses and italics of the word *Jisraël* ("Israel"). [GFD, LSW, JSR]

431 (in *Faith* 67). In Swedenborg's first edition, the remainder of this section is marked off by quotation marks at the beginning of each line. On the significance of this device, see note 424. Two earlier manuscripts on which Swedenborg may have drawn in compiling these interpretations are *Revelation Explained* (= Swedenborg 1994–1997a) §316:16 and *Draft on the Inner Meaning of Prophets and Psalms* (= Swedenborg 1996i, 2:21–234). However, the interpretation given here does not entirely match either of those earlier interpretations. [GFD, LSW]

432 (in *Faith* 68). "The deeds of caring they did not do" to which Swedenborg refers here are listed in Matthew 25:42–43: "I was hungry and you gave me no food, I was thirsty and you gave me nothing to drink, I was a stranger and you did not welcome me, naked and you did not give me clothing, sick and in prison and you did not visit

me" (New Revised Standard Version). For additional commentary on Matthew 25:31–46, see *Secrets of Heaven* 4661–4664, 4807–4810, 4954–4959, 5063–5071; *Revelation Explained* (= Swedenborg 1994–1997a) §§600:5, 817:12. [LSW, SS]

Notes to *Faith* Chapter 10, §§69–72

433 (in *Faith* 70). In the current section, Swedenborg argues on the basis of his experience in the spiritual world that people who have convinced themselves of a faith divorced from caring have no truth whatever. Elsewhere in Swedenborg's theological writings this proposition is given more analytical treatment. His basic analysis is that those who are not engaged in caring lives may be able to speak true things from external memory, but inwardly they neither accept them as true nor even understand them, so that they themselves do not actually have the truth. Further, Swedenborg says, any understanding they may have of anything that in itself is true is corrupted by evil motives, with the result that the "truth" they have is twisted into falsity that supports those evil motives. For more on this topic, see *Secrets of Heaven* 1072, 4767, 7950, 9300; *Divine Providence* 14; *True Christianity* 391; *Revelation Explained* (= Swedenborg 1994–1997a) §§434:15, 714:9. [LSW]

Notes to *Supplements* Chapter 1, §§1–7

434 (in *Supplements* 1). *Last Judgment* was published by Swedenborg in London in 1758. [Editors]

435 (in *Supplements* 1). On "the spiritual world," see note 141. [Editors]

436 (in *Supplements* 1). On Swedenborg's use of the word "church" to denote any of various spiritual eras in the history of humankind, see note 5. [Editors]

437 (in *Supplements* 3). On the Latin word *caelum*, here translated "heavens," see note 139. [Editors]

438 (in *Supplements* 3). New heavens and a new earth (or "new land") are mentioned in Isaiah 65:17; 66:22; Revelation 21:1. The belief that at the end of the world all people will be resurrected in reconstituted physical bodies has been common to many Christians throughout the ages. It is based on various passages of the Bible, including Job 19:25–27; Daniel 12:2; John 5:28–29; Acts 24:15; 1 Thessalonians 4:16; Revelation 20:13. Compare also 1 Corinthians 15:35–55. It also appears in some form in more than one major Christian creed. For example, the Apostles' Creed refers to the resurrection of the flesh, or physical body; the final lines of the Athanasian Creed refer to all people rising again "with their bodies." [SS, JSR, LHC]

439 (in *Supplements* 3). On "the Word" as used in Swedenborg's theological writings, see note 11. [Editors]

440 (in *Supplements* 3). On the spiritual meaning of the Bible as compared to its literal meaning, see notes 11 and 17. [Editors]

441 (in *Supplements* 3). Beliefs of this sort about the soul actually stemmed from long before Swedenborg's time. Ether, a very rare vapor supposedly more refined than other matter, was sometimes believed to be the material of which spirits are composed. Thus the Greek physician Galen (129–around 216 C.E.) taught that the human soul is ultimately derived from the ethereal (upper atmospheric) regions, whence eternal spirit is inhaled and refined (Galen 1968). Furthermore, the word for "spirit" in biblical Hebrew,

רוּחַ (*rûaḥ*), can mean not only spirit but breath or wind; see Brown, Driver, and Briggs 1996, under רוּחַ, definition 2.a. Likewise, the ancient Greek word for spirit, πνεῦμα (*pneûma*), can also mean breath or wind. The notion—apparently somewhat overstated here—that souls, spirits, and angels are simply wind seems to be based on the combined force of these associations. Compare note 298. [GMC, JSR, LHC, SS, DNG]

442 (in *Supplements* 3). In Swedenborg's theological works "angels" are people who have been born in the material world, died, gone through a transitional process in the spiritual world as described in *Heaven and Hell* 491–520, and arrived in heaven to stay. "Spirits" refers to one of two classes of beings. One class consists of people who have died recently and are still in the "world of spirits," a realm located between heaven and hell. All who die initially enter this realm and live there while awaiting transition to their final destination, which may be heaven or hell, depending upon whether they are good or evil. The other class consists of evil spirits who have in fact reached their final home—that is, hell. These spirits of hell are also referred to as "devils," "satans," and "demons." Both angels and spirits are described as real and tangible to the spiritual senses, though they are made, not of physical matter, but of spiritual substance. For more on the nature of spirits and the world of spirits, see *Secrets of Heaven* 320–323, 1880–1881, 5852; *Heaven and Hell* 421–444, 453–469; *Divine Love and Wisdom* 140–145. See also note 141 on the spiritual world. [LSW]

443 (in *Supplements* 4). The Latin word here translated "somewhere-or-other" is *Pu;* the word is the transliterated form of the Greek indefinite adverb πού *(poú)*, meaning "somewhere." It is used by Swedenborg to express an uncertain location, approximately in the sense of "limbo" (see *True Christianity* 769, where the two terms are equated; and see *True Christianity* volume 2 [= Swedenborg [1771] 2012], page 548 note 444 for discussion of the term *limbo* itself). Though it may be translated in any of several ways, it appears in the Latin in the same sense in *Supplements* 6; *Divine Love and Wisdom* 350; *Marriage Love* 28, 29, 182:5; *True Christianity* 29:2, 769, 771. See also Helander 2004, 137–138. [SS]

444 (in *Supplements* 4). On the idea of souls before the Last Judgment and the resurrection not being able to see, hear, or speak, see note 299. [Editors]

445 (in *Supplements* 4). The term "first creation" here refers to a literal interpretation of the creation of the world, and humans on earth, as presented in the first two chapters in Genesis. In this interpretation Adam, the first human being, was created by God approximately 6,000 years ago, a figure determined by calculations based on the genealogies in Genesis 5, 11:10–32, together with additional genealogical information scattered throughout the Bible and various ancient historical records. Although many researchers compiled chronologies in this fashion, perhaps the most famous was that of Irish archbishop James Ussher (1580–1656), whose conclusions were published in his influential seventeenth-century work *Annals of the Old Testament* (Ussher 1650–1654). It is difficult to know whether Swedenborg himself shared this common belief; he nowhere challenges it directly, though he does seem to have accepted some form of an alternate theory that people existed before Adam; see *Spiritual Experiences* (= Swedenborg 1998–2013) §3390, and *True Christianity* volume 2 (= Swedenborg [1771] 2012), page 489 note 28. For other references to this timeframe, see *Heaven and Hell* 415; *Marriage Love* 29, 39, 182:5; *True Christianity* 693:5. [LSW, SS]

Notes to *Supplements* Chapter 2, §§8–13

446 (in *Supplements* 8). On the term "new church" as used in Swedenborg's writings, see note 5. [Editors]

447 (in *Supplements* 9). For more on the nature and location of these pseudo-heavens, see *Supplements* 16–19; *Last Judgment* 65–72; *Revelation Explained* (= Swedenborg 1994–1997a) §§391–392, 394, 397, 497; *Draft of Five Memorable Occurrences* (= Swedenborg 1996e) §24. [LSW]

448 (in *Supplements* 10). Swedenborg's frequent description of the heavens as three in number agrees with Christian tradition, which is based primarily on 2 Corinthians 12:2. These three he delineates as the central or third heaven, also called the heavenly heaven; the intermediate or second heaven, also called the spiritual heaven; and the outermost or first heaven, also called the natural heaven. These heavens can be pictured as levels one above the other or as distinct regions one within the other. See *Secrets of Heaven* 9594; *Heaven and Hell* 29–40; *Divine Love and Wisdom* 202. The "lowest heaven" mentioned here is the first or earthly heaven. Swedenborg indicates that those who live in this heaven are "people who live good moral lives . . . and believe in the Divine with no particular interest in learning" (*Heaven and Hell* 33). In other words, they are simple, good people who are focused primarily on outward actions and who don't reflect on the motives and beliefs behind those actions. Since they typically focus on outward actions and largely ignore internal matters, in Swedenborg's account they were easily attached to spirits in the pseudo-heavens who lived good lives outwardly but were evil inwardly (see *Last Judgment* 70; *Revelation Unveiled* 330). For more on the lowest heaven and its relationship with the other two heavens, see *Secrets of Heaven* 4240, 4279, 4286:2, 9741; *Heaven and Hell* 31, 33, 270–271; *Revelation Explained* (= Swedenborg 1994–1997a) §449. On the overall layout of the spiritual world, see note 141. [LSW]

449 (in *Supplements* 12). Swedenborg's statement here that revelations for the new church were given after the Last Judgment happened and not before cannot be taken too strictly or literally. He states elsewhere that this final judgment was completed in the year 1757 (see *Last Judgment* 45; *Revelation Unveiled* 791:2, 865:1, 886:1). However, the eight-volume work *Secrets of Heaven,* in which he first revealed the bulk of his theological concepts, was published in the years 1749 to 1756—prior to the date he gives for the accomplishment of the Last Judgment. [LSW]

450 (in *Supplements* 12). This work, referred to in this edition by the short title *The Lord,* was published by Swedenborg in Amsterdam in 1763. [Editors]

Notes to *Supplements* Chapter 3, §§14–31

451 (in *Supplements* 14). On Swedenborg's use of "Babylon" to refer to the Roman Catholic Church, see note 148. [Editors]

452 (in *Supplements* 14). On the Lord as the sun of heaven, the warmth from the sun being divine love and the light of the sun being divine wisdom, see *Secrets of Heaven* 1521–1534, 3636, 8812, 10809; *Heaven and Hell* 116–140; *Divine Love and Wisdom* 83–102; *Soul-Body Interaction* 4–6; *Revelation Explained* (= Swedenborg 1994–1997a) §401. Swedenborg says in *Divine Love and Wisdom* 93–98 that although the Lord does appear as a sun to angels, that sun is not actually God, but is "the first emanation from his love and wisdom" (*Divine Love and Wisdom* 97). [LSW]

453 (in *Supplements* 14). For more on space and apparent distances in the spiritual world, see *Heaven and Hell* 191–199. [Editors]

454 (in *Supplements* 14). This work, referred to in this edition by the short title *Sacred Scripture,* was published by Swedenborg in Amsterdam in 1763. [Editors]

455 (in *Supplements* 15). "The sheep" as used here is a reference to Matthew 25:31–46, in which Jesus speaks of the sheep as those people who did good works (performed caring actions on behalf of others) and who therefore go to eternal life, and the goats as those people who did not do good works and who therefore go to eternal punishment. In the specific context of the Last Judgment, Swedenborg defines them in *Supplements* 31 as "individuals from previous centuries who had been held [in the lower regions] and protected by the Lord so that they would not be overcome by the malignant aura that flowed out from the dragon [on which see *Supplements* 16] and so that their caring would not be suffocated by it." [LSW, JSR]

456 (in *Supplements* 18). On "the world of spirits" and its place in Swedenborg's overall conception of the spiritual world, see note 141. [Editors]

457 (in *Supplements* 19). On Swedenborg's view of the human mind as having various levels, see note 180. [Editors]

458 (in *Supplements* 19). "Devils" is used here to refer generally to individual evil spirits in hell, who according to Swedenborg's theology were once human beings living in the material world. On the overall layout of the spiritual world and the regions in which its various inhabitants live, see note 141. [LSW]

459 (in *Supplements* 19). The reference here is not racial, but rather to the blackness associated with soot from a fire. Compare *Heaven and Hell* 585; *Divine Love and Wisdom* 357; *Revelation Unveiled* 153:12. On Swedenborg's high regard for Africans, see *Supplements* 73 and note 510. [LSW]

460 (in *Supplements* 20). *Heaven and Hell* was published by Swedenborg in London in 1758. [Editors]

461 (in *Supplements* 21). On "spiritual love" and "earthly love," see note 413. [Editors]

462 (in *Supplements* 23). According to Swedenborg's descriptions in *New Jerusalem* 4 and *Revelation Unveiled* 260, the various heavens are arranged in levels one above the other. The pseudo-heavens were situated in the world of spirits, which, in Swedenborg's topography of the spiritual world, forms a level below the lowest heaven. For more on the levels of heaven, see note 448. For more on clouds in the spiritual world, see *Last Judgment* 28; *Divine Love and Wisdom* 147; *Revelation Unveiled* 24; *True Christianity* 776; *Revelation Explained* (= Swedenborg 1994–1997a) §§36, 594, 906. On spiritual clouds serving a protective function, see *Secrets of Heaven* 6849, 8816. For more on the spiritual significance of clouds, see *Secrets of Heaven* 1043, 5922:6–9, 8106; *Revelation Unveiled* 642. [LSW]

463 (in *Supplements* 23). For more on how objects that appear in the spiritual world reflect the character of spirits and angels there, see *Secrets of Heaven* 10194; *Heaven and Hell* 488, 585; *Revelation Unveiled* 835; *Spiritual Experiences* (= Swedenborg 1998–2013) §§4788–4790; *Revelation Explained* (= Swedenborg 1994–1997a) §659:5. On the concept of correspondence in Swedenborg's theology, see note 169. [LSW]

464 (in *Supplements* 24). The Latin is *colligaverunt se in facies inferni,* literally, "they bound themselves into faces of hell." The translation "bundles" is based on emending

facies, "faces," to *fasces,* "bundles," presuming an allusion to the householder's command in the parable cited in *Supplements* 10, *colligate ea in fasciculos ad comburendum ea,* "bind them in bundles for burning" (Matthew 13:30). [GFD]

465 (in *Supplements* 28). It is a common theme in Swedenborg's theological writings that though overly literal interpretations of Scripture lead people to believe that God is angry and sends people to hell, the truth is that God is never angry or wrathful and never sends anyone to hell, but acts toward all people, the good and the evil alike, from pure love and mercy. According to Swedenborg, it is evil itself, rather than God or any angel, that brings pain and destruction upon those who engage in it. See, for example, *Secrets of Heaven* 245, 588, 592, 696, 1683, 8632, 10431; *Heaven and Hell* 545–550; *Revelation Unveiled* 525; *True Christianity* 650–653; *Revelation Explained* (= Swedenborg 1994–1997a) §647. Compare also *Sacred Scripture* 94. [LSW]

466 (in *Supplements* 29). In the later parts of *Spiritual Experiences* (= Swedenborg 1998–2013), Swedenborg recorded in much greater detail what he saw of the Last Judgment in the spiritual world. For some examples, see §§5034–5058, 5060–5074, 5202–5203, 5258–5267, 5347–5356 in that work. [LSW]

467 (in *Supplements* 30). On "the sheep," see note 455. [Editors]

468 (in *Supplements* 31). "The ones who woke up and came out of their graves" is a reference to Matthew 27:52–53; see also Ezekiel 37:12–13; Daniel 12:1–2; and Swedenborg's commentary on these passages in *Secrets of Heaven* 8018. "The souls of those who had been killed because of their testimony for Jesus" is a reference to Revelation 6:9–11; see also Revelation 12:17. And "those who were part of the first resurrection" is a reference to Revelation 20:5–6. [LSW, GFD]

Notes to *Supplements* Chapter 4, §§32–38

469 (in *Supplements* 32). On ether and the soul, see note 298. [Editors]

470 (in *Supplements* 33). The philosophers of the Enlightenment period were especially intrigued with the question of the difference between animals and humans, and ultimately the assertion that there was any difference at all became a shibboleth that distinguished believers from atheists. Descartes had argued in the 1600s that animals were essentially automata (Descartes [1637] 1952, 59), and other philosophers took the next step in this line of thinking, asserting that humans were only a special form of machine; see, for example, the notorious *L'Homme machine* (The Human as Machine [= La Mettrie [1747] 1994]) by the atheist writer Julien Offray de La Mettrie (1709–1751). A parallel line of thinking concluded that since animals did not have souls, humans could not possess souls either. (For a biblical basis for this view, see Ecclesiastes 3:19.) Swedenborg condemns these trends of thought in *Secrets of Heaven* 4760:2, 5114:5, and other passages. For further discussion of the general topic of animals during the Enlightenment, see Senior 2007 and *True Christianity* vol. 1 (= Swedenborg [1771] 2006), page 688 note 67. For more on Swedenborg's assessment of animals, see *Secrets of Heaven* vol. 2 (= Swedenborg [1749–1756] 2013), page 520 note 43. For extended passages in Swedenborg's works on the difference between animals and humans, see *Marriage Love* 151b:3–5; *Soul-Body Interaction* 15; *True Christianity* 48:8–13; *Revelation Explained* (= Swedenborg 1994–1997a) §§1196:2–1202 (where the discussion is continued serially in the later subsections of each section); *Dynamics of the Soul's Domain* (= Swedenborg [1740–1741] 1955) part 2, §§337–347; *The Old Testament Explained* (= Swedenborg 1927–1951) §§916–921. [SS, JSR, FLS]

471 (in *Supplements* 34). Although the biblical text sometimes refers to them not as angels but as "men" or "holy ones" or the like, angels appear to Abraham in Genesis 18:2; to Gideon in Judges 6:11–22; and to Daniel in Daniel 8:15–17; 10:5–7; 12:5–7. One or two angels appear in or near the tomb of Jesus in Matthew 28:2–5; Mark 16:5; Luke 24:4 (compare Luke 24:23); and John 20:12. Angels are mentioned more than sixty times in the Book of Revelation; John explicitly mentions *seeing* angels in Revelation 5:2; 7:1, 2; 8:2; 10:1, 5; 14:6; 15:1; 18:1; 19:17; 20:1. Swedenborg's point is that the Bible presents these angels as human beings. For Jesus showing his followers that he was human after the Resurrection by being touched and eating, see Matthew 28:8–9; Luke 24:36–43; John 20:24–28. For Jesus vanishing from their sight, see Luke 24:30–32. [JSR, LSW]

472 (in *Supplements* 35). Nineteen years before 1763, the date of the publication of *Supplements,* would be 1744. The exact point of commencement of Swedenborg's daily, waking, ongoing interaction with angels and spirits is variously stated in his writings. If the variations are taken at face value, the dates that he mentions for this commencement all fall within the range 1743–1745. To cite just a few representative examples: (1) In a diary passage apparently written in early 1746, Swedenborg states that his interaction with spirits and angels dates *a medio Aprilis 1745,* "from mid-April 1745" (*Spiritual Experiences* [= Swedenborg 1998–2013] §[8a]). (2) In two later passages, one in a theological manuscript of early 1763 and one in a letter of November 11, 1766, he assigns the commencement a date of 1744 (for the manuscript, see *Draft on Divine Wisdom* chapter 7, item 1 = §95 [Mongredien's numbering] [= Swedenborg 1994–1997c, 480]; for the letter, see Acton 1948–1955, 627). (3) In a still later letter to a British follower, Thomas Hartley (1708–1784), on August 5, 1769, he states that his sight was "opened into the spiritual world" in 1743 (Acton 1948–1955, 679). In other words, as the years passed, Swedenborg saw the commencement of his interaction as having occurred earlier and earlier. Some of this variation may derive from his changing assessment of which event constituted the true beginning of his spiritual experiences. See Tafel 1877, 1118–1127, for a list of the relevant passages, with discussion. For a detailed account of the onset of Swedenborg's spiritual experiences, see Acton 1927, 26–118. [JSR, GFD, SS]

473 (in *Supplements* 35). In the first Latin edition, the word here translated "seen" *(Visa)* is set in large and small capitals, presumably for special emphasis. For more on various types of visions in comparison to Swedenborg's spiritual experiences, see *Secrets of Heaven* 1786, 1882–1885, 1966–1983; *The Lord* 52; *Divine Providence* 134a–135; *Revelation Explained* (= Swedenborg 1994–1997a) §575. [LSW, JSR]

474 (in *Supplements* 38). Swedenborg is here referring to the Lord as the sun of heaven, on which see note 452. [LSW]

475 (in *Supplements* 38). In referring to the "fire" of the sun here, Swedenborg does not mean ordinary earthly fire, which he calls "common fire"; he means what he calls "elementary fire," which he believed had its origin in a release of so-called actives from the breakdown of elementary particles in the sun. For a discussion of these types of fire as they appear in his scientific works, see *True Christianity* volume 2 (= Swedenborg [1771] 2012), page 495 note 61. [SS]

Notes to *Supplements* Chapter 5, §§39–47

476 (in *Supplements* 40). During the Enlightenment, Britain was widely admired for the various freedoms it enjoyed relative to the Continent. For example, Swedenborg's

contemporary Voltaire characterizes Britain as a place where happiness obtains because "everyone has freely enjoyed the right of speaking his mind" (Voltaire [1764] 1962, 356). This freedom was seen as applying in religious matters in particular; as Voltaire adds in his *Letters Concerning the English Nation:* "An Englishman, as a free man, goes to Heaven by whatever road he pleases" (Voltaire [1733] 2003, 22). [SS]

477 (in *Supplements* 42:1). According to Swedenborg's explanation in *Spiritual Experiences* (= Swedenborg 1998–2013) §5092, cities in the spiritual world resembling those on earth arise from the mental activity of the spirits present with every person on earth. Since those spirits hold the contents of everything in the memory of the individual with whom they are associated, including their mental images of houses, buildings, and streets, similar cities appear in the spiritual world based on those mental images. [SS]

478 (in *Supplements* 42:1). Although Swedenborg was a Swede, he was familiar with London; he lived there on nine occasions for a cumulative total of seven years, including the last seven months of his life. The Latin passage here translated "is [like] the part of London, England, where the merchants are concentrated, which is called the Exchange" is *ubi in Londino Angliae Conventus mercatorum, qui vocatur Exchange.* By "merchants" here (Latin *mercatores*) Swedenborg may mean merchants in general or stockbrokers in particular; by "Exchange" he may mean either the Royal Exchange, a vibrant shopping and social district with merchandise from around the world, or the group of one hundred and fifty brokers then meeting in Jonathan's coffee house and soon afterward to become the London Stock Exchange. In any event, the area of London to which he refers is clear, and is the same in both cases: the area around Cornhill, due north of what was then the London Bridge. [JSR]

479 (in *Supplements* 44). On the teaching referred to as "faith alone," see note 209. [Editors]

480 (in *Supplements* 45). "Holy Supper" (Latin *Sancta Caena*) is Swedenborg's preferred term for Holy Communion or the Eucharist. For an extended discussion, see *True Christianity* 698–752. [JSR]

481 (in *Supplements* 45). For the source of this exhortation, see note 313. [Editors]

482 (in *Supplements* 46:1). This "particular British man" has not been conclusively identified. [SS]

483 (in *Supplements* 46:2). In the spiritual world as described by Swedenborg, the paths and roads on which spirits are seen traveling are determined by their beliefs and their faith, whether true or false, especially as their thoughts are driven by their underlying loves and motives. For more on this phenomenon, see *Secrets of Heaven* 10422; *Heaven and Hell* 479:5, 534; *Divine Providence* 60; *Revelation Explained* (= Swedenborg 1994–1997a) §§206, 569:9, 940. [LSW]

484 (in *Supplements* 47). Swedenborg here without explanation diverts his discussion from British figures to touch on a German theologian, Philipp Melanchthon (1497–1560), one of the earliest and ablest followers of Luther. Melanchthon's *Loci Communes Rerum Theologicarum* (Common Theological Topics) was the first systematic presentation of Lutheran theology and was soon widely accepted as definitive; see Melanchthon 1521 and, for a translation, [Melanchthon] [1543] 1992. However, unlike Luther, Melanchthon "recognized the essential nature of the [Holy] Spirit's work in salvation both in inducing the will to exercise saving faith and in enabling it so to do, at the same time insisting that the will is free to respond and to co-operate" (Watkin-Jones 1929, 259–260). This may explain

why Melanchthon appears here after the British writer featured in *Supplements* 46, who had similar views on the inflow and working of the Holy Spirit. Full Lutheran monergism, the belief that humankind is saved solely through the action of the Holy Spirit, was finally established when the Formula of Concord was promulgated in 1577; it held that "the human creature . . cannot believe and accept [the Word] on the basis of its own powers but only through the grace and action of God the Holy Spirit" (Kolb and Wengert 2000, 494). [SS, GFD]

Notes to *Supplements* Chapter 6, §§48–55

485 (in *Supplements* 50). Compare Revelation 19:14, in which the armies of heaven are described as "wearing fine linen, white and pure," and Revelation 15:6, 19:8, in which heavenly beings are described as wearing "pure bright linen." In explaining these and similar passages in the Bible, Swedenborg interprets both "white linen" and "bright linen" as a symbol of divine truth. See *Secrets of Heaven* 5319, 5954; *Revelation Unveiled* 814; *True Christianity* 686; *Revelation Explained* (= Swedenborg 1994–1997a) §§950:1, 951:1–7. [LSW, SS]

486 (in *Supplements* 53). There is no §52 in the first edition. [GFD]

487 (in *Supplements* 54). John Calvin (1509–1564) was the founder of the Reformed or Calvinist branch of Protestant Christianity. For a much fuller and less complimentary account of Calvin in the spiritual world, see *True Christianity* 798. [GFD, SS]

488 (in *Supplements* 54). Martin Luther (1483–1546) was the founder of the branch of Protestant Christianity that bears his name. [JSR]

489 (in *Supplements* 54). On Philipp Melanchthon, see note 484. [Editors]

490 (in *Supplements* 55). Swedenborg subsequently published an account of Luther in the spiritual world in *True Christianity* 796. For some of Swedenborg's unpublished accounts of Luther, see *Spiritual Experiences* (= Swedenborg 1998–2013) §§5103–5106, 5911–5916, 6039–6042; *Draft of "Supplements"* §§32–37 [Rogers's numbering] = §§31–36 [Potts's numbering] (= Swedenborg 1997a, 70–73). [GFD, LSW]

Notes to *Supplements* Chapter 7, §§56–60

491 (in *Supplements* 56). On problematic material in Swedenborg's theological works, see the translator's preface, pages 4–6. [Editors]

492 (in *Supplements* 58). "Babylon" here refers to Roman Catholicism. See note 148. For Swedenborg's view of leaven or yeast, see *Secrets of Heaven* 2342: "Yeast symbolizes evil and falsity that renders heavenly and spiritual qualities impure and profane." He is also alluding to Christ's command "Beware of the yeast of the Pharisees and Sadducees" (Matthew 16:6; New Revised Standard Version; and compare Mark 8:15; Luke 12:1). [RS]

493 (in *Supplements* 59). "Twenty years previously" apparently refers to twenty years previous to 1758, the year that is Swedenborg's usual time frame for looking back on the Last Judgment. This implied reference to 1738 and certain facts given about this pope elsewhere in Swedenborg's works confirm that he is referring to Clement XII (1652–1740), who was pope from July 12, 1730, until February 6, 1740. These facts are: (1) overt references to the year 1738 as part of the pope's tenure, for which see *Draft of "Supplements"* §§61, 102 [Rogers's numbering] = §§60, 102 [Potts's numbering] (= Swedenborg 1997a, 82, 95); (2) a reference to the blindness this pope suffered in old age, for which see *Spiritual Experiences* (= Swedenborg 1998–2013) §5272; *Draft of "Supplements"* §102 [in both

Rogers's and Potts's numbering] (= Swedenborg 1997a, 95); (3) a reference to the identity of his successor, for which see *Draft of "Supplements"* §103 [in both Rogers's and Potts's numbering] (= Swedenborg 1997a, 96). Swedenborg is especially positive toward Clement because he connects him with a movement, albeit unsuccessful, to allow the laity free access to Scripture (see *Revelation Unveiled* 734). (Swedenborg's reference to 1738 rather than to the complete range of Clement's tenure is likely owing to the fact that Swedenborg was in Rome in 1738 and knew firsthand that Clement was pope at the time.) [JSR, GFD, SS]

494 (in *Supplements* 59). The pope after Clement XII (see note 493) was Benedict XIV (1675–1758). He was best known for resolving a number of thorny issues in the church's relationships with secular rulers. While he did improve the church's financial position and reform the education of priests, the most obvious result of his papacy was a decline in the church's authority. For Swedenborg's report on his career in the spiritual world, see *Spiritual Experiences* (= Swedenborg 1998–2013) §§5833, 5841, 5843–5844, 5846–5847; *Revelation Explained* (= Swedenborg 1994–1997a) §114:9; and *Draft of "Supplements"* §103 [in both Rogers's and Potts's numbering] (= Swedenborg 1997a, 96). For a more positive view of his papacy, see Haynes 1970. [GFD, SS]

495 (in *Supplements* 60). Louis XIV (1638–1715), popularly known as "the Sun King," reigned for seventy-two years, a record in Europe. A firm believer in the divine right of kings, he used his immense authority to unite a feudal and fragmented region into a single nation and the leading power in Europe. He is noted for his Catholic piety, for his suppression of French Protestantism in the revocation of the Edict of Nantes in 1685, and for the vast extravagance of his court at Versailles. [GFD, SS]

496 (in *Supplements* 60). By "the present king of France," Swedenborg refers to Louis XV (1710–1774), who reigned from 1715 to 1774. He attempted to follow the absolutist model set by Louis XIV, which depended largely on personality cult. Unfortunately, though Louis XV was "intelligent and reasonably diligent about state business, . . . he was a shy and almost pathologically private person" (Van Kley 1996, 137). His personal reserve and his insistence on governing alone, without the assistance of any powerful minister of state, proved a fatal combination: under his rule France descended into increasing political and religious dissension. This may be why Swedenborg reports, at this end of this passage, that Louis XIV found Louis XV susceptible to his counsel during a paranormal visit. See also note 497. [SS, JSR]

497 (in *Supplements* 60). The primary purpose of the papal bull *Unigenitus,* issued in 1713, was the refutation of Jansenism, a movement within Catholicism. Among the bull's strictures was a condemnation of the Jansenist teaching that all people should have full access to Scripture, a matter of great weight with Swedenborg; see *Revelation Unveiled* 734, where Swedenborg actually cites the bull as an example of the restriction of access to Scripture. The bull was requested of the pope by Louis XIV (see note 495), the main aims of whose rule included the extirpation of heresy and the unification of the French under a single national church and a centralized government. However, the bull proved quite divisive in France. In fact, the resulting disputes continued long after the death of Louis XIV in 1715 and were, as that king indicates further on in Swedenborg's account here, "detrimental to the French nation." It can even be said that the controversy over the bull contributed to the French Revolution (1789–1799). During the period when these consequences were playing out, Louis XV (see note 496) did in effect (as hinted here) oppose the bull by aligning himself with the lower French clergy, which had Jansenist

leanings. Furthermore, in the year before *Supplements* was published, Louis XV declined to intervene when the French parliament decreed an end to the activities of the Jesuits in France, who had always been implacable foes of the Jansenist camp. A few more details about this incident of the two kings and the Bull *Unigenitus* can be found in *Spiritual Experiences* (= Swedenborg 1998–2013) §5980. On the role of the Bull *Unigenitus* in the century leading up to the French Revolution, see Van Kley 1996 and Swann 1995. For more on the struggle between the Jansenists and the Jesuits, see Van Kley 1975. [SS, GFD, JSR]

Notes to *Supplements* Chapter 8, §§61–67

498 (in *Supplements* 65). As mentioned in note 141, Swedenborg divides the spiritual world into three main areas, which, listed in descending vertical order, are heaven, the world of spirits, and hell. The "lower earth" is the lowest area of the world of spirits; as such it contains people who have died but have not yet gone to their final home in either heaven or hell (see *Heaven and Hell* 513; *Revelation Unveiled* 845:2; *Secrets of Heaven* 4728). For other memorable occurrences that Swedenborg experienced in the lower earth, see *True Christianity* 332–333. Swedenborg's descriptions give the impression that it is a kind of underground world or system of caves beneath the surface of the world of spirits. [JSR]

499 (in *Supplements* 65). Presumably Swedenborg refers to Francis Xavier (1506–1552), who with Ignatius Loyola (1491–1556) and four lesser-known young men founded the Society of Jesus ("the Jesuits") in 1534. Xavier was canonized in 1622. [GFD, SS]

500 (in *Supplements* 67). Geneviève (419 or 422–512) is the patron saint of Paris, famed for her piety, her austere way of life, and her many works of charity. Swedenborg visited the church housing her relics when he was in Paris in January 1737 (Tafel 1877, 98). [SS]

Notes to *Supplements* Chapter 9, §§68–72

501 (in *Supplements* 68). The Qur'an explicitly denies that Jesus was the Son of God in many passages, especially Surah 5:75 and following, which not only calls those who believe such things infidels, but offers several arguments against the idea that God could have a son at all. Though Islam does accept the miracle of the Virgin Birth as a special sign from God to humankind (Surah 19), the result of that birth is acknowledged only to be a child without a human father, not an offspring of God. Furthermore, any connection of Jesus with God in the role of his Son is strictly ruled out by the fact that one of the greatest crimes in Islam is to equate anything or anyone with God, since God is the greatest of all; this is the crime of "association," termed *shirk* in Arabic. Islam does teach that Jesus was one of many prophets who were precursors to Muhammad, and it could be said that it even teaches that Jesus was the greatest of these *pre-Islamic* prophets; but Muhammad has a distinct status as the Messenger or Apostle of the one God, Allah, and no Muslim could regard Jesus as greater than Muhammad. Swedenborg's statements here are all the more striking because in an unpublished manuscript written around 1741, *Draft Introduction to a Rational Psychology,* Swedenborg copied out an extensive quotation from a French translation of a book by the world traveler Giovanni Francesco Gemelli Careri (1651–1725) that includes the assertion that Muslims do *not* believe that Christ is the Son of God (Swedenborg 1984b, 258–259, referencing Gemelli Careri 1719,

387–392). However, misinformation regarding Islam was rampant in Europe up to and beyond Swedenborg's day, and it would seem he simply chose another source to rely on than Gemelli Careri. For extensive discussion of the origins of such misinformation in Europe from the twelfth century up to the middle of the fourteenth century, see Daniel 1993. [GMC, SS]

502 (in *Supplements* 68). Swedenborg is here referring to the Lord appearing before the angels as the sun of heaven, on which see note 452. [Editors]

503 (in *Supplements* 69). Further identification of this individual is not possible, but in the seventeenth century alone approximately a million Europeans were captured and enslaved by Algerian Corsairs, also known as Barbary pirates (Tinniswood 2010, xviii). Such enslaved individuals then might well convert to Islam, willingly or unwillingly. The Barbary pirates were active from the 1500s through the early 1800s and conducted slaving raids on coasts as far away as Ireland and Iceland. Furthermore, some historically verifiable accounts read much like the brief biography of the individual mentioned here by Swedenborg. For example, the Netherlander Jan Janszoon van Harlem (1570–after 1641), also known as Murad Reis, was similarly captured, and he too converted to Islam. He eventually became President and Grand Admiral of the Corsair republic of Salé in North Africa. Thousands of other Europeans—called "renegadoes"—became Corsairs in the 1600s. For colorful accounts of this phenomenon, with bibliographies, see Wilson 2003; Tinniswood 2010. [SS]

504 (in *Supplements* 70). The reference here is not racial. Compare *Supplements* 19 and see note 459. [Editors]

505 (in *Supplements* 71). On Swedenborg's statement here that there is something from the Bible in Islam, see note 304. [Editors]

506 (in *Supplements* 71). On Swedenborg's statement here that the Lord is recognized as the Son of God in Islam, see note 501. [Editors]

507 (in *Supplements* 72:3). For fuller explanations of Swedenborg's statement here on heavenly love being possible only within a monogamous relationship and not within a polygamous relationship, see *Marriage Love* 333–335, 345–347. [LSW]

508 (in *Supplements* 72:3). This passing reference to the lasciviousness of the Middle East hints at a long-established European stereotype that seems to have arisen from (a) some knowledge of Islamic polygamy and divorce, (b) distorted tales of Muslim household life (specifically, the so-called harem), and (c) the legend of the multiple houris, or beautiful companions, promised in Muslim scriptures to those who reach heaven in the afterlife. Though this stereotype was in evidence as early as medieval times, it was not until the early 1700s that it gained wide currency. The reasons for this change include the defeat of the Ottoman Empire in 1683, which resulted in a view of Middle Eastern culture as degenerate rather than powerful, and the publication in 1704–1717 of the Arabic story series *The Thousand and One Nights*, translated by Antoine Galland (1646–1715). On these and other causes for the increasing predominance of the stereotype in the Enlightenment, see Madar 2011, 32; Yeazell 2000, 4–5. Another reason for the stereotype that is unrelated to Muslim culture was (d) the belief, widespread in Europe in Swedenborg's time and before, that warm climates encouraged sexual promiscuity; see Schick 1999, 214–215, who quotes an example from *Spirit of the Laws* (= Montesquieu [1748] 1949, 223–224) a 1748 work by Montesquieu (1689–1755). Swedenborg himself assigns this cause to the supposed sexual obsession of Middle Easterners in *Second Sketch for "Marriage Love"* (= Swedenborg 1975 = Swedenborg

1996g) §46: "Those who are in warm countries, more than those who are in cold countries, burn with libidinous heat." For further general discussion of such sexual stereotyping of the population of the Middle East, see Schick 1999. For historical analysis of the European understandings of Islam from the 1100s through the mid-1300s, see Daniel 1993, 158–185; and for stereotypes of the harem during the Renaissance period, Madar 2011, especially pages 1–10. On houris as they are actually represented in Islamic literature, see Rustomji 2009, 94–95, 111–114. [SS, SÅH]

Notes to *Supplements* Chapter 10, §§73–78

509 (in *Supplements* 73). The reference of this passage is to pagans in general. Sun worship has been found all around the world since antiquity: notable examples include ancient Mesopotamia, Egypt, Greece, Rome, and Mesoamerica. For a discussion of this, see the *Encyclopedia of Religion* 1987, 14:132–143. Moon worship, though less prevalent than sun worship, has also been found around the world; examples include ancient Mesopotamia, Egypt, Greece, and the Americas (*The Encyclopedia of Religion* 1987, 10:83–90). [RS]

510 (in *Supplements* 73). In several passages—most of them here in *Supplements* but also in *Spiritual Experiences* and *True Christianity*, especially §§837–840—Swedenborg describes the spirits and angels who had lived their earthly lives in continental Africa, particularly the inland regions (see *Supplements* 76 and *Spiritual Experiences* [= Swedenborg 1998–2013] §4777), as excelling in spiritual perception and interior judgment. [RHK, JSR]

511 (in *Supplements* 77). On "correspondence," see note 169. [Editors]

Notes to *Supplements* Chapter 11, §§79–82

512 (in *Supplements* 79). On the problematic and offensive nature of much of the content of §§79–90, see the translator's preface to this volume, pages 5–6. On Swedenborg's references to Jews and Judaism specifically, see note 204. [Editors]

513 (in *Supplements* 79). A similar description of one of these cities occurs in *Secrets of Heaven* 940. Both passages are notable for their further similarity to an entry for July 23 in Swedenborg's travel journal of 1733, in which he mentions passing through the Jewish quarters in Prague (Tafel 1877, 39). [SS]

514 (in *Supplements* 82:1). For a discussion of the meaning of the term *Canaan*, see the appendix on pages 529–530. [Editors]

515 (in *Supplements* 82:1). The most explicit allusion in this passage is to Zechariah 8:23: "In those days ten men from nations of every language shall take hold of a Jew, grasping his garment and saying, 'Let us go with you, for we have heard that God is with you'" (New Revised Standard Version). However, the theme of Gentiles becoming servants of Jews in coming ages can be found in many Bible passages, including Isaiah 14:1–2; 49:22–23; 60:1–18. [LSW, GFD]

516 (in *Supplements* 82:2). The parallel passage in *True Christianity* 845:1 notes that the birth of the Messiah in Bethlehem was prophesied in Psalms 132:6 and Micah 5:2. The claim that Jews of Swedenborg's time do not know the location of Bethlehem is also found in a passage in *Spiritual Experiences* (= Swedenborg 1998–2013) §4832a in a somewhat tempered form: "Now it is hardly known [by Jews] where Bethlehem is located." So it is possible that Swedenborg is only remarking on supposedly lost geographical knowledge. However, compare John 7:27, where an alternate tradition is hinted at, to

the effect that no one knows where the Messiah will come from. What Christians saw as prophecies of the Messiah's birthplace in the cited passages in Psalms and Micah were not understood in that sense by all Jewish readers; there is no evidence of a connection between Bethlehem and the Messiah's birth in other Jewish literature until the fourth century, well into the Christian era (Freed 2004, 79; Brown 1979, 513). [SS, JSR]

517 (in *Supplements* 82:2). Though there is no mention in Moses' speech in Deuteronomy 32 of Moses being angry at the people for not being allowed to enter the Holy Land with them, Moses does blame the people for this in three passages earlier in the same book: Deuteronomy 1:37; 3:23–27; 4:21. For the story in which God decrees that Moses and his brother Aaron will not enter the Holy Land due to their own failure to follow the Lord's instructions and give the glory to the Lord, see Numbers 20:1–13. [LSW]

Notes to *Supplements* Chapter 12, §§83–85

518 (in *Supplements* 83). The Latin here translated "thickheaded" is *obesae naris,* literally, "of a thick nose," a phrase from Horace *Epodes* 12:3. Occasionally in classical Latin the nose represents the power of discernment. Compare *Divine Love and Wisdom* 383. [SS]

519 (in *Supplements* 83). The Quaker movement arose in the mid-seventeenth century; it was based on a rejection of the institutions of church and clergy as obstacles to simple devotion to Christian principles. It adopted a formal organizational structure in 1667–1671. From its beginnings in northern England, it spread rapidly to the rest of Great Britain, to the European continent, and to North America. Its current self-designation is "the Religious Society of Friends," and it is known for "silent meetings"—gatherings without formal liturgy in which worshipers sit in silence until they are led to speak by the Holy Spirit, or "the Inner Light." The exact historical reason the derogatory term "quakers" was originally applied to the Friends is not clear, but early members of the society ascribed it to the trembling they experienced when filled with the Holy Spirit, and Swedenborg's discussion in *Supplements* 84 suggests that he accepts that explanation. Their quaking during worship was said to have begun with the rise of the society about 1650 and to have mostly ceased by the time of the restoration of Charles II in 1660 (see, for example, Leslie 1697, 290). [GFD, SS]

520 (in *Supplements* 84). On the quaking ascribed to Friends (Quakers), see note 519. For a slightly more detailed statement describing how the full tremors experienced by Quakers progress to a minor movement on the left side of the spiritual body, see *Spiritual Experiences* (= Swedenborg 1998–2013) §3767. [JSR]

521 (in *Supplements* 84). Certainly Swedenborg was aware that Quakers in his day had a reputation for probity, and at one point he accepted that common assessment. In a passage apparently written on October 27, 1748, he says with reference to his opinion of the Quakers before that time: "I had thought of [Quakers] as honest in life, and upright, for I had never heard otherwise" (*Spiritual Experiences* [= Swedenborg 1998–2013] §3733). That said, rumors of sexual promiscuity and other irregularities attached to many of the nonconforming Christian movements that arose in the 1600s (Hill 1975, 306–323), and Quakers were associated with those excesses (Wright 2011, 289–294). Furthermore, the Quaker practice of marrying "by declaration before the meeting" rather than in an Anglican ceremony, which was the civil standard, led to the assumption that Quaker women and men married and divorced on a whim. This may

have something to do with Swedenborg's accusing Quaker spirits of "wife sharing" in *Spiritual Experiences* 3768, 3794–3796. The overriding error that Swedenborg saw in the general practice of Quakers, however, was their reliance on being led by the Holy Spirit rather than the Lord. This raised the possibility that they would be taken advantage of by evil spirits masquerading as the Holy Spirit, per Swedenborg's description in *Spiritual Experiences* 3781:

> From . . . the practices of the Quakers, it is clear how dangerous it is on this planet, when spirits speak with people, or people listen to spirits operating in them. . . . They are not only persuaded that it is the holy spirit [speaking], but are also aroused and incited toward wicked acts. For almost the whole world of spirits is wicked, and fanatical, and eager with all their effort to obsess mankind.

The charge that Quakers were possessed by evil spirits was common during the late 1600s; see, for example, Leslie 1697, 282–309. [SS]

522 (in *Supplements* 84). The founder of Quakerism was the British evangelist George Fox (1624–1691). Compare similar accounts in *Spiritual Experiences* (= Swedenborg 1998–2013) §3771 and *Draft of "Supplements"* §59 [Rogers's numbering] = §58 [Whitehead's numbering] (= Swedenborg 1997a, 80) of the Quaker "chief" or "founder" disclaiming all knowledge of the evil practices of his followers. On Fox's historically attested attitude toward marriage (compare note 521), see Tual 1988, 168–170. Like Swedenborg, he disapproved of both celibacy and adultery. [SS]

523 (in *Supplements* 84). The Quaker leader William Penn (1644–1718) encountered such resistance to his attempts to legitimize Quakerism in England that he sought to create a haven for Quakers in the Americas. One result of his efforts was that in 1681 a charter for land including what is now Pennsylvania was granted by the British king Charles II (1630–1685). The grant was intended both to resolve tension between the English church and the Quakers and to repay debts owed by the Crown to Penn's father, after whom the new territory was named. For Swedenborg's very brief account of Penn, see *Spiritual Experiences* (= Swedenborg 1998–2013) §3814. In keeping with Swedenborg's characterization of Penn here, and in contrast to the promiscuity alleged against Quakers by Swedenborg (see note 521), the historical Penn believed that "the satisfaction of our Senses is low, short, and transient" and that true marriage was found in a meeting of minds (Penn 1726, 1:826, as quoted in Tual 1988, 166). [GFD, SS]

Notes to *Supplements* Chapter 13, §§86–90

524 (in *Supplements* 86). By the traditional account, the Moravian church was started by John Hus (around 1372–1415) in Bohemia in the late fourteenth century in reaction to many of the features of Catholicism against which Luther would protest some hundred years later. Hus was burned at the stake in 1415, but his followers continued as an underground movement that spread to parts of Germany and Poland. In 1722 a group from Moravia was involved in the founding of the village of Herrnhut ("The Lord's Watchful Care") in eastern Germany, which prospered under the leadership of Count Nikolaus von Zinzendorf (see note 530). For a discussion of the historicity of the connection between the church of Hus and that of Zinzendorf, see Peuker 2015, 15–17. Swedenborg's interest in the Moravians seems to date from the period in 1744 when he lodged in the

home of a London Moravian, John Paul Brockmer. He attended some of the services of the Moravian church on Fetter Lane and at one point seems to have considered joining the church (Sigstedt 1981, 189–190). His printers in London, John Lewis (actively printing 1739–1755) and Mary Lewis (actively printing 1755–1776) were also Moravians (Davies 2013, 415). Swedenborg seems to have been attracted at first (in 1744) to the piety of the Moravians, but eventually (by the late 1750s) he came to dislike their theology for the reasons he sketches in *Supplements* 88. For his fuller critique of their beliefs as he understood them, which is repeated in various forms several times in *Spiritual Experiences* (= Swedenborg 1998–2013), see, for example, §§4785, 4791–4792, 4806a, 5988:2–3, 5995:2 in that work. [GFD, SS]

525 (in *Supplements* 86). In opposition to the Church of Rome, the Moravians modeled their church practices strictly on the Bible in a deliberate attempt to emulate the primitive church. Brother Řehoř (Gregor or Gregory; died 1473), a leader of the phase of the Moravian church known as the Old Brethren (1457–1495), explained the movement's position in this way: "We have determined once for all to be guided by the Gospel and the example of the Lord Jesus Christ and the Holy Apostles in meekness, poverty, patience, and the love of enemies" (quoted in Motel 1960, 269). For example, the Moravians to this day celebrate the lovefeast, a symbolic and communal sharing of food mentioned as early as Jude verse 12. Swedenborg himself at one point in 1748 described the Moravian church as one "with whom an image of the primitive Church had been preserved" (*Spiritual Experiences* [= Swedenborg 1998–2013] §3492). [SS]

526 (in *Supplements* 86). There are many evidences in the Epistles that the members of the early Christian church referred to one another with the term *brother;* see, for example, Philemon verses 7, 20; James 4:11. (A similar use of *sister* is evidenced in such passages as Romans 16:1; 2 John verse 13.) In emulation of this practice, the early group in Bohemia from which the Moravians derived called itself the "Bohemian Brethren" or "Unity of the Brethren"; the eighteenth-century revival group was known as the *Herrnhuter Brüdergemeine* or "Herrnhut Brotherhood"; and the official name of the present-day Moravian church is *Unitas Fratrum,* "Unity of the Brethren." For biblical passages in which terms such as *brother, sister,* and *companion* are used in the Bible as a whole, see note 394. [GFD, SS]

527 (in *Supplements* 86). Jesus is referred to as a lamb nearly thirty times in the New Testament; see, for example, John 1:29, 36; 1 Corinthians 5:7; Revelation 5:6–14. Hebrews 4:16 speaks of approaching "the throne of grace," referring to the heavenly throne of Jesus. The name "Lamb" has traditionally been popular among Moravians as a name for Jesus Christ. In one of his sermons, Zinzendorf (see note 530) said:

> The Saviour's intrinsic Name, which expresses his Essence, none knows. This very thing yields us Room, in the mean time, to give Him Names without End. . . . The favourite Name [used by writers] under the New Testament is Lamb. (Gambold 1751, 112–113)

The account in *Spiritual Experiences* (= Swedenborg 1998–2013) §4810 clarifies why Swedenborg sees a ruse in the Moravians' preference for such terms:

> When they talk about the Lord with others, they do not say that the Lord is the Only God, but that the Father is God, and that the Lord is His son. Thus they

> avoid calling the Lord, God, and also hide what they believe. Otherwise they would be reckoned as among the Socinians. For this reason they frequently say "Lamb of God."

The Socinians were a sect that held that Jesus was a human being without divinity. Swedenborg also accused the Moravians of sympathy with a similar theological position, that of the Arians; see *Supplements* 88 and note 529. [SS]

528 (in *Supplements* 87). Swedenborg is apparently speaking somewhat loosely here, according to the general Protestant view of Paul's writings. Paul never speaks of "faith alone" in his letters. However, various passages such as Romans 3:27–28 and Ephesians 2:8–9 are interpreted in Protestantism as referring to faith alone. [LSW, GFD]

529 (in *Supplements* 88). The Alexandrian priest Arius (around 250–around 336 C.E.) insisted that the Son was not equal to the Father (see John 14:28), and was sufficiently emphatic on the point that he was understood to regard the Son as entirely human. He was condemned as a heretic at the First Council of Nicaea in 325. The three negative attributes of Moravian theology listed here are opposed to the "three essential principles of the church" Swedenborg identifies in *Divine Providence* 259:3: "belief in the divine nature of the Lord, belief in the holiness of the Word, and the life that we call 'charity.'" It should be noted that in this and other respects, Moravian beliefs in the spiritual world as described by Swedenborg here differ sharply from those described in the then current doctrinal statements of the Moravian church and the writings of their early leader, Zinzendorf (on whom see *Supplements* 89 and note 530). Against the first charge, Moravians did in fact maintain that Jesus was the incarnation of God. As Zinzendorf declared: "Jesus did not for a single hour go about on the earth when he was not at the same time the God of all the world" (quoted in Atwood 1997, 28 note 9). With respect to the second charge, regarding the Bible, Zinzendorf was known to say, "Holy Scripture is in my and the Brethren's eyes the true Word of God" (quoted in Freeman 1998, 144). (For discussion of Zinzendorf's view of Scripture, see Freeman 1998, 124–161.) However, there seems to have been some truth to Swedenborg's charge with respect to the Moravian congregations themselves. One author speculates that "antibiblical statements" made by Moravians in the 1740s were "yet another form of the provocative behavior employed by some Moravians to show the assurance of their salvation to others" (Peuker 2015, 72). For discussion, see Peuker 2015, 71–73. On the third charge, regarding a life of caring, Zinzendorf did follow the Augsburg Confession of the Lutherans in maintaining that "whoever believes will by faith itself be led to good works and fruits" (paraphrased by Zinzendorf and quoted in Freeman 1998, 209, apparently from Augsburg Confession article 20 [= Kolb and Wengert 2000, 53–57]). For this reason a key motto for the Moravians was: "We can give nothing before we have something" (Freeman 1998, 208–209); in other words, the caring acts of a Christian are subsequent to and thus subordinate to faith, not united with and simultaneous to it, as Swedenborg holds. [SS, GFD]

530 (in *Supplements* 89). Count Nikolaus von Zinzendorf (1700–1760) was a German aristocrat who welcomed Protestant refugees from eastern Europe to his own lands in Saxony, where a Moravian religious community was established. His own religious beliefs were inclusive and eclectic, drawing on sources such as Lutheranism and Moravianism, but one consistent theme in them was an avoidance of arid, rationalized doctrine in preference for a *Herzensreligion,* a "theology of the heart." [SS]

531 (in *Supplements* 89). Zinzendorf certainly left himself open to this criticism. One of the Moravians' contemporary critics quotes one of his sermons as follows:

> In case those People, that do not die *Herrnhuters,* did only think thus within themselves at the Time of their Death: "It has been my fault; they [the Herrnhuters] are . . . the Saviour's People, they are his Brethren; let my Soul die the Death of these righteous People, and let my End be like theirs," they would possibly meet with Mercy on the Day of Judgment. (Rimius 1759, 47 note 5, with orthographical edits, quoting a sermon preached by Zinzendorf at Herrenhaag, November 22, 1744, page 14)

Despite this rhetorical claim of an exclusive right to salvation, Zinzendorf's theology was remarkably ecumenical overall; it was part of a movement now referred to as Philadelphianism, which sought to transcend the boundaries of denominations and sects and unite all true believers in Christ. On this aspect of Zinzendorf's theology, see Peuker 2015, 12–14, and Freeman 1998 generally. [SS]

532 (in *Supplements* 89). On the claim that Zinzendorf believed that Jesus was "just an ordinary human being," see note 529. The statement that Zinzendorf "thought whatever he pleased" about the conception of Jesus by God is probably a reflection of the indifferentist principle established among the Herrnhuter: that "incidentals," or matters not regarded as essential to faith, should not be subject to determination by the corporate church; in other words, that individuals were free to believe as they wished on such matters (Freeman 1998, 6, 15, 247–249 with note 13). Swedenborg's report is ironical: the point under discussion is no matter of indifference to Christians. The mention of "talking the way Jews did" about the Lord's divinity is presumably a reference to belief among non-Christians that Jesus was merely human. [SS]

533 (in *Supplements* 90). In Swedenborg's works, the word *confirmatio,* "confirmation," often carries with it the implication that the person who feels it has been willingly persuaded that something is true although it is actually false; it is opposed to *perceptio,* "perception," which often implies the simple, intuitive, and spontaneous perception of truth. A passage in *Spiritual Experiences* (= Swedenborg 1998–2013) §4792:2 spells out the sense of the present passage more clearly: "This feeling [the Moravians have] is not a perception of truth but a feeling of the confirmation of their doctrine." The "sensation" referred to here may be an allusion to *Gefühl,* "feeling," "religious sentiment," an important concept in the Zinzendorfian/Moravian "religion of the heart." As Zinzendorf said in one of his sermons, "To have a feeling in the heart, and to believe, are the same thing" (Gambold 1751, 61, as quoted in Sawyer 1961, 84). For more on Zinzendorf and the theology of the heart, see the chapter by that title in Atwood 2004, 43–75. [SS]

Appendix

The Reference of the Word Canaan in the Bible and in Swedenborg's Theology

LEE S. WOOFENDEN

In the biblical narrative, the land of Canaan is named for one of the four sons of Noah's son Ham. In the Hebrew table of nations, Ham represents the inhabitants of northeastern Africa and of Palestine reaching as far north as western Syria. Ham's other three sons (see Genesis 10:6; 1 Chronicles 1:8) were Cush (associated with ancient Ethiopia, the region south of Egypt in present-day Sudan), Mizraim (associated with Egypt), and Put (regional association uncertain; traditionally Libya). In an incident recorded in Genesis 9:10–27, Noah cursed his grandson Canaan as a consequence of Ham's actions, setting the stage for Israel's later conquest of Canaanite territory.

The sons of Canaan recorded in Genesis 10:15 and 1 Chronicles 1:13–16 represent the clans that made up the land of Canaan, stretching along the Mediterranean coast from the region around Gaza on the south to the region around Hamath (present-day Hama on the Orontes River in western Syria) on the north, and constrained by the Mediterranean Sea on the west and the Dead Sea and Jordan River on the east, though some Canaanite settlements did spill over to the east side of the Jordan.

In Genesis 15:18 the Lord promises Abraham an expansive version of this territory: "To your descendants I give this land, from the river of Egypt to the great river, the river Euphrates" (New Revised Standard Version)—the Euphrates being the primary river of Assyria. In later biblical usage, therefore, "the land of Canaan" comes to mean the territory of the Israelite nation.

Swedenborg, along with several ancient Jewish commentaries, takes the Lord's pronouncement to mean that Israelite territory extended from the Nile River to the Euphrates River (see, for example, *Secrets of Heaven*

5196; *Revelation Unveiled* 444; *Revelation Explained* [= Swedenborg 1994–1997a] §569:4–5). However, though there is some variation in the wording of "the river of Egypt" in the original Hebrew, and there have been several alternate identifications of it, scholars now generally believe it refers to the Wadi El-Arish, an ephemeral riverbed that drains much of the Sinai Peninsula, emptying into the Mediterranean Sea at the present-day city of Arish, southwest of the Gaza Strip. This is the most common understanding of the Mediterranean terminus of the southern boundary of Israelite territory as delineated in such passages as Numbers 34:3–5; Joshua 15:2–4; and Ezekiel 47:19; 48:28. There is no biblical or archaeological evidence that the nation of Israel ever controlled the rest of the Sinai Peninsula, and certainly not all the way to the Nile River, which remained under Egyptian control.

The northern boundary of the tribal territory of Israel delineated in such passages as Numbers 34:7–9, Joshua 19:24–39, and Ezekiel 47:15–17, 48:1 is somewhat uncertain, but seems to extend up toward the coastal cities of Tyre and Sidon in the earlier version, and as far as the present-day city of Laboueh, Lebanon (the most likely meaning of "Lebo-Hamath" in Numbers 34:8; Ezekiel 47:15, 20; 48:1; and elsewhere), in the Ezekiel version. The biblical account does say in 1 Kings 4:21 and 2 Chronicles 9:26 that in its heyday during the reign of King Solomon, Israel controlled territory extending to the Euphrates.

Regardless of the exact boundaries between them, the trio of Israel (Canaan), Assyria, and Egypt is symbolically important in biblical passages such as Isaiah 11:10–16; 19:18–25. For Swedenborg's interpretation of the land of Canaan as the church, or the spiritual component in a person, Assyria as the rational component, and Egypt as the natural or factual knowledge component, see, for example, *Secrets of Heaven* 1462, 1585, 6047:4–5; *Heaven and Hell* 307:3; *New Jerusalem* 5; *Revelation Unveiled* 503; *True Christianity* 200; *Revelation Explained* 503:3–6, 654.

Works Cited in the Notes

A list of the works of Swedenborg that are mentioned in the endnotes to this volume can be found on pages 112–119.

Acton, Alfred. 1927. *An Introduction to the Word Explained.* Bryn Athyn, Pa.: Academy of the New Church.

———. 1948–1955. *The Letters and Memorials of Emanuel Swedenborg.* 2 vols. Bryn Athyn, Pa.: Swedenborg Scientific Association.

Acton, Elmo C. 1983. "The Ancient Word." In *Ancient Church Conference at the Academy of the New Church, Bryn Athyn, Pennsylvania, August 27–September 1, 1975.* Bryn Athyn, Pa.: General Church Press.

Adler, Mortimer J. 1982. *The Angels and Us.* New York: Collier.

Alfelt, Lennart O. 1969. "Swedenborg's Library: An Alphabetical List." *The New Philosophy* 72:115–126.

Alighieri, Dante. 1970. *Inferno.* 2 vols. In *The Divine Comedy,* translated by Charles S. Singleton. Princeton: Princeton/Bollingen.

Aquinas, Thomas. 2012. *Summa Theologiae.* Translated by Laurence Shapcote and edited by John Mortensen and Enrique Alarcón. Vols. 13–20 in Latin/English Edition of the Works of St. Thomas Aquinas. Lander, Wyo.: The Aquinas Institute for the Study of Sacred Doctrine.

Archaeology Study Bible. 2017. Wheaton, Ill.: Crossway.

Aristotle. 1984. *The Complete Works of Aristotle.* Rev. ed. Edited by Jonathan Barnes. 2 vols. Princeton: Princeton University Press.

Atwood, Craig D. 1997. "Sleeping in the Arms of Christ: Sanctifying Sexuality in the Eighteenth-Century Moravian Church." *Journal of the History of Sexuality* 8:1, 25–51.

———. 2004. *Community of the Cross: Moravian Piety in Colonial Bethlehem.* University Park, Pa.: Pennsylvania State University Press.

Barthel, Manfred. 1984. *The Jesuits: History and Legend of the Society of Jesus.* Translated and adapted by Mark Howson. New York: William Morrow.

Benin, Stephen D. 1993. *The Footprints of God: Divine Accommodation in Jewish and Christian Thought.* Albany: State University of New York Press.

Beyer, Bryan E. 2007. *Encountering the Book of Isaiah: A Historical and Theological Survey.* Grand Rapids, Mich.: Baker Academic.

The Book of Common Prayer and Administration of the Sacraments and Other Rites and Ceremonies of the Church. 1711. London: Charles Bill and Thomas Newcomb.

Borsch, Frederick Houk. 1967. *The Son of Man in Myth and History.* Philadelphia: Westminster Press.

Boyle, Robert. 1675. *Some Considerations Touching the Style of the Holy Scriptures; Extracted from Several Parts of a Discourse, Concerning Divers Particulars Belonging to the Bible, Written Divers Years Since to a Friend.* 4th ed. London: Henry Herringman.

Brown, Francis, S. R. Driver, and Charles A. Briggs. 1996. *The Brown-Driver-Briggs Hebrew and English Lexicon.* Reprint, with Strong's numbering added, Peabody, Mass.: Hendrickson Publishers, Inc.

Brown, Raymond E. 1979. *The Birth of the Messiah: A Commentary on the Infancy Narratives in Matthew and Luke.* Garden City, N.Y.: Doubleday.

Burns, Norman T. 1972. *Christian Mortalism from Tyndale to Milton.* Cambridge: Harvard University Press.

Byrne, Peter. 1989. *Natural Religion and the Nature of Religion: The Legacy of Deism.* London: Routledge.

Calvin, John. [1559] 1854. *Commentary on the Book of the Prophet Isaiah.* Translated by William Pringle. 4 vols. Edinburgh: Calvin Translation Society.

Catechism of the Catholic Church. 2000. 2nd ed. Libreria Editrice Vaticana.

Collier, Katharine B. 1934. *Cosmogonies of Our Fathers: Some Theories of the Seventeenth and the Eighteenth Centuries.* New York: Columbia University Press.

Colpe, Carsten. 1972. "ὁ υἱὸς τοῦ ἀνθρώπου." In vol. 8 of *Theological Dictionary of the New Testament,* edited by Gerhard Kittel and Gerhard Friedrich and translated by Geoffrey W. Bromiley. Grand Rapids, Mich.: Wm. B. Eerdmans.

Concordia Pia et Unanimi Consensu Repetita Confessio Fidei. 1756. Edited by Adam Rechenberg. Leipzig: Johan Grosse.

Cross, Frank Moore. 1973. *Canaanite Myth and Hebrew Epic: Essays in the History of the Religion of Israel.* Cambridge: Harvard University Press.

Daniel, Norman. 1993. *Islam and the West: The Making of an Image.* Rev. ed. Oxford: Oneworld.

Davies, Keri. 2013. "'The Swedishman at Brother Brockmer's': Moravians and Swedenborgians in Eighteenth-Century London." In *Philosophy, Literature, Mysticism: An Anthology of Essays on the Thought and Influence of Emanuel Swedenborg,* edited by Stephen McNeilly. London: Swedenborg Society.

Descartes, René. [1637] 1952. *Discourse on the Method of Rightly Conducting the Reason.* Translated by Elizabeth S. Haldane and G.R.T. Ross. In vol. 31 of *Great Books of the Western World.* Chicago: Encyclopedia Britannica.

———. [1641] 1984. *Meditations on First Philosophy.* In vol. 2 of *The Philosophical Writings of Descartes,* translated by John Cottingham, Robert Stoothoff, and Dugald Murdoch. Cambridge: Cambridge University Press.

Edwards, Paul, ed. 1967. *The Encyclopedia of Philosophy.* 8 vols. New York: Macmillan.

Emerton, Norma E. 1984. *The Scientific Reinterpretation of Form.* Ithaca, N.Y.: Cornell University Press.

The Encyclopedia of Religion. 1987. Edited by Mircea Eliade. New York: Macmillan.

Freed, Edwin D. 2004. *The Stories of Jesus' Birth.* Understanding the Bible and Its World. London: T. & T. Clark.

Freeman, Arthur J. 1998. *An Ecumenical Theology of the Heart: The Theology of Count Nicholas Ludwig von Zinzendorf.* Bethlehem, Pa.: The Moravian Church in America.

Füssel, Stephan, and Benedikt Taschen. 2009. *The Bible in Pictures: Illustrations from the Workshop of Lucas Cranach (1534).* London: Taschen.

Galen. 1968. *Galen on the Usefulness of the Parts of the Body* (De Usu Partium). Translated with commentary by Margaret Tallmadge May. Ithaca, N.Y.: Cornell University Press.

Gambold, J., ed. 1751. *Maxims: Theological Ideas and Sentences, out of the Present Ordinary of the Brethren's Churches.* London: J. Beecroft.

Gemelli Careri, Giovanni Francesco. 1719. *Voyage du tour du monde.* Translated by L.M.N. Paris.

Goldhill, Simon. 2005. *The Temple of Jerusalem.* Cambridge: Harvard University Press.

Hare, Douglas A. 1990. *The Son of Man Tradition.* Minneapolis: Fortress Press.

Haynes, Renée. 1970. *Philosopher King: The Humanist Pope Benedict XIV.* London: Weidenfeld & Nicolson.

Helander, Hans. 2004. *Neo-Latin Literature in Sweden in the Period 1620–1720.* Uppsala: Uppsala University.

Henry, Matthew. [1708–1710] 1991. *Matthew Henry's Commentary on the Whole Bible.* 6 vols. Peabody, Mass.: Hendrickson.

Hill, Christopher. 1975. *The World Turned Upside Down: Radical Ideas during the English Revolution.* New York: Penguin.

Hunter, M. J., Geoffrey Sheperd, Henry Hargreaves, W. B. Lockwood, C. A. Robson, Kenelm Foster, and Margherita Morreale. 1969. "The Vernacular Scriptures." Chapter 9 in *The Cambridge History of the Bible,* vol. 2: *The West from the Fathers to the Reformation,* edited by G.W.H. Lampe. Cambridge: Cambridge University Press.

Janz, Denis R. 2008. *A Reformation Reader: Primary Texts with Introductions.* 2nd ed. Minneapolis: Fortress Press.

Josephus. 1997. *Antiquities of the Jews.* In *The Life and Works of Flavius Josephus,* edited and translated by William Whiston. Philadelphia: John C. Winston.

———. 1998. *Antiquities of the Jews.* In *The Complete Works of Flavius Josephus,* translated by William Whiston. Nashville: Thomas Nelson.

Kittel, Rudolf, ed. 1950. *Biblica Hebraica.* Stuttgart: Privileg. Wurtt. Bibelanstalt.

Kolb, Robert, and Timothy J. Wengert, eds. 2000. *The Book of Concord: The Confessions of the Evangelical Lutheran Church.* Translated by Charles Arand, Eric Gritsch, Robert Kolb, William Russell, James Schaaf, Jane Strohl, and Timothy J. Wengert. Minneapolis: Fortress Press.

Kors, Alan Charles, ed. 2003. *Encyclopedia of the Enlightenment.* 4 vols. Oxford: Oxford University Press.

La Mettrie, Julien Offray de. [1747] 1994. *Man a Machine; and, Man a Plant.* Translated by Richard A. Watson and Maya Rybalka, with an introduction and notes by Justin Leiber. Indianapolis: Hackett.

Laudan, Rachel. 1987. *From Mineralogy to Geology.* Chicago: University of Chicago Press.

Lawlor, Robert. 1982. *Sacred Geometry.* London: Thames & Hudson.

Leslie, Charles. 1697. *The Snake in the Grass: Or, Satan Transform'd into an Angel of Light, Discovering the Deep and Unsuspected Subtilty Which Is Couched under the Pretended Simplicity, of Many of the Principal Leaders of Those People Call'd Quakers.* 2nd ed. London: Charles Brome.

Lovejoy, Arthur O. 1960. *The Great Chain of Being: A Study of the History of an Idea.* 2nd ed. New York: Harper & Row. First printing: 1936, Cambridge: Harvard University Press.

Lucretius. 2001. *On the Nature of Things.* Translated by Martin Ferguson Smith. Indianapolis: Hackett Publishing.

Luther, Martin. [1520] 1955–1986. "The Babylonian Captivity of the Church, 1520." In vol. 36 of *Luther's Works,* American Edition, edited by Jaroslav Pelikan and Helmut T. Lehman. Philadelphia: Muehlenburg and Fortress.

———, trans. 1522. *Das newe Testament.* Wittenberg: Melchior Lotther.

Maccoby, Hyam. 1992. *Judas Iscariot and the Myth of Jewish Evil.* New York: Free Press.

MacCulloch, Diarmaid. 2003. *The Reformation.* New York: Penguin Group.

Madar, Heather. 2011. "Before the Odalisque: Renaissance Representations of Elite Ottoman Women." *Early Modern Women: An Interdisciplinary Journal* 6:1–41.

Matton, Sylvain. 1988. "Une Lecture alchimique de la Bible: Les *Paradoxes chymiques* de F. Thybourel." *Chrysopoeia* 2:401–422.

McCain, Paul Timothy, Robert Cleveland Baker, and Gene Edward Veith, eds. 2006. *Concordia: The Lutheran Confessions. A Reader's Edition of "The Book of Concord".* Translated by William Hermann Theodore Dau and Gerhard Friedrich Bente. 2nd ed. St. Louis, Mo.: Concordia.

McCormick, John F. 1940. *Scholastic Metaphysics.* Chicago: Loyola University Press.

Melanchthon, Philipp. 1521. *Loci Communes Rerum Theologicarum.* Basel: A. Perri.

[———]. [1543] 1992. *Loci Communes.* Translated by J.A.O. Preus. St. Louis, Mo.: Concordia.

Meslier, Jean. 1830. *Le Bon Sens du Curé J. Meslier, suivi de son testament.* Paris: Guillaumin.

Metzger, Bruce M., and Michael D. Coogan, eds. 1993. *The Oxford Companion to the Bible.* Oxford: Oxford University Press.

Migne, J.-P. 1863. *Patrologiae Cursus Completus, Bibliotheca Universalis, Integra, Uniformis, Commoda, Oeconomica, Omnium SS. Patrum, Doctorum Scriptorumque Ecclesiasticorum, sive Latinorum, sive Graecorum, . . . Series Latina.* Paris: Migne.

Montesquieu [Charles-Louis de Secondat, Baron de la Brède et de Montesquieu]. [1748] 1949. *The Spirit of the Laws.* Translated by Thomas Nugent. New York: Hafner.

Motel, Heinz. 1960. "The Relation of the Old and Renewed Moravian Church to Reformation." *Transactions of the Moravian Historical Society* 17:2.

Muller, Richard A. 1985. *Dictionary of Latin and Greek Theological Terms, Drawn Principally from Protestant Scholastic Theology.* Grand Rapids, Mich.: Baker Book House.

Odhner, Hugo Lj. 1933. "The History of the 'Animal Spirits,' and of Swedenborg's Development of the Concept." *The New Philosophy* 36:218–223, 234–249.

Oldroyd, David R. 1996. *Thinking about the Earth: A History of Ideas in Geology.* London: Athlone.

The Oxford Dictionary of the Christian Church. 2005. Edited by F. L. Cross. 3rd ed., rev., edited by E. A. Livingstone. London: Oxford.

Penn, William. 1726. "Some Fruits of Solitude, in Reflections and Maxims, Relating to the Conduct of Human Life." In *A Collection of the Works of William Penn: To Which Is Prefixed a Journal of His Life. With Many Original Letters and Papers Not Before Published.* 2 vols. London: The Assigns of J. Sowle.

Peters, Edward. 1980. *Heresy and Authority in Medieval Europe: Documents in Translation.* Philadelphia: University of Pennsylvania Press.

Peuker, Paul. 2015. *A Time of Sifting: Mystical Marriage and the Crisis of Moravian Piety in the Eighteenth Century.* University Park, Pa.: Pennsylvania State University Press.

Pinto-Correia, Clara. 1997. *The Ovary of Eve: Egg and Sperm and Preformation.* Chicago: University of Chicago Press.

Plato. 1997. *Complete Works.* Edited by John M. Cooper and D. S. Hutchinson. Indianapolis: Hackett.

Polman, Andries Derk Rietema. 1961. *The Word of God According to St. Augustine.* Grand Rapids, Mich.: Eerdmans.

Potts, John Faulkner. 1888–1902. *The Swedenborg Concordance. A Complete Work of Reference to the Theological Writings of Emanuel Swedenborg; Based on the Original Latin Writings of the Author.* 6 vols. London: Swedenborg Society.

Principe, Lawrence M., and William R. Newman. 2001. "Some Problems with the Historiography of Alchemy." In *Secrets of Nature: Astrology and Alchemy in Early Modern Europe,* edited by William R. Newman and Anthony Grafton. Cambridge, Mass.: MIT Press.

Pugh, Ben. 2014. *Atonement Theories: A Way through the Maze.* Eugene, Ore.: Cascade Books.

Rimius, Henry. 1759. *The History of the Moravians, from Their First Settlement at Herrenhaag in the County of Budingen, Down to the Present Time, Etc.* 2nd ed. Vol. 2. London: John Wilkie.

Rustomji, Nerina. 2009. *The Garden and the Fire: Heaven and Hell in Islamic Culture.* New York: Columbia University Press.

Sacré, Dirk. 2014. "The Pronunciation of Latin." In *Brill's Encyclopedia of the Neo-Latin World: Macropedia,* edited by Philip Ford, Jan Bloemendal, and Charles Fantazzi. Leiden: Brill.

Sawyer, Edwin Albert. 1961. "The Religious Experience of the Colonial American Moravians." *Transactions of the Moravian Historical Society* 18:1, 1–227.

Schaff, Philip, ed. 1931. *The Creeds of Christendom.* 3rd ed. 3 vols. New York: Harper and Row. Reprinted in 2007 by Baker Books, Grand Rapids, Mich.

Schaffer, Simon. 1999. "Enlightened Automata." In *The Sciences in Enlightened Europe,* edited by William Clark, Jan Golinski, and Simon Schaffer. Chicago: University of Chicago Press.

Schick, Irvin Cemil. 1999. *The Erotic Margin: Sexuality and Spatiality in Alteritist Discourse.* London: Verso.

Schmidt, Sebastian, trans. 1696. *Biblia Sacra sive Testamentum Vetus et Novum ex Linguis Originalibus in Linguam Latinam Translatum.* Strasbourg: J. F. Spoor.

Schmithals, Walter. 1997. *The Theology of the First Christians.* Translated by O. C. Dean, Jr. Louisville, Ky.: Westminster John Knox Press.

Schneider, Michael S. 1995. *A Beginner's Guide to Constructing the Universe: The Mathematical Archetypes of Nature, Art, and Science.* New York: Harper Perennial.

Scholem, Gershom. 1946. *Major Trends in Jewish Mysticism.* New York: Schocken.

Senior, Matthew, ed. 2007. *A Cultural History of Animals in the Age of Enlightenment.* Oxford: Berg.

Sewall, Frank. 1888. *The New Metaphysics; or, The Law of End, Cause, and Effect; with Other Essays.* London: James Speirs.

Shipley, Joseph T. 1984. *The Origins of English Words: A Discursive Dictionary of Indo-European Roots.* Baltimore: Johns Hopkins University Press.

Sigstedt, Cyriel Odhner. 1981. *The Swedenborg Epic: The Life and Works of Emanuel Swedenborg.* London: Swedenborg Society. First edition: 1952, New York: Bookman Associates.

Smith, C.U.M., Eugenio Frixione, Stanley Finger, and William Clower. 2012. *The Animal Spirit Doctrine and the Origins of Neurophysiology.* Oxford: Oxford University Press.

Smoley, Richard. 2005. "The Inner Journey of Emanuel Swedenborg." In *Emanuel Swedenborg: Essays for the New Century Edition on His Life, Work, and Impact,* edited by Jonathan S. Rose and others. West Chester, Pa.: Swedenborg Foundation.

Spinoza, Benedict de. [1667] 2006. *The Essential Spinoza: Ethics and Related Writings.* Translated by Samuel Shirley and edited by Michael L. Morgan. Indianapolis: Hackett.

Swann, Julian. 1995. *Politics and the Parlement of Paris under Louis XV, 1754–1774.* Cambridge: Cambridge University Press.

Swedberg, Jesper. 1694. *Then Swenska Psalm-Boken: Med the stycker som ther til höra och på föliande blad opteknade finnas.* Stockholm: Burchard.

Swedenborg, Emanuel. [1763] 1859. *Doctrina Novae Hierosolyma de Fide.* Edited by S. H. Worcester. New York: American Swedenborg Printing and Publishing Society.

———. 1859–1873. *Index Biblicus.* Vols. 1–3 edited by J. F. Immanuel Tafel, vol. 4 edited by Achatius Kahl, and vol. 5 edited by R. L. Tafel. London: Swedenborg Society.

———. 1927–1951. *The Word of the Old Testament Explained.* Translated and edited by Alfred Acton. 10 vols. Bryn Athyn, Pa.: Academy of the New Church.

———. 1942. *On Miracles.* Translated by Alfred Acton. *New Church Life* 62:400–411.

———. 1947. *Miracles and Signs.* Rev. ed. Translated and edited by P. H. Johnson. London: Swedenborg Society.

———. [1740–1741] 1955. *The Economy of the Animal Kingdom, Considered Anatomically, Physically, and Philosophically.* Translated by Augustus Clissold. 2 vols. Bryn Athyn, Pa.: Swedenborg Scientific Association. First edition of this translation: 1845–1846, London: W. Newbery, H. Bailliere, and Boston: Otis Clapp.

———. [1744–1745] 1960. *The Animal Kingdom, Considered Anatomically, and Philosophically.* Translated by James John Garth Wilkinson. 2 vols. [Bryn Athyn, Pa.]: Swedenborg Scientific Association. First edition of this translation: 1843–1844, London: W. Newbery.

———. 1971. *The Spiritual Diary of Emanuel Swedenborg.* Vol. 5. Translated by James F. Buss. New York: Swedenborg Foundation and The Academy of the New Church.

———. 1975. *On Marriage II.* In *Small Theological Works and Letters of Emanuel Swedenborg,* translated and edited by John E. Elliott. London: Swedenborg Society.

———. 1976a. *The Economy of the Animal Kingdom, Considered Anatomically, Physically, and Philosophically, Transaction III.* Translated by Alfred Acton. Bryn Athyn, Pa.: Swedenborg Scientific Association. First edition of this translation: 1918, Philadelphia: Swedenborg Scientific Association.

———. 1976b. *Three Transactions on the Cerebrum.* Translated by Alfred Acton. 2 vols. Bryn Athyn, Pa.: Swedenborg Scientific Association. First edition: 1938, Philadelphia: Swedenborg Scientific Association.

———. 1984a. *The Animal Spirit.* In *Psychological Transactions and Other Posthumous Tracts 1734–1744.* Translated by Alfred Acton. 2nd ed. Bryn Athyn, Pa.: Swedenborg Scientific Association.

———. 1984b. *Correspondences and Representations.* In *Psychological Transactions and Other Posthumous Tracts 1734–1744,* translated by Alfred Acton. 2nd ed. Bryn Athyn, Pa.: Swedenborg Scientific Association.

———. [1734] 1988. *The Principia; or, The First Principles of Natural Things.* Translated by Augustus Clissold. 2 vols. Bryn Athyn, Pa.: Swedenborg Scientific Association. First edition of this translation: 1846, London: W. Newbery.

———. 1994–1997a. *Apocalypse Explained.* Translated by John C. Ager, revised by John Whitehead, and edited by William Ross Woofenden. 6 vols. West Chester, Pa.: Swedenborg Foundation.

———. 1994–1997b. *The Athanasian Creed.* Translated by Samuel Worcester and revised by John C. Ager. In vol. 6 of *Apocalypse Explained,* edited by William Ross Woofenden. West Chester, Pa.: Swedenborg Foundation.

———. 1994–1997c. *On Divine Love and Divine Wisdom.* Translated by Samuel Worcester and revised by John C. Ager. In vol. 6 of *Apocalypse Explained,* edited by William Ross Woofenden. West Chester, Pa.: Swedenborg Foundation.

———. 1996a. *Appendix to "The White Horse."* In *Miscellaneous Theological Works,* translated by John Whitehead and edited by William Ross Woofenden. West Chester, Pa.: Swedenborg Foundation.

———. 1996b. *Canons of the New Church.* In vol. 1 of *Posthumous Theological Works,* translated by John Whitehead and edited by William Ross Woofenden. West Chester, Pa.: Swedenborg Foundation.

———. 1996c. *Coronis, or Appendix, to "True Christian Religion."* In vol. 1 of *Posthumous Theological Works,* translated by John Whitehead and edited by William Ross Woofenden. West Chester, Pa.: Swedenborg Foundation.

———. 1996d. *The Doctrine of Charity.* In vol. 1 of *Posthumous Theological Works,* translated by John Whitehead and edited by William Ross Woofenden. West Chester, Pa.: Swedenborg Foundation.

———. 1996e. *Five Memorable Relations.* In vol. 2 of *Posthumous Theological Works,* translated by John Whitehead and edited by William Ross Woofenden. West Chester, Pa.: Swedenborg Foundation.

———. 1996f. *Invitation to the New Church.* In vol. 1 of *Posthumous Theological Works,* translated by John Whitehead and edited by William Ross Woofenden. West Chester, Pa.: Swedenborg Foundation.

———. 1996g. *On Marriage* (De Conjugio). In vol. 2 of *Posthumous Theological Works,* translated by John Whitehead and edited by William Ross Woofenden. West Chester, Pa.: Swedenborg Foundation.

———. 1996h. *Sketch of the Coronis, or Appendix, to "True Christian Religion."* In vol. 1 of *Posthumous Theological Works,* translated by John Whitehead and edited by William Ross Woofenden. West Chester, Pa.: Swedenborg Foundation.

———. 1996i. *Summaries of the Internal Sense of the Prophetical Books, the Psalms of David, and the Historical Parts of the Word.* In vol. 2 of *Posthumous Theological Works,* translated by John Whitehead and edited by William Ross Woofenden. West Chester, Pa.: Swedenborg Foundation.

———. 1997a. *The Last Judgment.* In *Three Short Works,* translated by N. Bruce Rogers. Bryn Athyn, Pa.: General Church of the New Jerusalem.

———. 1997b. *Nine Questions.* In *Four Doctrines, with the Nine Questions,* translated by John Faulkner Potts and edited by William Ross Woofenden. West Chester, Pa.: Swedenborg Foundation.

———. 1997c. *The Sacred Scripture or Word of the Lord from Experience.* In *Three Short Works,* translated by N. Bruce Rogers. Bryn Athyn, Pa.: General Church of the New Jerusalem.

———. 1998–2013. *Emanuel Swedenborg's Diary, Recounting Spiritual Experiences during the Years 1745 to 1765.* Vols. 1–3 translated by J. Durban Odhner; vol. 4 translated by Kurt P. Nemitz. Bryn Athyn, Pa.: General Church of the New Jerusalem.

———. [1771] 2006. *True Christianity.* Translated by Jonathan S. Rose. Vol. 1. West Chester, Pa.: Swedenborg Foundation.

———. [1749–1756] 2008. *A Disclosure of Secrets of Heaven Contained in Sacred Scripture, or the Word of the Lord, . . . Together with Amazing Things Seen in the World of Spirits and in the Heaven of Angels.* Translated by Lisa Hyatt Cooper. Vol. 1. West Chester, Pa.: Swedenborg Foundation.

———. [1771] 2012. *True Christianity.* Translated by Jonathan S. Rose. Vol. 2. West Chester, Pa.: Swedenborg Foundation.

———. [1749–1756] 2013. *A Disclosure of Secrets of Heaven Contained in Sacred Scripture, or the Word of the Lord, . . . Together with Amazing Things Seen in the World of Spirits and in the Heaven of Angels.* Translated by Lisa Hyatt Cooper. Vol. 2. West Chester, Pa.: Swedenborg Foundation.

Tafel, R. L. 1877. *Documents Concerning the Life and Character of Emanuel Swedenborg.* Vol. 2, parts 1 and 2. London: Swedenborg Society.

Taylor, Charles. 1989. *Sources of the Self: The Making of the Modern Identity.* Cambridge: Harvard University Press.

Theological Dictionary of the Old Testament. 1986. Edited by G. Johannes Botterweck and Helmer Ringgren and translated by John T. Willis. Vol. 5. Grand Rapids, Mich.: William B. Eerdmans.

Tinniswood, Adrian. 2010. *Pirates of Barbary: Corsairs, Conquests, and Captivity in the 17th-Century Mediterranean.* New York: Riverhead Books.

Tual, Jacques. 1988. "Sexual Equality and Conjugal Harmony: The Way to Celestial Bliss. A View of Early Quaker Matrimony." *The Journal of the Friends' Historical Society* 55:6, 161–174.

Ussher, James. 1650–1654. *Annales Veteris Testamenti.* 2 vols. London: Flesher and Bedell.

Van Dam, Cornelis. 1997. *The Urim and Thummim: A Means of Revelation in Ancient Israel.* Winona Lake, Ind.: Eisenbrauns.

Van Kley, Dale. 1975. *The Jansenists and the Expulsion of the Jesuits from France 1757–1765.* New Haven: Yale University Press.

Van Kley, Dale K. 1996. *The Religious Origins of the French Revolution: From Calvin to the Civil Constitution, 1560–1791.* New Haven: Yale University Press.

Voltaire. [1764] 1962. *Philosophical Dictionary.* Translated by Peter Gay. New York: Harcourt, Brace, & World.

———. 1994. *Dictionnaire philosophique.* Edited by Christiane Mervaud. Oxford: Voltaire Foundation.

———. [1734] 2003. *Philosophical Letters: Letters Concerning the English Nation.* Translated by Ernest Dilworth. Mineola, N.Y.: Dover.

Waquet, Françoise. 2001. *Latin or the Empire of a Sign: From the Sixteenth to the Twentieth Centuries.* Translated by John Howe. London: Verso.

Watkin-Jones, Howard. 1929. *The Holy Spirit from Arminius to Wesley.* London: Epworth Press.

Watts, Isaac. 1733. *Philosophical Essays on Various Subjects.* London: Richard Ford and Richard Hett.

White, Samuel. 1709. *A Commentary on the Prophet Isaiah, Wherein the Literal Sense of His Prophecy's Is Briefly Explain'd.* London: Arthur Collins.

Wilson, Catherine. 2008. *Epicureanism at the Origins of Modernity.* Oxford: Oxford University Press.

Wilson, Peter Lamborn. 2003. *Pirate Utopias: Moorish Corsairs and European Renegadoes.* 2nd rev. ed. Brooklyn, N.Y.: Autonomedia.

Wright, Stephen. 2011. *An Investigation into the Possible Transfer of Theology and Practice from Continental Anabaptists to the First Quakers.* Dissertation, University of Birmingham, U.K.

Wuellner, Bernard. 1956. *Dictionary of Scholastic Philosophy.* Milwaukee: The Bruce Publishing Co.

Yeazell, Ruth Bernard. 2000. *Harems of the Mind: Passages of Western Art and Literature.* New Haven: Yale University Press.

Young, Edward J. 1965. *The Book of Isaiah: The English Text, with Introduction, Exposition, and Notes.* 3 vols. Grand Rapids, Mich.: William B. Eerdmans.

Index to Preface, Introduction, and Notes

The following index, referenced by page number, covers material in the preface, the note on editions and translations, the introduction, and the scholars' notes. References to the Bible in this material are listed under the heading "Scripture references." (References to the Bible that appear in the translation proper are treated in a separate index.) For topics in Swedenborg's footnotes, see the index to the translation.

A

Abelard, Peter, 458 note 69
Åbo, 71, 103
Abraham, 529
Accommodation *(theological term)*, 484–485 note 228
Adam, 513 note 445
Adolf Frederick, 88, 89
Aesop, 480 note 199
Africans, 523 note 510
Ages of humankind, 496 notes 302 and 303
Alchemy, 481 note 207
Algerian Corsairs (Barbary pirates), 522 note 503
Alnander, Samuel Johansson, 73–75
Amsterdam, 9 and note 2, 56–57 note 55, 76 note 88, 93. *See also* The Netherlands
    as publishing center, 42, 56–57, 76–77, 76 and note 88, 86, 90
The Ancient of Days, 485 note 237
The ancient Word, 29, 492–493 note 281, 493 notes 282 and 283, 495 note 295
"Angelic Wisdom about" *(phrase used in titles)*, 447–448 note 4, 463 note 100, 465 note 110, 498 note 322
    indicating philosophical rather than theological works, 79 and note 92, 82 note 98
    Marriage Love as part of the "Angelic Wisdom" series, 81 note 96
    as used in titles of works, 22, 78–82, 79 note 91
Angelic Wisdom about Divine Omnipotence, Omnipresence, Omniscience, Infinity, and Eternity, 22, 79 note 91, 80
Angelic Wisdom about Life, 22, 78, 79 note 91, 80

Angels, 33. *See also* Heaven; *names of angels*
    from Africa, 523 note 510
    ancient people communicating with, 475 note 168
    angel guardians, 466 note 118
    angels' understanding of the Bible, 465 note 112, 481–482 note 212, 487 note 245
    appearing in the Bible, 517 note 471
    archangels, 486 note 242
    believed by some to be made of ether, 495 note 298
    as differentiated from spirits, 513 note 442
    as an embodiment of the Lord, 491–492 note 275
    as expressions of caring, 508 note 398
    having been people on earth, 488 note 251, 513 note 442
    of the highest heaven looking like children, 482 note 217
    as human, 451 note 13, 508 note 398, 517 note 471
    place in the spiritual world of, 469–470 note 141
    reading Scripture, 28
    states of, 511 note 426
    Swedenborg claiming companionship with, 29
Animal spirit, 487 note 247
Animals
    as automata, 516 note 470
    Enlightenment views *vs.* Swedenborg's views on, 516 note 470
    as representations, 479 note 194
Annals of the Old Testament, 513 note 445

Anointing, with oil, 479 note 192
Anonymity, Swedenborg's, 43, 49
    his efforts to preserve, 42–43
        in Europe *vs.* in Sweden, 64
        as reason for his move to London from Amsterdam to publish, 76–77
        ultimately unsuccessful, 64–65 note 66
    sacrificed, 57, 62 note 61, 65, 71 and note 77, 91
Anselm of Canterbury, 458 note 69
Apostles' Creed, 512 note 438
Appearances, 511 note 426. *See also* Correspondence
Aquinas, Thomas, 458 note 69
Arianism (Arians), 526–527 note 527
Aristotle, 463 note 97, 476 note 170, 483 note 219, 491 note 269, 495 note 295
Arius, 527 note 529
Athanasian Creed, 466–467 note 119, 512 note 438
    acceptance of, 461 note 91
    alternate readings in, 468 note 133
    authorship of, 468 note 132
    Commentary on the Athanasian Creed, 52, 461 note 91
    quoted and reworded by Swedenborg, 27
    Swedenborg's references to, 462–463 note 96
Athanasius, 468 note 132
Atheism, 472–473 note 153, 494–495 note 293
Atonement, 458 note 69
Augsburg Confession, 527 note 529. *See also The Book of Concord*
Augustine, 461 note 85, 502 note 351
Aura, 467 note 122
Automata (robots), 504 note 368
    animals as, 516 note 470

B

Babylon, in the Book of Revelation, 3 note 7, 471 note 148, 509 note 410
Basic Principles of Nature, 496 note 302
Basilisk, 510 note 416
Bayley, Jonathan, 11
Becoming (*philosophical concept*), 483 note 219
Being (*philosophical concept*), 483 note 219
Benedict XIV (*pope*), 520 note 494
Bentley, Richard, 494–495 note 293
Benzelius, Carl Jesper, 71 note 77
Benzelius, Erik (the younger), 70–71, 70 note 75
Benzelius, Henrik, 70 and note 75
Benzelius, Jacob, 70 and note 75
Benzelstierna, Lars Larsson, 71, 95, 103
Beronius, Magnus, 103
Bethlehem, 465 note 115, 523–524 note 516

Beyer, Gabriel, 36–37 note 21, 69, 73, 81 note 96, 88, 93, 95, 96, 447–448 note 4
The Bible, 4, 482 note 214. *See also* Sacred Scripture; The Word; *individual Bible books*
    access to the Bible as a central plank of the Reformation, 493–494 note 284
    angels being with us when we read, 465 note 112
    angels' understanding of, 487 note 245
    as basis of the Moravian church, 526 note 525
    being studied for cabalistic or alchemical wisdom, 481 note 207
    being written about the Lord alone, 455 note 41
    Bible books with an inner meaning, 449–451 note 11
    biblical figures representing the Christian church, 469 note 138
    calculating the date of creation from, 513 note 445
    Catholic laity as forbidden to read, 493–494 note 284, 519–520 note 493, 520–521 note 497
    correspondence in, 492–493 note 281
    criticism of, 471–472 note 152, 473 note 155, 474 note 162
    as divinely inspired, 473 note 158, 474 note 163
    "the Four Sets of Teachings" being addressed to those who understand the Bible literally, 3
    in heaven, 481–482 note 212
    Hebrew Bible, 477 note 183, 496 note 300
    historical-grammatical school of Bible criticism, 72
    literal meaning of (*see* Literal meaning)
    literary style of, 471–472 note 152, 474 note 162
    as opening heaven, 474–475 note 164
    the possibility of convincing even earthly-minded people about the Bible's value, 27–28
    references to the Bible in the Qur'an, 496–497 note 304
    as representing the five churches, 448 note 5
    the shorter works of 1763 being addressed to the biblically literate, 4
    spirits' misuse of, 487 note 246
    spiritual meaning of (*see* Inner [spiritual] meaning)
    Swedenborg's Bible indexes, 41–42
    Swedenborg's biblical canon, 449–451 note 11
    the Ten Commandments as the first part of the Bible to be written, 501 note 345

Bishop, British. *See under* Clergy: British clergy
Bishops, Swedish. *See also* Clergy: Swedish clergy
    in office in 1760, 103
    of 1760–1772 listed, 103
    Swedenborg's connections with, 70–71
    as target of Swedenborg's book promotion, 70–72, 91, 94
Björnståhl, Jakob Jonas, 87 note 106
Black, spirits who appear black, 515 note 459
Blasphemy, 467–468 note 128
Board of mines, Swedish, 59–60
    Swedenborg asking leave from, 38–39
    Swedenborg's membership on, 58, 74 note 83, 487–488 note 249
Body
    belief in resurrection of the physical body, 512 note 438
    belief in reunion of body with soul at Last Judgment, 496 note 299
    interaction between soul and body, 486 note 243
Bohemian Brethren (Herrnhut Brotherhood; Unity of the Brethren), 526 note 526. *See also* Moravian church
Bonde, Gustaf, 58, 62, 64, 88
The Book of Common Prayer, 462–463 note 96, 497 note 313
The Book of Concord, 462–463 note 96, 503 note 353. *See also* Augsburg Confession; Formula of Concord
The Book of Jasher, 493 note 283
The Book of the Wars of Jehovah, 493 note 283
"Born from eternity," 461 note 85
Boyle, Robert, 471–472 note 152, 494–495 note 293
The brain, 483 note 223
Breastplate, of the high priest of the Israelites, 478 note 188
Bride and bridegroom, as metaphors in the Bible, 470 note 143, 479 note 190
Britain (Great Britain), 20, 39 note 26, 48, 51–52, 53 and note 48, 54–55 note 50, 55, 56, 58, 69, 80, 94. *See also* England; London
    religious freedom in, 517–518 note 476
The British, 20, 35, 36, 39 note 26, 48. *See also* England
    believed by Swedenborg to be influenced by their leaders, 52–53
    British clergy (*see* Clergy: British clergy)
    British elite the initial target of Swedenborg's marketing, 48–50, 52–54
    disappointing response of, 44–45, 50–54, 91
    spiritual receptivity of, 20
    Swedenborg's estimate of their spirituality, 50, 53
    their condition after judgment described in *Supplements,* 4
Brockmer, John Paul, 525–526 note 524
Broman, Erland Carlsson, 60, 61
"Brother," used to refer to fellow church member, 526 note 526
Burghers, Swedish House of, 40

C

Calvin, John, 458 note 69, 481 note 208
    briefly treated in *Supplements,* 36 and notes 19–20
    treated at length in *True Christianity,* 36 notes 19–20, 519 note 487
Calvinism, 519 note 487
Canaan, extent of, 470 note 144, 529–530
Caring. *See also* Faith; Love; Neighbor
    angels as expressions of, 508 note 398
    the "deeds of caring," 511–512 note 432
    defined, 24
    faith as the form of caring, 508 note 398
    faith divorced from caring as having no truth, 512 note 433
    faith not existing apart from caring, 29, 33
    its importance in Swedenborg's theology, 2, 24, 33, 34, 471 note 148
    reflections, good deeds, and obligations related to, 505–506 note 377
Catechism, 503 note 353
Causation, theory of, 476 note 170, 483 note 219
Chadwick, John, 12
Charles (*prince of Sweden*), 88
Charles II (*king of England, Scotland, and Ireland*), 524 note 519, 525 note 523
Charles XII (*king of Sweden*), 39, 71
Chastity, 503 note 357
Cherubs, 466 note 118
Children, religious instruction of, 503 note 353
Christ. *See also* Jesus Christ; The Lord; The Messiah
    imputation of merit of, 25–26, 460 note 81
    satisfaction theory of atonement of, 458 note 69
Christianity (Christians), 5, 22 note 9, 31, 53. *See also* The church; Clergy; *specific denominations*
    biblical basis of, 494–495 note 293
    Christianity as the fourth church era, 494 note 291
    Christians as "People of the Book," 496–497 note 304

Christianity *(continued)*
    the church as being destroyed by the faith of contemporary Christianity, 33–34
    "the church" meaning Christianity in general, 448 note 6
    essential principles of, 2, 9 note 3, 23–24, 527 note 529
    faith as lacking in final days of Christian era, 452 note 18
    the faith of contemporary Christianity blocking interaction with angels, 33
    "the Four Sets of Teachings" addressing eighteenth-century objections to Christianity, 4
    ignorance of spiritual matters in the Christian church, 475 note 168
    The Lord addressing core issues of, 26–27
    as one of five churches, 448 note 5
    Swedenborg's criticism of the Christian church, 452 note 18
    Swedenborg's summation of true Christian faith, 508 note 400
Christology, The Lord addressing core issues of, 26–27
The church. *See also* Clergy; *specific denominations*
    as being destroyed by the faith of contemporary Christianity, 33–34
    as bride of Christ (the Lord), 470 note 143, 479 note 190
    Christianity as the fourth church era, 494 note 291
    "church militant," "church triumphant," "church penitent," 504 note 369
    as corrupted before the Lord's Coming, 460 note 78
    the earliest church, 492 note 277
    the early church, 492 note 277
    end of, 448 note 5, 452 note 20, 476 note 173, 494 note 291, 494 note 292
    essential principles of, 2, 9 note 3, 23–24, 527 note 529
    the five churches, 448 note 5, 496 note 303
    four stages of, 496 note 303
    its leadership targeted by Swedenborg, 52, 70–71
    meaning Christianity in general, 448 note 6
    meaning the Lord's kingdom on earth, 499 note 331
    the new church, 448 note 5, 470 note 142, 514 note 449
        the New Jerusalem meaning a new church, 20, 22–23 and note 11
        as now to be established, 22, 23, 26, 90
    teaching about the Trinity to be foremost in, 26
    works of 1763 written to serve, 22, 23
    the old church as having come to an end, 22, 23, 29
    Protestantism considered the "old church," 22–23 note 10
    referred to as "the beautiful land," 511 note 430
    rewards of a career in, 500 note 334
    states of the, 479 note 193
    Swedenborg's criticism of the Christian church, 452 note 18
    Swedenborg's view that without caring there is no, 2
    symbolic (representative) church, 491 note 273
    use of term *the church* by Swedenborg, 22–23 notes 9 and 10
    as where the Word is known, 461 note 84
Cicero, Marcus Tullius, 495 note 295
Circumcision, 509–510 note 413
Cities, in the spiritual world, 518 note 477
Clarke, Samuel, 494–495 note 293
Classification, of minerals, 487–488 note 249
Clement XII, 519–520 note 493, 520 note 494
Clergy, 36–37 note 21, 83. *See also* The church
    as Swedenborg's target audience, 50 note 43, 71, 80, 81, 83, 92, 94–96
    British clergy
        British bishop with whom Swedenborg conversed in the afterlife, 20, 53–54, 53 note 48
        rejecting Swedenborg's works, 54, 77, 91
        as Swedenborg's target audience, 48–55, 54–55 note 50, 80, 81
    Swedenborg's view of, 452 note 18
    Swedish clergy, 68 note 72, 72 note 78 (*see also* Bishops, Swedish)
        Estate of the Clergy, 68 and note 72
        House of the Clergy, 40, 68 note 73, 88, 94–95
        mixed reaction to Swedenborg's works from, 72 note 78
        Swedenborg's correspondence with, 71 and note 77
        as Swedenborg's target audience, 57–65, 66, 68–70, 72 note 78, 80, 91, 95
Clouds, spiritual significance of, 515 note 462
Clowes, John, 11
Coleridge, Samuel Taylor, 10 note 5
Colophon, of Book of Deuteronomy, 477 note 183
Coming of the Lord, as predicted in Isaiah, 478 note 186

Commandments, the Lord's, 500–501 note 342
Commentary on the Athanasian Creed, 52, 461 note 91
Communion, 497 note 313. *See also* Holy Supper
Composers of Proverbs, 493 note 282
Comrie, Alexander, 85
Confirmation *vs.* perception, 528 note 533
Cookworthy, William, 11
Copenhagen, 88. *See also* Denmark
Correspondence, 485 note 232, 511 note 426
   defined, 475–476 note 169
   Genesis 1–11 as correspondential, 480 note 202
   knowledge of, 479 note 197
   in the spiritual world, 508 note 406, 515 note 463
   in the Word, 492–493 note 281
Council of Nicaea, 481 note 208, 527 note 529
Council of Trent, 506 note 386
Covenant, 501–502 note 348
Cowherd, William, 11
Creation
   date of creation of the world, 513 note 445
   of the universe, 482–483 note 218
Cronstedt, Axel Fredrik, 60, 62
Cross-references, Swedenborg's, 51, 75–78, 92, 97–100, 99 figure 2, 100 figure 3
Cubit, 476 note 174
Cuno, Johann Christian, 54–55 note 50, 93

D

Dagon, 510 note 414
Dante Alighieri, 509 note 410
Darkness, predicted in the Book of Revelation, 494 note 292
Daughters, in Bible passages, 479 note 192
"Day"
   meaning a coming of the Lord for judgment, 454 note 36
   meaning the Lord's Coming to set up a new church, 454 note 37
   meaning the Lord's Coming when there is nothing left of the church, 454 note 35
De Rerum Natura, 472–473 note 153
Deism (Deists), 80–81, 472–473 note 153
Denmark (Danes), 36, 56–57 note 55, 88, 89, 96
   Swedenborg distributing books in, 94
Derham, William, 494–495 note 293
Descartes, René, 472–473 note 153, 495 note 298, 516 note 470
The Devil, 457 note 62, 464 note 102
Devils (demons), 457 note 62, 464 note 102, 513 note 442, 515 note 458
Dick, William C., 10

The Diet. *See* The Riksdag
Diodorus Siculus, 479–480 note 198
Disciples, 462 note 92
The Divine, the emanating divine presence, 451 note 15. *See also* God; The Lord
Divine design, 500 note 337
Divine love and wisdom, 500 note 337
   connection of the heart and lungs with, 468 note 130
   as spiritual warmth and light, 448 note 7, 514 note 452
Divine Love and Wisdom
   empirical focus of, 4
   mentioned by Gjörwell, 86, 87
   mentioned in preface to *The Lord,* 22, 79 note 91, 80
   presented to royalty, 88
   publication of, 1 and note 1
   referred to as a *transactio,* 80
   referring to *Life,* 32
   referring to *Sacred Scripture,* 30
   referring to *The Lord,* 27
   subject of human form in, 463 note 100
   subject of human will and understanding in, 498 note 322
   targeting nontheological readers, 79, 82 note 98, 92
Divine Providence
   identifying essential principles of the church, 2, 9 note 3, 23–24, 527 note 529
   mentioned by Gjörwell, 86, 87
   mentioned in preface to *The Lord,* 22, 79 note 91, 80
   mentioning Paul, 36–37 and note 21
   presented to royalty, 88
   referred to as a *transactio,* 80
   referring to *Faith,* 34
   referring to *Life,* 32
   referring to *Sacred Scripture,* 30
   referring to *Supplements,* 37
   referring to *The Lord,* 27
   subject of human form in, 463 note 100
   targeting nontheological readers, 79, 82 note 98, 92
Diviners, 492 note 280
Draft Introduction to a Rational Psychology, 521–522 note 501
Draft of "The Lord," 50–51, 51 note 46, 97
Draft on the Inner Meaning of Prophets and Psalms, 451 note 16, 465 note 111, 491 note 272
Dragon, in the Book of Revelation, 510 note 420
Drottningholm, 88, 89, 91

Dura mater, 483 note 223
The Dutch, 35. *See also* The Netherlands
   their condition after judgment described in *Supplements,* 4

E

The earthly, 485 note 229, 486 note 243, 505 notes 373 and 374
   definition of, 476–477 note 180
   earthly love, 509–510 note 413
   earthly meaning of the Bible, 29, 452 note 17 (*see also* Literal meaning)
   earthly memory, 507–508 note 397
   the possibility of convincing even earthly-minded people about the Bible's value, 27–28
Earthly truth, 506 note 380
The East, 480 note 205
Edict of Nantes, 520 note 495
Ehrenpreus, Carl Didrik, 59
Elliott, John, 10
Emmanuel *(Hebrew name),* 454 note 38, 461 note 86
Empiricism
   consistent with the Bible, in Swedenborg's view, 4
   dialoguing with faith in *The Old Testament Explained,* 4 note 8
Enchiridion, 503 note 353
Engeström, Johan, 103
England, 54–55 note 50, 56–57 note 55, 58, 60, 77, 89, 90, 91 note 109, 96. *See also* Britain; The British
Enlightenment era, 472–473 note 153
   freedoms in Britain during, 517–518 note 476
Ephraim, 489 note 254
Epicureanism, 472–473 note 153
The Epistles, 36–37 note 21, 449–451 note 11
Equilibrium, between heaven and hell, 499 note 324
Ernesti, Johann August
   accusing Swedenborg of "naturalism," 73 and note 80, 83
   calling Swedenborg's system Sabellian, 83 note 101
   review of *Revelation Unveiled* by, 82 note 98
   review of *Secrets of Heaven* by, 72–73
   review of shorter works of 1763 by, 82—84, 88
   Swedenborg's identity known to, 83 note 99
Essence *(philosophical term),* 507 note 389
Ether, 495 note 298, 512–513 note 441

Evil, 452–453 note 22, 500 note 337. *See also* Hell
   as bringing pain upon the doer, 516 note 465
   evil spirits (*see* Spirits, evil)
   flowing out of hell, 458 note 66
   heaven being closed to people who live evil lives, 482 note 213
   importance of abstaining from evil actions, 30–32, 34
   turning one's back on, 505 note 375
Exinanition, 464 note 106

F

Fables, 480 note 199
Faith, 4 note 8. *See also* Faith; Faith alone; Truth
   being an inner recognition of truth, 32–33, 506 note 385
   blind faith shutting down the mind, 33 note 17
   coming to life only when our sins have been forgiven through repentance, 31
   "faith apart from truth" as part of Roman Catholicism and Protestantism, 33
   faith divorced from caring as having no truth, 512 note 433
   the faith of contemporary Christianity blocking interaction with angels, 33
   as the form of caring, 508 note 398
   given priority over works (caring) in Protestantism, 24, 29, 30, 31
   the Hebrew word for, 506 note 384
   knowledge not the same as faith, 33
   lacking in final days of Christian era, 452 note 18
   not existing apart from caring, 29, 33
Faith. See also Faith; Shorter works of 1763
   being based on the Bible, 2–3
   as a critique of the concept of "faith alone," 3
   as described in Swedenborg's other works, 34
   editions and translations of, 9–11
   mentioned in preface to *The Lord,* 21
   as negative epilogue to *The Lord, Sacred Scripture,* and *Life,* 2
   as one of the "four sets of teachings," 2, 10
   presented to royalty, 88
   publication of, 1 and note 1
   purpose of, 32–34, 92
   referring to *Life,* 32
   referring to *The Lord,* 27
   significance of full title of, 19–20
   topic of, 1–2
   using fewer biblical allusions than companion works, 32

Faith alone, 471 note 148, 481 notes 208 and 209, 498 note 316, 499 note 328. *See also* Faith; Justification; Protestantism; Salvation
    biblical symbols Swedenborg links to those who believe in salvation by faith alone, 32
    dragon in the Book of Revelation as having to do with, 32, 510 note 420
    in Lutheran and Anglican churches, 497 note 312
    Paul never speaking of, 527 note 528
    prevalent belief in faith as the solitary factor in our salvation, 2, 24, 29, 31, 34, 471 note 148

Falsity, convincing oneself of, 490–491 note 268
Feasts, Jewish, 470 note 145
Filenius, Petrus, 71, 72 note 78, 103
Fire
    elementary fire, 517 note 475
    sacred fire, 496 note 302
The Flood, 480 note 202
Form *(philosophical term),* 507 note 389
Formula of Concord, 518–519 note 484. *See also* The Book of Concord
Forssenius, Anders, 103
The Four Doctrines. *See* "The Four Sets of Teachings"
"The Four Sets of Teachings" ("the four teachings"). *See also* Shorter works of 1763
    audience of, 3
    being based on the Bible, 2–3
    as cornerstone of new religious edifice, 23
    each labeled a "teaching for the New Jerusalem," 19–20 (*see also* "Teachings for the New Jerusalem")
    only subset of his works referred to by Swedenborg, 19
    order of, 20
    overview of, 1–3 and note 3, 23
    publication history of, 9–11
    traditionally titled "the Four Doctrines," 2, 19
"Four Treatises," 2 note 3. *See also* "The Four Sets of Teachings"
Fox, George, 525 note 522. *See also* Quakerism
France, 55, 56–57 note 55, 89, 94, 95, 96. *See also* French Revolution; Louis XIV; Louis XV
    Edict of Nantes, 520 note 495
    identified as "noble Catholic nation," 494 note 289
    under the rule of Louis XV, 520 note 496, 520–521 note 497
Frederick I *(king of Sweden),* 48 note 40, 61
Frederick II *(king of Prussia)*
    Sweden's opponent in Seven Years' War, 55
Frederick V *(king of Denmark),* 88
Frederick Adolf, 88
Freedom of a Christian, 33 note 18
French Revolution, 520–521 note 497. *See also* France

G

Galen, 512–513 note 441
Galland, Antoine, 522–523 note 508
Gemelli Careri, Giovanni Francesco, 521–522 note 501
Genesis, historical accuracy of, 480 note 202, 492–493 note 281, 493 note 283
Geneviève *(patron saint of Paris),* 521 note 500
Gentiles, 523 note 515
George of Saxony, 509 note 410
German *(language),* 46, 82
Germany (Germans), 35, 36–37 and notes 19 and 21, 42, 49, 72, 82, 89, 94, 96
    Germans treated in a separate chapter in *True Christianity,* 36 note 19
Gjörwell, Carl Christoffer, 49 note 42, 84 note 103, 89 note 107
    on presentation of Swedenborg's works to Danish king, 88
    reviewing Swedenborg's works of 1763, 87
        factual error in review, 87 note 106
        modeling his review on another's, 87 note 105
    on Swedenborg's visit to the Swedish royal family, 89
    on Swedenborg's works of 1758, 74–75
    on Swedenborg's works of 1763 and 1764, 86
    visit to Swedenborg by, 89–91
Glorification (transformation), of the Lord, 452–453 note 22, 457 note 63. *See also* Jesus Christ; The Lord
    defined, 449 note 8
God. *See also* The Divine; The Lord
    as fully human, 486–487 note 244
    Islamic beliefs about, 521–522 note 501
    names of, 447 note 2, 449 note 9, 453 note 25, 485 note 237, 489 note 261, 496 note 301
    never sending people to hell, 516 note 465
"God with us," 454 note 38
Gold, frankincense, and myrrh, 481 note 206
Golden Age, 496 note 302
Goodness, 30
    good deeds, 498 note 318
    levels of, 498 note 317

The Gospels, 473 note 158
Göteborg (Gothenburg), 69, 70, 93, 95, 103
Gotland, 103
Great Northern War, 55. *See also* Sweden
Greek myths, 480 note 199
Gustav *(prince of Sweden)*, 57, 88
Gyllenborg, Carl, 60, 61
Gyllenborg, Fredrik, 60, 61

H

Halenius, Engelbert, 71, 103
Hanover, 55
Harlem, Jan Janszoon van (Murad Reis), 522 note 503
Hårleman, Carl, 60, 61
Harley, Doris H., 12
Härnösand, 103
Harrison, George, 10
Hart, John, 43 note 34
Hartley, Thomas, 54–55 note 50, 89, 517 note 472
Hatzel, Louis von, 64
Hayward, Tilly B., 10
Heart, theology of, 527 note 530, 528 note 533. *See also* Zinzendorf, Nikolaus von
Heart and lungs, 498 note 322, 500 note 340
 the Lord's divine love and wisdom connected with, 468 note 130
Heaven, 453 note 23, 513 note 442. *See also* Angels; *Heaven and Hell;* The heavenly; Spirits; The spiritual world
 and church as bride of the Lord, 479 note 190
 closed to people who live evil lives, 482 note 213
 communities in heaven, 487 note 246
 equilibrium between heaven and hell, 499 note 324
 ignorance of, 475 note 168
 levels of, 514 note 448, 515 note 462
 the lowest heaven, 514 note 448
 opened to people by reading the Word, 474–475 note 164
 as passing God's divine truth on to humans, 477 note 184
 pseudo-heavens (*see* Pseudo-heavens)
 Swedenborg's concept of, 469–470 note 141
 the three heavens, 514 note 448
 the Word existing in, 28, 451 note 14
Heaven and Hell, 47, 447 note 1. *See also* Works of 1758
 Alnander's notice about, 73–75
 continued in *Supplements,* 18
 discussed by Swedenborg and Tessin, 57
 Gjörwell's notice about, 74–75
 initially distributed to British clergy and nobility, 48
 its order in the works of 1758, 20
 mentioned in preface to *The Lord,* 21
 reporting on angels and spirits, 29
 Supplements referring to, 4
 Swedenborg wishing to import into Sweden fifty copies of, 57–58, 62, 63, 67, 69–70, 93
The heavenly, 485 note 229. *See also* Heaven; The spiritual
 definition of, 476–477 note 180
 the heavenly marriage, 479 note 190, 499 note 332
 people having no mental room for heavenly things, 51
Hebrew *(language)*, 453 note 25, 506 note 384
 God's name in the Hebrew Bible, 449 note 9
 letters in, 457 note 59, 490 note 266
 pronunciation of, 490 note 265
Hell, 464 note 102, 513 note 442. *See also* Evil; *Heaven and Hell;* Spirits, evil
 being cast into, 469 note 138
 being conquered by the Lord, 457 note 61, 458 note 66
 equilibrium between heaven and, 499 note 324
 evil flowing out of, 458 note 66
 hells, 452 note 21
 as powerful before the Lord's Coming, 460 note 78
 satans and devils (demons) in, 457 note 62, 513 note 442
 Swedenborg's concept of, 469–470 note 141
Hellfire, 503 note 355
Heredity, Swedenborg's view of, 463 note 97
Heresy, 490 note 267. *See also* Arianism; Sabellians; Socinians
Heresy trial, of Swedenborg's supporters, 69
Herod the Great, 470–471 note 146
Herrnhut, 525–526 note 524, 528 notes 531 and 532. *See also* Moravian church
Hesiod, 495 note 295
Hieroglyphics, 479–480 note 198
Hindmarsh, Robert, 10, 11, 12
Historical-grammatical school, of Bible criticism, 72
Hofaker, Ludwig, 9
Holbach, Baron d', Paul-Henri Dietrich, 472–473 note 153
Holberg, Ludvig, 73 note 81
Holland, 77, 89, 90, 96. *See also* The Netherlands

Holtius, Nicolaas, 85
The Holy Roman Empire, 55
The Holy Spirit. *See also* The Trinity
 blasphemy against, 467–468 note 128
 defined in *The Lord,* 27
 as emanating divine presence, 451 note 15
 its role in salvation, 518–519 note 484
 as member of the Trinity, 447 note 2
 in Quaker thought, 524 note 519, 524–525 note 521
Holy Supper, elements in, 500 note 336. *See also* Communion
Homer, 504 note 368
Höpken, Anders Johan von, 58, 62, 63, 66, 88
 memorial concerning Swedenborg by, 65
Houris, 522–523 note 508
House of Lords, British, 39 note 26, 50
Human, the human form, 463 note 100
Humanity, Swedenborg's definition of, 486–487 note 244
Hus, John, 525–526 note 524. *See also* Herrnhut; Moravian church

I
Ignatius Loyola, 495 note 297, 521 note 499
Imputation of merit of Christ, Swedenborg's disagreement with concept of, 25–26, 460 note 81. *See also* Sin
The Incarnation, 452–453 note 22, 458 note 66, 463 note 99, 527 note 529
Index Biblicus, 465 note 111
Indexlike statements, 98–100. *See also* Cross-references
Inflow, 486 note 243
 from higher to lower, 505 note 374
Inner (spiritual) meaning, of the Bible, 29, 45, 459 note 75, 488 note 252
 angels as perceiving, 465 note 112, 487 note 245
 being unveiled, 28–29
 Bible books with, 449–451 note 11
 defined, 452 note 17
 in the first chapter of Genesis, 41
 Sacred Scripture as focused on, 3
 spiritual meaning of the prophets, 451 note 16
 Swedenborg claiming revelation of, 27
 Swedenborg's emphasis on literal and spiritual meanings of the Bible, 3 and note 6
Iota, 457 note 59
Isaiah and Jeremiah Explained, 465 note 111
Islam, 522 note 503. *See also* Muhammad; Muslims; Qur'an
 Islamic beliefs about Jesus and God, 521–522 note 501
 stereotypes of Middle Eastern sexuality in Enlightenment Europe, 522–523 note 508
Israel
 biblical territory of, 529–530
 history of, 489 note 254

J
Jansenism, 520–521 note 497
Jehovah. *See also* God
 history of the name, 449 note 9
 root of word, 496 note 301
Jehovah Sabaoth, 453 note 25. *See also* God
Jehovih, 449 note 9. *See also* God
Jerusalem, degeneracy of leaders of, 470–471 note 146
Jesus Christ, in Swedenborg's theology, 460 note 83. *See also* Christ; The Incarnation; The Lord; The Messiah; The Son
 appearing to Swedenborg, 447 note 3
 beliefs about conception of, 528 note 532
 called "Lamb," 526–527 note 527
 calling Jehovah "Father," 461 note 90
 core issues about Jesus addressed in *The Lord,* 26–27
 as doing the will and works of the Father, 461 note 89
 as the embodiment of divine truth, 459–460 note 77
 glorification (transformation) of, 449 note 8, 452–453 note 22, 457 note 63
 heredity of, 452–453 note 22, 463 note 97
 his being "emptied out," 464 note 106
 his nature as part of the divine Trinity discussed in the shorter works of 1763, 26, 29
 importance of believing in the divinity of, 2
 as the incarnation of God, 527 note 529
 Islamic beliefs about, 521–522 note 501
 lineage of, 478 note 186
 as manifestation of the Divine, 447 note 2
 meaning of sufferings of, 25
 miracles of, 479 note 193
 representing the Word, 457–458 note 64
 as sent into the world by the Father, 461 note 88
Jewels, in the spiritual world, 485 note 232
Jews (Judaism), 22 note 9, 35, 523 note 515. *See also* Hebrew; Israel; Jerusalem; Torah
 Jewish feasts, 470 note 145
 Jewish mysticism, 481 note 207
 Jews' knowledge of Bethlehem, 523–524 note 516
 as "People of the Book," 496–497 note 304
 Swedenborg's attitude toward, 5, 480 note 204

Jezreel, 459 note 72
John the Baptist, as representing Jesus, 460 note 83
Johnson, P. H., 12
Josephus, Flavius, 478 note 188
Jot, 457 note 59, 474 note 163
Jove, name of, 496 note 301
Judas Iscariot, 456 notes 46 and 47, 459 note 74
Justification, 508 note 404. *See also* Faith alone; Salvation

K
Kalmar, 103
Karlstad, 103
Kiörning, Olof, 103

L
Lagerlöf, Nils, 103
"Lamb," as a name for Jesus Christ, 526–527 note 527
Lamberg, Erik, 93, 103
La Mettrie, Julien Offray de, 516 note 470
Last Judgment, 470 note 142, 516 note 466
    belief in reunion of soul and body at, 496 note 299
    change in world and churches after, 22–23 notes 10 and 11
    having already come about, 23, 26, 34, 50, 62–63
    having been carried out on Protestants, 34–35
    as having occurred before 1758, 519–520 note 493
    as having occurred in 1757, 469 note 137, 514 note 449
    not occurring in the physical world, 34
    as reorganization of the spiritual world, 453 note 23
    revelations for the new church given after, 514 note 449
    shown by *Supplements* to have changed the world and the church, 34
    Swedenborg's interpretation of, 452 note 20
    Swedenborg's report of the Last Judgment mentioned by reviewer, 84–85
    seen as dangerous, 63
Last Judgment, 47, 469 note 137. *See also* Shorter works of 1758; Works of 1758
    Alnander's notice about, 73–75
    Gjörwell's notice about, 74–75
    its order in the works of 1758, 20
    its relation to *Supplements,* 3 and note 7, 18
    mentioned in preface to *The Lord,* 21

Latin, 51, 52, 85, 101. *See also* Neo-Latin
    its importance as a common language, 49 and note 42
    Swedenborg's fluency in, 49
    Sweden's Latin consistently gender-neutral, 4
    vs. European vernaculars as language of Bible, 493–494 note 284
    word for sky in, 469 note 139
The law, 485 note 233
    meaning of the term in Romans 3:28, 25
The Law and the Prophets, 455–456 note 43
Leaven. *See* Yeast
Leipzig, 72
Letters Concerning the English Nation, 517–518 note 476
Levels
    closing the spiritual level, 505 note 374
    the foundation as the final level, 482–483 note 218
    of heaven, 514 note 448, 515 note 462
    of a human being, 476–477 note 180
    of life, 488 note 250
    of the Lord and reality, 463 note 98
    of meaning in the Bible, 452 note 17, 459 note 75
    of substance, 464 note 105
Lewis, John, 43, 44, 45–46, 525–526 note 524
Lewis, Mary, 48 and note 38, 525–526 note 524
Lidén, Johan Hinric, 89
Life, 488 note 250
    as divine love, 448 note 7
    meaning of term in Swedenborg's theology, 81 and note 97
    religion being about how we live, 30
    Swedenborg's two planned books about life, 78–79, 81–82
Life. *See also* Shorter works of 1763
    being based on the Bible, 2–3
    being based on the Ten Commandments, 3
    as described in Swedenborg's other works, 32
    editions and translations of, 9–11
    its relation to *Sacred Scripture,* 3
    laying out mechanism of salvation, 31, 92
    mentioned in preface to *The Lord,* 21
    as one of the "four teachings," 10
    presented to royalty, 88
    publication of, 1 and note 1
    purpose of, 30–32, 92
    significance of full title of, 19–20
    significance of its coda, 32
    teaching that our motivation is centrally important, 31

Life (continued)
  Ten Commandments as subject of, 19, 30, 31, 81
  topic of, 1–2
Life after death
  losing our outer facade after death, 502–503 note 352
  our nature remaining the same after death, 479 note 191
  theories on, 496 note 299
Light
  heavenly *vs.* earthly, 485 note 229
  intellectual, 53
  Swedenborg claiming spiritual light granted to him, 35
Limbo, 513 note 443
Linen, in Bible passages, 519 note 485
Linköping, 70–71, 103
Literal meaning, of the Bible (the Word), 29, 474–475 note 164, 476 note 172, 481–482 note 212, 484 note 225
  based on historical events, 492–493 note 281
  defined, 452 note 17
  as holy and divine to the smallest detail, 474 note 163
  protecting the inner meaning, 459 note 75
  Swedenborg's emphasis on literal and spiritual meanings of the Bible, 3 and note 6
  the Word lacking literal meaning in heaven, 451 note 14
Literary style, of Swedenborg's time, 471–472 note 152
Loci Communes Rerum Theologicarum, 518–519 note 484
London, 43, 44, 46, 48, 96. *See also* Britain; England
  "Exchange" in, 518 note 478
  as publishing center, 29, 42, 54, 56–57, 64, 74, 75, 76–77 and notes 87 and 88, 86, 90, 96
  Royal Society of London, 91
  Swedenborg's long association with, 76 note 88
  Swedenborg's printers in, 525–526 note 524
The Lord, 21, 22. *See also* Jesus Christ; God; The Son
  appearing through an angel, 491–492 note 275
  conquest of hell by, 457 note 61, 458 note 66
  the divine and human natures of, 452–453 note 22, 463 note 99, 465 note 108
  following his commandments, 500–501 note 342
  glorification (transformation) of, 449 note 8, 452–453 note 22, 457 note 63

  the Lord's Coming predicted in Isaiah, 478 note 186
  the Lord's union with us, 465 note 108, 468 note 135, 474–475 note 164
  the Lord's words in the Gospels, 473 note 158
  meaning of the term, 447 note 2, 466–467 note 119
  names of, 449 note 9, 526–527 note 527 (*see also under* God)
  providing people with the means of learning truth, 482 note 214
  the Resurrection of, 452–453 note 22, 457 note 60
  as the sole subject of the Word, 27
  as the sun of heaven, 514 note 452
The Lord
  addressing core issues of Christianity, 26–27
  being based on the Bible, 2–3
  as described in Swedenborg's other works, 27
  editions and translations of, 9–10
  its relation to *Sacred Scripture,* 3
  main principles presented in the work, 24–26, 92
  mentioned in preface to *The Lord,* 21
  as one of the "four teachings," 10
  preface to, 21–22, 80
  presented to royalty, 88
  publication of, 1 and note 1
  purpose of, 24–27
  significance of full title of, 19
  teaching that the Word is solely about the Lord, 27
  topic of, 1–2
The Lord's Prayer, taught to children, 503 note 353
Louis XIV, 84, 85–86, 87, 520 notes 495 and 496, 520–521 note 497
Louis XV, 84, 85–86, 520 note 496, 520–521 note 497
Love. *See also* Caring; Divine love and wisdom
  dominant love, 460 note 82
  life as divine love, 448 note 7
  role of love in spiritual rebirth, 498 note 322
  spiritual and earthly, 509–510 note 413
The lovefeast, 526 note 525. *See also* Moravian church
Lovisa Ulrika, 57, 64–65 note 66, 88
Loyola, Ignatius. *See* Ignatius Loyola
Lucretius (Titus Lucretius Carus), 472–473 note 153
Ludwig IX *(landgrave of Hesse-Darmstadt),* 94, 95
Ludwig Rudolf *(duke of Brunswick-Lüneburg),* 48 note 40

Lund, 70, 103
University of, 87 note 106
The lungs, 483 note 222. *See also* Heart and lungs
Luther, Martin, 33 note 18, 481 note 208, 493–494 note 284, 502 note 351, 503 note 353, 509 note 410, 518–519 note 484, 519 note 488, 525–526 note 524
associated with penal substitution theory of atonement, 458 note 69
briefly treated in *Supplements,* 36 and notes 19–20
in the spiritual world, 519 note 490
treated at length in *True Christianity,* 36 notes 19–20
Lutheranism, 519 note 488
division of the Ten Commandments in, 502 note 351
justification by faith in, 481 note 209 (*see also* Faith alone)
Lutheran theological treatise, 518–519 note 484
Lütkeman, Gabriel Timoteus, 103

M

Machines, people as, 516 note 470
Magi, 492 note 280
Manifestation *(philosophical concept),* 483 note 219
Mann, Charles H., 10
Marriage
chastity in, 503 note 357
the heavenly marriage, 479 note 190, 499 note 332
the hellish marriage, 499 note 332
monogamy in, 503 note 358, 522 note 507
Quaker marriage, 524–525 note 521, 525 note 522
Marriage Love, 503 note 356
containing list of Swedenborg's works, 21 note 8, 78 note 90
as part of the "Angelic Wisdom" series, 81 note 96
sent to Beyer, 96
sent to Oetinger, 94
Masoretes, 477 note 183
Materialistic monism, 472–473 note 153
Meaning, inner (spiritual). *See* Inner (spiritual) meaning
Meaning, literal. *See* Literal meaning
Melanchthon, Philipp
briefly treated in *Supplements,* 36 and notes 19–20
differing from Luther in question of human will, 518–519 note 484

treated at length in *True Christianity,* 36 notes 19–20
Memorials, written by Swedenborg to the Swedish government, 41, 65–67, 68 and note 72, 69
Memory, outer (earthly) *vs.* inner, 507–508 note 397
Mennander, Carl Fredrik, 71, 95, 103
Meslier, Jean, 473 note 155
The Messiah, prophecies about the birth of, 523–524 note 516. *See also* Christ; Jesus Christ
Messiter, Husband, 89
Metamorphoses, 496 note 302
Michael *(archangel),* 486 note 242
Middle Easterners, sexual stereotyping of, 522–523 note 508
Mina *(unit of money),* 497 note 309
Minerals, formation of, 487–488 note 249
Miracles, 479 note 193
Miscellaneous Observations (work by Swedenborg), 58
Monergism, 518–519 note 484
Money, love of, 500 note 335
Montesquieu, 522–523 note 508
Moon worship, 523 note 509
Moravian church, 525–526 note 524, 526 note 526, 527 note 530, 528 note 533. *See also* Herrnhut; Zinzendorf, Nikolaus von
biblical basis of, 526 note 525, 527 note 529
the lovefeast, 526 note 525
Swedenborg's view of, 525–526 note 524, 527 note 529
using "Lamb" for name of Jesus, 526–527 note 527
Moravians, 36
their condition after judgment described in *Supplements,* 4, 35
Moses, 524 note 517
as author of the first five books of the Bible, 501 note 345
Motivation, 31
Muhammad, 4, 521–522 note 501. *See also* Islam; Qur'an
Muslims, 5. *See also* Islam; Qur'an
their condition after judgment described in *Supplements,* 4, 35

N

Natural religion, 494–495 note 293
Naturalism, 495 note 294
Ernesti accusing Swedenborg of, 73 and note 80, 83
increasing identification of God with nature, 472–473 note 153

Nazirite, 484 note 226
Neighbor, levels of, 507 notes 394 and 395
Neo-Latin, 490 note 264. *See also* Latin
Nerves, fluid believed to flow through, 487 notes 247 and 248
The Netherlands, 42, 55, 64, 87, 88, 91 note 109, 94. *See also* Amsterdam; The Dutch; Holland
The new church. *See under* The church
New heaven and new earth, 469 note 140, 512 note 438
The New Jerusalem, 90
   as bride of Christ, 470 note 143
   meaning a new church, 20, 22–23 and note 11
New Jerusalem, 78. *See also* Shorter works of 1758; Works of 1758
   Alnander's notice about, 73–75
   final chapter of, 50 note 43
   Gjörwell's notice about, 74–75
   its order in the works of 1758, 20
   mentioned in preface to *The Lord,* 21
Nicene Creed, 466–467 note 119
Nicolai Klimii Iter Subterraneum, 73 and note 81
Nobility, 72 note 78
   as Swedenborg's target audience, 50 note 43, 80, 94
   British
      as Swedenborg's target audience, 48, 50, 53
   Swedish, 39 and note 26, 66
      Estate of the Nobility
         partisanship in, 66, 68 and note 70
         Swedenborg as being able to present his works to, 67–69
      power of, 40
      Swedenborg discussing his works with, 61–62
      as Swedenborg's target audience, 57–65
      tiers of, 39
      titles of, 39
Nordencrantz, Anders, 64 note 66, 66–67, 68 note 72
Numbers, spiritual meanings of, 488 note 252
Nyrén, Carl, 72 note 78

O

Octavo, 43. *See also* Quarto
   defined, 43 note 35
   translation of *Supplements* in, 11
Oelreich, Niklas von, 58, 74 note 84
Oetinger, Friedrich Christoph, 36–37 note 21, 94
The Old Testament Explained, 4 note 8, 41 and note 30

On the Babylonian Captivity of the Church, 509 note 410
Opusculum (Latin word), 80
Osander, Olof Petri, 103
Other Planets, 47. *See also* Shorter works of 1758; Works of 1758
   Alnander's notice about, 73–75
   its order in the works of 1758, 20
   mentioned in preface to *The Lord,* 21
Ottoman Empire, 522–523 note 508
Outer (earthly) memory, 512 note 433
Ovid, 480 note 199, 496 note 302

P

Paris, 96
Paul the Apostle
   mentioned fleetingly in *Supplements,* 36
   never speaking of "faith alone," 527 note 528
   Swedenborg's overall treatment of, 36–37 notes 21–22
Peasants, Swedish House of, 40
Penn, William, 525 note 523. *See also* Quakerism
Penny, Stephen, 44, 45
"The People of the Book," 496–497 note 304
Permission, laws of, 468 note 131
Philadelphianism, 528 note 531. *See also* Zinzendorf, Nikolaus von
Pius IV, 493–494 note 284
Plato, and metaphor of the cave, 509 note 408
Pleura, 483 note 222
Plotinus, 479–480 note 198
Poland, 94
Popes, 4
Portugal, 55
Potts, John Faulkner, 10
Pound, British, 56 and note 53
Prague, 523 note 513
Privy Council (*Riksråd*), 40
Problematic material, in the shorter works of 1763, 4–6
Profanation, 459 note 75
Program statement, 24 and note 13
Promiscuity
   as encouraged by warm climates, 522–523 note 508
   rumors of promiscuity in nonconforming Christian movements, 524–525 note 521, 525 note 523
Proof-texting, 32. *See also* Text-proofing
Prophecy, before the time of Abram, 492 note 277
The prophetic books of the Word. *See* The Word: prophetic books of

The prophets
  representing Israel's sins, 25
  representing the Word, 457–458 note 64
Protestantism (Protestants), 33 note 18, 35, 83, 481 note 209, 509 note 410. *See also specific denominations and leaders*
  considered heretical by Swedenborg, 490 note 267
  faith given priority over works (caring) in, 24, 29, 30, 31
  five shorter works of 1763 confronting Protestant thought, 92
  identified with Philistia, 471 note 148
  the Last Judgment having been carried out on Protestants, 34–35
  place of leading Protestant reformers in the afterlife, 36
  Protestantism considered the "old church," 22–23 note 10
  Protestants as believing in salvation by faith alone, 24, 31, 471 note 148
  the Reformation, 481 note 208, 493–494 note 284
  Swedenborg giving the works of 1758 to Protestant British lords, 54
  Swedenborg seeing "faith apart from truth" in Protestantism, 33
  Swedenborg's criticism of "faith alone" and conception of the Trinity in, 481 note 208
  as topic in *Supplements*, 3
Provo, Peter, 10
Prussia, 55
Psalms, Book of, 458 note 67
Pseudo-heavens, 514 notes 447 and 448, 515 note 462
  dispersed during reorganization of heaven, 453 note 23
  formed by Protestants before the Last Judgment, 35
Pu, 513 note 443

Q

Quakerism (Quakers), 5
  in the Americas, 525 note 523
  background of, 524 note 519
  beliefs about Quakers in Swedenborg's day, 524–525 note 521
  the condition of Quakers after judgment described in *Supplements*, 4, 35
  founder of, 525 note 522
  Quaker marriage, 524–525 note 521, 525 note 522
  Quaker worship, 524 note 519
Quaking, 524 note 520
Quarto, 43, 47, 67, 74, 76 note 86. *See also* Octavo
  defined, 43 note 35
  reviewers remarking on Swedenborg's printing in, 74, 75, 86
  translation of *Supplements* in, 11
Qur'an, 521–522 note 501. *See also* Islam; Muhammad; Muslims
  references to the Bible in, 496–497 note 304

R

Raphael *(archangel)*, 486 note 242
Reason, 494–495 note 293 *See also* Understanding
Rebirth, spiritual (regeneration), 498 note 322
Reformed (Calvinist) tradition, justification by faith in, 481 note 209. *See also* Faith alone; Protestantism
Reformed (Protestant) tradition, doctrine of justification by faith in, 498 note 316. *See also* Faith alone; Protestantism
Řehoř, Brother, 526 note 525
Religious eras, 452 note 20. *See also* The church
The Resurrection, 452–453 note 22, 457 note 60. *See also* Jesus Christ; The Lord
Resurrection, of the physical body, 512 note 438
Reuterholm, Hedvig, 60, 61
Revelation, Book of. *See also Revelation Explained; Revelation Unveiled*
  Babylon in, 3 note 7, 471 note 148, 509 note 410
  dragon in, 510 note 420
  predictions of darkness in, 494 note 292
Revelation Explained, 3 note 6
  decreasing cross-references to *Secrets of Heaven* in, 51, 97–100
  possible reasons it was not published, 56, 77
  referred to in *Draft of "The Lord,"* 51 note 46
  referring to the works of 1758, 51
Revelation Unveiled, 79, 82 note 98
  each British bishop being sent a copy of, 54–55 note 50
  referring to *Faith*, 34
  referring to *Life*, 32
  referring to *Sacred Scripture*, 30
  referring to *The Lord*, 27
Reviews and notices of books in the eighteenth century, 43–44

Reviews and notices of Swedenborg's works, 82, 86
  by Alnander, 73–75
  by Ernesti, 72–73, 82–84, 82 note 98, 88
  by Gjörwell, 74–75, 84 note 103, 86–87, 87 and notes 105–106
  of *Revelation Unveiled*, 82 note 98
  of *Secrets of Heaven*, 44–48, 48 note 39, 72–75
  of the works of 1758, 48, 72–75
  of the works of 1763, 82–88
Rhyzelius, Andreas Olai, 71, 73, 103
The Riksdag (Swedish parliament or Diet), 58, 63, 67, 71, 91. *See also* Nobility: Swedish; Sweden
  composition of, 39–40
  deputations of, 69
  Estate of the Clergy, 68 and note 72
  Estate of the Nobility, 66–69, 68 and note 70
  House of the Burghers, 40
  House of the Clergy, 40, 68 note 73, 88, 94–95
  House of the Peasants, 40
  as a possible target of Swedenborg's distribution, 67–69 and notes 70 and 73, 70
  Privy Council *(Riksråd)*, 40
  probably never addressed by Swedenborg, 41
  Secret Committee, 40, 41
  Secret Exchange Deputation, 67
  sessions of, 40, 41 note 27, 58
  Swedenborg's memorials to, 41, 65–67, 68 and note 72, 69
  Swedenborg's role in, 39–41
Rivers, as boundaries, 529–530
Robsahm, Carl, 66, 68 note 73
Rogers, N. Bruce, 9, 10
Roman Catholicism, 35, 481 note 208. *See also* names of popes; specific councils
  Catholic ban on vernacular Bibles, 493–494 note 284
  Catholic clergy as targets of Swedenborg's distribution efforts, 94
  Catholic piety of Louis XIV, 520 note 495, 520–521 note 497
  Catholics discouraged from reading the Bible, 519–520 note 493, 520–521 note 497
  "church penitent" in, 504 note 369
  considered heretical by Swedenborg, 490 note 267
  considered the "old church," 22–23 note 10
  Counter-Reformation, 493–494 note 284, 495 note 297
  decline in authority of, 520 note 494
  division of the Ten Commandments in, 502 note 351
  in France, 494 note 289
  Inquisition, 493–494 note 284
  Moravian church formed in opposition to, 525–526 note 524, 526 note 525
  Roman Catholic Church as the Babylon of Revelation, 3 note 7, 471 note 148
  Roman Catholic clergy as the Babylon of Revelation, 509 note 410
  Swedenborg seeing "faith apart from truth" in, 33
  as topic in *Last Judgment*, 3 and note 7
  veneration of relics in, 506 note 386
Rowlatt, J. C., 11
Royal Library, in Stockholm, 75, 86, 90, 95
Royal Society, of London, 91
Royal Society of Sciences (Royal Swedish Academy of Sciences), 95
Russia, 35, 55, 94

S

Sabaoth, 453 note 25
Sabellians, 83 and note 101. *See also* Heresy
Sacred Scripture, in Swedenborg's view. *See also* The Bible; The Word
  "the Four Sets of Teachings" being based on, 2–3
  not to be taken merely literally, 25
  spiritual meaning of (*see* Inner [spiritual] meaning)
  understanding of Scripture threatened with extinction, 29
Sacred Scripture. *See also* Shorter works of 1763
  being based on the Bible, 2–3
  as described in Swedenborg's other works, 30
  discussing how to deal with people such as Deists, 80–81
  editions and translations of, 9–11
  its focus on Bible's spiritual meaning, 3
  its relation to *The Lord* and *Life*, 3
  its relation to *True Christianity*, 1 note 1
  mentioned in preface to *The Lord*, 21
  the nature of the Word as described in, 27–28
  as one of the "four teachings," 10
  presented to royalty, 88
  publication of, 1 and note 1
  purpose of, 27–30, 92
  significance of full title of, 19
  topic of, 1–2

Saints, Protestant views on, 506 note 386
Salvation, 460 note 81, 463 note 99, 481 notes 208 and 209, 499 note 328, 508 note 404. *See also* Faith alone
  all those being saved who live by principles similar to the Ten Commandments, 31, 32
  biblical symbols Swedenborg links to those who believe in salvation by faith alone, 32
  coming from the Lord, 24
  depending on whether the good we do is genuine, 30
  Holy Spirit's work in, 518–519 note 484
  as including non-Christians, 6, 31
  Life laying out mechanism of salvation, 31, 92
  Protestants as believing in salvation by faith alone, 24, 31, 471 note 148
  role Swedenborg believes faith plays in, 31
  Secrets of Heaven as revealing the way to salvation, 50
  Swedenborg criticized for teaching against Protestant teachings about, 83
  Swedenborg praised for laboring in the cause of, 54–55 note 50
Sap, 487 note 248
Satans, 457 note 62, 513 note 442. *See also* Hell
Schmidt, Sebastian, 493 note 282
Scholasticism, 507 note 389
Schröder, Göran Claes, 103
Schröder, Karl Gustaf, 103
Scripture references
  Genesis 1, pages 451 note 13, 491 note 274
  Genesis 1, 2, page 513 note 445
  Genesis 1–3, page 496 note 302
  Genesis 1–11, page 480 note 202
  Genesis 1:5, page 491 note 274
  Genesis 1:8, 13, 19, 23, 31, page 491 note 274
  Genesis 3:22–24, page 466 note 118
  Genesis 4:25, page 454 note 38
  Genesis 5, page 513 note 445
  Genesis 6:3, page 467 note 127
  Genesis 8:21, page 504 note 367
  Genesis 9:10–27, page 529
  Genesis 10:6, page 529
  Genesis 10:15, page 529
  Genesis 11:10–32, page 513 note 445
  Genesis 15:18, page 529
  Genesis 18:2, page 517 note 471
  Genesis 19:7, page 507 note 394
  Genesis 29:32–33, page 454 note 38
  Genesis 41:52, page 489 note 254
  Genesis 46:20, page 489 note 254
  Genesis 48, page 489 note 254
  Exodus 12:1–28, page 470 note 145
  Exodus 12:46, page 456–457 note 56
  Exodus 17:8–16, page 458 note 68
  Exodus 20, page 501 note 345
  Exodus 20:1–17, page 485 note 233
  Exodus 20:2–11, page 502 note 351
  Exodus 20:12–17, page 502 note 351
  Exodus 23:14–17, page 470 note 145
  Exodus 25:10–40, page 478–479 note 189
  Exodus 26, page 478–479 note 189
  Exodus 28, page 478–479 note 189
  Exodus 28:30, page 478 note 188
  Exodus 30:1–10, page 478–479 note 189
  Exodus 31:18, page 501 note 345
  Exodus 32:27, page 507 note 394
  Exodus 34:18, 22–24, page 470 note 145
  Exodus 34:21–22, page 478–479 note 189
  Exodus 34:28, page 501 note 346
  Exodus 36:8–38, page 478–479 note 189
  Exodus 37, page 478–479 note 189
  Exodus 38:21, page 473–474 note 161
  Exodus 39:1–31, page 478–479 note 189
  Exodus 40:9–11, page 479 note 192
  Leviticus 1–7, page 478–479 note 189
  Leviticus 8:8, page 478 note 188
  Leviticus 23, page 478–479 note 189
  Leviticus 23:4–21, 33–43, page 470 note 145
  Leviticus 27:30–32, page 502 note 350
  Numbers 1:50, 53, page 473–474 note 161
  Numbers 6:1–21, page 484 note 226
  Numbers 7:1, page 479 note 192
  Numbers 9:12, page 456–457 note 56
  Numbers 16:22, page 467 note 126
  Numbers 20:1–13, page 524 note 517
  Numbers 21:14, page 493 note 283
  Numbers 27:18, page 467 note 126
  Numbers 27:21, page 478 note 188
  Numbers 28:9–10, 16–31, page 478–479 note 189
  Numbers 29:12–39, page 478–479 note 189
  Numbers 31:1–12, page 458 note 68
  Numbers 34:3–5, page 530
  Numbers 34:7–9, page 530
  Numbers 34:8, page 530
  Deuteronomy 1:37, page 524 note 517
  Deuteronomy 3:23–27, page 524 note 517
  Deuteronomy 4:13, page 501 note 346
  Deuteronomy 4:21, page 524 note 517
  Deuteronomy 5:6–15, page 502 note 351
  Deuteronomy 5:6–21, page 485 note 233
  Deuteronomy 5:16–21, page 502 note 351
  Deuteronomy 8:15, page 510 note 417
  Deuteronomy 9:10, page 501 note 345
  Deuteronomy 10:4, page 501 note 346

Scripture references *(continued)*
    Deuteronomy 14:22–23, page 502 note 350
    Deuteronomy 16:1–17, pages 470 note 145, 478–479 note 189
    Deuteronomy 16:16, page 470 note 145
    Deuteronomy 18:10, page 492 note 280
    Deuteronomy 18:14, page 492 note 280
    Deuteronomy 23:17, page 479 note 192
    Deuteronomy 32, page 524 note 517
    Deuteronomy 32:7–8, page 492 note 277
    Deuteronomy 33:8, page 478 note 188
    Joshua 6, page 458 note 68
    Joshua 8:1–29, page 458 note 68
    Joshua 10, page 458 note 68
    Joshua 11, page 458 note 68
    Joshua 13:22, page 492 note 280
    Joshua 15:2–4, page 530
    Joshua 19:24–39, page 530
    Judges 3:7–31, page 458 note 68
    Judges 4, page 458 note 68
    Judges 6:1–7:25, page 458 note 68
    Judges 6:11–22, page 517 note 471
    Judges 11:1–12:40, page 458 note 68
    Judges 11:40, page 479 note 192
    Ruth 4:11, page 465 note 115
    1 Samuel 1:20, page 454 note 38
    1 Samuel 5, 6, page 510 note 414
    1 Samuel 6:2, page 492 note 280
    1 Samuel 8:15, 17, page 502 note 350
    1 Samuel 13–14, page 458 note 68
    1 Samuel 14:41–42, page 478 note 188
    1 Samuel 17, page 458 note 68
    1 Samuel 28:3–25, page 488 note 251
    1 Samuel 28:6, page 478 note 188
    1 Samuel 30, page 458 note 68
    2 Samuel 1:24, page 479 note 192
    2 Samuel 5:5–25, page 458 note 68
    2 Samuel 7:6, page 473–474 note 161
    2 Samuel 8:1–14, page 458 note 68
    2 Samuel 10, page 458 note 68
    2 Samuel 12:25, page 454 note 38
    2 Samuel 22:11, page 466 note 118
    1 Kings 4:21, page 530
    1 Kings 8:29, page 470 note 145
    1 Kings 9:3, page 470 note 145
    1 Kings 14:21, page 470 note 145
    1 Kings 20, page 458 note 68
    1 Kings 22:1–40, page 458 note 68
    2 Kings 3, page 458 note 68
    2 Kings 9:1–10:17, page 459 note 72
    2 Kings 18:9–19:36, page 458 note 68
    2 Kings 24:1–17, page 458 note 68
    1 Chronicles 1:8, page 529
    1 Chronicles 1:13–16, page 529
    1 Chronicles 2:50–51, 54, page 465 note 115
    1 Chronicles 4:4, page 465 note 115
    1 Chronicles 17:5, page 473–474 note 161
    2 Chronicles 6:6, page 470 note 145
    2 Chronicles 7:16, page 470 note 145
    2 Chronicles 9:26, page 530
    2 Chronicles 33:7, page 470 note 145
    Ezra 2:63, page 478 note 188
    Nehemiah 7:65, page 478 note 188
    Job 19:25–27, page 512 note 438
    Psalms 18:10, page 466 note 118
    Psalms 22:1, page 465 note 107
    Psalms 22:18, page 456 note 53
    Psalms 32:2, page 490 note 263
    Psalms 34:20, page 456–457 note 56
    Psalms 41:9, page 456 notes 46 and 47
    Psalms 51:5, page 504 note 367
    Psalms 69:21, page 456 note 54
    Psalms 85:11, page 489 note 259
    Psalms 109:6–8, page 456 note 47
    Psalms 109:8, page 456 note 47
    Psalms 110:1, page 458 note 65
    Psalms 122:8, page 507 note 394
    Psalms 132:6, page 523–524 note 516
    Psalms 133:1, page 507 note 394
    Ecclesiastes 3:19, page 516 note 470
    Isaiah 2:6–21, page 469 note 140
    Isaiah 3:2, page 492 note 280
    Isaiah 3:16, 17, page 479 note 192
    Isaiah 4:4, page 479 note 192
    Isaiah 10:24–34, page 477–478 note 185
    Isaiah 11:1–10, page 478 note 186
    Isaiah 11:5, page 489 note 259
    Isaiah 11:6, page 478 note 186
    Isaiah 11:10–16, page 530
    Isaiah 14:1–2, page 523 note 515
    Isaiah 14:12, page 457 note 62
    Isaiah 14:29, page 510 note 418
    Isaiah 19:18–25, page 530
    Isaiah 31:1–3, page 499 note 327
    Isaiah 44:6, page 463 note 98
    Isaiah 48:12, page 463 note 98
    Isaiah 49:22–23, pages 510 note 417, 523 note 515
    Isaiah 51:23, page 471 note 147
    Isaiah 52:2, page 471 note 147
    Isaiah 53:10, page 456 note 49
    Isaiah 53:12, pages 456 note 52, 464 note 106
    Isaiah 57:16, page 467 note 127
    Isaiah 60:1–18, page 523 note 515
    Isaiah 61:1, page 456 note 45
    Isaiah 62:1–5, page 470 note 143
    Isaiah 65:17, pages 469 note 140, 512 note 438

Scripture references *(continued)*
    Isaiah 66:22, pages 469 note 140, 512 note 438
    Jeremiah 7:29, page 484 note 226
    Jeremiah 47:1, 2, 4, page 510 note 415
    Lamentations 4:20, page 456 note 50
    Ezekiel 1, page 466 note 118
    Ezekiel 10:1, 20, page 466 note 118
    Ezekiel 10:15, page 466 note 118
    Ezekiel 14:7, page 484 note 226
    Ezekiel 23:2–17, page 503 note 360
    Ezekiel 37:12–13, page 516 note 468
    Ezekiel 37:26–28, page 473–474 note 161
    Ezekiel 47:15, 20, page 530
    Ezekiel 47:15–17, page 530
    Ezekiel 47:19, page 530
    Ezekiel 48:1, page 530
    Ezekiel 48:28, page 530
    Daniel 2:31–35, page 496 note 303
    Daniel 4:5, page 467 note 125
    Daniel 4:8, page 467 note 125
    Daniel 5:11–12, 14, page 467 note 125
    Daniel 7:9, 13, 22, page 485 note 237
    Daniel 8:9, page 511 note 430
    Daniel 8:15–17, page 517 note 471
    Daniel 10:5–7, page 517 note 471
    Daniel 11:16, 41, page 511 note 430
    Daniel 12:1–2, page 516 note 468
    Daniel 12:2, page 512 note 438
    Daniel 12:3, page 486 note 241
    Daniel 12:5–7, page 517 note 471
    Hosea 1–3, page 470 note 143
    Hosea 1:4, 5, 11, page 454 note 31
    Hosea 4:1, page 454 note 32
    Joel 2:1–11, page 469 note 140
    Joel 3:1, page 454 note 32
    Amos 5:18–27, page 469 note 140
    Micah 5:2, pages 465 note 115, 523–524 note 516
    Zechariah 8:23, page 523 note 515
    Zechariah 9:13, page 489 note 255
    Zechariah 12:10, page 457 note 57
    Tobit 12:15, page 486 note 242
    Matthew 1:1–17, page 478 note 186
    Matthew 1:22–23, page 461 note 86
    Matthew 1:23, page 454 note 38
    Matthew 2:1–12, pages 480 note 205, 492 note 280
    Matthew 2:3–6, page 457 note 58
    Matthew 3:3, page 457 note 58
    Matthew 3:10, page 508 note 399
    Matthew 5:46, page 507 note 396
    Matthew 7:15–20, pages 33 note 18, 508 note 399
    Matthew 7:24–27, page 500–501 note 342
    Matthew 7:26, page 504 note 366
    Matthew 9:6, page 459 note 70
    Matthew 10:34–36, page 457 note 58
    Matthew 11:25, page 461 note 90
    Matthew 12:33, page 508 note 399
    Matthew 12:48–50, page 507 note 394
    Matthew 13:11–15, page 457 note 58
    Matthew 13:30, page 515–516 note 464
    Matthew 13:43, page 486 note 241
    Matthew 15:11, page 501 note 344
    Matthew 15:18, page 501 note 344
    Matthew 16:6, page 519 note 492
    Matthew 16:24, page 459 note 70
    Matthew 19:28, page 462 note 92
    Matthew 21:21, page 506 note 379
    Matthew 23:8, page 507 note 394
    Matthew 25:1–12, page 479 note 191
    Matthew 25:1–13, page 499 note 326
    Matthew 25:31–46, pages 511–512 note 432, 515 note 455
    Matthew 25:42–43, page 511–512 note 432
    Matthew 26:50, page 456 note 49
    Matthew 26:64, page 462 note 94
    Matthew 27:46, page 465 note 107
    Matthew 27:52–53, page 516 note 468
    Matthew 28:2–5, page 517 note 471
    Matthew 28:8–9, page 517 note 471
    Matthew 28:19, page 466–467 note 119
    Mark 1:14, 15, page 460 note 83
    Mark 2:11, page 459 note 70
    Mark 2:18–20, page 470 note 143
    Mark 8:15, page 519 note 492
    Mark 8:34, page 459 note 70
    Mark 10:33–34, page 457 note 60
    Mark 11:23, page 506 note 379
    Mark 14:36, page 461 note 90
    Mark 15:28, page 456 note 52
    Mark 15:34, page 465 note 107
    Mark 16:5, page 517 note 471
    Mark 16:19, pages 457 note 60, 485 note 235
    Luke 1:80, page 460 note 83
    Luke 3:8–9, page 460 note 83
    Luke 3:23–38, page 478 note 186
    Luke 5:24, page 459 note 70
    Luke 6:46, page 500–501 note 342
    Luke 6:46–49, page 500–501 note 342
    Luke 8:5–8, page 504 note 363
    Luke 9:23, page 459 note 70
    Luke 12:1, page 519 note 492
    Luke 13:6–9, pages 500 note 341, 508 note 399
    Luke 18:31–33, page 457 note 60

Scripture references *(continued)*
    Luke 22:37, page 456 note 52
    Luke 23:28, page 479 note 192
    Luke 23:34, page 461 note 90
    Luke 24:4, page 517 note 471
    Luke 24:23, page 517 note 471
    Luke 24:30–32, page 517 note 471
    Luke 24:36–43, page 517 note 471
    Luke 24:36–49, page 458 note 67
    Luke 24:44, page 458 note 67
    Luke 24:50–51, page 457 note 60
    John 1:14, page 473–474 note 161
    John 1:29, page 459 note 70
    John 1:29, 36, page 526–527 note 527
    John 3:12, page 471–472 note 152
    John 3:13, page 457 note 60
    John 3:17, page 461 note 88
    John 3:17–18, page 485–486 note 239
    John 3:21, page 504 note 362
    John 5:8, page 459 note 70
    John 5:28–29, page 512 note 438
    John 5:36, page 461 note 89
    John 5:38, page 462 note 95
    John 6:62, page 457 note 60
    John 6:63, page 488–489 note 253
    John 7:27, page 523–524 note 516
    John 7:39, pages 449 note 8, 468 note 129
    John 8:37, page 462 note 95
    John 8:42, page 461 note 88
    John 10:25, 32, page 461 note 89
    John 10:36, page 461 note 88
    John 11:41, page 461 note 90
    John 12:47, page 462 note 93
    John 12:47–48, page 485–486 note 239
    John 13, page 456 note 46
    John 13:2, page 497 note 313
    John 14:10, page 461 note 89
    John 14:15, 21, 23–24, page 500–501 note 342
    John 14:28, page 527 note 529
    John 15:9–10, 14, page 500–501 note 342
    John 16:28, page 461 note 88
    John 17:12, page 456 note 48
    John 17:18, page 461 note 88
    John 19:5, page 459–460 note 77
    John 19:28, page 456 note 54
    John 19:30, page 456 note 54
    John 19:36, page 456–457 note 56
    John 19:37, page 457 note 57
    John 20:12, page 517 note 471
    John 20:17, page 457 note 60
    John 20:24–28, page 517 note 471
    John 20:27, page 506 note 379
    Acts 1:9, page 457 note 60
    Acts 1:15–20, page 497 note 313
    Acts 1:16, page 507 note 394
    Acts 1:16–20, page 456 note 47
    Acts 2:22–24, page 457 note 60
    Acts 7:44, page 473–474 note 161
    Acts 8:9–24, page 492 note 280
    Acts 13:6–12, page 492 note 280
    Acts 24:15, page 512 note 438
    Romans 3:27–28, page 527 note 528
    Romans 3:28, pages 25, 37, 449–451 note 11
    Romans 3:31, pages 37, 449–451 note 11
    Romans 6:8–9, page 457 note 60
    Romans 8:6, page 488–489 note 253
    Romans 16:1, page 526 note 526
    1 Corinthians 5:7, page 526–527 note 527
    1 Corinthians 7, page 503 note 357
    1 Corinthians 11:17–34, page 497 note 313
    1 Corinthians 13:12, page 465 note 113
    1 Corinthians 15:26, 54–55, page 457 note 60
    1 Corinthians 15:35–55, page 512 note 438
    2 Corinthians 3, page 501–502 note 348
    2 Corinthians 3:5–6, pages 475 note 165, 488–489 note 253
    2 Corinthians 12:2, page 514 note 448
    Ephesians 2:8–9, page 527 note 528
    Ephesians 4:8–10, page 457 note 60
    Ephesians 5:23–27, page 470 note 143
    Philippians 2:14–15, page 486 note 241
    Colossians 2:9, page 466–467 note 119
    1 Thessalonians 4:16, page 512 note 438
    1 Timothy 5:1–2, page 507 note 394
    Philemon verses 7, 20, page 526 note 526
    Hebrews 2:14–15, page 457 note 60
    Hebrews 4:16, page 526–527 note 527
    Hebrews 8, page 501–502 note 348
    James 1:6, page 506 note 379
    James 2:15, page 507 note 394
    James 2:17, page 500 note 339
    James 4:11, page 526 note 526
    2 John verse 13, page 526 note 526
    Jude verse 9, page 486 note 242
    Jude verse 12, page 526 note 525
    Revelation 1:9, page 507 note 394
    Revelation 1:17, page 463 note 98
    Revelation 1:18, page 457 note 60
    Revelation 2:8, page 463 note 98
    Revelation 3, page 51 note 46
    Revelation 3:5, page 504 note 370
    Revelation 3:12, pages 26, 504 note 370
    Revelation 3:20, page 499 note 323
    Revelation 5:2, page 517 note 471

Scripture references *(continued)*
    Revelation 5:6–14, page 526–527 note 527
    Revelation 6:9–11, page 516 note 468
    Revelation 6:12, page 494 note 292
    Revelation 7:1, 2, page 517 note 471
    Revelation 7:4–8, page 476 note 178
    Revelation 8:2, page 517 note 471
    Revelation 8:12, page 494 note 292
    Revelation 9:2, page 494 note 292
    Revelation 10:1, 5, page 517 note 471
    Revelation 12, page 510–511 note 424
    Revelation 12:3, page 502 note 349
    Revelation 12:3–4, page 510 note 420
    Revelation 12:7, page 486 note 242
    Revelation 12:17, page 516 note 468
    Revelation 13, page 511 note 425
    Revelation 13:1, page 502 note 349
    Revelation 14:6, page 517 note 471
    Revelation 15:1, page 517 note 471
    Revelation 15:5, page 473–474 note 161
    Revelation 15:6, page 519 note 485
    Revelation 16:10, page 494 note 292
    Revelation 17:3, page 481 note 211
    Revelation 17:4–18, page 509 note 410
    Revelation 18:1, page 517 note 471
    Revelation 18:8–10, 15–19, page 469 note 138
    Revelation 18:23, page 494 note 292
    Revelation 19:8, page 519 note 485
    Revelation 19:10, page 77
    Revelation 19:11–19, page 481 note 211
    Revelation 19:14, page 519 note 485
    Revelation 19:17, page 517 note 471
    Revelation 19:20, page 469 note 138
    Revelation 20:1, page 517 note 471
    Revelation 20:5–6, page 516 note 468
    Revelation 20:10, 14–15, page 469 note 138
    Revelation 20:12–13, page 496 note 299
    Revelation 20:13, page 512 note 438
    Revelation 20:14, page 457 note 60
    Revelation 21, pages 22, 26
    Revelation 21–22, page 448 note 5
    Revelation 21:1, pages 35, 512 note 438
    Revelation 21:2, pages 26, 470 note 143
    Revelation 21:3, page 473–474 note 161
    Revelation 21:4, page 457 note 60
    Revelation 21:9, page 470 note 143
    Revelation 22, page 26
    Revelation 22:9, page 507 note 394
    Revelation 22:13, page 463 note 98
Searle, Arthur H., 10
Secret Committee, 40, 41. *See also* The Riksdag
Secret Exchange Deputation, 67. *See also* The Riksdag

Secrets of Heaven, 41, 42 note 32, 47, 447 note 3, 485 note 231, 514 note 449
    compared to Swedenborg's previous printed output, 42
    copies of *Secrets of Heaven* sent to Beyer, 93
    disappearing cross-references to, 51, 75–78, 92, 97–100
        graph showing, 100 figure 3
        table showing, 99 figure 2
    efforts to promote, 44–46, 48 and note 39, 64
    included in list in *Marriage Love,* 78 note 90
    John Lewis's pamphlet about, 45–46
    omitted from list in *The Lord,* 78
    possible reason it was unfinished, 47
    reason for anonymous publication of, 42–43
    as revealing the way to salvation, 50
    review of volume 1 in 1750, 46–47
    reviews of entire series of, 72–75
    unsatisfactory response to publication of, 44–46, 91
    the works of 1758 as topical indexes of, 47, 74–78, 98
Seneca, Lucius Annaeus, 495 note 295
Sensation *(religious sentiment),* 528 note 533
Senses, physical, 476 note 179
September-Testament, 509 note 410
Sequential *vs.* simultaneous arrangement, 484 note 227
Serenius, Jacob, 71, 103
Seven Years' War, 76
    impact on Swedenborg's publishing, 55–57
    role of Sweden in, 55
    severity of, 55 note 51
Seward, Samuel S., 10
Shaddai, 453 note 27
Sheep and goats, in the Bible, 511 note 427, 515 note 455
Sherlock, Thomas, 53 note 48
Shorter works of 1758, Swedenborg's, 447 note 1. *See also* Works of 1758; *individual titles*
    mentioned in preface to *The Lord,* 21, 22–23
    order of, 20 and note 7
    referred to as a single volume, 84 and note 103
    referred to as "digests" by Tilas, 63
Shorter works of 1763, Swedenborg's. *See also* Works of 1763; *individual titles*
    addressing topics central to Christianity, 18, 92
    apparently sent out for review, 82
    appearing after a five-year gap in publishing, 18, 19
    audience of, 4
    coming at a turning point in Swedenborg's theological publishing, 17

Shorter works of 1763 *(continued)*
  composition and printing order of, 9 and note 3, 101–102
  constituting a new approach, 17
  discussing Jesus' nature as part of the divine Trinity, 26, 29
  editions and translations of, 9–12
  first mention of *Secrets of Heaven* in, 78
  Gjörwell's publications about, 86–87
  mentioned in preface to *The Lord,* 21
  order of, 20, 101–102
  problematic material in, 4–6
  providing clues to Swedenborg's plans after 1758, 75
  publication of, 1 and note 1
  purpose of, 21–37
  reviews and notices about, 82–88
  short titles of, 447–448 note 4
  why neglected, 37
Simultaneous *vs.* **sequential arrangement,** 484 note 227
Sin. *See also* Imputation of merit of Christ
  Jesus' action with respect to our sins, 25
  Jesus' forgiveness of sins meaning imputation of merit, 26
  our faith coming to life when our sins have been forgiven through repentance, 31
Skara, 38, 70, 103
Sky, Latin word for, 469 note 139
Slavery, in the seventeenth century, 522 note 503
Small Catechism, 503 note 353
Society of Jesus (Jesuits), 495 note 297, 520–521 note 497, 521 note 499
Socinians, 526–527 note 527
The Son, in Swedenborg's theology. *See also* Jesus Christ; The Lord
  not being a separate person from the Father, 25
  references to "Son of God" and "Son of Humanity" explained in *The Lord,* 27 and note 15
Son of Humanity, 454–455 note 39, 459–460 note 77
  blasphemy against, 467–468 note 128
"Son of perdition," meaning Judas Iscariot, 456 note 47
Sophia Albertina, 88
The soul
  as "animal spirit," 487 note 247
  belief in reunion with body at Last Judgment, 496 note 299
  beliefs about, 512–513 note 441
  Enlightenment debate about possession of, 516 note 470
  interaction between soul and body, 486 note 243
  Latin word for, 507 note 390
  as not divesting itself of its characteristics at death, 90
  Swedenborg's rejection of generally held view of, 34
Soul-Body Interaction
  published in both Latin and English, 54–55 note 50
  published in London, 76 note 87
The Soul's Domain, 39 and note 25
Sower, parable of, 504 note 365
Spain, 55, 89, 94, 96
Spinoza, Benedict de, 472–473 note 153
Spirit, Hebrew and Greek words for, 512–513 note 441
Spirit of the Laws, 522–523 note 508
Spirits. *See also* Angels; Heaven
  belief that spirits are made of ether, 512–513 note 441
  definition of, 513 note 442
  as having been people on earth, 488 note 251, 513 note 442
Spirits, evil, 469–470 note 141, 488 note 251, 513 note 442, 524–525 note 521. *See also* Hell
The spiritual, 486 note 243, 505 note 374. *See also* The heavenly; The spiritual world
  Swedenborg claiming spiritual light was granted to him, 35
Spiritual awakening, Swedenborg's, 447 note 3, 517 note 472
Spiritual Experiences, 20, 54
  dating of passages in, 44 note 36, 53 note 48
Spiritual love, 509–510 note 413
Spiritual meaning, of the Bible. *See* Inner (spiritual) meaning
Spiritual trial, 463–464 note 101
Spiritual truth, 506 note 380
The spiritual world. *See also* Heaven; Hell; The world of spirits
  being reorganized by the Lord at the time of the Last Judgment, 452 note 20, 453 note 23
  cities in, 518 note 477
  correspondence in, 505 note 373, 508 note 406, 515 note 463
  correspondence to, 475–476 note 169
  "lower earth," 521 note 498
  paths and roads in, 518 note 483
  space and distances in, 515 note 453
  Swedenborg's concept of, 469–470 note 141, 499 note 324

Stadium *(unit of distance)*, 476 note 175
Star of Bethlehem, 481 note 206
Stars, as stationary, 491 note 269
Statues, earthly individuals appearing like statues to angels, 505 note 373
Stockholm, 60 note 59, 61, 63, 68 note 71, 72 note 78, 75, 86, 88, 90
Stoicism, 495 note 295
Strängnäs, 71, 103
Substance *(philosophical term)*, 464 note 105, 513 note 442
Sun
    in heaven as the Lord, 514 note 452
    sun worship, 523 note 509
Supplements, 470 note 142. *See also* Shorter works of 1763
    brief treatment of Luther, Melanchthon, and Calvin in, 36
    containing sequels to two published works, 3, 18
    coverage of groups and regions as uneven, 35–36
    as described in *Divine Providence*, 37
    editions and translations of, 11–12
    its relation to *Last Judgment* and *Faith*, 3–4 and note 7
    partially copied into *True Christianity*, 36 note 19
    on placement and condition of different groups in the spiritual world, 494 note 286
    presented to royalty, 88
    publication of, 1 and note 1
    purpose of, 34, 92
    referred to under two separate titles, 84
    showing how the Last Judgment changed the world and the church, 34
    structure of, 3–4
Survey
    copies of *Survey* sent to Beyer, 93, 95
    preface to, 21 note 8
    published in both Latin and English, 54–55 note 50
Swedberg, Albrecht, 39
Swedberg, Anna, 70–71
Swedberg, Jesper, 70, 73, 468 note 133
    influence of his printing activities on Swedenborg, 38
Sweden, 17, 39 note 26, 48 note 40, 56–57 note 55, 58, 64–65 note 66, 68, 70, 71 and note 77. *See also* Board of mines, Swedish; Nobility: Swedish; Swedes; *names of Swedish royal persons; specific place-names*
    as area in which Swedenborg distributed books, 68, 69, 80, 91, 94
    in Great Northern War, 55
    its role in Seven Years' War, 55, 56
    restrictions on publishing in, 42
    reviews of Swedenborg's books in, 82, 86
    Swedenborg's anonymity in, 57, 64, 65
    Swedish clergy (*see* Bishops, Swedish; Clergy: Swedish clergy)
    Swedish currency, 56 and note 53
    effect of Seven Years' War on, 55, 91
    Swedish parliament (*see* The Riksdag)
Swedenborg, Emanuel
    anecdotes about his clairvoyance, 62 note 61
    anonymity of, 42–43, 49, 57, 62 note 61, 64–65 and note 66, 71 and note 77, 76–77, 91
    being commanded by the Lord to offer nine works to the public, 21, 22
    being offered position on the Secret Exchange Deputation, 67
    Bible indexes of, 41–42
    biblical canon of, 449–451 note 11
    changing his publication program after 1762, 72
    claiming companionship with angels, 29
    claiming that spiritual light had been granted to him, 35
    claiming that the inner meaning of the Bible had been revealed to him, 27
    claiming that the Lord had been revealed to him, 21, 22
    contemporary reviews and notices of his works (*see* Reviews and notices of Swedenborg's works)
    criticized for teaching against Protestant teachings about salvation, 83
    declaring his publishing program, 21–23 and note 8
    dedicating works to various illustrious personages, 48 note 40
    demonstrating care for others in his life, 49 note 41
    diary of, 517 note 472
    ennoblement of, 39 and note 26
    as experiencing consciousness of the afterlife, 17, 41
    finances of, 55 note 52, 56 note 53
    having difficulty finding an audience, 17
    heresy trial of supporters of, 69

Swedenborg, Emanuel *(continued)*
   his accounts of seeing the dragon of Revelation, 510 note 420
   his accounts of the Last Judgment, 63, 84–85
   his attitude toward Catholicism, 33, 506 note 386
   his attitude toward gender, 5 and note 10
   his attitude toward religions, 5–6
   his correspondence with Swedish clergy, 71 note 77
   his criticism of the Christian church, 452 note 18
   his cross-references to his other works (*see* Cross-references; Indexlike statements)
   his drive to publish, 37–39
   his fluency in Latin, 49
   his interaction with royalty, 88–91
   his nervous stammer, 41
   his promotional efforts, 67, 93–96
      targeting British clergy and nobility, 48–55, 54–55 note 50, 80, 81
      targeting Swedish clergy and nobility, 57–72, 72 note 78, 80, 91, 95
   his role in government, 39–41
   his view of politics, 65–66
   his view of the Moravian church, 525–526 note 524, 527 note 529
   his writings as divinely revealed, 481 note 210
   impact of war and inflation on his work, 55–57
   Jesus Christ appearing to, 447 note 3
   meeting Athanasius in the spiritual world, 468 note 132
   misapprehensions regarding Islam, 521–522 note 501
   mission of, 448 note 5
   named Swedberg at birth, 17 note 1
   nontheological publications of, 38–39 (*see also* individual titles)
   as not content to rest on achievements, 17
   overseeing the printing of his theological works, 9 note 2
   praised for laboring in the cause of salvation, 54–55 note 50
   presentation of theology of, 466–467 note 119
   as prolific writer, 38–39 and notes 23 and 24, 42
   proposed works of, 21–22, 78–82, 79 note 91, 447–448 note 4, 463 note 100, 465 note 110, 489 note 258, 498 note 322
   referred to as a baron in Britain, 39 note 26
   reporting conversation about promotion of *Secrets of Heaven*, 44–45
   reporting to others about the deceased, 60–62 and note 62
   as a respected scientist and philosopher, 17
   spiritual awakening of, 447 note 3, 517 note 472
   as supervisor of Sweden's mining industry, 487–488 note 249 (*see also* Board of mines, Swedish)
   theological publications of (*see also* individual titles)
      generally appearing at regular intervals, 17
      having two distinct phases, 19
      lacking during one stretch of almost five years, 17
      not intended only for the elite, 48–49
      table of, 18 figure 1
      works of 1758 (*see* Shorter works of 1758; Works of 1758)
      works of 1763 (*see* Shorter works of 1763; Works of 1763)
   travels of, 90–91 and note 109, 518 note 478, 519–520 note 493, 521 note 500, 523 note 513, 525–526 note 524
   turning to publishing shorter works, 76
   understanding of the universe expressed in conceptual pairings, 5 and note 10
   writing memorials to the Swedish government, 41, 65–67, 68 and note 72, 69

Swedes, 36. *See also* Sweden

T

The tabernacle, 473–474 note 161, 478–479 note 189
Tafel, J.F.I., 11
"Taking up," as concept in interpretation of Bible passages, 459 note 70
Talent *(unit of money),* 497 note 309
"Teachings for the New Jerusalem" *(phrase used in titles).* See also "The Four Sets of Teachings"
   meaning of phrase, 22
   as theological rather than philosophical, 79 and note 92
   as used in titles of works, 22, 78–82, 79 note 91
The Ten Commandments, 473–474 note 161, 485 note 233
   all religions having something akin to, 31
   all those being saved who live by principles similar to, 31, 32
   deeper meaning of, 31
   division of, 502 note 351

The Ten Commandments *(continued)*
   as the first part of the Bible to be written, 501 note 345
   Life as based on, 3
   the Lord as not doing away with, 25
   only God being able to uproot the evils specified by, 31
   as subject of *Life*, 19, 30, 31, 81
   taught to children, 503 note 353

Tessin, Carl Gustaf, 50 note 43, 58–59, 60–61, 62, 63 and note 64, 72 note 78, 88
   political career of, 57
   visit to Swedenborg by, 57–58

Text-proofing, 2–3. *See also* Proof-texting

The Thousand and One Nights, 522–523 note 508

Tilas, Daniel, 59–61 and note 59, 62–63

Tithes, 502 note 350

Torah, 477 note 183. *See also* The Bible: Hebrew Bible; Moses

"Translation," as term was used in Swedenborgian publishing, 10 note 4, 11–12

The Trinity. *See also* The Holy Spirit; The Son
   the prevalent belief in three persons in the Trinity, 29, 481 note 208
   in Swedenborg's theology
      Jesus' nature as part of the divine Trinity discussed in the shorter works of 1763, 26, 29
      the Lord and God being one in the Trinity, 27, 29
      second person of the Trinity not having existed forever, 461 note 85
      there being no trinity of persons in God, 25, 26, 447 note 2, 466–467 note 119

True Christianity, 21 note 8
   discussing wide application of principles found in *Life*, 32
   its relation to *Sacred Scripture*, 1 note 1
   Luther, Melanchthon, and Calvin treated at length in, 36 notes 19–20
   significance of increased reference to Paul in, 37
   Swedenborg's plan to distribute, 69

Truth. *See also* Faith
   as adapted to our understanding, 484–485 note 228
   earthly and spiritual, 506 note 380
   "faith apart from truth" part of Roman Catholicism and Protestantism, 33
   faith being an inner recognition of, 32–33, 506 note 385
   faith divorced from caring as having no truth, 512 note 433
   heaven as passing God's divine truth on to humans, 477 note 184
   the Hebrew word for, 506 note 384
   how we learn truth, 482 note 214
   Jesus as the embodiment of divine truth, 459–460 note 77
   the Lord as the source of, 477 note 184

Tulk, Charles Augustus, 10 and note 5

U

Ulrika Eleonora, 39, 60, 61

Understanding, 498 note 322. *See also* Reason
   as connected with the lungs, 500 note 340

Unigenitus, papal bull, 520–521 note 497

Union, the Lord's union with us, 465 note 108, 468 note 135, 474–475 note 164

Universe
   structure of, 500 note 337
   Swedenborg's view of the creation of, 482–483 note 218

Uppsala. *See also* Sweden
   bishops of, 70, 103
   University of, 43 note 33, 59, 73

Urim and Thummim, 478 note 188

Ussher, James, 513 note 445

V

Västerås, 71, 103

Växjö, 103

Visby, 103

Visions, types of, 517 note 473

Voltaire, 55 note 51, 471–472 note 152, 473 note 155, 517–518 note 476

W

Wallerius, Nils, 43 note 33, 90 and note 108

War, in the Bible, 509 note 411

Warren, Samuel M., 11

Watts, Isaac, 496 note 299

Werner, Gustav, 9

White Horse, 47. *See also* Shorter works of 1758; Works of 1758
   Alnander's notice about, 73–75
   Gjörwell's notice about, 74–75
   its order in the works of 1758, 20
   mentioned in preface to *The Lord*, 21

Whitehead, John, 12

Wilkinson, James John Garth, 11

Will, 498 note 322
   as connected with the heart, 500 note 340
   as the core of our being, 460 note 82
   free will, 518–519 note 484

William VIII *(regent of Hesse-Kassel),* 48 note 40
Worcester, John, 10–11
Worcester, Samuel H., 9–11
The Word, in Swedenborg's theology. *See also* The Bible; Sacred Scripture
    the ancient Word, 29, 492–493 note 281, 493 notes 282 and 283, 495 note 295
    authorship of and inspiration for, 473 note 158
    being about the Lord and the church, 29
    as existing in heaven, 28, 451 note 14
    heaven opened to people by reading, 474–475 note 164
    importance of believing in the holiness of, 2
    its light being almost snuffed out, 29
    its many paired expressions explained in *Sacred Scripture,* 29
    Jesus and the prophets representing, 457–458 note 64
    lacking literal meaning in heaven, 451 note 14
    literal meaning of (*see* Literal meaning)
    The Lord teaching that the Word is solely about the Lord, 27
    the nature of the Word as described in *Sacred Scripture,* 27–28
    not to be taken lightly, 30
    prophetic books of, 451 note 16, 458 note 67, 477 note 182
        Swedenborg's studies of, 465 note 111
    spiritual meaning of (*see* Inner [spiritual] meaning)
    Swedenborg's emphasis on literal and spiritual meanings of, 3 and note 6
    Swedenborg's use of the term, 20 note 4, 449–451 note 11
    violence done to, 457–458 note 64, 459–460 note 77, 476 note 172, 480 note 204
Works (deeds)
    believed to contribute nothing to salvation, 24
    believing in the Lord is doing what he says, 2, 500–501 note 342
    the "deeds of caring," 511–512 note 432
    in Moravian theology, 527 note 529
    the "sheep" as those who do good works, 515 note 455

Works of 1758 *(as opposed to "the shorter works of 1758"),* 48, 63, 68, 78, 79 note 92, 85, 86, 97. *See also* Shorter works of 1758; *individual titles*
    Alnander's notice about, 73–75
    bound as a single volume, 84 note 103
    distributed without cost by Swedenborg, 49–50
    Gjörwell's notice about, 74–75
    order of, 20
    published by Mary Lewis, 48 note 38
    referred to in *Revelation Explained,* 51
    reviews of, 72–75
    Swedenborg wishing to import into Sweden fifty copies of, 57–58, 62, 63, 67, 69–70, 93
    as topical indexes of *Secrets of Heaven,* 47, 74–78, 98
    unsatisfactory response to, 50–54, 91
Works of 1763 *(as opposed to "the shorter works of 1763"),* 39, 86, 88. *See also* Shorter works of 1763; *individual titles*
The world of spirits, 469–470 note 141, 499 note 324, 502–503 note 352, 513 note 442, 515 note 462
Worship
    Quaker worship, 524 note 519
    of the sun and moon, 523 note 509
Worship and Love of God, 73–75
Wretman, Joachim, 56–57 note 55

X
Xavier, Francis, 521 note 499

Y
Yeast, 519 note 492
Yodh, 457 note 59

Z
Zinzendorf, Nikolaus von, 525–526 note 524, 526–527 note 527, 527 notes 529 and 530, 528 note 533. *See also* Herrnhut; Moravian church
    theology of, 528 notes 531 and 532
Zwingli, Ulrich, 481 note 208

Index to Scriptural Passages in the Shorter Works of 1763

The following index refers to passages from the Bible cited in the translations of *The Lord, Sacred Scripture, Life, Faith,* and *Supplements*. The numbers to the left under each Bible book title are its chapter numbers. They precede verse numbers with the following designations: bold figures indicate verses that are quoted; italics show verses that are paraphrased or only partially quoted; figures in parentheses indicate verses that are merely referred or alluded to. Biblical references that are enclosed in brackets indicate allusions in the text for which the present edition provides references. The numbers to the right are section numbers in *The Lord, Sacred Scripture, Life, Faith,* and *Supplements*. Subsection numbers are separated from section numbers by a colon. (Passages from the Bible cited in the preface, introduction, and scholars' notes can be found under the heading "Scripture references" in the separate index of those elements.)

GENESIS

[1 27]	*Supplements* 32
3 *4–5*	*Supplements* 61
3 *15*	*The Lord* 19:7
3 *15*	*Supplements* 62
3 **24**	*Sacred Scripture* 97:2
5 (21–24)	*Sacred Scripture* 21
6 **3**	*The Lord* 50:2
14 *18*	*Sacred Scripture* 101:3
14 *18–20*	*Sacred Scripture* 101:3
[17 (5, 15)]	*Sacred Scripture* 90:1
[19 (1–29)]	*Supplements* 26
21, 26 (chapters cited)	*Faith* 50
38 [(2, 16)]	*Supplements* 82:2
41 **8**	*The Lord* 48:4
45 **27**	*The Lord* 47:2
48 *5, 11,* and following	*Sacred Scripture* 79:2

EXODUS

12 *48*	*Faith* 54
19 *10, 11, 15*	*Life* 59
19 *12, 13, 20–23*	*Life* 59
19 *16, 18*	*Life* 59
20 *2–17*	*Life* 59
[20 **12**]	*Sacred Scripture* 67:1
[20 **13**]	*Sacred Scripture* 67:4
[20 **14**]	*Sacred Scripture* 67:3
[20 **15**]	*Sacred Scripture* 67:2
[20 **16**]	*Sacred Scripture* 67:5
24 *1, 2*	*Life* 59
24 (4–10)	*Life* 60
24 **8, 9, 10**	*The Lord* 39
25 *1–end*	*Life* 59
25 *16*	*Life* 59
25 *17–21*	*Life* 59
25 *18–21*	*Sacred Scripture* 97:3
25 *22*	*Sacred Scripture* 97:3
25 *22*	*Life* 59
26 (1)	*Life* 61
26 *1, 31, 36*	*Sacred Scripture* 46
[26 (1–13)]	*Sacred Scripture* 42
26 *1–end*	*Life* 59
26 *31*	*Sacred Scripture* 97:3

26 *33*	*Life* 59	9 *15–end*	*Life* 59		
28 **3**	*The Lord* 48:1	10 (33)	*Life* 60		
28 **6, 15–21, 30**	*Sacred Scripture* 44:2	10 *35, 36*	*Life* 59		
[28 (30)]	*Sacred Scripture* 42	14 *14*	*Life* 59		
31 *3*	*The Lord* 48:1	14 *18*	*Sacred Scripture* 51:2		
31 *18*	*Life* 59	14 (33)	*Life* 79:3		
32 (*12, 14*)	*Sacred Scripture* 51:2	15 *38, 39*	*Life* 2		
32 *15, 16*	*Life* 59	15 (39)	*Life* 79:3		
34 *13*	*Sacred Scripture* 101:1	16 **22**	*The Lord* 49:1		
34 (28)	*Life* 61	21 **14, 15**	*Sacred Scripture* 103:1		
34 *29–35*	*Life* 59	21 (*14, 15, 27–30*)	*Sacred Scripture* 103:1		
[36 (*8–17*)]	*Sacred Scripture* 42	21 **27, 28, 29, 30**	*Sacred Scripture* 103:2		
37 *9*	*Sacred Scripture* 97:3	22 *13, 18*	*Sacred Scripture* 101:2		
40 *17–28*	*Life* 59	22 *40*	*Sacred Scripture* 101:1		
40 *20*	*Life* 59	23 *1, 2, 14, 29, 30*	*Sacred Scripture* 101:1		
40 *38*	*Life* 59	23 *3, 5, 8, 16, 26*	*Sacred Scripture* 101:2		
		23 (*7, 18*)	*Sacred Scripture* 103:2		

LEVITICUS

6 (*9*)	*The Lord* 9	23 (*7–10, 18–24*)	*Sacred Scripture* 101:2
6 (*14*)	*The Lord* 9	23 (*19*)	*Sacred Scripture* 51:2
6 (*25*)	*The Lord* 9	24 *1, 13*	*Sacred Scripture* 101:2
7 (*1–11*)	*The Lord* 9	24 (*3, 15*)	*Sacred Scripture* 103:2
7 (*37*)	*The Lord* 9	24 (*3–9, 16–24*)	*Sacred Scripture* 101:2
[8 (*8*)]	*Sacred Scripture* 42	24 *17*	*Sacred Scripture* 101:2
10 *6*	*Sacred Scripture* 49:4	25 *1, 2, 3*	*Sacred Scripture* 101:1
14 (*2*)	*The Lord* 9	27 (*18*)	*The Lord* 49:1
16 *2–14 and following*	*Life* 59		

DEUTERONOMY

18 **5**	*Life* 2	1 *33*	*Life* 59
18 *5*	*Life* 39	2 **30**	*The Lord* 48:2
19 **37**	*Life* 2	4 *11*	*Life* 59
20 (*5*)	*Life* 79:3	4 (*13*)	*Life* 61
20 **8**	*Life* 2	4 (*13, 23*)	*Life* 60
21 *5*	*Sacred Scripture* 35	5 (*2, 3*)	*Life* 60
21 *10*	*Sacred Scripture* 35	5 *6–21*	*Life* 59
22 **31**	*Life* 2	[5 **16**]	*Sacred Scripture* 67:1
26 *3–46*	*Life* 2	[5 **17**]	*Sacred Scripture* 67:4
26 (*26*)	*Life* 61	[5 **18**]	*Sacred Scripture* 67:3
		[5 **19**]	*Sacred Scripture* 67:2

NUMBERS

		[5 **20**]	*Sacred Scripture* 67:5
2 *1–end*	*Life* 59	5 *22–23*	*Life* 59
5 **14**	*The Lord* 48:5	6 **4, 5**	*The Lord* 45:2
5 (*29–30*)	*The Lord* 9	7 *5*	*Sacred Scripture* 101:1
6 *1–21*	*Sacred Scripture* 49:4	9 (*5, 6*)	*Sacred Scripture* 51:9
6 (*13, 21*)	*The Lord* 9	9 (*9*)	*Life* 60
7 *89*	*Sacred Scripture* 97:3; *Life* 59	9 *10*	*Life* 59

INDEX TO SCRIPTURAL PASSAGES

10 (4)	*Life* 61
10 *5*	*Life* 59
10 **16**	*Faith* 54
12 *3*	*Sacred Scripture* 101:1
18 *15–19*	*The Lord* 15:3
24 *16*	*Sacred Scripture* 51:2
31 **9, 25, 26**	*The Lord* 9
32 (chapter cited)	*Supplements* 82:2
32 (7, 8)	*Sacred Scripture* 101:3
32 **20–35**	*Sacred Scripture* 51:9
33 *13–17*	*Sacred Scripture* 79:2
33 *21*	*Sacred Scripture* 85
33 (28)	*Sacred Scripture* 2:2
34 **9**	*The Lord* 48:1

JOSHUA

3 *1–17*	*Life* 59
3 (11)	*Life* 60
4 *5–20*	*Life* 59
6 *1–20*	*Life* 59
10 **12, 13**	*Sacred Scripture* 103:3

JUDGES

16 **17**	*Sacred Scripture* 49:3
[16 (23)]	*Supplements* 44

1 SAMUEL

3 *1–8*	*Sacred Scripture* 29
[5 (chapter cited)]	*Supplements* 44
5, 6 (chapters cited)	*Faith* 52
5 *1–4*	*Life* 59
5 (1–12)	*Sacred Scripture* 23:2
6 *19*	*Life* 59
15 (29)	*Sacred Scripture* 51:2
17 (chapter cited)	*Faith* 52
17 (26, 36)	*Faith* 51
20 *5, 12–41*	*Sacred Scripture* 29

2 SAMUEL

1 **17, 18**	*Sacred Scripture* 103:3
1 (20)	*Faith* 51
6 *1–19*	*Life* 59
6 (2)	*Life* 59
6 *6, 7*	*Life* 59
22 **2, 3**	*The Lord* 34:2, 38
22 (2–3)	*The Lord* 34:4

1 KINGS

[6–7 (chapters cited)]	*Sacred Scripture* 42
6 *7, 9, 29, 30*	*Sacred Scripture* 47
6 *19 and following*	*Life* 59
6 *23–28*	*Sacred Scripture* 97:3
6 *29, 32, 35*	*Sacred Scripture* 97:3
8 *3–9*	*Life* 59
8 *9*	*Life* 59
8 (21)	*Life* 60
17 *21*	*Sacred Scripture* 29
18 *34*	*Sacred Scripture* 29
20 *37–38*	*The Lord* 15:7
22 *11*	*The Lord* 15:7

2 KINGS

1 *8*	*The Lord* 15:8
2 **15**	*The Lord* 51:5
2 *23, 24, 25*	*Sacred Scripture* 35
22 **8, 11**	*The Lord* 9
23 *24*	*The Lord* 9

1 CHRONICLES

[5 (1)]	*Sacred Scripture* 79:2

PSALMS

2 **6, 7, 8, 12**	*The Lord* 6
2 **7, 12**	*The Lord* 19:5
8 **5, 6**	*The Lord* 6
15 **1, 2, 3, and following**	*Life* 84:1
18 **4, 14, 37, 39, 40, 42**	*The Lord* 14:6
18 **9, 10**	*Sacred Scripture* 97:4
18 **31**	*The Lord* 45:2
18 **43**	*The Lord* 14:6; *Sacred Scripture* 86
19 **14**	*The Lord* 34:2, 38
19 (14)	*The Lord* 34:4
24 **7–8**	*The Lord* 33:5
24 **7–10**	*The Lord* 38
24 *8, 10*	*The Lord* 14:9
29 **3–9**	*Sacred Scripture* 18:4
30 (5)	*Supplements* 13
31 **5**	*The Lord* 38, 49:1
32 **2**	*The Lord* 48:5
32 (2)	*Sacred Scripture* 90:1
33 **10**	*Sacred Scripture* 86
35 (19)	*The Lord* 10

36 **6**	*Sacred Scripture* 85	108 **8**	*Sacred Scripture* 79:2
37 **6**	*Sacred Scripture* 85	110 *1*	*The Lord* 35:5
41 (13)	*The Lord* 39	110 **1, 2, 4**	*The Lord* 6
44 **14**	*Sacred Scripture* 86	110 **1, 5, 6**	*The Lord* 14:8
45 (2–17)	*The Lord* 44	110 **4**	*Sacred Scripture* 101:3
45 **3, 5, 6, 7**	*The Lord* 14:7	110 (4)	*The Lord* 10
47 **3, 8, 9**	*Sacred Scripture* 86	110 **4, 5**	*The Lord* 19:7
51 **8**	*Sacred Scripture* 87:1	114 **7**	*The Lord* 39
51 **10–12**	*The Lord* 49:1	119 **7, 164**	*Sacred Scripture* 85
51 **17**	*The Lord* 49:2	122 (1–7)	*The Lord* 64:7
59 (5)	*The Lord* 39	122 (4–5)	*The Lord* 44
60 **7**	*Sacred Scripture* 79:2	130 **7, 8**	*The Lord* 34:2, 38
65 (8)	*Supplements* 13	130 (7, 8)	*The Lord* 34:4
67 **3–4**	*Sacred Scripture* 86	132 **1–9**	*The Lord* 6
68 (8)	*The Lord* 39	132 **2, 3, 5, 6**	*The Lord* 39
72 **2**	*Sacred Scripture* 85	132 2, 5	*The Lord* 14:9
72 **7, 8**	*The Lord* 4	132 **6, 7**	*The Lord* 41
72 **18, 19**	*The Lord* 39	132 (7, 8)	*Life* 59
78 **8**	*The Lord* 48:5	132 (8–18)	*The Lord* 44
78 9	*Sacred Scripture* 79:2	137 (4, 5, 6)	*The Lord* 64:7
78 **35**	*The Lord* 34:2, 41	139 **7**	*The Lord* 50:2
78 (35)	*The Lord* 34:4, 39	142 **3**	*The Lord* 48:4
78 **39**	*The Lord* 47:2	143 **4**	*The Lord* 48:4
78 **41**	*The Lord* 40	143 **7**	*The Lord* 48:4
80 **1**	*Sacred Scripture* 97:4	146 **4**	*The Lord* 47:2
80 **17, 18, 19**	*The Lord* 27:2		
82 **6**	*The Lord* 10	ISAIAH	
85 **11**	*Sacred Scripture* 85	1 **4**	*The Lord* 40; *Sacred Scripture* 86
89 **3, 4, 5, 19, 20, 21, 24, 25,**		1 **10–18**	*Life* 30:1
26, 27, 28, 29, 35, 36, 37	*The Lord* 44	1 **16, 18**	*Life* 113
89 **14**	*Sacred Scripture* 85	1 **21**	*Sacred Scripture* 85
89 **25, 26, 27**	*The Lord* 19:6	1 **27**	*Sacred Scripture* 85
89 **25, 26, 27, 29**	*The Lord* 6	2 **2, 11, 12, 20**	*The Lord* 4
89 (29)	*The Lord* 10	2 **3**	*The Lord* 39
90 (6)	*Supplements* 13	3 (1, 2, 8)	*Sacred Scripture* 51:9
90 **14, 15**	*Sacred Scripture* 87:1	3 (9)	*The Lord* 64:2
96 **11**	*Sacred Scripture* 87:1	3 **18**	*The Lord* 4
96 **13**	*The Lord* 14:10	4 **2**	*The Lord* 4
97 **3, 4, 5, 6**	*The Lord* 14:7	4 **2, 3**	*The Lord* 64:7
99 **1**	*Sacred Scripture* 97:4	4 **5**	*Sacred Scripture* 33
101 **6, 7, 8**	*Life* 84:1	5 (3–6)	*Sacred Scripture* 51:9
104 **29**	*The Lord* 47:2	5 **16**	*Sacred Scripture* 85
104 **30**	*The Lord* 49:1	5 **19**	*The Lord* 40
106 **4, 5**	*Sacred Scripture* 86	5 **21**	*Life* 30:2
106 **33**	*The Lord* 50:2	5 **30**	*The Lord* 4

INDEX TO SCRIPTURAL PASSAGES

7 **14**	*The Lord* 6, 19:3	23 (17, 18)	*Life* 79:3
7 **18, 20, 21, 23**	*The Lord* 4	24 (15)	*The Lord* 39
9 **2**	*Sacred Scripture* 111	24 **21, 23**	*The Lord* 4
9 **2, 3**	*Sacred Scripture* 86	24 **23**	*Sacred Scripture* 14:3
9 **6**	*The Lord* 19:4	24 (23)	*The Lord* 64:7
9 **6, 7**	*The Lord* 6, 38	25 **3**	*Sacred Scripture* 86
9 **7**	*Sacred Scripture* 85	25 **7**	*Sacred Scripture* 86
10 **3, 20**	*The Lord* 4	25 **9**	*The Lord* 4, 6, 30:2, 38
10 **5, 6**	*Sacred Scripture* 86	26 **1**	*The Lord* 4
10 **20**	*The Lord* 40	26 **9**	*The Lord* 49:1
10 **24–34**	*Sacred Scripture* 15:1	27 **1, 2, 12, 13**	*The Lord* 4
11 *1*	*The Lord* 19:7	28 (1)	*Sacred Scripture* 79:8
11 **1, 2**	*The Lord* 38, 50:1	28 **5**	*The Lord* 4, 38
11 **1, 2, 5, 10**	*The Lord* 6	28 **6**	*The Lord* 49:1
11 **1, 4, 5**	*The Lord* 51:4	29 **10**	*The Lord* 48:5
11 (1–10)	*Sacred Scripture* 15:2	29 **14, 15**	*Life* 30:2
11 *5*	*Sacred Scripture* 85	29 **18**	*The Lord* 4
11 **10**	*Sacred Scripture* 86	29 **19**	*The Lord* 40
11 **10, 11**	*The Lord* 4	29 **23**	*The Lord* 39
11 **11, 13–16**	*Sacred Scripture* 15:2	29 (23)	*The Lord* 39
12 **1, 4**	*The Lord* 4	29 **24**	*The Lord* 48:1
12 *3*	*Sacred Scripture* 2:4	30 **11, 12**	*The Lord* 40
12 **6**	*The Lord* 40	30 **25, 26**	*The Lord* 4
13 **6, 9, 13, 22**	*The Lord* 4	31 **1, 2, 3**	*Life* 30:2
13 **9–11**	*Sacred Scripture* 14:3	31 **7**	*The Lord* 4
14 **6**	*Sacred Scripture* 86	32 **15**	*The Lord* 49:1
14 **29**	*Faith* 53	33 **5**	*Sacred Scripture* 85
15 **2**	*Sacred Scripture* 35	33 **11**	*The Lord* 48:5
16 **1, 5**	*The Lord* 6	33 **15, 16**	*Life* 84:1
17 (3)	*Sacred Scripture* 79:8	33 **20**	*The Lord* 64:7
17 **4, 7, 9**	*The Lord* 4	34 **1**	*Sacred Scripture* 86
17 (6)	*The Lord* 39	34 **8**	*The Lord* 4
17 **7**	*The Lord* 40	34 **16**	*The Lord* 51:4
17 (14)	*Supplements* 13	35 **10**	*Sacred Scripture* 87:1
18 **7**	*Sacred Scripture* 86	37 **7**	*The Lord* 48:2
19 **14**	*The Lord* 48:5	37 **16**	*The Lord* 45:2
19 **18, 19, 23, 24**	*The Lord* 4	37 **20**	*The Lord* 45:2
20 **2, 3**	*The Lord* 15:4	37 (32)	*The Lord* 64:7
20 **2–3**	*Sacred Scripture* 16, 35	38 *16*	*The Lord* 47:2
20 *3*	*The Lord* 16:1; *Sacred Scripture* 29	40 **3, 5, 10**	*The Lord* 30:2, 38
20 **6**	*The Lord* 4	40 **3, 5, 10, 11**	*The Lord* 6
21 (10, 17)	*The Lord* 39	40 **13**	*The Lord* 50:2
21 **11, 12**	*Supplements* 13	41 **14**	*The Lord* 34:2
22 **5**	*The Lord* 4	41 (14)	*The Lord* 34:4
22 **13**	*Sacred Scripture* 87:1	41 **16**	*The Lord* 40

42 1	*The Lord* 50:1	[49 (5)]	*The Lord* 34:4
42 **1, 6, 7, 8**	*The Lord* 6	49 **7**	*The Lord* 34:2, 38, 40
42 *13*	*The Lord* 14:9	49 (7)	*The Lord* 34:4
42 **5**	*The Lord* 49:1	49 *8*	*Life* 60
42 **6**	*Sacred Scripture* 86	49 **22**	*Sacred Scripture* 86
42 *6*	*Life* 60	49 (22, 23)	*Sacred Scripture* 51:8
42 **6, 7, 8**	*The Lord* 30:3, 38	49 **26**	*The Lord* 34:2, 38, 39
43 **1, 3**	*The Lord* 34:2, 38, 40	49 (26)	*The Lord* 34:4
[43 (1, 3)]	*The Lord* 34:4	51 **3**	*Sacred Scripture* 87:1
43 (3, 11, 14, 15)	*The Lord* 34:4	51 **11**	*Sacred Scripture* 87:1
43 **9**	*Sacred Scripture* 86	52 **1, 2, 6, 9**	*The Lord* 64:4
43 **11**	*The Lord* 34:2, 38, 45:3	52 **6**	*The Lord* 4
43 (11)	*The Lord* 34:4	53 (chapter cited)	*The Lord* 16:4
43 *14*	*The Lord* 38, 40	53 **1–12**	*The Lord* 6
43 **14, 15**	*The Lord* 34:2	53 **3 to end**	*The Lord* 15:1
43 *15*	*The Lord* 38, 40	53 [4, 6, 11]	*The Lord* 16:4
44 **2, 6**	*The Lord* 38	53 *7*	*The Lord* 12
44 **3**	*The Lord* 49:1	54 **5**	*The Lord* 34:2, 38, 40, 41, 45:3
44 **6**	*The Lord* 34:2, 36:2, 45:3	54 (5)	*The Lord* 34:4, 39
44 *6*	*The Lord* 34:4	54 **6**	*The Lord* 49:2
44 (6)	*The Lord* 34:4	54 *8*	*The Lord* 34:2, 38
44 **8**	*The Lord* 45:2	54 (8)	*The Lord* 34:4
44 **24**	*The Lord* 34:2	54 (13)	*Faith* 5
[44 (24)]	*The Lord* 34:4	55 **3, 4**	*The Lord* 43
44 **24, 26**	*The Lord* 64:6	55 **4, 5**	*Sacred Scripture* 86
44 (24, 26)	*Sacred Scripture* 51:8	55 **5**	*The Lord* 40
45 **3**	*The Lord* 39	56 **1**	*Sacred Scripture* 85
45 **5, 6**	*The Lord* 45:2	57 (3)	*Life* 79:3
[45 (11)]	*The Lord* 34:4	57 **15**	*The Lord* 49:2
45 **11, 15**	*The Lord* 38, 40	57 **16**	*The Lord* 50:2
45 **11**, (15)	*The Lord* 34:2	58 **2**	*Sacred Scripture* 85
45 (14)	*The Lord* 34:4	59 **16, 17, 20**	*The Lord* 14:3
45 **14, 15**	*The Lord* 34:2, 45:3	59 **19, 20**	*The Lord* 50:1
45 (14, 18, 21, 22)	*The Lord* 34:4	59 **20**	*The Lord* 34:2
45 (15)	*The Lord* 39	59 **21**	*The Lord* 51:4
45 **21**	*The Lord* 34:2	60 **9**	*The Lord* 40
45 **21, 22**	*The Lord* 34:2, 38, 45:3	60 **16**	*The Lord* 34:2, 38, 39
47 **4**	*The Lord* 34:2, 38, 40	61 **1**	*The Lord* 50:1
47 (4)	*The Lord* 34:4	61 **1, 2**	*The Lord* 4
47 **9**	*The Lord* 4	61 **3**	*The Lord* 49:2
48 **1, 2**	*The Lord* 39	62 **1, 2, 3, 4, 11, 12**	*The Lord* 64:2
48 *12*	*The Lord* 36:2	63 **1, 4, 8**	*The Lord* 6
48 **17**	*The Lord* 34:2	63 **1–9**	*The Lord* 14:2
48 *17*	*The Lord* 38, 40	63 **4**	*The Lord* 4
48 (17)	*The Lord* 34:4	63 **4, 6, 8**	*The Lord* 33:5
49 **5**	*The Lord* 34:2, 38	63 (8)	*The Lord* 34:4

[63 **10**]	*The Lord* 50:2	9 **24**	*Sacred Scripture* 85
63 **11, 12, 14**	*The Lord* 50:2	9 **25**	*The Lord* 4
65 (17)	*The Lord* 62:2	10 (1, 2, 18)	*The Lord* 53
65 **17, 18, 19, 25**	*The Lord* 64:3	10 **15**	*The Lord* 4
65 (18)	*Sacred Scripture* 51:8	11 (1, 6, 9, 11)	*The Lord* 53
66 **10**	*Sacred Scripture* 87:1	11 (3)	*The Lord* 39
66 (10–14)	*The Lord* 64:7	11 **23**	*The Lord* 4
66 (20, 22)	*Sacred Scripture* 51:8	12 (14, 17)	*The Lord* 53
66 (22)	*The Lord* 62:2	13 (1, 6, 9, 11, 12, 13, 14, 15, 25)	*The Lord* 53
JEREMIAH		13 *1–7*	*The Lord* 15:4; *Sacred Scripture* 16
1 (4, 11, 12, 13, 14, 19)	*The Lord* 53	13 (9, 10, 14)	*The Lord* 64:8
2 (1, 2, 3, 4, 5, 9, 19, 22, 29, 31)	*The Lord* 53	13 (12)	*The Lord* 39
2 *13*	*Sacred Scripture* 2:4	13 (27)	*Life* 79:3
3 (1, 6, 10, 12, 14, 16)	*The Lord* 53	14 (1, 10, 14, 15)	*The Lord* 53
3 (2, 6, 8, 9)	*Life* 79:3	14 (16)	*The Lord* 64:8
3 **16, 17, 18**	*The Lord* 4	15 (1, 2, 3, 6, 11, 19, 20)	*The Lord* 53
3 **17**	*The Lord* 64:7	16 (1, 3, 5, 9, 14, 16)	*The Lord* 53
3 (18)	*Sacred Scripture* 51:8	16 *2, 5, 8*	*The Lord* 15:4
4 (1, 3, 9, 17, 27)	*The Lord* 53	16 **9**	*Sacred Scripture* 87:1, 2
4 **2**	*Sacred Scripture* 85	16 (9)	*The Lord* 39
4 **4**	*Faith* 54	16 **14**	*The Lord* 4
4 **9**	*The Lord* 4	17 (5, 19, 20, 21, 24)	*The Lord* 53
4 (15)	*Sacred Scripture* 79:8	17 (13)	*Sacred Scripture* 2:4
5 (1)	*The Lord* 64:8	18 (1, 5, 6, 11, 13)	*The Lord* 53
5 (7)	*Life* 79:3	18 **17**	*The Lord* 4
5 (11, 14, 18, 22, 29)	*The Lord* 53	19 (1, 3, 6, 12, 15)	*The Lord* 53
6 (4, 5)	*Supplements* 13	19 (3, 15)	*The Lord* 39
6 (6, 7)	*The Lord* 64:8	19 **6**	*The Lord* 4
6 (6, 9, 12, 15, 16, 21, 22)	*The Lord* 53	20 (4)	*The Lord* 53
6 **22**	*Sacred Scripture* 86	21 (1, 4, 7, 8, 11, 12)	*The Lord* 53
7 (1, 3, 11, 13, 19, 20, 21)	*The Lord* 53	22 (2, 5, 6, 11, 16, 18, 24, 29, 30)	*The Lord* 53
7 **2, 3, 4, 9, 10, 11**	*Life* 91	22 **3, 13, 15**	*Sacred Scripture* 85
7 (3)	*The Lord* 39	23 (2)	*The Lord* 39
7 (17, 18, and following)	*The Lord* 64:8	23 (2, 5, 7, 12, 15, 24, 29, 31, 38)	*The Lord* 53
7 **32, 34**	*The Lord* 4	23 **5**	*Sacred Scripture* 85
7 *34*	*Sacred Scripture* 87:1, 2	23 *5*	*The Lord* 19:7
8 (1, 3, 12, 13)	*The Lord* 53	23 (5)	*Sacred Scripture* 51:8
8 (6, 7, 8, and following)	*The Lord* 64:8	23 **5, 6**	*The Lord* 38
8 **12**	*The Lord* 4	23 **5, 6, 7, 12, 20**	*The Lord* 4
9 (3, 6, 7, 9, 13, 15, 17, 22, 23, 24, 25)	*The Lord* 53	23 **5–6**	*The Lord* 6
9 (10, 11, 13, and following)	*The Lord* 64:8	23 **14**	*Life* 79:2
		23 (14)	*The Lord* 64:2
9 (15)	*The Lord* 39	24 (3, 5, 8)	*The Lord* 53

24 (5)	*The Lord* 39	35 **15**	*Life* 30:1
25 (1, 3, 7, 8, 9, 15, 27, 29, 32)	*The Lord* 53	36 (1, 6, 27, 29, 30)	*The Lord* 53
		37 (6, 7, 9)	*The Lord* 53
25 **10**	*Sacred Scripture* 87:1, 2	37 (7)	*The Lord* 39
25 **14**	*Life* 2	38 (2, 3, 17)	*The Lord* 53
25 (15, 27)	*The Lord* 39	38 (17)	*The Lord* 39
26 (1, 2, 18)	*The Lord* 53	39 (15, 16, 17, 18)	*The Lord* 53
27 (1, 2, 4, 8, 11, 16, 19, 21, 22)	*The Lord* 53	39 (16)	*The Lord* 39
		39 **16, 17**	*The Lord* 4
28 (2, 12, 14, 16)	*The Lord* 53	40 (1)	*The Lord* 53
29 (4, 8, 21, 25)	*The Lord* 39	42 (7, 9, 15, 18, 19)	*The Lord* 53
29 (4, 8, 9, 19, 20, 21, 25, 30, 31, 32)	*The Lord* 53	42 (9, 15, 18)	*The Lord* 39
		43 (8, 10)	*The Lord* 53
29 (23)	*Life* 79:3	43 (10)	*The Lord* 39
30 (1, 2, 3, 4, 5, 8, 10, 11, 12, 17, 18)	*The Lord* 53	44 (1, 2, 7, 11, 24, 25, 26, 30)	*The Lord* 53
		44 (2, 7, 11, 25)	*The Lord* 39
30 (2)	*The Lord* 39	45 (1, 2, 5)	*The Lord* 53
30 **3, 7, 8**	*The Lord* 4	46 (1, 23, 25, 28)	*The Lord* 53
30 **9**	*The Lord* 43	46 **5, 10**	*The Lord* 14:4
31 (1, 2, 7, 10, 15, 16, 17, 23, 27, 28, 31, 32, 33, 34, 35, 36, 37, 38)	*The Lord* 53	46 **10, 21**	*The Lord* 4
		47 (1)	*The Lord* 53
		47 **1, 2, 4**	*Faith* 53
31 (6, 18)	*Sacred Scripture* 79:8	47 **4**	*The Lord* 4
31 **6, 27, 31, 38**	*The Lord* 4	48 (1)	*The Lord* 39
31 *9*	*Sacred Scripture* 79:2	48 (1, 8, 12, 30, 35, 38, 40, 43, 44, 47)	*The Lord* 53
31 (9)	*Sacred Scripture* 2:4		
31 *20*	*Sacred Scripture* 79:2	48 (37)	*Sacred Scripture* 35
31 (23)	*The Lord* 39	48 **44, 47**	*The Lord* 4
31 **27, 31, 33**	*Sacred Scripture* 51:8	48 **45, 46**	*Sacred Scripture* 103:3
31 **31, 33, 34**	*Faith* 5	49 (2, 5, 6, 7, 12, 13, 16, 18, 26, 28, 30, 32, 35, 37, 38, 39)	*The Lord* 53
32 (1, 6, 14, 15, 25, 26, 28, 30, 36, 42)	*The Lord* 53		
		49 **8, 26, 39**	*The Lord* 4
32 (14, 15, 36)	*The Lord* 39	49 **26**	*The Lord* 14:5
32 **19**	*Life* 2	50 (1, 4, 10, 18, 20, 21, 30, 31, 33, 35, 40)	*The Lord* 53
33 (1, 2, 4, 10, 11, 12, 13, 17, 19, 20, 23, 25)	*The Lord* 53		
		50 **4, 20, 27, 31**	*The Lord* 4
33 (4)	*The Lord* 39	50 (18)	*The Lord* 39
33 **10, 11**	*Sacred Scripture* 87:1, 2	50 (19)	*Sacred Scripture* 79:8
33 **14, 15, 16**	*The Lord* 4	50 (19, 20)	*Sacred Scripture* 51:8
33 **15**	*Sacred Scripture* 85	50 **34**	*The Lord* 34:2, 38
33 *15, 16*	*The Lord* 38	50 (34)	*The Lord* 34:4
33 **15–16**	*The Lord* 6	51 **5**	*The Lord* 40
34 (1, 2, 4, 8, 12, 13, 17, 22)	*The Lord* 53	51 **11**	*The Lord* 48:2
34 (2, 13)	*The Lord* 39	51 **17**	*The Lord* 47:2
35 (1, 13, 17, 18, 19)	*The Lord* 53	51 **18**	*The Lord* 4
35 (13, 17, 18, 19)	*The Lord* 39		

51 (25, 33, 36, 39, 52, 58)	The Lord 53	10 (19, 20)	The Lord 39
51 (33)	The Lord 39	11 **1, 24**	The Lord 52
		11 (2, 4, 15)	The Lord 28
LAMENTATIONS		11 **19**	The Lord 49:1
1 (8, 9, 17)	The Lord 64:8	11 *19*	Life 86:6
4 **21**	Sacred Scripture 87:1	[11 (19)]	Life 112
		11 (22)	The Lord 39
EZEKIEL		12 (2, 3, 9, 18, 27)	The Lord 28
1, 9, 10 (chapters cited)	Sacred Scripture 97:5	12 *3–7,* **11**	The Lord 15:5
1, 10 (chapters cited)	The Lord 52	12 *6,* **11**	The Lord 16:1, 16:4
1 (4)	Sacred Scripture 97:5	12 (18, 19)	The Lord 64:8
1 (5)	Sacred Scripture 97:5	12 **27**	The Lord 4
1 (6)	Sacred Scripture 97:5	13 (2, 17)	The Lord 28
1 (7)	Sacred Scripture 97:5	13 **3**	The Lord 48:5
1 (8, 9)	Sacred Scripture 97:5	13 **5**	The Lord 4
1 (10, 11)	Sacred Scripture 97:5	14 (3, 13)	The Lord 28
1 (12)	Sacred Scripture 97:5	15 (2)	The Lord 28
1 **12, 20**	The Lord 48:3	15 (6, 7, 8)	The Lord 64:8
1 (13, 14)	Sacred Scripture 97:5	16 (1–63)	The Lord 64:8
1 (15–21)	Sacred Scripture 97:5	16 (2)	The Lord 28
1 (22, 23)	Sacred Scripture 97:5	16 **15, 26, 28, 29, 32, 33, 35, and following**	Life 79:3
1 (24, 25)	Sacred Scripture 97:5	16 (46, 48)	The Lord 64:2
1 (26)	Sacred Scripture 97:5	17 (2)	The Lord 28
1 (27, 28)	Sacred Scripture 97:5	18 **5**	Sacred Scripture 85
2 (1, 3, 6, 8)	The Lord 28	18 **31**	The Lord 49:1
3 (1, 3, 4, 10, 17, 25)	The Lord 28	20 (3, 4, 27, 46)	The Lord 28
3 *12, 14*	The Lord 52	20 **32**	The Lord 48:2
3 **14**	The Lord 48:4	21 (2, 6, 9, 12, 14, 19, 28)	The Lord 28
4 (1, 16)	The Lord 28	21 **7**	The Lord 48:4
4 *1–15*	The Lord 15:7; Sacred Scripture 16	21 **25, 29**	The Lord 4
4 (1 to end)	The Lord 64:8	22 **3, 4**	The Lord 4
4 **4, 5, 6**	The Lord 16:2	22 (18, 24)	The Lord 28
4 **13, 16, 17**	The Lord 16:3	23 (1–49)	The Lord 64:8
5 (1)	The Lord 28	23 (2, 36)	The Lord 28
5 *1–4*	The Lord 15:5; Sacred Scripture 16, 35	23 **2–17**	Life 79:2
5 (9 to end)	The Lord 64:8	24 (2, 16, 25)	The Lord 28
6 (2)	The Lord 28	24 **25, 26, 27**	The Lord 4
7 (2)	The Lord 28	25 (2)	The Lord 28
7 **6, 7, 10, 12, 19**	The Lord 4	26 (2)	The Lord 28
7 **18**	Sacred Scripture 35	27 (2)	The Lord 28
8 *3 and following*	The Lord 52	28 (2, 12, 21)	The Lord 28
8 (4)	The Lord 39	28 *10*	Faith 54
8 (5, 6, 8, 12, 15)	The Lord 28	28 **12, 13, 14, 16**	Sacred Scripture 97:4
9 (3)	The Lord 39	28 **12–13**	Sacred Scripture 45
		[28 (12–13)]	Sacred Scripture 42

29 (2, 18)	*The Lord* 28	**DANIEL**	
29 *18*	*Sacred Scripture* 35	2 *3*	*The Lord* 48:4
29 **21**	*The Lord* 4	2 **28**	*The Lord* 4
30 **2, 3, 9**	*The Lord* 4	2 (31–35)	*Sacred Scripture* 117
30 (2, 21)	*The Lord* 28	2 **44**	*The Lord* 42
30 (3)	*The Lord* 38	4 **8**	*The Lord* 48:1
31 (2)	*The Lord* 28	4 **13, 23**	*The Lord* 40
31 **15**	*The Lord* 4	[5 **11–12, 14**]	*The Lord* 48:1
31 *18*	*Faith* 54	7 (1, 2, 7, 13)	*The Lord* 52
32 (2, 18)	*The Lord* 28	7 *3*	*The Lord* 52
32 **7, 8**	*Sacred Scripture* 14:3	7 (7, 20, 24)	*Life* 61
32 *19*	*Faith* 54	7 *9*	*Sacred Scripture* 49:5
33 (2, 7, 10, 12, 24, 30)	*The Lord* 28	7 **13**	*The Lord* 26:1
33 **14, 16**	*Sacred Scripture* 85	7 **13, 14, 27**	*The Lord* 6, 42
34 (2)	*The Lord* 28	7 **14**	*Sacred Scripture* 86
34 **11, 12**	*The Lord* 4	7 (14)	*The Lord* 10
34 **17, 18, 21, 22,** and following	*Faith* 68	7 **15**	*The Lord* 48:4
		7 **22**	*The Lord* 4
34 **23, 24**	*The Lord* 43	8 (chapter cited)	*Faith* 61
35 (2)	*The Lord* 28	8 *1 and following*	*The Lord* 52
36 (1, 17)	*The Lord* 28	8 (2)	*The Lord* 52
36 **15**	*Sacred Scripture* 86	8 **2–14**	*Faith* 65
[36 (26)]	*Life* 112	8 [(2–14)]	*Faith* 63:4
36 **26, 27**	*The Lord* 49:1	8 **14**	*Supplements* 13
36 **26, 27**	*Life* 86:6	8 (17)	*The Lord* 28
36 **33**	*The Lord* 4	8 **17, 19, 26**	*The Lord* 4
37 (3, 9, 11, 16)	*The Lord* 28	[8 (20)]	*Faith* 66
37 **5, 6, 9, 10**	*The Lord* 47:2	8 **26**	*Supplements* 13
37 (16)	*Sacred Scripture* 79:8	9 (21)	*The Lord* 52
37 **23–26**	*The Lord* 43	9 **24–25**	*The Lord* 6
38 (2, 14)	*The Lord* 28	9 **25**	*The Lord* 64:6
38 **14, 16, 18, 19**	*The Lord* 4	10 (1, 7, 8)	*The Lord* 52
39 (1, 17)	*The Lord* 28	10 **14**	*The Lord* 4
39 **8, 11, 22**	*The Lord* 4	11 **35**	*The Lord* 4
39 **17–21**	*Sacred Scripture* 15:3	12 **1**	*The Lord* 4
40–48 (chapters cited)	*The Lord* 52	12 **4, 9, 11, 13**	*The Lord* 4
40 *2*	*The Lord* 52		
40 (4)	*The Lord* 28	**HOSEA**	
41 *18, 19, 20*	*Sacred Scripture* 97:3	1 (chapter cited)	*Sacred Scripture* 79:7
43 (2)	*The Lord* 39	1 *2–9*	*The Lord* 15:6; *Sacred Scripture* 16
43 *5*	*The Lord* 52	1 **4, 5, 11**	*The Lord* 4
43 (7, 10, 18)	*The Lord* 28	2 **16, 18, 21**	*The Lord* 4
44 (2)	*The Lord* 39	2 *19*	*Sacred Scripture* 85
44 (5)	*The Lord* 28	3 (chapter cited)	*Sacred Scripture* 79:7
44 *9*	*Faith* 54	3 *1–2*	*The Lord* 15:6
48 (5)	*Sacred Scripture* 79:8	3 *2, 3*	*Sacred Scripture* 16

INDEX TO SCRIPTURAL PASSAGES

3 5 — *The Lord* 4, 43
4 (7, 10, 11) — *Life* 79:3
4 9 — *Life* 2
4 12 — *The Lord* 48:5
4 (17, 18) — *Sacred Scripture* 79:8
5 3 — *Sacred Scripture* 79:6
5 4 — *The Lord* 48:5
5 **5, 9, 11, 14** — *Sacred Scripture* 79:3
6 **1, 2** — *The Lord* 4
6 **4** — *Sacred Scripture* 79:3
6 **10** — *Sacred Scripture* 79:6
7 (1, 11) — *Sacred Scripture* 79:8
8 (9, 11) — *Sacred Scripture* 79:8
9 **3** — *Sacred Scripture* 79:4
9 **7** — *The Lord* 4, 48:5
9 (11, 12, 13, 16) — *Sacred Scripture* 79:8
10 (11) — *Sacred Scripture* 79:8
11 (3) — *Sacred Scripture* 79:8
11 **8** — *Sacred Scripture* 79:7
12 **1** — *Sacred Scripture* 79:5
12 (1, 8, 14) — *Sacred Scripture* 79:8
13 (1, 8, 14) — *Sacred Scripture* 79:8
13 **4** — *The Lord* 34:2, 38, 45:3
13 (4) — *The Lord* 34:4

JOEL

1 **15** — *The Lord* 4
1 **16** — *Sacred Scripture* 87:1
2 **1, 2, 10** — *Sacred Scripture* 14:3
2 **1, 2, 11** — *The Lord* 4
2 **11** — *The Lord* 14:5
2 (11) — *The Lord* 38
2 **17** — *Sacred Scripture* 86
2 **28, 29** — *The Lord* 49:1
2 **29, 31** — *The Lord* 4
3 **1, 2, 14, 18** — *The Lord* 4
3 **15** — *Sacred Scripture* 14:3
3 **17–21** — *The Lord* 64:7
3 **18, 20** — *Sacred Scripture* 51:8

AMOS

2 **16** — *The Lord* 4
3 **14** — *The Lord* 4
4 **13** — *The Lord* 49:1
5 **18, 20** — *The Lord* 4
5 (18, 20) — *The Lord* 38
5 **24** — *Sacred Scripture* 85
6 **12** — *Sacred Scripture* 85
8 **3, 9, 13** — *The Lord* 4
8 **10** — *Sacred Scripture* 35
9 **11** — *The Lord* 43
9 **11, 13** — *The Lord* 4

OBADIAH

verses **8, 12, 13, 14, 15** — *The Lord* 4
(verse 19) — *Sacred Scripture* 79:8

JONAH

1 **17** — *Sacred Scripture* 29
3 (9) — *Sacred Scripture* 51:2
4 (2) — *Sacred Scripture* 51:2

MICAH

1 (7) — *Life* 79:3
1 **16** — *Sacred Scripture* 35
2 **4** — *The Lord* 4
2 **11** — *The Lord* 48:5
4 **1, 2, 8** — *The Lord* 64:7
4 **1, 6** — *The Lord* 4
4 **2** — *The Lord* 39
5 **2** — *The Lord* 37:3
5 **2, 4** — *The Lord* 6, 38
5 **10** — *The Lord* 4
7 **4, 11, 12** — *The Lord* 4
7 **9** — *Sacred Scripture* 85

NAHUM

1 (15) — *Sacred Scripture* 51:8
3 (4) — *Life* 79:3

HABAKKUK

2 **3** — *The Lord* 4
3 **2** — *The Lord* 4
3 **3** — *The Lord* 40

ZEPHANIAH

1 **7, 8, 10, 12, 14, 15, 16, 18** — *The Lord* 4
1 (7, 14, 15, 18) — *The Lord* 38
1 **8, 15, 16** — *The Lord* 14:5
2 **2, 3** — *The Lord* 4
2 **9** — *Sacred Scripture* 86
2 (9) — *The Lord* 39

3 **8, 11, 16, 19, 20**	*The Lord* 4	13 **1, 2, 4**	*The Lord* 4
3 **14, 15, 16, 17, 20**	*The Lord* 64:5	13 **2**	*The Lord* 48:6
		13 (4)	*The Lord* 15:8

HAGGAI

		14 **1, 4, 6, 7, 8, 9, 13, 20, 21**	*The Lord* 4
1 **14**	*The Lord* 48:2	14 **3, 4**	*The Lord* 38
		14 **3, 4, 5, 6, 9**	*The Lord* 14:5

ZECHARIAH

		14 **7**	*Supplements* 13
1 **6**	*Life* 2	14 (8, 11, 12, 21)	*The Lord* 64:7
1 *8 and following*	*The Lord* 52	14 **9**	*The Lord* 45:3
1 *18*	*The Lord* 52		
2 *1*	*The Lord* 52	## MALACHI	
2 **10, 11, 12**	*Sacred Scripture* 51:8	2 **15**	*The Lord* 49:1
2 **10–11**	*The Lord* 6	2 **16**	*The Lord* 48:5
2 **11**	*The Lord* 4	3 **1**	*The Lord* 30:4
3 *1 and following*	*The Lord* 52	3 *1*	*Life* 60
3 **9, 10**	*The Lord* 4	3 **1, 2**	*The Lord* 6
4 *1 and following*	*The Lord* 52	3 (2, 4)	*The Lord* 64:7
4 **6**	*The Lord* 50:2	3 **2, 17**	*The Lord* 4
5 *1, 6*	*The Lord* 52	3 (4)	*Sacred Scripture* 51:8
6 *1 and following*	*The Lord* 52	4 **1, 5**	*The Lord* 4
6 (1–8)	*Sacred Scripture* 12:2	4 **5**	*The Lord* 6, 38
6 **8**	*The Lord* 49:1		
7 **12**	*The Lord* 51:5	## MATTHEW	
8 **3**	*The Lord* 64:7	1 **18–25**	*The Lord* 21
8 **19**	*Sacred Scripture* 87:1	1 (18–25)	*The Lord* 29:2
8 *20–23*	*The Lord* 64:7	[1 (18–25)]	*Supplements* 72:1
8 **22**	*Sacred Scripture* 86	1 **22–23**	*The Lord* 6
8 **23**	*The Lord* 4; *Sacred Scripture* 51:8	1 (22–23)	*The Lord* 19:3
8 (23)	*Life* 61	2 (1, 2, 9, 10, 11)	*Sacred Scripture* 23:3
9 **9–10**	*The Lord* 6	3 **3**	*The Lord* 30:2
9 (10)	*Sacred Scripture* 79:8	3 **4**	*The Lord* 15:8
9 *11*	*Life* 60	3 **8**	*Life* 104
9 *13*	*Sacred Scripture* 79:2	[3 *8*]	*Life* 101
9 **16**	*The Lord* 4	3 *10*	*Life* 93
10 **3**	*Faith* 68	3 **11**	*The Lord* 51:4
10 **3, 4**	*Sacred Scripture* 51:8	3 **16**	*The Lord* 51:4
10 **7**	*Sacred Scripture* 79:2	3 **17**	*The Lord* 19:10
11 **11**	*The Lord* 4	4 (1–11)	*The Lord* 12
12 **1**	*The Lord* 49:1	4 **4**	*Sacred Scripture* 69
12 **3, 4, 6, 8, 9, 11**	*The Lord* 4	4 **16**	*Sacred Scripture* 111
12 (3, 6, 9, 10)	*The Lord* 64:7	4 **17**	*The Lord* 18:4
12 **8**	*The Lord* 43	4 (23)	*The Lord* 42
12 **10**	*The Lord* 49:1	5 **3**	*The Lord* 49:2; *Sacred Scripture* 51:4
13 **1**	*The Lord* 43	5 **8**	*Sacred Scripture* 57; *Life* 17
13 *1*	*Sacred Scripture* 2:4	5 **8, 48**	*Life* 84:2

INDEX TO SCRIPTURAL PASSAGES

[5 (17)]	*The Lord* 8	12 **31, 32**	*The Lord* 50:2
5 **17**, (18)	*The Lord* 9	12 **33**	*Life* 104
5 **17, 19**	*The Lord* 17:2	12 **34, 35**	*Life* 28
5 **18**	*The Lord* 11; *Sacred Scripture* 90:2	12 **35**	*Life* 51
5 **19**	*Life* 104	12 *39*	*Life* 79:3
5 **19, 20**	*Life* 2	12 (39)	*Sacred Scripture* 51:9
5 **20**	*Life* 84:2	12 **43, 44, 45**	*The Lord* 48:6
5 *21, 22*	*Life* 73	12 (43, 44, 45)	*The Lord* 48:7
[5 (22)]	*Sacred Scripture* 67:4	12 *46–49*	*The Lord* 35:4
5 **23–26**	*Life* 73	13 **3–8**	*Life* 90
5 **27, 28**	*Life* 78	13 **3–9, 23**	*Life* 2
5 (43–47)	*Faith* 21	13 *14, 15*	*Sacred Scripture* 60
6 **24**	*Life* 28	13 (19–23, 37)	*Life* 90
7 **1, 2**	*Sacred Scripture* 51:5	13 **24–30, 37–40**	*Supplements* 10
7 **7, 8**	*Sacred Scripture* 51:3	13 *33*	*Sacred Scripture* 29
7 **12**	*The Lord* 9; *Life* 73	13 **37**	*The Lord* 27:1
7 **19**	*Life* 104	13 **57**	*The Lord* 15:3
7 *19*	*Life* 93	14 (33)	*The Lord* 19:10, 41
7 **19, 20**	*Life* 2	15 **11**	*Life* 51
7 **21**	*Life* 2	15 (24)	*The Lord* 20
7 **21, 22, 23**	*Life* 30:3	15 (25)	*The Lord* 41
7 *22, 23*	*Life* 2	15 **31**	*The Lord* 39
7 **24**	*Life* 104	16 (4)	*Life* 79:3
7 *24*	*Life* 39	16 (24)	*Life* 99
7 **24**, 26	*Life* 2	16 (25)	*Life* 99
7 (26)	*Life* 91	16 **27**	*The Lord* 25; *Life* 2, 105
8 (4)	*The Lord* 9	16 (28)	*The Lord* 42
8 **11, 12**	*Life* 65	17 **1–5**	*Sacred Scripture* 48
8 (16)	*The Lord* 48:7	17 **1–8**	*The Lord* 35:6
8 **20**	*The Lord* 27:2	[17 (2)]	*Sacred Scripture* 42
8 (29)	*The Lord* 19:10	17 (2 and following)	*Sacred Scripture* 98
9 (15)	*Sacred Scripture* 87:2	17 **5**	*The Lord* 19:10
9 (18)	*The Lord* 41	18 **11**	*The Lord* 27:1
9 (35)	*The Lord* 42	19 **16, 17**	*The Lord* 45:2
10 (1)	*The Lord* 48:7	19 **28**	*The Lord* 25; *Sacred Scripture* 51:7
[10 (28)]	*Sacred Scripture* 67:4	20 (18, 19)	*The Lord* 24
10 (38)	*Life* 99	20 **28**	*The Lord* 27:1
10 (39)	*Life* 99	21 **11**	*The Lord* 15:3
10 (40)	*The Lord* 20	21 (21, 22)	*Sacred Scripture* 51:3
11 **3, 4, 5**	*Sacred Scripture* 17:4	21 *33–44*	*Life* 2
11 **13**	*The Lord* 9	21 **40, 41**	*Life* 65
[11 *13*]	*The Lord* 21	21 **43**	*Life* 2, 65, 104
[11 (27)]	*Sacred Scripture* 9	22 *37*	*Life* 86:6
12 **8**	*The Lord* 27:1	22 **37, 39, 40**	*The Lord* 9
12 (28)	*The Lord* 42	[22 *40*]	*Life* 31

22 **41–46**	*The Lord* 35:5	28 **18, 20**	*The Lord* 46:6
22 **44**	*The Lord* 6	28 **19**	*The Lord* 46:6
22 (44)	*The Lord* 14:8	28 **20**	*The Lord* 46:6, 51:2
23 **8, 9, 10**	*Sacred Scripture* 51:6		
23 **25–26**	*Sacred Scripture* 40:2	MARK	
23 **25–28**	*Life* 30:1	1 *1*	*The Lord* 19:8
23 **26**	*Life* 113	1 *3*	*The Lord* 30:2
23 (27, 28)	*Sacred Scripture* 51:9	1 *4*	*The Lord* 18:4
23 (37, 39)	*The Lord* 64:8	1 *8*	*The Lord* 51:4
24 **3, 30**	*The Lord* 26:1	1 *10*	*The Lord* 51:4
24 (14)	*The Lord* 42	1 *11*	*The Lord* 19:10
24 (30)	*Sacred Scripture* 25	1 (12–13)	*The Lord* 12
24 **29, 30**	*Sacred Scripture* 112:2	1 **14, 15**	*The Lord* 18:4; *Life* 103
24 **29, 30, 31**	*Sacred Scripture* 14:1	1 (14, 15)	*The Lord* 42
24 **44**	*The Lord* 25	1 (23–28)	*The Lord* 48:7
25 (chapter cited)	*Faith* 61	1 (40)	*The Lord* 41
25 *1*	*Life* 61	2 **8**	*The Lord* 50:1
25 **1–12**	*Sacred Scripture* 17:1	2 **10**	*The Lord* 27:1
25 **1–12**	*Life* 2	2 **19**	*Life* 17
25 **14–31**	*Life* 2	2 (19, 20)	*Sacred Scripture* 87:2
25 **31, 33**	*The Lord* 25	2 **28**	*The Lord* 27:1
[25 (31–40)]	*Supplements* 10	3 (11)	*The Lord* 19:10
25 **31–46**	*Life* 2	3 **28, 29, 30**	*The Lord* 50:2
25 (31–46)	*Faith* 68	3 *31–35*	*The Lord* 35:4
25 [(32–33)]	*Faith* 64:2	4 **3–8**	*Life* 90
25 (41–46)	*Supplements* 10	4 (14–20)	*Life* 90
25 [41–46]	*Supplements* 16:2	5 (22)	*The Lord* 41
[26 (14–16, 47–68)]	*The Lord* 16:5	6 *4*	*The Lord* 15:3
26 *28*	*Life* 60	6 **12**	*The Lord* 18:4
26 *34*	*Sacred Scripture* 29	7 (25)	*The Lord* 41
26 (36–44)	*The Lord* 12	8 **12**	*The Lord* 50:1
26 *39–44*	*Sacred Scripture* 29	8 (31)	*The Lord* 24
26 **45**	*The Lord* 24	8 **34, 35**	*Life* 99
26 **52, 54, 56**	*The Lord* 11	8 (38)	*Life* 79:3
26 *61*	*Sacred Scripture* 29	9 (1)	*The Lord* 42
26 **63, 64**	*The Lord* 19:8, 26:2	[9 *2*]	*Sacred Scripture* 42
26 **64**	*Sacred Scripture* 49:2	9 (2 and following)	*Sacred Scripture* 98
[27 (1–61)]	*The Lord* 16:5	9 *2–8*	*The Lord* 35:6
27 (33–56)	*The Lord* 12	9 *7*	*The Lord* 19:10
27 (43, 54)	*The Lord* 19:10	9 (17–29)	*The Lord* 48:7
28 *1*	*Sacred Scripture* 29	9 (37)	*The Lord* 20
[28 (1–10)]	*The Lord* 16:5	10 (2, 3, 4)	*The Lord* 9
28 (9)	*The Lord* 41	10 (17)	*The Lord* 41
28 **18**	*The Lord* 32:4, 46:6	10 **17–22**	*Life* 66:1
[28 *18*]	*The Lord* 60	10 (21)	*Life* 99
28 **18, 19, 20**	*The Lord* 46:1	10 **33, 34**	*The Lord* 24

10 45	The Lord 27:1	2 **10, 11**	The Lord 34:2
11 **22**	Life 17	2 (10, 11)	The Lord 34:4
12 (19)	The Lord 9	2 **22, 23, 24, 27, 39**	The Lord 9
12 **29, 30**	The Lord 45:2	2 **30, 31, 32**	Sacred Scripture 86
12 *35, 36, 37*	The Lord 35:5	2 **40**	The Lord 32:1
12 **36**	The Lord 51:5	2 **52**	The Lord 32:1
12 (36)	The Lord 14:8	3 **3**	The Lord 18:4
13 *3, 4*	The Lord 14:5	3 *4*	The Lord 30:2
13 *11*	The Lord 51:4	[3 (8)]	Life 101
13 **26**	The Lord 26:1	3 **8, 9**	The Lord 18:4; Life 2
13 **31**	Sacred Scripture 2:3	3 *16*	The Lord 51:4
13 **35**	Supplements 13	3 *21*	The Lord 51:4
14 **21, 49**	The Lord 11	3 *22*	The Lord 19:10
14 *26*	The Lord 14:5	4 (1–13)	The Lord 12
14 (32–41)	The Lord 12	4 **16–21**	The Lord 11
[14 (43–65)]	The Lord 16:5	4 *18*	The Lord 50:1
[14 *61, 62*]	The Lord 26:2	4 *24*	The Lord 15:3
14 **62**	The Lord 27:2; Sacred Scripture 49:2	4 (33, 36)	The Lord 48:7
		4 (43)	The Lord 20, 42
14 *62*	The Lord 19:8	5 *24*	The Lord 27:1
[15 (15–37)]	The Lord 16:5	5 **32**	Life 103
15 (22–38)	The Lord 12	5 (34, 35)	Sacred Scripture 87:2
15 **28**	The Lord 11	6 *5*	The Lord 27:1
15 (39)	The Lord 19:10	6 (17, 18)	The Lord 48:7
15 (43)	The Lord 42	6 **20**	Sacred Scripture 51:4
[16 (1–8)]	The Lord 16:5	6 **37**	Sacred Scripture 51:5
16 **19**	The Lord 35:10	6 **43, 44**	Life 28
[16 *19*]	The Lord 60	6 **45**	Life 51
16 (19)	Sacred Scripture 49:2	6 *46*	Life 39
		6 **46–49**	Life 2, 104
LUKE		7 **16**	The Lord 15:3
1 **14**	Sacred Scripture 87:1	7 (21)	The Lord 48:7
1 **17**	The Lord 51:5	7 **46–50**	Life 51
1 **26–35**	The Lord 19:2	8 (1, 10)	The Lord 42
1 (26–35)	The Lord 29:2	8 (2, 29)	The Lord 48:7
[1 (26–38)]	Supplements 72:1	8 **5–8**	Life 90
1 (32–33)	The Lord 19:4	8 (11–15)	Life 90
1 (33)	The Lord 42	8 **20, 21**	The Lord 35:4
1 **35**	The Lord 40	8 **21**	Life 2
1 **41**	The Lord 51:5	8 *21*	Life 39
1 **46, 47**	The Lord 34:2	8 **54, 55**	The Lord 47:2
1 **47**	The Lord 49:1	9 (2, 11, 60)	The Lord 42
1 (47)	The Lord 34:4, 39	9 (22)	The Lord 24
1 **67**	The Lord 51:5	9 (24)	Life 99
1 **68, 69**	The Lord 39	9 (28 and following)	Sacred Scripture 98
1 **78**	The Lord 30:4	9 *28–36*	The Lord 35:6

9 (39, 42, 55)	*The Lord* 48:7	[21 **10, 11, 25**]	*Supplements* 25
9 (48)	*The Lord* 20	21 *14*	*The Lord* 51:4
9 *35*	*The Lord* 19:10	21 (20, 21, 22)	*The Lord* 64:8
9 *56*	*The Lord* 27:1	21 **27**	*The Lord* 26:1
9 **58**	*The Lord* 27:2	21 (31)	*The Lord* 42
10 (11)	*The Lord* 42	21 **36**	*The Lord* 25
10 (16)	*The Lord* 20	21 *37*	*The Lord* 14:5
10 **18**	*The Lord* 13	[22 *3*]	*Supplements* 45
10 **21**	*The Lord* 50:1	22 (18)	*The Lord* 42
10 *30–37*	*Life* 2	22 **37**	*The Lord* 11
11 (24, 25, 26)	*The Lord* 48:7	22 *39*	*The Lord* 14:5
[12 (5)]	*Sacred Scripture* 67:4	22 (39–46)	*The Lord* 12
12 *10*	*The Lord* 50:2	[22 (47–71)]	*The Lord* 16:5
12 **11, 12**	*The Lord* 51:4	[23 (26–56)]	*The Lord* 16:5
12 *40*	*The Lord* 25	23 (28, 29, 30)	*The Lord* 64:8
13 **3, 5**	*The Lord* 18:4; *Life* 103	23 (33–49)	*The Lord* 12
13 *6 and following*	*Life* 2	23 (51)	*The Lord* 42
13 (11)	*The Lord* 48:7	[24 (1–35)]	*The Lord* 16:5
13 **25, 26, 27**	*Life* 30:3	24 **6–7**	*The Lord* 24
13 **25–27**	*Life* 2	24 **25, 26, 27**	*The Lord* 11
13 **29**	*Life* 65	24 **26**	*The Lord* 13, 35:7
13 **33**	*The Lord* 15:3	24 (31)	*The Lord* 35:10
14 (27)	*Life* 99	24 **39, 40**	*The Lord* 35:9
16 *8*	*Life* 17	24 **41, 42, 43**	*The Lord* 35:10
16 **16**	*The Lord* 9	24 *44*	*The Lord* 14:11
[16 *16*]	*The Lord* 21	24 **44**–(45)	*The Lord* 11
16 (16)	*The Lord* 42	24 **47**	*The Lord* 18:4
16 **17**	*The Lord* 10; *Sacred Scripture* 90:2	24 **51**	*The Lord* 35:10
16 **19, 20**	*Sacred Scripture* 40:3		
16 *19–31*	*Life* 2	**JOHN**	
16 **29, 31**	*The Lord* 9	[1 *1*]	*The Lord* 37:3
17 *10*	*Life* 30:3	1 **1, 2**	*Sacred Scripture* 98
17 (15, 16)	*The Lord* 41	1 **1, 2, 3**	*Sacred Scripture* 2:3
17 **21**	*Sacred Scripture* 78	1 **1, 2, 3, 4, 5, 14**	*The Lord* 1
18 **8**	*Faith* 69	1 *1, 9*	*Sacred Scripture* 109
18 *11–14*	*Life* 30:3	1 *5*	*Sacred Scripture* 109
19 (11)	*The Lord* 42	[1 *9*]	*Sacred Scripture* 2:1
19 **10**	*The Lord* 27:1	1 **11, 12, 13**	*The Lord* 18:5
19 *12–25*	*Life* 2	1 **12**	*The Lord* 32:6
19 *13*	*Life* 61	1 *12*	*Life* 17
19 (41–44)	*The Lord* 64:8	1 **12, 13**	*Life* 17
20 (28, 37)	*The Lord* 9	1 (12, 13)	*Life* 51
20 *36*	*Life* 17	1 *13*	*Life* 17
20 *41–44*	*The Lord* 35:5	1 **14**	*Sacred Scripture* 98
20 (42)	*The Lord* 14:8	[1 **14**]	*The Lord* 2
20 **42–43**	*The Lord* 6	[1 **14**]	*The Lord* 37:3

INDEX TO SCRIPTURAL PASSAGES

[1 (14)]	*Sacred Scripture* 62	4 (42)	*The Lord* 34:4
1 *17*	*The Lord* 9	5 (16–26)	*The Lord* 22
1 **18**	*The Lord* 32:5	5 **19**	*The Lord* 32:2, 3
1 *18*	*The Lord* 19:7	5 **21**	*The Lord* 32:3
1 (18, 34, 49)	*The Lord* 19:10	5 **22, 27**	*The Lord* 25
1 **27, 30**	*The Lord* 37:3	5 **23**	*The Lord* 32:5
1 **29**	*The Lord* 15:1	5 (23, 24, 36, 37, 38)	*The Lord* 20
[1 *29*]	*The Lord* 17:1	5 **25**	*The Lord* 32:6
1 *32, 33*	*The Lord* 51:4	5 (25)	*The Lord* 19:10
1 **41**	*The Lord* 19:8	5 **26**	*The Lord* 32:3
1 **45**	*The Lord* 9	5 **29**	*Life* 2, 105
2 **4**	*The Lord* 35:4	5 **30**	*The Lord* 32:2
2 *19*, **21**	*The Lord* 30:4	5 **37**	*The Lord* 32:5
2 *19*, **21**	*Sacred Scripture* 47	5 (38)	*The Lord* 27:2
3 **5**	*The Lord* 49:1	5 **39**	*The Lord* 11
3 *13*	*The Lord* 31, 35:11	5 *46*	*The Lord* 14:11
3 (14)	*The Lord* 9	6 **27**	*The Lord* 27:1; *Sacred Scripture* 69
3 **15**	*The Lord* 32:6	6 **28, 29**	*The Lord* 32:6
3 **16**	*The Lord* 32:6	6 **29**	*Life* 48
3 **17**	*The Lord* 27:1	6 (29, 39, 40, 44, 57)	*The Lord* 20
3 (17, 34)	*The Lord* 20	6 **33, 35**	*The Lord* 32:6
3 **17–18**	*The Lord* 25	6 **33, 35, 41, 50, 51**	*The Lord* 31
3 (17–18)	*Sacred Scripture* 51:7	6 **40**	*The Lord* 32:6
3 **18**	*The Lord* 32:6	6 (45)	*Faith* 5
3 (18)	*The Lord* 19:10	6 **46**	*The Lord* 32:5
3 **19**	*The Lord* 1	6 **47**	*The Lord* 32:6
3 **19, 20, 21**	*Life* 50	[6 *47*]	*The Lord* 60
3 (19, 20, 21)	*Life* 24	6 **53**	*The Lord* 27:1
3 **19–21**	*Life* 2	6 *56*	*Sacred Scripture* 89
3 **21**	*Life* 17	6 **62**	*The Lord* 35:11
3 *21*	*Life* 39	6 **63**	*The Lord* 51:4; *Sacred Scripture* 2:2, 39, 69
3 **27**	*Sacred Scripture* 114; *Life* 17		
3 **29**	*Sacred Scripture* 87:2	6 *63*	*Sacred Scripture* 17:4
3 **31**	*The Lord* 31	[6 *63*]	*Sacred Scripture* 2:1
3 **34, 35**	*The Lord* 50:1	6 (63)	*Life* 99
3 **35**	*The Lord* 32:4	6 **68**	*Sacred Scripture* 2:3
3 **36**	*The Lord* 32:6	6 **69**	*The Lord* 19:8
3 *36*	*The Lord* 55:5	7 (16, 18, 28, 29)	*The Lord* 20
4 **7, 10, 13, 14**	*Sacred Scripture* 2:2	7 (19, 51)	*The Lord* 9
4 **14**	*Sacred Scripture* 69	7 **24**	*Sacred Scripture* 51:5
4 **23**	*The Lord* 49:1	7 **29**	*The Lord* 31
4 **24**	*The Lord* 50:2, 51:4	7 **33**	*The Lord* 35:11
[4 (24)]	*Supplements* 74	7 **37, 38**	*The Lord* 32:6; *Sacred Scripture* 2:3
4 **25**	*The Lord* 19:8		
4 (34)	*The Lord* 20	7 **37, 38, 39**	*The Lord* 51:1
4 **42**	*The Lord* 34:2	7 **39**	*The Lord* 51:3

7 *40, 41*	*The Lord* 15:3	12 *49–50*	*The Lord* 32:2
7 **48–49**	*The Lord* 10	[13 *3*]	*The Lord* 60
8 *1*	*The Lord* 14:5	13 **17**	*Life* 2, 104
8 *5*	*The Lord* 9	13 **18**	*The Lord* 11
8 *12*	*The Lord* 32:6	13 **20**	*The Lord* 32:5
8 (16, 18, 29, 42)	*The Lord* 20	13 (20)	*The Lord* 20
8 (17)	*The Lord* 9	13 **21**	*The Lord* 50:1
8 **19**	*The Lord* 32:5	[13 (27)]	*Supplements* 45
8 **24**	*The Lord* 3, 32:6	13 **31, 32**	*The Lord* 13, 35:7
8 **28, 29**	*The Lord* 32:2	14 **5, 6**	*The Lord* 51:2
8 (37)	*The Lord* 27:2	14 **6**	*The Lord* 32:6; *Sacred Scripture* 2:3
8 **42**	*The Lord* 31	[14 *6*]	*Sacred Scripture* 2:1
8 (44)	*Sacred Scripture* 51:9	14 **7**	*The Lord* 32:5
8 **58**	*The Lord* 30:1	14 **7–11**	*The Lord* 32:4
[8 *58*]	*The Lord* 37:3	14 **10**	*The Lord* 32:2
9 **4**	*Supplements* 13	[14 *10*]	*The Lord* 1, 60
9 (4)	*The Lord* 20	14 **10, 11**	*The Lord* 35:8
9 **31**	*Life* 2	14 **15, 21–24**	*Life* 2
9 (38)	*The Lord* 41	14 **16–19**	*The Lord* 51:1
10 **29, 30**	*The Lord* 32:4	14 **16–19, 26–28**	*The Lord* 51:2
[10 *30*]	*The Lord* 1, 60; *Supplements* 72:1	14 **20**	*The Lord* 32:4, 32:6, 35:8, 61:1; *Life* 102
10 **34**	*The Lord* 10	14 **20, 21**	*Sacred Scripture* 89
10 (36)	*The Lord* 19:10	14 **20, 21, 23**	*Sacred Scripture* 57
10 **37, 38**	*The Lord* 32:4	14 **21**	*Life* 39
11 (3, 5, 36)	*Sacred Scripture* 40:4	14 **21, 23**	*Life* 102
11 (4)	*The Lord* 19:10	14 **21, 24**	*Life* 38
11 (11)	*Sacred Scripture* 40:4	14 **23**	*Life* 17
11 **25, 26**	*The Lord* 32:6	14 (24)	*The Lord* 20
11 **27**	*The Lord* 19:8	15 **1, 2**	*Life* 2
11 (41, 42)	*The Lord* 20	15 **1–5**	*The Lord* 32:6
12 (2)	*Sacred Scripture* 40:4	15 **1–6**	*Life* 29
12 **23, 28**	*The Lord* 35:7	15 **4**	*Life* 102
12 **24**	*Life* 99	15 **4, 5**	*The Lord* 35:8
12 (25)	*Life* 99	15 **4, 5, 6**	*The Lord* 61:1
12 **27, 28**	*The Lord* 13	15 **5**	*Sacred Scripture* 114; *Life* 17, 102
12 **31**	*The Lord* 13	15 **5, 7**	*Sacred Scripture* 89
12 **34**	*The Lord* 10	15 **7**	*Sacred Scripture* 51:3
12 **36**	*The Lord* 32:6	15 **7, 10**	*Life* 102
12 *36*	*Life* 17	15 **8**	*Life* 2
12 **36, 46**	*The Lord* 1	15 **10**	*Life* 38
[12 **36, 46**]	*The Lord* 2	15 **14**	*Life* 104
12 (44, 45, 49)	*The Lord* 20	15 **14, 16**	*Life* 2
12 **45**	*The Lord* 32:5	15 (21)	*The Lord* 20
12 **46**	*The Lord* 32:6	15 **25**	*The Lord* 10
12 **47, 48**	*The Lord* 25	15 **26**	*The Lord* 51:1
12 (47–48)	*Sacred Scripture* 51:7		

16 (5)	*The Lord* 20	20 **31**	*The Lord* 19:8
16 *5, 16*	*The Lord* 35:11	21 *15, 16, 17*	*Sacred Scripture* 29
16 **7**	*The Lord* 51:1		
16 **8, 10**	*Sacred Scripture* 85	GALATIANS	
16 **11**	*The Lord* 13	[4 (4)]	*The Lord* 3
16 **13**	*The Lord* 51:1		
16 **14, 15**	*The Lord* 51:1	REVELATION	
16 **15**	*The Lord* 32:4	1 *2*	*The Lord* 52
16 **27**	*The Lord* 31	1 *7*	*The Lord* 26:1
16 **28**	*The Lord* 31, 35:11	1 **8, 11**	*The Lord* 36:2
[16 *28*]	*The Lord* 37:3	1 (8, 11, 17)	*Sacred Scripture* 98
16 **32**	*The Lord* 32:2	1 *10*	*The Lord* 52
16 **33**	*The Lord* 13	1 (13)	*The Lord* 26:1
17 **1, 5**	*The Lord* 13, 35:7	1 **13, 17**	*The Lord* 36:2
17 *2*	*The Lord* 32:4	1 *13* (and following)	*The Lord* 27:2
17 (3, 8, 21, 23, 25)	*The Lord* 20	1 (13–16)	*Sacred Scripture* 98
17 *5*	*The Lord* 1, 30:1	1 *14*	*Sacred Scripture* 49:5
[17 *5, 24*]	*The Lord* 37:3	1 *16*	*The Lord* 35:6
17 **7**	*The Lord* 32:3	2 **1, 2, 4, 5**	*Life* 2
17 **10**	*The Lord* 32:4, 35:8	2 *5, 16, 21, 22*	*Life* 103
[17 *10*]	*The Lord* 29:2, 60	2 **7**	*Life* 99
17 **11, 13**	*The Lord* 35:11	2 **7, 11, 29**	*The Lord* 51:5
17 **12**	*The Lord* 11	2 **8**	*The Lord* 36:2
17 **21**	*The Lord* 32:4	2 (8)	*Sacred Scripture* 98
17 *22, 23*	*The Lord* 61:1	2 **8, 9**	*Life* 2
17 **22, 23, 26**	*Life* 84:2	2 **11**	*Life* 99
17 *23*	*The Lord* 32:6	2 **12, 13, 16**	*Life* 2
[18 (1–14)]	*The Lord* 16:5	2 **17**	*Life* 99
18 **9**	*The Lord* 11	2 **18, 19**	*Life* 2
19 *1–5*	*The Lord* 16:7	2 **26, 28**	*Life* 99
[19 (1–30)]	*The Lord* 16:5	3 **1, 2, 3**	*Life* 2
19 (7)	*The Lord* 9	3 *1, 6, 13, 22*	*The Lord* 51:5
19 (17–37)	*The Lord* 12	3 (3)	*Life* 103
19 *24*	*The Lord* 11	[3 (4–5)]	*Supplements* 33
19 **25, 26, 27**	*The Lord* 35:4	3 **5**	*Life* 99
19 **28**	*The Lord* 11	3 **7, 8**	*Life* 2
19 **30**	*The Lord* 11	3 **12**	*Life* 99
19 **36, 37**	*The Lord* 11	[3 (12)]	*The Lord* 61:1
[20 (1–18)]	*The Lord* 16:5	3 **14, 15, 19**	*Life* 2
20 *17*	*The Lord* 35:11	3 **15, 16**	*Life* 71
20 (19, 26)	*The Lord* 35:10	3 **20**	*Life* 57
20 *20*	*The Lord* 35:9	3 **21**	*Life* 99
20 (21)	*The Lord* 20	4 *1*	*The Lord* 52
20 **22**	*The Lord* 51:1	4 **2, 3, 10**	*The Lord* 41
20 **27, 28**	*The Lord* 35:9, 41	4 **5**	*The Lord* 51:5
20 **29**	*Faith* 10	5 *1*	*The Lord* 52

5 **1, 3, 5, 6, 7, 8, 14**	*The Lord* 41	17 4	*Sacred Scripture* 44:4
5 **6**	*The Lord* 51:5	17 5	*Life* 79:1
5 9	*Sacred Scripture* 86	17 **14**	*The Lord* 42
6 *1*	*The Lord* 52	18 **2**	*The Lord* 48:6
[6 **1–8**]	*Sacred Scripture* 12:1	18 **3**	*Life* 79:1
7 [**4–8**]	*Sacred Scripture* 11	19 **2**	*Life* 79:1
7 **17**	*Sacred Scripture* 2:4	19 **10**	*The Lord* 7, 51:5
[9 **1–3, 7–11**]	*Sacred Scripture* 13:1	19 **11–18**	*Sacred Scripture* 9
9 *17*	*The Lord* 52	19 (11–18)	*Sacred Scripture* 25
10 **11**	*Sacred Scripture* 86	19 **16**	*The Lord* 42
11 (8)	*The Lord* 64:2	19 (19)	*Sacred Scripture* 25
11 **11**	*The Lord* 49:1	20 **12, 13**	*Life* 2
11 **16, 17**	*The Lord* 37:3	20 **13**	*Life* 105
11 (19)	*Life* 60	21 (chapter cited)	*The Lord* preface;
12 (chapter cited)	*Faith* 57; *Supplements*		*Sacred Scripture* 43
	16:2	21, 22 (chapters cited)	*The Lord* 61:1
12, 13 (chapters cited)	*Faith* 55	21 *1*	*Supplements* 8, 9, 18
12 **1–8, 13–17**	*Faith* 58–59	[21 *1*]	*The Lord* 65
12 *3*	*Sacred Scripture* 44:4; *Life* 61	21 **1, 2, 3, 5**	*The Lord* 62:1
[12 *4*]	*Faith* 56	21 *1, 2, 5*	*Supplements* 12
13 (chapter cited)	*Faith* 60	21 **2**	*The Lord* 63
13 *1*	*Sacred Scripture* 44:4	[21 (2)]	*The Lord* 61:1
13 (1)	*Life* 61	21 (2, 9)	*Sacred Scripture* 87:2
13 (1–10)	*Faith* 60	[21 *5*]	*The Lord* 65
13 (2, 4, 11)	*Faith* 60	21 *6*	*The Lord* 36:2
12 (10–12)	*Supplements* 30	21 (6)	*Sacred Scripture* 98
13 (11–18)	*Faith* 60	21 **9, 10**	*The Lord* 63
13 (15)	*The Lord* 48:7	21 *10*	*The Lord* 52
13 **18**	*Faith* 60	[21 **11–12, 16–21**]	*Sacred Scripture* 10
14 **8**	*Life* 79:1	[21 (14, 19)]	*Sacred Scripture* 42
14 **13**	*The Lord* 51:5; *Life* 2, 105	21 **17, 18, 19, 20**	*Sacred Scripture* 43
14 **14**	*The Lord* 26:1	21 (18–21)	*Sacred Scripture* 36
16 *11*	*Life* 103	22 *1*	*Sacred Scripture* 2:4
16 (13, 14)	*The Lord* 48:7	22 **12**	*Life* 2, 105
17, 18, 19 (chapters cited)	*Faith* 55	22 **12, 13**	*The Lord* 36:2
17 **1, 2**	*Life* 79:1	22 (13)	*Sacred Scripture* 98
17 *3*	*The Lord* 52	22 **17**	*The Lord* 51:5
17 (3)	*Sacred Scripture* 25	22 (17)	*Sacred Scripture* 87:2
17 (3, 7)	*Life* 61	22 **19**	*Sacred Scripture* 13:4

Table of Parallel Passages

The following table indicates passages in *The Lord, Sacred Scripture, Life, Faith,* and *Supplements* that parallel passages in Swedenborg's other theological works. Parallel passages, also called repeated passages, are portions of text that Swedenborg appears to have copied from one place to another—usually from an earlier work into a later one, but sometimes even from one part of a work to another. Because he copied material quite frequently in this manner, a passage may have more than one parallel. The study of such parallels is of special interest because the content of one version may shed light on the slightly different content of another. Furthermore, a comparison of parallels may reveal how Swedenborg has reshaped his material in transposing it. Such reshaping can sometimes be seen to have occurred even when a later passage is presented as a direct quotation from an earlier work.

The table draws on John Faulkner Potts's *Swedenborg Concordance* (1902, London: Swedenborg Society), 6:859–864, and on the tables of parallel passages in various editions of Swedenborg's works. The content of these tables has been selectively imported, since some of them adhere to a broader definition of a parallel passage than the table here. The source editions are: *Tria Opuscula: De Scriptura Sacra seu Verbo Domini, ab Experientia; De Ultimo Judicio; De Praeceptis Decalogi,* edited by N. Bruce Rogers, B. Erikson Odhner, Prescott A. Rogers, and others (1997, Bryn Athyn, Pennsylvania: Academy of the New Church), ccviii–ccxvii; *Three Short Works: The Sacred Scripture of Word of the Lord from Experience, The Last Judgment, The Precepts of the Decalogue,* translated by N. Bruce Rogers (1997, Bryn Athyn, Pennsylvania: General Church of the New Jerusalem), ccxxxii–ccxli; *Quatuor Doctrinae Novae Hierosolymae,* edited by N. Bruce Rogers, ([1763] 2014, Bryn Athyn, Pennsylvania: Academy of the New Church), cv, clxxxv–clxxxvi, ccxli, cclxxvii; *Four Doctrines of the New Jerusalem,* translated by N. Bruce Rogers, ([1763] 2014, Bryn Athyn, Pennsylvania: General Church of the New Jerusalem), cxxxiii, cclvii–cclviii, cccxlix, cdlxxxvii–cdlxxxviii; *Sapientia Angelica de Divino Amore et de Divina Sapientia,* edited by N. Bruce Rogers ([1763] 1999, Bryn Athyn, Pennsylvania: Academy of the New Church), cxcix; *Angelic*

Wisdom Regarding Divine Love and Wisdom, translated by N. Bruce Rogers ([1763] 1999, Bryn Athyn, Pennsylvania: General Church of the New Jerusalem), ccxliii; *Sapientia Angelica de Divina Providentia,* edited by N. Bruce Rogers ([1764] 2003, Bryn Athyn, Pennsylvania: Academy of the New Church), cclxxxvii; *Angelic Wisdom Regarding Divine Providence,* translated by N. Bruce Rogers ([1764] 2003, Bryn Athyn, Pennsylvania: General Church of the New Jerusalem), cccxlviii; *Apocalypsis Revelata,* edited by N. Bruce Rogers ([1766] 2010, Bryn Athyn, Pennsylvania: Academy of the New Church), 2:ccclxxxiii–ccclxxxiv; *The Apocalypse Revealed,* translated by N. Bruce Rogers ([1766] 2010, Bryn Athyn, Pennsylvania: General Church of the New Jerusalem), 2:cdlxxxvii–cdlxxxviii; *Delitiae Sapientiae de Amore Conjugiali,* edited by N. Bruce Rogers ([1768] 1995, Bryn Athyn, Pennsylvania: Academy of the New Church), cdxv–cdxvii; *Married Love,* translated by N. Bruce Rogers ([1768] 1995, Bryn Athyn, Pennsylvania: General Church of the New Jerusalem), dlvii–dlix; *Vera Christiana Religio,* edited by Freya H. Fitzpatrick ([1771] 2009, Bryn Athyn, Pennsylvania: Academy of the New Church), 2:cdxxxi–cdxxxix.

Reference numbers in this table correspond to Swedenborg's section numbers; subsection numbers are separated from section numbers by a colon. Numbering of passages from *Spiritual Experiences* follows the numbering in *Experientiae Spirituales,* edited by J. Durban Odhner (1983–1997, Bryn Athyn, Pennsylvania: Academy of the New Church, 6 vols.).

The Lord	Parallel Passage
56	*Revelation Explained* 1091:2
60	*Divine Providence* 263:1
61	*Divine Providence* 263:2–3
64	*Revelation Unveiled* 880; *True Christianity* 782
64:1	*New Jerusalem* 6

Sacred Scripture	Parallel Passage
1	*True Christianity* 189
2	*True Christianity* 190
3	*True Christianity* 191
4	*True Christianity* 192–193
5	*True Christianity* 194
6	*True Christianity* 195
9	*True Christianity* 196
10	*True Christianity* 197
14	*True Christianity* 198
17	*True Christianity* 199
18:1–3	*True Christianity* 200:1–3
20	Draft of "Sacred Scripture" 7:1–2 (Potts's numbering) = 17 (Hayward's numbering); *True Christianity* 201
21	Draft of "Sacred Scripture" 7:3 (Potts's numbering) = 18

TABLE OF PARALLEL PASSAGES

	(Hayward's numbering); *True Christianity* 202	52	*True Christianity* 228
		53	*True Christianity* 229
22	*Draft of "Sacred Scripture"* 7:4 (Potts's numbering) = 19 (Hayward's numbering); *True Christianity* 204	54	*True Christianity* 227
		55	*True Christianity* 229
		56	*True Christianity* 230
		57–58	*True Christianity* 231
23	*Draft of "Sacred Scripture"* 7:5 (Potts's numbering) = 19 (Hayward's numbering); *True Christianity* 205	60	*True Christianity* 232
		61	*Draft of "Sacred Scripture"* 9 (Potts's numbering) = 24 (Hayward's numbering); *Revelation Unveiled* 255:5–6; *True Christianity* 233
24	*Draft of "Sacred Scripture"* 7:6 (Potts's numbering) = 20 (Hayward's numbering); *True Christianity* 206		
		62–63	*True Christianity* 234
		64	*True Christianity* 235
25	*Draft of "Sacred Scripture"* 7:8 (Potts's numbering) = 21 (Hayward's numbering); *True Christianity* 207	65–66	*True Christianity* 237
		67	*True Christianity* 236
		68–69	*True Christianity* 239
26:1–2	*True Christianity* 208	70	*True Christianity* 240
26:3–5	*Spiritual Experiences* 3605.5; *Draft of "Sacred Scripture"* 1; *Revelation Unveiled* 255:2–4; *True Christianity* 277	71	*True Christianity* 241:1–2
		72	*True Christianity* 241:3
		73–75	*True Christianity* 242
		76	*True Christianity* 243
27–28	*True Christianity* 210	79	*True Christianity* 247
29	*True Christianity* 211	80–81	*True Christianity* 248
33	*True Christianity* 213	82–83	*True Christianity* 249
37–39	*True Christianity* 214	84	*True Christianity* 250
38	*Marriage Love* 314:2	85–86	*True Christianity* 251
40–41	*True Christianity* 215	87	*True Christianity* 252
42	*True Christianity* 216	88	*True Christianity* 253
43	*True Christianity* 217	90	*Draft of "Sacred Scripture"* 4 (Potts's numbering) = 14 (Hayward's numbering); *True Christianity* 278
44	*True Christianity* 218		
45	*True Christianity* 219		
46	*True Christianity* 220		
47	*True Christianity* 221	90:1	*Spiritual Experiences* 4671
48	*True Christianity* 222	91–92	*True Christianity* 254
49	*True Christianity* 223	93	*True Christianity* 255
50	*True Christianity* 225	94	*True Christianity* 256
51:1–7, 9	*True Christianity* 226		

95	*True Christianity* 257
96a	*True Christianity* 258
96b	*True Christianity* 259
97	*Revelation Unveiled* 239:2–6; *True Christianity* 260
98	*True Christianity* 261
99	*True Christianity* 109:1
100	*True Christianity* 263
101	*True Christianity* 264
102	Draft of "Sacred Scripture" 15:1 (Potts's numbering) = 36 (Hayward's numbering); *True Christianity* 279:1–2
103	Draft of "Sacred Scripture" 15:2–4 (Potts's numbering) = 37 (Hayward's numbering); *True Christianity* 265
104	Draft of "Sacred Scripture" 17:1 (Potts's numbering) = 40 (Hayward's numbering); *True Christianity* 267
105	Draft of "Sacred Scripture" 17:1 (Potts's numbering) = 40 (Hayward's numbering); *True Christianity* 268
106	Draft of "Sacred Scripture" 17:1 (Potts's numbering) = 41 (Hayward's numbering)
107	Draft of "Sacred Scripture" 17:2 (Potts's numbering) = 41 (Hayward's numbering); *True Christianity* 269
108	Draft of "Sacred Scripture" 18:2 (Potts's numbering) = 46 (Hayward's numbering)
109	*True Christianity* 269
110–111	Draft of "Sacred Scripture" 17:3–4 (Potts's numbering) = 42–43 (Hayward's numbering); *True Christianity* 270
112	Draft of "Sacred Scripture" 17:5 (Potts's numbering) = 44 (Hayward's numbering); *True Christianity* 271
113	*True Christianity* 272
115	*True Christianity* 273
116	*True Christianity* 274
117	Draft of "Sacred Scripture" 15:5 (Potts's numbering) = 38 (Hayward's numbering); *True Christianity* 275
118	*True Christianity* 276

Life	**Parallel Passage**
19	*Life* 69
43	*New Jerusalem* 28, 29, 32; *True Christianity* 397
53–55	*Revelation Unveiled* 529; *True Christianity* 282, 283
56	*True Christianity* 286
57	*True Christianity* 285
59	*True Christianity* 284
60	*True Christianity* 285
67	*True Christianity* 309–311
69	*Life* 19
111	*Revelation Explained* 1009:2; *Marriage Love* 153a:2, 494:2; *True Christianity* 316

Faith	**Parallel Passage**
34	Draft of "Supplements" 366 (Rogers's numbering) = 358 (Potts's numbering)
34–36	*Revelation Unveiled* 67; *Survey* 116; *True Christianity* 2
39	Draft of "Supplements" 367 (Rogers's numbering) = 359–360 (Potts's numbering)

42	*True Christianity* 391:2
43	*True Christianity* 391:3
59	*Revelation Unveiled* contents of Revelation 12

Supplements	Parallel Passage
32	*True Christianity* 693:3, 792
34	*Marriage Love* 30; *True Christianity* 793
36	*True Christianity* 793
37	*True Christianity* 794
39	*True Christianity* 806
40	*True Christianity* 807
41	*True Christianity* 808
42	*True Christianity* 809
43	*True Christianity* 811
44	*True Christianity* 810
45	*True Christianity* 812
48	*True Christianity* 800–801
49	*Draft of "Supplements"* 24 (Rogers's numbering) = 23 (Potts's numbering); *True Christianity* 802
50	*True Christianity* 804
51	*True Christianity* 805
51:2	*Draft of "Supplements"* 22 (Rogers's numbering) = 21 (Potts's numbering)
56	*True Christianity* 817
57	*True Christianity* 818
59	*True Christianity* 820:1
61	*True Christianity* 822
63	*True Christianity* 823
64	*Draft of "Supplements"* 60 (Rogers's numbering) = 59 (Potts's numbering); *True Christianity* 824:1
65	*True Christianity* 824:2
66	*Spiritual Experiences* 5834; *Draft of "Supplements"* 69 (Rogers's numbering) = 68 (Potts's numbering); *True Christianity* 102:3, 824:2, 827
67	*Spiritual Experiences* 6091; *Draft of "Supplements"* 62–63 (Rogers's numbering) = 61–62 (Potts's numbering); *True Christianity* 826
68	*True Christianity* 828
69	*True Christianity* 829
70	*True Christianity* 830
73	*True Christianity* 835
74	*Divine Love and Wisdom* 11; *True Christianity* 836
76	*True Christianity* 840
79	*True Christianity* 841
80	*Draft of "Supplements"* 249, 257 (Rogers's numbering) = 252, 260 (Potts's numbering); *True Christianity* 842
81	*Draft of "Supplements"* 251–252 (Rogers's numbering) = 254–255 (Potts's numbering); *True Christianity* 843
82	*Draft of "Supplements"* 312 (Rogers's numbering) = 292–293 (Potts's numbering); *True Christianity* 844–845
82:2	*Draft of "Supplements"* 254 (Rogers's numbering) = 257 (Potts's numbering)

Index to the Shorter Works of 1763

Reference numbers in this index correspond to Swedenborg's section numbers in *The Lord, Sacred Scripture* (here abbreviated as *SS*), *Life, Faith,* and *Supplements (Supp)*. Subsection numbers are separated from section numbers by a colon.

A

Action (deeds; doing; works). *See also* Sin
    abstaining from evil and doing good as though on our own, *Supp* 46:2–3
    acting as though we are on our own, *Life* 22, 101, 104, 107
    action and thought working together, *Life* 1, 47
    civic, moral, and spiritual good works, *Life* 12
    the connection between caring and doing good, *Life* 9; *Faith* 13, 68
    the desire to do good leading to a desire for truth, *Faith* 13
    the desire to do what is good developing in our will, *Faith* 33
    giving an account of our deeds, *Life* 105
    good actions (deeds) as coming from the Lord
        to the extent that we are in the Lord, *Life* 21
        not from ourselves, *Life* 58, 72; *Supp* 46:2
        in spiritual people, *Life* 16, 50
    good actions of earthly people coming from themselves, *Life* 16, 108
    good deeds compared to different kinds of gold, *Life* 10
    knowledge coming to life for us only when we act on it, *Life* 27
    the Lord teaching good and loving actions, *Life* 73
    loving to do good because it is good, *Faith* 21
    our being judged according to our deeds, *Life* 31
    our being unable to do anything good on our own, *Life* 17, 24, 29, 31, 58
    our deeds (actions) being good to the extent that
        they come from God (the Lord) and not from ourselves, *Life* 9–11, 13, 29
        they come from love of our neighbor, *Life* 72
        we are purified from our evils, *Life* 30:1
        we turn our backs on evil deeds, *Life* 21, 24, 72, 114; *Supp* 16:2
    religion being about doing what is good, *Life* 31
    salvation and works (*see under* Salvation)
    the sequence of will, understanding, and bodily action, *Faith* 15–16
    thinking coming from the understanding and actions coming from the will, *Life* 42
    truths as the means by which the good we do becomes manifest, *Life* 39
    turning our backs on evil deeds because they are sins (*see under* Evil)
    uniting with the good others do and not with their personality, *Faith* 21
    wisdom dwelling with good actions that come from love, *SS* 74
    the Word showing that religion is about how we live and that the religious way to live is to do good, *Life* 2
    works making us part of the church, *Life* 2
Adultery. *See also* Chastity; Fornication; Marriage
    adultery being the height of wickedness, *Life* 74
    different meanings of "adultery," *Life* 74, 78, 79
    the sixth commandment, on adultery, *Life* 74–79
    those who do not regard adultery as a sin not being Christian or having any religion, *Life* 77
    turning our backs on adultery (as a sin), *Life* 75–77, 89
Africans
    African spirits scoffing at the religious beliefs of European spirits, *Supp* 78
    Africans having deeper natures than people of other religions, *Supp* 73, 75
    Africans in the spiritual world, *Supp* 73–78
    Swedenborg's interaction with, *SS* 108; *Supp* 77–78
    angelic spirits communicating with Africans, *Supp* 76
Ancient times (people), *SS* 20, 23:1–2, 102, 117
The ancient Word, *SS* 102, 103. *See also* The Word
Angels. *See also* Heaven; Human; Life after death; Spirits
    an angel appearing to be Moses teaching Jews in the spiritual world, *Supp* 80
    angel guardians, *SS* 26:2–5, 97:2–5
    angelic spirits communicating with Africans, *Supp* 76

Angels *(continued)*
  angels and human beings
    angels (and spirits) being people (human beings), *SS* 70; *Faith* 19:2; *Supp* 5, 34, 74
    angels being present when we read the Word, *Lord* 37:2; *SS* 64:1, 67
    goodness united to truth making love and wisdom for angels and for us, *Life* 32:2
    how humans become angels, *Lord* 33:2; *Supp* 5
    our companionship (union) with angels
      through correspondence, *SS* 67:6
      through the Word, *SS* 49:5, 63, 67:6, 68, 69, 114
    the people of the earliest church talking with angels, *SS* 21
    the spiritual meaning making the Word spiritual for us and for angels, *SS* 5
  angels and spirits
    believed to be made of wind, *Supp* 3
    everything visible in the spiritual world corresponding to the feelings of, *Faith* 63:2, 3; *Supp* 23
    the Holy Spirit being the Lord's presence with us through, *Lord* 46:4
    the light in which spirits and angels live coming from the Lord as the sun, *Supp* 20
    reading the Word, *SS* 70
    Swedenborg being granted companionship with, *SS* 70, 93, 116:1; *Faith* 3
  angels and wisdom (*see under* Wisdom)
  angels breathing just as we do, *Lord* 51:3; *Faith* 19:2
  angels focusing on the spiritual (heavenly) meaning of the Word, *Lord* 37:2; *SS* 26:1
    heavenly angels focusing on the heavenly meaning and spiritual angels focusing on the spiritual meaning, *SS* 63, 64:1, 65, 67
  angels having a human form, *Lord* 32:8
  angels having the same Word that we have in the world, *Lord* 2
  angels of the heavenly kingdom (heavenly angels), *SS* 6:1, 63, 64:1, 65, 67, 86
  the angels of the lowest heaven being the "sheep," *Supp* 10
  angels of the spiritual kingdom (spiritual angels), *SS* 6:1, 63, 64:1, 65, 67, 86
  angels teaching us after death, *SS* 93, 116:1; *Life* 49, 65; *Faith* 30
  Catholics who become angels, *Supp* 58
  children in heaven being raised by angels, *Supp* 58
  the emanations that radiate from angels, *Lord* 46:3
  the life of angels as an embodiment of caring and their form as an embodiment of faith, *Faith* 31
  reckonings being carried out by angels before the Last Judgment, *Supp* 26, 27
  the speech of angels, *SS* 90:2
  Swedenborg's conversation with an angel regarding faith divorced (separated) from caring, *Faith* 41–43
  the threeness in angels, *Lord* 46:3
Animals, differences between humans and, *Life* 15, 86:1, 86:5; *Supp* 33. *See also* Beasts
Arians, *Supp* 88. *See also* Heresies
Aristotle, *SS* 115:3
The ark of the covenant, the law in, *Lord* 9; *SS* 46; *Life* 55, 60. *See also* Covenant; The Ten Commandments
Athanasian statement of faith, *Lord* 21, 29:1, 35:1–2, 55:6; *Life* 3
  asserting that God and a human being in the Lord are one person, *Lord* 60
  the doctrinal statement rewritten, *Lord* 58
  on the Lord's human nature, *Lord* 59
  text of the doctrinal statement, *Lord* 56
  on "a trinity of persons," *Lord* 57, 58
Atonement, *Lord* 18:1. *See also* The Crucifixion; Redemption

B

Babylon, *Faith* 49, 55; *Supp* 58. *See also* Control
Baldness, *SS* 35. *See also* Hair
Battle (fight). *See also* Trials
  doing battle with evils, *Lord* 33:1; *Life* 66:2, 93–100
  the Lord alone fighting within us against evils, *Life* 96
  the Lord's suffering on the cross being his last battle, *Lord* 12, 14:12, 33:3, 34, 35:3, 65
  trials being battles against hell, *Lord* 33:1; *Life* 98
Beasts, of the dragon in the Book of Revelation, *Faith* 60. *See also* Animals
Being. *See also* Essence
  the complete series of being, becoming, and achieving full manifestation, *SS* 28
Belief (conception; notion). *See also* Athanasian statement of faith; Conviction; Doubt; Faith alone; Heresies; Thought
  African spirits scoffing at the religious beliefs of European spirits, *Supp* 78
  belief in the Lord, *Lord* 17:2, 32:6–7, 35:2, 55:5; *Life* 48, 51; *Faith* 34, 36
  beliefs of the present-day faith, *Faith* 39
  beliefs of the true Christian faith, *Faith* 35
  beliefs that seem to require faith only, *Life* 47–49
  false beliefs (misconceptions), *Supp* 3, 33, 46
    arising from not thinking intelligently, *Lord* 19:1; *Faith* 46, 47
    being led out of, *SS* 92, 93

Belief *(continued)*
  false beliefs *(continued)*
    the belief that no one can fulfill the law, *Life* 63:1–2, 64
    the belief that the Father sent the Son to make satisfaction for the human race, *Faith* 38, 39, 42, 44
    convincing ourselves of false beliefs as condemning (harming) us if genuine truth is destroyed, *SS* 92–96a
    engendered by a faith divorced from caring, *Faith* 45
    about God, *Supp* 74
    about the Last Judgment, *Supp* 3–5
    about life after death, *SS* 116:2; *Supp* 32, 33
    about the Lord, *Lord* 15:1, 18:1–3, 19, 65; *Faith* 44; *Supp* 89
      the Lord bearing our damnation, *Lord* 18:1, 2; *Faith* 44
      the Lord fulfilling the law, *Lord* 8, 11, 18:1–2
      the Lord's suffering on the cross, *Lord* 15:1, 18:1–2, 65
    about salvation (*see under* Salvation)
    about sin, *Lord* 15:1
    about the soul, *Supp* 32, 33
      body and soul being reunited on the day of the Last Judgment, *Supp* 72:2
      the soul being a breath (air; breeze), *Supp* 3, 4, 6, 72:2
Body. *See also* Hair; Heart; Heart and lungs; Human; Sight; Soul
  the belief that body and soul are reunited on the day of the Last Judgment, *Supp* 72:2
  the divine nature in the Lord being like the soul within the body, *Lord* 29:1–2, 32:7, 34:4, 35:2, 35:11
  the inner meaning within the outer meaning compared to a soul within a body, *SS* 4, 5, 9, 10
  Jesus' body or human side being made divine, *Lord* 29:2
  the Lord's rising after death with his whole body, *Lord* 35:9–10
  the spiritual body, *Supp* 3, 36
The Book of Jasher, *SS* 103:3. *See also* The ancient Word
Breath. *See also* Heart and lungs
  all of heaven's breathing originating with the Lord, *Lord* 51:3
  angels breathing just as we do, *Lord* 51:3; *Faith* 19:2
  the belief that the soul is a breath (air; breeze), *Supp* 3, 4, 6, 72:2
  "spirit" or "soul" meaning the life that depends on breathing, *Lord* 47:1

Britain. *See also* London
  the British in the spiritual world, *Supp* 39–47
    the British community, *Supp* 41
    British preachers (elders) in the spiritual world who believe in faith alone, *Life* 7; *Supp* 42:2–3, 44, 45
    their governance, *Supp* 40
    their location in the spiritual world, *Supp* 40
  the intellectual light resulting from freedom in Britain, *Supp* 40
Business, the Dutch being devoted to a spiritual love of, *Supp* 48:3, 49:2, 51:1. *See also* Occupation; Usefulness

C

Calvin, John, *Supp* 54. *See also* Protestants; The Reformation
Canaan, *SS* 102; *Supp* 82. *See also* Middle East
Caring (charity). *See also* Faith; Love
  caring as love for our neighbor, *Faith* 20, 22
  Christian charity, *Life* 114
  the connection between caring and doing good, *Life* 9; *Faith* 13, 68
  faith and caring
    acting together to do useful things, *Faith* 17, 19:2
    angels being embodiments of, *Faith* 31
    caring as the essence of faith, *Faith* 22, 69
    caring becoming manifest through faith, *Faith* 17
    a caring faith in those who have turned toward the Lord and away from evils, *Faith* 23, 30
    the church existing by means of its faith and love (caring), *SS* 77; *Faith* 69
    damnation resulting from a lack of faith and caring, *Faith* 68
    faith coming from caring, *Faith* 31, 32, 68
      spirits who are devoted to, *Supp* 42:2
    falsity destroying faith and caring, *Faith* 29
    given by the Lord to the extent that we turn our backs on evil deeds because they are sins, *Supp* 49:2
    knowledge about goodness and truth as a resource for forming a caring faith, *Faith* 27, 31–33
    needing to be lived, *Supp* 49
    our intelligence depending on our caring faith, *Faith* 29
    the priority between caring and faith, *Faith* 31
    rams and sheep meaning people devoted to (a faith prompted by) caring, *Faith* 61, 67
    a saving faith being found only in people who are caring, *Faith* 24
    the union of, *Faith* 18, 19, 29, 43, 67; *Supp* 46

Caring *(continued)*
    faith divorced from caring (*see under* Faith)
    spiritual love being caring, *Faith* 51
    spiritual love coming only from a life of caring, *Supp* 21
    spiritual warmth being caring, *Faith* 32
    wanting to be of use as the origin of caring, *Faith* 14
Catholic Church. *See* Roman Catholic Church
Caves, in the spiritual world, *Life* 26. *See also* The spiritual world; The world of spirits
Chastity, loved by those who turn their backs on adultery, *Life* 89. *See also* Adultery
Children, *Life* 64; *Supp* 58, 77
Christ, *Lord* 55:1. *See also* Jesus; The Lord
Christianity (the Christian church; Christians). *See also* The church; The Reformation; Religion; *and names of specific denominations*
    beliefs distinctively Christian, *Life* 77, 111
    beliefs of the true Christian faith, *Lord* 29:1, 55:2–4; *Faith* 34–37
    the Book of Revelation dealing with the state of the Christian church, *Lord* 62:1; *Faith* 55
    Christian charity, *Life* 114
    the Christian church called "the church militant," *Life* 98
    Christians who read the Word (and worship the Lord) being at the center of the heavens (the world of spirits), *SS* 105:3, 106; *Supp* 48:1
    the early Christian church having no knowledge of correspondences, *SS* 24
    false teachings of the Christian church regarding the doctrine of faith alone, *Life* 4; *Faith* 55
    heresies in Christianity, *SS* 92
    introducing children to the Christian religion by teaching them the Ten Commandments, *Life* 64
    the universal interaction between European countries and the nations outside the church, *SS* 108
The church, *SS* 108; *Life* 106. *See also* Christianity; Jewish religion; The new church; Preachers; Religion; Teachings; Worship; *and names of specific denominations*
    all names in the Word having to do with matters of (heaven and) the church, *SS* 15:1, 2; *Faith* 49
    the belief that deeds have nothing to do with salvation or the church, *Faith* 68
    a body of teaching being the source of a church, *SS* 43
    the Christian church called "the church militant," *Life* 98
    the church being the church because of the Lord, *Lord* 55:4–5
    the church being within us, *SS* 78
    the church existing by means of its faith and love (caring), *SS* 77; *Faith* 69
    the church functioning as the heart and lungs in the human being that makes up heaven, *SS* 105
    the church having divorced faith from caring, *Life* 9
    a church where the Word is read and the Lord is known, *SS* 104, 110
    the end of the church, *Lord* preface, 15:2; *SS* 112; *Faith* 49, 55
        the Lord coming into the world at, *Lord* 3, 5, 33:3
    goodness united to truth making a person a true member of the church, *Life* 32:2
    heaven and the church being called the Lord's kingdom, *Lord* 42
    "a human being" meaning a church, *Lord* 16:7
    Jerusalem meaning the church, *Lord* 63, 64; *Supp* 79
    the marriage of the Lord and the church (*see under* Marriage)
    the people of the earliest church talking with angels, *SS* 21
    rituals in the ancient churches being based on correspondences, *SS* 20:2
    the state of (the world and) the church
        being changed by the Lord's Coming, *SS* 99
        compared to times of day, *Supp* 13
        before and after the Last Judgment, *Supp* 2, 8, 11, 13
    the tabernacle representing heaven and the church, *SS* 46
    the Word
        being entirely about the Lord (heaven) and the church, *SS* 112:1; *Faith* 65
        the church depending on our understanding of, *SS* 76, 77, 79, 114
        the Lord as the supreme prophet representing the church and, *Lord* 15:8, 16:5
        people of every religion being dependent on the union of the Lord and heaven with the church through the Word, *SS* 105
    prophets
        meaning the body of teaching the church draws from the Word, *Lord* 15:8, 28
        representing the Word and the church, *Lord* 15:2, 15:4–8
    providing enlightenment for people outside the church, *SS* 106, 114
    the spiritual meaning of the Word
        being opened at the close of the church, *SS* 9
        having to do with the church, *SS* 80
        uniting the Lord to the church, *SS* 18:1
    works making us part of the church, *Life* 2

Cicero, *SS* 115:3
Circumcision, *Faith* 51, 54
City. *See also* The civic; Communities
   cities in the spiritual world, *Supp* 42–43, 51:1, 79
   a city meaning a body of teaching, *Lord* 64:1 and note a, 64:4
The civic. *See also* City
   civic, moral, and spiritual good works, *Life* 12
   civic, rational, and spiritual law, *Life* 12
   morality and civic-mindedness depending on spiritual goodness, *Life* 13, 14
   obeying the law for civic and moral reasons but not religious reasons, *Life* 63:1–2, 64
The civil
   the Ten Commandments as civil, moral, and spiritual laws, *Life* 53
The close of the age, the Lord's predictions about, *SS* 14; *Supp* 10
Clothing, in the spiritual world, *Supp* 50, 77
Commandments, *Life* 31, 104. *See also* The Ten Commandments
Communities. *See also* City
   the British community in the spiritual world, *Supp* 41
   communities in the world of spirits, *Supp* 21, 57
   the communities of heaven, *SS* 107, 113; *Supp* 21
   our connection to a community in the spiritual world, *Supp* 21, 57
Control. *See also* Governance; Power
   control in marriage *vs.* mutual love, *Supp* 51:2
   the love of controlling others, *Faith* 49, 55; *Supp* 61–63
Conviction. *See also* Belief; Doubt; Heresies
   convincing ourselves of false beliefs, *SS* 91–96a; *Faith* 11
Correspondence
   correspondences in
     the Book of Job, *SS* 20:2
     Egyptian hieroglyphs and ancient fables, *SS* 20:2
     the Jewish religion, *SS* 20:2, 22, 23:4
     rituals in the ancient churches, *SS* 20:2
     the world of spirits, *Faith* 56
   correspondences in the spiritual world, *Faith* 63:2, 3; *Supp* 21, 23, 50, 57, 77
   everything on earth corresponding to something spiritual, *SS* 20, 23
   the knowledge of correspondences, *SS* 7, 20, 21–24, 102, 117
     being necessary to see the spiritual meaning of the Word, *SS* 9, 10, 56
   the Lord speaking in correspondences while on earth, *SS* 17, 20:3, 40:2, 3; *Life* 66:2
   our union with angels through correspondence, *SS* 67:6
   the people of the earliest church talking with angels using correspondences, *SS* 21
   the Word composed using correspondences, *SS* 8, 20:3, 40, 51:1, 91, 117
Covenant, *Life* 57, 60. *See also* The ark of the covenant
Cravings (urges), *Life* 90. *See also* Evil
   the cravings of our evils clogging the deeper levels of our earthly mind, *Life* 86:4, 5
   distancing ourselves from our cravings by fighting against evils, *Life* 66:2, 91
   our cravings remaining with us after death, *Life* 63:2
The Crucifixion, *Lord* 59. *See also* Atonement; Glorification; Jesus; The Lord; Trials
   the Lord's suffering on the cross, *Lord* 3, 13, 17:2, 26:2, 51:3; *Faith* 35
   being his last battle, *Lord* 12, 14:12, 33:3, 34, 35:3, 65
   beliefs about, *Lord* 15:1, 18:1–2, 65
   the Lord's divine and human natures being united by, *Lord* 34

D

Damnation, *Life* 69. *See also* Hell; Salvation
   all religions agreeing that we are damned if we do not refrain from sins, *Life* 64
   all who live by the laws of the Ten Commandments being saved, and all who do not being damned, *Life* 65
   the belief that the Lord bore our damnation, *Lord* 18:1, 2; *Faith* 44
   convincing ourselves of false beliefs as condemning (harming) us if genuine truth is destroyed, *SS* 92–96a
   damnation resulting from a lack of faith and caring, *Faith* 68
   the Lord never condemning anyone to hell, *Lord* 25; *SS* 94; *Faith* 45, 46
   people with religion knowing that those who live a good life are saved and those who live an evil life are damned, *Life* 1, 3, 4, 7
Daniel, Book of. *See also* Prophetic books; The Word
   the battle between the ram and the goat in Daniel chapter 8, *Faith* 61, 65–67
David
   the Lord being called David, *Lord* 37:1, 37:3, 42–45:1, 55:1
   the Lord not acknowledging himself to be the son of David, *Lord* 35:5
Day
   "day" and "time" meaning the Lord's Coming, *Lord* 4, 5
Death. *See also* Life after death
   a good life being called life and an evil life being called death, *Life* 8
   the Lord conquering death and hell through battles, *Lord* 12

Death *(continued)*
    the Lord providing a means of reformation to save us from eternal death, *Life* 69
    the Lord's Coming saving humankind from eternal death, *Lord* 3, 18; *Faith* 39

Deception, to be rejected as a sin, *Life* 82–84. *See also* False witness; Falsity; Honesty

The Devil, our freedom to turn toward, *Life* 19, 20, 69. *See also* Evil; Hell

The disciples, *Lord* 18:4–5

Divine goodness. *See also* Divinity
    divine goodness and divine truth
        emanating from the Lord, *SS* 19; *Life* 32:1
        the Lord being, *SS* 100
        the marriage of, *SS* 88
    divine goodness coming from the Lord's divine love, *SS* 19; *Life* 32:1
    the heavenly kingdom of heaven receiving divine goodness, *Life* 32:1
    the heavenly meaning of the Word having to do with divine goodness, *SS* 80

Divine love. *See also* Divinity
    divine goodness coming from the Lord's divine love, *SS* 19; *Life* 32:1
    divine wisdom and divine love, *Lord* 1; *SS* 3:2; *Life* 32:1; *Supp* 20
    the Lord being divine love, *Supp* 14, 21
    the spiritual sun being divine love, *Supp* 20
    spiritual warmth being divine love, *Life* 86:3

Divine Love and Wisdom, *Lord* preface, 65; *SS* 32, 83
    references to *Divine Love and Wisdom*, *Life* 36

Divine Providence, *Lord* preface, 46:2; *SS* 32, 83

Divine truth. *See also* Divinity
    divine goodness and divine truth
        emanating from the Lord, *SS* 19; *Life* 32:1
        the marriage of, *SS* 88
    divine truth being present in the literal meaning, *SS* 38:2, 97:3
    divine truth coming from the Lord's divine wisdom, *SS* 19; *Life* 32:1
    divine truth in its outermost form, *SS* 44:1, 44:4, 49:3–5
    enlightenment as necessary for seeing the divine (genuine) truth in a body of teaching, *SS* 50, 57
    the Holy Spirit being divine truth that comes from the Lord, *Lord* 51:4–5
    judgment being executed according to the divine truth in the Word, *Lord* 25
    the life of the Lord's wisdom being divine truth, *Lord* 51
    the light in heaven being divine truth radiating from the Lord, *SS* 106, 109
    light meaning divine truth, *Lord* 2
    the Lord becoming divine truth or the Word even on the outermost level, *SS* 98, 99
    the Lord being divine truth, *SS* 57, 78
        and divine goodness, *SS* 100
        and divine wisdom, *Lord* 1, 51:3
    the power of divine truth against falsity and evil, *SS* 49:1
    seeing divine truths in the Word, *SS* 41
    the spiritual kingdom of heaven receiving divine truth, *Life* 32:1
    the spiritual meaning having to do with divine truth, *SS* 80
    the Word being divine truth, *Lord* 1, 2, 27:2; *SS* 2:1, 3:1, 76, 78, 106, 114; *Supp* 12

Divine wisdom. *See also* Divinity
    divine truth and divine wisdom
        the Lord being, *Lord* 1, 51:3
        the Word being, *Lord* 1
    divine wisdom and divine love, *Lord* 1; *SS* 3:2; *Life* 32:1; *Supp* 20
    spiritual light being divine wisdom, *Life* 86:3; *Supp* 14

The Divine-Human One, *Lord* 28, 32:5. *See also* Jesus; The Lord; The Son of God

Divinity, *Lord* 46:5, 55:2–4. *See also* Divine goodness; Divine love; Divine truth; Divine wisdom; The Divine-Human One; The Lord's divine nature
    the divinity of the Word, *Lord* 1; *SS* 1, 4, 6:2, 18:4, 19, 32, 90; *Supp* 62
    everything divine that emanates from Jehovah God tending to take on a human form, *Lord* 32:8
    the Lord making his human nature divine, *Lord* 20, 29:2, 32:1–4, 33, 35, 36:1; *Supp* 75

Doubt, caused by a literal reading of the Word, *SS* 18. *See also* Belief; Conviction

Dragons
    the dragon in the Book of Revelation, *Faith* 55–60; *Supp* 16:2, 28
    spirits who are devoted to faith alone looking like dragons, *Faith* 56

The Dutch
    the Dutch being devoted to a spiritual love of business, *Supp* 48:3, 49:2, 51:1
    the Dutch being taught after death, *Supp* 49
    the Dutch holding firmly to their religious principles, *Supp* 49, 50
    the Dutch in the spiritual world, *Supp* 48–55
    the fate of irreligious Dutch people in the Last Judgment, *Supp* 53

E

The earth (world). *See also* The earthly; The spiritual world
    acknowledging the Lord alone as God (Lord) of heaven and earth, *Lord* 65; *Supp* 76
    everything on earth corresponding to something spiritual, *SS* 20, 23:1

The earth *(continued)*
  the first heaven and the first earth, *Supp* 9, 10, 18
  the Lord coming into the world (*see* The Lord's Coming)
  the Lord having power over heaven and earth, *Supp* 59
  the Lord making a new church in both the spiritual and the earthly worlds, *Lord* 62:2
  the new heaven and the new earth, *Lord* 62, 64:3, 65
  our self-importance as focused on ourselves and the world, *SS* 115:2
  outer thinking being in the earthly world and inner thinking being in the spiritual world, *Supp* 39
  the Son of God being born into the world, not from eternity, *Lord* 19
  the spiritual world having everything we see in the earthly world, *Faith* 63:1; *Supp* 37
  the state of the world and the church
    compared to times of day, *Supp* 13
    before and after the Last Judgment, *Supp* 2, 8, 11, 13, 30
  the Word being earthly in the world but spiritual in the heavens, *Lord* 2
The earthly. *See also* The earth; The heavenly; The spiritual
  the attitude of earthly-minded people toward the Word, *SS* 3:1, 4, 18:4
  earthly love as either subservient to or opposing spiritual love, *Supp* 21
  the earthly meaning of the Word (*see* Literal meaning of the Word)
  good actions of earthly people coming from themselves, *Life* 16, 108
  the heavenly, the spiritual, and the earthly emanating from the Lord, *SS* 6
  the Lord flowing from the spiritual into the earthly, *Life* 110
  love of our occupations being an earthly type of love, *Faith* 25
  moral earthly individuals, *Life* 108, 109
  our having an earthly mind and a spiritual mind, *Life* 86; *Faith* 32
  our having heavenly, spiritual, and earthly levels, *SS* 68
  people devoted to earthly love being in hell, *Supp* 21
  the root of evil remaining in place in earthly individuals, *Life* 108
  storing knowledge about goodness and truth in our earthly memory, *Faith* 26
  "uncircumcised" meaning having only earthly love, *Faith* 51, 54
  the Word being earthly in the world but spiritual in the heavens, *Lord* 2

Earthquakes, in the spiritual world during the Last Judgment, *Supp* 25
Enlightenment. *See also* Truth
  enlightenment as a perception as to whether something is true, *Faith* 5
  enlightenment as necessary for seeing the divine (genuine) truth in a body of teaching, *SS* 50, 57
  enlightenment coming from the Lord, *SS* 50, 57, 91; *Supp* 11
  our enlightenment and reformation depending on communication with heaven, *Supp* 12
  the Word providing enlightenment
    for everyone, *SS* 110, 111
    for people outside the church, *SS* 106, 114
Enoch, preserving the knowledge of correspondences, *SS* 21
Ephraim, inner meaning of, *SS* 79
Essence, *Faith* 18:2. *See also* Being
Eternity. *See also* Life after death
  beliefs about a Son of God born from eternity, *Lord* 19
  the Lord from eternity, *Lord* 1, 19, 30, 31, 54, 55:1, 59
Evil. *See also* Cravings; Goodness; Hell; Sin; Spirits
  abstaining from evil and doing good as though on our own, *Supp* 46:2–3
  all societies knowing that it is evil to steal, commit adultery, murder, and bear false witness, *Life* 53
  the belief that we go to hell if we do evil and to heaven if we do good, *Life* 1, 3, 4, 7, 94
  a caring faith in those who have turned toward the Lord and away from evils, *Faith* 23, 30
  the Christian teaching that living an evil life does not damn those who have been justified by faith alone, *Life* 4
  concern for reputation and wealth as preventing evil behaviors, *Life* 92
  the cravings of our evils clogging the deeper levels of our earthly mind, *Life* 86:4, 5
  doing battle with evils, *Lord* 33:1; *Life* 66:2, 93–100
  the effects of the evil we practice, *Life* 44
  everyone being capable of turning away from evils through the Lord's power, *Life* 31, 58
  evil and falsity (*see under* Falsity)
  evil and goodness as opposites, *Life* 8, 70, 71
  evil hating truth, *Life* 45; *Faith* 30
  evil people having an intellectual faith, *Life* 46
  evil people visiting a heavenly community, *Life* 49
  an evil will removing the Word's truth from the understanding, *SS* 116:2
  evils being replaced by good when they are set aside, *Life* 70, 95

Evil *(continued)*
  to the extent that we are not purified from our evils our deeds are not good or devout and we are not wise, *Life* 30
  a good life being called life and an evil life being called death, *Life* 8
  inherited evil being a love of controlling others, *Supp* 61, 63
  living an evil life as condemning us, *SS* 92
  only Christians turning their backs on evils because they are sins, *Life* 111
  our being kept in freedom to turn toward evil or goodness while in this world, *Life* 19, 20, 69
  our evils keeping the Lord from coming in to us, *Life* 18
  our inability to resist evils on our own, *Life* 66:2, 96, 110, 112
  our not having faith if we are leading an evil life, *Life* 44, 49
  our self-centeredness (self-importance) being evil, *SS* 115, 116:1–2; *Life* 92, 93
  the root of evil remaining in place in earthly individuals, *Life* 108
  seeing evil as hideous and loathing it, *Life* 95
  turning one's back on evils but not because they are sins, *Life* 108, 111; *Supp* 10
  turning our backs on evil deeds (evils) because they are sins, *Life* 22, 65, 73, 92; *Faith* 12; *Supp* 45
    despite a belief in faith alone, *Faith* 72
    to the extent that we do so
      knowledge about goodness and truth become part of our faith, *Faith* 27
      the Lord opens our spiritual mind, *Life* 86:4
      our deeds (actions) are good, *Life* 21, 24, 72, 114; *Supp* 16:2
      our devout thoughts and words are devout, *Life* 25, 26
      our spiritual mind is open with respect to our will, *Life* 86:2; *Faith* 32
      we are given faith and caring by the Lord, *Supp* 49:2
      we are spiritual, *Life* 52
      we are wise, *Life* 27
      we are (with and) in the Lord, *Life* 21, 24, 25, 48
      we have faith, *Life* 45, 52, 91
      we love what is true, *Life* 34, 37, 41
Experience, *Life* 76. *See also* Knowledge

F

Fables, *SS* 20:2, 21, 117. *See also* Parables
Faith. *See also* Caring; *Faith;* Faith alone
  the belief that the Lord transferred the sins of the faithful to himself, *Lord* 15:1
  faith and caring (*see under* Caring)
  faith and intellect (intelligence; understanding)
    the dogma that the intellect (understanding) must be subject to faith, *Faith* 4, 39
    evil people having an intellectual faith, *Life* 46
    faith and life being distinct from each other in the same way that understanding and will are distinct, *Life* 42
    faith divorced from intellect being a blind faith, *Faith* 71
    faith in the understanding being alive if it has goodness from the will, *Life* 46
    our intelligence depending on our caring faith, *Faith* 29
  faith and truth (*see under* Truth)
  faith depending on our power to be receptive, *Life* 107
  faith divorced (separated) from caring, *Faith* 9, 18:2, 19:2, 44–48; *Supp* 26
    the absurd notions engendered by, *Faith* 45
    the beasts of the dragon in the Book of Revelation having to do with, *Faith* 60
    the Christian religion based on, *Faith* 55
    the church having divorced faith from caring, *Life* 9
    the dragon in the Book of Revelation meaning, *Faith* 56, 57, 59
    as no faith at all, *Faith* 69
    people devoted to, *Faith* 70; *Supp* 28
    goats meaning, *Faith* 61–68; *Supp* 10
    symbolized by Philistines, *Faith* 49–53
    after the Reformation, *SS* 24
    Swedenborg's conversation with an angel regarding, *Faith* 41–43
  faith not accomplishing anything good or useful by itself, *Faith* 17
  kinds of faith, *Lord* 18:3; *Life* 50
    blind faith, *Faith* 1, 8, 9, 46, 71
    dead faith compared to living faith, *Life* 46, 47
    spiritual faith compared to nonspiritual faith, *Life* 49, 50
  knowledge about goodness and truth
    becoming part of our faith to the extent that we turn our backs on evils because they are sins, *Faith* 27
    faith depending on, *Faith* 28, 29
    as a resource for forming a caring faith, *Faith* 27, 31–33
  life and faith (*see under* Life)
  the Lord as the focus of faith that saves, *Lord* 32:7
  love and faith (*see under* Love)
  our faith saving us when we have ceased to sin, *Life* 51
  our having faith to the extent that we turn our backs on evils because they are sins, *Life* 45, 52, 91

Faith *(continued)*
 our understanding of the Word determining our truth, faith, love, and life, *SS* 78
 summaries of views about faith, *Faith* 34–37, 38–43

Faith, *Lord* preface, 65. *See also* Faith; Faith alone
 references to *Faith, Life* 64

Faith alone, *Supp* 87. *See also* Belief; Conviction; Faith
 belief in salvation through faith alone, *Lord* 18:2; *Life* 4, 91; *Faith* 42; *Supp* 54, 55
 the belief that faith alone does everything, *Faith* 39
 beliefs that seem to require faith only, *Life* 47–49
 British preachers (elders) in the spiritual world who believe in faith alone, *Life* 7; *Supp* 42:2–3, 44, 45
 the Christian teaching that living an evil life does not damn those who have been justified by faith alone, *Life* 4
 spirits who believe in faith alone, *Faith* 56; *Supp* 42:2–3, 47
 those who turn their backs on evils because they are sins despite a belief in faith alone, *Faith* 72

False witness (lying), *Life* 87–91. *See also* Deception; Falsity; Honesty

Falsity. *See also* Deception; False witness; Truth
 convincing ourselves of false beliefs, *SS* 60, 91–96a; *Faith* 11
 evil and falsity
  coming from hell, *Lord* 33:1
  our self-importance as evil and giving rise to falsity, *SS* 115
  the power of divine truth against, *SS* 49:1
  trials being battles against, *Lord* 33:1
  the union of evil and falsity being called "the hellish marriage," *Life* 33
 falsity destroying faith and caring, *Faith* 29
 seeing false things as true, *Faith* 71

The Father. *See also* God; Jehovah; The Lord; The Son; The Son of God; Trinity
 the belief that the Father sent the Son to make satisfaction for the human race, *Faith* 38, 39, 42, 44
 the belief that the Son of God is distinct from the person of the Father, *Lord* 19:1
 the Father and the Son being one in the Lord, *Lord* 46:1
 the Father as an element of the trinity within the Lord, *Lord* 55:1
 the Lord alone being meant by "the Father, the Son, and the Holy Spirit," *Lord* 46:6
 the Lord being divine because of Jehovah the Father and human because of the Virgin Mary, *Lord* 35:1
 the Lord being one with the Father, *Lord* 1, 29:2, 32:7, 35:3, 35:8, 35:11
 the Lord being sent into the world by the Father, *Lord* 20
 the Lord calling Jehovah "Father," *Lord* 20
 the Lord doing the will of the Father, *Lord* 20
 the Lord having been conceived by God the Father, *Supp* 89
 the Lord uniting his human nature to the divine nature of the Father, *Lord* 17:1
 the Lord's divine nature being the Father, *Lord* 32:7, 57
 the Lord's human nature from his mother being material and his human nature from his Father being substantial, *Lord* 35:2
 the Lord's state of glorification being his union with the Divine called "the Father," *Lord* 35:3, 35:8
 our believing in the Lord who is both Father and Son, *Lord* 32:6
 the trinity of Father, Son, and Holy Spirit, *Lord* 57

Feasts, *Lord* 64:1

Feelings, *Faith* 63:2, 3; *Supp* 23

Flame, the inmost level of the Word compared to, *SS* 42

Forgiveness, *Lord* 18:2–3, 65

Form
 the union of essence and form, *Faith* 18:2

Fornication, *Life* 79. *See also* Adultery

Foundation
 the foundations of the wall of the New Jerusalem in Revelation 21 meaning the truths of the literal meaning, *SS* 43
 the literal meaning being the foundation, container, and support of the spiritual and heavenly meanings, *SS* 30–33, 35, 36, 38:2
 what is last being a foundation, container, and support, *SS* 27

Fox, George, *Supp* 84. *See also* Quakers

France. *See* Geneviève; Louis XIV; Parisians; Versailles

Freedom, *Life* 57
 freedom and reason being the Lord's within us, *Life* 101
 the intellectual light resulting from freedom in Britain, *Supp* 40
 the Lord giving us freedom and the power to reason, *Life* 102
 our being kept while in this world in a freedom to turn toward
  evil or goodness, *Life* 19, 69
  heaven or hell, *Life* 19, 20, 69
  the Lord or the Devil, *Life* 19, 20, 69
 our thinking and doing freely whatever we love, *Life* 1

Freedom (*continued*)
    reformation as impossible without freedom and reason, *Life* 101

G

Garden, the mind compared to, *Life* 86:3, 86:5
Garden of Eden, *SS* 45, 97:4
Geneviève (*saint*), *Supp* 67
Gladness
    "joy" having to do with goodness and "gladness" having to do with truth, *SS* 87
Glorification, *Lord* 16:6, 17:1, 59, 64:1. *See also* The Crucifixion; Jesus; The Lord; The Lord's divine nature; Resurrection
    the Lord being divine truth and divine wisdom after his glorification, *Lord* 51:3
    the Lord coming into the world to glorify his human nature, *Lord* 3, 14:12, 26:2, 34:1, 65; *SS* 99; *Faith* 35
    the Lord glorifying his human nature, *Lord* 12, 13, 20, 33:2, 33:4, 35:5–9
    the Lord's state of glorification being his union with the Divine called "the Father," *Lord* 35:3, 35:8
Goal, means, and result, *SS* 28, 67:6; *Life* 14
Goats. *See also* Sheep
    fights between sheep and goats, *Faith* 63:4, 65–67
    the separation of the "sheep" and the "goats" during the Last Judgment, *Supp* 10
    symbolic meaning of goats, *Faith* 61–68; *Supp* 10, 16:2
God, *Lord* 64:1; *Life* 3, 47, 53. *See also* The Father; Gods; Jehovah; The Lord; Trinity; Worship
    acknowledging the Lord as God, *Life* 66:2
    of heaven and earth, *Lord* 61:1, 65
    belief in God as believing in the Lord and revering the Word, *SS* 92
    belief in one God, *Lord* 55:3; *Supp* 68, 73, 74
    the faith that is God's compared to the faith that is our own, *Lord* 18:3
    God becoming human on the first level and the last level, *Lord* 36
    God being justice itself, love itself, mercy itself, and goodness itself, *Lord* 18:1
    God being one, *Lord* 45, 57; *SS* 88
        in person and in essence, *Lord* 54, 55:6, 60, 65; *Supp* 49:2, 72:1
    God being the Lord, *Lord* 54, 60, 65; *Supp* 49
    "God" meaning the Lord with respect to his divine truth, *SS* 88
    Jehovah being God of heaven and earth, *SS* 2:1
    the Lord being God, *Lord* 45; *Faith* 35
        from eternity, *Lord* 1, 19:1
        and having power over heaven and earth, *Supp* 59
    and a human being, *Lord* 55:3, 60
    in respect to both his human nature and his divine nature, *Lord* 34
    the Lord having been conceived by God the Father, *Supp* 89
    the love of controlling others ultimately being a desire to be called upon and worshiped as God, *Supp* 61, 63
    misconceptions about God, *Supp* 74
    our deeds (actions) being good to the extent that they come from God (the Lord) and not from ourselves, *Life* 9–11, 13, 29
    our not knowing about God if there were no Word, *SS* 114, 115:2–3
    people in the spiritual world who know nothing (are unwilling to hear) about God, *SS* 116
    the Son of God as the second person of the Godhead, *Lord* 19:1
    Swedenborg's conversations with Muslims in the spiritual world regarding the one God, *Supp* 72:1
    thinking in terms of three gods, *Lord* 57
    the trinity within God, *Supp* 72:1
Gods, those who want to be worshiped as, *Supp* 62–64. *See also* God; Idolatry
Gold, good deeds compared to different kinds of, *Life* 10. *See also* Stones, precious
Goodness, *Lord* 18:1. *See also* Evil; Love; Truth
    belief in the Lord means leading a good life, *Faith* 36
    doing good (*see also under* Action)
    evil and goodness as opposites, *Life* 8, 70, 71
    evils being replaced by good when they are set aside, *Life* 70, 95
    faith in the understanding being alive if it has goodness from the will, *Life* 46
    a good life being called life and an evil life being called death, *Life* 8
    goodness and truth, *SS* 44, 100
        the desire to do good leading to a desire for truth, *Faith* 13
        everything in the universe originating in, *Life* 43:1
        goodness as the underlying reality and truth as its manifestation, *Life* 43:2
        goodness having to do with the will and truth with the understanding, *Life* 36, 43:1
        goodness loving what is true, *Life* 39, 40, 65; *Faith* 13
        goodness needing to be united to truth, *Life* 32:2, 37
        knowledge about (*see under* Knowledge)
        the Lord being goodness itself and truth itself, *Life* 38

Goodness *(continued)*
  goodness and truth *(continued)*
    the marriage of, *SS* 80–82, 85, 88, 114; *Life* 43:2
    as one in the Lord, *Life* 33
    our goodness and truth making us human, *SS* 100
    our having truth to the extent that we have goodness, *Life* 52
    paired expressions in the Word as having to do with, *SS* 84–88
    the relationship between goodness and loving what is true, *Life* 38, 44; *Faith* 30
    truths as the means by which the good we do becomes manifest, *Life* 39
    the union of, *Life* 33, 41, 44; *Faith* 18:1, 29
    the kind of goodness we practice determining our citizenship, *Life* 12
    learning about what is good taking place in our understanding, *Faith* 33
    love for (focus on) what is good leading to faith, *Life* 36, 45
    our being kept in freedom to turn toward evil or goodness while in this world, *Life* 19, 20, 69
    our coming into goodness that is the opposite of the evil on which we turn our backs, *Life* 21, 24, 70, 75, 82–84, 88, 89
    our deeds (actions) being good to the extent that
      they come from God (the Lord) and not from ourselves, *Life* 9–11, 13, 29
      they come from love of our neighbor, *Life* 72
    we are purified from our evils, *Life* 30:1
    we turn our backs on evil deeds, *Life* 21, 24, 72, 114; *Supp* 16:2
    our thinking well and behaving well when we are focused on goodness, *Life* 47
    people with religion knowing that those who live a good life are saved and those who live an evil life are damned, *Life* 1, 3, 4, 7
    spiritual goodness, *Life* 13
    uniting with the good others do and not with their personality, *Faith* 21
The Gospels, *SS* 2:1, 17:3. *See also* Matthew, Gospel of; The Word
Governance, of the British in the spiritual world, *Supp* 40. *See also* Control; Power

H

Hair, meaning divine truth in its outermost forms, *SS* 49:3–5. *See also* Baldness
Heart, meaning the will, *Life* 51. *See also* Body
Heart and lungs. *See also* Body; Breath
  the church functioning as the heart and lungs in the human being that makes up heaven, *SS* 105
  correspondences to the heart and lungs, *SS* 107; *Life* 46; *Faith* 19
  the Word without its literal meaning compared to the heart and lungs without pleura and ribs, *SS* 33
Heaven, *Life* 47. *See also* Angels; Heaven and Hell; The heavenly; Heavenly meaning of the Word; Hell; Life after death; Salvation; Spirits; The spiritual world
  the angels of the lowest heaven being the "sheep," *Supp* 10
  the belief that we go to hell if we do evil and to heaven if we do good, *Life* 1, 3, 4, 7, 94
  children in heaven being raised by angels, *Supp* 58
  communication with heaven, *SS* 102; *Supp* 12
  the communities of heaven, *SS* 107, 113; *Supp* 21
  everyone in heaven believing in one God, *Lord* 55:3
  the experience of Catholic saints in heaven, *Supp* 66
  the first heaven and the first earth, *Supp* 9, 10, 18
  heaven appearing like one human being, *SS* 105
  heavenly communities (*see* the communities of heaven)
  the heavens being divided into two kingdoms, *SS* 34; *Life* 32:1
  heaven's light (*see under* Light)
  heaven's warmth being love, *Life* 15
  human beings as the foundation, container, and support of the heavens, *SS* 34
  the Last Judgment
    restoring communication with heaven, *Supp* 12
    taking place when the power of hell was stronger than the power of heaven, *Lord* 61:2, 65
  the light in heaven (*see under* Light)
  the Lord and heaven
    all of heaven's breathing originating with the Lord, *Lord* 51:3
    enlightenment coming from the Lord through heaven, *Supp* 11
    heaven and the church being called the Lord's kingdom, *Lord* 42
    heaven being heaven because of the Lord, *Lord* 61:1
    the Lord as the sun of heaven, *SS* 106, 109; *Supp* 20
    the Lord being God and having power over heaven and earth, *Supp* 59
    the Lord coming into the world to bring heaven and earth into order, *Lord* 14:1
    the Lord's presence in the angelic heavens increasing during the Last Judgment to protect the inhabitants, *Supp* 23

Heaven *(continued)*
    the Lord and heaven *(continued)*
        the only source of true teachings being through heaven from the Lord, *Lord* 63
        only those who acknowledge the Lord alone as God of heaven and earth being able to enter heaven, *Lord* 61:1
        the whole heaven acknowledging the Lord alone, *Lord* 61:1
    Moravians visiting the third heaven, *Supp* 87
    Muslims who go to heaven, *Supp* 69
    the new heaven and the new earth, *Lord* 62, 64:3, 65
    the opening of our spiritual mind admitting (connecting) us to heaven, *Life* 86:4; *Faith* 32
    our becoming spiritual when our will is raised into heaven, *Life* 15
    our being halfway between heaven and hell, *Supp* 57
    our being kept in freedom to turn toward heaven or hell while in this world, *Life* 19, 20, 69
    our being unable to be in heaven and in hell at the same time, *Life* 18, 28
    our reformation depending on our understanding being raised into heaven, *Life* 15
    our understanding (intellect) as able to be in heaven, but not our will unless we turn our backs on evils because they are sins, *Life* 86:2; *Faith* 32
    our union with heaven, *SS* 104
    people devoted to spiritual love being in heaven, *Supp* 21
    people of every religion being dependent on the union of the Lord and heaven with the church through the Word, *SS* 105
    the pseudo-heavens, *Supp* 9, 10, 18, 20, 23, 57
    the tabernacle representing heaven and the church, *SS* 46
    those who acknowledge the Lord alone as God (Lord) of heaven and earth, *Supp* 76
    those who were connected outwardly with heaven but inwardly with hell, *Supp* 18
    the Word and heaven
        the belief that mere knowledge of the Word leads to heaven, *SS* 61
        Christians who read the Word being at the center of the heavens, *SS* 105:3, 106
        communication with heaven through the Word, *SS* 5, 64:2, 96a, 108, 113
        Sacred Scripture being entirely about heaven and the church, *Faith* 65
        studying the Word from love of truth and of one's neighbor as leading to heaven, *SS* 61:3
        union with heaven through the Word, *SS* 64:2; *Life* 3
        the Word being earthly in the world but spiritual in the heavens, *Lord* 2
        the Word in heaven, *SS* 70, 71, 114
            the writing style of, *SS* 71, 72, 74, 90
        the Word uniting us to the Lord and opening heaven, *SS* 3
    the world of spirits as an intermediate space between heaven and hell, *Faith* 63:3; *Supp* 18, 20, 57

Heaven and Hell, *Lord* preface. *See also* Heaven; Hell
    references to *Heaven and Hell, Lord* 25, 26:2, 32:8, 36:1, 61:2; *SS* 6:1 note a, 7, 20, 34, 49:1, 64:2, 85, 100, 105:1, 106, 107; *Life* 8, 20, 32:1, 77, 101 note a; *Supp* 20, 32, 38, 48:2
    Swedenborg reporting his spiritual experiences in *Heaven and Hell, SS* 70

The heavenly (what is heavenly). *See also* The earthly; Heaven; Heavenly meaning of the Word; The spiritual
    angels of the heavenly kingdom (heavenly angels), *SS* 6:1, 63, 64:1, 65, 67, 86
    the heavenly kingdom of heaven receiving divine goodness, *Life* 32:1
    the heavenly marriage (*see under* Marriage)
    the heavenly, the spiritual, and the earthly emanating from the Lord, *SS* 6
    marriage love being a heavenly love, *Supp* 51:2, 72:3
    our having heavenly, spiritual, and earthly levels, *SS* 68
    what is earthly corresponding to what is heavenly, *SS* 7

Heavenly meaning of the Word, *SS* 19. *See also* Heaven; The heavenly; Inner meaning of the Word; Literal meaning of the Word; The Word
    the earthly, spiritual, and heavenly meanings of the Ten Commandments, *SS* 67
    heavenly angels being focused on the heavenly meaning, *SS* 63, 64:1, 65, 67
    the heavenly meaning as the first level of the Word, *SS* 31
    the heavenly meaning having to do with divine goodness, *SS* 80
    the heavenly meaning having to do with the Lord, *SS* 80
    the inmost level of the Word compared to a flame because of the heavenly meaning, *SS* 42
    the literal meaning as a container for the spiritual and heavenly meanings, *SS* 30–33, 35, 36, 38:2, 40

Heavenly meaning of the Word *(continued)*
the spiritual and heavenly meaning(s)
being in heaven's light, *SS* 58
being in the earthly meaning, *SS* 37, 38:2, 39, 63, 65, 80
in the details of the Word, *SS* 58, 80
unfolding from the earthly meaning, *SS* 63, 65, 66

Hell, *Life* 3, 47. *See also* Damnation; The Devil; Evil; Heaven; *Heaven and Hell;* Life after death; Spirits; The spiritual world
the belief that we go to hell if we do evil and to heaven if we do good, *Life* 1, 3, 4, 7, 94
communication with hell opening during the Last Judgment, *Supp* 25
evil and falsity coming from hell, *Lord* 33:1
evil spirits casting themselves into hell, *Lord* 25
the hell of Catholics who want to be called upon as gods, *Supp* 62–64
hellfire, *Life* 67
irreligious Protestants being cast into hell after death, *Supp* 17
the Last Judgment taking place when the power of hell was stronger than the power of heaven, *Lord* 61:2, 65
the Lord
coming into the world to subdue the hells, *Lord* 3, 26:2, 34:1, 65
conquering death and hell through battles, *Lord* 12
defeating the hells, *Lord* 13, 14, 20, 33:2, 33:4, 35:3
fighting and overcoming the hells, *Lord* 18:2; *Faith* 35
never condemning anyone to hell, *Lord* 25; *SS* 94; *Faith* 45, 46
our being halfway between heaven and hell, *Supp* 57
our being kept in freedom to turn toward heaven or hell while in this world, *Life* 19, 20, 69
our being unable to be in heaven and in hell at the same time, *Life* 18, 28
people devoted to earthly love being in hell, *Supp* 21
the rise of the hells before the Lord's Coming, *Lord* 33:3
those who have a love of controlling others being in hell, *Supp* 61
those who were connected outwardly with heaven but inwardly with hell, *Supp* 18
trials being battles against hell, *Lord* 33:1; *Life* 98

Heresies, *SS* 52, 92. *See also* Arians; Belief; Conviction

Hieroglyphics, *SS* 20:2

Holiness. *See also* The Holy One of Israel; The Holy Spirit; The Holy Supper
the holiness of the tabernacle, *Life* 55
the holiness of the Ten Commandments, *Life* 54–56, 59
the holiness of the Word, *Lord* 7; *SS* 1, 3:1, 4, 18, 81, 90

The Holy One of Israel, *Lord* 22, 37, 40, 45:1, 55:1; *SS* 88

The Holy Spirit. *See also* Trinity
the belief that an inflow of the Holy Spirit unites faith and caring in us without our involvement, *Supp* 46
fanatical spirits who believe they are the Holy Spirit, *Supp* 83–85
the Holy Spirit
being divine truth that comes from the Lord, *Lord* 51:4–5
being the emanating divine nature, *Lord* 46:2, 57
being the Lord, *Lord* 51:2–3, 54
being the Lord's presence with us through angels and spirits, *Lord* 46:4
being the same as the Lord, *Lord* 46
being the spirit of the Lord's mouth, *SS* 2:1
as an element of the trinity within the Lord, *Lord* 55:1
the Lord alone being meant by "the Father, the Son, and the Holy Spirit," *Lord* 46:6
the spirit of the prophets being called the Holy Spirit, *Lord* 51:5
the trinity of Father, Son, and Holy Spirit, *Lord* 57

The Holy Supper
the prayer that is read to people who are taking the Holy Supper, *Life* 4–7; *Supp* 45

Honesty. *See also* False witness; Theft
our loving honesty to the extent that we turn our backs on theft (deception) as a sin, *Life* 82–84, 89
qualities associated with honesty, *Life* 83

Human (human beings; people; us). *See also* Angels; Body; The Divine-Human One; The Lord's human nature; The Son of Humanity; Soul; Spirits
all the people who have ever lived and died being gathered in the spiritual world, *Supp* 3, 5
angels and human beings (*see under* Angels)
the belief that the Lord made atonement for the human race, *Lord* 18:1
the belief that we are saved by believing that the Son was sent to make satisfaction for the human race, *Faith* 38, 39, 42, 44, 45

Human *(continued)*
   the communities of the heavens together leading one human life, *Supp* 21
   differences between humans and animals, *Life* 15, 86:1, 86:5; *Supp* 33
   the divine and human natures in the Lord being one in the way the soul and the body is one human being, *Lord* 29:1–2, 34:4, 35:11
   every community of heaven being like a human being, *SS* 107
   God as a human being, *Lord* 36; *Supp* 74
   heaven appearing like one human being, *SS* 105
   "a human being" meaning a church, *Lord* 16:7
   human beings as the foundation, container, and support of the heavens, *SS* 34
   the human form
      of angels, *Lord* 32:8
      of everything divine that emanates from Jehovah God, *Lord* 32:8
      of everything good and true that emanates from the Lord, *SS* 100
   the Lord
      being human, *Lord* 55:3; *SS* 100, 116:1; *Supp* 34
      coming into the world to save humankind, *Lord* 3, 14:1–3, 14:7, 17:1, 18:1, 33:3; *Faith* 34, 35, 39
   the Lord's human nature (*see under* The Lord's human nature)
   our being human after death, *Supp* 3, 5, 6, 32–34
   our goodness and truth making us human, *SS* 100
   people of other religions being taught in the spiritual world that the Lord was born as a human, *Supp* 75
   the prophets being called "children of humanity" or "sons of humanity," *Lord* 28
   the Word being a divine work for the salvation of the human race, *SS* 32
Husbands, *Supp* 51:2, 71. *See also* Marriage

I

Idolatry, *Lord* 33:3; *SS* 22, 23, 117. *See also* Gods
Ignorance, *Faith* 9. *See also* Knowledge; Wisdom
Images, created by the ancients based on their knowledge of correspondences, *SS* 23:1–2. *See also* Correspondence
Imputation, *Lord* 18:2–3, 65. *See also* Merit
Inflow, *SS* 61:2, 82; *Life* 110; *Supp* 46. *See also* The Lord
Inner meaning (spiritual meaning) of the Word.
   See also Heavenly meaning of the Word; Literal meaning of the Word; Parables; The Word
   angels focusing on the spiritual (heavenly) meaning, *Lord* 37:2; *SS* 26:1, 63
   the earthly, spiritual, and heavenly meanings of the Ten Commandments, *SS* 67
   the inner meaning
      convincing even earthly-minded people, *SS* 4
      the inner meaning within the outer meaning compared to a soul within a body, *SS* 4, 5, 9, 10
      the inner meanings of words being the same in the prophetic books as in the Gospels, *SS* 17:3
      the Lord revealing an inner meaning of the Word to Swedenborg, *SS* 4, 112:1
      the Lord's words and the miracles he performed having an inner meaning, *SS* 17:4
   the spiritual and heavenly meanings
      being in heaven's light, *SS* 58
      being in the earthly meaning, *SS* 37, 38:2, 39, 63, 65, 80
      the literal meaning being the container of, *SS* 30–33, 35, 36, 38:2, 40
      unfolding from the earthly meaning, *SS* 63, 65, 66
   the spiritual meaning
      awareness of, *SS* 17:2
      being about the Lord and his kingdom, *SS* 26
      being given only to those focused on truths from the Lord, *SS* 26, 56
      being opened at the close of the church, *SS* 9
      being revealed, *SS* 18, 20, 25; *Faith* 55, 57; *Supp* 3
      Bible passages that are unintelligible except through, *SS* 9–13, 15, 16, 84:2, 97:5; *Faith* 55, 57
      the Book of Revelation promising, *SS* 25
      the earthly-minded not knowing that there is a spiritual meaning in the Word, *SS* 18:4
      every detail of the Word containing a spiritual meaning, *SS* 13:1, 13:4, 16, 17:4, 58
      having to do with divine truth, *SS* 80
      having to do with the church, *SS* 80
      heaven's light showing us, *SS* 41
      the intermediate level of the Word compared to a light because of, *SS* 42
      a knowledge of correspondences being necessary to see, *SS* 9, 10, 56
      the Lord guarding, *SS* 56
      the Lord's parables containing, *SS* 17; *Life* 2; *Supp* 10
      making the Word divinely inspired and holy, *SS* 18
      making the Word spiritual for us and for angels, *SS* 5
      not being evident in the literal meaning, *SS* 13:4, 14:2

Inner meaning of the Word *(continued)*
   the spiritual meaning *(continued)*
      spiritual angels being focused on, *SS* 63, 64:1, 65, 67
      what the spiritual meaning of the Word is, *SS* 5
   the Word
      being in communication with heaven through the spiritual meaning, *SS* 5
      having a spiritual meaning throughout, *SS* 9
      having an earthly meaning and a spiritual meaning, *Lord* 2

Inner nature (inner self). *See also* Nature
   concealing our inner nature to earn rank or money, *Life* 68
   the inner nature of outwardly religious spirits being revealed during the Last Judgment, *Supp* 19, 23, 24
   our inner nature revealing itself after death, *Life* 110, 111; *Supp* 39, 53
   the spirit being the inner self, *Supp* 39

Intellect. *See* Understanding
Intelligence. *See* Understanding
Islam, *SS* 117
   the Islamic practice of polygamy, *Supp* 71, 72:3
   Muslims
      the location of Muslims in the spiritual world, *Supp* 68
      and Muhammad in the spiritual world, *Supp* 68–72
      Muslims who go to heaven, *Supp* 69
      recognizing the Lord as a son of God and as the wisest of all, *Supp* 68, 71
      recognizing the Lord as the greatest prophet, *Supp* 68
   a person identified as Muhammad always appearing to Muslims in the spiritual world, *Supp* 69
   the Qur'an, *Supp* 69, 70
   Swedenborg's conversations with Muslims in the spiritual world regarding the one God, resurrection, and marriage, *Supp* 72
   the Ten Commandments as Islamic religious practice, *Supp* 71

J

Jehovah, *Lord* 32:8. *See also* The Father; God; The Lord
   Jehovah being called Redeemer and Savior, *Lord* 34:2–4, 38, 55:1
   Jehovah being God of heaven and earth, *SS* 2:1
   Jehovah being the Lord from eternity, *Lord* 30, 31, 54, 55:1
   Jehovah proclaiming the Ten Commandments in a miraculous fashion, *Life* 53, 55:1, 59
   Jehovah speaking through the prophets, *Lord* 52–54; *SS* 2
   Jehovah talking with the prophets, *Lord* 52
   Jesus (the Lord's human side) having been conceived by Jehovah and born of the Virgin Mary, *Lord* 19:2–3, 20, 21, 29:2, 30:1, 59
   the Lord being called Jehovah, *Lord* 14:9–10, 22, 30:2, 35:2, 37:1, 37:3, 38, 45:1; *SS* 88
   the Lord being called King and Jehovah's Anointed, *Lord* 37:1, 37:3, 42, 45:1, 55:1
   the Lord being divine because of Jehovah the Father and human because of the Virgin Mary, *Lord* 35:1
   the Lord being Jehovah, *Lord* 34, 53; *SS* 2:1
   the Lord calling Jehovah "Father," *Lord* 20

Jerusalem. *See also* Middle East; New Jerusalem; The Temple in Jerusalem
   cities in the spiritual world that before the Last Judgment were called Jerusalem, *Supp* 79
   the holy Jerusalem meaning a new church, *Lord* 63, 64; *SS* 10
   Jerusalem meaning the church, *Lord* 63, 64; *Supp* 79
   the new church being established among people outside Jerusalem, *Lord* 64:3

Jesuits (Society of Jesus), *SS* 116:2; *Supp* 56. *See also* Xavier, Francis

Jesus, *Lord* 21, 29:2, 55:1. *See also* The Crucifixion; The Divine-Human One; Glorification; The Lord; The Lord's Coming; The Lord's divine nature; The Lord's human nature; Mary; The Son of God

Jewels. *See* Stones, precious

Jewish people. *See also* Jewish religion
   the ancient Jews having no knowledge of correspondences, *SS* 23:4
   Jewish spirits' belief that the Messiah will come and lead them into the land of Canaan, *Supp* 82
   Jews in the spiritual world, *Supp* 79–82

Jewish religion (church), *Lord* 16:6. *See also* Jewish people
   everything in the Jewish religion being based on correspondences, *SS* 20:2, 22, 23:4
   the Jewish church understanding "the Son of God" to be the Messiah, *Lord* 19:8

Job, Book of, *SS* 20:2. *See also* Prophetic books; The Word

Joy
   "joy" having to do with goodness and "gladness" having to do with truth, *SS* 87

Judgment, *Lord* 25; *SS* 85; *Life* 31. *See also* The Last Judgment

Justice, *Lord* 18:1, 18:3, 65; *SS* 85

K

Killing
- the fifth commandment, on killing, *Life* 67–73
- hostility, hatred, and vengefulness as kinds of killing, *Life* 67–69, 72, 73
- our having love for our neighbor to the extent that we turn our backs on killing, *Life* 70, 89
- the three levels of "killing," *Life* 67

King, the Lord being called, *Lord* 37:1, 37:3, 42, 45:1, 55:1

Kingdom
- comparisons from the three kingdoms of nature, *SS* 66
- heaven and the church being called the Lord's kingdom, *Lord* 42
- the heavens being divided into two kingdoms, *SS* 34; *Life* 32:1
- the spiritual meaning of the Word being about the Lord and his kingdom, *SS* 26:1

Knowledge. *See also* Ignorance; Perception; Recognition; Scholars; Truth; Understanding; Wisdom
- knowledge about goodness and truth
  - becoming part of our faith to the extent that we turn our backs on evils because they are sins, *Faith* 27
  - being stored in our earthly memory, *Faith* 26
  - faith depending on, *Faith* 28, 29
  - as a resource for forming a caring faith, *Faith* 27, 31–33
- knowledge coming to life for us only when we act on it, *Life* 27
- the knowledge of correspondences, *SS* 7, 20, 21–24, 102, 117
  - being necessary to see the spiritual meaning of the Word, *SS* 9, 10, 56
- our being able to know only about things we have experienced, *Life* 76
- our inborn eagerness for knowledge, *Faith* 25, 26
- wisdom not depending on mere knowledge, thinking, and understanding, *Life* 44

L

Lamp, a body of teaching compared to, *SS* 52, 54, 59, 91. *See also* Light

Last (final). *See also* The Last Judgment; Last Judgment
- every work of God being complete and perfect in its final stage, *SS* 28
- everything containing something first, intermediate, and last, *SS* 27, 28, 38:2
- what is last being a foundation, container, and support, *SS* 27

The Last Judgment. *See also* Last; Last Judgment
- the belief that body and soul are reunited on the day of the Last Judgment, *Supp* 72:2
- changes in the spiritual world following the Last Judgment, *Supp* 57
- cities in the spiritual world that before the Last Judgment were called Jerusalem, *Supp* 79
- communication with hell opening during the Last Judgment, *Supp* 25
- earthquakes in the spiritual world during the Last Judgment, *Supp* 25
- the event of the Last Judgment being revealed, *Supp* 5
- the fate of irreligious Dutch people in the Last Judgment, *Supp* 53
- the inner nature of outwardly religious spirits being revealed during the Last Judgment, *Supp* 19, 23, 24
- the Last Judgment being carried out on those who were outwardly moral but not inwardly spiritual, *Faith* 64; *Supp* 28
- the Last Judgment on Catholics, *Supp* 56
- the Last Judgment on Protestants, *Supp* 2, 15–22
- the Last Judgment restoring communication with heaven, *Supp* 12
- the Last Judgment taking place in the spiritual world, *Supp* 3, 5, 7, 8
- the Last Judgment taking place when the power of hell was stronger than the power of heaven, *Lord* 61:2, 65
- the light in the world of spirits and on earth after the Last Judgment, *Supp* 30
- the location of Jews in the spiritual world before and after the Last Judgment, *Supp* 79
- the Lord coming into the world to carry out a last judgment, *Lord* 3, 5, 14:10
- the Lord's presence in the angelic heavens increasing during the Last Judgment to protect the inhabitants, *Supp* 23
- misconceptions about the Last Judgment, *Supp* 3–5
- the New Jerusalem coming after the judgment, *Lord* preface, 62:1
- the plots of those affected by the Last Judgment, *Supp* 27
- reckonings being carried out by angels before the Last Judgment, *Supp* 26, 27
- revelations (secrets) being given after the Last Judgment, *Lord* 61:2, 65; *Supp* 12
- the salvation of the "sheep" after the Last Judgment, *Supp* 30–31
- the separation of the "sheep" and the "goats" during the Last Judgment, *Supp* 10
- signs that preceded the Last Judgment, *Supp* 23–25, 27
- the spirits affected by the Last Judgment looking like a great dragon, *Supp* 28
- the state of the world and the church before and after the Last Judgment, *Supp* 2, 8, 11, 13, 30

The Last Judgment *(continued)*
    what happened during the Last Judgment, *Supp* 27–29
Last Judgment, *Lord* preface. *See also* Last; The Last Judgment
    the purpose of the supplement to *Last Judgment*, *Supp* 2
    references to *Last Judgment*, *Lord* preface, 61:2, 62:2; *SS* 105:3; *Faith* 64:2; *Supp* 1, 7, 9, 10, 14, 56
The Law and the Prophets, *Lord* 8, 19:9. *See also* Moses
Laws. *See also* The Ten Commandments
    civic, rational, and spiritual law, *Life* 12
    the law in the ark, *Lord* 9; *SS* 46; *Life* 55
    "the Law" meaning everything Moses wrote in the Pentateuch, *Lord* 8, 9
    laws of religion being for God's sake and the sake of our salvation, *Life* 53
    the laws of the Ten Commandments, *Life* 53, 63:3, 64, 65
    the Lord fulfilling the law, *Lord* 8, 11, 14:11, 18:1–2, 65
    the meaning of "the law," *Lord* 8, 10; *Life* 55
Life. *See also* Life; Life after death
    action and thought working together in order to be part of our life, *Life* 1
    a good life being called life and an evil life being called death, *Life* 8
    knowledge coming to life for us only when we act on it, *Life* 27
    life and faith
        becoming one, *Life* 42, 44
        being distinct from each other in the same way that understanding and will are distinct, *Life* 42
        British clergy being focused on teachings about faith, while the British laity is focused on teachings about how to live, *Supp* 45
        faith and caring needing to be lived, *Supp* 49
        our having faith to the extent that we have life, *Life* 52
        our not having faith if we are leading an evil life, *Life* 44, 49
    the life of the Lord's wisdom being divine truth, *Lord* 51
    the life of those who have been regenerated being called spiritual life, *Lord* 49
    living by our religion, *Supp* 76
    the Lord's words being life, *SS* 2, 17:4
    love being our life, *Supp* 21
    our gaining life by means of the Word, *SS* 3:2
    our life not changing after death, *Life* 8; *Supp* 32
    our life varying depending on our state, *Lord* 48
    our understanding of the Word determining our truth, faith, love, and life, *SS* 78
    people with religion knowing that those who live a good life are saved and those who live an evil life are damned, *Life* 1, 3, 4, 7
    religion being about how we live and the religious way to live being to do good, *Life* 2, 8
    the spirit and life in the literal meaning of the Word, *SS* 39
    "spirit" meaning "life" (*see* Spirit: meanings of "spirit")
    what we love constituting our life, *Life* 1
Life, *Lord* preface, 65. *See also* Life
    references to *Life*, *Faith* 12, 16, 22, 23, 37, 40; *Supp* 45, 76
Life after death, *Life* 3, 47. *See also* Angels; Death; Eternity; Heaven; Hell; Life; Spirits; The spiritual world; The world of spirits
    angels teaching us after death, *SS* 93, 116:1; *Life* 49, 65; *Faith* 30
    the Dutch being taught after death, *Supp* 49
    irreligious Protestants being cast into hell after death, *Supp* 17
    misconceptions about life after death, *SS* 116:2; *Supp* 32, 33
    our being human after death, *Supp* 3, 5, 6, 32–34
    our cravings remaining with us after death, *Life* 63:2
    our inner nature revealing itself after death, *Life* 110, 111; *Supp* 39, 53
    our life not changing after death, *Life* 8; *Supp* 32
    our natures not changing after death, *SS* 17:2
    our shedding our outward characteristics after death, *Life* 45, 63:2–3, 68
    our spiritual mind enabling us to live after death, *Life* 86:1
    recognizing truth after death, *Faith* 30
Light. *See also* Lamp
    heaven's light (the light in heaven)
        being divine truth radiating from the Lord, *SS* 106, 109
        being divine wisdom, *SS* 73
        being greatest in the center, *SS* 14, 106
        being spiritual light, *Faith* 3
        being truth, *Life* 15
        our comprehending spiritual matters when we are lifted mentally into, *Faith* 3
        our understanding as able to be raised into heaven's light even if we are not spiritual, *Life* 15
        revealing true appearances, *Supp* 44
        showing us the spiritual meaning of the Word, *SS* 41
        the spiritual and heavenly meanings being in, *SS* 58
    the intellectual light resulting from freedom in Britain, *Supp* 40

Light *(continued)*
    the intermediate level of the Word compared to a light because of the spiritual meaning, *SS* 42
    light from the people in the middle of a heavenly community spreading to everyone in the community, *SS* 107
    the light in the world of spirits and on earth after the Last Judgment, *Supp* 30
    the light in the world of spirits being greatest in the center, *Supp* 14, 20
    the light in which spirits and angels live coming from the Lord as the sun, *Supp* 20
    light meaning divine truth and the Word, *Lord* 2
    location in the spiritual world depending on receptivity to light from the Lord, *Supp* 48:1, 73
    the Lord being the light that came into the world, *Lord* 1
    spiritual light
        being divine wisdom, *Life* 86:3; *Supp* 14
        entering our understanding to the extent that we are able to perceive it, *Supp* 14
        the light of heaven being, *Faith* 3
        radiating spiritual light reaching an outermost circumference, *Supp* 14, 20, 48:1

Literal meaning (earthly meaning) of the Word, *SS* 5, 6:2. *See also* Heavenly meaning of the Word; Inner meaning of the Word; The Word
    the decorated surfaces inside the Temple representing the literal meaning, *SS* 47
    divine truth being present in the literal meaning, *SS* 38:2, 97:3
    doubt caused by a literal reading, *SS* 18
    the earthly, spiritual, and heavenly meanings of the Ten Commandments, *SS* 67
    the foundations of the wall of the New Jerusalem in Revelation 21 meaning the truths of the literal meaning, *SS* 43
    a knowledge of the literal meaning leading people to think they are part of the church, *SS* 76
    the literal meaning
        being a container of the spiritual and heavenly meanings, *SS* 30–33, 35, 36, 38:2, 40
        being divine truth in its outermost form, *SS* 44:1
        being in communication with heaven and opening it, *SS* 96a
        being made up of semblances of truth, *SS* 40, 51:1, 91, 95
        being the source of a body of teaching, *SS* 43, 50, 53, 55, 59
        bringing angels and humans together, *SS* 49:5, 63, 67:6, 68, 69
        as the covering of the deeper levels, *SS* 30, 40, 45
        protecting the real truths within, *SS* 97
    the Lord being present with us in the literal (earthly) meaning, *SS* 50, 53, 58
    the Lord teaching and enlightening us through the literal meaning, *SS* 50
    our being reformed and reborn through truths from the literal meaning, *SS* 49:1
    our union with the Lord (and with heaven) taking place in the literal meaning, *SS* 62, 64:2
    precious stones corresponding to the literal meaning, *Supp* 81
    the prophets representing violence done to the literal meaning, *SS* 35
    the spirit and life in the literal meaning, *SS* 39
    the spiritual and heavenly meanings being in the earthly meaning, *SS* 37, 38:2, 39, 63, 65, 66, 80
    the spiritual meaning not being evident in the literal meaning, *SS* 13:4, 14:2
    truths of the literal meaning being meant by the precious stones in the Garden of Eden, *SS* 45, 97:4
    the Urim and Thummim meaning the good and true elements of the literal meaning, *SS* 44
    the veils and curtains of the tabernacle symbolizing the literal meaning, *SS* 46
    the Word
        being in its fullness in the literal meaning, *SS* 37, 49:5, 53, 62
        having an earthly meaning and a spiritual meaning, *Lord* 2
        in its literal meaning being the emanating divine influence at the outermost level, *Supp* 62
        in its literal meaning giving many names to a single entity, *Lord* 55:1–2
        its outermost level compared to a ruby and a diamond because of the earthly meaning, *SS* 42
        misconceptions that arise when it is understood only in its literal meaning, *Supp* 3

London, two cities in the spiritual world that are similar to, *Supp* 42–43. *See also* Britain

The Lord. *See also* Christ; The Crucifixion; The Divine-Human One; Divinity; The Father; Glorification; God; The Holy Spirit; Jehovah; Jesus; *The Lord;* The Lord's Coming; The Lord's divine nature; The Lord's human nature; Messiah; The Son; The Son of God; The Son of Humanity; Trinity; Worship
    acknowledging the Lord as God, *Life* 66:2
    the Athanasian statement of faith asserting that God and a human being in the Lord are one person, *Lord* 60
    belief in the Lord, *Lord* 17:2, 32:6–7, 35:2, 55:5; *Life* 48, 51; *Faith* 34, 36

The Lord (*continued*)

beliefs about the Lord (*see also under* Belief)
a caring faith in those who have turned toward the Lord and away from evils, *Faith* 23, 30
Christians who read the Word and worship the Lord being at the center of the world of spirits, *Supp* 48:1
the church being the church because of the Lord, *Lord* 55:4–5
a church where the Word is read and the Lord is known, *SS* 104, 110
the commandments of love for the Lord and for our neighbor, *Life* 31
divine goodness and divine truth emanating from the Lord, *SS* 19; *Life* 32:1
divine love and divine wisdom emanating from the Lord, *SS* 3:2
divine wisdom and divine love being one with each other and one in the Lord, *Lord* 1
doing the Lord's commandments, *Life* 104
enlightenment coming from the Lord, *SS* 50, 57, 91; *Supp* 11
everyone being capable of turning away from evils through the Lord's power, *Life* 31, 58
to the extent that we turn our backs on evil deeds because they are sins
we are given faith and caring by the Lord, *Supp* 49:2
we are (with and) in the Lord, *Life* 21, 24, 25, 48
freedom and reason being the Lord's within us, *Life* 101
God being the Lord, *Lord* 54, 60, 65; *Supp* 49
good actions of spiritual people coming from the Lord, *Life* 16, 50
the good things we do coming not from ourselves but from the Lord, *Life* 58, 72; *Supp* 46:2
goodness and truth as one in the Lord, *Life* 33
the heavenly, the spiritual, and the earthly emanating from the Lord, *SS* 6
inflow from the Lord, *SS* 61:2, 82; *Life* 110
location in the spiritual world
being determined by one's acknowledgment of the Lord and of the oneness of God, *Supp* 68
depending on receptivity to light from the Lord, *Supp* 73
the Lord alone fighting within us against evils, *Life* 96
the Lord and heaven (*see under* Heaven)
the Lord and hell (*see under* Hell)
the Lord and his disciples teaching repentance and the forgiveness of sins, *Lord* 18:4–5
the Lord and the Word (*see under* The Word)
the Lord and truth (*see under* Truth)
the Lord becoming our Savior through trials, *Lord* 33:5
the Lord being at once God and a human being, *Lord* 55:3
the Lord being called
David, *Lord* 37:1, 37:3, 42–45:1, 55:1
the God of Israel and the God of Jacob, *Lord* 37:1, 37:3, 39, 45:1
the Holy One of Israel, *Lord* 22, 37, 40, 45:1, 55:1; *SS* 88
Jehovah, *Lord* 14:9–10, 22, 30:2, 35:2, 37:1, 37:3, 38, 45:1
King and [Jehovah's] Anointed, *Lord* 37:1, 37:3, 42, 45:1, 55:1
Lord and God, *Lord* 41, 45:1, 55:1
Savior and Redeemer, *Lord* 33:4, 39
the Shepherd, *Faith* 61
the Lord being divine goodness and divine truth, *SS* 100
the Lord being divine love, *Supp* 14, 21
the Lord being divine truth and divine wisdom, *Lord* 1, 51:3
the Lord being God, *Lord* 45; *Faith* 35
from eternity, *Lord* 1, 19:1
and having power over heaven and earth, *Supp* 59
of heaven and earth, *SS* 104
the Lord being goodness itself and truth itself, *Life* 38
the Lord being human, *SS* 100, 116:1; *Supp* 34
the Lord being love itself, mercy itself, and goodness itself, *SS* 94
the Lord being one with the Father, *Lord* 1, 29:2, 32:7, 35:3, 35:8, 35:11
the Lord being revealed to Swedenborg, *Lord* preface
the Lord being the Messiah or Christ, *Lord* 42
the Lord being the quintessential (greatest) prophet, *Lord* 15:2–3, 15:8, 16:5
the Lord being the Redeemer and Savior, *Lord* 3, 5, 38, 45:3, 65; *Life* 47
the Lord being the Son of God (*see* The Son of God)
the Lord being the Son of Humanity (*see* The Son of Humanity)
the Lord calling Jehovah "Father," *Lord* 20
the Lord carrying our iniquities (sins), *Lord* 15:1–2, 16:4, 16:7, 65
the Lord doing everything, *Life* 48
the Lord doing the will of the Father, *Lord* 20
the Lord establishing a new church, *Lord* preface, 3, 5, 20, 26:2, 62:2
the Lord existing before his coming into the world, *Lord* 37:3
the Lord from eternity being Jehovah, *Lord* 30

The Lord (continued)
- the Lord fulfilling the law, *Lord* 8, 11, 14:11, 18:1–2, 65
- the Lord gaining divine power when he fulfilled the whole Word, *Lord* 27:2
- the Lord giving us freedom and the power to reason, *Life* 102
- the Lord giving us the ability to respond, *Life* 102–105
- the Lord having been conceived by God the Father, *Supp* 89
- the Lord loving us and dwelling with us, *Life* 102
- the Lord making a new church in both the spiritual and the earthly worlds, *Lord* 62:2
- the Lord not acknowledging himself to be the son of David, *Lord* 35:5
- the Lord not bringing destruction on anyone, *Supp* 28
- the Lord not calling Mary "mother," *Lord* 35:4
- the Lord opening our spiritual mind when we turn our backs on evils because they are sins, *Life* 86:4
- the Lord rising after death with his whole body, *Lord* 35:9–10
- the Lord shedding everything human he received from his mother, *Supp* 66
- the Lord speaking in correspondences while on earth, *SS* 17, 20:3, 40:2, 3; *Life* 66:2
- the Lord speaking through the prophets, *Lord* 37:2
- the Lord taking up our iniquities (sins), *Lord* 15:1–2, 17
- the Lord teaching and enlightening us through the literal meaning, *SS* 50
- the Lord teaching good and loving actions, *Life* 73
- the Lord's Coming (*see* The Lord's Coming)
- the Lord's constant presence and wish to come in, *Life* 57
- the Lord's divine nature (*see* The Lord's divine nature)
- the Lord's glorification (*see* Glorification)
- the Lord's human nature (*see* The Lord's human nature)
- the Lord's human substance or essence becoming just like his divine substance or essence, *Lord* 35:11
- the Lord's kingdom, *Lord* 42; *SS* 26:1
- the Lord's merit and righteousness (justice), *Lord* 18:3, 65
- the Lord's parables, *SS* 17; *Life* 2; *Supp* 10
- the Lord's presence in the law (Ten Commandments), *Life* 55:2–3
- the Lord's role in our salvation (*see under* Salvation)
- the Lord's state of being brought low, *Lord* 35:3, 59
- the Lord's trials, *Lord* 15:1–2, 33, 35:3, 59, 65
- the Lord's words and the miracles he performed having an inner meaning, *SS* 17:4
- the Lord's words being life, *SS* 2, 17:4
- "love" really meaning love for the Lord, *Faith* 22
- the marriage of the Lord and the church (*see under* Marriage)
- misconceptions about the Lord (*see under* Belief)
- a mutual relationship with the Lord, *Life* 103–105
- Muslims recognizing the Lord as the greatest prophet, *Supp* 68
- names of the Lord, *Lord* 22, 36:2, 37, 45:1, 55:1; *SS* 88
- the only source of true teachings being through heaven from the Lord, *Lord* 63
- only the Lord as able to regenerate us, *Life* 112
- only the Lord as able to set aside the compulsions to evil of our deeper nature, *Life* 110
- our being kept in freedom to turn toward the Lord or the Devil while in this world, *Life* 19, 20, 69
- our being unable to turn our backs on evils because they are sins unless we acknowledge and turn to the Lord, *Life* 66:2
- our evils keeping the Lord from coming in to us, *Life* 18
- our freedom to turn toward heaven or hell coming from the Lord, *Life* 20
- our good deeds as coming from the Lord to the extent that we are in the Lord, *Life* 21
- our loving the Lord to the extent that we focus on goodness and love what is true, *Life* 38
- our union with the Lord (*see under* Union)
- people of other religions being taught in the spiritual world that the Lord was born as a human, *Supp* 75
- Protestants occupying the central area of the spiritual world because they read the Word and worship the Lord, *Supp* 14, 20, 22
- radiating spiritual light from the Lord reaching an outermost circumference, *Supp* 14, 20
- "spirit" meaning the Lord's life and the Lord himself, *Lord* 50
- those who acknowledge the Lord alone as God (Lord) of heaven and earth, *Lord* 65; *Supp* 76
- those who worship nature having thinking that comes from themselves rather than from heaven and the Lord, *SS* 1
- the trinity in the Lord, *Lord* 46:2, 46:3, 46:6, 55:1
- what the prophets said about the Lord, *Lord* 3
- the worship of saints as diverting worship from the Lord, *Supp* 64

The Lord, *Lord* preface. *See also* The Lord
- references to *The Lord*, *SS* 2:2, 10, 32, 35, 43, 62, 88, 89, 98; *Life* 79:3; *Supp* 12, 76

The Lord's Coming, *Lord* 6. *See also* Jesus; The Lord
"day" and "time" meaning the Lord's Coming, *Lord* 4, 5
how the Lord's Coming changed the state of the church, *SS* 99
idolatry before the Lord's Coming, *Lord* 33:3
the Lord being sent into the world by the Father, *Lord* 20
the Lord coming into the world
to bring heaven and earth into order, *Lord* 14:1
to carry out a last judgment, *Lord* 14:10
to found a new church, *Lord* 20, 26:2
to fulfill the Word, *SS* 98, 111
to glorify his human nature (*see* Glorification)
to save humankind, *Lord* 3, 14:1–3, 14:7, 17:1, 18:1, 33:3; *Faith* 34, 35
to subdue the hells, *Lord* 17:1, 26:2, 34:1, 65
when the church was at an end, *Lord* 33:3
the Lord's Coming being called "the gospel of the kingdom," *Lord* 42
the Lord's Coming saving humankind from eternal death, *Lord* 3, 18; *Faith* 39
the name "the Son of Humanity" being used when the subject is the Lord's Coming, *Lord* 23, 26
prophecies about the Lord's Coming, *Lord* 14, 19:5–7, 21, 64:2–5; *SS* 15:2, 101:2
the rise of the hells before the Lord's Coming, *Lord* 33:3
the timing and purpose of the Lord's Coming, *Lord* 3, 5

The Lord's divine nature. *See also* Divinity; Glorification; The Lord; The Lord's human nature
the divine and human natures in the Lord being one, *Lord* 21, 29:1–2, 34:4, 35:2, 35:11
the divine nature being indivisible, *Lord* 57
the divine nature in the Lord being like the soul within the body, *Lord* 29:1–2, 32:7, 34:4, 35:2, 35:11
the Holy Spirit being the emanating divine nature, *Lord* 46:2
the human nature that came from the Lord's divine nature being the Son of God, *Lord* 32:7
the Lord being divine because of Jehovah the Father and human because of the Virgin Mary, *Lord* 35:1
the Lord being Jehovah and God in respect to both his human nature and his divine nature, *Lord* 34
the Lord making the human nature divine from the divine nature within himself, *Lord* 32
the Lord's divine and human natures being united by his suffering on the cross, *Lord* 34
the Lord's divine nature being from his own divine nature from eternity and his human nature being from Mary in time, *Lord* 59
the Lord's divine nature being the Father, *Lord* 32:7, 57

The Lord's human nature. *See also* Jesus; The Lord; The Lord's divine nature
the Athanasian statement of faith on the Lord's human nature, *Lord* 59
the divine and human natures in the Lord being one, *Lord* 21, 29:1–2, 34:4, 35:2, 35:11
"the Holy One of Israel" meaning the Lord in his divine-human nature, *Lord* 40
the Lord being divine because of Jehovah the Father and human because of the Virgin Mary, *Lord* 35:1
the Lord being Jehovah and God in respect to both his human nature and his divine nature, *Lord* 34
the Lord from eternity, or Jehovah, taking on a human nature to save us, *Lord* 31
the Lord glorifying his human nature (*see* Glorification)
the Lord making his human nature divine, *Lord* 20, 29:2, 32:1–4, 33, 35, 36:1, 59; *Supp* 75
the Lord taking off the human nature that he received from his mother, *Lord* 16:6, 35, 59; *Supp* 66
the Lord uniting his human nature to the divine nature of the Father, *Lord* 17:1
the Lord's divine and human natures being united by his suffering on the cross, *Lord* 34
the Lord's divine nature being from his own divine nature from eternity and his human nature being from Mary in time, *Lord* 59
the Lord's divine-human nature being the Son, *Lord* 57
the Lord's human nature being called Son of Humanity, *Lord* 55:1
the Lord's human nature from his mother being material and his human nature from his Father being substantial, *Lord* 35:2
the Lord's human side being conceived by Jehovah the Father and born of the Virgin Mary, *Lord* 19:2–3, 20, 30:1, 59
the Lord's human side being the Son of God, *Lord* 19:2–3, 19:9–10, 20, 32:7, 55:1, 59
the Son, or the Lord's divine-human nature, being the Redeemer and Savior, *Lord* 34:3

Louis XIV *(king of France)*, *Supp* 60

Love, *Lord* 18:1, 18:5. *See also* Caring; Goodness; Will
communities in the world of spirits corresponding to different kinds of love, *Supp* 21, 57
control in marriage *vs.* mutual love, *Supp* 51:2

Love *(continued)*
    goodness united to truth making love and wisdom for angels and for us, *Life* 32:2
    heaven's warmth being love, *Life* 15
    love and faith
        the church existing by means of its, *SS* 77
        geographical regions in the spiritual world being related to, *Supp* 48:2
        love bringing forth faith, *Faith* 13
        love for (focus on) what is good leading to faith, *Life* 36, 45
    love and truth (*see under* Truth)
    love being our life, *Supp* 21
    love being the underlying reality and our thinking being its manifestation, *Life* 48
    love belonging to the will, *Life* 48
    the love of controlling others, *Faith* 49, 55; *Supp* 61–63
    love of our occupations being an earthly type of love, *Faith* 25
    "love" really meaning love for the Lord, *Faith* 22
    marriage love being a heavenly love, *Supp* 51:2, 72:3
    our calling "rational" whatever agrees with our will or love, *Life* 15
    our thinking and doing freely whatever we love, *Life* 1
    people devoted to earthly love being in hell, *Supp* 21
    the source of everything in the spiritual world being a sun that is pure love, *Supp* 38
    spiritual love, *Faith* 51; *Supp* 21, 48:3, 49:2, 51:1
    true marriage love being with one spouse, *Supp* 77
    what we love constituting our life, *Life* 1
    wisdom dwelling with good actions that come from love, *SS* 74
Lower earth, *Supp* 65. *See also* The world of spirits
Lungs. *See* Heart and lungs
Luther, Martin, *Supp* 54, 55. *See also* Protestants; The Reformation

M

Marriage. *See also* Adultery; Husbands; *Marriage Love;* Polygamy; Wives
    control in marriage *vs.* mutual love, *Supp* 51:2
    marriage love being a heavenly love, *Supp* 51:2, 72:3
    the marriage of goodness and truth, *SS* 80–83, 85, 88, 114; *Life* 43:2
    the marriage of the Lord and the church
        in the details of the Word, *SS* 80, 82, 87:2, 88, 89, 114
        the marriage of one husband and one wife corresponding to, *Supp* 71
        a marriage of the Lord and the church within us, *SS* 83
    our being ignorant of the chastity of marriage if we have not turned our backs on the lechery of adultery as a sin, *Life* 76
    our loving marriage to the extent that we turn our backs on adultery, *Life* 75
    Swedenborg's conversations with Muslims in the spiritual world regarding marriage, *Supp* 72:3
    true marriage love being with one spouse, *Supp* 77
    the union of evil and falsity being called "the hellish marriage," *Life* 33
    the union of goodness and truth being called "the heavenly marriage," *Life* 33, 41
Marriage Love. See also Marriage
    references to *Marriage Love, Life* 74, 77
Mary. *See also* Jesus
    Jesus (the Lord's human side) having been conceived by Jehovah and born of the Virgin Mary, *Lord* 19:2–3, 20, 21, 29:2, 30:1, 59
    the Lord being divine because of Jehovah the Father and human because of the Virgin Mary, *Lord* 35:1
    the Lord not calling Mary "mother," *Lord* 35:4
    the Lord taking off the human nature that he received from his mother, *Lord* 16:6, 35, 59; *Supp* 66
    the Lord's divine nature being from his own divine nature from eternity and his human nature being from Mary in time, *Lord* 59
    the Lord's human nature from his mother being material and his human nature from his Father being substantial, *Lord* 35:2
    Swedenborg's interaction with Mary in the spiritual world, *Supp* 66
Masoretes, *SS* 13:4
Matter
    the Lord's human nature from his mother being material and his human nature from his Father being substantial, *Lord* 35:2
Matthew, Gospel of, *Faith* 61; *Supp* 16:2. *See also* The disciples; The Gospels; The Word
Melanchthon, Philipp, *Supp* 47, 54. *See also* Protestants; The Reformation
Memory, *Faith* 26. *See also* The mind
Mercy, *Lord* 18:1
Merit
    the belief that the Lord's merit is imputed to us, *Lord* 18:2–3, 65
    the Son's merit, *Faith* 38, 39, 42, 44, 45
Messiah, *Lord* 19:8, 55:1; *Supp* 82. *See also* The Lord
Middle East, the knowledge of correspondences in, *SS* 21, 23:3. *See also* Canaan; Jerusalem

The mind. *See also* Memory; The rational; Reason; Thought; Understanding
- the cravings of our evils clogging the deeper levels of our earthly mind, *Life* 86:4, 5
- the mind compared to a garden, *Life* 86:3, 86:5
- the spiritual mind
  - enabling us to live after death, *Life* 86:1
  - guile and trickery united with theft infecting our spiritual mind, *Life* 81, 85
  - the opening of, *Life* 86:2, 86:4; *Faith* 32
- our having an earthly mind and a spiritual mind, *Life* 86; *Faith* 32
- truth taking root in the spiritual mind, *Life* 90
- will and understanding together making the mind, *Life* 43, 85

Miracles, *SS* 17:4; *Life* 53, 55:1, 55:3, 59

Monarchs. *See* King; Kingdom

The moral. *See also* The earthly; The heavenly; The spiritual
- all societies knowing that it is evil to steal, commit adultery, murder, and bear false witness, *Life* 53
- civic, moral, and spiritual good works, *Life* 12
- the Last Judgment being carried out on those who were outwardly moral but not inwardly spiritual, *Faith* 64; *Supp* 28
- moral earthly individuals compared to moral spiritual individuals, *Life* 109
- moral individuals who turn their backs on evils but not because they are sins, *Life* 108, 111; *Supp* 10
- obeying the law for civic and moral reasons but not religious reasons, *Life* 63:1–2, 64
- outward morality as not real morality, *Life* 111
- the Ten Commandments as civil, moral, and spiritual laws, *Life* 53
- whether we are moral and civic individuals depends on whether we have spiritual goodness, *Life* 13, 14

Moravians, *Supp* 86–90. *See also* Protestants
- Nikolaus von Zinzendorf, *Supp* 89
- religious beliefs and practices of Moravians, *Supp* 86–89
- Swedenborg's conversations with Moravians in the spiritual world, *Supp* 86

Moses, *Lord* 9, 14:11; *SS* 103; *Supp* 80. *See also* The Law and the Prophets

Muhammad. *See also* Islam; Qur'an
- Muslims and Muhammad in the spiritual world, *Supp* 68–72
- a person identified as Muhammad always appearing to Muslims in the spiritual world, *Supp* 69

Muslims. *See* Islam

Mysteries
- Moravians' religious mysteries, *Supp* 86–89
- spiritual mysteries being revealed, *SS* 6:2, 20, 32, 70, 80; *Supp* 7, 72:2

N

Names
- all names in the Word having to do with matters of (heaven and) the church, *SS* 15:1, 2; *Faith* 49
- names of the Lord, *Lord* 22, 36:2, 37, 45:1, 55:1; *SS* 88

Nations
- "nations" having to do with goodness and "peoples" having to do with truth, *SS* 86

Nature
- comparisons from the three kingdoms of nature, *SS* 66
- our inner nature (*see* Inner nature)
- those who worship nature, *SS* 1

Nazirites, *SS* 49:2–4

Neighbor
- caring as love for our neighbor, *Faith* 20, 22
- the commandments of love for the Lord and for our neighbor, *Life* 31
- loving our neighbors for the service we offer them, *Faith* 21
- our deeds (actions) being good to the extent that they come from love of our neighbor, *Life* 72
- our having love for our neighbor to the extent that we turn our backs on killing, *Life* 70, 89
- studying the Word from love of truth and of one's neighbor as leading to heaven, *SS* 61:3
- usefulness being our neighbor in a spiritual sense, *Faith* 20
- what "our neighbor" is, *Faith* 20

The new church. *See also* The church
- the holy Jerusalem meaning a new church, *Lord* 63, 64; *SS* 10
- the Lord establishing a new church, *Lord* preface, 3, 5, 20, 26:2, 62:2
- the new church being established among people outside Jerusalem, *Lord* 64:3
- New Jerusalem meaning a new church, *Lord* preface; *SS* 43
- prophecies about the establishment of a new church, *Lord* 61:1, 62:1, 64:2–8
- revelations for the new church being given after the Last Judgment, *Supp* 12
- teachings for the new church, *Lord* preface, 65

New Jerusalem, meaning a new church, *Lord* preface. *See also* Jerusalem

New Jerusalem, Lord preface
- references to *New Jerusalem, Lord* 12; *SS* 10; *Life* 100, 101 note a; *Faith* 37, 40

O

Occupation, love of one's, *Faith* 25. *See also* Business; Usefulness

Omnipotence, Omnipresence, and Omniscience, *Lord* 46:2

Opposites
> evil and goodness as opposites, *Life* 8, 70, 71
> heaven and hell being opposites, *Life* 18
> opposite, or negative, inner meanings, *Lord* 2
> our coming into goodness that is the opposite of the evil on which we turn our backs, *Life* 21, 24, 70, 75, 82–84, 88, 89

Other Planets, *Lord* preface

P

Parables, *SS* 17; *Life* 2, 90; *Supp* 10. *See also* Fables; Inner meaning of the Word; Literal meaning of the Word

Parisians, *Supp* 67

Penn, William, *Supp* 84. *See also* Quakers

Peoples
> "nations" having to do with goodness and "peoples" having to do with truth, *SS* 86

Perception, *SS* 58; *Faith* 5; *Supp* 14. *See also* Knowledge; Recognition

Philistia, *Faith* 49, 53, 55

Philistines, *Faith* 49–53

Polygamy, *Supp* 71, 72:3, 77. *See also* Marriage

Pope, *Supp* 59, 60. *See also* Roman Catholic Church; Saints, Catholic; Unigenitus

Power. *See also* Control; Governance
> the Lord gaining divine power when he fulfilled the whole Word, *Lord* 27:2
> the Lord having power over heaven and earth, *Supp* 59
> Nazirites representing the Lord's power through the outermost forms of truth, *SS* 49:2–4
> the power of the Ten Commandments, *Life* 56, 59
> the Word being in its fullness, holiness, and power in the literal meaning, *SS* 49

Prayer, read to people who are taking the Holy Supper, *Life* 4–7; *Supp* 45. *See also* The church; Religion; Worship

Preachers (clergy; priests). *See also* The church; Religion
> British clergy being focused on teachings about faith, while the British laity is focused on teachings about how to live, *Supp* 45
> British preachers (elders) in the spiritual world who believe in faith alone, *Life* 7; *Supp* 42:2–3, 44, 45

Pronouncements, *SS* 103

Prophecies, about the Lord's Coming, *Lord* 14, 19:5–7, 21, 64:2–5; *SS* 15:2, 101:2. *See also* Prophets

Prophetic books, of the Old Testament, *SS* 13:4. *See also* Daniel, Book of; Job, Book of; Prophets; The Word
> the inner meanings of words being the same in the prophetic books as in the Gospels, *SS* 17:3
> the prophetic books being unintelligible except through the spiritual meaning, *SS* 15, 16, 51:1

Prophets. *See also* Prophecies; Prophetic books
> Jehovah speaking through the prophets, *Lord* 52–54; *SS* 2
> Jehovah talking with the prophets, *Lord* 52
> the Lord as the quintessential (greatest) prophet, *Lord* 15:2–3, 15:8, 16:5
> the Lord speaking through the prophets, *Lord* 37:2
> Muslims recognizing the Lord as the greatest prophet, *Supp* 68
> the prophets being called "children of humanity" or "sons of humanity," *Lord* 28
> the prophets carrying the iniquities of the people, *Lord* 16:1–3
> the prophets foretelling
>> the establishment of a new church, *Lord* 64:2–8
>> the Lord's Coming, *Lord* 14, 19:5–7, 21, 64:2–5; *SS* 15:2, 101:2
>> a new heaven and a new earth, *Lord* 62:2, 64:3
> the prophets having visions, *Lord* 52
> the prophets representing
>> the body of teaching the church draws from the Word, *Lord* 15:8, 28; *SS* 35
>> the Lord as the Word, *Lord* 28
>> violence done to the literal meaning of the Word, *SS* 35
> the Word and the church, *Lord* 15:2, 15:4–8
> the spirit of the prophets being called the Holy Spirit, *Lord* 51:5
> the suffering of the prophets, *Lord* 15:2, 15:4–7
> what the prophets said about the Lord, *Lord* 3
> the Word being given to the prophets, *SS* 102:2

Protestants. *See also* Calvin, John; Christianity; The church; Luther, Martin; Melanchthon, Philipp; The Reformation; *and names of specific denominations*
> how the Last Judgment was carried out on Protestants, *Supp* 2, 15, 16–22
> irreligious Protestants being cast into hell after death, *Supp* 17
> Protestants' location in the spiritual world, *Supp* 14, 20, 22, 48:1
> the separation of Protestants and Catholics in the spiritual world, *Supp* 56

Purpose. *See* Goal, means, and result

Q

Quakers, *Supp* 83–85
Qur'an, *Supp* 69, 70. *See also* Islam

R

Rank, concealing our inner nature to earn money or, *Life* 68. *See also* Reputation; Wealth
The rational, *Life* 12, 15. *See also* The mind; Thought; Understanding
Reason, *SS* 116:3; *Life* 101, 102. *See also* The mind; Thought; Understanding
Rebirth, through truths from the literal meaning of the Word, *SS* 49:1. *See also* Reformation; Regeneration
Receptiveness, *Life* 102, 106, 107. *See also* Responsiveness
Recognition. *See also* Knowledge; Perception
   faith as an inner recognition that something is true, *Faith* 2, 11–13, 24, 30
   the inner recognition that occurs in the light of truth from the Word, *Faith* 10
   the misconception that faith is thinking that something is true without a recognition that it is true, *Faith* 9, 10, 31
   those who have a longing (love) for truth recognizing whether something is true, *Faith* 3–5
Redemption. *See also* Atonement; Salvation
   beliefs about redemption, *Lord* 15:1
   the name "the Son of Humanity" being used when the subject is the Lord's redeeming, saving, reforming, or regenerating us, *Lord* 23, 27
   the Redeemer and Savior
      being the Lord, *Lord* 3, 5, 33:4, 38, 39, 45:3, 65; *Life* 47
      being the Son, or the Lord's divine-human nature, *Lord* 34:3
      Jehovah being called, *Lord* 34:2–4, 38, 55:1
Reformation, *Life* 112. *See also* Rebirth; The Reformation; Regeneration
   the church's teachings in regard to reformation, *Life* 106
   faith seeming to come before caring during the stage of reformation, *Faith* 31
   the Lord providing a means of reformation to save us from eternal death, *Life* 69
   the name "the Son of Humanity" being used when the subject is the Lord's redeeming, saving, reforming, or regenerating us, *Lord* 23, 27
   our being reformed and reborn through truths from the literal meaning of the Word, *SS* 49:1
   our enlightenment and reformation depending on communication with heaven, *Supp* 12
   our reformation depending on our understanding being raised into heaven, *Life* 15
   reformation as impossible without freedom and reason, *Life* 101
The Reformation, *SS* 24, 110. *See also* Calvin, John; Luther, Martin; Melanchthon, Philipp; Protestants; Reformation
Regeneration, *Lord* 23, 27, 49; *Life* 112; *Faith* 31. *See also* Rebirth; Reformation
Religion. *See also* Christianity; The church; Islam; Jewish religion; Prayer; Preachers; Protestants; Teachings; Worship; *and names of specific denominations*
   African spirits scoffing at the religious beliefs of European spirits, *Supp* 78
   all newly arrived spirits being kept at first in their original religion, *Supp* 59
   all religions agreeing that we are damned if we do not refrain from sins, *Life* 64
   all societies with religion having laws similar to the Ten Commandments, *Life* 65
   Babylon as a religion corrupted by a love of control over others, *Faith* 49, 55
   delusional spirits who confirm people's beliefs about their religion, *Supp* 90
   the Dutch holding firmly to their religious principles, *Supp* 49, 50
   the fate of irreligious Dutch people in the Last Judgment, *Supp* 53
   the inner nature of outwardly religious spirits being revealed during the Last Judgment, *Supp* 19, 23, 24
   irreligious people turning their backs on evils because they are harmful, *Life* 111
   irreligious Protestants being cast into hell after death, *Supp* 17
   the law (Ten Commandments) being a summary of everything that constitutes religion, *Life* 54, 56
   laws of religion being for God's sake and the sake of our salvation, *Life* 53
   living by our religion, *Supp* 76
   obeying the law for civic and moral reasons but not religious reasons, *Life* 63:1–2, 64
   people having had religious knowledge from the earliest times and all over the world, *SS* 117
   people of every religion being dependent on the union of the Lord and heaven with the church through the Word, *SS* 105
   people of other (non-Christian) religions in the spiritual world, *Supp* 14, 73–75
   people whose understanding has been closed because of their religion, *Faith* 48
   people with religion knowing that those who live a good life are saved and those who live an evil life are damned, *Life* 1, 3, 4, 7

Religion *(continued)*
    Philistia as religion corrupted by pride in one's own intelligence, *Faith* 49, 53, 55
    the Protestants on whom the Last Judgment was carried out being outwardly but not inwardly religious, *Supp* 16–22
    religion being central to our nature, *Supp* 69
    religious beliefs and practices of Moravians, *Supp* 86–89
    religious beliefs and practices of Quakers, *Supp* 85
    religious groups in the human being that makes up heaven, *SS* 105:2–3
    those who do not regard adultery as a sin not having any religion, *Life* 77
    using the intellect to test religious ideas, *Supp* 46:2
    what religion is about
        doing what is good, *Life* 2, 8, 31
        how we live, *Life* 2, 8
        shown by the Word, *Life* 2

Repentance, *Lord* 17:3, 18, 65; *Life* 103. *See also* Salvation; Sin

Reputation, *Life* 35, 92. *See also* Rank; Wealth

Responsiveness, *Life* 102–106

Resurrection, *Lord* 35:9–10; *Supp* 72:2. *See also* Glorification

Revelation, Book of. *See also* Revelations; The Word
    the Book of Revelation dealing with the state of the Christian church, *Lord* 62:1; *Faith* 55
    the Book of Revelation promising the spiritual meaning of the Word, *SS* 25
    the dragon in the Book of Revelation, *Faith* 55–60; *Supp* 16:2, 28
    the foundations of the wall of the New Jerusalem in Revelation 21 meaning the truths of the literal meaning, *SS* 43
    the inner meaning of Revelation chapter 12, *Faith* 58–59
    the inner meaning of Revelation chapter 13, *Faith* 60
    the new heaven and the new earth in Revelation, *Lord* 62:1, 64:3, 65
    Revelation 21 and 22 foretelling the establishment of a new church at the close of the former one, *Lord* 61:1, 62:1
    the spiritual meaning of passages in Revelation, *SS* 9–13
    White Horse explaining the spiritual meaning of passages in Revelation 19, *SS* 9

Revelations, for the new church being given after the Last Judgment, *Supp* 12. *See also* Revelation, Book of

Roman Catholic Church, *SS* 24. *See also* Christianity; The church; Pope; Saints, Catholic
    Catholics forbidden from reading the Word, *Faith* 8
    Catholics in the spiritual world, *Supp* 56–60
        their location, *Supp* 56
        their saints, *Supp* 61–67
        their separation from Protestants, *Supp* 56
    Catholics in the world of spirits being governed by a supposed pope, *Supp* 59
    Catholics who become angels, *Supp* 58
    Catholics who have a love of controlling others, *Supp* 62
    the hell of Catholics who want to be called upon as gods, *Supp* 62–64
    the Last Judgment on Catholics, *Supp* 56

S

Sacred Scripture, *Lord* preface, 3, 65
    references to *Sacred Scripture,* *Lord* 14:12; *Life* 14, 15, 62, 66:2, 87; *Faith* 65; *Supp* 14, 48:1, 76, 81, 82:1
    Sacred Scripture showing that the whole Sacred Scripture is written about the Lord, *Lord* 7

Sacrifices, *SS* 101

Saints, Catholic, *Supp* 59, 61–67. *See also* Roman Catholic Church

Salvation, *Lord* 35:2. *See also* Damnation; Heaven; Redemption
    the Lord's role in our salvation
        the Lord becoming our Savior through trials, *Lord* 33:5
        the Lord coming into the world to save humankind, *Lord* 3, 14:1–3, 14:7, 17:1, 18:1, 33:3; *Faith* 34, 35
        the Lord from eternity, or Jehovah, taking on a human nature to save us, *Lord* 31
        the Lord transferring salvation to us after we practice repentance, *Lord* 18:2
        our being saved by a faith focused on the Lord, *Lord* 32:7
        our being saved by belief in the Lord, *Faith* 34, 36
        our salvation depending on good and loving actions that come from the Lord and truths of our faith that come from the Lord, *Lord* 18:5
        salvation not being possible apart from the Lord, *Lord* 33:4; *SS* 104
    misconceptions about salvation
        belief in salvation through faith alone, *Lord* 18:2; *Life* 4, 91; *Faith* 42; *Supp* 54, 55
        the belief that salvation depends on believing the teachings of the church, *Life* 91
        the belief that salvation does not depend on obeying the Ten Commandments, *Life* 91
        the belief that we are saved by believing that the Son was sent to make satisfaction for the human race, *Faith* 38, 39, 42, 44, 45

Salvation *(continued)*
> misconceptions about salvation *(continued)*
>> the Christian teaching that living an evil life does not damn those who have been justified by faith alone, *Life* 4
>> the misconception that deeds have nothing to do with salvation, *Faith* 68; *Supp* 46:1
>> the name "the Son of Humanity" being used when the subject is the Lord's redeeming, saving, reforming, or regenerating us, *Lord* 23, 27
>> our faith saving us when we have ceased to sin, *Life* 51
>> recognition of the Lord and salvation not being possible without the Word, *SS* 111
> the Redeemer and Savior
>> being the Lord, *Lord* 3, 5, 33:4, 38, 39, 45:3, 65; *Life* 47
>> being the Son, or the Lord's divine-human nature, *Lord* 34:3
>> Jehovah being called, *Lord* 34:2–4, 38, 55:1
> religion and salvation
>> laws of religion being for God's sake and the sake of our salvation, *Life* 53
>> people with religion knowing that those who live a good life are saved and those who live an evil life are damned, *Life* 1, 3, 4, 7
> salvation and works (actions; deeds)
>> all who live by the laws of the Ten Commandments being saved, and all who do not being damned, *Life* 65
>> the belief that we go to hell if we do evil and to heaven if we do good, *Life* 1, 3, 4, 7, 94
>> good works that come from ourselves as not saving us, *Life* 11, 30:3
>> our salvation depending on works, *Life* 2
>> the salvation of the "sheep" after the Last Judgment, *Supp* 30–31
>> a saving faith being found only in people who are caring, *Faith* 24
>> the Word being a divine work for the salvation of the human race, *SS* 32

Samson, *SS* 49:2–4

Scholars (the learned), *SS* 61:1, 115:2–3, 116:1; *Supp* 46, 47. *See also* Knowledge; The mind

Secrets of Heaven
> references to *Secrets of Heaven, Lord* 64:1 note a; *SS* 44:3, 46

Seed, *Life* 90

Selfhood (sense of autonomy; what is our own). *See also* Self-importance
> abstaining from evil and doing good as though on our own, *Supp* 46:2–3
> acting as though we are on our own, *Life* 22, 101, 104, 107

> the faith that is God's compared to the faith that is our own, *Lord* 18:3
> our being unable to do anything good on our own, *Life* 17, 24, 29, 31, 58
> our inability to cleanse and purify ourselves from evil by our own strength, *Life* 112
> our seeming to use our own strength when we fight against evil, *Life* 96
> repentance depending on a sense of autonomy, *Life* 103
> turning our backs on evil because it is sinful, in apparent autonomy, *Life* 22; *Supp* 46:3

Self-importance (self-centeredness). *See also* Selfhood
> our being blinded by our self-importance, *SS* 60
> our self-centeredness as the taproot of our life, *Life* 93
> our self-centeredness (self-importance) being evil, *SS* 115, 116:1–2; *Life* 92, 93
> our self-importance as focused on ourselves and the world, *SS* 115:2
> our sense of self-importance corrupting our understanding, *Lord* 17:3
> our will as involving a sense of our own self-importance (self-aggrandizement), *SS* 115, 116
> those focused on their self-importance being closed to inflow from the Lord, *SS* 61:2

Seneca, *SS* 115:3

Sequential arrangement, *SS* 38, 65

Series
> everything that is complete containing a series of three, *SS* 28

Sheep. *See also* Goats
> the angels of the lowest heaven being the "sheep," *Supp* 10
> fights between sheep and goats, *Faith* 63:4, 65–67
> the Lord being called the Shepherd, *Faith* 61
> rams and sheep meaning people devoted to (a faith prompted by) caring, *Faith* 61, 67
> the salvation of the "sheep" after the Last Judgment, *Supp* 30–31
> the separation of the "sheep" and the "goats" during the Last Judgment, *Supp* 10

Sight. *See also* Visions
> the eyes of the spirit being opened, *Lord* 52; *Supp* 34, 35
> not the Father, but only the Divine-Human One as able to be seen, *Lord* 32:5

Simultaneous arrangement, *SS* 38, 65

Sin. *See also* Action; Evil; Repentance
> all religions agreeing that we are damned if we do not refrain from sins, *Life* 64
> breaking the laws of the Ten Commandments as a sin against God, *Life* 53, 63:3, 64
> false beliefs about sin, *Lord* 15:1

Sin *(continued)*
    the imputation of merit meaning the forgiveness of sins that follows repentance, *Lord* 18:2–3, 65
    the Lord and his disciples teaching repentance and the forgiveness of sins, *Lord* 18:4–5
    the Lord carrying (taking up) our iniquities (sins), *Lord* 15:1–2, 16:4, 16:7, 17, 65
    our faith saving us when we have ceased to sin, *Life* 51
    our loving honesty to the extent that we turn our backs on theft (deception) as a sin, *Life* 82–84, 89
    our loving truth to the extent that we turn our backs on lying because it is a sin, *Life* 88
    the prophets carrying the iniquities of the people, *Lord* 16:1–3
    rejecting sins making us love truths more, *Life* 41
    repentance as the only means by which sin can be taken away, *Lord* 17:3
    resisting evil behaviors as sins, *Life* 92
    turning our backs on adultery as a sin, *Life* 76, 77
    turning our backs on evils because they are sins (*see under* Evil)

The Son. *See also* The Father; Jesus; The Lord; The Son of God; The Son of Humanity; Trinity
    the belief that we are saved by believing that the Son was sent to make satisfaction for the human race, *Faith* 38, 39, 42, 44, 45
    the Father and the Son being one in the Lord, *Lord* 46:1
    the Lord alone being meant by "the Father, the Son, and the Holy Spirit," *Lord* 46:6
    the Lord calling himself "the Son," "the Son of God," or "the Son of Humanity," depending on the subject of the discourse, *Lord* 22
    our believing in the Lord who is both Father and Son, *Lord* 32:6
    the Son's merit, *Faith* 38, 39, 42, 44, 45
    the trinity of Father, Son, and Holy Spirit, *Lord* 57

The Son of God. *See also* The Divine-Human One; Jesus; The Lord; The Son; The Son of Humanity
    attributes of the Son of God
        being the human nature that came from the Lord's divine nature, *Lord* 32:7
        being the Jesus who was conceived by Jehovah the Father and born of the Virgin Mary, *Lord* 21
        being the Lord's divine-human nature, *Lord* 34:3, 57
        being the Lord's human side, *Lord* 19:2–3, 19:9–10, 20, 55:1, 59
        born into the world, not from eternity, *Lord* 19
        an element of the trinity within the Lord, *Lord* 55:1
    false beliefs about the Son of God, *Lord* 19
    the Jewish church understanding "the Son of God" to be the Messiah, *Lord* 19:8
    the Lord as the Divine-Human One being called "the Son of God," *Lord* 28
    the Lord calling himself "the Son," "the Son of God," or "the Son of Humanity," depending on the subject of the discourse, *Lord* 22
    Muslims recognizing the Lord as a son of God and as the wisest of all, *Supp* 68, 71

The Son of Humanity, *Lord* 16:7. *See also* The Lord; The Son; The Son of God
    the Lord calling himself "the Son," "the Son of God," or "the Son of Humanity," depending on the subject of the discourse, *Lord* 22
    the Lord's human nature being called Son of Humanity, *Lord* 55:1
    the name "the Son of Humanity" being used in certain contexts, *Lord* 23–26
    the prophets being called "children of humanity" or "sons of humanity," *Lord* 28
    "the Son of Humanity" meaning the Lord as the Word, *Lord* 23, 27, 28, 50:2

Soul. *See also* Body; Spirit
    the divine nature in the Lord being like the soul within the body, *Lord* 29:1–2, 32:7, 34:4, 35:2, 35:11
    the evils of our self-centeredness being harmful to our souls, *Life* 93
    the inner meaning within the outer meaning compared to a soul within a body, *SS* 4, 5, 9, 10
    misconceptions about the soul, *Supp* 32, 33
        the belief that body and soul are reunited on the day of the Last Judgment, *Supp* 72:2
        the belief that the soul is a breath (air; breeze), *Supp* 3, 4, 6, 72:2
    "spirit" or "soul" meaning the life that depends on breathing, *Lord* 47:1

Speech, *SS* 90:2; *Life* 15

Spirit. *See also* The Holy Spirit; Soul; The Spirit of Truth; Spirits; The spiritual
    the eyes of the spirit being opened, *Lord* 52; *Supp* 34, 35
    meanings of "spirit" ("soul")
        an individual's life, *Lord* 47
        the life of the Lord's wisdom, *Lord* 51
        the life of those who have been regenerated, *Lord* 49
        the life that depends on breathing, *Lord* 47:1
        the Lord's life and the Lord himself, *Lord* 50
        the variable attitude we take toward life, *Lord* 48
        what "spirit" means in the Word, *Lord* 46:7
    the spirit and life in the literal meaning of the Word, *SS* 39
    the spirit being the inner self, *Supp* 39

Spirit *(continued)*
    the spirit of the prophets being called the Holy Spirit, *Lord* 51:5

The Spirit of Truth, being the Lord, *Lord* 51:2–3

Spirits. *See also* Angels; Heaven; Hell; Life after death; Soul; Spirit; The spiritual; The spiritual world; The world of spirits
    all newly arrived spirits being kept at first in their original religion, *Supp* 59
    angels and spirits (*see under* Angels)
    communication with heaven through the Word misused by spirits living underneath the heavens, *SS* 64:2
    delusional spirits who confirm people's beliefs about their religion, *Supp* 90
    evil spirits casting themselves into hell, *Lord* 25
    evil spirits inflicting spiritual trials on us, *Lord* 33:1
    fanatical spirits who believe they are the Holy Spirit, *Supp* 83–85
    the Last Judgment being carried out on spirits who were outwardly moral but not inwardly spiritual, *Faith* 64; *Supp* 28
    the spirits affected by the Last Judgment looking like a great dragon, *Supp* 28
    spirits who are devoted to a faith that comes from caring, *Supp* 42:2
    spirits who believe in faith alone, *Faith* 56; *Supp* 42:2–3, 47
    spirits who made pseudo-heavens for themselves between heaven and hell, *Supp* 9, 10, 18, 20, 23, 57

The spiritual. *See also* The earthly; The heavenly; Spirit; Spirits; The spiritual world
    angels of the spiritual kingdom (spiritual angels), *SS* 6:1, 63, 64:1, 65, 67, 86
    the civic and the spiritual (*see under* The civic)
    divine love and wisdom as the source of everything spiritual in the spiritual world, *Supp* 20
    everything on earth corresponding to something spiritual, *SS* 20, 23:1
    faith and the spiritual
        blind faith not being a spiritual faith, *Faith* 1
        the faith of spiritual people being truth, *Life* 50
        spiritual faith compared to nonspiritual faith, *Life* 49, 50
    good actions of spiritual people coming from the Lord, *Life* 16, 50
    the heavenly, the spiritual, and the earthly emanating from the Lord, *SS* 6
    the Last Judgment being carried out on those who were outwardly moral but not inwardly spiritual, *Faith* 64; *Supp* 28
    the life of those who have been regenerated being called spiritual life, *Lord* 49
    the Lord flowing from the spiritual into the earthly, *Life* 110
    moral earthly individuals compared to moral spiritual individuals, *Life* 109
    our becoming spiritual
        through trials, *Lord* 33:2
        when our will is raised into heaven, *Life* 15
    our being spiritual to the extent that we turn our backs on evils because they are sins, *Life* 52
    our having heavenly, spiritual, and earthly levels, *SS* 68
    our needing to be spiritual for truth and love to be united in us, *Life* 15
    our will as unable to be lifted into heaven's warmth if we are not spiritual, *Life* 15
    spiritual angels (*see* angels of the spiritual kingdom)
    the spiritual body, *Supp* 3, 36
    spiritual goodness containing the essence of what is good, *Life* 13
    the spiritual kingdom of heaven receiving divine truth, *Life* 32:1
    spiritual light (*see under* Light)
    spiritual love, *Faith* 51; *Supp* 21, 48:3, 49:2, 51:1
        people devoted to spiritual love being in heaven, *Supp* 21
    the spiritual meaning of the Word (*see* Inner meaning of the Word)
    the spiritual mind (*see under* The mind)
    spiritual mysteries being revealed, *SS* 6:2, 20, 32, 70, 80; *Supp* 7, 72:2
    the spiritual perspective that flows into people who have a longing for truth, *Faith* 5
    spiritual warmth, *Life* 86:3; *Faith* 32
    the Word being earthly in the world but spiritual in the heavens, *Lord* 2

The spiritual world. *See also* The earth; Heaven; Hell; Life after death; Lower earth; Spirit; Spirits; The world of spirits
    all the people who have ever lived and died being gathered in the spiritual world, *Supp* 3, 5
    apparent distances in the spiritual world, *Supp* 14, 42:2–3, 44, 45
    caves in the spiritual world, *Life* 26
    changes in the spiritual world following the Last Judgment, *Supp* 57
    children being taught in the spiritual world, *Supp* 77
    cities in the spiritual world, *Supp* 42–43, 51:1, 79
    correspondences in the spiritual world, *Faith* 63:2, 3; *Supp* 21, 23, 50, 57, 77
    divine love and wisdom as the source of everything spiritual in the spiritual world, *Supp* 20
    earthquakes in the spiritual world during the Last Judgment, *Supp* 25

The spiritual world *(continued)*
    everything in the spiritual world being spiritual in essence, *Supp* 38
    governance of the British in the spiritual world, *Supp* 40
    the Last Judgment taking place in the spiritual world, *Supp* 3, 5, 7, 8
    location in the spiritual world
        the arrangement in the spiritual world of people from different religions, *Supp* 14, 20, 22, 56, 73, 79, 86
        being determined by one's acknowledgment of the Lord and of the oneness of God, *Supp* 68
        of the British, *Supp* 40
        depending on receptivity to light from the Lord, *Supp* 73
        geographical regions in the spiritual world being related to faith and love, *Supp* 48:2
    the Lord making a new church in both the spiritual and the earthly worlds, *Lord* 62:2
    Muhammad in the spiritual world, *Supp* 70
    our inner nature revealing itself in the spiritual world, *Supp* 39
    outer thinking being in the earthly world and inner thinking being in the spiritual world, *Supp* 39
    people of other religions being taught in the spiritual world that the Lord was born as a human, *Supp* 75
    precious stones in the spiritual world, *SS* 44:4; *Supp* 81
    representations in the spiritual world, *Supp* 44
    saints living as ordinary people in the spiritual world, *Supp* 64
    the source of everything in the spiritual world being a sun that is pure love, *Supp* 38
    specific groups in the spiritual world
        Africans, *Supp* 73–78
        the British, *Supp* 39–47
        Catholic saints, *Supp* 61–67
        the Dutch, *Supp* 48–55
        Jesuits, *Supp* 56
        Jews, *Supp* 79–82
        Moravians, *Supp* 86–90
        Muslims, *Supp* 68–72
        people of other religions, *Supp* 73–75
        Quakers, *Supp* 83–85
        Roman Catholics, *Supp* 56–60
        those who were canonized, *Supp* 63
    specific individuals appearing in the spiritual world
        an angel appearing to be Moses teaching Jews, *Supp* 80
        a person identified as Muhammad always appearing to Muslims, *Supp* 69
        a spirit who says she is Geneviève appearing to a community of Parisians, *Supp* 67
    the spiritual world having everything we see in the earthly world, *Faith* 63:1; *Supp* 37
    Swedenborg's experiences in the spiritual world, *Life* 49; *Supp* 35, 37
    Swedenborg's interactions in the spiritual world
        with Africans, *Supp* 77–78
        with an angel regarding faith divorced (separated) from caring, *Faith* 41–43
        with Calvin, *Supp* 54
        with Catholic saints from the lower earth, *Supp* 65
        with Louis XIV, *Supp* 60
        with Mary, *Supp* 66
        with Melanchthon, *Supp* 47
        with Moravians, *Supp* 86
        with Muslims, *Supp* 72
        with a pope, *Supp* 59
        with scholars, *Supp* 46
        with Xavier, *Supp* 65
Stars, *SS* 95:3. *See also* Sun
Stones, precious, *SS* 42, 44:4, 45, 97:4; *Supp* 81. *See also* Gold
Substance
    the Lord's human nature from his mother being material and his human nature from his Father being substantial, *Lord* 35:2
Sun. *See also* Stars
    the apparent motion of the sun as a semblance of truth, *SS* 95:2–3
    the earth's sun compared to the sun of heaven, *SS* 109
    the Lord as the sun of heaven, *SS* 106, 109; *Supp* 20
    the source of everything in the spiritual world being a sun that is pure love, *Supp* 38
    the spiritual sun being divine love and its light being divine wisdom, *Supp* 20
Supplements, *Lord* preface
    the purpose of the supplement to *Last Judgment*, *Supp* 2
    references to *Supplements*, *Lord* 62:2; *Faith* 64:2
Swedenborg, Emanuel
    the Lord being revealed to Swedenborg, *Lord* preface
    the Lord revealing an inner meaning of the Word to Swedenborg, *SS* 4, 112:1
    Swedenborg being granted companionship with angels and spirits, *SS* 70, 93, 116:1; *Faith* 3
    Swedenborg's experiences in the spiritual world, *Life* 49; *Supp* 35, 37
    Swedenborg's interactions in the spiritual world (*see under* The spiritual world)
    Swedenborg's publications, *Lord* preface (*see also* specific titles)

T

Tabernacle, *SS* 46; *Life* 55. *See also* The ark of the covenant

Teaching. *See also* Teachings
- angels teaching us after death, *SS* 93, 116:1; *Life* 49, 65; *Faith* 30
- the Dutch being taught after death, *Supp* 49
- the Lord teaching by means of the Word, *SS* 26:2, 50

Teachings (body of teaching). *See also* The church; Religion; Teaching
- a body of teaching
  - being drawn from the literal meaning of the Word, *SS* 43, 50, 53, 55, 59
  - being the source of a church, *SS* 43
  - a city meaning, *Lord* 64:1 and note a, 64:4
  - compared to a lamp, *SS* 52, 54, 59, 91
  - enlightenment as necessary for seeing the divine (genuine) truth in, *SS* 50, 57
  - as necessary to understand the Word, *SS* 50–52, 54, 91
  - people seeing and explaining the Word through their, *SS* 54
- British clergy being focused on teachings about faith, while the British laity is focused on teachings about how to live, *Supp* 45
- Jerusalem meaning the church in regard to its teachings, *Lord* 63, 64
- the misconception that salvation depends on believing the teachings of the church, *Life* 91
- the New Jerusalem meaning a new church in regard to its teachings, *SS* 43
- the only source of true teachings being through heaven from the Lord, *Lord* 63
- prophets meaning the body of teaching the church draws from the Word, *Lord* 15:8, 28; *SS* 35
- teachings for the new church, *Lord* preface, 65
- using the Word to support false religious teachings, *SS* 52, 60
- why these teachings have not been known before, *Lord* 61, 65; *SS* 25
- worship being defined by teachings, *Lord* 64:1

The Temple in Jerusalem, *Lord* 64:1; *SS* 47. *See also* Jerusalem

Ten, meaning all, *Life* 56, 61, 62

The Ten Commandments (the law). *See also* The ark of the covenant; Commandments; Laws
- breaking the laws of the Ten Commandments as a sin against God, *Life* 53, 63:3, 64
- individual commandments
  - the fifth commandment, on killing, *Life* 67–73
  - the sixth commandment, on adultery, *Life* 74–79
  - the seventh commandment, on theft, *Life* 80–86
  - the eighth commandment, on bearing false witness, *Life* 87–91
- Jehovah proclaiming the Ten Commandments in a miraculous fashion, *Life* 53, 55:1, 59
- the law
  - in the ark, *Lord* 9; *SS* 46; *Life* 55
  - being a summary of everything that constitutes religion, *Life* 54, 56
  - being the means of the Lord's union with us and our union with the Lord, *Life* 54, 57
  - the belief that no one can fulfill the law, *Life* 63:1–2, 64
  - called a covenant (and a testimony), *Life* 57, 60
  - "the law" meaning the Ten Commandments, *Lord* 8
  - the Lord's presence in, *Life* 55:2–3
  - obeying the law for civic and moral reasons but not religious reasons, *Life* 63:1–2, 64
- the rich man in the Bible who kept the commandments, *Life* 66:1
- the Ten Commandments
  - all societies with religion having laws similar to, *Life* 65
  - being called the "Ten Words," *Life* 55:3, 56, 61, 62
  - as civil, moral, and spiritual laws, *Life* 53
  - the earthly, spiritual, and heavenly meanings of, *SS* 67
  - the holiness of, *Life* 54–56, 59
  - as Islamic religious practice, *Supp* 71
  - living by the principles of, *SS* 92; *Life* 65
  - the misconception that salvation does not depend on obeying, *Life* 91
  - people of other religions who acknowledge one God and have religious principles similar to, *Supp* 73
  - the power of, *Life* 56, 59
  - teaching children the, *Life* 64
- the two tablets of the law, *Lord* 9; *SS* 46; *Life* 55:1, 56–60, 62
  - the first tablet having to do with God, *Life* 56, 57, 62
  - the second tablet being for us, *Life* 56–58, 62

Theft. *See also* Deception; Honesty
- guile and trickery united with theft infecting our spiritual mind, *Life* 81, 85
- our loving honesty to the extent that we turn our backs on all kinds of theft because they are sins, *Life* 82, 84, 89
- the seventh commandment, on theft, *Life* 80–86
- the three levels of "theft," *Life* 80

Thought. *See also* Belief; The mind; The rational; Reason; Understanding
  action and thought working together, *Life* 1, 47
  to the extent that we turn our backs on evil deeds because they are sins, our devout thoughts and words are devout, *Life* 25, 26
  love being the underlying reality and our thinking being its manifestation, *Life* 48
  our apparent ability to think independently depending on our power to be receptive, *Life* 107
  our loving the truth in our understanding when we think on the basis of what is good, *Life* 44
  outer thinking being in the earthly world and inner thinking being in the spiritual world, *Supp* 39
  thinking belonging to the understanding, *Life* 42, 48
  those who worship nature having thinking that comes from themselves rather than from heaven and the Lord, *SS* 1

Three, *SS* 28, 29

Time
  "day" and "time" meaning the Lord's Coming, *Lord* 4, 5

Trees
  a person compared to a tree, *Life* 46, 93; *Faith* 16, 17, 31, 32

Trials (tests). *See also* Battle; The Crucifixion
  evil spirits inflicting spiritual trials on us, *Lord* 33:1
  the Lord's trials, *Lord* 12, 15:1–2, 33, 35:3, 59, 65
  our becoming spiritual through trials, *Lord* 33:2
  trials being battles against hell (what is evil and false), *Lord* 33:1; *Life* 98

Trinity, *Lord* 60. *See also* The Father; The Holy Spirit; The Lord; The Son
  the Athanasian statement of faith on "a trinity of persons," *Lord* 57, 58
  early Christians dividing Divinity into three persons but believing the three to be one, *Lord* 55:2–4
  thinking in terms of three gods, *Lord* 57
  the threeness in angels, *Lord* 46:3
  the threeness or trinity in the Lord, *Lord* 46:2, 46:3, 46:6, 55:1
  the trinity of Father, Son, and Holy Spirit, *Lord* 57
  the trinity within God, *Supp* 72:1

Truth, *Lord* 18:5. *See also* Enlightenment; Falsity; Goodness; Knowledge; Wisdom
  convincing ourselves of false beliefs as condemning (harming) us if genuine truth is destroyed, *SS* 92–96a
  enlightenment as necessary for seeing the divine (genuine) truth in a body of teaching, *SS* 50, 57
  evil hating (destroying) truth, *Life* 44, 45; *Faith* 30
  faith and truth
    faith apart from truth, *Faith* 8
    faith as an inner recognition that something is true, *Faith* 2, 11–13, 24, 30
    faith as dependent on truth, *Faith* 2
    faith entering the discussion when the truth is not believed, *Faith* 7
    the faith of spiritual people being truth, *Life* 50
    the misconception that faith is thinking that something is true without a recognition that it is true, *Faith* 9, 10, 31
    as one and the same, *Faith* 6, 11, 21, 29
    people devoted to a faith divorced from caring as having no truth, *Faith* 70
  goodness and truth (*see under* Goodness)
  having enlightenment as having a perception whether something is true, *Faith* 5
  heaven's light being truth, *Life* 15
  ignorance of the truth protecting dogmatism, *Faith* 9
  an inner perception allowing us to recognize what is true, *SS* 58
  the Lord and truth
    the Lord being divine truth, *SS* 57, 78
    the Lord being (goodness itself and) truth itself, *Lord* 51:3; *Life* 38
    the Lord flowing into truths and bringing them to life, *SS* 82
    Nazirites representing the Lord's power through the outermost forms of truth, *SS* 49:2–4
  love and truth
    desiring (loving) the truth because it is true, *SS* 58, 91
    the love of truth inside a good life, *Faith* 30
    loving truth as the only way to arrive at wisdom, *Life* 89
    loving truth for the sake of goodness, *Life* 38
    loving what is true for the sake of reputation, *Life* 35
    our loving the Lord to the extent that we focus on goodness and love what is true, *Life* 38
    our loving the truth in our understanding when we think on the basis of what is good, *Life* 44
    our loving truth to the extent that we turn our backs on lying because it is a sin, *Life* 88
    our loving what is true to the extent that we turn our backs on evils because they are sins, *Life* 34, 37, 41

Truth *(continued)*
  love and truth *(continued)*
    our needing to be spiritual for truth and love to be united in us, *Life* 15
    those who have a longing (love) for truth recognizing whether something is true, *Faith* 3–5
  our ability to grasp spiritual truths, *Faith* 3
  recognizing truth after death, *Faith* 30
  rejecting sins making us love truths more, *Life* 41
  the seed in the field meaning truth, *Life* 90
  seeing false things as true, *Faith* 71
  semblances of truth not being harmful in themselves, *SS* 94, 95, 97:1
  truth taking root in the spiritual mind, *Life* 90
  the truth we believe residing in our understanding, *Life* 44, 45
  wisdom as being enlightened by the Lord and seeing truths in the light of truths, *SS* 91
  the Word and truth
    angel guardians meaning the protection of the truths of the Word, *SS* 97:2–5
    distorting the truths of the Word, *SS* 24, 26, 56, 60, 61:2, 77, 79, 97:1, 111; *Faith* 67
    drawing a body of teaching containing genuine truth from the literal meaning of the Word, *SS* 55
    the foundations of the wall of the New Jerusalem in Revelation 21 meaning the truths of the literal meaning, *SS* 43
    the inner recognition that occurs in the light of truth from the Word, *Faith* 10
    judgment being executed according to the divine truth in the Word, *Lord* 25
    the literal meaning being made up of semblances of truth, *SS* 40, 51:1, 91, 95
    the literal meaning protecting the real truths within, *SS* 97
    seeing divine truths in the Word, *SS* 41
    semblances of truth in the Word becoming falsities if we convince ourselves of them, *SS* 91, 92
    the spiritual meaning being given only to those focused on truths from the Lord, *SS* 26, 56
    the spiritual meaning being revealed because a body of teaching based on genuine truth is being revealed, *SS* 25
    studying the Word from love of truth and of one's neighbor as leading to heaven, *SS* 61:3
    the truth of the Word taking root, *Life* 90
    truths of the literal meaning being meant by the precious stones in the Garden of Eden, *SS* 45, 97:4
    the Urim and Thummim meaning the good and true elements of the literal meaning, *SS* 44
    the Word being divine truth, *Lord* 2, 27:2; *SS* 2:1, 3:1, 76, 78, 106, 114; *Supp* 12
    the Word being truth depending on how it is understood, *SS* 77

U

Understanding (intellect; intelligence). *See also* Knowledge; The mind; The rational; Reason; Thought; Will
  faith and intellect (*see under* Faith)
  false beliefs arising from not thinking intelligently, *Lord* 19:1; *Faith* 46, 47
  the intellectual light resulting from freedom in Britain, *Supp* 40
  learning about what is good taking place in our understanding, *Faith* 33
  our ability to grasp spiritual truths, *Faith* 3
  our loving the truth in our understanding when we think on the basis of what is good, *Life* 44
  our sense of self-importance corrupting our understanding, *Lord* 17:3
  our understanding being raised into heaven, *Life* 15
  our understanding receiving what is true and what is wise, *SS* 83
  people whose understanding has been closed because of their religion, *Faith* 48
  Philistia as religion corrupted by pride in one's own intelligence, *Faith* 49, 53, 55
  the sequence of will, understanding, and bodily action, *Faith* 15–16
  spiritual light entering our understanding to the extent that we are able to perceive it, *Supp* 14
  thinking belonging to the understanding, *Life* 48
  those who have pride in their own intelligence (wisdom) convincing themselves of falsities, *SS* 91, 92
  the truth we believe residing in our understanding, *Life* 44, 45
  using our intellect in regard to spiritual matters, *Supp* 5
  using the intellect to test religious ideas, *Supp* 46:2
  what people are like after death who attribute everything to their own intelligence, *SS* 118
  will and understanding (*see under* Will)
  the Word and the understanding
    all spiritual understanding (intelligence) coming from the Word, *Lord* 2; *SS* 114, 115:2–3, 117
    an evil will removing the Word's truth from the understanding, *SS* 116:2

Understanding *(continued)*
   the Word and the understanding *(continued)*
      our understanding of the Word determining the church, *SS* 76, 77, 79, 114
         its truth, *SS* 77
         the Lord's presence and union with us, *SS* 78
         our truth, faith, love, and life, *SS* 78
      understanding the Word according to one's abilities, *SS* 72, 91

Unigenitus *(papal bull)*, *Supp* 60

Union
   "covenant" meaning union, *Life* 60
   our union with the Lord, *SS* 62, 64:2; *Life* 102
      belief in the Lord as the union with him that gives us salvation, *Faith* 36
      the Lord's union with us and our union with the Lord, *Lord* 35:8; *Life* 54, 57; *Faith* 22
      taking place in the literal meaning of the Word, *SS* 62, 64:2
      through the Word, *SS* 69, 76, 78, 105
   the union of
      caring and faith, *Faith* 18, 19, 29, 43, 67
      essence and form, *Faith* 18:2
      goodness and truth, *Life* 40, 44, 65; *Faith* 18:1, 29
      understanding and will, *SS* 83; *Life* 42–44, 86:6; *Faith* 18:1
   union with angels through correspondence, *SS* 67:6
   union with heaven, *SS* 104

The Urim and Thummim, *SS* 44

Usefulness, *Faith* 14, 16, 17, 19:2, 20, 21, 25. *See also* Business; Occupation

V

Versailles, *Supp* 60

Visions, the prophets having, *Lord* 52. *See also* Sight

W

Warmth
   heaven's warmth, *Life* 15
   spiritual warmth, *Life* 86:3; *Faith* 32

The Wars of Jehovah, *SS* 103. *See also* The ancient Word

Wealth, *Life* 66:1, 68, 92. *See also* Rank; Reputation

White Horse, *Lord* preface
   White Horse explaining the spiritual meaning of passages in Revelation 19, *SS* 9

Will. *See also* Love; Understanding
   the desire to do what is good developing in our will, *Faith* 33
   the evil we practice residing in our will, *Life* 44
   the heart meaning the will, *Life* 51
   love belonging to the will, *Life* 48
   our becoming spiritual when our will is raised into heaven, *Life* 15
   our calling "rational" whatever agrees with our will or love, *Life* 15
   our will as involving a sense of our own self-importance (self-aggrandizement), *SS* 115, 116
   our will receiving what is good and receiving love, *SS* 83
   will and understanding
      being our two faculties of life (abilities), *SS* 83, 115; *Life* 43:1
      everything in us originating in our will and our understanding, *Life* 43:1
      faith and life being distinct from each other in the same way that understanding and will are distinct, *Life* 42
      faith in the understanding being alive if it has goodness from the will, *Life* 46
      goodness having to do with the will and truth with the understanding, *Life* 36, 43:1
      needing to act together, *Faith* 15
      our understanding (intellect) as able to be in heaven, but not our will unless we turn our backs on evils because they are sins, *Life* 86:2; *Faith* 32
      the sequence of will, understanding, and bodily action, *Faith* 15–16
      thinking coming from the understanding and actions coming from the will, *Life* 42
      together making the mind, *Life* 43, 85
      the understanding corresponding to the lungs and the will to the heart, *Life* 46
      the union of, *SS* 83; *Life* 42–44, 86:6; *Faith* 18:1
      will as the underlying reality of our life and understanding as its manifestation, *Life* 43:2
      the will leading the understanding, *SS* 115; *Life* 15, 44
   what our will intends as all that we are, *Lord* 18:3

Wind, the belief that spirits and angels are made of, *Supp* 3

Wisdom. *See also* Ignorance; Knowledge; The rational; Reason; Truth; Understanding
   angels and wisdom
      goodness united to truth making love and wisdom for angels and for us, *Life* 32:2
      Swedenborg's planned works on angelic wisdom, *Lord* preface, 32:8, 36:1; *SS* 32, 83, 100; *Life* 15, 107
      the wisdom of angels, *SS* 74; *Faith* 4
      the Word as the source of, *Lord* 2; *SS* 73, 114
      the Word containing all of, *SS* 75
   divine wisdom (*see* Divine wisdom)
   to the extent that we turn our backs on evil deeds because they are sins, we are wise, *Life* 27

Wisdom *(continued)*
    the life of the Lord's wisdom, *Lord* 51
    loving truth as the only way to arrive at wisdom, *Life* 89
    our being unwise to the extent that we are not purified from our evils, *Life* 30:1, 2
    wisdom as being enlightened by the Lord and seeing truths in the light of truths, *SS* 91
    wisdom dwelling with good actions that come from love, *SS* 74
    wisdom not depending on mere knowledge, thinking, and understanding, *Life* 44

Wives, *Supp* 51:2, 71. *See also* Marriage

The Word (Sacred Scripture). *See also* The ancient Word; Daniel, Book of; The Gospels; Job, Book of; Matthew, Gospel of; Prophetic books; Revelation, Book of
    all names in the Word having to do with matters of (heaven and) the church, *SS* 15:1, 2; *Faith* 49
    angels and spirits reading the Word, *SS* 70
    angels being present when we read the Word, *Lord* 37:2; *SS* 64:1, 67
    angels having the same Word that we have in the world, *Lord* 2
    a body of teaching as necessary to understand the Word, *SS* 50–52, 54, 91
    Catholics forbidden from reading the Word, *Faith* 8
    Christians who read the Word and worship the Lord being at the center of the world of spirits, *Supp* 48:1
    a church where the Word is read and the Lord is known, *SS* 104, 110
    the divinity of the Word, *Lord* 1; *SS* 1, 4, 6:2, 18:4, 19, 32, 90; *Supp* 62
    the earthly meaning of the Word (*see* Literal meaning of the Word)
    finding enlightenment in the Word, *Lord* 2; *SS* 106, 110, 111, 114
    the heavenly meaning of the Word (*see* Heavenly meaning of the Word)
    the historical books of the Word, *Lord* 14:11
    the inner meaning of the Word (*see* Inner meaning of the Word)
    Jehovah speaking the Word through prophets, *Lord* 52, 53; *SS* 2
    the Law and the Prophets meaning the whole Sacred Scripture, *Lord* 8
    "the law" meaning everything in the Word, *Lord* 10
    light meaning the Word, *Lord* 2
    the literal meaning of the Word (*see* Literal meaning of the Word)
    the Lord and the Word
        the Lord becoming divine truth or the Word even on the outermost level, *SS* 98, 99
        the Lord being present throughout the Word, *SS* 57
        the Lord being the Word, *Lord* 1, 15:2, 37; *SS* 47, 62, 73, 78, 100
        the Lord coming into the world to fulfill the Word, *SS* 98
        the Lord coming into the world to fulfill the Word, make it whole, and restore it, *SS* 111
        the Lord fulfilling all things of the Word, *SS* 49:1, 2; *Supp* 13
        the Lord fulfilling the law meaning that he fulfilled all of the Word, *Lord* 8, 11, 65
        the Lord gaining divine power when he fulfilled the whole Word, *Lord* 27:2
        the Lord representing the Word, *Lord* 15:8, 16:5; *SS* 48
        the Lord speaking the Word with the Gospel writers, *SS* 2:1
        the Lord teaching the Word, *Lord* 20, 27:1; *SS* 26:2
        the marriage of the Lord and the church in the details of the Word, *SS* 80, 82, 87:2, 88, 89, 114
        names of the Lord in the Word depending on the subject of the discourse, *Lord* 22, 23
        our union with the Lord through the Word, *SS* 3, 62, 64:2, 69, 76, 78, 105
        prophets representing the Lord as the Word, *Lord* 28
        recognition of the Lord and salvation not being possible without the Word, *SS* 111
        "the Son of Humanity" meaning the Lord as the Word, *Lord* 23, 27, 28, 50:2
        the whole Word having been spoken by the Lord, *Lord* 53
        the Word being the Lord, *Lord* 2, 45:1; *SS* 2:4
        the Word (Sacred Scripture) being entirely about the Lord, *Lord* 2, 7, 8, 11, 14:11, 19:9, 37, 45:1, 55:5, 65; *SS* 62, 89, 112:1
        the Word uniting the Lord to the church, *SS* 18:1
    the marriage of goodness and truth in the details of the Word, *SS* 80–82, 85, 88, 114
    the misconception that spiritual knowledge is possible without the Word, *SS* 115
    our companionship (union) with angels through the Word, *SS* 49:5, 63, 67:6, 68, 69, 114
    our gaining life by means of the Word, *SS* 3:2
    our not knowing about God if there were no Word, *SS* 114, 115:2–3
    paired expressions in the Word as having to do with goodness and truth, *SS* 84–88
    people seeing and explaining the Word through their body of teaching, *SS* 54

The Word *(continued)*
    the perversion (abuse) of the Word, *Lord* 15:2, 16:6, 65
    the prophetic books of the Word (*see* Prophetic books)
    prophets meaning the body of teaching the church draws from the Word, *Lord* 15:8, 28; *SS* 35
    the prophets representing the Word and the church, *Lord* 15:2, 15:4–8
    Protestants occupying the central area of the spiritual world because they read the Word and worship the Lord, *Supp* 14, 20, 22
    reading the Word with reverence, *SS* 19
    secrets from the Word having been revealed after the Last Judgment was carried out, *Lord* 61:2, 65
    seeming contradictions in the Word, *SS* 51:1, 51:9
    seeming repetitions in the Word, *SS* 81, 84–87
    spirit and life in the Word, *SS* 69, 77
    the spiritual meaning of the Word (*see* Inner meaning of the Word)
    those who worship nature having contempt for the Word, *SS* 1
    the three levels of meaning in the Word, *SS* 6:2, 31; *Life* 87
    using the Word to support false religious teachings, *SS* 52, 60
    the Word and heaven (*see under* Heaven)
    the Word and the understanding (*see under* Understanding)
    the Word and truth (*see under* Truth)
    the Word being
        concerned with heavenly matters throughout, *SS* 18:2, 3
        earthly in the world but spiritual in the heavens, *Lord* 2
        given to the prophets, *SS* 102:2
        the source of angels' wisdom, *Lord* 2; *SS* 73, 114
    the Word compared to a garden, *SS* 96b
    the Word composed using correspondences, *SS* 8, 20:3, 40, 51:1, 91, 117
    the Word containing all angelic wisdom, *SS* 75
    the Word containing secrets, *Lord* 14:11
    the Word showing that religion is about how we live and that the religious way to live is to do good, *Life* 2
    the Word's holiness, *Lord* 7; *SS* 1, 3:1, 4, 81
    the writing style of the Word, *SS* 8
        in heaven, *SS* 71, 72, 74, 90
        those who evaluate the Word by its writing style, *SS* 1, 3:1

The world of spirits. *See also* Lower earth; The spiritual world
    Catholics in the world of spirits, *Supp* 59
    communities in the world of spirits, *Supp* 21, 57
    correspondences in the world of spirits, *Faith* 56
    fights between sheep and goats in the world of spirits, *Faith* 63:4
    the light in the world of spirits, *Supp* 20, 30, 48:1
    the location of Christians in the world of spirits, *Supp* 48:1
    Luther in the world of spirits, *Supp* 55
    the world of spirits as an intermediate space between heaven and hell, *Faith* 63:3; *Supp* 18, 20, 57

Worship, *Lord* 64:1; *SS* 116:3; *Supp* 64. *See also* The church; The Lord; Religion

Writing style, of the Word, *SS* 1, 3:1, 8, 71, 72, 74, 90

X

Xavier, Francis, *Supp* 65. *See also* Jesuits

Z

Zinzendorf, Nikolaus von, *Supp* 89. *See also* Moravians

Biographical Note

EMANUEL SWEDENBORG (1688–1772) was born Emanuel Swedberg (or Svedberg) in Stockholm, Sweden, on January 29, 1688 (Julian calendar). He was the third of the nine children of Jesper Swedberg (1653–1735) and Sara Behm (1666–1696). At the age of eight he lost his mother. After the death of his only older brother ten days later, he became the oldest living son. In 1697 his father married Sara Bergia (1666–1720), who developed great affection for Emanuel and left him a significant inheritance. His father, a Lutheran clergyman, later became a celebrated and controversial bishop, whose diocese included the Swedish churches in Pennsylvania and in London, England.

After studying at the University of Uppsala (1699–1709), Emanuel journeyed to England, the Netherlands, France, and Germany (1710–1715) to study and work with leading scientists in western Europe. Upon his return he apprenticed as an engineer under the brilliant Swedish inventor Christopher Polhem (1661–1751). He gained favor with Sweden's King Charles XII (1682–1718), who gave him a salaried position as an overseer of Sweden's mining industry (1716–1747). Although Emanuel was engaged, he never married.

After the death of Charles XII, Emanuel was ennobled by Queen Ulrika Eleonora (1688–1741), and his last name was changed to Swedenborg (or Svedenborg). This change in status gave him a seat in the Swedish House of Nobles, where he remained an active participant in the Swedish government throughout his life.

A member of the Royal Swedish Academy of Sciences, he devoted himself to studies that culminated in a number of publications, most notably a comprehensive three-volume work on natural philosophy and metallurgy (1734) that brought him recognition across Europe as a scientist. After 1734 he redirected his research and publishing to a study of anatomy in search of the interface between the soul and body, making several significant discoveries in physiology.

From 1743 to 1745 he entered a transitional phase that resulted in a shift of his main focus from science to theology. Throughout the rest of his life he maintained that this shift was brought about by Jesus Christ, who appeared to him, called him to a new mission, and opened his perception to a permanent dual consciousness of this life and the life after death.

He devoted the last decades of his life to studying Scripture and publishing eighteen theological titles that draw on the Bible, reasoning, and his own spiritual experiences. These works present a Christian theology with unique perspectives on the nature of God, the spiritual world, the Bible, the human mind, and the path to salvation.

Swedenborg died in London on March 29, 1772 (Gregorian calendar), at the age of eighty-four.